XIII   FRANCOIS MARIE AROUET = VOLTAIRE
XIV   ELECTOR GEORGE LEWIS OF HANOVER → KING GEORGE I

29   TWO POUNDS OF MEAT WAS A FRUGAL MEAL !?!
145 ABOLISHING TORTURE
140 TRUE ASSESSMENT OF F. THE GREAT
555 IT PAYS TO BE DIPLOMATIC !

TOP SHELF

Frederick
the
Great

Robert B. Asprey

FREDERICK
THE
GREAT
The Magnificent Enigma

TICKNOR & FIELDS
New York 1986

Library of Congress Cataloging-in-Publication Data

Asprey, Robert B.
Frederick the Great: the magnificent enigma.

Bibliography: p.
Includes index.
1. Frederick II, King of Prussia, 1712–1786.
2. Prussia (Germany) — Kings and rulers — Biography.
3. Prussia (Germany) — History — Frederick II, the
Great, 1740–1786. I. Title.
DD404.A75   1986   943.053'092'4 [B]   86-5993
ISBN 0-89919-352-8

Printed in the United States of America

P 10 9 8 7 6 5 4 3 2 1

To dear Belle — and to Sammy, who always will be

CONTENTS

Book Six

The Seven Years' War, 1756–1763 · 425

Book Seven

The Ruler and the Realm, 1763–1786 · 561

ILLUSTRATIONS AND MAPS

Illustrations

Maps

INTRODUCTION

A.D. 1712.

The western world was Europe, a much smaller Europe. Russia was not yet part of it; Czar Peter was not yet great; Versailles was not old. Kingdoms and empires had but begun the long climb to nationhood; man had not yet become free to wrestle with the problems of freedom. Lemuel Gulliver had not begun to travel; François Marie Arouet was not yet Voltaire; Jean Jacques Rousseau was seven years old.

This world belonged largely to emperors, kings, nobles, and priests. They made war as they made love: Scarcely one affair ended before another began. The first world war — the War of the Spanish Succession — was still being fought. It would cinder down in the hearths of Utrecht in 1713 and of Rastadt in 1714. The Northern War, in which Sweden faced a five-power coalition, continued, and so long as religions, crowns, lands, oceans, and trade existed, there would be no lack of new conflicts in the political jungle that was Europe of this day.

The European periphery for the most part consisted of political crudities: Italy, a mosaic of petty kingdoms, city-states, republics, and ducal territories — altogether some thirteen million people variously owned and frequently fought over by Spain, France, and Austria; the Balkans, still tribal, controlled in part by Hungary and Austria, in part by Turkey, which, though recently defeated in a war with Austria, remained of real and constant concern to that power, and also to Russia; Hungary, a kingdom of sprawling feudal and tribal estates paying reluctant fealty to Charles VI, Habsburg ruler of Austria and Emperor of the Holy Roman Empire; Poland, a great kingdom once, now a torn, generally impoverished country of vast feudal estates yielding insolent homage to an elected king, August II, who was also Elector of Saxony, a ruler who preferred submissive Saxon subjects to rebellious, hard-drinking Polish aristocrats seemingly bent on their own political destruction; Sweden, once undisputed master of the north, savaged two decades earlier by Russia, Poland, and Denmark (later joined by Hanover and Prussia), defended brilliantly by fiery young King Charles XII, but now being led to defeat and humiliation by that same king, who failed to recognize his limitations and was paying the price; Prussia, home of the Hohenzollerns, more accurately Brandenburg-Prussia — not a giant like Russia or Austria, but an athlete (as Lord Acton put it), that by war, marriage, inheritance, and diplomacy had acquired a collection of separate territories scattered from the Rhine to the Vistula, from the Baltic to the borders of Bohemia, diverse lands ruled by the Elector of Brandenburg, also King *in* Prussia, Frederick I; Hanover, a rich and powerful collection of homogeneous estates ruled by Elector George Lewis, who would soon become King George I of England; Denmark, waiting greedily with its Baltic allies to profit from Sweden's defeat; Holland, a collection of seven territories constituting the United Provinces and ruled by the States-General, a political entity distinct from the Spanish Netherlands, ruled now by the Austrian Habsburgs.

The great powers of Europe were France, Austria, and Spain, and, playing a larger role now, England. Despite the disastrous War of the Spanish Succession, France was still the most powerful European kingdom, far more homogeneous and wealthier than any except England. The Versailles court, fashioned by Louis XIV, had dictated royal protocol for as long as man could remember. Minor rulers, and some not so minor, such as the Prussian King Frederick I, plunged their lands into debt and even bankruptcy in attempting to emulate French splendor. European royalty, almost without exception, wore French dress, practiced French manners, spoke the French language, wore French wigs. But France was in decline, King Louis old and ailing, soon to die, his heir a sickly boy. Spain, allied with France through marriage and the maritime trade challenge posed by England and Holland, was also in trouble, laboring "in decrepitude, insolvent, incoherent, tracing her genealogies and telling her beads."[1] In contrast, Whig England was wide awake, rich, powerful, ambitious, its ships penetrating to the remote corners of the earth, its overseas colonies expanding, trade flourishing.

England's traditional allies were Holland and Austria; the three formed the Grand Alliance, which had all but defeated France and would soon be strained by Britain's defection and separate peace with Versailles. Holland was slowing. Its influence in European affairs, especially its economic influence, had sharply declined, the result primarily of internecine political dissensions that had sapped her strength and brought about a sluggish, generally frightened, and frequently impotent diplomacy. Austria had also faded; its treasury was empty, its dominions were disorganized, its ruler increasingly resentful of his British ally.

If France and England were the strongest of the great powers, Austria was by far the most complex, certainly the most infuriating. Its

Habsburg, devoutly Catholic, ruler, Charles VI, owned a vast con-
glomerate of hereditary lands and acquired territories that included
Austria, Hungary, Bohemia, large parts of Italy, and the Spanish Netherlands — altogether some twenty-four million people. Charles was also
Holy Roman Emperor, which in theory made him ruler of a large portion of central Europe, the German empire. In fact this empire long
since had been moribund, a political anomaly defined by a seventeenth-
century historian, Samuel Puffendorf, as "an unclassifiable body comparable to a monster."

The Holy Roman Empire was neither holy nor Roman; Voltaire would
even deny it empire status. It was a perhaps inevitable growth from
ruins left by Charlemagne centuries earlier. Founded by Otto the Great
in the tenth century, it had evolved into a Habsburg vanity of more
shadow than substance. Its charter emerged in 1356 in a formal document, the Golden Bull. By this time the great emigration east had spilled
from old Germany, the Rhineland, to cross the Elbe, subdue and assim-
ilate the Slavs there, push on and across the Oder, and settle as far as
to the lower reaches of the Vistula. A powerful nobility had grown up
during these two migratory centuries, and in 1356 Emperor Charles IV
was forced to recognize their rights.

The Golden Bull recognized seven *Kurfürsten,* or electoral princes,
of the Empire. Three were spiritual rulers, the powerful and very rich
Archbishops of Mainz, Cologne, and Trier. Four were secular, equally
powerful and rich, the Duke of Saxony, the Count Palatine of the Rhine,
the Margrave of Brandenburg, and the King of Bohemia. Though
swearing fealty to the emperor, the electors, along with most minor
princes, remained autonomous rulers responsible for the administration of their realms, for maintaining their own defense, and conducting
their own foreign relations. When need arose, they were responsible
for electing a new emperor. They or their representatives sat in a House
of Electors, part of the Reichstag or Diet at Ratisbon. In addition to
the electorates, the empire included an extraordinary collection of principalities, dukedoms, baronies, bishoprics, and fiefdoms — in the eighteenth century they numbered 330 — whose lords held Imperial charters and who were represented in the Reichstag in the House of Princes.
In the fifteenth century the emperor granted Imperial charters to a
number of trading centers, and these came to be represented at Ratisbon in the House of Free Cities.

The Reichstag proved obdurate to Imperial authority from the beginning, and subsequent events did little to remedy the defects of de-
centralized rule, which generally allowed provincial interests to override those of the Imperial weal. No standing Imperial army existed, nor
could the emperor levy military contributions without approval of the
provincial estates. Instead, he had to rely on his own armies for con-

solidating and defending far-flung territories, and in fending off various enemies from his home realms — challenges that kept his treasury depleted if not empty. When he had to seek military aid from the electors, he often had no money for subsidies and had to pay them in the form of increased privileges. Each such barter or treaty, and there were many, further diluted Imperial authority. A major blow occurred with the immense religious upheaval of the Reformation. The resultant Thirty Years' War (1618–1648) established finally the Protestant Church as co-shareholder with the Roman Catholic Church in God's estate.

By the turn of the eighteenth century some electors had gained such privileges and had otherwise prospered by their own devices to such a degree that, rather than being Imperial vassals, they were partners in a loose political confederation. When the confederation served their needs, they were partners; when Imperial policy stood at odds to their own ambitions, usually territorial aggrandizement, they were opponents.

The two most powerful electorates were Brandenburg-Prussia and Hanover. They were Protestant powers. Hanover, more properly the duchy of Lüneburg-Kalenberg, was the parvenu electorate of the Empire, having been nominated to that status only in 1692 and only because Duke Ernest August had supported the emperor militarily against the Turks. Formal admission to the Electoral College required another sixteen years and more military support by the duke's son and successor, George Lewis, in the War of the Spanish Succession. Hanover comprised about eighty-five hundred square miles and perhaps 750,000 subjects, who seemed to accept the duke's despotic rule without complaint. Its promotion to electorate status further sapped Imperial authority. Not only was Hanover a strongly Protestant dukedom, but it was allied by religion and especially by marriage to strongly Protestant Prussia. As in Prussia's case, the vassal now loomed as an uncomfortably strong rival whose strength would sharply increase two years later, when Queen Anne of England died and the Whig Party, acting within the authority of the Act of Settlement, placed Elector George Lewis on the English throne as King George I.

Brandenburg was the older electorate. A frontier territory, or "march," dating from the ninth century, it had expanded over the centuries, acquiring diverse territories that included East Prussia, the base of the Order of Teutonic Knights. Although suffering numerous setbacks, it had continued to expand, a process occasioned by treaty, outright aggression, and, not least, inheritance through dynastic marriages.

Brandenburg-Prussia had emerged from the Thirty Years' War as a Protestant power of considerable dimensions. Although this prolonged and extremely cruel war had laid waste large parts of the kingdom, Elector Frederick William, known always as the Great Elector, in time repaired the ravages and made a number of important if incipient ad-

ministrative, military, and economic reforms. Among other vital innovations, he challenged the theretofore sacrosanct privileges of his feudal nobility, he partially centralized the administration, and he raised
and maintained a standing army. The Great Elector died in 1688. His
son and successor, Elector Frederick III, though limited in many ways,
at first used his military legacy well. In 1700 he lent the hard-pressed
Emperor Leopold the services of eight thousand Prussian troops in return for a sort of crown: the following year Frederick became King *in*
(not *of*) Prussia, a prepositional subtlety that did not long survive its
intention of preserving Imperial authority within the actual Empire.
This was another of those appointments which sapped further the emperor's already weakened authority by strengthening a potential rival,
a fact plainly seen by wily old Prince Eugene of Savoy, who, informed
of the treaty, said: "The emperor should hang the minister who gave
him such perfidious counsel." [2]

Eugene's admonition seemed unduly harsh. Crowned at Königsberg
in 1701 (his delightfully uninhibited wife pinched snuff during the
elaborate ceremony), King Frederick very nearly spent his kingdom into
bankruptcy by trying to emulate the splendors of the French court at
Versailles. But no one paid much attention. In 1712 the Berlin court,
with its fat, foppish little king, was not taken very seriously in Europe.
In 1712 Prussia was still a minor power of little interest to the giants
around her.

BOOK ONE

A Prince of the Blood

1712–1730

Impressions received in childhood cannot be erased from the soul.

— *Frederick the Great*

I

SUNDAY, JANUARY 24, 1712.

He was born to the sound of cannon and bells, an easy baby, requiring only three and a half hours of labor. When at noon the court chamberlain formally announced that Crown Princess Sophia Dorothea had safely delivered a prince, gunners shivering on Berlin's high walls thrust glowing sticks of punk to primed touchholes; young bell pullers in city churches quickly sweated through winter woolens in a futile bid of bells against guns.

A few days later he was christened Frederick, a name that, as his grandfather King Frederick I wrote to a friend, "has always brought good fortune to my House." This small, misshapen Prussian king was a stickler for ceremony: later historians called him Frederick the Ostentatious, and in the christening of his eight-day-old grandson he lived up to the name. Wearing a tiny gold crown and dressed in a robe of silver and diamonds, its flowing train held by six countesses, the newborn was carried to the court chapel under a canopy supported by two margraves accompanied by many ladies and gentlemen, a truly regal procession flanked by a double row of ornately uniformed Swiss guards. When the tower clock chimed three, the king, followed by his mad wife, Queen Sophia Louisa; Crown Prince Frederick William, the father; and Prince Leopold of Anhalt-Dessau, personally carried the baby into the splendidly illuminated room, cold despite hundreds of burning candles. There, under a magnificent gold-embroidered canopy attended by senior army generals and state ministers, the king placed the infant on a table holding a gold basin. On his being baptized Frederick, Prince of Prussia and Orange, organ music boomed from the rafters while "all bells of the city rang and the cannon on the city walls, accompanied by drums and trumpets, fired three times." That evening, as the prince slept, the court sat to a magnificent table, and great celebrations filled the city.[1]

He was a sickly little fellow, the source of great anxiety to parents

and nurses, and especially to his grandfather the king. Not least of King
Frederick's worries had been his daughter-in-law's inability to produce
a surviving male heir. Crown Princess Sophia Dorothea earlier had borne
two sons who died in infancy. When a third prince failed to materialize, the king panicked to the extent of taking on a third wife and bravely
if unsuccessfully attempting to produce his own male heir.

So Frederick's survival was particularly important to the House of
Hohenzollern.* The baby delighted the king, who frequented the nursery, annoying the nurses by hovering anxiously over the frail heir. When
Frederick's teeth came through, King Frederick regarded the event as
predestined and a blessing to his House. His attentions ended thirteen
months later. On a February night his insane wife, in a fit of religious
frenzy and convinced that she was being divorced to be married to the
Sultan of Morocco, burst through a glass door into his apartments.
Bloody and disheveled, wearing only a white shift, she flung herself on
the dozing monarch. Mistaking her for "the White Lady," who traditionally appeared just before the death of a Hohenzollern, Frederick
lapsed into a coma and shortly died. His son Frederick William now
became king, and the infant Frederick was Crown Prince of Prussia.

The baby Frederick demanded and received considerable attention.
He was a small, nervous, sickly infant — the result, it was said, of neu-
rotic and related blood in his tiny veins, or perhaps of the cannon fire
that had punctuated his christening. He was cared for by two friendly
souls, a lady-in-waiting who was governess, Frau von Kamecke, and a
chief nurse, Madame de Roucoulle, a widow who had also nursed his
father and who would remain "Mother" to Frederick for many years.

Mainly because of the ministrations of Madame de Roucoulle, Frederick survived a number of serious illnesses, not an easy feat in that
day of primitive medicine when the body's evil humors had to be purged
by frequent bloodlettings. Although he grew stronger, he remained delicate, which probably explained an early air of thoughtful sadness. His
elder sister, Crown Princess Wilhelmina, later wrote that he had an
"angelic temper," and witnesses like Charles Whitworth, the British
envoy in Berlin, were impressed by both children. "The Prince gives
very great hopes, both as to his temper and person," he reported in
1716, when Frederick was four, "and the eldest Princess is one of the
finest children I ever saw; she dances charmingly, and much surpasses
her age in all her carriage and sense."[2]

Several major influences molded the young prince. The most comfortable was undoubtedly the nursery, and integral to that was Wilhel-

---

* The family name of Margrave Frederick I, who was appointed Elector of Brandenburg in
1415, was Hohenzollern, the name of his ancestral castle in the duchy of Swabia, not far
from Lake Constance. (Schevill, *Elector*.)

mina. Three years her brother's senior, she was never far from young Frederick, and they grew even closer as their loyalty to the king and queen began to waver. Naturally precocious, Wilhelmina began reading at an unusually early age, a practice passed on to Frederick, along with a preference for French culture and manners. She also became an accomplished actress who could faint at will and was not above using hot stones dipped in turpentine to induce artificial fevers — tricks that did not fail to impress her younger brother. Her active imagination, fed by the queen's numerous and openly expressed prejudices, unfortunately brought spite and malignancy to the fore. At a very early age Frederick and Wilhelmina both were swimming in the murky waters of Court cabals and intrigues. As a later French historian put it, "Their mutual affection was fortified by the hatred they bore to the rest of the world."[3]

Some of the blame must be laid to their mother. Sophia Dorothea was a determined, prolific, formidable, and extremely ambitious woman, known with good reason to foreign envoys as Olympia. An accomplished troublemaker, she forever walked an emotional tightrope strung between one pole planted in the fertile ground of her own grand plans and another pole that bent dangerously in the soft slough of reality to forever frustrate those plans.

A Hanoverian princess and the daughter of George, Elector of Hanover, Sophia had been raised with her brother, George August, the future King George II of England, in the formal Hanover court at Herrenhausen. During one of the elector's frequent military campaigns, her mother had been seduced by the dashing Count Philip von Königsmarck. The affair ended messily, with the count's mysterious disappearance — and presumed murder — the dissolution of the marriage, and the erring wife's banishment to the remote castle of Ahlden, in neighboring Lüneburg. Here the tragic "Princess of Ahlden," forbidden to see her two children or to receive visitors of noble rank, remained under guard until her death, thirty-two years later.

The effect of this scandal on eleven-year-old George and nine-year-old Sophia Dorothea can well be imagined. They were thenceforth consigned to governors, tutors, and lackeys until their respective marriages eleven years later. Their father never remarried, contenting himself with a string of mistresses. He was not a good father, not even an interesting one, and Sophia was probably delighted to escape to the Berlin court in 1705, even though escape entailed being the consort of the loutish Crown Prince Frederick William.

Sophia was a pretty woman then, blond, comely, and well proportioned, with a generous bosom. She was gracious, at home in the arts, and professed an interest in the sciences. But she dipped at learning rather than immersing herself. Haughty and vain, moody and temperamental, Sophia attempted to skim off the cream of knowledge while disdaining the milk. The result was a superficially cultured person ill fitted to serve as Frederick William's mate. Their basic incompatibility was exacerbated by Sophia's belief that the House of Hanover was infinitely superior to the House of Hohenzollern. King Frederick I, her father-in-law, may have dressed his court in splendid imitation of Versailles, but its *nouveau* splendor paled in comparison with the cultured, traditionally polished, and opulent Herrenhausen court. In Sophia's mind no question existed as to which was superior, an understandable but awkward loyalty that transferred itself to the English court when her father became King George I in 1714.

Even before this impressive elevation, Sophia had decided to marry her daughter Wilhelmina to her Hanoverian nephew, Frederick, in keeping with the tradition of marriages between the Hanoverian and Hohenzollern Houses. Letters and gifts were exchanged with Cousin Frederick from the time Wilhelmina was two. To complicate matters, Sophia decided that her own crown prince, Frederick, would marry an English princess, presumably Emily, and at an early age Frederick received a ring made from Emily's hair. These marital projects were seconded not only by her own court, but also to a considerable degree by her husband, King Frederick William; by her father, King George I; and, not least, in time by the children themselves.

This was the genesis of the great marriage plot that would so dangerously divide the Berlin court. The Austrian court could not tolerate the thought of these Protestant Houses being further united; such a union would make Prussia a partner of France and England, opposing the Austrian emperor.

Frederick William at times would argue passionately for the marriage plans. Dynastic marriages traditionally played a vital and sometimes decisive role in diplomacy, and frequently helped to cement a political alliance. Although the Prussian king leaned politically toward Austria and the Holy Roman Empire — he was after all German born and bred and, as Elector of Brandenburg, a vassal of Emperor Charles VI — he remained only too aware of the bond, formed by blood and the Protestant religion, between Prussia and Hanover, one politically strengthened by the accession of his father-in-law (his own blood uncle) to the rich and powerful English throne, and by their mutual interests in the Northern War, then being fought. What the king did oppose was his wife's ostentatious bias in favor of the Hanover court and culture. She often expressed disapproval of his barrackslike life, insisted on raising their children in the French rather than German manner, and was constantly meddling in political affairs in her determined efforts to bring about the marriages she had planned.

The relationship was curious. When on good terms, they used diminutives — he called her Fiechen, and she called him Wilke. Physically

King Frederick William, an iron-handed ruler of two million subjects, a short, fat, and very rude Hohenzollern monarch who would soon become an outrage of a man

Queen Sophia Dorothea, a determined, prolific, formidable, and extremely ambitious woman, known with good reason to foreign envoys as Olympia

they seemed compatible; she would bear fourteen children, ten of whom survived. But in other ways they were hopelessly incompatible, living in separate worlds even on those occasions when they were together in the royal palace at Potsdam or in the bleak lodge of Wusterhausen during the hunting season. In Berlin, Sophia maintained her own court, Monbijou, with a niggardly annual allowance of eighty thousand thalers.* Not only did she have to pay normal expenses and provide clothing and linen for the entire family, but she had to pay for gunpowder and shot fired on partridge drives. In return she was allowed to sell any game not eaten at the royal table. Despite her limited budget, she patterned Monbijou after the grand court of her youth, with its predominant and extravagant French influence, its costly objets d'art, and magnificent library. The atmosphere was neither happy nor healthful. Sophia was consumed by ambitions and vanities; she saw herself as mother of both the future Queen of England and King of Prussia, and in trying to bring this about she indulged in constant scheming and intrigue that would have been dangerous even had it been subtle. It was anything but subtle: she could not keep her mouth closed; her confidants and servants were frequently disloyal; and the eventual result was disastrous.

The difference in style between the king and his queen was extreme. At Monbijou and at the palace of Charlottenburg, young Frederick lived in a pseudo-French world. For as long as he could remember he heard not only the virtues of this world, which would increase once he married into the civilized English court; he heard his mother's constant criticism of his father and his father's companions and way of life. In Frederick's early years the contrast between his mother's luxurious court and his father's spartan court must have been very confusing. In time

* This was an age of thalers, crowns, ducats, écus, florins, guilders, livres, and pounds. I have in general used the thaler value because it was similar to that of the crown and écu and because it seemed futile to try to calculate today's dollar value, the more so because the thaler was almost exactly the equivalent in silver content to the much later American silver dollar. The real value of money, however, is what it buys, and here we are on slightly more rewarding ground. In 1730 a loaf of bread cost a few pfennige (ten pfennige = one groschen; thirty groschen = one thaler), a pound of butter cost four groschen, a pound of beef one groschen and six pfennige, two young chickens two groschen and six pfennige, a pound of sugar six groschen, a whole deer three thalers two groschen, and a wild boar four thalers. A wispel of rye, twenty-four bushels, cost twenty-two thalers, a good riding horse two hundred fifty to three hundred thalers or more, a cavalry horse from forty to eighty thalers, an artillery horse around sixty thalers. A collected set of Plutarch's *Lives* (ten volumes) cost ten thalers. So when a regimental commander bought a tall recruit for a thousand thalers, or when King Frederick gave a departing ambassador two thousand thalers, we are talking of a lot of bread, butter, beef, pigs, chickens, deer, and wine (and volumes of Plutarch).

Measures, weights, and distances presented a further problem because this was an age of wispels, roggens, quintals, scheffels, puds, centers, füsse, rute, long German miles, French leagues, and toises. I have converted these into bushels, pounds, American miles, and so on.

he came to understand and accept the difference, and there is no doubt which manner he preferred. At an extremely early age Frederick began to detest the king his father and everything the king his father stood for.

2

FREDERICK WILLIAM, father of Frederick the Great, Elector of Brandenburg and King in Prussia, is a difficult man to characterize: a religious despot who nightly reveled with drunken and loutish cronies (army generals for the most part), who wrote and spoke in the most outlandish and vulgar terms, who washed twelve times a day and changed body linen as often as mind, who increasingly flared into violent and destructive temper and recovered in deep remorse, an iron-handed ruler of two million subjects, a short, fat, and very rude Hohenzollern monarch, who would soon become an outrage of a man.

His parents must share much of the blame for failing to curb his childhood tantrums. His father had been intent only on gaining a kingship, then on enjoying its pomp and circumstance. He was said to have arisen early "so as to prolong his enjoyment of the kingly state"[1]: the splendid court with hundreds of liveried lackeys, elegant carriages, yachts, over a thousand richly caparisoned horses, an army of coachmen, footmen, grooms, huge stud farms, richly uniformed Swiss guards, his own luxurious jackets and velvet cloaks held with gold-and-diamond buttons (and cut to hide a twisted spine — he had been dropped as a child by a careless nurse). His life rarely included the bumptious son, whose education, though carefully prescribed by father, was a matter for governors, subgovernors, and tutors.

Queen Sophia Charlotte, though closer to him, led far too active a life to devote much time to his care and was also much too indulgent to discipline him effectually. His tutor, Lieutenant General Count Alexander von Dohna, was the major influence, though not altogether a healthful one. Frederick William's curriculum embraced reading, writing, arithmetic, and geography, with heavy doses of religion. He was taught primarily in French, but he learned enough Latin to translate at sight from the Bible into French and German. He was also taught the clavier and the flute and was early grounded in rigorous physical and military exercises. Dohna's own position was none too secure, and his constant fear of court cabals, along with his mounting criticism of the king's extravagance, made a deep and unfortunate impression on the young prince. At the age of eight, Frederick William kept a personal account of expenditures. ("So young and such a miser!" his mother complained.)[2] Dohna was also responsible for Frederick William's love of the army, an enthusiasm originally encouraged by the king. As a young man, he spent a considerable part of his considerable income on maintaining a company of young noblemen at Wusterhausen. He was soon given a regiment by his father and spent long hours drilling it to his satisfaction. From it he formed a special company that was composed only of large soldiers, or "big men," variously procured for significant sums. Known as the Crown Prince's Guard, the company was the origin of the Potsdam giants, an obsession that would make him a laughingstock in later life. When not on the parade ground or reveling with regimental cronies, he was in the field shooting stags and wild boars and birds, all of which he slaughtered in prodigious and shocking quantities. The king did not entirely approve of this rough, martial life, and in a few years replaced Dohna with a much more civilized tutor, Major General Count Albrecht Konrad Finck von Finckenstein. The count, a descendant of men who had settled in Prussia centuries earlier, in the days of the Teutonic Order, had served in the Great Elector's army and was the veteran of numerous battles.

By this time Frederick William was a thoroughly rude youngster. He loathed the French language and the graces seemingly inseparable from it, both the language and graces being slavishly respected in his father's court. Women made him nervous, and as he matured, the affliction showed in his coarse and sometimes brutal treatment of them. His mother's gentle admonitions might have rubbed off on him in time, but she died when he was seventeen. The following year, 1706, he married his first cousin Sophia Dorothea of Hanover. He was one year younger than his bride.

Frederick William was twenty-five when he succeeded to the Prussian throne. He had served with the Duke of Marlborough and Prince Eugene of Savoy and had witnessed their famous victory against the French at Malplaquet in 1709. The army had since become his life. It was already acknowledged in other courts that he had "little knowledge of anything but the barracks, and knows no other form of social intercourse but giving and obeying orders."[3] Such harsh criticism was reasonably accurate. His father had spent five million thalers on his own prolonged coronation; Frederick William spent twenty-five hundred thalers and couldn't wait for it to end. He had long since come to regard the army as the touchstone of greatness. He cared nothing for court society or for ministers and diplomacy, and his contempt was solidified by the intrigues and deceits he had witnessed in youth.

In 1713, after giving the king an elaborate and very expensive funeral, he stripped the formal and elegant court to bare essentials and began to prepare for war. "The good days are over," the Saxon envoy informed his court; "now there is talk of imprisonment at hard labor if it is believed — and it is frequently believed — that this or that one is not doing his duty." Frederick William disbanded an ineffective militia, formed seven new regiments of foot, and introduced new and severe military regulations that he believed necessary if he was to build the finest army in Europe. In 1717 a visiting aristocrat wrote from Berlin, "I see here a court that has nothing brilliant and nothing magnificent except its soldiers." [4]

The new king was a short man, less than five feet five inches, but fit and healthy, with a soldierly bearing, a fair and somewhat florid complexion that would not tan, an oval head, high forehead, and slightly bulbous blue eyes. When not in uniform, he wore a simple brown coat with English cuffs and a red waistcoat with a small golden border; a three-cornered hat with narrow golden rim and gold tassels topped a small blond wig; trouser legs were tucked into knee-length boots. At Wusterhausen, his principal hunting lodge, he wore a green shooting suit with a hunting knife strapped to his side, and in cold weather a simple blue cloak. In office and chambers he wore an apron and protective linen sleeve covers.

Early in his reign he acted energetically, quite often effectively. His father had sent grandly dressed ambassadors to the Utrecht peace negotiations to present impressive but improbable Prussian demands. Although Frederick William, like other European members of the Grand Alliance, greatly resented England's secret peace with France, he bowed to reality. England and Wales counted six million subjects and Scotland another million; Habsburg Austria counted ten million; France twenty million. Prussia, with not many more than two million subjects, tenth in size, twelfth in population, was not yet strong enough to call the European tune. The Great Elector, his grandfather, had returned empty-handed from the Saint-Germain negotiations in 1679; his father had returned empty-handed from Ryswick in 1697. The young king now chose to deal directly with France, was willing to take a bone instead of a haunch: a piece of the Upper Gelder instead of the principality of Orange.

This was only a beginning. Frederick William's desire to consolidate, strengthen, and enlarge his kingdom was always evident, indeed understandable, in view of long, exposed borders and rapacious neighbors. Although he maintained a careful neutrality in the Northern War, in 1714 he hastened to exploit the opportunity created by the Russian threat to Swedish Pomerania. By accepting guardianship of that province, he soon brought Prussia into the war. To a friend he explained "that he must absolutely have a foot on the sea in order to participate in world commerce"; moreover, "he would never suffer a foreign power in Germany, be it Sweden, be it France."[5] The next year he refused French mediation, turned his kingdom over to Queen Sophia (while carefully providing for the care of the crown prince), and joined his army at Stralsund, where Prussian, Saxon, Danish, and English forces waged a brilliant and successful campaign against the Swedish army. Prussia eventually won the important Baltic port of Stettin and environs — "the foot on the sea" that the king desired and for which he finally paid Sweden two million crowns.

Every European monarch and petty ruler shared the Prussian king's goal, but few possessed the will to forgo ostentatious luxury in favor of enlarging the army and filling the treasury. Those were Frederick William's priorities. He inherited an army of thirty-eight thousand; by 1719 it would number nearly fifty-seven thousand; by his death in 1740 it would be over eighty-three thousand. He sought strength from other pursuits. He had begun the involved and, as it turned out, immensely prolonged task of Prussian law reform. He concerned himself with important economic ventures. He would bring in thousands of religious refugees, subsidize them, and settle them in wastelands, what he called *wüste Stellen,* which over the years they turned into viable farming communities. He studied Prussian administration and in time introduced sweeping reforms essential to his concept of centralized despotism. He worked like an ox, from five in the morning to late at night. He concerned himself with the minutest details of every aspect of his sprawling kingdom. He traveled frequently, hard, and fast, with the smallest of retinues, often surprising civil officials and military commanders in distant provinces. He built roads, bridges, canals, schools, whole villages, even communities in East Prussia, which had been scourged by famine and plague a few years before his accession. He pared court and administrative expenses to the bone, and his treasury — barrels of silver thalers kept in the basement of the Berlin palace — was soon comfortably expanding, if not yet overflowing.

Unfortunately, Frederick William's defects heavily outweighed his strengths. He suffered a common enough malady, a gigantic inferiority complex, which he sought to hide under a crude, gruff, often cruel manner. When he lost his temper, as he often did, he spared no one. A fit and strong man early in his reign, he was a bully who did not shrink from using physical violence to obtain absolute obedience, at home and abroad, to his will and to his will alone.

Religious bias, combined with authoritarianism, led him to practice a mystical and dualistic concept of government. In his mind the kingdom was not only a being, but an omnipotent being; the individual was completely subordinated to its requirements. Frederick William frequently pointed out that he was a mere mortal, "the first sergeant" of the kingdom, the commander-in-chief and financial adviser to a severe taskmaster that demanded unswerving obedience, a master that drove him to frantic lengths in pursuit of inexorable duty. A subject had no rights, only duties. "No reasoning, obey orders," as he put it. Although he did not physically beat the queen and his generals, he threatened Sophia at least once with imprisonment in fortress Spandau and at least once with death; he either ignored or dismissed errant generals. If his children disobeyed the royal will and were caught, they were beaten. He dismissed wayward ministers and civil officials summarily and without pension, sometimes jailing them for long periods, on occasion arbitrarily hanging them. If the king suspected an ordinary subject of not working hard enough, he was apt to whack him with the "sergeant's cane," a heavy stick he always carried. He had a pathological hatred of idleness. On occasion he would grab a passing woman and harshly order her home, where she should be working; he went so far as to publish a ukase that forced all Berlin market women to spin or weave in idle moments.[6]

Ironically, in view of his mystical ranting about serving the state, he refused personal discipline. He was and he remained the king, a complete autocrat upholding Louis XIV's famous maxim *L'état c'est moi*. In his words: "We are king and master and can do what we like." He once wrote, "I need render account to no one as to the manner in which I conduct my affairs." Momentary passion frequently ruled royal behavior. "What he desires, he desires vehemently," one foreign ambassador succinctly noted; and if he failed to achieve that desire, he reverted to the adult equivalent of childhood tantrums. He could never control his passion for hunting and shooting; he ate and drank far too much, smoked far too many pipes of strong tobacco. He early began to suffer from severe attacks of colic and gout, and his health continued to deteriorate, as did his mind.

Owing to a youth spent in and around formal courts, he loathed foppery in any form, but he erred in confusing it with manners and intellect, often at great cost. Holding that "all learned men are fools," he despised esoteric studies, scorned all art, all books, all paintings, and all science, and whenever possible humiliated the learned members of the Academy of Sciences so proudly founded by his father.

Owing to a loathing of French language and manners, Frederick William made a fetish of being German, and this often blinded him to realities of European politics at a particularly crucial time in Prussian history. His distrust of the Hanoverians, of his uncle King George I of England, and of his cousin, later King George II, further blinded him. Yet the more he leaned toward Emperor Charles VI and the Holy Roman Empire, the more confused and contradictory became his position. As Elector of Brandenburg, he had sworn fealty to the emperor;

as King in Prussia his attempts to mold a powerful and homogeneous kingdom could not but conflict with Austrian insistence on subservient satellites of the Empire.

Owing to his father's dangerous extravagance, Frederick William became the most parsimonious monarch in the world. Having pared court and administrative staffs to the bone, he paid miserable salaries to those who remained, although a few favorites enjoyed enormous incomes. Any reforms that demanded large expenditures were virtually abandoned — legal reforms, for example — because he would not pay sufficient salaries to attract competent and honest judges and advocates. His subjects labored under heavy and inequitable taxes that the nobility for the most part were not required to pay, a common situation in the Europe of the day. In all dealings his motto was *ein Plus machen* (Show a profit). He sold favors with the fervor of a corrupt cardinal, the money going into the army recruiting chest. No official could authorize cash expenditures without the king's personal approval. He normally turned down such requests, sometimes in rude verse form:

> I cannot grant your request,
> I have a hundred thousand people to support.
> I cannot shit money,
> Frederick William, King in Prussia.[7]

Owing to a love of the army, which he deemed necessary both to preserve and to enlarge his kingdom, he built the finest force in Europe, but he made numerous enemies by spending vast sums and by violating neighboring borders in pursuit of the coveted tall men to fill the ranks of the Potsdam Grenadier Guards. No effort was spared to secure these unfortunate brutes. Rulers protested repeatedly, war was threatened more than once, but to little avail. He even tried unsuccessfully to "breed" giants within his kingdom.

Owing to love of power, the king all but excluded civil ministers, including some very able ones, from his immediate court. Those admitted to the royal presence were so intimidated by the monarch's vicious temper, scurrilous innuendoes, and blustering threats that they rarely stood their ground. Frederick William tolerated no cabinet decisions, depended on no single minister. He often annotated ministerial reports and proposals with a rude reprimand and crude drawing of a gallows. Whether in Berlin or Potsdam or Wusterhausen, his "parliament" of cronies, mostly veteran generals of the Rhine and Danube campaigns, met almost every night for the famed Tabaks-Kollegium, or Tabagie, an institution begun by his father during a plague epidemic on the theory that tobacco smoke would ward off the fatal disease. The group puts one in mind of the ancient Goths of Germany who debated everything twice, "once drunk and once sober: — Drunk — that their councils might not want vigor; — and sober — that they might not want discretion."[8] Here among pots of beer and bread, cold meats and cheese, tobacco, pet bear cubs and monkeys, and polluted streams of court gossip, coarse jokes, and childish, often cruel horseplay; here among games of piquet, ombre, and backgammon; here among the sweat and stench of smoking, drinking, belching, farting old men, Frederick William found relaxed contentment while picking those brains he momentarily needed — though what he heard was not often the truth.

These hard-drinking army friends who hunted with the king in the day and gossiped with him until late at night were nearly all feudal aristocrats, each intent on feathering his own nest in the eyrie of the Holy Roman Empire, whose interests frequently coincided with the aristocrats' own. Called the Imperialists, this body of twelve to twenty informal but influential advisers was averse to any form of alliance — political, military, or matrimonial — with England, and if convictions ever wavered, Austrian gold soon appeared to allay any doubt.

Crown Prince Frederick was introduced to the Tabagie at an early age. The king was very proud of the boy's military education and frequently summoned him to the nightly session, where he or one of the elder Prussian generals would put the youngster through army drill.

3

FREDERICK WILLIAM was not a good father to any of his vast brood unless being so was of momentary expedience — to annoy the queen by showing tender affection to Wilhelmina, or to favor another prince in order to make Frederick conform to the royal will. Believing that children should be rarely seen and almost never heard, he insisted that his own be raised in *bürgerlich,* or middle-class, style, and not have their heads filled with royal affectations. Something of his parental attitude emerges in a letter written to Prince Leopold of Anhalt-Dessau, who himself had several daughters, after Princess Louise Ulrica's birth in 1720: "It is the time of girls, and yesterday another one came into the world. I will establish a convent for which my dear prince could also furnish some nuns — one must either drown them or make nuns out of them. They certainly won't all get husbands." He was slightly more tolerant of his sons, but only as long as each conformed to his image of a proper prince. Even as an infant Frederick did not often conform, and he was not very old when he began to develop his love-hate relationship with the king.

The basis of this unpleasant and incredibly sad relationship is not too difficult to understand. To a king, a crown prince was often more a necessity than a desire. Frederick was vital to the survival of the House of Hohenzollern. Necessity is also easier to resent than desire. Throughout history kings have resented princes: Irish kings used to blind their sons to prevent being tumbled from their thrones. Turkish sultans locked their sons in cages to prevent their becoming contaminated by court plots, a universal danger fervently expressed by Brutus:

> And therefore think him as a serpent's egg,
> Which, hatch'd, would, as his kind, grow mischievous,
> And kill him in the shell.[1]

If a crown prince was a necessary extension of ego, he was even more an object of scrutiny, even more the dough to be molded into the father's loaf. To the physically strong and bellicose Prussian king, Frederick seemed a gross insult, a sickly joke. The father could not tolerate the child's weakness and frequent illnesses, and he constantly ranted, raved, and shouted at this misbegotten spawn who one day would steal *his* crown from *his* head.

Frederick faced increasing paternal fury as he grew into early childhood. His father often stormed into the nursery or had the child brought to him to examine as if he were some sort of backward worm. The king was never satisfied; as the infant grew, his dissatisfaction increased. He soon began to manhandle the prince royal, cuffing and poking him, and when this drew only tortured silence and a casting down of brimming eyes, the king would shout and hurl abuse and blows while demanding that Frederick speak up. But Frederick only trembled until the storm blew over or until he escaped the royal presence. Wilhelmina observed many of these scenes and later recalled that "the king could not bear my brother; he abused him whenever he laid eyes on him, so that Frederick became obsessed with a fear of him which persisted even after he had reached the age of reason."

The relationship deteriorated further as the king continued to press the dough to his own mold. He put his son into uniform at the age of five. Characteristically, in a day when other princelings wore colonel's rank in the cradle, the Crown Prince of Prussia became a mere noncommissioned officer charged with drilling a group of nobles his own age. That year he learned the fifty-four movements that constituted the Prussian drill, and he also began to master the Lutheran catechism. He attended military reviews at the king's side, and on Sundays marched his cadet corps to church. When one day the king saw his son beating a toy drum, he became so excited at this martial display that he summoned the court painter, Antoine Pesne, to record the scene.

When Frederick was seven the king turned over his education to two trusted soldiers. Named as governor was sixty-six-year-old Lieutenant

General Count Finck von Finckenstein, who had tutored Frederick William. As subgovernor the king appointed Colonel Christoph von Kalkstein, a young Swedish officer whom he had encountered at the battle of Malplaquet, and who subsequently entered Prussian service. He was thirty-six, a man of cultivated taste and education, but, according to Wilhelmina, also "coarse and violent." As civil tutor the king named a thirty-year-old French Huguenot, Jacques Egide Duhan de Jandun, whose intelligence and bravery had impressed him at the siege of Stralsund.*

Frederick William's "Instructions" to Count von Finckenstein have survived; they were based on his own father's lengthy instructions for Frederick William's education, but with significant changes. The count was to supervise a regimen that would ensure proper moral, mental, and physical upbringing. Crown Prince Frederick would arise early; in the king's opinion, too much sleep made children dumb. Religious education was paramount: "My son together with all his servants will start and end the day by saying prayers on their knees . . . followed by reading a chapter from the Bible." Frederick would learn to revere, esteem, and obey his parents and to feel "brotherly love" and "perfect confidence" toward his father. The king wished his son to be submissive but not servile. More curiously, "You are to make him afraid of his mother, but of me, never." He must be impressed with a proper love and fear of God "as the foundation and only basis of our temporal and eternal welfare." He was to have nothing to do with such false religions as atheism, Arianism, Socinianism, which are absurd and "which can so easily corrupt a young mind. . . . On the other hand, a proper abhorrence of Papistry and insight into its baselessness and nonsense is to be communicated to him." He was not to waste time learning Latin. Ancient history was also *verboten*, "except very superficially." In Frederick William's quaint phrase, his son and heir was not to be educated to be "a king of yesterday."[2]

He was to learn to speak French and German "clearly and purely" and to write them with "a concise and elegant style." Nothing is more suitable and necessary for a great prince than to speak effectively "in a clear and pure accent"; he was to learn early "to inspire an army to a vigorous action." He was to study arithmetic, mathematics, geography, gunnery, and domestic economy from the ground up; also "contemporary history, and the history of the last hundred and fifty years is to be taught most carefully . . . particularly the history of his House, for which purpose the library and archives will be at his disposal, be-

---

* "It is rare," Frederick noted sardonically, "to engage a tutor in a trench." (Frederick the Great, *Oeuvres*, Volume 2, *Histoire de mon temps*, hereafter *Oeuvres*, Volume 2, *Histoire de mon temps*.)

cause a family example is always more impressive than a foreign one."
He was to learn the history of those Houses to which his own was
bound, such as England, Brunswick, Hesse.

In time his military education would become paramount. Once started
in mathematics and drawing, he was to learn what was necessary of
fortification, formation of camps, and other branches of military science "so that the prince, from childhood on, will act as officer and
general." Even more ominously, the king charged the military tutors
"in the highest measure to instill into my son a true love for the military
profession, and impress on him that nothing in the world can give a
prince such fame and honor as the sword, and that he would be the
most despicable creature on earth if he did not revere it and seek true
glory from it."

The governors were to pay careful attention to the prince's moral
habits. Frederick William had already perceived the six-year-old crown
prince's "inflated pride and the tendency for extravagance." As for expensive vanities, operas, plays, and other "dissipations," the tutors were
to "inspire him with disgust of them." He was not to be flattered; he
would be addressed as simply as possible and would learn all the virtues of modesty and humility. In 1718 his privy purse amounted to an
annual 360 thalers; in the next ten years it would grow to a niggardly
six hundred thalers, and every groschen had to be accounted for to the
king. Frederick was to learn "the greatest disgust possible" for laziness,
"one of the greatest of all vices." His tutors were never to leave him
alone, and they were to be very careful concerning the company he
kept. "Above all he was to be shielded from the depravity of whoring
and lust, which often came at puberty, failing which the governors
would pay with their heads."[3]

These rigorous instructions do not seem to have been so rigorously
carried out. Count Finckenstein not only wisely tempered them, but
won the crown prince's affection in the process. Frederick went often
to the count's mansion to play with his sons, who were about his age;
the friendships would extend to later years. Frederick also seems to
have liked Colonel von Kalkstein, whom he later referred to as "my
master, Kalkstein." But his real friend and confidant was Jacques Duhan, a sensitive and intelligent teacher, who, like Wilhelmina, soon
became a dominant influence in Frederick's youth.

At first all went reasonably well. Early reports from Finckenstein to the
king showed Frederick in a favorable light. He was earnestly studying,
he rode, drilled his cadet company, went shooting. Frederick had started
to write the king letters when he was five, a habit his tutors encouraged. Now he proudly reported that his cadets had shot well; he re-

warded them with a barrel of beer; he killed a hare, felled his first partridge. He complemented such news items with little missives, a few of which have survived. At the age of eight he submitted a treatise, "Rule of Life for a Prince of High Birth," which began: "His heart must be upright, his religion that of the Reformed Church; he must fear God in a particular manner, not like common people who do it for money or worldly goods. He must love his father and mother; he must be grateful."[4] It continued with an evangelical zeal that presumably brought tears of paternal delight. In a friend's *Album Amicorium* — a friendship diary — he loftily wrote in French above his signature: "The beginning of wisdom is the fear of God."* The king signaled his satisfaction on Frederick's ninth birthday by presenting him with a specially fitted room in the Berlin palace, a private armory holding every conceivable weapon and intended for the boy's enjoyment and further education.

The king's pleasure was short-lived. Frederick's outpourings should not have been taken so seriously. They represented much more what his tutors wanted the king to read than what the prince knew or believed or enjoyed. For Frederick's major influences remained Wilhemina and Duhan. Wilhemina represented Monbijou, Mummy, and Hanoverian aristocracy, and she continued to scorn the king's primitive manner of living. Duhan from the outset defied royal orders. He cut short tiresome religious sessions to teach his ward Greek and Roman classics; Frederick learned to read Italian and even a little Latin, a language expressly forbidden by the king. Together they read Fénelon's *Télémaque* and other romantic classics of the time, an excursion seriously at odds with the rules laid down by his father, who had informed Duhan that "the history of the Greeks and Romans is to be done away with; it can serve no useful purpose." Finckenstein and Kalkstein must have known of these and other violations. The king had some notion of them. On one occasion he caught Frederick reading Latin, a crime defended by a subtutor, who said it was necessary if the Prince was to understand the Bulla Aurea, or Golden Bull, the charter of Empire signed in 1356. In a fury the king characteristically snarled, "I'll Golden Bull you," beat the hapless man, then discharged him.[5] But the lessons continued.

Royal opposition served only to produce an atmosphere of conspiracy that intensified as the royal temper worsened. Despite the favorable signs alleged by Finckenstein, Frederick already loathed all that his father stood for, particularly the rude atmosphere of the Tabagie and the wanton slaughter of birds and animals. Instead, he had grown to love

*The entry is dated October 21, and on the reverse side Count Finckenstein certified that it was written and signed by the crown prince. (British Museum, Additional Manuscripts, 27310.)

These portraits of Crown Princess Wilhelmina at seven years of age and Crown Prince Frederick at age four were only recently identified in Buckingham Palace, where they had been hanging for over two and a half centuries. Charles Whitworth, the British ambassador in Berlin who commissioned them, reported in 1716, "The Prince gives very great hopes, both as to his temper and person, and the eldest Princess is one of the finest children I ever saw."

Le commencement de sagesse, est la crainte de l'Eternel.

Berlin le 21 d'Octobre

Friderich Prince Roial de Prusse

"The beginning of wisdom is the fear of God." — Crown Prince Frederick to an unknown friend, 1720

French literature and, in the tradition of his paternal grandfather and his mother, most things French. Influenced by Duhan, he adopted French mannerisms, spoke only that language except when his father forced him to speak German, and combed his hair in foppish fashion — "like a cockatoo," Frederick William complained.[6] Duhan later smuggled French clothes to the royal apartments, "soft silk robes, touching the floor like women's dresses."[7] He helped the prince begin a private library that in time would hold nearly four thousand volumes of eclectic, generally forbidden works; they were kept secretly in a house rented by the tutor. He bought his ward a flute and taught him how to play it. Frederick soon preferred it to the clavier. On royal hunts he carried it in his game bag and would sneak off to find a secluded glen in which to play it; he also preferred playing duets with one of his cadet non-commissioned officers to drilling with his company. Frederick William loathed these habits. "Fritz is a flute player and poet," he grumbled to his rowdy companions of the Tabagie.[8]

The king could find no harsher criticism to levy. A flute player and a poet was not what he had in mind as a successor, and he now set about to correct his son's errant ways.

4

BERLIN, 1723. The prime minister of Saxony, Field Marshal Count Karl Flemming, described it as a border fortress where everyone, soldiers and civilians, spoke only of military matters, "of march and countermarch, of file and rank." The king, he noted, was very gifted and highly intelligent but lacked the true principles of a monarch and ruled more by fear than affection. The eleven-year-old crown prince, he went on, "shows spirit, and although he is not as inclined toward the military profession as his father, he adapts himself to it in order to please the king."[1] Later that year King George of England visited Berlin and watched the crown prince, his grandson, drill the cadet corps of three hundred young aristocrats. George was "extremely well pleased with His Royal Highness's behavior, which was highly admired."[2]

But Frederick had already grown to prefer infinitely his mother's court, where the king could not so easily block the horizons of learning opened by Jacques Duhan, and where he was surrounded by people who openly mocked the king's pleasures. At Potsdam and Wusterhausen he opted whenever possible for Wilhelmina's company in preference to the hunt. He would play the flute, she the lyre, his *principesse* wooing her *principe,* a musical duet with Freudian overtones. By this time the two youngsters realized that they were becoming pawns in the struggle between Austria and Great Britain to win and hold the Prussian alliance; and if they did not yet understand the many nuances of the struggle, they could not fail to recognize the intrigues that filled the separate courts of their parents. In self-defense they played together, read together, invented mocking tales that poked fun at the king and his ministers, for whom they used private and pejorative names. At table they fidgeted and grimaced, giggled at private jokes. This was adolescent nonsense, a rudimentary flutter of the wings, incipient rebellion familiar to any parent.

Unfortunately Frederick William read it as patent disloyalty. He had for some years suspected that an international plot existed to kidnap and murder him, a fear that partially explains his weird tantrums.* Inept in European diplomacy, which was particularly complicated at this time, he transferred his frustrations to family, especially to the crown prince. Count Ulrich von Suhm, the Saxon envoy in Berlin, reported an extraordinary scene at a dinner in early 1724. The king suddenly pointed to the prince royal and told an intimate: "I should like very much to know what is passing in that little head. I know that he does not think as I do. There are people who try to instill quite contrary ideas into his head and encourage him to find fault with all that I do; they are scoundrels!" Having worked himself into mild fury, he turned to his son: "Fritz, listen carefully! Always maintain a good and large army; you can have no better friend, and without that friend you cannot stand. Our neighbors desire nothing so much as to see us topple. I know their intentions; you will learn to know them. Take my word for it; do not think of vanities; hold on to the real. Keep a good army and plenty of money. In those two things lie the glory and security of a prince." As he started this Hohenzollern exhortation, he began giving the boy little taps on the cheek, and as he continued talking these grew harder and harder, until at the end they were just short of blows.[3]

In the spring of 1725 a visiting nobleman and distinguished diplomat and general from Vienna, Count Friedrich Heinrich von Seckendorff, described Frederick William's own demanding schedule to his court and added that Crown Prince Frederick, despite his thirteen years, "had to follow this same regimen, and even though the king loves him dearly, he so tires him with early rising and constant activity through the day that he, despite his youth, looks old and stiff and walks as if he already were a veteran of numerous military campaigns." Although the visitor

---

* A Hungarian nobleman and *agent provocateur,* Clement, exposed an Austrian plot to kidnap Frederick William. This was fraudulent, and Clement was arrested, tried, and hanged in 1720.

understood the king's intention, it was obvious that "this way of life was opposed to the crown prince's inclination and would in time exercise exactly the contrary effect, because the crown prince's temperament is directed more on generosity, neatness, comfort and luxury, and he is also disinterested, liberal and compassionate." The writer had witnessed young Frederick receiving cash gifts from the burghers of Magdeburg and Stassfurth and forthwith turning the gold coins over to the poor.[4]

Not surprisingly, the severe routine did not have the effect desired by the king. Frederick cared no more than formerly for vigorous and robust sports. He preferred arts and sciences and the company of those versed in higher learning. His foppish ways continued to enrage the king, who on one occasion beat him for using a three-pronged silver fork instead of the standard two-pronged steel instrument. That autumn the king in a state of alarm issued new "Instructions" to Finckenstein and Kalkstein to see that their ward followed a daily schedule that would wean him from slothful ways. Thenceforth Frederick was awakened daily at six A.M. to say "private prayers" as laid down by the king. He dressed, washed without soap, and breakfasted by six-thirty. While he drank tea, a barber queued his hair without powder. Duhan then arrived to lead the young prince and servants in biblical readings and hymns for fifteen minutes. Another fifteen minutes went to private discussion with Frederick on "important problems of Christianity." Lessons followed until ten, when a Lutheran minister arrived to teach an hour of Christian religion. At eleven Frederick washed his hands, this time with soap, put on his uniform and reported to the king for dinner and a two-hour discussion. Three more hours of lessons followed, then physical exercise, usually riding or drilling, later fencing and swimming, at times long hunts in cold weather. After a short rest he supped, bade the king good night, said public prayers in front of the servants, and was asleep by ten-thirty. If he behaved to the king's pleasure, which he rarely seemed to do, he earned a half holiday on Wednesdays. On Sundays he rose at seven and escaped lessons but had to accompany the king to church.[5]

The stern course served only to increase Frederick's rebellion. More quarrels and beatings ensued. Count Konrad Alexander von Rothenburg, the French envoy in Berlin, would shortly report to his court "the alienation between father and son," which he feared "will increase still further."[6]

A large part of Frederick William's bad temper resulted from inept diplomacy. For some years he had been wrestling with the problem of alliance. On the one hand were the advantages to be gained from friendship with Austria. He was after all an elector of the Holy Roman Empire and owed certain fealty to Emperor Charles VI. But Charles, who was said to be serious even when he laughed, was in the uncomfortable position of having bred no surviving male heirs. Indeed, for some time he had bred nothing, but finally in 1717 a daughter, Maria Theresa, was born and survived. In an attempt to change Empire rules, he had some years earlier drawn up a document, called the Pragmatic Sanction, that would guarantee the Imperial succession to his daughter, and for years his emissaries had been hawking the document about Europe like demented insurance salesmen. A historian has called the Pragmatic Sanction "the cardinal error of his life," and he was right.[7] Prince Eugene of Savoy would have scrapped it in favor of a filled treasury and a good army. Charles could gain acceptance of the document from other rulers only by yielding on major political issues. It seemed to Frederick William that, as his father had been rewarded by being named King in Prussia for alliance at a crucial time, so now he should be rewarded by Imperial recognition of Prussian claims to two Rhenish duchies, Juliers and Berg — a recognition he fruitlessly sought up to his death. Most members of the Tabagie favored Prussian alliance with Austria.

On the other hand, Frederick William was related by blood to the Hanoverian and English courts and saw numerous advantages in an alliance with England, to which he was spiritually tied by the Protestant faith — particularly if that could be cemented by marrying his children into the English royal family and if the English court would guarantee Prussian claims not only to Juliers and Berg, but also to East Frisia and Mecklenburg. This was the union so heartily wished by the queen and by the "English party" at her court, of whom the important members were the ranking minister of foreign affairs, Baron Friedrich Ernst von Knyphausen; the English envoy Brigadier Dubourgay; and the French envoy Count Rothenburg.

The situation spelled unavoidable conflict. The Vienna court could not tolerate the thought of these Protestant Houses, Brandenburg-Prussia and Hanover, being further united. They had already allied in the War of the Spanish Succession, and had found common interest in the Northern War. If subsequent developments in the Baltic had caused a rift, it was on the verge of being healed by a diplomatic effort on England's part, an effort welcomed by Frederick William. The Austrian court correctly read this as a challenge, not only to Imperial supremacy, but perhaps even to Imperial survival.

For several years Frederick William had vacillated, but in 1725 Austria unexpectedly made peace with Spain. The treaty was announced in only general terms and led to intense speculation on its secret clauses, and with justification. France and England in particular were incensed with Spain's guarantee of Austrian trading privileges, which could easily lead to war. Rumors of another alliance, between Austria, Sweden, and Russia — the last two about to make war on Denmark — in return for Russia joining the Austrian-Spanish alliance, further confused the situation. Frederick William was as usual caught in the middle, dreading the religious implications of the Austrian alliance with Spain (a new Catholic League?), yet reluctant to trust either England or France.

At this crucial juncture General Count von Seckendorff arrived in Berlin from Vienna with orders from the emperor and Prince Eugene to win over the wavering Frederick William — cost what it may. Seckendorff, one of the most refreshing if unscrupulous diplomats (and certainly one of the most unfortunate generals) in European history, was fifty-three, short but ramrod straight, a North German Protestant who had been in Saxon service and was now in Austrian service. According to an acquaintance, Baron Karl Ludwig von Pöllnitz, a courtly gadabout of racy memoir fame, Seckendorff was "the most ambitious, most self-seeking, most presumptuous man in the world." He had served ably and bravely as co-commander of the Saxon army during the siege and capture of Stralsund, where he had greatly impressed King Frederick William, and where he and General Friedrich Wilhelm Grumbkow had become friends. The Prussian king had given him a valuable diamond ring for service in that campaign, and they remained in correspondence, the king unfailingly offering Seckendorff his "everlasting favor and friendship." Worldly and knowledgeable, thrifty, hardworking, and deeply religious, Seckendorff had struck common ground, his curiously hoarse voice vigorously defending the virtues of Protestantism and warning of dangers inherent in French expansionism — subjects only too dear to Frederick William. In 1717 the king wrote to congratulate him on taking his regiment into the field in Hungary: "You will shoot Turks while I shoot partridges." He had visited Potsdam in 1716 and again in 1723, when he was probably responsible for the resumption of diplomatic relations between Austria and Prussia. In the king's eyes the count was a true *Biedermann* — a man of honor — and now in 1725 Seckendorff quickly became a favorite. This was a somewhat exhausting experience: "Whoever spends a few weeks at this court and is constantly around its king," he complained to Prince Eugene, "can never be sufficiently astonished over the many alterations, resolutions, projects, fears, hopes, and various emotions." Recovering from "the unbelievable and unnecessary exertions" back at his Meuselwitz estate, he described to Eugene how he had attempted to assuage royal doubts of Imperial resolutions, and he also described Frederick William's thinking on a variety of sensitive subjects — very sound intelligence reports buttressed by personal observation of court, army, and economy, and by collaboration with General Grumbkow. In return for Grumbkow's continued cooperation, Seckendorff paid him thousands of thalers per year on behalf of the Vienna court, as well as additional sums to support what in time would become a formidable army of spies, informants, and *provocateurs*. Count von Seckendorff's popularity increased to the degree that, according to the English envoy, the king asked him to leave Austrian service and become a Prussian field marshal.[8]

But Frederick William's fear of increasing Austrian power, which among other things would jeopardize his claim to Juliers and Berg, continued to override Seckendorff's influence. England had agreed to accept the Prussian claim to the two duchies, and the French court was prepared to follow suit. Frederick William now believed that his best protection lay in strengthening the 1723 alliance with England. In September 1725, he traveled to Hanover, where his uncle and father-in-law King George I was then visiting, to discuss in detail the new threat caused by the Austrian-Spanish alliance. The two monarchs got on well, and George was a splendid host: Frederick William put on another two inches of stomach during his brief stay. A series of conferences shared by Prussian ministers and senior French ministers produced the League of Hanover — a triple alliance of Great Britain, France, and Prussia, which Holland, Sweden, and Denmark would soon be asked to join. The League was essentially defensive, each power guaranteeing the other's possessions and rights both in and out of Europe. It was, the Prussian king thought, a "safe" treaty, since it would not involve him in imbroglios from which he could expect no profit. The most important article, from his standpoint, was secret and confirmed the validity of his claim to Juliers and Berg.

Never very strong, the foundations underlying the League of Hanover soon began to crumble. Scarcely were the signatures dry on the parchment than Frederick William was besieged by dragons of doubt. A very big dragon was the much discussed marriage of his daughter Wilhelmina to Prince Frederick of Hanover, the English king's grandson. The Danish envoy, General Paul von Løvenørn, reported to his court that the Prussian king "will move heaven and earth to have a date set and the contract of marriage signed before the King of England returns to England."[9] King George, however, would put nothing in writing. Although it was believed that he had given his daughter, Queen Sophia of Prussia, positive assurances for both marriages — Wilhelmina's and Crown Prince Frederick's — he could not guarantee them without consent of Parliament, a consent that he was not ready to solicit.

Another dragon was the possible result of Frederick William's rash diplomacy. Baron Rüdiger d'Ilgen, his veteran minister of foreign affairs, objected to the treaty because he felt the risks outweighed advantages. Was the king not forsaking his sworn loyalty to emperor and

Empire? Did the king want his authority to be used to further English and Dutch commercial aspirations by attacking the Ostend Company — the trading company of Emperor Charles VI — and seizing Austrian ships, or by defending Gottorp on behalf of the weak King of Denmark? Were France and England not *using* the Prussian king to advance their own interests? Suppose that Austria went to war with the League: England was safe behind the Channel, France safe behind the elaborate belt of fortresses built by Marquis Sébastien de Vauban, the brilliant military engineer of Louis XIV. Only Brandenburg-Prussia lay open to invasion. And what if the Habsburgs were overthrown? Would a French or even an English emperor reign instead?

These and other doubts were swirling furiously through the king's tortured mind when Seckendorff again appeared in Berlin in the spring of 1726, his mission being "to influence the king and lead him to better thoughts, which must be accomplished naturally and not forced." [10]

Warmly welcomed, Seckendorff soon discovered that the king was frightened to death of war and had severe doubts that his allies in the Treaty of Hanover would adequately support him. His relations with his own family were worse than ever, and he could trust no one.

Here the king had another legitimate grievance, albeit one brought about by his own brutal behavior. As usual, political uncertainty had caused him to turn his wrath against his son. But Frederick was fourteen now, in many ways a very weary fourteen, and he had launched a counterattack. In late May, Count Rothenburg reported to the Versailles court that "the crown prince is loading me with favors and . . . told me a few days ago that he would give an exact account of all that the king his father said." The envoy added, "I shall be careful to commit myself to nothing, however precocious and cunning this young prince may be." Queen Sophia, who had been sending secret letters to her father and to her sister-in-law all along through Dubourgay's couriers, now also confided state secrets to Count Rothenburg in an effort to enlist him in her cause. She would shortly startle him by confiding the "measures which, in her opinion, should be taken if the king were to die mad." [11]

In short, Seckendorff found a bubbling pot of political and family dissension, to which he quickly added his own subtle but powerful ingredients to move the harassed king farther from England and France, convincing him that King George had no intention of letting the marriages take place. He soon converted Frederick William to the Austrian cause, at least enough so that the king stated his grievances, particularly the matter of Juliers and Berg, which the Vienna court promised to straighten out. Seckendorff's line was ably seconded by General Grumbkow, already in Austrian pay; by Baron d'Ilgen, whom Seckendorff had also bribed; and, indeed, by nearly everyone in the king's court, for Seckendorff was spending a great deal of money to enlist supporters. "It is inconceivable," Dubourgay reported to England, "in what an abject manner everybody in this place courts Seckendorff's favor and friendship. Even persons that one thought proof against any temptations by their known attachment to the queen cannot forbear falling in with the crowd."[12] In August, Seckendorff wrote to the emperor that he would need "substantial gifts" for d'Ilgen, Knyphausen, and Grumbkow should the treaty materialize, and tall men for four of Frederick William's favorite generals and colonels. He already had asked for tall men for the Prussian king, and now he wanted a letter authorizing the king to recruit giants in Austrian territories.

The upshot of Seckendorff's campaign was a political volte-face by Frederick William. Despite the most stringent efforts on the part of the queen, the Prussian king signed a new treaty with Austria that October. The Treaty of Wusterhausen was purely defensive, with each party guaranteeing the succession of the other's crown and pledging a certain number of troops in case the other signatory was attacked. The essence of the treaty was that in return for Prussia's guarantee of the Pragmatic Sanction, the emperor would do his utmost to uphold the Prussian claim on the Rhenish duchies, a claim reluctantly shaded by Frederick William, who agreed that after the death of the Elector Palatine, Juliers would go to the Prince of Sulzbach, Berg and Ravenstein to Prussia. Neither Seckendorff nor anyone else could totally allay Frederick William's suspicions concerning the Vienna court's sincerity, and the Prussian king carefully stipulated that the treaty would not be ratified until the Palatine-Sulzbach faction gave its agreement to this clause, which it had to do within six months. If it did not, then the entire alliance was null and void. Softening this ultimatum, however, was the king's obvious desire to abandon England and France in favor of an alliance with Austria.

5

CROWN PRINCE FREDERICK did not take kindly to his father's new alliance. He looked forward to marrying Princess Emily, not so much for the reasons pounded into him by his mother but rather as escape from his father's brutal treatment. Relations between them had continued to deteriorate. In that autumn of 1726 the fourteen-year-old heir had been confined to Potsdam for rigorous studies and discipline. Even his menu was prescribed: he was served a "frugal" table — "at noon a soup using no more than two pounds of meat, a fricassee, or fish, and then a roast, likewise for the evening meal."[1]

Frederick still showed Rothenburg his favor, reporting whenever possible all that came his way, including numerous proposals by Seckendorff and Grumbkow designed to win him to the Imperialist side. Rothenburg, who had no love for Frederick William — he once declared that he would rather become a Carthusian monk than remain long at the Prussian court, and he had been trying to get himself recalled for some years — had begun to form a third force. "The king is absolutely hated by every class in his kingdom," he reported inaccurately to Versailles. "In order to disarm the father we must form a party for the crown prince and attach a number of officers to him. . . . I think such a plan ought to succeed. In any case we should be fostering in the young prince views favorable to France."[2]

The French court enthusiastically endorsed Rothenburg's plan, and Frederick remained so enthusiastic over the traitorous relationship that Rothenburg had to caution him "to maintain great reserve" to avoid compromising himself. The envoy pretended never to speak to him, using Knyphausen, who was in French pay, as a go-between. He soon reported "a perfect understanding" between Frederick and Knyphausen; his own secret relationship prospered to such an extent "that I can already make use of his name to flatter or intimidate our friends and our enemies." Rothenburg sincerely believed that Prussia was on the verge of revolution, and he thought that its king would be declared insane and interned in a fortress.[3] Some evidence exists to show that Frederick and the queen shared this view, which certainly would have been an exciting prospect to the harassed heir.

Rothenburg extended his counterattack in late November. In a long and candid audience he laid some cards on the table, telling the king that he "was so beset by persons who infused into him notions directly contrary to his true Interest and Honor, that those who had both sincerely at heart could seldom get opportunity of approaching him, and confuting the idle Stories they invented to alienate him from his true friends." Dubourgay, who reported the scene, added that "I am told from a very sure hand that His Prussian Majesty stay'd alone in his Closet an hour and a half after Count [Rothenburg's] Audience, his head leaning all the time upon his hand, and full of the deepest thought, and afterwards he sent for his chief ministers, with whom he conferr'd a long time."[4]

Seckendorff was aware of this audience, and also of the queen's incessant arguments against the Austrian alliance, arguments listened to by the king for a reason more mercenary than political. Sophia's mother, the luckless Princess of Ahlden, had died and left her a considerable sum, reportedly over a million crowns. Frederick William desperately wanted this money and was trying to sweet-talk the queen out of it. In early December Seckendorff complained to his court that the queen "has more influence than ever; the king makes a great deal of her." Nonetheless, Seckendorff stuck close by the king through most of December, reassuring him that the emperor was doing everything possible to settle the Berg affair in Prussia's favor. He also made sure that the king heard rumblings of a palace revolution, and to further exacerbate the suspicions of the harried ruler, he had Grumbkow send Frederick William anonymous letters suggesting that "the queen was making him a cuckold, and that a plan was on foot to carry him off, imprison him, and place the crown prince upon the throne." Confronted with the letters, the queen easily proved her innocence, but Frederick William held "a great fear of those letters, and especially of the one that spoke of the crown prince." *

Seckendorff ended the year on a successful if exhausted note. He had rewarded Grumbkow with another bribe, an annual pension of a thousand ducats, and shortly afterward obtained an Imperial medal set with diamonds for the court jester Jakob Gundling. Now he was going to his nearby estate to recover from a surfeit of suppers that lasted late into the night, night after night, "not without excesses." [5]

The struggle for Frederick William's allegiance continued throughout 1727, first one side, then the other, gaining the upper hand. Queen Sophia remained a powerful influence — the king was still trying to get his hands on her inheritance — and was opposing Grumbkow so violently that in case of a revolution or the king's death, Seckendorff feared for the man's life; he went so far as to ask the emperor secretly to commission Grumbkow a lieutenant general in the Imperial army in case he required protection. As for himself, "My countenance is so hated by the queen that only with the greatest effort will she answer me at table." [6]

Seckendorff returned to Berlin in early February with a double mission. He was first to persuade the king to accept a protracted delay in the Berg negotiations, since the six-month period was rapidly running out. Should negotiations prove fruitless, Seckendorff was to employ his "usual discretion and dexterity" in persuading the king to accept an equivalent territory, perhaps the duchy of Kurland, perhaps lands that bordered Brandenburg-Prussia, which, considering the enmity between Austria and England, "from all appearance were about to become enemy lands." [7]

---

*Along with the earlier Clement affair, this was the genesis of the alleged "plot" that would emerge a few years later with such violent repercussions.

Frederick William received the envoy as warmly as usual and assured him that he had remained loyal to the emperor during Seckendorff's absence. The dragons of doubt were nonetheless still present. Seckendorff shortly reported that "the queen and crown prince have in part so intimidated the ministers, in part won them, that only Borcke remains patriotic." Seckendorff at once began putting matters right, bribing here, entertaining there. He needed more money, because once a week he had to entertain the Potsdam Guards officers, who, "being young, strong, and big, and being paid very little by the king, ate and drank voraciously — they would consume forty to fifty bottles of wine in an evening." The king always joined these parties, sometimes staying until midnight and usually drinking to excess. After one such evening Seckendorff noted, "I am not able to write much today."[8]

Nonetheless court affairs were so unsettled that Seckendorff waited until mid-February to bring up the notion of a territorial equivalent for Berg. He met with instant rebuff, particularly when it came to a substitution of lands that could be acquired by war, "for should war occur then in all conscience he [Frederick William] must receive further satisfaction [that is, territory]."[9]

War between England and Austria seemed imminent. Friction occasioned by overseas trade had caused an open rupture between England and Spain, followed by the Spanish siege of Gibraltar. England blamed Austria in large part for fomenting the crisis, and also accused the Vienna and Madrid courts of supporting a new Jacobite movement. This led to a diplomatic rupture with Vienna. To exacerbate the situation, both England and Holland insisted that the emperor close down his overseas trading company, the Ostend Company, under threat of his vessels' being seized wherever found.

The crisis put Frederick William in two minds. He was secretly delighted that the Vienna and London courts now approached him for support, yet at the same time he was frightened that war would cost him more than he would gain. Accordingly, he turned momentary broker by submitting a compromise peace plan to the involved powers. No one paid much attention to it, and in the event it was eclipsed by French mediation. But it is interesting because it called for the electors to maintain the peace of Germany. These princes, including the Elector of Hanover (King George) and the Elector of Bavaria (Charles Albert), were to declare neutrality "whereby a Third League," as the king personally explained to Dubourgay, "a kind of Moderator would be established between the Allies of Hanover and Vienna."[10]

Although the London court seemed to favor the plan, King George delayed a reply until consulting his allies, France and Holland. Their refusal to accept any such scheme greatly upset Frederick William. Meanwhile, Seckendorff, assisted by Grumbkow, Borcke, and many

minions, continued his propaganda drive, which included new promises concerning the duchy of Berg. In late March, Dubourgay glumly
reported that the Prussian king seemed determined "to joyn in the closest Measures with the Emperor, and to try all manner of ways to dis-
unite His [Britannic] Majesty and France."[11] The situation had worsened, Dubourgay warned, to the degree that Austria and Prussia were
considering an attack on Hanover. Frederick William was now keen to
march for the emperor's cause, Seckendorff reported at the end of March,
and had it not been for d'Ilgen's unwavering protests, "we would have
seen Prussian troops on the bank of the Elbe."[12]

At this crucial point Czarina Catherine I of Russia died, leaving affairs to a council of regents that would rule until Peter the Great's
twelve-year-old grandson ascended the throne as Peter II. It placed
Frederick William in another quandary. Unexpected events always upset the Prussian monarch, but Russia posed a particularly unsettling
enigma, and the czarina's death only added to his fears. Unable to pin
them down, much less master them, he smothered them in ill temper,
which worsened after a quarrel with August II, King of Poland and
also Elector of Saxony, over the arrest of a Prussian noncommissioned
officer for illegally recruiting soldiers in Saxony. The Vienna court did
not help matters: the six-month grace period had expired, and he was
no closer to having an Imperial guarantee to Berg.

It was not a good time for one who detested "complicated arrangements," for now England's first minister, Sir Robert Walpole, brought
about a peace of sorts between England and Austria. This spelled an
end, at least temporarily, to Frederick William's bargaining powers and
plunged him into deepest grief.

Another calamity followed: King George unexpectedly died. Only a
few months earlier Queen Sophia's mother had died, and now her father suddenly went — some said he was the victim of a curse. Despite
recent setbacks to the marriage alliance, Sophia was convinced that this
summer in Hanover she would have overcome her father's final doubts
and attained royal assent for the marriages. Now there would have to
be new and undoubtedly prolonged and unpleasant negotiations with
her brother, already crowned George II.

If Sophia grieved, Frederick William was shattered, even bursting
into tears in the presence of the British envoy. He had lost an anchor.
Deep within, he seems to have understood that Prussia's proper destiny
would have been realized through the League of Hanover, and he apparently believed, as Dubourgay reported, that his uncle, the English
king, would eventually have welcomed him back to the fold. But that
hope had suddenly vanished, and he was left to deal with George II,
his forty-four-year-old cousin, whom he despised. The antipathy was
mutual, reaching back to childhood at Schloss Herrenhausen. Though

five years younger than George August, Frederick William had been bigger and stronger and had once settled a quarrel by giving him a bloody nose, an act never forgotten by George and one that had caused Grandmother Sophia to banish her ragamuffin grandson back to the barbaric Berlin court. Frederick William later resented George's successful courtship of the beautiful Princess Caroline of Ansbach, who had refused to take him seriously. Time had not repaired hard feelings. Frederick William scornfully referred to the somewhat foppish George as "my brother the dancing master"; George in turn contemptuously called the Prussian king "my brother the drill sergeant."[13]

The combined weight of these vicissitudes proved too heavy for Frederick William. For years illness had succeeded illness, the inevitable result of his having abused body and mind by adhering to a schedule that would have killed most men. As early as the spring of 1725 Seckendorff had warned Prince Eugene that "according to all human calculations" the Prussian king could not live much longer. "From morning until late at night he is constantly active, from the early hours his mind is taxed with a host of different problems followed by unbelievably fatiguing rides, drives, walks, and talks, stuffs himself with heavy foods and strong drink (though not yet to the point of debauchery), sleeps little and at the same time restlessly, which taken with his vehement nature excites him to such a degree that in time evil results will probably follow." The Saxon envoy, Count von Suhm, pinpointed the mental problem. The Prussian king, who refused to rely on subordinates to run the affairs of state, was so occupied with petty details that he often forgot general policy concepts, both internal and foreign; when details conflicted with policy he was apt to change his mind and alter earlier orders, depending on the subject and his temper of the moment. His impulsive decisions, based on conflicting notions and false facts, so exhausted and hampered his thought processes "that he floated in a perpetual irresolution with no fixed notion on anything."[14]

The king sought refuge in heavier and heavier drinking bouts, enthusiastically encouraged by Seckendorff and Grumbkow. He had become so gross that three soldiers had to help him mount his horse. Wilhelmina described his step as so heavy "that it always sounded as if he wore thick boots." Heavy nightly drinking merely compounded painful bouts of colic (indigestion) and gout, not to mention incipient apoplexy and dropsy, the whole resulting in what Wilhelmina termed "severe nervous attacks," which were checked only in part by doses of ipecacuanha. These were manifested by bizarre, often violent actions, usually followed by long spells of profound melancholy. Now in spring of 1727 he entered into such a spell, and it was scarcely lessened by the black mourning garb of the entire court, nobility and servants, which created a constant atmosphere of Stygian gloom.

At this perigee of his reign the king took even more extremely to religion. His new vessel of belief was an old acquaintance, August Herman Francke, follower of Pietism, forerunner of Methodism. He had founded a model orphanage at Halle and believed "in the power of Grace combined with an understanding of the value of rational education and action." This was all dear to Frederick William's heart and he installed the sixty-year-old Francke at court. Wilhelmina later described the new regimen:

> This clergyman delighted in making scruples of conscience respecting the most innocent actions. He condemned every diversion, even hunting and music, as damnable. Nothing was to be spoken of but the word of God; any other discourse was prohibited. It was always he who acted the fine speaker at table, where he performed the office of lecturer, as in the dining room of convents. The King preached a sermon to us every afternoon; his valet began to sing a hymn, in which we all joined; we were forced to listen to this sermon with as much attention as if it had been that of an apostle. My brother [Frederick] and I were often inclined to laugh, and sometimes we could not help bursting out. But we were instantly overwhelmed with all the anathemas of the church, to which we were obliged to attend with a contrite and penitent air, which we found it difficult to affect. In short, the tedious Francke made us live like the monks of La Trappe.

Frederick William was so carried away by this religious wave that he spoke seriously of abandoning all earthly cares and abdicating in favor of the crown prince. At thirty-nine he was talking like King Lear:

> . . . 'tis our fast intent
> To shake all cares and business from our age;
> Conferring them on younger strengths, while we
> Unburthen'd crawl toward death.[15]

6

ALTHOUGH THE KING continued to grumble about the cares of monarchy, he had no real intention of abdicating in favor of his eldest son. Nearly everything about the young man, going on sixteen, displeased his father. Frederick's idle, effeminate ways had continued, and his seeming rejection of "manly virtues" was sufficient to have caused the royal fury. But added to that was the growth of his mind and his intense love of learning. His private and secret library was rapidly growing. He had personally catalogued it in the previous year, and the record shows that he was reading books by Descartes, Bayle, Locke, and Voltaire.

The prince was well on his way to becoming one of those "learned men" so despised by the king. Only recently Frederick William had summoned Lieutenant von Borcke and three other young officer-companions of Frederick and in his son's presence informed them that his son "had reached a dangerous age, and one which was subject to every bad inclination." The four officers were ordered "to keep an eye upon his conduct." They would answer "with their heads for the smallest excess or breach of propriety from which they had not turned the prince," warned the king.[1]

By January 1728 the rupture between father and son had become so serious that Frederick was not included in the royal party that departed for the Dresden carnival, guests of August II, King of Poland and Elector of Saxony. Although Frederick William had little use for August, whom he called the "clothes peg," Seckendorff and Grumbkow had suggested that a change would raise his spirits and also improve relations with neighboring Saxony.

The carnival promised to be exciting. King August was a man of many parts and almost no self-discipline. "He rushed from one exciting occupation to another," wrote the noted nineteenth-century German historian Leopold von Ranke, "from pleasure to pleasure, without the least regard to duty or to dignity; he delighted in a mixture of power and licentiousness." He ran the most lavish and sensual court in the German empire, a "voluptuous court in which the relations of the sexes were emancipated from all restraint and decorum."[2]

Large, cheerful, and robust, August at fifty-five was fast deteriorating but retained gargantuan appetites for women, wine, and food, in that order. He had sired 354 bastards, of whom he acknowledged only ten. This prolonged procreative effort, combined with immense physical strength — he liked to snap horseshoes with one hand — had earned him the appropriate soubriquet August the Strong. In pursuing one conquest he threw a bag of gold coins at the target's feet followed by pieces of a horseshoe to show that his strength was as great as his generosity. Told that the Duke d'Orléans had died in the arms of a voluptuous mistress, August sighed, "Ah, that I may die in this way." At a court as opulent as the Berlin court was spartan, he surrounded himself with favorites, whom he seduced when not engaged in drunken orgies. He was also famous for prodigious expenditures that would have shamed even Frederick William's profligate father, and news of his lavish preparations for the Prussian royal visit had early traveled to European courts. Dubourgay reported an expenditure of no less than 200,000 crowns: "Besides Italian comedians sent from Prague, Balls,

Masquerades and Hunting Matches, all other Diversions that can be thought of will be pursued on this occasion with the Elegance and Magnificence for which that Court is so renowned."[3]

No wonder young Frederick was sulking in Potsdam, where by royal order he would continue his studies and prayers. His complaints, however, reached Wilhelmina, who interceded with the Saxon envoy on her brother's behalf. Dubourgay duly reported that Count Flemming, the Saxon prime minister, who met the king outside Dresden, "finding that the Prince Royal was not with him, made such earnest instances that young Prince might partake of the Diversions preparing at Dresden . . . that His Prussian Majesty was prevailed upon to send immediately an estaffete to Potsdam with orders to the Prince to come to Berlin and after having got Cloathes made with all possible diligence to set out for Dresden."[4]

A surprised and delighted Frederick soon found himself in a new world of dashing courtiers and beautiful courtesans, tables elegantly laid with crystal, silver, and gold, lackeys by the score to serve exotic dishes and wines, lavish balls and splendid musicales and operas and elaborate military demonstrations complemented by all manner of royal sport, such as animal baiting (sows, foxes, and badgers being the luckless victims). His exuberance is clear in a letter to Wilhelmina written shortly after his arrival:

> Dearest Sister: In spite of so many diversions I think of you constantly and shall not forget you until I die. But wait . . . what do you want to hear about? The great world? Good. The King of Poland is of average height. He has very heavy eyebrows and a slight pug nose. He walks well, despite his lameness. He has esprit, is polite to everybody, and has considerable urbanity . . . is difficult to understand, particularly as he has lost so many teeth. Nevertheless his appearance is good and he is physically agile; he dances and does other things, just like a young man.

After describing the electoral prince and princess and offering the family tree of August's various bastards, Frederick continued:

> I have been heard as a musician. Richter, Buffardin, Quantz, Pisendel, and Weiss played with me. I admire them. They are the best artists at the Court. . . . Today Tartuffe is being played. I am about to go. Farewell. Love me as I love you. . . . I love you so much that I would gladly surrender my place to you . . .

Frederick was obviously interested in the "other things" that he mentioned. "The fair, white Saxon women," wrote Baron Pöllnitz, "have the most beautiful faces in the world. Most of them have fine figures, which is what strikes one most. . . . They are tall and slender, they

The famed Tabagie, begun by King Frederick I during a plague epidemic in the belief that tobacco smoke would keep the fatal germs from spreading

Both daughter and mistress of King Augustus, Countess Anna Orzelska was a raven-haired beauty who frequently dressed in male riding clothes. Crown Prince Frederick fell in love with her at the Dresden carnival of 1728.

dance well, dress richly, are lively and playful, gentle, but cunning and shrewd. . . . A separate volume would be necessary to describe all the amusements at Dresden."[5]

Frederick quickly turned to one of these amusements. The Polish king's favorite mistress of the moment was one of his illegitimate daughters, Countess Anna Orzelska, whose mother was a French milliner in Warsaw. The young countess had become the mistress of a soldier, Count Friedrich Rutowsky, one of August's bastards. In flamboyant disregard of incest but admirable display of fealty, Rutowsky brought her to court and recommended her charms to his royal master! A raven-haired beauty, the countess indulged in a number of idiosyncrasies, one of which was to dress frequently in male riding clothes. Whatever the costume, Frederick fell in love with her. His attentions, apparently reciprocated (she was understandably aware of future possibilities), aroused royal envy. But August, far too regal for awkward confrontation and in any event an excellent host, one night after dinner guided Frederick William and the crown prince to a beautifully decorated private salon. At a silent signal a servant rolled up a couch of velvet holding a girl, one Formera, whose natural beauty was enhanced by total nakedness. Frederick William at once rudely pushed his son from the room and later had Grumbkow inform August that another such incident would cause him to leave Dresden.

Frederick scorned his father's spoilsport attitude. What took place between the young prince, Countess Orzelska, and her intended replacement is not known with certainty, but smoke there was and, if Wilhelmina is to be believed, fire as well. Apparently the crown prince, as planned by August, transferred his affection to the lovely and willing Formera. Considering his age, inclinations, and later ways, he may also have found entertainment with young courtiers; the court was lascivious enough, and homosexuality common enough, to have readily permitted it.

So exciting was the Dresden air that even Frederick William began to loosen the moral stranglehold earlier maintained on his son. Dubourgay, who had spies at Dresden, reported at the end of January: "Yesterday upon leaving the comedy, the King and Prince Royal of Prussia went to . . . a masquerade ball, supper and dancing. Everything transpired with good order and plenty of magnificence, the dance continuing until three A.M. The King of Prussia excused himself from dining . . . retired early, and charged the Prince his son to look after the ladies, which he did admirably. The Prince by his soft manners and polish has endeared himself to everyone."[6] "Everyone" included the jaded Polish king, who having regained Countess Orzelska, rewarded Frederick with the Order of the Saxon Eagle, whose diamonds alone made it a particularly worthwhile decoration.

Father and son greatly enjoyed their Dresden stay and for once seem to have got along without rancor. The king's letters at times sound like Montesquieu's *Persian Letters:* he was greatly impressed, as he soon informed Seckendorff, with the magnificent and warm reception given him by August and the electoral prince and princess, all three of whom he liked very much; the magnificence of the court easily rivaled that of Versailles.

He and August, after numerous conferences, which may have included discussion of August's marrying Wilhelmina, signed a treaty of mutual defense, and Frederick William invited the Polish king to pay him a state visit that spring. When he discovered that August planned to arrive in Berlin with only a male entourage, he immediately protested, and the breaker of horseshoes finally agreed to bring "the Ladies."

Wilhelmina later wrote that "the king my father left Dresden highly satisfied with his journey, as likewise was my brother. They were both equally zealous in launching out before us in praise of the King of Poland and his court." The visit apparently gave Frederick William a new sense of his own importance, a desire to stand more on his own feet instead of being kicked around by such powers as Austria and England. But the euphoria occasioned by the *dolce vita* soon wore off as the king faced the usual problems: another Saxon protest against illegal recruiting; Sophia's increasingly serious quarrels with Seckendorff; her intercepted messages to Dubourgay, evidence of a disloyalty that caused Frederick William to warn her "that the loss of a wife should not be considered as at all more serious than that of a hollow tooth, which only hurts when it is extracted, but of which, a moment later, one is thankful to be free."[7]

The brief rapprochement with his son also soon ended. Prodded constantly by the queen, Frederick was again being argumentative and otherwise difficult; this time he fell into "a gloomy melancholy" that was accompanied by loss of weight, poor color, and fainting fits. According to Wilhelmina, her brother attributed his sorrow to the ill treatment he received from the king. In her opinion he was lovesick. "He had taken a fancy to dissipation since his visit to Dresden, and the poverty in which he was kept prevented him from indulging in it." In early April, however, his lassitude gave way to a serious illness and high fever that brought Dr. Stahl to Potsdam "in great haste."

Professor Georg Ernst Stahl of the University of Halle had revived the theory of animism, which he explained at great length in his book *Theoria medica vera* of 1708:

Illness was a salutary effort on the part of the soul to expel morbid matter from the body. . . . The supreme vital principle was represented by the universal soul, which was the cause of every form of life and came direct from God. When the soul left the body on death the body putrefied. Illness was the tendency of the soul (which became identified with nature) to re-establish order in bodily functions.[8]

After the usual treatment — bloodletting, emetics, enemas, and scores of pills — Stahl declared the prince out of danger but insisted on prolonged rest and regular diet. The intermittent fever, "generally preceded by a coolness in his hands and feet" and usually provoking nausea, persisted throughout April, and his condition at times grew very serious. Evidence is meager on which to base diagnosis. According to a Baron Johann Georg Zimmermann, a physician who first examined Frederick many years later, the prince had acquired a venereal disease that eventually led to a mutilation of the penis and sexual impotency, thus possibly explaining his later negative attitude toward women — a convenient theory embraced by at least two modern writers.[9] But there is no proof of this and considerable contrary evidence. Wilhelmina noted before April that Frederick frequently fainted, but this is not a symptom of venereal disease, nor did the king suggest it in a confidential letter to his close friend Prince Leopold of Anhalt-Dessau that described symptoms of consumption. None of the foreign envoys — Suhm, Dubourgay, or Rothenburg, each of whom usually had at least one royal physician in his pay — suggested anything of the sort to his court. The timing is also wrong; a chancre sufficiently toxic to need excision would not have appeared so soon. Frederick's subsequent love affair with Madame von Wreech (whom he allegedly made pregnant) and his frank comments to Grumbkow on women, sex, and marriage are scarcely compatible with sexual impotence.*

It seems more likely that a harsh regimen, extreme dissipation, and supreme melancholy had lowered his never strong resistance. Suhm reported to the Saxon court that Dr. Stahl, when reproached by the king for not curing the crown prince, replied that he could not cure in fifteen days an illness that had taken two years to come on.

Whatever the exact disease, it caused a sharp reversal in the king's attitude. Wilhelmina noted that "the king upbraided himself for having thrown his son into his present deplorable situation by numerous sorrows and vexations to which he had subjected him; and he endeavored to atone for the past by lavishing his caresses and kindness upon him."

---

* Zimmermann's charges have been demolished by Gaston Vorberg, among other authorities. Vorberg cites two sources who investigated the charges in detail at the time. Frederick's corpse was seen by more than twelve people, none of whom reported any mutilation. Four surgeons attended to the washing of the body. One of them, Gottlieb Engel, who had also attended the king during his last illness, later swore to Anton Büsching that Frederick's genitals were as completely normal as those of any other healthy man. (Vorberg, *Klatsch*.)

The king wrote to Prince Leopold that one must of course submit to God's will, but nevertheless "it is hard now that I perhaps could enjoy the fruit, since he begins to be reasonable, and must lose him in the flowering. Still, it is God's will. . . . When one's children are well, one does not know that one loves them." About two weeks after this sentimental effusion the king told Leopold that "my son walks around like a shadow and eats nothing; judging from experience I regard him as finished unless this shortly changes." A few days later the king reported an improvement, and Frederick was soon out of danger, though he faced a lengthy recuperation.

Frederick was still recovering when the Polish royal party descended on Berlin in the spring of 1728. August's entourage of three hundred included three countesses with servants, ten German princes, ministers (counts and barons), and cavaliers (knights), all with servants, and twenty-six court personnel, including a chaplain, two surgeons, six lackeys, four members of the royal bodyguard, six chefs, one *échanson* or wine cup bearer with assistant, one valet of silver plate, and three pastry cooks. The Polish prince royal's suite of another two hundred included numerous pages and lackeys, a tailor, a master of wigs, two chasseurs, eight coachmen and postilions, fifteen personal servants, ten Polish cavaliers, five German cavaliers, four privy secretaries, three palace officials, and additional coachmen, postilions, and a great many horses. To feed this horde the royal hunting master had to provide the kitchens *each day* with six deer, two grown and two young wild boars, six roebucks, twenty old and twenty young hares, forty wild ducks plus heathcocks, blackcocks, hazel hens, partridges, and woodcocks.[10]

King August was recovering from dangerously abscessed legs and was carried about in a sedan embroidered with velvet and chased with gold. He was extremely impressed with Frederick William's gigantic Potsdam Grenadiers, especially the file leader, Hohmann, who was over seven feet tall; he otherwise admired the Prussian king's vast collection of gold and silver objets d'art, which included enormous silver chandeliers from Augsburg, each of which had cost ten thousand thalers. Wilhelmina, whose curiosity was overflowing because of Frederick's tales and the talk of her own possible marriage to the Polish king, noted his "majestic presence," enhanced by "kindness and civility," but found him "much broken" for his years, the result of *les débauches terribles*. Nonetheless August threw himself into the "diversions" until his legs swelled so badly that he was confined to his apartments.

Crown Prince Frederick missed the earlier celebrations but did come to Berlin to assist at the general military review — a performance of some sixteen thousand troops at Templehof field — only to fall ill again. He recovered sufficiently to visit secretly Countess Orzelska, whose encouraging reception, according to Wilhelmina, completely cured him. Of more lasting influence were three fine musicians from the Dresden court, the German composer and lute virtuoso, Silvius Leopold Weiss; the first flautist, Pierre Gabriel Buffardin; and his student, Johann Joachim Quantz, who would soon become Frederick's personal teacher and who would in time compose some three hundred flute concertos for him.

The diversions ended in early June, and August departed after grandly presenting twenty-seven thousand thalers, "besides jewels to a very considerable value," to various courtiers. The two monarchs parted on ostensibly friendly terms, August having been very complimentary about the Prussian army. At Frederick William's invitation he left behind one of his bastards, Count Maurice (who would become the famous Marshal of Saxony), to study it further.

7

YOUNG FREDERICK'S illness and recuperation were followed by another severe decline in his relationship with the king. Characteristically, part of the trouble stemmed from the turbulent political situation. Seckendorff and Grumbkow had spent the spring and summer trying to bring the king closer to the Austrian alliance, but their blandishments had had only limited effect. In this autumn of 1728 the King of Prussia was as usual torn between loyalty to Austria and reconciliation with England. Friendship with the emperor had as yet earned him nothing and had caused a virtual rupture between the Potsdam and Versailles courts; Rothenburg had been recalled that summer and was not replaced by another ambassador. Rumors of peace further disturbed his mind, since general peace would vitiate the emperor's need for his support.

All the old issues between father and son had reasserted themselves, and new ones, like debauchery, possibly including homosexual relations with at least one companion, had cropped up. Frederick had adopted a royal page, Peter Christoph Karl von Keith, from whom he "soon became inseparable," Wilhelmina wrote. "Keith was intelligent, but without education. He served my brother from feelings of real devotion, and kept him informed of all the King's actions. . . . Though I had noticed that he was on more familiar terms with this page than was proper in his position, I did not know how intimate the friendship was." *

Religion had also caused quarrels. The chaplain charged with Frederick's religious instruction had attempted to steer clear of predestination, but Frederick was too intellectually adroit not to pursue it on his own, and he probably baited his father by reference to such forbidden works as Jacques Basnage's *Histoire de la religion des églises réformées.* Seckendorff's suggestion of a grand tour of Europe had also prompted an argument; the king refused to hear of it. The crown prince became so depressed that in July Rothenburg reported: "I have reason to believe that he is thinking of making his escape. I have been aware on previous occasions that the idea had crossed his mind." [1]

Matters came to a head that autumn at Wusterhausen, the "house in the desert" that Wilhelmina sarcastically described as a castle

> surrounded by moat and ramparts. The water in the moat was as black as the Styx. . . . There were two wings to the main building, each guarded by two black and two white eagles. The sentries consisted of ten or twelve large bears, who walked about on their hind legs, their front paws having been cut off. . . . We always dined in a tent, whatever the weather might be. Sometimes when it rained we sat up to our ankles in water. The dinner always numbered twenty-four persons, half of whom had to starve, for there were never more than six dishes served, and these were so meager that one hungry being might easily have eaten them up alone.

Despite her usual exaggeration, Wilhelmina had a point. For next to the army on the royal pedestal stood hunting, and not very comfortable hunting. The mildest form, in which even the queen joined, took place in spring and autumn around Potsdam, where falcons beat up to intercept giant herons, four to one, the victims being retrieved by the royal *Falkenmeister,* who grandly presented them to the king. The king and his chums rode to the hunt; the guests were carried in long, open "sausage wagons," each holding sixteen or twenty people. Eyewitness accounts of these outings describe a relatively harmless sport, which, with a huge fire, crisp clear weather, and roasting oxen, may have been enjoyable.

Far more rigorous were the wild boar hunts, generally held in Pomerania after the Berlin winter carnival. A hunt would begin at five A.M., when one rode or was hauled in an open wagon ten to fifteen miles to where an enormous square trap had been erected. Two or three hundred wild boars, some of them five or six hundred pounds, would be driven into this large enclosed area for dispatch by two-man teams armed with boar spears and hunting knives. The king was gored more than

---

* Just what is meant is open to question. Keith does not appear to have been physically attractive; he was described as slender, thin, somewhat pale, with light brown hair and a severe squint. (Koser, *Kronprinz.*)

once in this sport, as were many of his fellows. The hunt often lasted until late afternoon, and over the season thousands of boars were killed; four thousand in a few weeks was not uncommon. Typically the king sought profit from slaughter: tradesmen and others were forced to buy quantities of the meat. Shamefully he forced wealthy Orthodox Jewish merchants in Berlin to buy entire carcasses, which they donated to the king's hospital.

The real hunting chapter, however, was written at Wusterhausen, where without fail in late August the entire court retired for two months. Here the king maintained a pack of one hundred hounds managed by twelve huntsmen, each of whom had his own horse, which cost only thirty-five or forty thalers, since it was apt to be run to death.

The season normally began with a large partridge shoot, the feathered victims having been brought in from all over the kingdom. The king, accompanied by falconer and loader, shot daily. A contemporary observer, David Fassmann, recorded one day's bag as 160 partridges, nine hares, four pheasants, and a screech owl so beautiful that the king had its portrait painted. His personal bag in the autumn shoot amounted to about four thousand birds. The main event, however, was the *Parforcejagd,* the hunting of stags while riding to hounds. On such days the king ate dinner at nine in the morning and carried cold food; on occasion he hunted early and delayed dinner until midafternoon, much to Sophia's annoyance. A large stag hunt always marked the anniversary of the battle of Malplaquet. The participants returned to dine accompanied by the entire *Hautboist* band, with the huntsmen blowing horns while outside a cannon boomed. Large glasses of drink passed from hand to hand, and the occasion ended with the king dancing with old generals and other officers.

Crown Prince Frederick had always loathed Wusterhausen. The only sizable room, the smoking room, was reserved for the nightly Tabagie. At meals when the king was present, the crown prince and Wilhelmina sat quietly; when the king was hunting, however, Frederick became most unruly, tormenting the drunken old jester, Gundling, and being rude to other guests. He and the younger princes and princesses occupied tiny garret rooms. The house was so small that it was difficult to avoid either the king or his hearty, generally drunken companions. The perpetual hunting, shooting, and nightly drinking bored Frederick to death. During this miserable autumn of 1728 he unburdened himself to his confidant and possible lover, Lieutenant Friedrich von Borcke, to whom he frequently wrote. "Tomorrow I am obliged to hunt," he complained in one letter; "the next day is Sunday, and on Monday I am obliged to hunt again." As for the court: "We have here the most idiotic collection of people of all sorts and kinds, and ill-assorted, for neither the tempers, nor the ages, nor the inclinations of those who compose it agree, which prevents any connected conversation." Life was a matter of passing time: "I got up at five o'clock this morning, and it is now midnight. I am so weary of all that I see that I should like to efface it from my memory, as though it had never been." He held little hope for escape. Travel prospects were at a standstill: "We are not only making no headway, but we are losing ground." He found refuge only in books, flute, and friends: "Nobody loves and esteems you as I do. . . . Give me in return half the friendship I bear you." And again: "My wearisome affection breaks from me and discloses to you the feelings of a heart filled with you, and which cannot be satisfied save in knowing that you are fully convinced of the tender friendship with which it adores you."

Nor was the king easy to escape. "The king," Frederick told Borcke, "continues in a bad temper; he scolds everybody, is pleased with no one, not even with himself. . . . He is still terribly angry with me." Later he complained, "We have accursed scenes here every day; I am so tired of them that I had rather beg my bread than live any longer on this footing."[2]

Frederick was not being melodramatic. So vile had the relationship become that he wrote his father a formal, very subservient letter, complaining among other things that the king seemed to hate him. The reply was equally formal and referred to Frederick in the third person:

> He has a willful and wicked disposition; he does not love his father. A son who loves his father does the will of that father, not only in his presence, but also when he is not there to see. He knows perfectly well that I cannot endure an effeminate boy, who is without a single manly inclination, who cannot ride, nor shoot, and who, into the bargain, is dirty in his person, never has his hair cut, and curls it like an idiot. A fine gentleman, withal, haughty, never speaking to anyone except one or two people, not affable, and not popular. He makes grimaces with his face, as though he were mad. He does my will in nothing except under compulsion. He does nothing from filial love. He has no pleasure but to follow his own head. That is my answer.[3]

By early October the prolonged and unsatisfactory Vienna negotiations had thrown the Prussian king "into frequent fits of ill humor," as Dubourgay reported to London, "not to say violent passions, which all those about him, great and little, feel the effects of most severely."[4] The burning question concerned the emperor's guarantee of the duchy of Berg to Prussia. Even Seckendorff's honeyed words and Grumbkow's constant assurance of Austrian fidelity could not smooth over the Vienna court's dilatory and generally noncommittal responses. Once again the Prussian king began to suspect that the emperor was merely "amusing" him; he therefore would give Charles a worry by looking to England. He struck on the characteristically awkward device of or-

dering Sophia to write to the queen of England to find out what the
British monarchs intended in relation to the match between the Prince
of Wales and the Princess Royal of Prussia.

Frederick William at once felt better for having forced Sophia to
send this unusual and, from the standpoint of protocol, insulting demand to the English court. His son also mollified him in a somewhat
macabre scene at a dinner described in detail by Count Ulrich von Suhm,
the Saxon envoy, who sat next to the crown prince. Frederick as usual
complained about "the bondage in which he lived" and begged Suhm
to obtain King August's intercession and persuade his father to let him
travel. He drank more than usual, his voice rising as he recited his
myriad sufferings. Ignoring his mother's warning hisses, he kept looking at the king, interrupting his tirade to say "I love him nevertheless."
The frightened queen left the table, but Frederick, on taking leave of
the king, grasped the royal hand and covered it with kisses, then threw
his arms around the king's neck and sat in his lap while the guests
cheered. Embarrassed but obviously delighted, Frederick William gently
pushed him away. "Enough," he said, "enough. Only be an honest
lad."[5]

Shortly after this emotional scene, the king and crown prince visited
old Prince Leopold in Dessau. Frederick William's temper was further
softened by a favorable reply from Queen Caroline to Sophia's letter.
"I at once forwarded it to the king," Caroline wrote, "who to me appears very disposed for the marriage that you propose."[6] Frederick
also continued to behave himself. He wrote Prince Leopold a polite
thank-you letter, and when the old warrior sent him a riding horse and
some of his famous hounds as gifts, Frederick responded in terms that
would have done Nimrod proud. The situation improved even more in
December, when King George suddenly summoned *his* Frederick, Prince
of Wales, from exile in Hanover to the London court. This long overdue move may have resulted from a plan of the twenty-one-year-old
heir to elope with Wilhelmina, but more probably the English monarch
was forced to it by parliamentary rumblings.

Alas, all was in vain!

Queen Sophia and the English Party once again had underrated
Seckendorff's shrewd and effective diplomacy, which now, to nearly
everyone's astonishment, resulted in a new treaty with Austria, an
"eternal alliance" that was signed shortly before Christmas. It essentially reconfirmed the 1726 Treaty of Wusterhausen, and it placed Prussia
politically in Austria's orbit.

Still another shock awaited. By Christmas the Prussian king was again
wavering; he had "a thousand scruples" concerning the planned marriages, Dubourgay reported. One was the cost of the prince royal's
future court, another the amount of Wilhelmina's dowry. Frederick
William had sounded out the crown prince concerning Princess Caro-

line (Emily's younger sister, whose youth would delay the marriage), "but His Royal Highness broke out into such raptures of love and passion for the Princess Emily and shews so much impatience for the Conclusion of that Marriage, as gave the King of Prussia a great deal of Surprise and the Queen as much Satisfaction. The great and good Qualities of that young Prince, both of Person and Mind, deserve a distinct and particular account which I shall trouble Your Lordship with another day."[7]

8

DESPITE Queen Sophia's most forceful arguments, hammered home during several violent scenes, the king was now unalterably opposed to the marriages. As Baron Knyphausen pointed out, the king's ill humor was "occasioned by nothing else but His Prussian Majesty's covetousness, and his jealousy of the Prince Royal, who he conceives will be in some measure independent of him when married, the thought of which he cannot bear."[1]

The king continued to treat his son so harshly that Wilhelmina later felt no compunction in frankly describing events at Potsdam, where her father was suffering a violent attack of gout. "I was called nothing else by him but the 'English *canaille,*' and he ill treated me and my brother in a shocking manner. We were not allowed to leave him for one single moment during the whole day. We took all our meals near his bedside, and to torment us still more he let us have only those things to eat for which we had an absolute dislike." On one occasion he threw a full plate of food at Frederick; on another he chased both children in his wheelchair, cursing and trying vainly to strike them with his crutches. Dubourgay reported still another quarrel, when the king grabbed his son by the throat, and servants had to separate them. The incident made Frederick ill, but his father insisted on his hunting the next day, "and would not permit him, though in this severe cold weather, to be as warmly clad as the meanest of his Peasants is. God be praised, it did His Royal Highness no harm."[2] Frederick became so desperate to escape the kingdom that he sent Count von Finckenstein to Dubourgay with a secret message for the English monarchs, whom he begged to do everything possible to help him marry Princess Emily.

The crown prince gained some relief in mid-February, when the king fell ill again. This time his "Fit of Phrenzy [temporary insanity] . . . lasted so long, and was so very violent, that all about him were afraid he would never come to his right Senses again."[3] Recuperation lasted until early spring, but though the body healed, the temper did not. In one more attempt to reform his wayward son he appointed a forty-year-old lieutenant colonel, Friedrich Wilhelm von Rochow, as Frederick's *Hofmeister,* or chamberlain, and Lieutenant Baron Dietrich von Keyserling as master of horse. Although Rochow was a serious type, Dubourgay reported, Keyserling was a well-educated and widely traveled "young Gentleman of parts and good breeding" — a "lively" young man, the king called him.[4] In mid-March the king sent Rochow detailed instructions in his new capacity as "companion and friend" to Frederick. These covered again all the old grievances — the prince's frivolity, fecklessness, idleness, arrogance, and even disloyalty, not to mention his "effeminate, lascivious, and womanly activities."[5]

Meanwhile the battle for the Prussian king's alliance continued between Austria and England. For every step forward, the English party suffered two in reverse. Frederick William had finally decided to send Colonel von Kalkstein, Frederick's former subtutor, to London as envoy. Kalkstein was a staunch member of the English party; Borcke also had come around, having been bribed, and was now favoring the same party. As always, however, Count von Seckendorff was on hand to sabotage any such gains. Supported by quantities of Austrian gold, he continued to plant doubt and suspicion in the royal mind. His weapons until this point had been powerful enough, but now he unveiled a secret weapon, the Prussian resident secretary in London, one Benjamin Reichenbach, "a Person," as the important British minister Lord Townshend had earlier complained, "whose Behaviour is such, that neither the [English] King nor his Ministers can put the least confidence in him."[6] Reichenbach was a paid agent of Seckendorff and Grumbkow. For some time he had been reporting to the Prussian king what his employers told him to report. English archives contain copies of over forty of his letters, the originals of which were found in Grumbkow's effects. They were generally long, written in French, and employ a simple number code. They showed the three principals — Grumbkow, Reichenbach, and Seckendorff — to be extremely intelligent, at home in the classics, and complete masters of the Prussian king. They shed considerable light on the king's ambivalent behavior during this entire crucial period, particularly in his relationship with Grumbkow. They were highly incriminating and frequently treacherous. Grumbkow and Seckendorff furnished information, in part true and confidential, to Reichenbach, who exploited it in two ways: first, by furnishing confidential and controversial information to the opposition party in Parliament, thus stirring up trouble for King George; second, by reporting information to the Prussian king that could only exacerbate affairs in his court and enhance Austria's position.[7]

Here was a first-rate intelligence operation that already had proven effective. When Frederick William was on the point of accepting an English compromise regarding the marriages, Reichenbach reported "that the making of the Mariages was earnestly wished in England, and that he had been told our [English] Court proposed thereby to be reconciled with the Emperor through His Prussian Majesty's Mediation." Frederick William at once had greedily proposed new conditions that were to accompany any marriage agreement. These extraneous additions were unacceptable to King George, who now backed off from the affair. In turn, Frederick William canceled Kalkstein's assignment, and when George refused to submit the problem of Mecklenburg to a concert of states, the Prussian king threatened to call off the marriages altogether.

In less than a month, however, Frederick William was again favoring the marriages and was excited when King George arrived in Hanover, from where he at once summoned Dubourgay. But Dubourgay no more had reached the splendor of Schloss Herrenhausen when a new crisis exploded, one caused by Prussian recruiting. Prussian recruiting officers illegally at work in Hanover had been arrested and would not be released until ten Hanoverians who had recently been impressed into the Prussian army were freed. Frederick William, who learned of the arrests from newspapers and not through diplomatic channels, lost his temper and immediately ordered preparations for the Prussian army to march. To his surprise and even greater fury, various allies, such as King August, not only failed to respond to his martial cry but, as Dubourgay reported, pointed out that this was a "Quarrel which his Prussian Majesty had drawn upon himself by Practices contrary to the Laws and Constitutions of the Empire."[8]

Frederick William nonetheless seemed determined to have his war. In ensuing weeks orders went out to purchase horses for the heavy cannon, procure blacksmiths for work on artillery carriages, grind corn for magazines, and all the other measures necessary to put his army on the march. Dubourgay reported that the king would spend over 600,000 thalers in the first stages of mobilization; the Danish envoy reported that he had just returned from parade, "where everything breathes war"; a few days later he wrote that "preparations for war are redoubled from one day to the next."[9]

The crisis had driven the king into violent fits of rage. Queen Sophia confided to Dubourgay that for seven nights he had restlessly prowled "from Bed to Bed and from Chamber to Chamber like One whose Brains were turned and that at last He took a sudden Resolution to go to Wusterhausen at Two o Clock in the Morning, saying he hoped to find there a little Rest and Sleep. That on his Return he gave himself up entirely to Drink and was almost continually drunk, in which Condition he used to do such things as confirmed People more than ever in their Apprehensions." He was treating Frederick and Wilhelmina so brutally "that the Queen is in continued Fear of what may happen. The King will not suffer the Prince Royal to sit next to Him at Table, but obliges him to sit at the lower End where Things are so ordered that the poor Prince often rises without getting one Bit, insomuch that the Queen was obliged two Days ago to send by a trusty Servant a box full of Fowles and other Eatables for His Royal Highness's Subsistence."[10]

In mid-August Frederick William called senior generals and ministers to a council of war at Potsdam. Dubourgay, well informed of what took place, reported that "the resolution seems fixed and determined on this side to appear on the banks of the Elbe in less than three weeks with an army of fourty thousand men."[11]

Three factors dampened the king's bellicosity. One was the disapproval of Prince Leopold, who insisted that it be formally recorded in the council's minutes. Another was a formal French threat to intervene as guarantor of the Treaty of Westphalia "against any aggressor." A third was King George's apparent readiness for war and yet his conciliatory reply to Frederick William's various demands. In the ensuing critical days — Prussian troops were on the march — Knyphausen, backed by Prince Leopold, used these factors with great determination and skill in besting the martial demands of Borcke backed by Seckendorff, who was "arguing for war and claiming Vienna would back Prussia."[12] Knyphausen's reasoned logic won the day. In early September Frederick William agreed to arbitration by two minor German princes, who drew up a convention eventually accepted by both parties.

The quarrel between Prussia and England-Hanover plunged Queen Sophia into the depths of despair, but not so the crown prince, who cunningly converted it to his advantage. Frederick had been promoted to lieutenant colonel in early 1728, and he now

> appeared extremely satisfied with the Appearance of a War as if he was impatient for an opportunity of being in action. This conduct had [such] Success and Effect that the King of Prussia gave him the command of part of his tall Regiment and sent His Royal Highness to Brandenburg, from whence he had every day accounts of the manner in which the Prince governed himself; and that His Prussian Majesty might the better judge of his Son's ability in military affairs all Officers were ordered under pain of His Prussian Majesty's Displeasure not to give him any advice. The Prince behaved himself entirely to his Father's Satisfaction insomuch that he is now a greater Favorite than ever he had been from the time of his Birth.

Dubourgay wrote these words in mid-September and added:

Three days ago the King of Prussia went to Potsdam upon no other Business than to see the Prince Royal march into that Place at the head of his command. His Prussian Majesty being come a little too soon went a mile out of Town to meet the Prince. His Royal Highness, on seeing the King his Father, came up to him, and said that he had the Pleasure to bring back to His Majesty the two Battaillons he had committed to his care without their having suffered anything by Sickness or Desertion. He mentioned Sickness because it is here as great a Crime in a Commanding Officer to have men sick, as to have them desert.[13]

The pacific sky was quickly marred by Seckendorff, who arrived back in Berlin with no less than fifty thousand thalers to pay off the people who had incited Frederick William to war. He now promoted new trouble — first, by using the Mecklenburg border controversy; second, by trying to convince the King that Frederick should marry the Princess of Bevern. Frederick would have nothing to do with such a marriage, and the "marks of tenderness and affection" shown by his father abruptly vanished. In late October Dubourgay reported that father and son were "worse together than ever." Ill health — colic, diarrhea, and "a swelling in his knee with black spots around it" — scarcely improved the king's temper. In early December he was "in such a violent Agitation as is beyond anything that I have yet heard, no body dares come near him, and the Prince Royal has been treated in such a manner as I cannot for shame relate."[14] On one occasion the king attempted to strangle his son. On another he learned from a spy that the crown prince, while waltzing about in elegant French clothes, had called his uniform "a shroud." The king burst into his son's apartments, picked up a brocade gown, and threw it into the fire, heaping insults on the terrified prince.[15]

Frederick was also behaving more and more indiscreetly with the page Keith. The duo recently had been joined by Lieutenant Hans Hermann von Katte of the prestigious regiment of gensdarmes, where he was aide to Margrave Henry of Schwedt. Twenty-six years old, Katte was the scion of an ancient military family and an intimate of the former French envoy, Count Rothenburg. "A sensible and intelligent man," Seckendorff described him — but he also referred to Frederick's "special" and intimate relationship with Katte.[16] Wilhelmina later wrote that Katte's association with the polished Rothenburg, and

his travels, industry and study, had given refinement both to his mind and his manners. He was extremely cultivated, and a most agreeable social companion. His appearance was not attractive. He was very plain, with a dark complexion much marked by smallpox. His thick black eyebrows were drawn down low over his eyes, and met above his nose. This gave him a most unfortunate expression. Katte was very wild, and boasted of being very strong-minded. It was Katte's influence which destroyed

Lieutenant Hans Hermann
von Katte, Crown Prince Frederick's lover and friend — a
role that cost him his life

Cüstrin, where the repentant crown prince began to learn the
practical side of farming: how fields were ploughed, fertilized,
planted; crops harvested; grain stored and marketed

all religious belief in my brother. I had observed this in his conversations, and had also often argued with him about his fatalist views. He maintained that once being predestined to sin, it was impossible to escape from it.

Wilhelmina frequently blamed her brother's shortcomings on others. Frederick's religious beliefs had been wavering long before he met Katte, and he had also savored and liked the Calvinist tenet of predestination. Katte's mind instantly appealed to him. In addition to arts and music, the lieutenant was knowledgeable in mathematics and physics. Their love of intellectual pursuits shortly led each freely to express love for the other, as later attested by their mutual friend Lieutenant Baron Alexander von Spaen and by Katte himself. Katte entered Frederick's life at a time when he had taken all that he could from his father and desperately needed a stronger and wiser accomplice than Keith. The rakish, romantic Katte was just such an ally.

In late January 1730, the king beat Frederick so cruelly that he decided to attempt an escape, but this plan was reported by anonymous letter to the king. Surprisingly, the king treated the matter lightly, paid his son's theretofore secret debts of ten thousand thalers, and published an edict that forbade anyone, under "very severe penalties," to lend the prince money. This was possibly to influence Frederick favorably toward his desire to marry Wilhelmina to Margrave Frederick William of Schwedt, but Frederick refused to agree to what could be only an unfortunate match. On the other hand he was beginning to criticize the English monarchs for not exerting themselves "a little more to save him and his Sister from ruin and destruction," as Dubourgay reported. "If they had no thought about his Sister's welfare, and suffer'd her to be forced to take other engagements than those she had been made to hope and expect from her infancy, he must conclude they were as indifferent as to what became of him."[17]

9

KING GEORGE and his ministers were not as indifferent to the fate of Frederick and Wilhelmina as they were helpless to counter the constant turnabouts in Frederick William's turbulent mind. In early February 1730, Lord Townshend wrote to Dubourgay:

> I never saw both His Majesty and the Queen more concerned than they were at the Account you gave of the ill State of Health of the Queen of Prussia, and of the terrible Situation the Prince and Princess Royal were

in with respect to the violent proceedings of the King their Father. Both Their Majestys have all the Love and Tenderness imaginable for the Queen of Prussia, and for the Prince and Princess Royal, and are so far from having the least thought of abandoning the Prince or his Sister, that they are ready to do with the greatest Cordiality any thing in their Power for their Service, or to draw them out of their present Difficulties. The Queen has already suggested her Thoughts with all the affection possible; But as She has not received any Answer upon them, nor seen any objection to them, She knows not what further Step to take as yet.[1]

Townshend had no more than written these words than Dubourgay reported a new twist to affairs. Sophia, a plump woman further swelled by being five months with child, had become so ill that physicians believed "that the most favorable turn her illness can take is a miscarriage." Until now Frederick William had shown only slight concern over his wife's state, believing, as Grumbkow and Seckendorff cruelly insisted, that her illness was "feigned," and had continued to try to force her to accept Wilhelmina's betrothal to the Margrave of Schwedt. On learning the truth from Dr. Stahl "and the great Danger Her Prussian Majesty was in, he went directly to her Apartment where he expressed a sincere grief and affliction and promised he would not speak to her about the Princess Royal's Marriage till the first of March."[2]

Sophia's desperate state was further emphasized in a letter enclosed by Dubourgay. This was written by the Reverend Dr. Villa, a Protestant clergyman in Berlin who for some years had served as chaplain to the English envoy and had been teaching English to Wilhelmina while instructing her in the Anglican faith. Villa wasted few words in outlining the "deplorable situation" that

> has induc'd the friends to Her Majesty to send me to England with orders to lay before the King the desolate condition that the Royal Family is in, to implore his favor, and beg of him in pure humanity and Christian compassion to do something for 'em, that may relieve 'em in this distress. And as they have some hopes, that if His [Britannic] Majesty wou'd but name some man of distinction to goe immediately to Berlin to treat about the marriages, it might produce good effect.[3]

Here was a new and clever stratagem. Villa had attended Westminster College and was known both at court and in Whitehall. At Sophia's urging, he set off for London "like a carrier pigeon in extremity." He evidently pleaded his case effectively, for King George decided to send a special envoy, Sir Charles Hotham, to Berlin — though not without certain qualms and not with any particular hope of success.

Frederick William, though in worse temper than usual, welcomed Dubourgay's report of the new ambassador and asked a great many questions. Dubourgay, who knew Sir Charles, replied that "he was a

Gentleman of a very ancient family, of known Merit and Abilitys, That his Father was a General Officer in Spain, and that he himself was in the Army" — all of which was agreeable to the Prussian king, "as much altered in his Behaviour and Humor as it is possible to imagine. His Behaviour to ye Queen, Prince and Princess Royal of Prussia is very Tender and Affectionate, and General Seckendorff is very much neglected, not to say entirely slighted."[4]

Sir Charles Hotham is one of those figures who suddenly and unexpectedly appears on center stage of a historical drama, a deus ex machina who performs badly and returns to virtual anonymity when the play goes bust.

The baronet, a colonel in the Horse Grenadier Guards, belonged to an old Yorkshire family. His father, the fourth baronet, had been a colonel of dragoons and member of Parliament for Beverley; when he died in 1723, the title went to his son. The next year Sir Charles married Lady Gertrude, the eldest daughter of the Earl of Chesterfield, by whom he had three children. At the time of his Berlin mission he was thirty-seven, "*poli, généraux, et excessivement riche*," according to the French secretary in Berlin. He was no "figure of romance," according to another observer, "the fat face and thin nose of all Hothams giving him a rather birdlike mien, and between his eyebrows and eyelids lay little deposits of fat which lent his eyes a boyish aspect at once sleepy and swollen."[5] Reichenbach reported to Grumbkow from London "that he is a very pretty man, but without experience. . . . We will see a comedy."[6]

Reichenbach was correct; Hotham was not a diplomat. Even more curiously, he did not seem to want the job: he made it very clear to Lord Townshend that his commission would end "the Moment this Affair is brought to an Issue one way or the other."[7]

Sir Charles received the king's orders in early March. He was to leave for Berlin as soon as possible. There he would work with Knyphausen in arranging not only Wilhelmina's marriage to the Prince of Wales but, an indispensable condition, Crown Prince Frederick's marriage to Princess Emily. He was to deal firmly with the Prussian king, but if that king "should fly out at any time into Expressions not becoming our Minister to hear, You will support our Honour and Dignity with Resolution and Firmness."[8] Beyond arranging the marriages, Sir Charles was to bring the Prussian king back to the League of Hanover, and as ammunition against the Austrian enemy he was furnished with a number of intercepted letters between Grumbkow and Reichenbach that proved their treachery beyond any doubt.

The new envoy did not reach the continent until late March — "a very tempestuous passage," he noted. At the Hague the Dutch foreign minister warned him of worse waters ahead, "considering the excessive jealousy of the King of Prussia's temper, and how averse he was to take any Step, that might tend to give an Increase of Power to the Prince Royal's interests, which Seckendorff and Grumbkow would continually suggest must inevitably happen whenever the double Match is concluded."

More discomfiting information awaited Sir Charles in Hanover, where he was met by Dubourgay's secretary, Captain Guy Dickens, sent, at Sophia's express desire, to brief Hotham on the situation in the Prussian court. Hotham learned that things were not as rosy as he had been led to believe. The king's present good humor, Dickens explained, existed only because he expected Hotham to deal with a single marriage, that of Wilhelmina to the Prince of Wales. Dickens also warned of Knyphausen's extremely limited influence on the king.

Hotham nonetheless found a favorable court climate when he arrived on a Sunday in early April, and he was soon granted an audience at Charlottenburg. This culminated in a very drunken dinner party and a royal faux pas: "When Hotham left the table to pee," Grumbkow later wrote, "the king suddenly declared that the princess [Wilhelmina] was promised with the Prince of Wales, and His Majesty received the compliments of the table, and Borcke wept with joy." Hotham returned to find various dignitaries kissing the king's knees or coat skirts, according to custom, and his surprise increased when Frederick William announced that Wilhelmina "was ugly and freckled, but, with that exception, she was a good girl, and would be faithful and satisfy her husband . . . besides which, if they had chosen to take her three years previously, they would have found her prettier."

Although Dubourgay reported to Townshend that "everything passed very well" at this opening scene, his assessment was debatable. According to Grumbkow and Hotham, everyone drank enormously, coarse jokes spilled over the table, and the guests finally began to dance with each other, the servants happily joining in! The king returned to Potsdam that night and awakened in a vile temper, the result of a hangover and Lutheran conscience coupled with the hazy recollection of having talked too much. Hotham, who priggishly noted that he was "not accustomed to these exhibitions," reported that the king's action had become common knowledge in Berlin. A somewhat strained meeting followed with the ministers Knyphausen and Borcke, who assured Hotham that the king was ready to conclude a formal marriage contract; but no mention was made of the double marriage, nor did Hotham introduce the delicate subject in a subsequent and noncommittal royal audience. Instead, he postponed the entire negotiation by dispatching a courier to London to report Prussian proposals and to request additional instructions.

The double marriage, however, remained very much on the Prussian king's mind, and he was certain that Hotham had orders to arrange it. As he privately informed Seckendorff, he would have nothing to do with it; and when he came to Berlin, Hotham reported, he left Crown Prince Frederick in Potsdam *"de peur que le vente anglois nelle touchat"* (lest the English wind affect him).

The king was even beginning to doubt the advisability of Wilhelmina's marriage; this was the result of Reichenbach's reporting. In addition to describing the contempt in which King George and Queen Caroline held their son the Prince of Wales, Reichenbach reported the prince's drinking and whoring — all accurately enough. But he also suggested that the Hanoverians were not very firmly seated on the throne of England. He spoke of Princess Emily "as an ambitious, haughty, capricious, cynical woman." This and more venom had been poisoning Frederick William's mind. As he told Borcke and Knyphausen, he could not tolerate a haughty English princess as a daughter-in-law: "She will never accustom herself to the simplicity and economy that are necessary in Prussia; she will be extravagant. On her account it will become obligatory to reduce the army, and the royal household and the state will walk backwards, like crabs."[9]

The delicate negotiations, nonetheless, continued in early May, when fresh instructions reached Sir Charles from Whitehall. He now dropped all subterfuge, telling Frederick William that King George wanted a double marriage and was willing to make Princess Emily the *Stadhoudler*, or Regent, of Hanover, which would greatly ease Frederick William's financial burden. Although surprised, the king was very civil and said that he needed a few days to think over the proposition. Unfortunately Sir Charles did not leave it at that. Grumbkow's and Seckendorff's machinations were maddening, and Knyphausen's reluctance to use the intercepted letters to expose these villains was particularly frustrating. Hotham now acted:

> I thought this a proper opportunity of producing the intercepted Letters, and said I was sorry to acquaint His Majesty, that as to one of his Ministers he had acted so infamous a part towards us that I hoped his opinion would have little Weight with him: and then I laid the whole Scene of Villainy between Grumbkow and Reichenbach, and made him sensible that without any regard to truth, Reichenbach writ nothing but what was dictated to him from hence by Seckendorff and Grumbkow.

Alas, poor Hotham — we knew him well. If he had read pertinent portions of dispatches sent by earlier envoys, if he had discussed the Prussian king's abnormal mentality with Knyphausen or Dubourgay, he would not have acted so rashly. When Frederick William failed to explode in wrath over his perfidious minister, Hotham "endeavored as

much as I could to stir up his Indignation against Grumbkow by painting him in his true Color, being very sensible how much my Success
depended upon his Ruin, but am sorry to tell Your Lordship that it did
not seem to me to make all the Impression I wished for." Frederick
William did promise to recall Reichenbach, but when Hotham offered
him the incriminating letters, he asked the envoy to hold them until
further notice.

Hotham's discomfiture was intensified a week later by the royal reply to the English proposition. Borcke told Hotham that, although
Frederick William was grateful for the offer, he could not accept, "because it would appear to the world as if he was either not able or
willing to maintain his Son, whose Absence might also have this ill
Effect, with respect to the Prince himself, that he might be look'd upon
as a Stranger amongst his Subjects, and would be unacquainted with
the Maxims by which he ought one day to govern this Country." Borcke
added that Crown Prince Frederick would not be ready to marry for at
least ten years, and that when he was, Princess Emily's dowry should
consist of some of the English king's German estates. As for Wilhelmina's marriage, the Prussian king wanted England's guarantee to the
emperor that France would not attack the Low Countries or the Empire in case war broke out in Italy. When Hotham fiercely attacked the
absurdity of these counterproposals, Frederick William replied that he
would welcome Wilhelmina's immediate marriage and would agree to
a future date for Frederick's marriage, providing England guaranteed
the eventual succession of Juliers and Berg to Prussia.

At this crucial stage Sir Charles received a confidential emissary from
the crown prince. Frederick would never forget the infinite obligations
he had to the English king and queen, but "he begg'd for God's Sake,
that how unreasonable soever the propositions from his Father might
be, the [English] King would not reject them immediately: for tho' he
was determined to lose his life sooner than marry any body but the
Princess [Emily], yet if this Negotiation was entirely broke off, his Father would use all manner of Extremitys to oblige him and his Sister to
contract other Engagements."

Frederick followed this message later in the month with two letters
sent to Hotham in great secrecy. In the first he wrote:

> I am being treated in an unheard-of manner by the king, and I know that
> at present he is plotting terrible things against me, concerning certain
> letters [to the English court] that I have written this past winter. . . .
> Frankly and in a word the true and secret reason that the King refuses
> to agree to this [my] marriage is that he wishes always to keep me in an
> inferior status, and forever to bait me when the fancy strikes him, thus
> he will never agree to it. If you consider that this princess [Emily] would
> be treated similarly, you will easily understand that I would be very sad
> to remain forever in the same state that I am in.

Far better, Frederick wrote, to let Wilhelmina's marriage come off now; once it did, Frederick would escape to England and marry Princess Emily.

1 0

THE ENGLISH COURT'S reaction to these latest developments had not reached Sir Charles when the Prussian king departed for Saxony. King August had prepared a magnificent celebration in honor of his newly reorganized army, patterned after the Prussian force. The camp at Radewitz had cost August over three million thalers to build, and operating costs were enormous — every twenty-four hours the bakery produced seven thousand loaves of bread, each weighing over two pounds! Magnificent military maneuvers and demonstrations during the day were followed by stage comedies and diverse entertainments at night, the guests imbibing vast quantities of food and drink all the while.

This was the setting for the next phase of the marriage negotiations. In mid-June, Sir Charles, who had followed the Prussian king to Saxony, presented the English court's reply to Frederick William's new demands. King George refused to consider any extraneous political matters, he could not guarantee the succession of Juliers and Berg, and he insisted on the double marriage. Frederick William replied that his son at eighteen was too young to marry — he would have to be at least thirty, "finding it likewise necessary that this Prince tries to previously distinguish himself in the world, and to acquire the qualities requisite to establishing a family." Hotham submitted that the Prussian king would never come around; indeed, that he allegedly had decided to marry Wilhelmina to the Prince of Weissenfels. Accordingly, he wrote, "I look upon my Negociation as ended [and] I humbly hope His Majesty will think proper to recall me immediately."

But on this same day Hotham dictated another "most secret" dispatch to Lord Newcastle (who had replaced Townshend), one of such sensitivity that he ordered Guy Dickens to carry it personally to London. Crown Prince Frederick, he reported, had been toying with the idea of escaping from the kingdom for some time. In Berlin he had illegally borrowed a thousand thalers from a moneylender and, through his confederates von Keith and von Spaen, had considered ordering a carriage in Leipzig, a plan evidently abandoned as premature. The king may have learned of this notion, for at Radewitz he continued to treat his son abominably. The Danish envoy, Løvenørn, reported that on one occasion he accused Frederick in the presence of half a dozen Prussian officers not only of lying but of intending to kill him, not by a direct attack, "since you are too cowardly," but rather by stabbing him in the back. Another quarrel had led the king repeatedly to strike his son. Regarding the cringing, weeping prince, the king said contemptuously, "Had I been treated so by my father, I would have blown my brains out, but this fellow has no honor, he takes all that comes." Soon after this episode Frederick asked Count Hoym, a Saxon minister, to provide horses for two officers who wished to travel incognito to Leipzig. Hoym refused and, probably at Keith's urging, Frederick dropped the plan.

He next turned to his English friends. Some days earlier, Hotham reported, the prince royal had eluded spies and escorts to hustle Guy Dickens into his tent. He told Dickens "that he could no longer bear the outrageous treatment he every day met with from his Father, and therefore was resolved to make himself easy as soon as ever he could, and thought he had now a very favourable opportunity to do it." Frederick was referring to the forthcoming inspection trip with his father to Ansbach and the Rhine territories, from where he was to go to Stuttgart, which, since it was not far from Strasbourg, would enable him to proceed to Paris. He planned to stay there about six weeks and then go to England. The reason he intended to stay some while in France was to avoid casting his father's suspicion on his mother as being privy to his plan. Frederick was also worried about Wilhelmina and hoped that King George would help to protect her. He himself would try to devise some method to ensure her safety, but in any event, wrote Hotham, "he was resolved to put his design in execution. He said further that his measures were well taken, and that he wanted for nothing that might facilitate his Escape; and desired I would write to our Court to dispose the Court of France to grant him their Protection." Hotham cautiously and presciently noted that "it is possible the thing may miscarry, by the Prince's being watched too narrowly, or by some other unforeseen accident; but there is no room to doubt of the Prince's having taken a fixed resolution, and that even he will run great hazards to free himself from the oppression he is at present under."

The final part of Hotham's mission occurred in Berlin, where in early July Guy Dickens returned with the English court's response. King George did not agree to Hotham's proposal to abandon the mission; indeed, he continued "to look upon the strictest Union between the two Royal Families as not only highly essential to the Interests of both, but also of the greatest Importance to the Protestant Religion itself" and was willing to negotiate a deferred second marriage. Hotham was to explain to Frederick William that King George had found his terms "a trifle vague" — in short, *when* did Frederick William propose to approve his son's marriage and to *which* English princess?[1] While

Frederick William and the crown prince traveled to the Rhine, Hotham was to go to London for further instructions. His return to Berlin would coincide with that of the Prussian king from the Rhine. In view of these arrangements, Crown Prince Frederick was to be advised to defer the execution of his plan.

Hotham then met with Frederick William, who swore that he would always prefer Frederick to marry an English princess, the one most suitable in age when the time came, which would be no later than ten years. This was a reasonable enough answer, and it might conceivably have satisfied the English court. Whether the king's promise was repeated to the crown prince is not certain, but it is certain that no one could look forward to another ten years of the treatment that Frederick had been receiving. We know that Guy Dickens, through Katte's connivance, secretly met with Frederick at Potsdam to inform him of his royal uncle's advice to abstain from any precipitate action, at least until the air had cleared; Dickens would arrange for him secretly to receive funds for his debts. While evading a specific promise not to escape, Frederick hastily accepted the offer, shrewdly asking for seventeen thousand thalers, though he owed only nine thousand.

One detail remained before Hotham's departure. Dickens had been promoted to envoy status and was to be formally presented at the Berlin court. Hotham had been newly supplied with an original and highly incriminating letter from Grumbkow to Reichenbach, one he took along to the audience on July 10. After presenting Dickens to the king, whom he found "in very good humour," he handed over the incriminating letter, no doubt expecting a reaction favorable to him.

> He took the Letter from me, cast his Eye upon it, and seeing it to be Grumbkow's Hand, said to me with all the Anger imaginable: *Monsieur, j'ai eu assez de ces choses là* [Sir, I have had enough of those matters], threw the Letter upon the Ground, and immediately turning his back went out of the Room and shut the door upon us. Your Lordship will easily imagine that Captain Guy Dickens and I were not a little astonished at this most extraordinary Behaviour. I took up the Letter he had thrown upon the Floor and, returning home, immediately wrote one to His Prussian Majesty.

Hotham had acted impetuously, and now he behaved stupidly. He had been instructed that if the Prussian king "should fly out at any time into Expressions not becoming our Minister to bear, You will support our Honour and Dignity with Resolution and Firmness." In Hotham's mind the King of Prussia had trampled on that "Honour and Dignity" and must now be treated "with Resolution and Firmness," which Hotham proceeded to do in a very blunt letter asking for horses: he would depart for England at once.

King Frederick William also had acted impetuously and *very* stu-

pidly, and Hotham's letter threw him into a terrible funk. He ordered
Borcke to deliver a thinly veiled apology and an invitation to dinner
the following day. Crown Prince Frederick secretly notified Hotham of
this royal embarrassment and begged him not to break off the negotiations. But Hotham trampled on all this as if it were a grape in the
vineyard of wrath, nor did further heartfelt appeals from Borcke change
his attitude.

Sir Charles Hotham's departure from Berlin marked a watershed in
the history of the marriage negotiations, and in so doing stands as a
monument to a momentous shift in relations between Prussia and England. Leopold von Ranke's conclusion can be read in two ways:

> England was too powerful not to have in the end overshadowed her
> weaker ally, or dragged it along in her wake by her natural preponder-
> ance. . . . If the peculiar genius and character of England, which just
> then began to give birth to various great and splendid works, had been
> allowed to exercise an open and authorized influence in Berlin, it may be
> doubted whether the genuine German spirit would not have been stifled
> and obliterated. Prussia would at all events have acquired a totally dif-
> ferent character and aspect.[2]

In more immediate terms, Hotham's departure ended the hope of
Crown Prince Frederick for a reversal of fortune. He was now forced
to turn to his own devices, and as a result he very nearly forfeited his
life.

I I

FREDERICK decided to escape, come what may. He secretly summoned Katte to a night rendezvous in the palace garden at Potsdam,
where he outlined the plan: Katte would join him later in the trip and
they would flee to France, the Versailles court having offered sanctuary. Katte demurred. He had not yet received permission to leave his
regiment for recruiting duty and wanted to delay. Frederick brushed
off all objections by explaining that a cause should not be abandoned
because of difficulties; indeed, difficulties made it more attractive. When
Katte remained adamant, Frederick agreed to a postponement, and they
arranged to keep in touch through Rittmeister Hans Friedrich von Katte,
a cousin temporarily stationed at Erlangen.

But the next morning Frederick changed his mind and informed Katte
by secret letter to meet him at Cannstatt, from where they would flee
to France. He also sent him a large chest of incriminating letters and a
thousand ducats raised in part by his selling the semiprecious stones he
had pried from the Order of the Saxon Eagle and replaced with glass.

Saturday, July 15. The royal convoy departed early, the crown prince traveling in a carriage with General Wilhelm von Buddenbrock and Colonel Arnold von Waldow, sexagenarian members of the Tabagie, and the younger (and suspicious) chamberlain, Lieutenant Colonel Friedrich von Rochow. The weather was stormy, but the royal party soon reached Meuselwitz, Count Seckendorff's estate outside Altenburg, to enjoy a weekend of lavish hospitality. Seckendorff joined the party and the carriages continued in better weather through a picturesque country of winding roads, soft valleys, and small streams, a pastoral setting occasionally blemished by avenues of man-made gibbets, each holding the bird-pecked corpse of a dangling highwayman, mute testimony to hazards of travel in 1730.

Altenburg, Gera, Saalfeld, Coburg, Bamburg, Erlangen, Nuremberg — normally the medieval towns with their diverse tradespeople would have fascinated the inquisitive crown prince, but only at Ansbach, his sister Frederica's court, did Frederick come to life. Here Rittmeister Katte delivered a letter from Hans Hermann von Katte. Frederick's excitement was short-lived. Katte had not yet been given leave. Frederick burned the letter and wrote to him to remain quiet until he received further word. A few days later he wrote to Katte of continued ill treatment by the king. He was determined to escape, but not to France; rather, he would go to the Hague, where Katte would find him disguised as Count d'Alberville. He also sent a secret message to Keith at Wesel, instructing him to join them in Holland. Frederick tried to enlist Rittmeister Katte in the plan, asking him to secure horses and meet him in the Mannheim area. The cavalry officer wisely declined, warned Frederick of Gypsy robbers waiting in every wood, and also warned Rochow to keep a careful eye on his charge. About this time Frederick persuaded a royal page, Lieutenant Keith's younger brother, to help him. Though terrified, the lad secretly bought cloth at Augsburg, which Frederick had made into two cloaks at Ludwigsburg; his own was bright red.

Friday, August 4. The party was heading for Mannheim on the Rhine. Tension must have filled the crown prince's carriage. The previous day Frederick had flaunted his new red cloak, drawing only a quiet warning from Rochow, who said the king must not see it. The prince by now had decided to make his break somewhere around Mannheim, but suddenly the king halted the convoy to bed down in barns around the tiny village of Steinsfurt. At Frederick's instructions young Keith slipped into the village to purchase horses.

Frederick rose about two A.M., dressed, and stole from the barn, but Rochow's vigilant valet observed him. Rochow found him on the village green, red cloak about him, waiting for Keith. When the terrified page appeared, leading two saddle horses, Rochow curtly dismissed him. But now Buddenbrock, Waldow, and Seckendorff were on the scene. Rochow covered as best he could, and the party soon left for Mannheim.

Sunday, August 6. Frederick was not yet beaten. The previous evening in Mannheim, he had slipped a note to Keith to hire two post horses for another attempt. The earlier experience, however, had shattered the young page; now, having heard a sermon of hellfire and damnation in the local church, he threw himself at the king's feet and confessed all. The king immediately charged Frederick's escorts with getting him to Wesel, to Prussian territory, dead or alive.

The grim party continued on to Darmstadt that afternoon, but not before the king had observed some French officers paying court to the Elector Palatine. The suspicious royal mind at once converted their presence to part of his son's escape plan — possibly even a plot to murder Frederick William! Still, he kept his own counsel, greeting the errant youth at Darmstadt with "I thought you would be in Paris by now."[1] Frederick replied that he could easily have been had he so wished.

Tuesday, August 8. At Frankfurt-on-Main, where the party boarded the royal yacht for the trip down the Rhine, the king received an express message from Rittmeister Katte, who enclosed an intercepted letter from Frederick to his accomplice. This erased any doubt of Frederick's intentions. When the king boarded the yacht and saw his son, he struck him across the nose with his cane. Backing away and with blood pouring from his nose, Frederick sobbed, "Never did a Brandenburg face suffer the like of this."[2]

Although Frederick had not yet been formally arrested, the king's intention was obvious. Aides who took the prince ashore at Bonn were charged in his hearing to return him aboard "living or dead." Suddenly realizing his dangerous position, he sought out his old enemy Count Seckendorff and begged for help, not so much for himself as for involved friends. He also smuggled a note to Lieutenant Keith at Wesel: "Save yourself; all is discovered."

Saturday, August 12. The king convened a formal hearing at Wesel, where he exhorted the crown prince "to do God, his lord and father the honor to confess in all duty and conscience the details of his intended desertion." Finding the prince arrogant and uncooperative, he lost his temper and drew his sword, evidently intending to run the youth through. This was too much for the Wesel commandant, General Konrad von Mosel, who leaped between them, shouting, "Sire, cut me to death, but spare your son." The king backed off but at once placed Frederick under formal arrest, stripped him of his sword, and put him under sentry guard in Mosel's house. Not wishing to see the crown prince again, he ordered an aide, Colonel Christoph von Derschau, to interrogate him further.[3] Derschau, described by Wilhelmina as "a thorough scoundrel, and as true a son of Satan as ever walked this earth," quickly caught Frederick in a web of contradictions and lies.

Frederick was in very serious trouble. As far as the king was concerned, his son, a colonel, had been about to desert, without question the most heinous crime in the kingdom. But Frederick William meanwhile had learned of Keith's flight from Wesel and presumed escape to England, and of Katte's participation. These events, and the presence of French officers at Mannheim, convinced him that Frederick's intended escape was part of a sinister Anglo-French plot against himself and Prussia, one in which Queen Sophia and Crown Princess Wilhelmina were also inextricably involved.

Saturday, August 19. Possibly on Seckendorff's advice, Frederick sent the king an importunate letter, stating that he had had no intention of going to England and asking for his release. The king's fury only increased when he read this and a new interrogation report from Derschau, who had discovered more inconsistencies. Orders went to old General von Buddenbrock to take the prisoner to Cüstrin fortress on the Oder. The party, which included Waldow and Rochow and suitable armed escort, left in the middle of the night. The carriages were to stop only for calls of nature, and then only in open fields with no shelter. They were to avoid Hanover territory. In Frederick's presence the warders were ordered "to kill the prisoner rather than let him be taken."[4]

The news reached Berlin within a few days. The king had written a terse note to Madame von Kamecke, asking her to pass a similar note to the queen once she had been prepared for the devastating news, which, as Guy Dickens soon reported to London, "has put the whole Town under the greatest consternation." Dickens went on, "Your Lordship may easily imagine the terror and anguish, which a tender and affectionate Mother must be under, at such a stabbing piece of news, and indeed, notwithstanding all Madam Kamecke's care and circumspection, the poor Queen is inconsolable."[5]

The poor queen had very good reason to be inconsolable, but not alone for young Frederick's fate. The king had also ordered Katte to be put "under the closest confinement." Although the lieutenant had been warned and had made preparations to escape, he had not realized the gravity of the situation, or he did not care, or he preferred the drama of arrest to the ignominy of flight with an uncertain future. Whatever the reason, he delayed departure until it was too late and he was arrested. But he had already sent Countess von Finckenstein the chest of incriminating letters and cash that Frederick had sent to him, and she quickly put these into Queen Sophia's hands.

The queen immediately contacted Guy Dickens, "pressing me with all the earnestness imaginable to send Your Lordship an account, with all the expedition possible, of her present melancholy and deplorable situation" so that the King and Queen of England will know "that her whole trust and confidence is in them," and that they "will not forsake her, in this her very great distress and affliction."[6] Unknown to Dickens there remained the chest of several hundred letters, many of which proved the mother and daughter's complicity in the marriage plot, and also contained outspoken criticism of the king, material evidence that in Frederick William's present rage might well cost them their lives. Their answer was to burn the documents and replace them with forged letters of innocuous content, an ingenious if herculean solution accomplished within the ten days before the king's return to Berlin.

Frederick William arrived in Berlin late on a Sunday, brusquely informed his pregnant queen that her son was dead, and sent her to fetch the chest of letters. Snatching the chest from her, he disappeared but shortly returned. The terrified princesses ran to kiss his hand. Seeing Wilhelmina, "he became black with rage," struck her, and undoubtedly would have beaten her but for the queen and her sisters, who formed a protective cordon. The king eventually calmed down, telling the frightened court that Frederick was not dead but that "by all holy angels" he would kill him. He added that Wilhelmina was "the cause of all the trouble" and would pay for it with her head.[7]

He certainly was out for blood. He submitted the unfortunate Katte to no less than five detailed interrogations in fourteen days, and was dissuaded only with great difficulty from putting him on the rack; Dickens reported that "the torturing Engines were constantly set before him at every Examination." The interrogations proved disappointing, because Katte at first refused to involve anyone but himself in the escape attempt. Frederick, when interrogated at Mittenwalde by a special commission headed by General von Grumbkow, stressed that neither his mother nor his sister was involved in the slightest way. To the king's further fury, Frederick had recovered his composure, would not be caught up in contradictions, and showed himself "merry and gay" throughout the proceedings, which, as Grumbkow reported to Seckendorff, he seemed to regard more as debate than inquisition. The letters seized by the king revealed nothing untoward, nor did he seem to suspect that they had been forged.[8]

Lack of evidence only increased his temper, as did a severe attack of gout. Anyone remotely connected with the crown prince or with Katte was suspect and in trouble. A French diplomat warned his court that he was in physical danger. A French count who had lent Frederick money and who fled Berlin was nailed in effigy to the gallows. The king brutally beat Wilhelmina and confined her to her apartments, where she remained isolated and humiliated. He sent a former trusted diplomat to a remote border post. Knyphausen was relieved of all offices and honors, and died a broken man a year or so later. Frederick's chums at Potsdam, Lieutenants Baron Alexander von Spaen and Johann Ludwig von Ingersleben, were arrested and court-martialed. The page, Keith, was sent to Spandau fortress prison. The king sequestered Frederick's carriages and horses, he gave Frederick's cavalry regiment to Prince William, and he seized the secret library of nearly four thousand volumes and had it sold anonymously. He jailed or banished a host of tainted people: Frederick's and Wilhelmina's favorite servants; the bookseller who had helped the prince build his library; Duhan, who had taught Frederick for twelve years. Abused and damned by weakness and melancholy, he struck defenseless targets. A girl in Potsdam, Elizabeth Ritter, with whom Frederick had carried on a harmless flirtation, was believed to have seduced the prince. The poor thing was medically examined, found to be a virgin, but nonetheless was publicly whipped and sent to Spandau prison.

Retribution only drove the king to further absurdities. He told General Reinhold von Ginkel, the Dutch envoy, that he suspected the entire royal family, including Queen Sophia and "every man about him except Grumbkow," of concurring "directly or indirectly" in Frederick's action. Wild-eyed, he cursed the governments of England and France and went on to proclaim "such wicked designs" that Ginkel feared for the lives of the Prussian royal family and of Guy Dickens. "If the King of Prussia continued in the mind he was at present," Ginkel told Dickens, "we should see here as wicked and bloody scenes as any that had been heard of since the Creation of the World." [9]

One such scene was shortly to occur. The setting would be Cüstrin fortress prison, to which the king already had sent his son under heavy guard.

12

FREDERICK was taken to Cüstrin in early September. The crown prince was given prison garb of coarse brown cloth and occupied a cell with no furniture or candlelight. He ate prison rations, two meals served by an officer, the meat cut so that he would need no knife; a servant emptied a waste bucket three times a day; officers and servants remained silent in his presence: no books, no flute, no visitors, no news of the outside world except that gleaned from a single grated cell window, a tiny aperture looking on to the prison yard and to the smelly marshes of the sluggish River Oder. But as was the case with earlier harsh strictures, awareness of human mortality brought some relief. He soon obtained books, pen, paper, candles, and probably a better diet than that ordained by the king. When told that his daily budget had been reduced to eight groschen, he replied, "Starvation for starvation, I prefer Cüstrin to Potsdam."

Nearly two weeks of this stark regimen had passed when it was broken by an auditor, Christian Otto von Mylius — "a very bad man," Wilhelmina noted — who conducted a "special inquisition" based on 185 "articles" prepared by the king. The first 178 concerned various events of the previous year and details of Frederick's intended flight. The last seven were "conscience" questions. Asked whether he wished to have his life spared, Frederick replied, "I submit myself to the king's mercy." He replied similarly when asked whether he would renounce the throne. In a separate statement he apologized for the sorrow he had caused the king, pledged complete submission to royal "grace and will," and begged forgiveness — a petition that the king tore furiously to bits.[1]

In early October the prisoner requested another hearing. The king granted it but told Grumbkow, "When this rogue asks about me, my wife, and my children, you will tell him that no one thinks of him any longer, that my wife wishes to hear nothing of him, that Wilhelmina is in disgrace, a prisoner in Berlin, and will be exiled to the country. Knyphausen has been consigned to the devil."[2]

Frederick appeared contrite enough and told Grumbkow that, rather than suffer life imprisonment, he would renounce the throne; indeed, would even prefer death. Pressed for details of the conspiracy that the king believed to exist, the prince denied everything. Frederick William did not believe him. "The little scoundrel defends himself with unsurpassable cleverness and determination, always refusing to admit that he intended to desert." In the king's speech and writings Frederick was variously a "scoundrel," "villain," "blackguard," and "good-for-nothing." "God spare all decent parents from such offspring," he wrote to Prince Leopold. "It is a great pity, yet before God and man my conscience is clear. I have warned him, punished him mildly and severely — all to no avail."

The king's desire for positive proof of a foreign conspiracy continued to be thwarted, but enough information had been obtained from Katte and Frederick to incriminate the Dutch, French, and English courts. "There is no doubt that England knew everything but advised against desertion," the king told Leopold. England remained the major villain.

He flatly refused that court's overtures to renew the marriage alliance. "No further thought is to be given to any marriage, double or single, between the Royal families of England and Prussia," Dickens was informed.[3]

Frederick remained the primary domestic villain. General Ginkel, who saw the king frequently in these turbulent days, reported that "his Prussian Majesty's hatred against the Prince was not only increased but that he was grown very jealous of his Son's Parts and Talents, which had remarkably appeared in all his Examinations."[4] The King next ordered Frederick, Katte, and lesser fry to be tried by court-martial. Whatever hope he had of thus breaking his son was in vain; the latter wrote philosophically to Wilhelmina, "Chi ha tempo ha vita" (Who has time has life).

The military court met at Köpenick castle in late October. Headed by seventy-year-old Lieutenant General Count Achaz von Schulenburg, it consisted of three generals including Grumbkow, three colonels including Derschau, three majors, three captains, and three auditors or judge advocates including von Mylius. A week later Schulenburg pronounced its sentences: Lieutenant von Ingersleben was to serve a further six months in prison; Lieutenant von Spaen was to be cashiered and placed in fortress arrest (which was not so severe as criminal arrest) for three years; Lieutenant von Keith was to be hanged in effigy; Lieutenant von Katte was to be cashiered and imprisoned for life. The military court did not deem itself entitled to judge the case of the crown prince, which was a royal family affair.

The sentences infuriated Frederick William. "You were supposed to pronounce justice, not glide over it with a featherduster," he scribbled on the report. The judges had shown themselves disloyal, he later complained: "I thought I had selected men of honor who would not forget their duty, who would not worship the rising sun [Crown Prince Frederick], and would consult only their consciences and the honor of their king." Nonetheless he approved the first three sentences because there was little else he could do, but he judged Katte's punishment as too lenient. Not only was Katte an officer in the king's army, Frederick William wrote, but an officer of the royal bodyguard, the gendarmes, "therefore owing me a special personal loyalty." Instead, the wretch had "intrigued with the rising sun" and with foreign ambassadors. Katte deserved to be torn to death by red-hot pincers and then hanged. As for the crown prince, the court would reconvene, try him for desertion, and return its verdict forthwith.[5]

When the court refused either to try the crown prince or reverse its sentence on Katte, the king summarily decreed that the latter would be executed by beheading (as opposed to hanging, in deference to his distinguished family). Frederick would be forced to watch the execution, a scene planned by the king in minute detail, his purpose being to break Frederick's will and thus prepare him for spiritual redemption.[6]

Katte's sentence raised storms of protest, to no avail. His father, a lieutenant general and commandant of Königsberg, had earlier petitioned the king for mercy. Frederick William expressed regret but pointed out that "your son is a scoundrel, mine too; we can neither of us help it."[7] To further pleas from Katte's father and grandfather, the king remained adamant. *"Fiat justitia et pereat mundus,"* he decreed: Let justice be done though the world perishes.[8]

A detachment of cavalry escorted Lieutenant von Katte to Cüstrin in early November. Johann Müller, chaplain of the regiment of gendarmes, rode with the condemned man, an unpleasant journey during which he exhorted the young officer to penance and more penance. Katte behaved well. He had written farewell letters to his father and grandfather, asking forgiveness. He had also written to Frederick, absolving him from any blame but begging him to come to terms with the king.

At Cüstrin fortress the chaplain of the garrison joined the party. He spent most of the night praying and singing hymns with the victim. Early next morning, escorted by garrison soldiers, the party entered the prison compound below Frederick's cell.

The tower clock tolled five. Light had broken on a gray and cold day, and the smell of Oder bogs filled the damp cell. Warders suddenly flung open the iron door and ordered the royal prisoner to the small barred window. A surprised Frederick at once recognized Katte. "What is he doing here?" he asked his warders. No one answered. In silence he watched his friend walk slowly but with dignity, hat tucked under one arm, the other arm free, soldiers on either side, and behind him two mumbling chaplains.

Frederick suddenly realized what was happening. Frantically he sent an appeal to the general of the fortress, asking for a stay of execution so that he could beg the king to spare Katte's life. His words bounced off blank faces. The group continued across the prison yard.[9]

Katte suddenly looked up. Frederick's eyes fastened on him. He touched fingers to his lips and called in French, "My dear Katte, a thousand pardons, please." Katte saluted: "My prince, there is nothing to apologize for." The words were spoken, one chaplain related, "with no little emotion or sorrow."

The grim procession continued to a raised platform built on a bastion that overlooked the somber river. Frederick watched it halt by a little heap of sand. Katte stood motionless, his pocked face in familiar profile as an officer formally intoned the death sentence. Katte shook hands with the officers, removed his wig, opened his shirt at the neck, knelt to receive the sword's edge. "Lord Jesus," he prayed — but when an attendant tried to blindfold him, he brushed aside the binding. Eyes open, he again prayed, "Lord Jesus . . ."

Death interrupted prayer; blood jetted as his head fell to the sand.

Frederick already had fainted.

BOOK TWO

The Actor

1730–1740

All the world's a stage,
And all the men and women merely players.
They have their exits and their entrances;
And one man in his time plays many parts . . .
— *Shakespeare,* As You Like It

FREDERICK soon regained consciousness. Refusing either succor or sympathy, the eighteen-year-old prisoner hugged the tiny window of the cell, blue-gray eyes fixed dully on Katte's headless, shrouded body. That afternoon townsfolk came and took the pieces for burial. Frederick remained at the window, staring at the blood-spattered sand, refusing food or conversation.

By evening he had developed a high fever and lay moaning on the rack that served as his bed. Chaplain Johann Müller, who was to supervise Frederick's spiritual redemption, brought a cooling potion. Frederick awakened, recognized the man of Christ, and thought that he was being given poison. "I had a hard time convincing him otherwise," Müller reported to the king. In desperation, he drank first. Frederick followed and lapsed into delirious sleep.[1]

Müller appeared the next morning to find his ward in a better frame of mind. He had brought Katte's farewell letter to Frederick, and the two tearfully read it. Müller noted that Frederick seemed impressed by Katte's plea for reconciliation with the king. The dead man's words launched them on a theological discussion in which the Lutheran minister began to try to dissuade the prince from such dangerous Calvinist beliefs as predestination. Frederick showed himself eager and contrite. His zeal, combined with seemingly genuine humility, so impressed Müller that only two days after Katte's execution he informed the king that his son had undergone a remarkable change of attitude. Müller wanted the king to encourage the prince; otherwise, he might lapse into incurable melancholy.

King Frederick William also had been doing some hard thinking. Throughout October his attitude toward his errant son had hardened to such an extent that he wished to disinherit him. He turned a deaf ear to reports of Frederick's and Wilhelmina's severe illnesses, and he ignored Queen Sophia's despondency. Diplomats continued to report both harsh words and measures, general fears of what one called "a tragical Event." General Løvenørn, the Danish envoy, who sometimes hunted with the king, reported that he spoke "of the Prince in his usual Terms of Bitterness and Hatred, calling his Royal Highness all the infamous names he could think of." Løvenørn did not believe that the boy would be put to death, but neither would he be released, and "therefore the Prince must inevitably perish, it being impossible for him to hold out long under such inhuman Treatment."[2]

But several factors were working in Frederick's favor. One was pressure on the king from other courts to pardon the crown prince. Although the king refused to answer a host of petitions submitted by other rulers on Frederick's behalf, and in general blustered to his cronies about invasion of Prussian privacy, the collective voice of royal disapproval haunted his already tortured mind. So did critical rumblings from the army. More pressure was brought by Seckendorff, to whom Sophia had early turned for help. Recognizing the possibility of placing the royal family in his debt, he had obtained a letter from Emperor Charles asking the Prussian king to show extreme leniency to Frederick. Seckendorff did not at once present this letter. Instead, he and Grumbkow, who instantly jumped on the bandwagon, used drunken Tabagie sessions to talk up the idea of a quasi-pardon, suggesting that in return Frederick must swear to a new oath of loyalty and must follow this by working in a humble capacity in the local Cüstrin administration.

By October's end the king had decided to pardon Frederick, a decision reinforced by the emperor's letter, which Seckendorff now delivered. It was further prompted by the outcry that followed Katte's execution, criticism so widespread and voluble that the king decreed that any subject thenceforth discussing the matter would have his tongue cut out.

Chaplain Müller brought Frederick the good news only three days after Katte's death. Frederick was not one to overlook such a reprieve, and Müller continued to report his religious zeal, evident contrition, and enviable humility: the crown prince had been sending for him at six A.M. and frequently was keeping him until noon. Frederick had practically donned a hair shirt when General von Grumbkow appeared a week later. The king had chosen him to head a special "oath commission," and the wily general had arrived a day early in order to have a private talk with Frederick. Exactly what passed is not known, but it is obvious that each needed the other. From now on Grumbkow would often serve as buffer between father and son.

On the following day, a Sunday, Frederick swore before the stern commissioners "to obey unfailingly the orders of the king," speaking, as decreed by the king, "loud and clear, no muttering or anything like that." After signing the written oath, he walked from the jail to a church service whose simple Lutheran content so moved him (as his father was told) that, on cue and in front of dignitaries and townsfolk, he burst into tears.[3] After this lachrymose display, he went to the large and comfortable town house where he was to live during parole, and there he wrote the king the first of many sycophantic letters, admitting disobedience and asking full pardon and permission to return to court. The king replied that he would remain in Cüstrin to learn domestic administration and economics. Too many rulers, the king explained, turned their countries over to court favorites and ministers, who "put everything into confusion"; most princes are miserable administrators and "in spite of holding the most beautiful lands, they fail to utilize them correctly and instead ruin themselves by going into debt."

Frederick was allowed a sword, but no uniform; instead, he wore a light gray frock coat with narrow silver cordings. Sentries were not to salute him, nor was he permitted beyond the walls of the small fortress town. He was comfortable enough physically. Servants looked after him and his companions, the chamberlain Gerhard Heinrich von Wolden and two young aristocrats, Karl Dubislav von Natzmer and Wilhelm von Rohwedel. They were to live simply — no oysters or plump capons from Hamburg, no pâté from Strasbourg, no delicacies from anywhere — and conversation theoretically was limited to matters at hand; no talk of war or politics. Frederick could not have a flute, and he could correspond only with his parents. He was permitted three books: the German Bible, a hymn book and Johann Arndt's *True Christianity*.

Having failed the army course, so to speak, the crown prince would take the civilian course. "He must spend the entire day at the Chamber of War and Domains, which will inform him of all matters," Frederick William told Prince Leopold. "If he will not readily learn them, they will be repeated a thousand times so that he must retain them. If he should become a man of honor, which I very much doubt, it will be his good fortune."

The Chamber of War and Domains for the Cüstrin area was headed by President Christian Ernst von Münchow and run by Director Christoph Werner Hille. As *Auskultator,* or listener, Frederick by royal order was to sit at a small desk "quite low down" the board table and take notes on which to base later discussions with his chief tutor, Hille. He would attend morning sessions from seven to eleven-thirty, and from three to five in the afternoon. Although the king warned the chamber against his son's "noxious and deceitful character," he soon became popular with its members and with the local people.

Frederick began rehabilitation with mixed feelings. One day Hille would report to Grumbkow his ward's bad temper; the next day he was "happy as a bullfinch." A new storm soon broke, however, and it was caused largely by Frederick. Forced to silence by day, he vented his intelligence in the evening, flitting from topic to topic, including religion and the forbidden Calvinist doctrine of predestination. Chaplain Müller only recently had reported Frederick's conversion from this heretical doctrine, but now Wolden reported his awakened interest in it. The king replied that if the wretch was going to go to the devil, so be it; "but meanwhile the three of you must always refute his error with quotations from the holy Scriptures. . . . You will learn in time to know your pious ward better and better and that there is nothing good in him except his tongue — nothing is wrong with that."[4]

The prince refused to eat crow, and Wolden reported that "he believes he acted better in speaking his heartfelt belief clearly and plainly rather than deceiving God and the King through hypocrisy." The King's angry reply contained all the old grievances. Not only did his *Bösewicht,* or rogue son, refuse to have his hair cut, but he walked like a ballet dancer: he "stands on tiptoe and won't plant his feet firmly, he holds himself bent over . . . he won't look an honest man in the eyes . . . he is shockingly untidy and physically dirty, eats like a pig with his nose always on the plate, is constantly making funny faces, and behaves very stupidly." At Christmas the king sarcastically scrawled on a report of his son's illness, "As he is predestined, all will go well with him; if there were any good in him he would die, but I am convinced that he won't because ill weeds don't die."

Matters would probably have got out of hand once again but for Grumbkow, to whom Hille hastily turned. The general persuaded Frederick to renounce the hated doctrine in a humble letter to the king, and this restored a peace of sorts.

Life at Cüstrin was not physically onerous. President von Münchow had allowed Frederick to enjoy forbidden fruit during imprisonment, and he now turned a blind eye as townspeople and friends vied in keeping the royal larder stocked with delicacies from neighboring estates and from abroad. Hille was a well-educated man with an open mind and a good sense of humor, but he had no use for arrogant royalty and had been ordered to drill the fundamentals of economics, finance, commerce, and farming into his subject's not always receptive skull. Wolden, Rohwedel, and Natzmer were lenient warders, but with the exception of the last, Frederick had little in common with them. Confined to the stifling bureaucratic chamber by day, confined to the house by night, he soon became bored and even quarrelsome.

Seeing no way out, at least for the present, Frederick perforce relied on his own talents for amusement. Hille was at once impressed with his sense of humor and wrote to Grumbkow that he taught Frederick more easily through wit than by rote. The student had never yielded his love of belles lettres, and Hille sourly noted that "while the crown prince did not know whether his forefathers had won Magdeburg in a card game or otherwise, he has the rules of Aristotle's *Poetics* at his fingertips and has spent the last two days gnawing his fingernails to the quick while putting German verse into French."[5] But Hille also observed that Frederick loved hard work — as long as it interested him.

The most surprising development in this period grew from another of the king's strictures. Frederick was not to speak "of war and peace or any other political matters," yet Hille soon reported that he regarded "matters of state as much more elegant and important than those of finance." His major ally here was Natzmer. Scion of an ancient Pomeranian family and son of a famous field marshal, the twenty-six-year-old warder was a long-time admirer of Frederick, to whom he had dedicated his university dissertation. Well educated, well traveled, well connected, and a francophile to boot, he was a friend of princes and diplomats. "Almost a fop," Wilhelmina sniffed, and Hille refused to take him seriously, writing to Grumbkow of "the little politician Natzmer, who makes me laugh with his unrealistic [diplomatic] embassies and negotiations." He instantly appealed to Frederick, who took him very seriously, and the two were soon involved in lengthy political discussions that often ran into the small hours.

Frederick continued one discussion in a long letter to Natzmer that would have brought howls of rage from the king, since it indirectly attacked his foreign policy. Frederick proposed no less than a new "system" if Prussia were to prosper. Her awkward physical position — she was open to attack from all sides — made it incumbent on the ruler to maintain "good relations with all the kings, the emperors, and the principal electors," because war with these neighbors could only be disadvantageous. The ruler could not stop here, however, "for when one does not advance, one retreats," and the ruler must constantly work for the further aggrandizement of the House of Hohenzollern. He must do whatever possible to "sew on again each of the detached pieces," be it Polish Prussia (western Poland), which had been taken by force from the Teutonic Order, be it the duchy of Mecklenburg, "where one has only to wait patiently the extinction of the ducal line in order to take possession without further ceremony," be it Juliers and Berg, which, joined to the present Cleves estates, could garrison thirty thousand Prussian soldiers and thereby furnish a powerful western bulwark to the kingdom. "I advance from country to country," he wrote, "from conquest to conquest, like Alexander proposing new worlds to conquer." Time did not permit discussion either of the legality or mechanics of such conquests; he wished only to prove the "political necessity" of acquiring these provinces, a necessity if the King of Prussia was "to cut a striking figure among the great men of the world and play one of the great roles, neither giving nor maintaining the peace by any other reason than love of justice, and not by fear, or, if the honor of the House demanded war, being able to pursue it with vigor." Frederick demanded that his House totally lift itself "from the dust in which it has been lying, in order to make the Protestant religion flourish in Europe and the Empire; that it would become the resource of the afflicted, the supporter of widows and orphans, the provider of the poor, and the scourge of the unjust." [6]

It was a very long winter, with no alteration of the spartan regimen. Notified that Wolden had refused an invitation for Frederick to dine out, the king scribbled, "Correct; he is not to dine away from his house. This is not the place for music or dance." In late March, Wolden asked whether Frederick could attend the wedding of Münchow's daughter: "Refused; a man under arrest ought to be in prison."

Spring brought no relief. A request for light clothing was brusquely treated. "He has never worn such before, nor is it a Brandenburg-Prussian habit, but rather French." A project conceived by Frederick, undoubtedly with Natzmer's help, for marriage with an Austrian archduchess horrified Grumbkow, who ordered it burned before the king saw it. The only resolution, Grumbkow wrote to Hille, was a meeting between father and son. Until then, the errant prince would remain at Cüstrin. The king showed no sympathy but rather pleasure when told that Frederick was bored. He still did not trust him; the test would continue to be run.

All very well, replied Hille, but boredom was making the crown prince very ill tempered. "At times it is astonishing," he informed Grumbkow, "how much he resembles a thundering Jupiter [their code word for the king]. . . . His distrust increases in proportion to his vanishing hopes." Wolden warned Grumbkow that Frederick desperately needed more to do, that boredom was affecting his health, that he was nervous and upset, and that Dr. Stahl seemed to fear a nervous breakdown. "As for us monks, we shall soon all die if this way of life continues."

Owing largely to Grumbkow's work, a hole was made in the paternal dam of penance in early May. A letter from the king informed Frederick of Wilhelmina's engagement to the Hereditary Prince Frederick of Bayreuth. Frederick William added that it was time for Frederick to marry, and he would soon send Grumbkow with a list of prospective brides. This twist stemmed from the Vienna court, where Prince Eugene had decided that Frederick must marry the Empress of Austria's niece, Princess Elizabeth of Brunswick-Bevern, in order to bind the crown prince to Habsburg interests. Grumbkow turned up in Cüstrin in June to hawk this particular piece of matrimonial goods and won tentative agreement from Frederick, but "on condition that the bride would be neither dumb nor disagreeable." Meanwhile his letters to the king dripped with sycophancy, but to no apparent effect. In late May the king wrote to Wolden that the crown prince must become accustomed to leading a quiet life, "for if I had done what he did I would be ashamed to show my face to anyone. . . . He shall obey only my will, get rid of those French and English manners, think only as a Prussian, be faithful to God and his father, and have a German heart." In late June the ever-patient Wolden wrote to the king that his son hoped he would stop by Cüstrin when traveling to Prussia. But Frederick William had no desire to see his son: "I shall know when that wicked heart has changed and become genuine and not full of hypocrisy."

Frederick evidently was to remain in the wilderness.

14

FREDERICK'S first break came in August 1731, nine months after his release from prison. Due mainly to Grumbkow's intervention, the king interrupted an inspection trip to visit Cüstrin, a cloud of self-righteousness whirling down on a plain of sycophancy. "As soon as I have looked into the whites of his eyes," he wrote to Wolden, "I shall know whether he has improved or not." The test came at von Münchow's house on the king's forty-third birthday. Frederick fell at his father's feet with all the fervor of Thomas à Becket prostrating himself before King Henry II. The king told him to stand, then subjected him to stern review of his evil ways. Frederick again flung himself at the royal feet, again was bidden to rise. The king questioned him closely, and he admitted that he had wanted to escape to England. Had he thought of the consequences? his father asked. His mother would have suffered the greatest misfortune; Wilhelmina would have been imprisoned for life. Finally, "I would have invaded Hanover and burned and ravaged it even at the cost of my life and kingdom." Asked if he had corrupted Katte or vice versa, Frederick replied, "I corrupted him." Frederick William said, "I am glad to hear you tell the truth for once."[1]

The interview continued. Did the prince still hate the army; did he still regard his uniform as a shroud? (Oh no, sire.) Did the prince still embrace such Calvinist heresies as predestination? (Oh no, sire.) Slightly mollified, the inquisitor launched into self-deprecation: "I can quite understand that my company displeases you. I have no French manners; I am neither witty nor foppish. I am a German prince, and I shall live and die a German prince." The crown prince had better try to do the same. There was not much hope for him, the king rambled on, but there was some — and with the idea of nursing that wee bit, the king was willing to forgive what was past.

A sort of pardon.

Frederick fell to the floor, this time in tears, and fervently kissed the king's boots. Frederick William raised his son, held him briefly to his breast. Frederick followed him from the chamber and at the royal carriage again fell to the ground. Tears welled in Frederick William's eyes as he lifted his son, embraced him, and promised ultimate benediction.

Frederick seemed genuinely touched. Later he told Hille that this was the first sign of love his father had ever shown him.

Frederick's world now changed for the better. In the mornings he sat next to President Münchow at meetings of the chamber, where he frequently offered opinions on matters at hand. He could go where he wished in the afternoon, and he quickly traded the onerous council air for open fields and fragrant forests of neighboring crownlands and estates, where he began to learn the practical side of farming — how fields were ploughed, fertilized, planted; crops harvested; grain stored and marketed; cows calved; beer brewed; wool shorn and spun; how flax was turned to cloth; animals slaughtered; meat smoked. When work palled, he could hunt and fish; crown commissioners and estate owners everywhere vied in capturing him for elaborate meals and entertainments.

He was scarcely free. He was not allowed to spend nights away from Cüstrin; he could invite no woman to table (or bed); his reading was still prescribed; and he was allowed neither music nor dance. His request again to wear a uniform brought a lengthy and insulting refusal. As long as Frederick preferred French flutes, fops, and females to a company of grenadiers, which he regarded as *canailles,* he was not worthy to wear a uniform. Once he learned how to conduct himself and his affairs, once he was done with rogues and whores and stopped wasting money on trinkets and bagatelles, once he learned to show his father proper respect and obedience, then and only then would he again become a Prussian soldier.

Grumbkow was doing his best to heal the relationship. Shortly after the king's visit he had prepared formal instructions that spelled out Frederick's future behavior. He was to stop all the nonsense that so irritated the king. He would be humble and contrite and would ask the king's advice on various matters. He would no longer call the king "Papa" but rather "Majesty," as Frederick William had called his father. Grumbkow's strictures extended to the smallest detail, and it is evident from correspondence that Frederick paid the closest attention to the advice.[2]

The king on his part sent Frederick horses, a carriage, and new clothes, and also responded warmly to detailed reports on neighboring crown lands. Here new outbuildings were needed; there a brewery must be repaired; here a wood could be cleared and turned into profitable grazing land; there the sandy and chalky soil needed fertilizing. Not only was the reformed dilettante spending most of his waking hours examining estates and talking to farmers, foresters, stewards, bailiffs, brewers, and local officials, but he became a veritable Nimrod, chasing deer and stags about the land and even practicing marksmanship. His letters reeked of the humility, obedience, and flattery demanded by the king: "Finally, I shall do everything possible to apply myself to all economic matters, and through incessant industry and humble respect, obedience and submission, make myself worthy of seeking my most gracious father's favor."

Frederick reported a great deal to his father but omitted certain details. In late September, in accordance with the king's wish, he had entertained Prince Charles of Brunswick, who was passing through. He failed to add that to make up for drinking only very little, they had made a lot of noise and thoroughly torn up an inn. He probably did not mention the presence of a new valet, Michael Gabriel Fredersdorff, a private soldier but an oboist and flautist whom Frederick had heard play one evening in Frankfurt; he was transferred to Cüstrin on orders of Lieutenant General Count Kurt Christoph von Schwerin, who liked the crown prince and did everything possible for him. Fredersdorff was four years older than Frederick, clever, well mannered, tall, and strikingly handsome. The two hit it off; he may have been used to smuggle letters between Frederick and Wilhelmina.

Frederick had earlier reported shooting ducks with Colonel von Wreech at nearby Tamsel estate. He did not, however, mention the colonel's wife, the beautiful twenty-three-year-old Louise Eleanor, with whom he promptly fell in love and who became pregnant in September. Judging from extant letters and poems, Frederick was responsible; at least Colonel von Wreech later denied being the father. There is no doubt that the juices were flowing strongly in Frederick's nineteen-year-old body at this time. Lieutenant General Count von Schulenberg visited him in October and reported to Grumbkow that he had grown larger and was healthy and cheerful. So animated was his friendship with Louise that the count felt it necessary to deliver a homily on morals: Frederick must not devote himself to women, because "the slight pleasures gained cause a million displeasures." The prince bluntly refused the advice. His father had lived it up as a youth, he told Schulenburg, and he would do likewise. He was not worried about the pox (syphilis), which everyone got and which could be cured. He went on to suggest that the count himself had just enjoyed an extracurricular fling in Vienna, and when that was hotly denied, Frederick said that he must have "the gift of continence, but I assure you that I do not."[3]

The romance continued through the winter. Frederick wrote to Louise's mother of her daughter's insurpassable "beauty, her majestic air, her bearing, and her entire deportment." In late February, Seckendorff reported the alarming situation to Prince Eugene, but by then it was finished. Frederick already had sent her his portrait, which he hoped would cause her to think of him and say, "He was not a bad fellow but he bored me because he loved me too much and often annoyed me with his clumsy love." Louise duly delivered a daughter, whom the king believed to be Frederick's. "He is very pleased," Grumbkow wrote to Seckendorff, "hoping that he will do the same for la Bevern [Princess Elizabeth]."[4] Frederick somewhat enigmatically denied the charge. But a few years later he would write to Voltaire of this "little wonder of nature" who had taught him love and poetry "with taste and delicacy." "I did well enough in love but poorly in poetry."

While Frederick was frolicking from forest to field and from brewery to bed in Cüstrin, preparations for Wilhelmina's marriage were being made in Berlin. From the somewhat meager list of candidates (nominated by Grumbkow and Seckendorff at the Austrian court's suggestion), Wilhelmina had selected Margrave Frederick of Brandenburg-Kulmbach, the Hereditary Prince of Bayreuth. The decision infuriated Queen Sophia, who had continued secret negotiations with the English court and still hoped for a double marriage. "I no longer own you as my daughter," she allegedly told Wilhelmina. Nor did the margrave particularly please the Prussian king, who, Wilhelmina wrote, got the unfortunate prospect drunk every day "to test his character and accustom him to drink," and who found him far too refined and effeminate. He would have preferred the uncouth Duke of Weissenfels, but since the Austrian court approved of Margrave Frederick, he ordered an elaborate wedding and secretly arranged for the presence of his son Frederick.

The crown prince did not attend the wedding in late November, but he did appear suddenly at an elegant ball a few nights later. Wilhelmina found him "so much altered that I should scarcely have known him again." He had become very stout, "very broad in the shoulders, and his head seemed sunk between them: he was no longer so handsome." He responded to Wilhelmina's impassioned embraces and words with distinct coolness, and when she presented her husband, Frederick refused to speak to him. She partially recovered on learning that von Grumbkow had advised Frederick to seem aloof in order to impress the king, but nevertheless the relationship between brother and sister was beginning to change.

If Wilhelmina had lost a brother, the king had gained a crown prince. When four hundred couples sat to dinner, Frederick and the king dined elsewhere, "in a select circle," where the father reportedly treated his son with great affection. The two appeared the following day at a military review, "where Crowds of People of all Ranks," Guy Dickens reported to London, "flock'd to see His Royal Highness, and gave the most open demonstrations of their pleasure and satisfaction, at this seeming mark of a thorough Reconciliation between the King of Prussia and his Son."[5] A few days later a group of senior generals, headed by Prince Leopold, petitioned the king to return Frederick to the army. He was easily convinced, and at a banquet given by Seckendorff the crown prince appeared in the uniform of the Infantry Regiment Goltz, which he would soon command.

Total submission, blind obedience. That is what the king demanded; that is what he got. A few days after Frederick's return to Custrin to serve the final months of his parole, he wrote to his father, "I know I have you alone to thank and in consequence will always have loyalty, respect, love, deference, and appreciation for you; I wish only that I had opportunity to convince my most gracious father of my sincerity." The king received his words "with great pleasure" and replied, "I also have confidence in you [and believe that] you will steadfastly continue in this way and leave yourself entirely in my hands; then you will learn that you have a father who loves you from the heart, and will love you always, and further will take care of you in every way."

Frederick hastened to exploit the reconciliation. His letters were stuffed with details calculated to win royal approval. He suggested that peasants bound to crownlands should plough only three times a week with two horses instead of daily with one horse, a suggestion endorsed by local crown officials. He submitted his household accounts to the last groschen and asked advice on how to manage his cook. In January he was in Marienwald, working out final arrangements for glass factories, and he sent some specimen glasses. He was delighted to hear that Wilhelmina was with child and hoped that his father might "live to enjoy the grandchild in complete health and happiness." A lieutenant came through Custrin with seventy remount horses: "I looked at them. They were in excellent shape and none was lame." He went to a pig shoot, killed twenty sows; a beef was slaughtered, and because he knew "how much my most gracious father likes it," he sent a piece for roasting. He

asked for and received a copy of the "Infantry Regulations" and assiduously studied them. He came down with three-day fever, and although he had learned to prefer beer, in accordance with paternal desires, he drank champagne because the doctors prescribed it. He hoped
that his most gracious father was not annoyed with all of his plans,
which were designed to make "my most gracious father a fair profit,
and when I hit on something I joyfully submit it; please be assured that
it stems from a really sincere intention."

The king lapped it up. His replies to Frederick were not only enthusiastic but cordial and warm, even loving. He sent the "Infantry Regulations" immediately. He approved a large number of proposed projects, complimented Frederick on his progress, thanked him for gifts,
sent him three riding horses, and promised an equipage: "Keep God
before your eyes and be obedient, and learn how to run your household
and make do with your income, and spend nothing until you consider
if you can't buy it more cheaply, and apply yourself to this so that I
can trust you with more."

Not all observers were as favorably impressed. Grumbkow privately
complained that Frederick was a troublemaker with but little judgment. General von Schulenburg feared that he was too much the romantic ruled solely by emotions and willing to accept only those companions who were intellectually inferior to him but who shared his
pleasures. He was leading a far too licentious life, was perhaps too
aware of his importance, and was not interested in good advice. His
desire to find the ludicrous side of everyone's nature and his inclination
to poke painful fun at people seemed dangerous qualities for a prince,
who should indeed discern human weaknesses but keep that knowledge to himself. Count von Seckendorff informed the Vienna court that,
although Frederick was a spendthrift, his greatest weaknesses were dis-
sembling and deceit — the count was master practitioner of
each — and that his numerous and passionate love affairs, arranged by
Natzmer, would undoubtedly cause trouble when the king learned of
them. "On the other hand his physical strength cannot sufficiently support his taste for wicked pleasures, and it follows that the crown prince
seeks more a frivolous renown from his romances than a sinful preference."[6] Hille agreed that Frederick was far too frivolous, and he also
criticized his contempt for the ordinary man, an aristocratic bias that
he blamed on Frederick's francophilia. The Cüstrin experience, Hille
wrote, had not altered this damaging passion for things French, a ju-
venile and unrealistic blindness that made Frederick prone to flattery
and in time would hurt him severely.* Wolden wrote to Grumbkow

* In a letter of October 7, 1732, Frederick related Hille's good qualities but criticized him for
being irreligious and for an insupportable arrogance and hatred (envy) of the aristocracy.
(Frederick der Grosse, Briefswechsel . . . mit Grumbkow.)

that the prince had strongly benefited in heart and mind from adversity, but he hoped that the king would live for a few more years so that the crown prince could mature. "My bet is that he will be one of the greatest princes produced by the House of Brandenburg."[7]

Frederick had to make a final submission if the new relationship with his father was to continue. The question of his marriage had been brewing since the previous spring. Although it was virtually common knowledge in Berlin that he would marry Princess Elizabeth of Brunswick-Bevern, Frederick had been wavering for some time, telling colleagues in the chamber that he was not willing to take a pig in a poke. He had told Schulenburg in October that if he were forced to marry, he would do so, but it would be strictly a marriage of convenience and he would go his own way afterward. Subsequently he had learned that Elizabeth was "not very pretty, speaks but little, and acts like a blockhead." Moreover the empress her aunt had so little money that she could not give Elizabeth much of a dowry. He would prefer to marry one of the Austrian archduchesses (presumably Maria Theresa) or the Russian czarina's niece, the beautiful Princess Anne of Mecklenburg, who claimed a dowry of two or three million rubles. If forced to marry Elizabeth, he wrote to Grumbkow, "I will disown her once I am king, and I doubt that the [Austrian] empress would be very pleased. I cannot tolerate a stupid wife; I must be able to talk sensibly with her or it is not for me."

The blow arrived one night in early February when a courier galloped into Cüstrin to hand Frederick a letter from the king. Having examined as many eligible princesses as possible, the king wrote, he had decided on the Empress of Austria's niece, seventeen-year-old Princess Elizabeth, who "is not ugly, but neither is she beautiful. . . . [She is] a God-fearing person which is all important." The king wanted nothing more than to see his son married and in the army; once he had spawned an heir, he could even go on his long-desired tour of European capitals.

Frederick meekly accepted the decision by letter but then wrote to Grumbkow, "I have always wanted to distinguish myself by the sword and have not wanted to obtain royal favor by any other means. Now I will have only the duty to fuck. I pity this poor person, for she will be one more unhappy princess in the world."

Pity soon turned to chagrin, then hysterical self-pity, as Frederick poured out his heart in a series of impassioned letters to Grumbkow. He sensed nothing good about his fiancée, to whom he variously referred as "this unpleasant creature," "the corpus delecti," "the abominable object of my desires," "my Dulcinea," "my mute," or "the person." He would rather marry "the biggest whore in Berlin than a person surrounded by religious hypocrites." Even Grumbkow's own daughter, he wrote tactlessly, without family or fortune, would be better than a

Princess Elizabeth Christina of Brunswick-Bevern, chosen bride for Crown Prince Frederick. "I pity this poor person," Frederick wrote before the marriage, "for she will be one more unhappy princess in the world."

Below: Frederick and his new wife *(left)*, with the Rheinsberg palace in the background. In the autumn of 1737 Frederick told a friend that a fitting epitaph for him would be "Here is one who lived for a year."

stupid princess. If she could be changed, which he doubted, then it was up to Grumbkow to intervene. Grumbkow's description of the king's pleasure in Frederick's acceptance and of the prospective bride — quite attractive but reserved and plain — changed nothing.

Frederick's ill-advised letter both frightened and angered Grumbkow. He had done his best in coping with a potentially explosive situation. He had assured Frederick that special tutors would teach the girl various graces before next winter's wedding, and he had stressed the many advantages that the marriage would bring to Frederick. But he sternly reminded his ward that he had accepted the king's decision without demur; the king with tears in his eyes had shown Frederick's letter to Grumbkow and said that this was the happiest day in his life. Now Frederick might ruin everything.

But Frederick was largely acting. He would soon make it up with Grumbkow and would continue to milk the situation for every conceivable advantage. In late February he arrived in Berlin and behaved with considerable decorum. The Brunswick court was already there, along with such luminaries as Grand Duke Francis of Lorraine (who would marry Archduchess Maria Theresa and become Emperor of the Holy Roman Empire). Frederick liked Francis and seemed to enjoy the many dinners, reviews, and even hunts that the king arranged for them. "He is the most charming prince," Frederick wrote to Wilhelmina. "He has all imaginable wit and a noble and easy bearing. . . . When we are together we must be both taken for fools, for we do nothing but laugh and joke." As for Princess Elizabeth: "The person is neither beautiful nor ugly, nor does she lack intelligence but is very poorly educated, bashful and without breeding. . . . You may judge for yourself if she is to my taste."

Early in March the two courts visited the king's bedchamber for the *preliminaires de fiançailles,* at which Frederick and Elizabeth pledged troth to each other but did not exchange rings. The ceremony left Frederick cold. Guy Dickens reported that he scarcely spoke to Elizabeth and avoided being alone with her. Frederick told Grumbkow that the girl had a good heart and he would not do her any harm, "but I shall never be able to love her." At the formal betrothal where they exchanged rings — hers was allegedly worth twenty-four thousand thalers — he made no secret of his feelings before three hundred guests. Once the ceremony ended, he abruptly turned from Elizabeth to converse at length with a young beauty said to be his current mistress.

Princess Elizabeth, undoubtedly a nervous wreck from the entire ghastly experience, returned to Brunswick to undergo a crash course in manners, deportment, conversation, and dancing. Frederick, newly appointed colonel in command of Regiment Goltz, left for regimental headquarters at Neu-Ruppin, a village some forty miles north of Berlin.

1 5

RUPPIN was Cüstrin with a regiment. The village of Neu-Ruppin (as opposed to Alt-Ruppin, a few kilometers away) loomed from a flat landscape of peat bogs, meadows, and marshlands interrupted by woods and lakes, and by rude farm cottages and narrow sandy roads used by ox carts to bring in the harvest. Villages and farms sat in the royal domain, an unsmiling authority upheld by bailiffs, accountants, and Infantry Regiment Goltz.

Frederick had been sent there primarily to ensure that his unit would become combat-ready in the fullest sense. He would resume the military education that had been so abruptly interrupted, and he would continue the civil education begun in Cüstrin; he was to draft new leases for local crownlands. The king had bought him a comfortable house at nearby Nauen, and here, joined by the chamberlain Wolden, Rohwedel, and his now-permanent valet Fredersdorff, he turned to the job at hand.

The army that Frederick rejoined in 1732 numbered over seventy-five thousand, which made it the fourth largest in Europe after the armies of France, Russia, and Austria. It was incontestably the best in appearance and drill. Its guiding genius, Prince Leopold of Anhalt-Dessau — known to the troops as *der Schnauzbart* (the Mustache) and to others as Old Dessauer — had introduced iron ramrods, which did not break like wooden ones and, when used by trained and disciplined troops, increased the speed of loading and thus the rate of fire. Perhaps as important, he had also improved the bayonet so that it remained attached to the musket during firing, and he had introduced marching in step (the *Gleichschritt*), which eventually led to the precision close-order drill so greatly admired by foreign visitors and so helpful in battlefield maneuverability.

King Frederick William had also played a major role in building the army. Shortly after his accession, he had introduced a comprehensive set of regulations that were quite extraordinary for the time. They covered life in garrison and field in detail; they prescribed a complicated manual of arms, drill, and maneuver; they specified the type of material, color, and cut of uniforms (including the number of buttons).

The king also weaned Prussia from a militia system and from dependence on foreign subsidies. Such was the financial profit from his hard civil rule that the army had nearly doubled since he ascended the throne; he would soon increase it further by introducing the "canton system" of regimental replacements. Aside from the hunt, the army was his ruling passion, and he was immensely proud of it and its reputation.

As Old Dessauer put it, "Friend and foe admire Your Majesty's infantry — your friends regard it as one of the wonders of the world; your foes admire it with trembling."[1]

Infantry Regiment Goltz, or Prussian Infantry Regiment Number 15, consisted of about seventeen hundred troops, of whom 50 were officers and perhaps 150 were noncommissioned officers. In addition to some fourteen hundred musketeers and grenadiers, the command included a quartermaster, an auditor, a lawyer, a chaplain, a surgeon-major and twelve surgeons, a drum major, six drummers and six fifers, a gunsmith, and a provost marshal. The regiment was divided into two battalions, one in and around Ruppin, the other at Nauen. Each battalion consisted of five musketeer companies, with twelve grenadiers in each company.

The troops did not live in barracks or eat in mess halls. They were billeted in private dwellings — houses and farms — anywhere from two to a dozen men in each, depending on the holding. A private soldier received two pounds of bread a day and one and a half pounds of meat a week, the cost of which was deducted from his monthly wage of two and a half thalers. Soldiers cooked their own meals in the household's fireplace or kitchen and each contributed a few more groschen a week to a general fund for supplementary rations.

Recruit training was tough. Close-order drill and the numerous "evolutions" and "maneuvers" cited in the king's voluminous "Regulations" took months to master. The manual of arms consisted of thirty-nine separate orders with 112 "motions" or movements that must have exhausted even the strongest youth. "It is necessary, in the first place," so read the "Regulations," "to observe that every man under arms, and particularly at the place of exercise, appears with a good grace, holds his head and body upright and unconstrained, keeps his feet in a proper position, and draws in his belly."

Considerable emphasis was given to musket fire and to the rapid loading and firing for which the Prussian army was famous:

> Every man must be taught to load quick, and to do all the firing motions properly. . . . The men must half cock their firelocks briefly, in coming down to level their firelocks; and take hold of their cartridges nimbly, which are to be roll'd up tight, and plac'd in the pouch with the tops downwards. As soon as the men have taken out their cartridges, they must bite the tops hastily off, so far, that the powder may fall into their mouths, then prime, shut their pans, and cast about to charge with quick motions, taking care, in casting about, not to spill any: they must then bring up their cartridges nimbly to the muzzle, shake the powder down the barrels, draw their rammers as quick as possible at two motions, shorten them, put them in the barrels, and ram the charge well down. . . . The rammers must then be nimbly recover'd, shorten'd, and return'd, one for another.[2]

Company drill was fairly relaxed for most of the year. For nine months, up to 40 percent of the command was furloughed to home farms or villages, which meant that the average Prussian peasant soldier spent up to three months a year on furlough without pay; the money saved went into the king's general recruiting fund. Soldiers who could not be furloughed — that is, foreigners who constituted from 30 to 40 percent of the entire army — enjoyed local leaves and liberties and could work on farms or in villages for wages. They were allowed to marry, and their wives could also work. Normally they had to perform garrison duties, drill ten or twelve days a month — short but exhausting sessions — and were required to stand watches and parades, including a Sunday church parade.

On duty they performed like automatons. King Frederick William demanded complete obedience and total subservience: "When one takes the oath to the flag one renounces oneself and surrenders entirely, even one's life and all, to the monarch in order to fulfill the Lord's will; and through this blind obedience one receives the grace and the confirmation of the title of soldier." An officer of that day, Varnhagen von Ense, later wrote:

> Order and punctuality were extended with implacable severity to the most insignificant matters. . . . Every accident was punished as if it were a crime. A slip in the manual exercises, an improperly polished button on the uniform, or water spots on spatterdashes [leggings] would draw down a severe caning. Caning in fact became so common that it was regarded as part of the service, and no drill passed without one.[3]

Any form of insubordination, any theft or drunkenness, was punished by flogging or, worse, by being made to run the gauntlet. The victim was stripped naked and forced to run between two lines of his fellows, who either beat him with all their strength or were beaten themselves by watchful sergeants. A man running the gauntlet only once was fortunate to escape with the skin torn from his back. Many a man condemned to running it more than once did not survive. This was company punishment only. For more serious crimes, particularly mutiny or desertion, the soldier was court-martialed and usually sentenced to be hanged, burned, broken on the wheel or otherwise tortured, beheaded, or shot.

Normal garrison routine changed abruptly in April of each year, the first of what were called the three drill months. By the time Frederick joined his regiment, all men on furlough had been recalled to bring the units to full strength. Uniforms, shoes, and weapons were being repaired or replaced, companies drilled from dawn to dusk, all in preparation for the general review of those regiments summoned to Berlin by the king in June.

Much of the routine was familiar to Frederick, who had practically teethed on a bayonet and had accompanied his father to military reviews for years. Daily drill and attendant administrative minutiae were scarcely exciting for the twenty-year-old crown prince, who had just been the toast of Berlin. Not long after taking command, he wrote dejectedly to Grumbkow that he must go to Potsdam to watch the giants drill (so that Regiment Goltz could emulate them at the general review): "New brooms sweep clean; I must emphasize my new character, and make one see that I am an *able* officer."

Grumbkow replied sympathetically. He wanted to keep Frederick stable at this delicate time, because the Vienna court wanted nothing more than his marriage to Princess Elizabeth. Prince Eugene already had sent Seckendorff twenty-five hundred ducats to "lend" Frederick, whose debts could not be repaid from the king's niggardly allowance of five hundred thalers per month. The task now was to keep him isolated but as content as possible while poor Elizabeth learned the necessary social graces. (Seckendorff hoped that in time her smallpox scars would disappear and that her neck would become less scrawny.) Mainly for these reasons the marriage was postponed to spring of 1733. Meanwhile Frederick was to be surrounded with companions who were sworn Imperialists. Seckendorff and Grumbkow tried unsuccessfully to have Count von Schulenburg replace Wolden as chamberlain; they did succeed in preventing both Natzmer and Keyserling from joining Frederick.

Seckendorff informed Frederick that the Vienna court was aware of his debts from the Cüstrin period and was prepared to advance five hundred ducats in monthly payments to avoid arousing the king's suspicions. The first payment, called a "book" in their secret correspondence, delighted the prince, who quickly realized that Seckendorff and Grumbkow had placed themselves in an awkward situation, because the king would have their heads if the "loan" were ever discovered. He soon asked for more "books" to pay for pâté de foie gras from Strasbourg, oysters and capons from Hamburg, Hungarian wines, and French champagne — so many "books" that Seckendorff quickly spent the allotted sum and requested Eugene to provide a secret "pension" of six thousand ducats a year for the crown prince. Frederick continued to take advantage of a good thing and in time even persuaded Seckendorff to arrange a pension and employment for his former tutor Duhan and a considerable sum of cash for strapped Wilhelmina — all at Vienna's expense.[4]

These presents did not cover all of Frederick's extraordinary expenses. He early complained that he could invite no more than four friends to dinner because of his sharply limited budget. The main problem was one that he shared with all regimental and company com-

manders. Sickness and age dictated an annual attrition rate of about
20 percent, which meant that each year a regiment had to recruit some
three hundred sound specimens. This in turn meant that regimental
and company commanders vied with each other in recruiting at home
and abroad. If commanders were to gain royal favor, at least some of
the recruits had to be "big men," bought abroad or kidnapped with
considerable difficulty and risk. A five-foot, ten-inch Rhinelander cost
about seven hundred thalers, a six-footer a thousand thalers, genuine
giants several thousand. When the king inspected individual regiments
at a general review, he took his pick of these men for the Potsdam
Grenadiers, and he usually paid the commander for them. It was vital,
however, for a commander to produce such recruits, and many a promising career had been summarily ended by failure to do so.

Crown Prince Frederick was not immune from the requirement to
enlist big men. Already in April one of his officers was under arrest in
Hesse-Cassel for illegal recruiting. In July Frederick was pressing the
king to pay him money owed for recruits from his regiment for the past
year, and he eventually got over fifteen hundred thalers. Simultaneously he asked Seckendorff to help him purchase some big men from
senior Austrian generals. He also wrote Captain Count Hans Christian
von Hacke at Potsdam that he had been forced to discharge thirty un-
desirables: "And how am I to replace them? I would like every bit as
much as Old Dessauer to give the king big men, but I have no
money. . . . Next year I shall have one recruit only to show the king
and my regiment will be a rabble." At about the same time he wrote to
the king that he had learned of a shepherd in Mecklenburg who was at
least six feet, four inches tall, and asked permission to kidnap him,
which the king readily granted. The attempt failed and the shepherd
was shot to death, but Frederick gained credit for trying.

16

IN THAT YEAR of 1732 another problem loomed larger in Frederick's
mind than either finances or recruits. This was his approaching marriage. That autumn he wrote to Wilhelmina, "I do not love the princess; on the contrary she is repugnant to me and our marriage cannot
be good, since we can have neither friendship nor compatibility." He
was forced to correspond with his fiancée, but his letters were short
and desultory, significantly lacking verses, which he normally inflicted
on friends.

When the king took him to task for not writing to Elizabeth as often as he should, he denied the charge and blamed the mail service, then exploded to Grumbkow that the king would force him to love "by blows of a stick, but since I do not have a donkey's nature I fear he will not succeed. . . . The truth is I lack material and often do not know how to fill the page." Frederick believed that the complaint had come from Elizabeth's mother — "the fat tripe-dealer," he called her — in order to put him under his future bride's thumb. It wouldn't work. Once married, he would be sovereign in his own house, and his wife would have nothing to say: "I believe that anyone who allows himself to be bossed by a woman is the biggest asshole in the world and unworthy of being called a man." That aside, it was all wrong to try to force him to love someone. "Love can never be forced. I love sex but in a very fickle way; I like the immediate pleasure, but afterward I despise it. Judge then if I am the stuff from which one makes good husbands. It makes me wild to become one, but I am making a virtue of necessity. I shall keep my word. I shall marry; but after that, goodbye and good luck."

Grumbkow again tried to put the best light on Elizabeth, writing that his daughter, who had recently visited her, found her greatly improved. Although she was still very shy in the presence of her despotic mother and blushed whenever spoken to, when the young women were by themselves, the general's daughter assured her father,

> she lacks neither intelligence nor judgment, and . . . she discusses all kinds of things very nicely, and is compassionate, apparently being very good-natured. She likes to have a good time and is considered a good dancer; she does not dress well and is very slovenly. I believe that if someone told her this she would soon change. . . . Berlin greatly pleases her and she wishes very much to return there, apparently desiring to get married.

Frederick remained unenthusiastic. When the king announced that after the carnival they would visit Elizabeth and her family in Brunswick, Frederick wrote to Grumbkow: "I confess that I feel no great impatience for the trip, knowing already what my mute friend will say to me. . . . [However] I shall act the part at Brunswick to the hilt." Father and son departed in February, Frederick having secretly borrowed money from Seckendorff for the trip. He proved as good an actor as always, and his father wrote Old Dessauer approvingly that "the lovers are very much in love."

The prince returned to Ruppin seemingly resigned to his matrimonial fate, perhaps even looking forward to the event, which possibly would permit him to travel outside the kingdom. Although Queen Sophia continued to work for a revival of the double marriage between the Prussian and English courts, Frederick was not very interested, having become nearly as disillusioned with the English court as was his father. Sophia's attempts to sabotage the current marriage plan by spreading highly critical pronouncements of Elizabeth's shortcomings met only with contempt on Frederick's part and if European politics had not intervened, the entire situation would have remained as the king intended.

King Frederick William was still loyal to Emperor Charles. The previous winter he had used his influence in the Diet to persuade the German states to accept the Pragmatic Sanction. In the summer of 1732 he had forced a meeting with the emperor in Bohemia. This was the last thing the Austrian court wanted. Austrian influence in European affairs had been steadily growing, at French and Spanish expense. By the 1731 Treaty of Vienna, the maritime powers, England and Holland, had guaranteed the Pragmatic Sanction. Seckendorff's active diplomacy had settled a number of differences within the Empire, and the Vienna court did not wish to upset anyone by meeting with the King of Prussia, who inevitably would demand payment for his support. Frederick William was pleased enough with his reception, but his political hopes were dashed; Prince Eugene bluntly said he would have to content himself with only a part of Berg, not including its capital, Düsseldorf.

Prince Eugene next added insult to injury by accepting a modified plan for a Prussian-English marriage that would have canceled Frederick's engagement. Wishing to curry favor with England, Eugene ordered Seckendorff to introduce it in the Tabagie. Seckendorff, who called this the most difficult mission ever given him by the emperor, approached Grumbkow, who refused to have any part in the scheme. The king was momentarily displeased with the Vienna court, which was actively encouraging persecution of Salzburg Protestants (of whom some twenty thousand would finally be resettled in Prussia at his expense). The new plan would open a Pandora's box and end in unalterable hatred of Prussia for Austria. "The king is not as stupid as you think," he told Seckendorff, who nonetheless brought up the subject in a Tabagie. Frederick William was first "taken aback," then "overcome," and very shortly "outraged." No one had ever seen him "in such a rage," and he denounced the Vienna court in terms formerly reserved for the English.[1]

Matters might have ended there but for the death of King August the Strong. Early in 1733, while traveling to Poland, the sixty-three-year-old monarch had summoned Grumbkow to Crossen to discuss his ambitious diplomatic plans. Acting on Frederick William's instructions to pump the Polish king for all he was worth, the general had turned the meeting into a prolonged drinking bout, from which neither participant ever fully recovered. Throughout January, August weakened so much that he told his confessor, "I have not at present strength to name my many and great sins."[2] His death brought a new political crisis.

France was vitally interested in Polish affairs. The new French envoy to Prussia, the Marquis de la Chétardie (only six years older than Crown Prince Frederick), had been doing his best to wean the Prussian king from Seckendorff's influence, and this now seemed possible. The Versailles court announced that the Polish crown would revert to the former King of Poland, Stanislaus Leszczynski, King Louis's father-in-law. Neither Russia nor Austria would accept this; their choice was the Saxon elector. Frederick William would back the elector only if he guaranteed Prussian claims to Berg and the duchy of Kurland. When the elector refused and when Russia backed away from earlier agreements, Frederick William withdrew support from the emperor. Seckendorff and Grumbkow furled political sails to weather the storm, and by May the Prussian king once again had become "the good and faithful ally of His Imperial and Catholic Majesty," as he put it in a formal note to Chétardie.[3]

But at this critical point, when war with France was imminent, Emperor Charles became ever more desirous of alliance with England and Holland. King George was not unwilling. He was concerned over Bourbon expansion and the concomitant threat to his beloved and relatively unprotected Hanover. However, in return for such an alliance, which would bring down Gallic wrath, he demanded a reversal of Prussian marriage plans. Crown Prince Frederick was to marry his daughter Princess Emily.

This was the situation in June 1733, when the Prussian king and his court, including Count von Seckendorff, traveled to Brunswick for Frederick's wedding. Their host was the Duke of Wolfenbüttel, Elizabeth's grandfather, who received them in the beautiful palace of Salzdahlum. But while royal coaches had rumbled through budding countryside, a courier was galloping from Vienna with an urgent letter from Prince Eugene to Seckendorff.

King Frederick William was still in bed when Seckendorff delivered Eugene's message. The Vienna court wanted Frederick William to cancel his son's marriage. Instead, Frederick would marry the English princess and Elizabeth would marry the Prince of Wales. The King flew into a violent rage. He refused even to consider what he called a dastardly plot. With that, the ceremony took place as scheduled. Frederick remained only a short time in the bridal suite before making a solitary promenade in the gardens. At midnight he wrote briefly to Wilhelmina: "At this precise moment, my dear sister, the ceremony is finished, and praise God that it is over. I hope that you will take it as a token of my friendship that I give you first news of it."

The ordeal was not quite over. Numerous reviews and presentations spotted the return trip to Berlin. There, Frederick installed Elizabeth in Schönhausen, a palace outside Berlin that was the king's present to her. In late June the crown prince drilled his regiment in the Berlin general review and then returned to Ruppin. His bride was to remain in Berlin until he found a suitable place for them to live.

17

AMONG FREDERICK'S wedding presents from the king was the income from Ruppin crown lands, a not overly generous gift, but the king also told his son to find an estate suitable for married life. Frederick discovered what he wanted at Rheinsberg, an old château overlooking lake, woods, and farmland. His personal survey went to the king in November. He found it "agreeable" and bought the property for seventy-five thousand thalers, of which twenty thousand came from Crown Princess Elizabeth's dowry. The king put up another twenty-five hundred thalers to pave the main street and marketplace of the nearby town, and to replace thatched roofs with tile. The work was to be completed in five years, and the inhabitants would also enjoy some tax relief and other privileges. The king also agreed to pay for extensive renovations of the château: "You must seek out some good architect or engineer who will build you something handsome and convenient."

A great deal of work had to be done on the old house and its neglected gardens and grounds. Early plans were drawn and the work supervised by the king's architect, but very little progress had been made before another major political crisis interrupted the work to take Crown Prince Frederick to his first war.

In September 1733, the Versailles court by judicious bribes had persuaded the Polish Diet to re-elect Stanislaus Leszczynski the new King of Poland. Stanislaus had arrived in Poland somewhat ignominiously —he traveled through Prussia disguised as a merchant — to accept the honor. It was short-lived, because Russia and Austria at once sent armies to Warsaw. Being practical men, the members of the Diet now elected August the Strong's heir as king. Stanislaus fled to Danzig, which the Russians, much against the wishes of Frederick William, besieged. When a French relief force failed to reach the port, Stanislaus escaped to Königsberg in Prussia, where he remained under Frederick William's protection. France, which had made a secret treaty with Spain in 1733, meanwhile declared war on Austria and invaded and seized the border duchy of Lorraine; another army, in concert with Spanish and Sardinian troops, marched on Austrian holdings in Italy. In October the French army in Lorraine crossed the Rhine to besiege and capture Kiel and move on to the Austrian fort of Philippsburg (southwest of Heidelberg), which the French commander, Marshal Duke of Berwick, put under siege.

Emperor Charles meanwhile had called Germany to arms. Its various princes responded carelessly, all but Frederick William. At first he was of two minds. He was not too sympathetic with the emperor, "who is in a curious situation, which is his own fault," as he wrote Dessauer. For a time he held out in order to make the best deal but, probably due to the urging of Seckendorff and Grumbkow, he suddenly volunteered to march an enormous army — some forty thousand troops — to the Rhine on the emperor's behalf (in return for Imperial guarantee of his territorial claims).

This bellicose offer thoroughly alarmed Emperor Charles, whose own army was far from mobilized. The Prussian army could march almost instantly and appear on the Rhine in virtually an independent role. The emperor could never let the mere Elector of Brandenburg outshine his arms to such a degree, and he also feared that Frederick William would simultaneously seize Juliers and Berg. He thus turned down the offer, asking for only the ten thousand troops called for in their defensive treaty of 1728. The rejection surprised and angered the king, who spilled out his ire in letters to Old Dessauer, Crown Prince Frederick, and Count von Seckendorff.

Crown Prince Frederick was not too worried about political niceties. Life at Ruppin was becoming boring, and his major desire was to go to war. The Prussian force of ten thousand foot and horse did not march until April 1734. The king's orders called for short marches, only a few miles a day, with the men resting every fourth day; the force was not to be divided (probably to preclude desertion) or used as a fortress garrison; at the end of the campaign it would take up winter quarters at Austrian expense.

Regiment Goltz was not included in the task force, and rumor had it that the regiment would not march to war until its commander had impregnated his wife. Perhaps under the false impression that this blessed event had occurred, the king relented in June and sent his son off suitably escorted by two generals and a colonel who received secret and detailed instructions concerning their charge. Frederick was not to participate in close combat, but was to serve honorably and bravely and set an example to his juniors. He would maintain his own headquarters and would live economically, with only eight courses for luncheon, but another two if he entertained a foreign general and another six if he entertained Prince Eugene. He was not to gamble, drink, or whore about; any violation of the king's instructions would be carried to Potsdam by

special courier. The assignment was largely educational. Frederick was
to learn how the men's shoes were made, how long they would last,
and similar facts, with special attention to supplying an army, to making camp, and the study of artillery. He would eventually pass on to
command matters.

Frederick left Berlin at the end of June. Although the battle did not
materialize, the crown prince took his duties seriously. He made a
number of forward reconnaissances from the allied camp at Wiesenthal
and reported regularly to the king. On one occasion his party came
under dangerous cannon fire; his companion, the Prince of Liechtenstein, reported that he handled himself with utmost composure, not
even interrupting a conversation he was having with some generals.

His father arrived a week later to teach his son something of the
military profession. But now the Philippsburg garrison surrendered,
thus ending the campaign. The Prussian king seems to have spent most
of his time either dining out or smoking and drinking beer with his
entourage in a specially built thatched Tabagie. Ill health and Austrian
perfidy had worsened his temper, and although he seemed delighted
that the crown prince had made a favorable impression on Austrian
commanders, he was as critical as ever of his son. Frederick was soon
begging Wilhelmina to "pray with me that we shall soon be free of
him." Cold, rainy weather made the king miserable, and a few days
later Frederick joyfully wrote Wilhelmina that "the fat one" was finally
departing.

Frederick escorted his father as far as Mainz before returning to the
allied camp, from where he would shortly take his regiment into winter
quarters near Heidelberg. This period was more social than military.
Royalty overflowed Eugene's camp, and princes vied with princes in
holding prolonged dinner parties, which usually led to extended drinking bouts. Frederick entertained frequently in his headquarters tent,
behind which had been constructed a large dining room with windows
and thatched roof. He and Old Dessauer visited the French camp and
were well received; Frederick later recruited three French officers whom
he met here into the Prussian army. He also received one Lieutenant
François Chasot, who had killed a French officer in a duel and had
escaped to the Austrian camp; he returned to Ruppin with Frederick.

Although old Prince Eugene was too cautious tactically, Frederick
discerned his moral force, which made the French fear him "more than
the entire military strength of the Empire united against them." He was
appalled at the "reigning confusion and disorder" of the Austrian
army — he considered it undisciplined, lacking morale.

Frederick was in camp outside Heidelberg when he learned that his forty-six-year-old father had suffered a massive apoplectic seizure on the journey home, finally arriving more dead than alive at Potsdam in mid-September.

Biographers have variously treated the effect of this crisis on Frederick. Admirers have suggested that he performed an emotional volte-face and that hatred of his father suddenly turned to love. If so, it quickly turned back again, as evident in his candid letters to close friends in subsequent years. Detractors have held that Frederick could scarcely wait for the "fat one" to die and only with difficulty hid his anticipation. This is closer to the mark.

On learning of the king's illness, Frederick could easily have hurried to Potsdam and the royal bedside. Instead, he remained in Heidelberg, a town he loathed, since "it was full of Jesuit seminaries and Catholic convents," a town in which he daily was growing more bored from general inactivity. His initial mood is clearly revealed in his letter to Wilhelmina. In early September Frederick wrote to her from Heidelberg that "we remain in our usual inactivity and amuse ourselves as best we can. An express was received here two days ago to look for Dr. Eller because the king is said to be very ill in his chest. We are given a very pessimistic diagnosis by the Dutch doctor, who was called and who believes it is dropsy. We shall have more news on Friday and I shall inform you of it. The good Lord, who directs everything in the world and who determines what is to come, will dispose of the matter according to his wisdom." A week later he wrote her a chatty letter about preparations for winter troop quarters and noted that "the news which we have of the king is very bad; he is in a sad situation and the belief is he will not live long. I have decided to console myself with whatever happens, for after all I am strongly convinced that during his lifetime I will have only a slim chance for happiness." Two weeks later he wrote: "According to all reports that I have received . . . the king approaches his end and will probably not live beyond this year, having fluid in the chest, no respiration, sleep, or appetite, and the legs fiercely inflamed even beyond the knees, though without pain." Wilhelmina replied: "In truth I wish you wouldn't return there [Potsdam] in these circumstances, for I very much dread his bad temper since I don't foresee his early death, this illness in my opinion being more a decline than decisive. The queen must be at her wit's end; this will be a furious blow for her, although in truth she would be happier from it."

In early October Frederick spent a few days with Wilhelmina and left only when a courier brought word from their mother that the king was dying. Frederick found him in a terrible state, stomach swollen to sixty-one inches, face yellow and mottled, stubby legs ulcerated and swollen with dropsy (as big as "two butter Tubbs," one observer recorded), which had affected his penis and testicles, preventing urination and adding to his agony. His breathing was tortured by a chest full of fluid.

The king allegedly received his son so tenderly that the young man burst into tears. Guy Dickens reported that the crown prince was with his father night and day and was so deeply grieved that doctors feared for his health and caused the king to send him to Ruppin. Although these are not firsthand reports, the information having come from spies who were probably also in Prussian pay and from palace bulletins, they undoubtedly have some substance. Frederick always professed filial devotion, particularly when he knew it would be reported to the king. He was also a consummate actor who turned tears on and off like a water tap. By his own admission the crisis was emotionally upsetting. Summoned back to Potsdam, he told Wilhelmina, "The doctors give him only fifteen days to live. I return there tomorrow and am trying to prepare myself in every way possible for this fatal event; for it concerns me to the depths of my soul."

Here is the real nub of the matter. The crisis upset him because it once again emphasized the gulf between the man of reason and the man of action. Frederick could gain the liberty he desired only by the king's death, but that liberty would disappear once he was king. This thought sobered and frightened him. It was scarcely the first time it had occurred to him, but as Dr. Johnson one day would say, "When a man knows he is to be hanged in a fortnight, it concentrates his mind wonderfully."

But the king refused to die. In between attacks of gout, asthma, and colic, in between bloodlettings and operations on his legs to drain fluid (two quarts of the red stuff with a nauseating odor came from his legs daily), he remained master in his house, firing pistols loaded with rock salt at any attendant who annoyed him. Only a lion "can be more furious than His Prussian Majesty is at present," Dickens reported.[1] He continued to rave in his usual self-righteous manner, now and again confiding in the crown prince, cursing all enemies of Prussia, particularly Austria and the Imperialists who had deceived him, and warning Frederick to "make a good use of my Mistakes and Errors and take care in whom you place your Confidence, that you may not be led astray as I have been." Frederick remained humble and obsequious, no doubt shedding appropriate tears by the sick bed, for after all the king could not live beyond fifteen days.

Fifteen days passed and the king was still alive. By the end of October he was beating his pages so hard that attendants feared he would suffer a heart attack. Frederick remained in attendance until the king sent him back to Ruppin. For two months he commuted to Potsdam and Berlin to attend the dying man, and for two months he easily accepted the obeisance paid him by army officers, civil officials, and foreign envoys both at Ruppin and Potsdam. He believed himself king. He treated certain envoys, such as Dickens, with contempt. He treated others, specifically the dashing, worldly Chétardie, with considerable warmth, making no secret of his desire to see Stanislaus back on the Polish throne. The French envoy reported to Versailles that he spoke as ruler and even conqueror, comparing himself with King Charles XII of Sweden.

Still the king did not die. At times he could scarcely breathe; he was almost constantly in agony; he endured fevers and chills; gallons of noxious humors flowed from ulcerated legs. Physicians came and went — those who told him he would live remained in attendance; those who held no hope were discharged. Almost no one believed that he would survive into the new year.

The king not only lived; he suddenly began to improve. And very soon it was obvious that he was not going to die. Early in the new year Frederick informed his sister that

> he is entirely recovered, he is walking, and is in better health than I. I dined with him yesterday and can assure that he eats and drinks like a horse. He will go to Berlin in eight days and I believe for certain that he will be riding in fifteen days. This is an extraordinary miracle. . . . To recover entirely from three mortal illnesses at the same time is superhuman, and one must believe that the good Lord has very good reasons to restore his life. Once again I must stand aside.

18

WITH THE KING back in harness, Frederick returned again to Ruppin, where he was extending the Nauen gardens, building a splendid vineyard, and renovating the nearby Rheinsberg château. It was scarcely an exciting life. Friends in Berlin pitied him, saying that there were no more than three officers at Ruppin who could write four reasonable words. He himself wrote that "any man who pursues only knowledge and lives without friends is a learned werewolf."[1]

Winter and spring nevertheless passed swiftly. Regiment Goltz needed considerable attention before the all-important spring review at Templehof plain near Berlin to which, as a senior regiment, it would be summoned. The ranks had to be brought to full strength. In early spring furloughed soldiers were recalled from farms; foreigners from towns and villages where they were employed. Gaps created by age, sickness, and desertion had to be filled. This meant recruiting at home and abroad.

Home recruiting had been made easier by the king's new canton system. Formerly anyone in the kingdom had been fair game for any regimental or company commander, infantry or cavalry. This had resulted in constant recruiting quarrels between unit commanders, to resentment among civilians in those districts more harshly treated than others, and also to lower morale of peasant lads taken away from familiar surroundings. In 1733 Frederick William divided the kingdom into military circles, or districts, and assigned a specific district, based on the number of fireplaces within, to each regiment. Each district was subdivided into cantons, which were assigned to each infantry, cavalry, or garrison company for replacement purposes. Eligible male children had to be enrolled on regimental lists at the age of ten and had to take the military oath once they had been confirmed in the Church and eaten of the Lord's Supper so that, in the king's words, "they would not profane the oath."[2] They were called for service as needed. In theory this was universal conscription; in fact it was not. Vast numbers of youngsters in numerous categories were exempted, leaving the sons of smaller craftsmen, servants, farm workers, and peasants to serve. The system did provide more and better recruits on a more reliable basis, and it also introduced an element of nationalism in the army. Recruiting abroad remained a year-round affair as difficult and expensive as ever, and Frederick, along with other regimental commanders, spent a great deal of money in trying to satisfy the king's insatiable appetite for beautiful big men.

New recruits had to be fitted with uniforms and equipment, trained in the incredibly complex close-order drill of the day, then exercised in the intricate maneuvers they would be expected to perform faultlessly at the grand review.

The spring review, also called the grand review, was usually held in June. Consisting of two parts, a general review of all regiments present and a special review of individual regiments, it was a harrowing experience for everyone, from the most senior regimental commander to the most junior private. The general review was held on an enormous drill field at Templehof; the 1733 review saw fifteen regiments, some twenty-five thousand foot and horse soldiers, on parade. The real value of the general review was psychological, intended as much to impress foreign envoys as anything else. It was a splendid show of power. "I never saw troops march with more order and state; it seemed as if they were all moved with one spring," Baron Pöllnitz noted. Some years earlier Seckendorff had been equally impressed; he reported to Prince Eugene that "it is certain that one cannot see troops of such good appearance, order and correctness anywhere else in the world."[3]

The special review served a different purpose. The king spent literally scores of hours after the general review with the luckless individual regiments. The designated regiment formed in the Tiergarten, each company deployed in four ranks so that the king could inspect each soldier in each rank. On his appearance, drums beat the command to present arms, and this was followed by the long and exhausting manual of arms. He then inspected ranks, stopping frequently, usually before recruits who were identified by a sprig of oak leaves tacked onto their uniforms, and asking, "My son, is everything all right? Are you satisfied in my army?" The recruit was not only free to voice any complaints but was encouraged to do so, according to David Fassmann, who wrote that the king would listen to a malcontent with endless patience — though whether he applied corrective measures was another matter. After the review the regimental commander had to call forth the tallest men, from which the king arbitrarily selected those he fancied for the Potsdam Guards. If there were no "beautiful" recruits, he was furious. But if there was good material and if the review had proven satisfactory, he would give the commander a little kiss to show his satisfaction.

The value of the special review was threefold: it allowed the king to satisfy himself personally as to a regiment's condition; it exposed him to troops who theoretically would appreciate the paternal interest shown and would respond by no longer wanting to desert; and it impressed regimental commanders with the importance of efficient recruiting procedures. The reviews were not confined to Berlin. Frederick William often held autumn reviews at Potsdam as well as in various provinces, scheduling his trips so that he inspected all regiments within a three-year period.

Like any regimental commander in 1735, Frederick wanted to make the best possible impression, but for more than one reason. He had tasted military action and liked it. He enjoyed the responsibility of command, the camaraderie, the challenges that daily presented themselves. The military portions of his frequent letters to the king show him to be an interested student of warfare, no matter the recent dull campaign on the Rhine. He believed that the forthcoming campaign would be more exciting. As early as May he began barraging the king with importunate letters asking permission to serve. Crown Princess Elizabeth wrote to the king on his behalf, and Frederick asked Old Dessauer and his sons to do the same. The king was not to be bludgeoned, however; he was annoyed that Prince Eugene had asked Prince William of Orange to join his campaign but not the Crown Prince of Prussia. His decision would not be made until after the June review.

This went off better than Frederick could have dreamed. "The king embraced the crown prince before the line," Count von Seckendorff's nephew, Baron Christoph Ludwig von Seckendorff, recorded in his journal.[4] "My review finished successfully yesterday," Frederick wrote to Wilhelmina. "The king was very pleased; I have been made a major general and have received permission to campaign once the army is assembled, permission vague and dubious enough."

In July he excitedly wrote to Wilhelmina that he would march within fifteen days. That plan fell through, and in August the king changed his mind, "with no effort at all," Frederick complained to his sister, "because he knows very well that I have no lever to force him to keep his word." His spirits revived in late August, when he wrote to her that the army was assembling and that he hoped to join it. Meanwhile he would wait peacefully in Ruppin, "where I spend my time as quietly as possible." He was reading and writing and finishing his first symphony.* He had planted a large garden and vineyard, his beloved Amalthée, which his architect, Georg von Knobelsdorff, graced with a temple "consisting of eight Doric columns supporting a dome above which is a statue of Apollo. Once it is built we shall make our sacrifices there and . . . their purpose will be as protectors of the fine arts."

But the man of action was never long dormant. At the end of August he wrote to the king that Prince Eugene probably intended to cross the Rhine: "My most gracious father can easily consider what a disgrace and cruel chagrin it would be for me to miss such an opportunity." A few days later he reminded the king of his earlier promise, and protested that "the whole world knows I am becoming a professional soldier, yet, when this opportunity exists to learn the profession correctly, I remain at home."

The king was not to be moved. He had already decided that Frederick was growing too partial to the Imperialist camp, whose luminaries had done nothing in recent years but deceive him, but he now replied that the political situation was so crucial that it would not be prudent for Frederick to go to war; nothing would happen on the Rhine, he went on, because the emperor lacked men, and there was nothing glorious in Frederick's watching Imperial idleness. As a sop he promised that the prince could march after the grand review next year. Meanwhile, "I would ask if you would like to take a working holiday of five or six weeks in Prussia in order to study and learn the local economy and provincial ways, and from that determine why things have gone wrong there; it could be very useful for you to learn everything about the towns, country, and administration, because one day you must rule this land and only evil will result if you rely simply on those specious reports submitted by self-seeking officials." If Frederick wished to make the trip, the king would send him full instructions and would order all

---

* Four of Frederick's symphonies were recorded by Kurt Redel and the Munich Pro Arte orchestra in 1981 under the Philips label.

provincial chambers to keep nothing from him. He would also inspect all the regiments and take necessary remedial action.

Frederick did not want to go to Prussia and was annoyed with the king's decision. "He told me that he had very secret reasons that prevented my going [on campaign]," he wrote to Wilhelmina. "I believe it, for I am convinced that he does not know them himself. To console me he wishes me to travel to Prussia, a place only slightly more civilized than Siberia." To the king he sent only an obsequious acceptance.

Once under way with the ebullient Lieutenant Chasot — the French officer who had traded armies during the Rhine campaign — as traveling companion, Frederick became enthusiastic. He liked a great deal of what he found. The open countryside, the pretty cities with suburbs spilling from them, colonists such as the Salzburg refugees hard at work, so many youngsters of eight to ten, he wrote to Colonel Camas, his old mentor, that within eight years "this kingdom will have more people than Switzerland or Franconia." But he also discovered a great deal wrong with civil and military affairs, and he did not hesitate to take corrective action and report in detail to the king. Some officials were not performing properly, schools were neglected, the people poor and in some cases on the verge of starvation. An interim report to the king, written from Marienwerder in late September, spoke favorably of two cavalry companies, "both very pretty, and though neither man nor beast is particularly large they are well-dressed men and a beautiful type of stocky horse." The regiments were in fine shape, and the king had nothing to fear for next year's review. In Danzig he inspected the Russian fieldworks and was given an account of the siege the previous year: "I have been over the field and swear that I had a better opinion of Marshal Münnich than to have believed him capable of such a foolish effort, badly conceived and badly executed." In Königsberg he got to know and like the fugitive King Stanislaus, who "possesses all the beautiful qualities in the world . . . a character neither arrogant in fortune nor abject in misfortune." He prepared a final report at Königsberg in mid-October, a frank and at times highly critical account. He was especially upset by the prevailing poverty and wrote to Grumbkow that "if the king does not decide to open the granaries toward the new year, you can count on it that half the people there will die of hunger, for the harvests of the last few years have been very bad."

The king eagerly read his son's long letters. "I have derived much satisfaction from your reports, because you have made such an intelligible and lucid presentation of the condition and order of both infantry regiments."

Frederick was still in Prussia when the War of the Polish Succession abruptly ended. As Frederick William had foreseen, the Austrians were in no position to mount a successful campaign. By October the emperor's regiments were being pushed from Italy, and across the Rhine Marshal Duke Charles Louis de Belle-Isle had outmaneuvered an Imperial army commanded by the Prussian king's old crony, General Count von Seckendorff. What Frederick William did not know was that for several months the politically influential Cardinal André de Fleury in Versailles had been negotiating a peace with the Austrian court. Preliminaries were announced in early October. The Saxon elector would become King August III of Poland. King Stanislaus would remain a king with a very limited kingdom, the duchy of Lorraine. Duke Francis of Lorraine, slated to marry Archduchess Maria Theresa, would eventually receive the duchy of Tuscany in Italy. These and other adjustments were made at Emperor Charles's expense, but in return France would guarantee the Pragmatic Sanction — and Austria would gain a breathing spell.

Peace left Prussia more isolated than ever. The Austrian and Russian courts were angry because Frederick William was protecting Stanislaus and continuing to treat him as king. He did not want the Saxon elector on the Polish throne. He severely criticized King Louis XV for selling out his own father-in-law's interests, and for a short period refused to give the French envoy an audience. If he was annoyed with King Louis he was furious with Emperor Charles, who had not even notified him of the impending peace. He, the King of Prussia, had had to learn it from newspapers. Nor did the emperor tell him of Maria Theresa's marriage to Duke Francis. Rather than displaying gratitude for Prussia's contribution to the war, the emperor had openly criticized him for withholding his army from the final campaign across the Moselle. Not content with all this, the emperor, on the pretext of Prussian troops' misbehavior in German countries, summarily forbade further Prussian recruiting in the Empire. Crown Prince Frederick was compelled to recall two lieutenants who were recruiting in Austria and Hungary and complained to the king that this was a great blow, since his best recruits came from Imperial lands. The king replied: "That is the thanks for the ten thousand men that I sent him and for all the deference which I have paid the Emperor. . . . So long as we are needed we are flattered, but when one believes that we are no longer needed, off comes the mask and we are shown no gratitude. The thoughts which must accordingly strike you will also enable you to guard against similar behavior in the future." The king's resentment of Austrian perfidy would grow. According to Baron von Seckendorff, who had replaced his uncle the count as Austrian envoy in Berlin, the king on one occasion worked himself into lachrymose rage and, indicating the crown prince, said, "Here is one who will avenge me." [5]

Ideas are always exciting (to some), and they can be dangerous, and in 1736 they were both. The religious schism that had torn Europe to pieces in the Thirty Years' War (1618–1648) had scarcely healed. Religious beliefs continued to play an important and at times vital role in political affairs. Roman Catholics still stood on one side of the spiritual chasm, Protestants on the other. In pursuing such practical matters as economics, land, and dynasties, neither would hesitate to cross to the other camp, but such transients carried with them specific religious biases. Neither territory was barren, however, for each camp was pitched on a plain of dogma. Thanks to greed within the Church and widespread ignorance and superstition, Western religion had grown into dogmatic and irrational forms that a few brave souls were now challenging throughout Europe and even in the North American colonies. Freethinking scientists and philosophers like René Descartes, John Locke, Isaac Newton, Gottfried Leibniz, Pierre Bayle, and Samuel Clarke had been dropping seeds of challenging thought that had steadily grown into dangerous ideas. Emperor Charles VI and King Louis XV would tolerate no heresy to Roman Catholic beliefs; King George II was sworn to be defender of the Protestant faith, a role shared by King Frederick William. But in each camp, Catholic and Protestant, there were those who were trying to replace dogmatic belief with belief based on reason.

One of these thinkers was Christian von Wolff, whom King Frederick William had expelled from Prussia in 1723 for "atheistical teachings." Wolff was a disciple of Leibniz and believed that all knowledge could be systematized. A prolific writer of what he modestly termed "reasonable thoughts," he seemed dangerously heterodox to many. He separated mind and body, the mental and the physical. He argued that the world was physical and could not admit miracles, and he also held to a cause and effect mechanism in the reasoning process. The function of the state, he held, was to provide the individual with opportunities to develop; it was not meant to dominate him. Wolff praised the ethics of Confucius for being based on human reason. Wolff's lasting influence was to be slight, but he did in his "stumbling way" begin the German enlightenment, or *Aufklärung*.[6]

His influence on Frederick would be enormous. As we know, the crown prince had concerned himself with John Calvin's doctrine of predestination in long talks with Chaplin Müller in the Cüstrin cell and had ostensibly allowed himself to be turned from this and other tenets odious to the king. But Frederick was like a savage converted to Christianity by some zealous missionary. He had lost faith in heathen beliefs without understanding new beliefs, and one of his doubts concerned the doctrine of the immortality of the soul. Materialist arguments had convinced him that this doctrine was founded upon a delusion arising from the innate pride of man. When in Berlin for the long carnival season, Frederick had discussed this with an older friend, Count Ernst

Christoph Manteuffel, a former Saxon minister who had "retired" to Berlin (where he secretly functioned as a spy for the Saxon court). Manteuffel told his young friend that he had been disturbed by similar doubts but that Wolff's philosophical teachings had dispelled them. Another close friend, Count Ulrich von Suhm, the frail and somewhat melancholy but immensely cultivated Saxon envoy whom Frederick called his dear Diaphane, enlarged on the subject and agreed to translate one of Wolff's treatises into French.

When Frederick at Ruppin received from Suhm the first chapter of the *Métaphysique,* in which Wolff demonstrates how man can be certain that he exists and has a soul, he wrote gratefully, "You have convinced me that I indubitably exist."

Leopold von Ranke marked this period of conversion as beatific, and he may have been right. The discovery of one's soul does not occur every day, and it is certainly exciting to learn that one is immortal. According to Ranke, Frederick's friends "now found him more gentle, frank, and generous, less harsh and contradictory than before." If so, this was still not Wolff's major contribution to Frederick's education. Wolff's chief function was that of a spark plug, igniting fuels of thought. Wolff is not easy to understand and his metaphysical arguments are elaborate, often tortuous. Frederick's sustained interest demanded a great deal of discipline and stimulated him to further reading on which to form comparative judgments. When Wilhelmina at this time spoke of her preference for Descartes, her brother loftily replied that he was "a great retailer of sophisms," good forty years ago, but his merit lay in exposition, whereas Newton and Wolff had perfected philosophy by proving that man was essentially a reasoning animal and that his salvation lay in the ability to reason from fact, not prejudice.

He was not as open with Suhm, nor even with Pastor Anthony Achard, whose sermons he had listened to in Berlin — no mean task, since the poor man had lost his teeth and was difficult to understand. Achard sent his published sermons to Ruppin with a request that the crown prince point out the weakest of their arguments for immortality. Frederick wrote to Suhm that, although Achard's work contained more sophisms than arguments, he still did not wish to joust with those who had studied and knew infinitely more than he. Instead, he continued to read Wolff avidly, and not only metaphysics. In studying one treatise in which Wolff developed Plato's argument that men will become happy when governed by philosophers, Frederick's thinking perforce turned to the ruler's role in the state, a difficult subject to which he would return. Frederick in time would reject Wolff's teachings, but their stimulus to his mind can never be denied nor can the influence of some of his humanitarian lessons.

Frederick's intellectual idyll abruptly ended that spring when furloughed troops returned from farms and villages to be drilled into shape for the spring review. In late April he apologized for not answering Suhm's last letters, but "the service of Mars" was occupying him entirely and he scarcely had time to eat or drink: "I am being summoned and I now hear the voices of six hundred men who wish to be drilled. I must go and get rid of them as soon as possible." His life was consumed by a trip to Potsdam, daily drill, and a visit of his young brother Henry in company of two officers. As these were people, he wrote to Suhm, "who have a better notion of their stomachs than their minds, I put them on a chapter of Duval's philosophy [Duval was his chef], which did wonders and stuffed them to the utmost." In Berlin, he found the king in a vicious mood, which Frederick put down to constipation but which made him fear the impending inspection even more. It apparently passed, however, without incident, and he soon left for another tour of Prussia.

Rheinsberg was ready for occupancy by the time of his return, but only in mid-August could he tell Suhm, "I am now going to retire to my blessed solitude, where I will give myself over completely to my studies. Wolff . . . will have his place; Rollin will have his hours, and what is left will be devoted to the gods of tranquillity and repose."

19

RHEINSBERG was Ruppin with a regiment and a court. "We have divided our activities into two categories," Frederick happily informed Suhm shortly after taking up residence. "The one is useful, the other agreeable. Studying philosophy and the history of languages are among the useful; the agreeable include music, the comedies and tragedies which we stage, the masquerades and the gifts that we give each other. But the serious occupations always take precedence over the others."

The old manor house rose mystically from the edge of a lake on the far side of the village. It was a big house, some 200 feet long and 150 deep, and it stood two stories high between two 60-foot towers. Surrounded by a moat and backed by a score of outbuildings, it overlooked lake and countryside, a bucolic scene in the Watteau tradition: cattle and horses grazing in grassy fields, peat bogs and yellow sand, lakes, birch and pine copses lingering under soft cloudy skies.

The architects had rebuilt the house and grounds to Frederick's specifications. Much of the work had been done on the cheap because of a frugal budget, but the result stood in striking contrast to the average country mansion. Though baroque and rococo prevailed, Frederick had gone for light and air, for bright, gilt-trimmed salons whose walls bore, instead of heavy portraits and battle scenes, serene paintings by Watteau and Lancret, works chosen personally by the crown prince.

His own apartments were striking. Located at the far end of a covered esplanade that overlooked the lake, they consisted of seven rooms, including a bedchamber in the tower. They were entered through an anteroom whose ceiling the court artist, Antoine Pesne, had painted in an allegorical style that would have displeased King Frederick William: Cupids and goddesses gamboled about intent on disarming a benevolent-looking Mars. Possibly as sop to the king, weapons done in gilt hung from the walls, as did portraits of their majesties. Perhaps more significant were the medallion profile busts of Hannibal, Pompey, Scipio, and Caesar that graced the doorways. Light reflected from six large windows by long wall mirrors sparkled on polished parquet floors. The anteroom led into Frederick's rapidly growing library, an octagon-shaped room with thick walls and three recessed windows. A frescoed ceiling by Pesne showed Minerva being offered a book with the names Horace and Voltaire on the pages. Directly above the library was Frederick's bedroom, its walls of green silk embossed with yellow and white parrots. A canopied bed stood between Corinthian columns.

Crown Princess Elizabeth arrived with an entourage as undistinguished as herself. Madame de Katsch was a sort of grand mistress, sixty years old, dignified and acerbic, lording it over a number of younger ladies-in-waiting. Elizabeth's education would soon be carried on by a "reader," or special tutor, Jean Deschamps, son of a French refugee, an educated and clever man who had studied under Wolff. Frederick's court included the chamberlain von Wolden; Major Johann von Senning, a military tutor and friend; a younger soldier, Major Ludwig von Stille, a university-educated military historian, a man of solid character, pious, fluent in English and French; his old guardian Colonel von Bredow, who would soon quarrel with von Wolden; a theologian, Charles Étienne Jordan, "a learned scholar" according to Frederick, a thirty-six-year-old Lutheran minister who had left the Church after his wife's death and who would live in Rheinsberg village with his children while serving the crown prince as private secretary and librarian; the architect Knobelsdorff, soon to be dispatched to Italy for study; the painter Pesne; his confidant Keyserling, always called Césarion, a thirty-eight-year-old nobleman, fluent in four languages ("which he sometimes spoke all at once," Voltaire noted), traveled and polished, a singer and composer, a heavy drinker, the frequent victim of painful and incurable gout, buoyant, and totally trusted by Frederick; twenty-one-year-old Chasot, now a captain, a "matador," his employer called him, who devoted one day to Diana, goddess of hunting, the next day to

Venus, goddess of love, a born wit and ghastly flautist; the valet Fredersdorff, more and more a royal confidant, treasurer, trusted friend; Baron Henri de La Motte Fouqué, one of Old Dessauer's officers on almost permanent loan to Frederick;* the composer Karl Heinrich Graun (Frederick later remarked that he really did his musical homework with Graun, whose composition *Timareta* was played at his wedding); twenty musicians, itinerant actors and singers who seemed to have caused endless trouble ("The musicians for the most part are ill tempered and quarrelsome. . . . The most difficult people of all, they sometimes require more care than governing a state," Frederick variously complained to Wilhelmina); various regimental officers from Ruppin; frequent guests such as the French poet Jean Baptiste Louis Gresset, the composer-flautist Johann Joachim Quantz, the Saxon diplomat Count Manteuffel; and several more lackeys to feed and look after the assemblage. "We have ample company here," Frederick told his sister, "with our table ordinarily of twenty-two to twenty-four settings."

He was delighted with his new retreat, which he sometimes called "my Sanssouci" but more often Remusberg, connecting it to a local legend that Remus, when exiled by his brother, Romulus, traveled across the Elbe to settle at Rheinsberg. Shortly after Elizabeth and her court arrived, he wrote, "The ladies spread an indescribable charm over our daily activities. Entirely apart from the pleasing affairs of heart, they are indispensable, and without them any conversation is dull." He was particularly taken with a Frau Luise von Brandt, whom he found witty and charming. So ebullient was Baroness Charlotte von Morrien that he called her Turbillon (Whirlwind) and praised her in his poems. A lady-in-waiting, the fifteen-year-old "kleine Tettau," was a favorite, rumored to be a mistress.

There remained Crown Princess Elizabeth. Berlin tutors had done their job, and Frederick found her considerably improved in social graces. He installed her in elegant apartments of her own, treated her kindly if passively, and probably did his best to get her with child, as he had tried to do earlier in Berlin. His biographers have speculated at length on the barren marriage; the usual conclusion is that the two did not have sexual relations. Elizabeth's letters were generally silent on the subject, but she did say that her failure to have children could be ascribed only to "divine will." She repeatedly wrote of her pleasure with life at Rheinsberg. As for Frederick, she informed her grandmother, "It can truly be said that he is the greatest prince of our time. . . . He is

---

*Fouqué eventually ran afoul of Old Dessauer because of his Frenchified ways and was forced to take service in the Danish army.

a scholar with massive intellect. He is just and obliging, can never harm anyone, is generous and moderate, disliking any excesses. . . . In short he is the Phoenix of our age, and I am blessed to be the wife of such a great prince with so many good qualities. Anyone who knows him must love him."[1]

These words do not sound like those of a frustrated woman, but every woman is not knowingly frustrated when denied sex. Yet Frederick had everything to gain and nothing to lose by producing a child. He never claimed to be a sexual athlete, despite salon rumors to the contrary. When Seckendorff once chided him about his numerous love affairs, he replied, "I am not as bold as is believed." Sex was a convenience, a release rather than prolonged enjoyment. And in Elizabeth's case, it was a duty. Rapprochement with his father depended as much on the king's desire for an uninterrupted succession of the House of Hohenzollern as on Frederick's seeming contrition and change of heart. The father had long since promised that once his son had produced an heir, he could travel outside the kingdom. The matter undoubtedly was mentioned between hunts and pigeon shooting during a brief — and from Frederick's view, unwanted — royal visit to Rheinsberg in September. The king presented the couple with a splendid great bed, and Frederick presumably reassured his father that he was doing his best to propagate; at least the king appeared to be satisfied and even paid outstanding debts of some forty thousand thalers.

There were other pressures on Frederick. One friend pointed out that if Frederick failed to produce an heir and his younger brothers did so, unfortunate complications could result. Grumbkow approached the subject through the side door, congratulating the prince on getting Elizabeth pregnant. Frederick replied laconically, "If my destiny is that of the rutting stags, you will have your wish in nine months." It was not to be, and it was the one blight on an otherwise sublime period for the crown prince. He did not appear to blame Elizabeth, and he later wrote, "I would be the most vile man in the world to say I didn't like her, for she is of the most gentle nature, docile, thoughtful, and agreeable, and does everything to please me. What is more, she cannot complain of my not having slept with her. I don't know why there has been no child."

The thought should not be ruled out that Frederick unconsciously may not have wanted an heir; he may have been influenced by the soul-searing relationship with his father. The historian Friedrich Meinecke has pointed out that Frederick's treatment of Elizabeth "indicated a fundamental weakness in him of the instinct for blood and family, and equally points to a fundamental strength of his purely individual will."[2] He did not seem to regard an heir as very important, except to please the king. To Voltaire he later expressed contempt for princes who are enamored with family trees. "Kings always find successors," he wrote to Grumbkow at this time, "and there is no instance where a throne has remained vacant." On the other hand, "a prince destined by God to the throne and who has three brothers should wish for heirs in order to eliminate a million inconveniences."

Frederick seems to have treated Elizabeth kindly, at times even tenderly (she was in Berlin when her father died in 1735, and he wrote the king from Ruppin asking permission to go to Berlin to console her). Their correspondence during his absences is gentle, at times affectionate. In 1739 he would write from Prussia, "Do not forget me, I beg you, and accept my warmest sentiments." Again, "I await very impatiently the moment of embracing you." Some evidence exists that Elizabeth was a born nagger, frequently complaining, never really an integral part of the Remusberg crowd. Whatever the case, she seems never to have been much more than a convenience to Frederick, who would shelve her at the first opportunity. Meanwhile, she was the price of Remusberg and the intellectual freedom so devoutly desired by its master.

The intellectual hallmark of the eighteenth century, the philosophical Enlightenment, stemmed largely from French and British writers, scientists, and philosophers, men who preached the controversial and often dangerous credo of science and wisdom over superstition and ignorance. Frederick's eclectic reading had included many skeptical authors. If he was not yet familiar with Newton and Locke, he had read Montaigne, Corneille, Bossuet, la Bruyère, Fléchier, Bourdaloue, Massillon, Molière, la Fontaine, Fénelon, Wolff, Boileau, Bayle, Racine, Gresset, Rollin, and Fontenelle. He would shortly be corresponding with Charles Rollin, whose *Ancient History* he greatly admired, and Fontenelle, among others.

He had also read — indeed, devoured — Voltaire. He had been thrilled by *The History of Charles XII* as well as by the *Henriade* (a not very good epic poem — "a political broadcast on an epic scale," in Will Durant's words). But its unremitting recital of religious crimes through the ages and its sympathetic treatment of Henry of Navarre appealed to Frederick, as did the carefully disguised controversial philosophy.

Voltaire's most recent work, a tragedy called *Alzire,* which was staged in Paris in January 1736, had been a great success, and in an unusual preface to it Voltaire called for a humanism that stemmed from his infatuation with Lockian philosophy. "This humanity," he wrote, "which should be the chief characteristic of every thinking being, will be found in nearly all my writings . . . [which show] a wish for the happiness of mankind, a horror of injustice and oppression; and this only has so far saved my works from the obscurity in which their defects should have buried them."[3]

Frederick knew that Voltaire was living at Cirey, a dilapidated country estate in Champagne, with his intellectual mistress Madame Gabrielle Emily du Châtelet. Shortly before moving to Rheinsberg he had written Voltaire a long and fulsome letter in which he mentioned his interest in Wolff's philosophy and his own intellectual and artistic ambitions, and in which he tendered a veiled offer of political sanctuary in Prussia should need arise.

As one of Voltaire's biographers has written, his words came at a time when Voltaire was most vulnerable: "[He] had been exiled, imprisoned, several times in danger of arrest, beaten, persecuted, spied on, his works regularly prohibited and burnt. He was well-nigh convinced by this time that not even the greatest literary fame, the protection of his eminent friends, the distant retirement of Cirey, his increasing wealth, would make it possible for him to write freely in France." [3] He replied to Frederick in a most flattering vein, delighted to find that "in the world there is a prince who thinks like a man, a royal philosopher who will make men happy." Voltaire thanked him for the invitation to come to Rheinsberg, which he could not then accept, and enclosed a long moral verse on the duties of a king.

The lengthy reply sent Frederick into raptures, and a voluminous correspondence developed in which each tried to outflatter the other. A modern French historian has noted that Voltaire in various letters saw in Frederick "a Caesar, an Augustus, a Marcus Aurelius, a Trajan, an Anthony, a Titus, a Julian, a Virgil, a Pliny, a Horace, a Mécène, a Cicero, a Catullus, a Homer, a Rochefoucauld, a Bruyère, a Boileau, a Solomon, a Prometheus, an Apollo, a Patroclus, a Socrates, an Alcibiades, an Alexander, a Henry IV, and a Francis I." [4] Frederick was no slouch: "You alone are able to combine the wisdom of a philosopher, the talents of an historian and the brilliant imagination of a poet in the same person."

In the main Frederick wanted to pick the critical brain of a man he regarded as a genius, and Voltaire wanted a guarantee of royal patronage should he need it. These aims were hinted at through pages of philosophical discussions in which Voltaire avoided any outright contradiction of Wolff's tenets but held for a more scientific approach, as befitted a student of Newton and Locke. In truth, neither correspondent was much of a philosopher and the exchange of thoughts was not very deep, but in those shallow waters the Prussian crown prince more than held his own. Mercifully, they soon lost interest in the subject.

Despite differences of thought, the relationship prospered. Frederick accompanied lengthy and frequent letters with valuable gifts, such as a cane topped by a miniature head of Socrates in gold. Voltaire responded at length, airing Madame du Châtelet's learned opinions, which seemed to make Frederick a part of Cirey. He still wanted Voltaire to come to Rheinsberg, but lacking that, "Cirey henceforth will be my

Delphi, and your letters, which I beg you to continue, my oracles."
Voltaire replied in revolting fulsomeness: "Louis XIV was a great king
. . . but never did he speak with your humanity. . . . Berlin under
your auspices will become the Athens of Germany and perhaps of Europe." Frederick soon persuaded the French author to correct his poems,
a task undertaken with no great enthusiasm but one softened by the
prince's continuing sycophancy: "If I were to approach the divine Emily I would say to her like the angel of the annunciation: You are blessed
among women for you possess one of the greatest men in the world."

This early correspondence, the beginning of a forty-two-year effort
that would number more than a thousand letters, is interesting for more
than the exchange of intellectual and artistic views. It is interesting for
what is lacking. Almost never do we read of Frederick's life at Rheinsberg, of regimental duties, his thoughts on Prussian internal affairs and
on European politics, even of his illnesses. While the crown prince was
writing to Voltaire "as an intellectual who happens to be heir to a
throne," he was otherwise living as heir to a throne, with intellect frequently confined to second place.

Although free from his father, "from Jupiter and his thunder," as he
acerbically put it, he was never free from his regiment, with its mani-
fold responsibilities. Late in 1736 he complained to the king that the
men were not getting enough to eat because of the high cost of rye, and
sickness would result. Could his most gracious father sell him some
flour at cut rates from the Spandau mill? There was also the estate to
look after and guests to entertain. Frederick was an excellent host and
doted on the company of intellectual friends. The French envoy, Chétardie, a polished and worldly man, loved to visit Rheinsberg; one guest
described the Rheinsberg court as Plato's Republic; even Grumbkow
compared its hospitality with that of the Germans of Tacitus. Frederick
complained in various letters of lacking time for studies, not surprising
in view of numerous hedonistic and at times sybaritic activities. In early
1736 he asked Grumbkow to send him eight hundred bottles of his
favorite champagne, a hundred of Volnay and a hundred of Pommard.
A modern French historian has written of the numerous balls, masquerades, and sometimes drunken and rowdy parties: "They gave rise
to such scandalous accounts being sent in by the Saxon envoy that the
Dresden archivist has shrunk from publishing them." [5] Perhaps this explains Frederick's poignant remark to Grumbkow in the autumn of
1737 that a fitting epitaph for him would be "Here is one who lived
for a year."

Frederick Meinecke concluded that Frederick's political interests "were
already formed before the development of his philosophical ideas. The

future ruler and statesman had a priority over the philosopher." The observation is valid to a certain extent. Despite his feigned indifference to world affairs, he had been keenly interested in them since the king's near-fatal illness. Grumbkow had been sending him the more important dispatches from Prussian envoys abroad, and had kept him informed of Prussia's current negotiations concerning claims to Juliers and Berg and other matters. His letters to Grumbkow from the autumn of 1735 show a growing interest in European politics. He was thus aware of Prussia's progressive isolation from the great powers (to which illegal Prussian recruiting had contributed not a little), not to mention Frederick William's prevalent antagonistic attitude which spared almost no kingdom. Guy Dickens reported that "as things are managed here, at present, I see few Powers who would not rather have this Court for an Enemy than a Friend. As an Enemy, experience has shown they are not to be feared, and as a Friend, They will be always false, useless, troublesome and burthensome."6

The king's maladroit diplomacy very much annoyed the crown prince, particularly in the matter of Juliers and Berg.

> I need no crystal ball to foresee that our plan for Juliers and Berg is doomed [he wrote to Grumbkow]. . . . I find it upsetting that all necessary measures are not taken to bring this project to a successful conclusion. . . . What alarms me the most is to see a certain lethargy on our side at a time when people have recovered from the terror of our arms and push their audacity to the point of despising us. . . . Our age is unfortunately more famous for negotiations than for military deeds. Militarily we are in a good condition but our negotiations lack vigor, as if lulled to sleep by a pernicious vertigo.

Frederick would push current negotiations by concentrating an army in Cleves in order to seize *both* duchies when the Elector Palatine died. "Afterward, if they [Austria] want to lead us to the conference table, all they will be able to do will be to make us give up Juliers, and we shall keep Berg; whereas, if we overrun only Berg, they will make us give up half of it." Prussia should not worry too much about Austrian reaction, since the excessive arrogance of this court was pushing it into decline. Indeed, its situation was critical, and the emperor's death would bring vast upheavals, with each kingdom grabbing what it could.

A problem closer to home was Frederick's lack of money. The king now allowed him fifty thousand thalers a year paid in quarterly installments. As Frederick later testified, he spent thirty thousand thalers a year on recruiting big men in order to satisfy the king. The remainder was spent on his wife's allowance and on servants' wages. For other domestic expenses, for vast quantities of food and wine consumed by his relatively large court, for extraordinary recruiting of the occasional giant, for improvements and furnishings at Remusberg, the crown prince relied on credit.

Once again he was heavily in debt, but the Vienna court was unwilling to increase its clandestine payments, despite urgent pleas. That winter Frederick had prevailed upon Suhm, about to depart for Saint Petersburg as Saxon envoy, to arrange a loan from the Russian court.*

Suhm had no more arrived in Saint Petersburg than Frederick was pressing him to send a book, *The Life of Prince Eugene;* "book" was their codeword for a loan. Suhm replied that, although the Russian court looked favorably on the request to subscribe to such a work, these affairs required time to negotiate. "Twelve copies of this book are required here," Frederick wrote urgently in March, meaning that he needed twelve thousand thalers. "Those who have ordered them harass me daily, as if I had a printing press in my house." With the help of Ernst Johann Biron, the Duke of Kurland, who was Czarina Anna's lover, Suhm finally arranged a preliminary loan from the Russian monarch and sent Frederick three thousand thalers. "It must be admitted that you are the finest librarian in the world," Frederick responded, but added glumly, "My friends await with the greatest impatience the dozen volumes of the Russian edition. You can't believe to what point they press me." Frederick again thanked him for the money: "Fifteen days more and I would have been lost."

No sooner had one crisis been temporarily checked than another arose. Frederick's relationship with the king was still tenuous. "Write me frankly whether the king has spoken of me or not," Frederick implored his brother William. The king did not often do so, but when he did it was usually in pejorative terms. Frederick did what he could to strengthen the relationship. If he wrote Apollo (Voltaire) from Olympian heights in the morning, he wrote Jupiter (the king) from the realm of Mars in the afternoon. Couriers brought the more tiresome details of Regiment Goltz to Potsdam — its drill, the health of the troops, the content of sermons read by the crown prince to his men, the size of recruits, the occasional prospect of acquiring a beautiful big man, diverse disciplinary problems. He continued to report fully on Ruppin's civil affairs, and he often sent game and fruit for the king's table.

His father frequently replied in kind but in that spring of 1737 the equilibrium was upset when Colonel von Bredow spread the rumor that Frederick had lapsed into atheism under the influence of Manteuffel and Suhm. Frederick's resolution in handling the new crisis speaks considerably for his growing maturity and also for the condition of his regiment. "You know that the accusation of atheism is the last refuge of slanderers," he wrote to Suhm, "and having said that there is noth-

---

* Frederick was very upset with Suhm's new assignment and accurately if rather tactlessly pointed out that with his weak constitution he would never survive the harsh life there. "Only men who can drink and fuck vigorously can survive in that barbaric court," he advised Suhm.

ing to add. The king flew into a rage, I kept a tight grip on myself, my regiment has done marvels [at the Berlin review]; and the manual of arms, some flour thrown on the soldiers' wigs, some men over six feet tall, and plenty of recruits have been stronger than those of my slanderers. All is currently quiet, no one speaks of religion anymore, of Wolden, of my persecutors, or of my regiment." He was nonetheless relieved at the outcome and now looked forward to country life and his beloved garden of Amalthée: "I am burning with impatience to see once again my vineyard, my cherries and melons; and there, in calm and free from all useless cares, I shall live only for myself."

20

"I AM STUDYING as hard as possible, doing everything in my power to acquire what I can of the diverse knowledge necessary to acquit myself of all that falls within my province; in short, I am working to improve myself and fill my mind with everything offered us by the outstanding personalities of antiquity and modern times." Thus Frederick wrote to Suhm in late 1737.

It was a wonderful time of life for the twenty-five-year-old crown prince. Knobelsdorff had returned from Italy with harsh artistic judgments and with fascinating sketches that Frederick studied hours on end.* He painted one of the few portraits made of the crown prince, and "dear Césarion" (Keyserling, now a count) carried it to Voltaire at Cirey, because Frederick was still not permitted to leave the kingdom. Césarion returned with Voltaire's portrait, thenceforth to peer down on Frederick's desk, some draft chapters of Voltaire's latest work, which some years later would become famous as *Le Siècle de Louis XIV*, and other literary odds and ends. Keyserling had been enormously impressed with the whirling intellects of Cirey, who devoted their days to intense study of history, philosophy, and science; who staged brilliant plays and fêtes; who represented everything in French intellectualism and enlightenment so admired by Frederick. Fired by Keyserling's enthusiasm, the crown prince soon began acquiring books on physical sciences; in time Knobelsdorff would build a tower to hold an air pump and other scientific equipment, with an observatory on the roof. As it

---

* Though he praised the remains of Greek art in Italy, Knobelsdorff loathed medieval and more recent Italian art. "A Christ ascending into heaven," he wrote, "in a cold Siberian atmosphere, whilst the spectators in the foreground are taken up with the capers of a boy possessed of a devil, is, because Raphael painted it, thought worth more than all the world besides." (Hamilton, *Rheinsberg*.)

turned out, Frederick did not show much aptitude for the physical sciences, but he nevertheless retained a lifelong interest in and respect for them.

Philosophy remained his chief intellectual interest, with history and literature running close seconds. Readings in French medieval history and romantic classics led to establishing the Order of Bayard, a semiserious society based on medieval traditions and devoted to the study of military history and leadership.* Its twelve members included Frederick (le Constant), Prince William (le Sabre), Prince Henry, Prince Ferdinand of Brunswick, Prince William of Brunswick, and some younger officers. Captain Fouqué (le Chaste) was Grand Master. The order's symbol was a sword inscribed *Sans peur et sans reproche*. The knights wore a sword-shaped ring inscribed *Vivent les sans-quartiers* (Death before surrender) and corresponded with each other in the old French knightly style. Not everyone was impressed. "It is a pity," Manteuffel reported to Dresden, "that this prince is surrounded with young officers only, the majority of whom are very giddy and ignorant."

Current events continued to concern the crown prince. Europe was again in ferment, the Russians fighting the Turks in the Ukraine, the Austrians fighting the Turks in Hungary. England was feuding with Spain, and Robert Walpole had his hands full trying to ward off the war demanded by William Pitt, who headed the fractious parliamentarians known as Cobham's Cubs.

Diplomatic offensives were running rampant over the European continent. Reports of alliance here, alliance there reached Frederick through dispatches from Prussian envoys, which Grumbkow forwarded from Berlin, and Suhm's letters were full of the Russian war. Frederick was thrilled with Field Mashal Münnich's capture of Oczakow: he must be the Alexander of this century, he replied. He was not impressed otherwise with the Russian army, which needed as many supply wagons as there were troops, nor did he find anything to admire in the Austrian effort in Hungary. When Emperor Charles abruptly relieved General Count von Seckendorff of command and imprisoned him, Frederick thought that it was just punishment "for all the wicked and evil acts that he had committed," as he wrote to Suhm.

Grumbkow had kept the prince informed of the king's diplomacy. Frederick William was still trying to use the present war to further his old claims to Juliers and Berg. When Austria declared war on Turkey, he offered to lend Emperor Charles money in return for a guarantee of his claims but was turned down. He next turned directly to the ailing

* Pierre de Terrail, Chevalier de Bayard (1475–1524), was famous for chivalrous deeds. Killed at the battle of Sesia, he was eulogized as *Chevalier sans peur et sans reproche*.

Elector Palatine with an offer of over a million thalers for the cession of Berg. This also was refused. He finally turned to the maritime powers, England and Holland, with no more satisfactory result. England was reluctant to take up the matter with the Vienna court, and both powers shared the fears of Rhenish princes about increased Prussian presence on the Rhine; they were also annoyed by Frederick William's continuing illegal recruiting of giants in their countries.

Worse was to come. Emperor Charles, influenced by Cardinal Fleury, placed what was exclusively an Empire problem before a conference of major powers, Austria, France, Holland, and England. The Quadrilleurs, as the Prussian king bitterly referred to them, decided that on the Elector Palatine's death the future possession of the two duchies would be subject to mediation, but that in the interim the Prince of Sulzbach would have "provisional possession." Frederick William was furious.

Active military preparations soon filled the kingdom. "We are drilling daily . . . war is the daily topic," Frederick wrote to Wilhelmina. The English envoy reported that if the king could not have Berg, he would indemnify himself from neighbors on the right or left, which caused the Austrian ambassador to fear for Silesia, whose borders were open to invasion. Spurred by such hawks as Lieutenant General Count von Schwerin ("They call him, here, the little Marlborough," Dickens reported, "and, in his own Opinion, he is not inferior to the great One"),[1] the king continued to protest the decision, even allowing Schwerin to threaten seizure of Silesia, Hanover, and Mecklenburg.

To no one's real surprise Frederick William finally acknowledged the decision but implied that in the event of the elector's death he would contest it militarily; he followed this statement by concentrating forty thousand troops in nearby Cleves, an action that terrified the Austrian court and caused it to seek even closer alliance with Versailles.

Crown Prince Frederick's anger at the vapid negotiations over Juliers and Berg had continued to spill over in his letters to Grumbkow. The previous November he had condemned the king for "sacrificing" his interest to other powers, which he would never do:

> I fear rather that I may be blamed for too great rashness and ardor. Heaven appears to have destined the king to make all the preparations which wisdom and prudence exact that we should make before beginning a war. Who knows whether Providence may not be reserving me to turn these preparations to glorious account and use them for the accomplishing of those designs for which the king's forethought intended them?

As for the outcome of the four-power conference on the fate of the Rhenish duchies, he would have informed the great powers "that the King of Prussia is like the noble palm tree, which can bend low but can quickly spring back to its proud height." Instead, the Prussian reply was feckless. Regarding Grumbkow's smug opinion that "a King of Prussia like a King of Sardinia must be a fox rather than a lion," Frederick replied, "I confess that I perceive in [the king's] reply a conflict between greatness and humiliation with which I can never agree. The answer is that of a man who has no desire to fight and yet pretends that he wants to." There were only two answers, he went on, either that of noble pride or that of total abjection. "I am not a sufficiently subtle politician," he continued, "to be able to make threats while giving way at the same time. I am young. I would perhaps follow the impetuosity of my temperament; under no circumstances would I take only half an action."

Frederick had already turned to his pen to mobilize public opinion against the decision of the major powers. He hoped particularly to influence Bavaria and even France, but the maritime powers, England and Holland, were his prime targets. By the spring of 1738 he had completed, in French, a book-length manuscript, *Reflections on the Present State of European Politics.*[2]

The work shows a rapidly maturing intellect. He had earlier concerned himself with Prussia's weak geographical position and the responsibility of its ruler to repair matters. Although this was superficial writing by a nineteen-year-old frustrated romantic, it nonetheless concerned what that writer believed to be the proper function of a ruler and his state, a *raison d'état* that had never seriously been defined by Frederick William except in the rather grubby phrase *ein Plus machen.* In seven years Frederick's seed had grown to a plant of permanent inquiry that found a real voice in the *Reflections,* a work that first stated his perpetual conflict between rule by reason and rule by force.

Reflections consisted of practical and theoretical portions. The late British historian George Gooch found its major importance in the former. The real threat to the balance of European power, in Frederick's opinion, was France. He had shared his father's indignation over French duplicity in ending the War of the Polish Succession. Despite a veneer of gentility, Cardinal Fleury was not to be trusted. He was pursuing an aggressive policy designed to enrich France — at the expense of Germany and Holland — in aiming at a universal monarchy. At the same time, Austria was attempting to monopolize the Imperial crown by making it hereditary to the Habsburgs, and because of disunity the German princes were ill prepared to frustrate either French or Austrian ambitions. Austria herself was weak, bogged down in a senseless war with the Turks. France was left with a virtually free hand in European affairs. It followed that only England and Holland, aided by northern

German states, could restore the balance of power and prevent France from gobbling up Europe. Prussia must wean herself from Austria, whose court time and again had broken its word in the matter of Juliers and Berg. Since neither Austria nor France wished to strengthen Protestant Prussia, the other defenders of the Protestant faith, England and Holland, should overlook various regional differences and support Prussia. Gooch concluded that Frederick's "appeal for Anglo-Prussian cooperation against the designs of France and Austria anticipates the grouping of the Seven Years' War."

Friedrich Meinecke judged the theoretical portion of *Reflections* to be more important, and we agree. Frederick was very impressed with the work of one of the pioneers of the Enlightenment, Baron de Montesquieu, whose *Persian Letters* had been a best seller when Frederick was nine. More recently Montesquieu had published a study of the Roman empire,[3] in Will Durant's words "a pioneer attempt at a philosophy of history . . . a classic of French prose."[4] Montesquieu daringly used causal analysis in attempting to identify historical laws as Newton had sought spatial laws:

> It is not Fortune who governs the world, as we see from the history of the Romans. . . . There are general causes, moral or physical, which operate in every monarchy, raise it, maintain it, or overthrow it. All that occurs is subject to these causes; and if a particular cause, like the accidental result of a battle, has ruined a state, there was a general cause that made the downfall of this state ensue from a single battle. In a word, the principal movement draws with it all the particular occurrences.

Although this view contrasted sharply with Frederick's notion of predestined events — or fatalism — he had advanced far enough in his thinking to examine and in part accept Montesquieu's premise. But he was also concerned with the "true interests of the kingdom" and he now concluded that by applying the laws of history as determined by causal analysis to the day-to-day interests of a state, a ruler could foresee the future: "It is a matter of wisdom to be able to know everything, to judge everything, and to foresee everything." Montesquieu maintained that rational analysis of history resulted in universal laws, and Frederick agreed: "The policy of great monarchies has never varied. Their fundamental principle has consisted in anticipating the stratagems of their enemies and in winning the contest of wits." Various factors influenced the principle, but the principle remained dominant to rulers: "It is a question of their ostensible glory; in a word, they *must* increase in size."

This conclusion scarcely fitted the humanitarianism of the Enlightenment, and Frederick, though accepting the fact of aggression, was forced to brand it a "false principle," the result of errant rulers. Where the first kings had been chosen by the people and remained responsible to them and to their welfare, later rulers had allowed unruly passions to introduce either limitless ambition or ruinous neglect, which in time brought down the sturdiest empires. Frederick left no doubt of the moral obligation of a prince to do his duty to his subjects, and here he was nudging the later demand for a social contract. He stopped well short, however, by *not* mentioning the right of a subject to depose a bad ruler. But Frederick in no way resolved the natural conflict between his virtuous interpretation of *raison d'état* and the ruler's (and kingdom's) own interest. Resolution being impossible, he turned to compromise. Power politics, he concluded, were permissible when based on legitimate and not supposed rights: "It is a shame and a humiliation to lose parts of one's territory; and it is an act of injustice and criminal robbery to conquer lands to which one has no legitimate right."

Who was to decide on what were legitimate and what supposed rights? Frederick concluded that the decision must be up to the ruler; this was the birth of his unshaken belief in authoritarian rule, or what has since been called benevolent despotism. As Plato had fallen into a trap by calling for rule by intellectuals — who would judge the judges? — so Frederick fell into a similar trap. A ruler may think his actions were virtuous when taken on behalf of his own interests, but other rulers may think to the contrary and, in contesting these actions, may well go to war. This was precisely the blueprint of the future. It was essentially a conflict between virtuous thought and expedient action, the moral versus the practical — and Frederick was neither the first nor the last ruler to be uncomfortably confronted with it.

The crown prince sent the manuscript of *Reflections* to Voltaire in the spring of 1738 and asked him to arrange for translation and anonymous publication in England so that the book would be received as the work of an Englishman wanting to mobilize public opinion in Britain. If possible, it should also be published in French in Holland for surreptitious circulation in France. The work greatly surprised Voltaire, who wrote that he and Madame du Châtelet had read it several times and regarded it as the best of Frederick's writings.

Another exchange of fulsome letters ensued, but the work was not published. Relations between England and Spain had steadily deteriorated. Sir Robert Walpole was hard pressed to refuse William Pitt's cries in Parliament to declare war on this ancient enemy. With war imminent, Walpole could not afford to antagonize France and would surely suppress publication in England. Moreover, as Voltaire pointed out, Frederick was arguing on behalf of a German empire, and his words would scarcely arouse favorable sentiment in England. At Voltaire's suggestion, Frederick shelved the work, a wise decision as it turned out. Unknown to the crown prince, his father's envoy at the

Hague had been secretly working with the Versailles court, a diplomatic effort that would soon result in a treaty by which the Prussian king secured a guarantee of his claim to Berg. Further, despite Frederick William's saber rattling, he had swung toward England, a move reciprocated by the English king and one that shortly would benefit the Crown Prince of Prussia.

21

PRUSSIA'S tense relations with the great powers had brought noticeable improvement in Frederick William's treatment of the crown prince. Following the 1738 review, the king had taken his son to a military inspection in Cleves before going on to Holland, to the castle of Loo in Geldern, where they were guests of the Prince of Orange, married now to one of Frederick's cousins, Princess Anne of England.

The prince seems to have enjoyed himself on this tour, though more through its diversity and frequent dissipations than through meeting outstanding people, and not least through recruiting a giant of six feet, four inches, for whom he paid six thousand thalers. He had met and would correspond with Count Schaumburg-Lippe, who had arranged his secret initiation into the Freemasons, an event described by another new acquaintance, Baron Jakob Friedrich Bielfeld. The latter would join the Rheinsberg group the next year and, like Wilhelmina, would later publish an intimate and frequently exaggerated and inaccurate account of his time with Frederick. Bielfeld described the crown prince as looking younger than his twenty-six years, an extremely genial person, short but with charming features and fine auburn hair, large blue eyes at once severe, sweet, and gracious. The king later complimented his son for being "rational, serious, not dangling about among the women as formerly."[1]

The relationship continued to improve. In October Frederick wrote to Suhm: "The news of the day is that the king is reading Wolffs philosophy three hours a day, God be praised! Thus we have reached the triumph of reason and I hope that the bigots with their gloomy intrigues will no longer be able to oppose good sense and reason." In December he told Camas, "I have found a marked change in the king's temper; he has become extremely gracious, gentle, affable, and fair; he has spoken of the sciences in praiseworthy terms; and I have been charmed and delighted at what I have seen and heard."

Had a twenty-six-year test of wills finally ended? It had not. The king was a sick man, showing "symptoms of a person in a great decay," as Guy Dickens reported, and his mind and temper were uncertain at best.[2] Severe attacks of dropsy and gout made him want to die, but he wanted the Elector Palatine to die first, and he was not yet reconciled to leaving his kingdom on earth to Frederick. Good temper quickly vanished. In late December the prince wrote to his sister "of scenes comparable to the destruction of Carthage. . . . I cannot tell you all I have had to endure from the king." More was to come in the new year. The king refused to release his son from the "Egyptian slavery" of Berlin. His extreme jealousy of Frederick caused several senior officers, Count von Schulenburg included, to flee to their regiments in order to avoid offending either father or son. Toadies like Grumbkow exploited the situation by filling the royal ear with tales of Frederick's alleged misconduct. Only a few weeks later Frederick again wrote to Camas:

> To my great regret, I must recant. All the beautiful signs of graciousness, kindness, and gentleness have disappeared as in a dream. The king's humor has soured so strongly, and his hatred of me has manifested itself in so many different ways, that if I weren't what I am I would have already requested my dismissal, and I would prefer a thousand times to beg my bread honorably elsewhere than to survive on the chagrin that I am forced to down here. The relentlessness with which the King attacks me . . . is the talk of the town . . . and what is more curious, I am still ignorant of my crimes unless it is that of being heir presumptive.

He had to guard himself constantly against courtiers ready to stab him in the back: "The least faux pas, the least imprudence, a bagatelle, a mere nothing exaggerated and amplified, will suffice for my condemnation." He could "never expect to be able to live in peace with a father so easy to irritate."

Ill treatment was only part of the trouble. Frederick had been spending money in his usual carefree way, not only on high living and improvements on Rheinsberg but on expensive big recruits to satisfy the king. He had expected a large loan from the Russian court, but Suhm had not brought it off.

He now received help from a totally unexpected quarter. Ever since the Prussian king's near death in 1735, the English court had wanted to worm its way back into Frederick's good graces. But the crown prince felt that King George, his uncle, had badly let down him and Wilhelmina, so Dickens's few approaches met with only indifference and contempt. As war with Spain and France threatened, England intensified its effort. The previous October, Dickens had been ordered to arrange a secret meeting, inform Frederick that he had no better friend in the world than Uncle George, that it was only at the English king's insistence that Emperor Charles had intervened on Frederick's behalf in the dark days of 1730, and that George, prompted alone by an "uncle's

Love and Affection," now stood ready to lend him whatever sums necessary to pay his debts. No strings were attached, except that Frederick had to pledge himself to complete secrecy and promise to handle the money in such a way that his father would not become suspicious.[3] Uncle George suggested an initial loan of two thousand pounds sterling, an immense sum of money — to anyone except the crown prince.*

Due to the extreme secrecy involved, Dickens did not contact Frederick until February 1739, when the prince's situation had grown so precarious that, as the envoy reported, "his Horses were obliged for three Days to feed upon nothing but Hay, his Highness having neither Money nor Credit to get them Oats." Dickens used a confidant, Colonel Count Friedrich Sebastian von Truchsess, who was also sworn to secrecy. No one other than Frederick, Dickens, or Truchsess was to know "one tittle of this Business," warned Lord Harrington. Frederick accepted the offer "with great Joy and Gratitude." He also reported that his debts were high and that he would need not only another two thousand pounds as soon as possible but an additional ten thousand thalers come autumn. These sums, he promised, "would set him on horseback"; the money would be very carefully managed, it would all be repaid in time, and he would be eternally grateful to Uncle George.[4] With these and other preliminaries out of the way, the complicated financial machinery and secret codes were set up, and Frederick received the first loan shortly after returning to Rheinsberg.

The first payment was like the first drink to an alcoholic. At Frederick's urging, Truchsess was soon again on the way to Rheinsberg to deliver another two thousand pounds. Frederick meanwhile had informed Dickens that "he was greatly mistaken in his Calculations"[5]: he owed four years of accumulated debts at home and abroad (Dickens reported a total of several hundred thousand thalers) and needed another six thousand pounds. In addition, he wanted an annual allowance of fifty thousand thalers, to begin in a few weeks. King George not surprisingly demurred, on the grounds that such large sums would attract the Prussian king's attention, but he finally agreed to an annual allowance of five thousand pounds in quarterly installments commencing in late March. The first payment was made in gold ducats sent from the Hague. Frederick asked for and received subsequent payments considerably ahead of schedule.† (By the time of his accession he owed

---

* Frederick was constantly and often heavily in debt. Thanks mainly to Voltaire's biased *Mémoires*, the legend grew that as king he did not have to repay these debts. This is false. (Granier, "Kronprinzlichen Schulden.") From 1749 to 1750 he repaid debts in the sum of 272,242 thalers. One debt incurred in 1738 was repaid with interest in 1782! (Preuss, *Friedrich . . . eine Lebensgeschichte*, Volume 1.)

† The code used was "books" for payments. In a November dispatch, Dickens somewhat frantically noted that he had given the "student" a few "brochures" in advance but that he now demanded "folios"!

Uncle George over twelve thousand pounds, which were promptly repaid with thanks.)

March was a good month for the crown prince. In addition to English gold he received the welcome news of Grumbkow's death. Grumbkow, by then a field marshal, had never fully recovered from his drinking bout with King August the Strong some years earlier. Though Frederick perforce had become allied with the man from 1730 on and had written to him frequently and frankly, he had never trusted him and now wrote to Wilhelmina: "Today is the funeral of the late Marshal Grumbkow whom nearly everyone remembers with loathing. I gain a limitless advantage by his death and flatter myself that we shall breathe again after a long storm." He enclosed a rude verse epitaph.

Grumbkow's death coincided with a diplomatic victory for Frederick William. Despite France's ostensibly pro-Austrian intervention in Empire affairs, Cardinal Fleury had been playing a double game: his aim was to detach Prussia from Austrian influence. A year earlier, Prussian and French envoys had begun secret talks, which led to a treaty that was signed in early April. It was not a great diplomatic achievement, since it guaranteed only Frederick William's claim to Berg minus its capital, Düsseldorf. Its true significance lay in Frederick William's defection from the House of Habsburg, thus starting a new phase in Prussian-French relations. Only four years earlier, when the emperor had spurned the Prussian king's offer of his entire army to fight the French, Frederick William had written to Seckendorff that, although he would remain loyal to the Emperor, his successor would ally with another country in order to heal the injuries inflicted by the Vienna court. Frederick William had now taken the first steps toward a new alliance, and there can be little doubt that this was the principal subject of subsequent talks that he held with the crown prince on foreign policy.

Frederick had been broadcasting his own hawkish desires ever since returning from Holland. Make no mistake, he wrote to the Prince of Orange: if France occupied the Rhenish duchies when the Elector Palatine died, the King of Prussia would go to war. To Suhm he confided that he would like to see the next army review not in Berlin but in the Rhine plains outside Düsseldorf. Voltaire learned that with the Elector Palatine's death "our march on Juliers and Berg will be an inevitable result."

In late 1739 the new French envoy, Marquis Guy Louis Henri de Valory, reported to Versailles that, although the crown prince on his accession would favor the arts and sciences, along with trade and agriculture, he would add to the paternal role that of the hero: "His true desire is for fame, indeed for martial fame; he is burning with the desire to follow in the footsteps of the Great Elector." Valory unknowingly echoed words written nearly a year earlier by Baron von Seckendorff.

When asked by his court whether the crown prince "liked the military," the baron replied, "Yes, and much more so than his father. His principle is to begin with a thunderbolt." [6]

◦▦◦

Frederick stayed at Rheinsberg in the spring of 1739, planning new improvements with Knobelsdorff, drilling with his regiment at Ruppin, writing long letters to close friends, working on a new and elegant edition of Voltaire's *Henriade,* relaxing with friends, sending the ailing king such gifts as a marinated salmon (a token of "love and obedience"), a lamb, lobsters, strawberries, cheeses — and many details of regimental activities.

He also resumed political studies, particularly those concerning the *raison d'état* and a ruler's responsibility. Frederick had criticized Voltaire for praising Machiavelli in *Le Siècle de Louis XIV;* Machiavelli was not a great man, he argued, but a "dishonest" man. More recently he had read Machiavelli's *The Prince,* which he found greatly at odds with the humanitarian doctrines of the Enlightenment. Machiavelli had written, in a time of warring Italian city-states, that "a Prince should have no other aim or thought, nor take up any other thing for his study, but war and its organization and discipline." This oft-quoted statement sounds terrifying when taken out of context, but it was a realistic assessment of a current political climate.

In May 1739, Frederick wrote to Voltaire: "At the moment I am busy with Machiavelli. I am taking notes on *The Prince,* and have already begun a work that will entirely refute his maxims, which are opposed to virtue and the true interests of princes. . . . Health and other duties permitting, I hope to send you the manuscript within three months." Voltaire as usual encouraged the work. A month later Frederick informed him that the project would take longer than he had anticipated. It would be his sequel to the *Henriade* and the noble sentiments of King Henry IV: "I am forging the thunderbolt that will annihilate Caesar Borgia."

◦▦◦

The 1739 spring review soon interrupted the Rheinsberg routine, but for once Frederick thoroughly enjoyed it. The king publicly complimented him on the splendid condition of Regiment Goltz, especially its new recruits (of whom he selected five, paying Frederick nearly 11,000 thalers for them). He went on to praise his son's good sense and understanding; he was satisfied to leave kingdom and army "to so deserving a son." The cup ran over when in a drunken moment he promised Frederick a present of 100,000 thalers (and finally gave him 40,000).

In Prussia a few weeks later he was still all charm. "Everything has changed since Grumbkow's death," Frederick wrote to Wilhelmina. "Thank heavens I could not be on better terms with the king than at present." On the spur of the moment, but "with all the grace in the world," the king gave him a stud farm worth an annual income of twelve thousand thalers.

In a good humor, Frederick sent Voltaire a eulogy of the king's work in Prussia. After pointing to the immense improvement of this land, which had been plague-stricken and impoverished since the turn of the century, he went on:

> All this is due to the king, who not only gave orders, but supervised their execution; who made the plans and alone carried them out; who spared no trouble nor pains, nor immense expenditures, neither promises nor rewards, to secure a happy existence for half a million thinking people. . . . I find something heroic in the King's generosity and labor in repeopling this desert and making it fertile and happy, and I believe that you would agree with my feelings.

22

FREDERICK spent the autumn of 1739 at Remusberg, his usual pleasure heightened by a host of guests, including the ebullient French diplomat Chétardie, who was en route to Saint Petersburg, and Lord Baltimore, who was traveling with Francesco Algarotti. Baltimore, Frederick wrote to Voltaire, was a very sensible and highly intelligent man keenly interested in the sciences.* Algarotti was a Venetian intellectual — poet, scientist, and critic — only a few months younger than Frederick. He had recently published an interpretation of Newton's mathematics "for the ladies" and had been highly praised by Voltaire. He and Frederick hit it off immediately and spent eight "unforgettable days" discussing "philosophy, the sciences, the arts, everything that is to the taste of gentlemen." Frederick found him full of fire, vivacity, and sensibility; he was soon nicknamed the Swan of Padua, and they remained in warm correspondence until Algarotti's return to Prussia.

Frederick had already plunged into writing what he called *The Re-*

---

* Baltimore may have introduced Frederick to Lord Chesterfield's and Jonathan Swift's works. In early December Frederick wrote to Algarotti of "the singular productions of Dr. Swift. His new, daring, and somewhat absurd ideas amuse me. I very much like this English Rabelais." He had also read Chesterfield's work on the make-up of ladies, which he found full of spirit with good jokes and humor. Frederick would soon correspond with Chesterfield, who became his ardent admirer and champion.

futation of The Prince of Machiavelli. He should have called it *The Condemnation,* because it is moral homily written, in his words, "to inspire mankind with horror by the false wisdom of this policy." In reality it was based on what Meinecke aptly termed "a secret dialogue with himself, and with the passionate impulses inside him."[1] He would remove the contradiction between interest and idea that had bothered him in the earlier *Reflections.* The judgment was not to be diluted by considerations of temporal environment, philosophical nuance, or political reality. Machiavelli had corrupted society, and it was time to refute him morally. Sounding like an accuser of Socrates, Frederick wrote in his preface:

> I venture to undertake the defense of humanity against this monster who desires to destroy it, to oppose reason and justice to sophistry and crime. I have always regarded *The Prince* as one of the most dangerous books in the world; an ambitious young man, too immature to distinguish good from evil, may only too easily be led astray by maxims that flatter his passions. That is bad enough in a private individual; it is far worse in reigning princes, who should set an example to their subjects, and by their goodness, magnanimity, and mercy be the living images of deity. The passions of kings are worse than flood, pestilence, and fire, for their consequences are more lasting.

This was a return to the opening theme of *Reflections,* in which he argued that the sovereign should be servant not master of his subjects, "the instrument of their happiness as his people are instruments of his glory." The good ruler is benevolent and virtuous, and Machiavelli was wrong to argue that goodness spells catastrophe: "The good king will be well served." He will make his people as virtuous as himself, his neighbors will imitate him "and the wicked will tremble."

A good prince will cultivate his mind before seeking such riotous and brutalizing pleasures as the hunt. (Take notice, King Frederick William.) "He should acquire learning less for the sake of knowledge than to enable him to exercise his mind in the society of wise and learned men so that he may learn to think justly and combine his ideas correctly." Ideally he should hold the same religious beliefs as his subjects, but if he does not, he will still be loved as long as he is honest, "for it is not by opinions but by actions that men are made happy." A good prince should also be as generous as possible but must always keep a secret treasury in case of war.

Regarding foreign policy, the most virtuous prince must on occasion break treaties and alliances, but he should do this honestly and advise his allies beforehand. Similarly he must sometimes go to war: "How great is the fame that awaits him who delivers his country from the invasion of an enemy, or who recovers rights and privileges that have been usurped by others."

Frederick regarded war as so important a subject that he devoted his final chapter to it. He specified three types of justifiable wars: wars of defense, wars of legitimate interest, and wars of precaution. The first two are the most just, since they are fought to preserve a monarchy's freedom and territory. But the third is also justified under certain circumstances:

> When the excessive greatness of a power seems ready to overflow and threatens to engulf the universe, it is the path of prudence to make dikes and to arrest the violent course of a torrent while it is still under control. One sees the gathering clouds and the lightning that heralds the storm. The sovereign whom it menaces, unable to avert it alone, should unite all threatened by the common peril. . . . It is better for a prince to enter on an offensive war . . . than to wait till the situation is desperate and a declaration of war can only postpone enslavement and ruin. . . . Thus all wars are just that aim at resisting usurpers, maintaining legitimate rights, safeguarding the liberty of the universe, and warding off the oppression and violence of ambitious men. Sovereigns who wage such wars need not reproach themselves for the shedding of blood. Necessity compels them to act, and in such circumstances war is a lesser evil than peace."

This is not the only instance where the teachings of Machiavelli inspired Frederick. In Meinecke's words, "His advice to the prince, to rule personally, to act as his own commander in the field, to accommodate himself to the situation, to despise flatterers, to ascertain the secret intentions of other rulers, and so forth, entirely coincided with [Frederick's] own ideas and certainly helped to bring his political thought to fruition at that time."

Frederick finished a rough draft and in September was correcting faults that he had overlooked "in the heat of composition." Only in December did he send the first twelve chapters to Voltaire, as usual asking for critical advice. Voltaire and Emily liked it enormously: it was a work for all men and all time; it should become "the catechism of kings and their ministers." Voltaire agreed to write an introduction to the work, which would have to be published anonymously; he would also edit it and see it through publication in Holland. Under his aegis it did appear, but in considerably altered form (and considerably altered circumstances) in September 1740, with the title *L'Anti-Macchiavel.*

While Frederick was working on the *Refutation,* European statesmen had been fashioning a sort of peace. Austrian and Russian arms had fared no better against the Turks in 1739. In September, with France mediating, Austria withdrew from the war after ceding large areas to the Turks.* Thus isolated, Russia followed suit and retained only the port of Azov in return for a heavy loss of men and gold.

But peace was short-lived. Cardinal Fleury's diplomatic offensive had succeeded beyond even his expectations: a new treaty with Austria in 1738, the following year a treaty with Prussia, and, with it, the friendship of Sweden and Poland. Intercession with Austria had also placed the Versailles court high in Turkish favor. As icing on the cake he next persuaded the Spanish termagant Elizabeth Farnese to accept a French bride for her younger son, Don Philip.

Fleury's success was Robert Walpole's failure. Deeming it vital to English interests to avoid war, Walpole had been working assiduously since 1737 to calm public anger against Spain. Expanding overseas commerce had mainly caused the friction. For some years the South Seas Company, a private company representing London traders, had been violating trade rights in Spanish America. Spain retaliated by forcibly searching English vessels, searches and seizures often being made by the notorious *guardacostas,* local coast guard ships similar to wartime privateers. Here was a natural target for parliamentary opposition, headed by William Pitt and Cobham's Cubs. In an effort to sabotage Walpole's negotiations with Spain in 1738, they had produced one Captain Robert Jenkins, who told excited parliamentarians that *seven years earlier* his ship had been boarded by *guardacostas* who had seized the cargo, tortured the crew, and mutilated him — and he held up a withered ear preserved in a bottle of alcohol.

Jenkins's dramatic appearance lashed public opinion to frenzy. Walpole was still powerful enough to withstand the pressure and negotiate the Convention of Pardo, a sensible compromise of conflicting Spanish and British claims. But he could not withstand the pressure from commercial interests. Prompted by Pitt, the South Seas Company refused to pay the agreed sum, nor would Spain pay compensation until she received British gold. London pamphleteers continued to agitate the affair, and in autumn of 1739 Walpole finally yielded. "It is your war," he told Lord Newcastle, "and I wish you the joy of it." [2]

Thus came about the War of Jenkins's Ear, "the first major conflict between European powers fought because of overseas disputes," the British historian Glyndwr Williams noted. Walpole's bitterness was not

---

* Frederick later wrote: "The war that they undertook was vanity and the peace which followed was that of weakness." Frederick blamed the minister Johann Christoph von Bartenstein and General Seckendorff for persuading Emperor Charles to enter the war against the Turks. "The cabals of the chiefs who were in opposition, and the jealousy of generals caused all operations to fail. The orders that the generals received from the court were either contradictory or obliged those generals to undertake impracticable operations. This domestic disorder became more fatal to Austrian arms than the strength of the infidels." (*Oeuvres,* Volume 2, *Histoire de mon temps.*)

assuaged by Admiral Edward Vernon's capture of Porto Bello on the Panamanian isthmus in November. Far bigger issues, he realized, were at stake. Britain had opened a hornet's nest. By forcing war with Spain, the British opposition had brought about Spanish rapprochement with France, and that would cause Britain to spend thousands of lives and millions of pounds in the next forty years. The conflict would not be resolved for another forty years after that — and then only with considerable loss of overseas holdings.

As the shadow of war hovered over Rheinsberg happiness, so did the shadow of death. Frederick would soon be called to Berlin, where, as he informed Wilhelmina, "I expect to find things . . . about the same as I left them: Now gout in the knees, now tightness of the chest; I foresee that we shall pass a sad winter."

Baron Pöllnitz sent the crown prince special reports from Potsdam. The king was in constant pain from severe gout, not to mention dropsy and shortness of breath with frequent vomiting. He sometimes recovered sufficiently to conduct state business in the mornings, but a relapse usually followed. He could not sleep and frequently held nightlong sessions of the Tabagie, insisting that old comrades smoke and tell stories; sometimes he dozed off, but if someone stopped talking he instantly awakened. To pass lonely and painful hours he made wooden boxes, furiously hammering on a special bed table. On occasion he would have some of the Potsdam giants march through the bedroom. The sight of them invariably made him feel better, and sometimes he would hug one or paint a portrait. When his breath failed, his grotesque body had to be carried to a bath chair. A task force of physicians and surgeons headed by Dr. Eller buzzed in and out of the sickroom, frequently taking a pint or so of blood from the exhausted patient to dispel the noxious humors that, they claimed, fomented illness. Simultaneously a task force of chaplains headed by Pastor Roloff sought to dispel noxious spiritual humors by preparing the king for a death that could not be far away. In November he insisted on moving to Berlin; he doubted that he would see Potsdam again.

In late January 1740 Frederick wrote his wife from Ruppin that he had learned the king could not recover: "God knows that I do not want my father to die, and I believe that I shall be more grieved by his death than many others who pretend to idolize him during his life; natural feeling is an instinct too powerful in me and I am not sufficiently strong to smother it."

The king nonetheless revived sufficiently to summon another Tabagie. When Frederick walked in, the old generals, contrary to custom, stood to receive him. The king lost his temper, had himself carried from the room, and ordered everyone to leave the palace for "paying homage to the Rising Sun." He soon calmed down and saw a great deal of Frederick; he wrote to Old Dessauer that "I have prepared myself for death and have told my eldest son everything I know that is still to be done." The tenor of these talks is suggested in a report by Guy Dickens:

> Our wrathful Monarch continues in the same way; he is angry with the [British] King our Master for making so formidable a figure [in the war against Spain]; he is angry with France because she does not join with Spain and declare war against us; he is angry with Holland because they seem disposed to augment their Forces by Sea and Land; he is angry with the Emperor and Russia for having made their Peace with the Turks, and lastly, he is angry with himself, because he finds that he wants Courage, as well as Opportunity, to put his mischievous Designs in Execution.[3]

This time, it seemed, the king was going to die. In March he told Old Dessauer that since Frederick did not enjoy hunting, he wanted the prince to take his pick of the royal hounds and hoped he would continue to derive much pleasure from the chase. Frederick advised Wilhelmina that she would not see the king again: "His illnesses are worsening so rapidly that I doubt whether he will last the coming week. He has given you his blessing and has spoken very well of you. At present his fever is so fierce that he can scarcely speak. . . . Keep calm and do not grieve too much, for there is no remedy for such things."

But somehow Frederick William continued to survive; he even allowed the crown prince to return to Ruppin to put his regiment in order for the spring review. In late April the king insisted on returning to Potsdam, but he sent a minister to Ruppin to discuss internal affairs with Frederick; two more ministers of foreign affairs, Count Heinrich von Podewils (Grumbkow's son-in-law) and Wilhelm Heinrich von Thulemeyer, followed to brief him on foreign affairs.

Frederick, learning that Wilhelmina was thinking of coming to Berlin, at once advised her to stay away from that madhouse. He himself had his hands full, he continued. The village of Rheinsberg had burned to the ground (without spreading to his estate) and the old chamberlain, Wolden, had died and had to be buried. It would do no good for Wilhelmina to turn up. Frederick had been spared from "galley service" only by troop demands and was vastly enjoying his liberty. Dr. Eller continued to report on the king's health, but in his replies Frederick seemed more concerned with his own health; only six days before the king's death he was asking Eller whether he could eat whey and lemon, and was impatiently awaiting the recipe for herbs and the diet that Eller had promised to send. Frederick now received a letter from his father with the salutation, the first time ever, "My beloved Son." He returned to Potsdam the following day expecting to find his father dead. Instead, the king was in the palace gardens, supervising the laying of a cornerstone for a blacksmith's cottage!

An emotional meeting was followed by lengthy conversations on the kingdom's internal and external affairs. Podewils and Frederick listened to the king explain the reasons for his alliance with England and Hanover in 1725 and his subsequent counteralliance with Austria. He warned Frederick of the Vienna court's intention to hold down Prussia, and he also warned that King George as Elector of Hanover was jealous of Prussia and must be watched. Frederick was to pursue vigorously the Prussian claim to Berg. Concerning Russia, there was little to say except that Prussia would lose more than it would win in any war with her — indeed, any war is more easily begun than ended. Frederick should avoid alliances that required him to splinter his army by sending auxiliary troops hither and yon.

The king next summoned various officers and officials to his deathbed. "Has God not graced me by having given me such a courageous and worthy son?" he asked them. Frederick rose, gripped the royal hand, and cried. The king embraced him and said, "My God, I die content, since I leave behind such a worthy son and successor."[4]

Frederick William went out well. A practical man, he had designed his own coffin, which was brought into his chambers. He dictated lengthy instructions for his post-mortem and funeral, which under no circumstances was to cost more than twenty thousand thalers; less if possible. He seemed fully resigned to death and even showed a flicker of humor. When a chaplain sang one of his favorite hymns, "Naked I came into this world, naked I shall fare hence," the king interrupted: "That isn't true; I shall be wearing my uniform." On Tuesday at five A.M. he summoned the court and surrendered the government to the crown prince. Then, as Frederick informed Voltaire, the king "tenderly took leave of my brothers, of the senior officers, and of me."[5] His chaplains remained with him, exhorting him to detailed confessions. As death approached, he asked for a hand mirror so that he could examine his face to see if it was changing.*

The king's stoicism greatly impressed Frederick, who wrote to Voltaire that "he died with the curiosity of a scientist as to what was happening to him at the moment of death, and with the heroism of a great man, leaving all of us sincere regrets over his loss and, in his courageous death, an example for his family to follow." To the new queen he wrote: "God took the king this afternoon at half past three. You were in his thoughts. His death has drawn real tears of compassion

---

* A post-mortem found decayed lungs and liver and a stone in the gall bladder. Nearly fourteen quarts of water were drained from the body. He had forbidden embalming and soon had to be buried in Potsdam's garrison church. (British Foreign Office, 90/47.)

from all of us. You would never believe with what firmness he died."
And to Wilhelmina: "The good Lord summoned our father yesterday
at three. He died with angelic firmness and without suffering too much."
Frederick was more candid with Voltaire: "My destiny has changed; I
have witnessed the last moments of a king, his agony, his death. In
succeeding to the throne, I assuredly did not need this lesson to be
disgusted with human vanity."

BOOK THREE

The First Silesian War

1740–1742

The times do not adapt themselves to men but men must adapt themselves to the times.

— *Frederick the Great*

23

MANY BIOGRAPHERS have written that the king's death, in 1740, plunged Frederick into deepest sorrow, but his actions, orders, and correspondence do not justify the assertion. However, he was no doubt more than a little frightened now by "the good luck of having the bad luck," as the envoy Valory put it. On the one hand, he had the authority he had so long desired; on the other, he was bound to cares remote from Parnassus. To Voltaire he wrote: "The infinite amount of work that falls on me since his death scarcely has left time for sorrow. I have always believed that after my father's death it was my duty to devote myself entirely to my country. Accordingly I have worked as hard as I can to make the most expeditious arrangements possible for the common good."

It is not difficult to empathize with King Frederick's initial pensive and melancholy mood. Although his father had left a strong and prosperous legacy, much work remained. He would have to complete or at least continue the task of internal consolidation and growth begun by the Great Elector. Frederick William had worked hard to convert disparate feudal holdings into a centralized monarchy, but his administrative, economic, agricultural, and legal reforms were only partially completed and in some instances scarcely begun. Roads were poor, the mail service fledgling; almost no industry existed; the kingdom suffered a trade deficit of 1.25 million thalers; schools and hospitals were in short supply; colonists were needed to populate wastelands, clear forests, and drain swamps, to farm, provide new skills, start new industries, increase trade. Altogether, an immense internal effort was needed if Prussia was to take her place in the sun.

The Prussian army, vital to survival and growth, left much to be desired. Its command structure was far too rigid. Of five field marshals only two, Old Dessauer (at sixty-four) and Schwerin (at fifty-six) were young enough to go to war; far too many of its thirty-five generals were either too old or physically unfit to campaign. Most junior officers lacked

Prince Leopold of Anhalt-Dessau,
"The Old Dessauer," guiding genius
of the Prussian army

Field Marshal Count Kurt Christoph
von Schwerin. "The salvation of the
state depends on your expedition; if
you do not carry it out according to
my will, you will pay with your head."
— Frederick to Schwerin, April 1757

General Hans Joachim von Zieten,
father of the Prussian hussars

education and, despite strict regulations, devoted too much time to whoring, drinking, and gambling. The army's appearance and reputation were impressive, but it was relatively small and almost untested on the battlefield, its cavalry far too bulky and immobile, its artillery ineffective and undermanned, its engineers and pioneers few in number. Although the infantry was well disciplined, Frederick found its commanders overly concerned with spit-and-polish, with unimportant details, with complicated parade ground "evolutions" that neglected the tactics and strategy necessary to win battles and wars. "The soldier polished his rifle and accouterments," Frederick later wrote, "the cavalier his bridle, saddle, and even his boots; the manes of horses were dressed with ribbons. . . . If peace had lasted beyond 1740, we would probably now have rouge and beauty spots."[1] Frederick William's reforms, aided and often inspired by Old Dessauer, had enlarged and greatly improved the army, but Frederick would have to carry on the work.

His legacy was particularly weak in the realm of foreign affairs. He faced a confused, changing, and potentially explosive European political situation at a time when Prussia was virtually isolated. Earlier that year the Russian minister, Count Heinrich Johann Friedrich Ostermann, had warned that "only a general war can end the present unnatural state of affairs."[2] Most statesmen agreed, and most of them realized that such a war would contravene the traditional system of Austria confronting France, with the maritime powers holding the balance. Now it would be England and Holland against France and Spain, the continental powers against the sea powers, with the Empire looking on. England already was at war with Spain; France and England were at loggerheads concerning overseas trade. But France was also bent on seducing the Bavarian elector from Empire control while winning over the Elector of Cologne and the King of Prussia. If Emperor Charles died, a war of succession would undoubtedly break out in central Europe. Frederick's frontiers everywhere lay open to invasion. His army provided one defense, alliances another. But no viable tradition of alliance existed. His father had never understood the complex nature of European politics, having seen the problem as one of Empire versus other powers rather than as one of achieving and maintaining a European power balance. One result was that he had swayed back and forth, allied now to Hanover and England, now to Austria, now to France, invariably humiliated by each, too frightened to use his army, his territorial claims rudely rejected. Frederick for some time had realized that Prussia as an Austrian satellite, as a satellite to any power, would continue to taste humiliation. As an independent power, however, Prussia could become a major factor in European politics and in time attract scattered and weak German principalities to her banner. It was up to him to keep his army ready, to forge the alliances necessary to survival and expansion.

Frederick faced massive problems but he had a lot working for him. The kingdom seemed delighted to have him. Valory had earlier reported to Versailles that "great things are expected from this prince."[3] Now the Hanoverian envoy told his court that "everyone has hopes and high expectations from their new king and seems to be completely revitalized and delighted."[4] The kingdom itself was also impressive. The royal dominions, though spread all over the place, comprised something over ten thousand square miles, about twice the size of Connecticut. His subjects numbered some two and a quarter million; the kingdom's annual income exceeded seven million thalers, of which six million was spent to support an army of eighty-one thousand men. The reserve treasury of silver coins in the basement of the Berlin palace amounted to nearly nine million thalers, and this did not count the splendid silver services and giant silver chandeliers, which if necessary could be melted into coin. Frederick could afford war at any moment; most rulers could not.

The total legacy fell into unique hands. Frederick was only twenty-eight, in general good health despite recurrent sieges of fever and indigestion, extremely intelligent and shrewd, and he possessed seemingly inexhaustible energy with which to realize the ambitions that swirled in his fecund mind. He had been waiting for the crown since 1734. Now it was his. Now he could lead Prussia from the shadow of his father's political ineptness. Now Prussia, now King Frederick II could become names admired and respected throughout the world. He had a major task before him, but very shortly events and the lessons of Machiavelli would lend themselves to at least partial accomplishment of it.

Not since the reign of Charles XII of Sweden had such energy claimed a throne. Scarcely had the old king breathed his last when Frederick ordered the Berlin gates closed to prevent the news from reaching foreign courts until military commanders, garrison regiments, and civil ministers had sworn personal allegiance to him.

The army came first. There was no question who commanded it. Frederick was touched when Old Dessauer came to court with condolences, and he at once confirmed the field marshal and his sons in their respective commands. But when the old prince supposed he would retain his traditional authority in the army, he was told abruptly that there was one authority in the army, and that was the king. When veteran Lieutenant General von der Schulenburg, long a friend and protector of the crown prince, came to Berlin to pay his respects, Frederick reprimanded him for leaving his command without orders.

The new king promised his generals the same reciprocal relationship they had enjoyed with his father but demanded more disciplined leadership and behavior. "Complaints have been laid against some of you of harshness, avarice, and insolence. See that they are silenced." Noncommissioned officers and enlisted men were to be treated "kindly and humanely." He ordered all regimental commanders to eliminate "the usual brutalities" that accompanied conscription, and he publicly punished violators "so that everyone can see that I will tolerate no such excesses."[5] He ordered better treatment for cadets who are "aristocrats and future officers, not mere peasants." At meals they were to be read either a bit of the history of Brandenburg or an excerpt from Feuquières's *Art of War.* Meals were to be improved, the kitchens "well ordered and clean." Instruction in engineering and French would be intensified. Beatings and similar punishments would cease; the cadet was to be instilled with "a love for the service."[6]

The ministers came next. Perhaps inspired by one of Voltaire's sycophantic odes — "You, Solomon of the north, more learned, more wise" — he explained that the crown was no longer to be enriched at the country's expense; he regarded the kingdom's best interests as identical with his own, but if a conflict developed, then the welfare of the country must come first.

Humanitarian ukases shot from Charlottenburg like Roman candles. To ameliorate the harsh effects of a late spring, he bought grain in Russia and Poland, opened royal granaries, and sold corn to bakers at reasonable prices. In Berlin he set up a new office, an inspectorate of the poor headed by his friend Charles Étienne Jordan, the former Lutheran minister. A decree went out to provincial administrators: "Our greatest care will be directed to advancing the welfare of the country and to making each subject comfortable and happy."[7] On learning of oppressive actions by a senior official in Prussia, he summarily dismissed the man and stripped him of honors.

The young king at once pledged himself to a policy of toleration, news that shocked repressive fellow rulers. He abolished the use of torture in criminal interrogations, and he soon would push major legal reforms begun but almost abandoned by his father. In settling a dispute with the Catholics, he reminded those concerned of the crown's traditional policy of religious toleration, and in a marginal note commented that "all religions must be tolerated . . . for in this country every man must go to heaven in his own way."[8] To the clergy's fury, he abolished dispensations for marriages in order to increase the population; on one occasion he said that the number of subjects was a king's real wealth. He authorized public speeches and forbade newspaper censorship except for political necessity. He invited the distinguished French mathematician Pierre Louis de Maupertuis* to head a reinvigorated Academy of Sciences and Letters, which was to be "not for show but for education."[9] Invitations were sent to Wolff,† Francesco Algarotti, the Swiss mathematician Leonhard Euler, and other distinguished intellectuals to come to Berlin as academy members at good salaries. He started two newspapers and promised to contribute to their columns. He opened a department of commerce and manufacturing that was to recruit skilled workers abroad by offering subsidies and exemption from taxes and military service for two years. He commissioned plans for a new opera house in Berlin and sent agents scurrying about Europe to attract suitable artistic talent. If Frederick was not intent on making his capital the Athens of the north, he at least was going to improve its cultural and academic image, and it was with pride that he announced these various projects to Voltaire.

The surprises continued. Once his father was buried, he disbanded the regiment of giants, which cost nearly 300,000 thalers a year to maintain (compared with 72,000 for a normal regiment), not to mention the vast sums spent on acquiring big men to keep its ranks full. The order was welcomed by every colonel and captain in the Prussian army, because it eliminated the effort and expenditure necessary to satisfy the former King's insatiable appetite. That aside, the saving allowed Frederick to form new units. His father had recommended in *The Political Testament* of 1722 that five new regiments should be established within six months of his death. Frederick raised the figure: "I have begun to expand the army by sixteen [infantry] battalions, five [hussar] squadrons, and one squadron of the royal bodyguard," he wrote to Voltaire in June — an increase of more than eight regiments of foot.

As Frederick had bluntly told Old Dessauer, there was to be only one authority in the kingdom. He had been expected to seek counsel not only from the field marshal but from his mother, now the dowager queen. He did no such thing. Although he always treated her with great respect and generously supported her court at Monbijou, he refused to discuss with her anything more important than a menu. He had never confided in his wife, now Queen Elizabeth, and was expected to divorce her. Instead, he installed her in her own residence, treated her with every courtesy, and thenceforth saw almost nothing of her. Wilhelmina had anticipated the change in status and warily began her first letter with "Sire" instead of her usual "My dear Brother." Frederick

---

* Maupertuis had become famous following his expedition to Lapland, where he confirmed one of Newton's postulates by measuring a degree of the meridian. He had sent Frederick his book, *La Figure de la Terre*, two years earlier.

† Frederick wrote Wolff that "philosophers should be the preceptors of the universe and the masters of princes. . . . Their task is to disclose; ours is to use." (*Oeuvres*, Volume 16.)

instructed her and his other sisters against such ceremony, but nevertheless their future correspondence lacked the earlier intimacy. His letters to his younger brothers were affectionate and correct but not particularly warm. Although he soon promoted them in military rank, he continued to comment on their studies and behavior in words strikingly similar to those used by the late king in reprimanding him. The critical aloofness that existed in his relations with nineteen-year-old Prince William and fourteen-year-old Prince Henry would in time lead to severe quarrels.

Frederick might easily have wreaked vengeance on senior generals and officials who had earlier harmed his interests. In most cases, he left them alone as long as they continued to perform satisfactorily. He did sack one minister, but he promoted forty-six-year-old Heinrich von Podewils to replace the terminally ill minister of foreign affairs, von Thulemeyer. He promoted Colonel von Derschau, once an archenemy — he had conducted Frederick's interrogation in 1730 — to major general and decorated two former opponents with the newly created Order of Merit. He recalled Captain Fouqué from Denmark, decorated him with the Order of Merit, promoted him to colonel, and gave him command of a regiment. He began to recruit foreign officers who had favorably impressed him during the Rhine campaign. He also repaid old debts. The Münchows of Cüstrin received well-deserved promotions, as did von Katte (father of his executed friend). He brought his former tutor, Duhan, to Berlin and gave him a modest pension. He recalled von Keith from English exile, made him a lieutenant colonel and equerry, and thereafter rarely saw him. He eagerly awaited Suhm's return to Berlin, where he would resign from Saxon service to replace Thulemeyer in the foreign office.

If Prussian officialdom was relieved at the relatively smooth transition, most of Frederick's cronies were disappointed. Hopes had run high at Rheinsberg for a new era of personal prosperity — of *Saus und Braus*, riotous living. When Baron Bielfeld knocked over a table and bent to pick up some coins, the architect Knobelsdorff exclaimed, "What? Pick up groschen when it will be raining ducats?"[10] The rains failed to appear. Only a lucky few benefited, and they were scarcely overwhelmed with favors. Fredersdorff was promoted to chamberlain and received a small estate near Rheinsberg. Algarotti would be ennobled and Keyserling promoted to colonel and aide; both were invited to reside at court to provide intellectual stimulation and comic relief. Five other officers were made aides with the rank of colonel. But this was scarcely the stuff of influential appointments, of enormous estates and pensions, which had been so eagerly anticipated.

"The fun is over," Frederick allegedly told Fredersdorff — and so it was, at least for a while.[11] He did increase the number of palace servants at Potsdam and drastically improved the cuisine, and he would soon order a costly dining service of gold from Paris, but he showed no sign of maintaining an opulent court in his grandfather's tradition. Indeed, he embraced economy with all the fervor and some of the contradiction of his father. Soon after Frederick William's death, Baron Pöllnitz found the new king distraught and in tears as he gave orders for the purchase of black mourning crape, but he recovered sufficiently to warn the baron against submitting a false expense account. "I would give a hundred gold coins," Pöllnitz told Count Manteuffel, "if I could have the old king back." [12] The minister of finance, August Friedrich von Boden, proved so pleasingly parsimonious in distributing funds that Frederick rewarded him with a magnificently furnished mansion and rich silver plate. To save time and money the king accepted homage from most dominions by simple proxy. Where he appeared personally, as in Prussia and Cleves, he traveled with a small equipage and insisted on minimum ceremony. His grandfather had taken two weeks to travel to Königsberg for his inauguration; Frederick took four days. When provincial committees requested portraits of the king and queen, he ordered them mass-produced in Berlin for a few pennies each. Manteuffel for one was appalled and suggested that the late king would soon seem a spendthrift in comparison with his son.

Frederick was already emulating his father in other ways. Even before the funeral, he began wearing a uniform — the once derided "shroud" — in preference to civilian clothing. "I get up at four A.M., drink mineral waters until eight (while reading dispatches), write until ten, inspect the troops until noon, write until five, then relax in good company," he informed Voltaire. In behavior he was aloof, generally suspicious, often querulous. His impetuous manner was all too familiar to veterans of the late king's inspections. During the trip to Königsberg in July, he inspected Schulenburg's cavalry regiment, found it unsatisfactory, and, as he wrote to his brother, Prince William, severely reprimanded the unfortunate general.* En route to Cleves, he stopped in Bayreuth to see Wilhelmina, a strained meeting, since her expectations greatly exceeded his largesse, as she sulkily recorded. On the road again he impetuously took young Prince William, Algarotti, and Fredersdorff on a caper across the Rhine to Strasbourg. Although they traveled under false passports, their identity soon became known, and the French populace began to demonstrate pleasure at the royal visit. The awkward reception accorded Frederick by Field Marshal Count François

---

*This letter, dated July 11, 1740, could have been written in part by Frederick William. ". . . Regiments Borcke, La Motte, Platten and Buddenbrock — not to mention Schwerin — are altogether superb, but I saw one of Schulenburg's squadrons which was disorder itself. I have written a very strong letter to the general; he will not forget that in a hurry."

Marie de Broglie, the governor, caused him to cut short the visit.* Was it a harmless lark? Perhaps. His father had once impetuously chased off to Hamburg solely to gorge on fresh oysters. He may also have hoped that the foray would bring a secret invitation to meet Cardinal Fleury. More likely he wanted to draw attention to himself — and he certainly succeeded. Podewils wrote bluntly, "You are alarming all of Europe and giving umbrage to everyone by your mysterious conduct." Whatever its ultimate purpose, the visit provided a pleasant enough interlude before a series of unexpected events that would put Frederick's political acumen to the test.

24

KING FREDERICK's diplomacy has been praised and damned through the centuries, a prolonged and vigorous historical debate that often bogs down in tiresome detail without getting to the nub of the matter.

Frederick was a child of the eighteenth century. It is futile to judge his political concepts, actions, and goals from either the physical or moral standards of later centuries. From the beginning of his reign, he played eighteenth-century politics with a deftness surprising for one of limited years and background. As his political correspondence — forty-six volumes — and other writings confirm, he held two ambitions, one long term and one short term. His immediate goal was to ensure Prussian claims to Juliers and Berg, East Frisia, and Mecklenburg — or satisfactory territorial equivalents — while giving away little or nothing in return, and at the same time to raise a question mark in foreign courts as to Prussia's future alliance, if any. His long-term goal was to raise Prussia to the status of a major power and attempt to revive the moribund German empire (the Holy Roman Empire) but with Protestant Prussia, not Roman Catholic Austria, as its natural leader.

He underestimated neither the difficulties nor the dangers that might arise from this policy. He knew that he faced powerful enemies who would do everything possible to keep Prussia in a minor role. He knew that his means were too limited to form and support the kinds of alliances that France and Britain so often used to achieve their ends. He knew that he was pitting himself against some very able and ruthless

---

* According to the Danish envoy, in a later audience Valory mentioned to King Frederick how surprised Marshal de Broglie was at his unannounced visit. "That I well believe," the king replied, and, in reference to one of Broglie's military disasters, added, "The man seems to be made only for surprises." (Volz, *Friedrich der Grosse im Spiegel*, Volume 1.)

ministers — Cardinal Fleury in France, Johann Christoph von Bartenstein in Austria, Lord Harrington in England, Count Ostermann in Saint Petersburg. He knew that today's ally could easily be tomorrow's enemy. He realized that survival and expansion would demand every possible political wile: his correspondence makes clear that from the beginning he practiced *Realpolitik* with severe Machiavellian overtones. All in all, he did a pretty good job of it.

France was the linchpin. Frederick had inherited a treaty of sorts with Versailles, and if that court would widen its guarantees to his various claims, the alliance would be agreeable to him. But Frederick suspected that Fleury was playing a waiting game. Once Emperor Charles died, French forces would move across the Rhine. Fleury was already believed to be making a secret treaty with the Electors of Cologne and Bavaria. He wanted the subservient Bavarian elector to become the next Holy Roman Emperor, thus giving France a continental supremacy similar to that of the golden days of King Louis XIV. Fleury would have to be carefully handled. One-armed Colonel Tilio von Camas, sent to Versailles as envoy extraordinary, received bold but precise instructions, along with the very large allowance of two thousand thalers per month. He was to do everything possible to heighten the envy that the French had of England. Fleury was to learn that Frederick expected better offers for his alliance than those made to his father. England was already making substantial offers, and if Frederick was to remain with France, then it must be on "solid foundations."

> Velvet words will be answered with velvet words, and facts with other facts [Frederick instructed]. The increase which will be made in my troops during your stay at Versailles will furnish you the occasion to speak lively and impetuously on my behalf; you may say that it should be feared that this increase would light a fire which would set Europe ablaze, that it was the way of the young to be daring, and that heroic ideas have always disturbed the peace of many nations. You may say that by nature I am partial to France, but that if I am neglected now this perhaps will be irreparable, and that contrariwise if I am won over, I will be able to render the French monarchy more important services than ever those rendered by Gustavus Adolphus.

Frederick sent Colonel von Münchow to Vienna to work with the envoy, Borcke, in trying to bring that court around. Borcke was instructed to exploit the favorable sentiments expressed by Minister Bartenstein and Chancellor Philip Ludwig von Sinzendorf on Frederick's accession. "The succession of Juliers and Berg will be the touchstone from which I will be able to perceive the sincerity of their feelings toward me."

Baron Axel von Mardefeld, his envoy in Saint Petersburg, was to tell that court that Frederick was completely disposed to renew old alliances with Russia and likewise to enter into new ones with her. Russia should make the first proposals. Frederick would prove amenable.

He was not amenable to renewing an alliance with Hanover. However, he sent another special envoy, Colonel Count Truchsess, to the English royal family and court, then in residence at Herrenhausen in Hanover. Truchsess was to be very cordial to the French ministers who were there and was to make much of Camas's mission to Versailles. "Mention with a show of jealousy that he is one of my intimates, that he possesses my confidence, and that he does not go to France to waste his time." Truchsess was to inform King George that his nephew Frederick would ally with England if he received better terms than those offered by France concerning his claims on Juliers, Berg, East Frisia, and Mecklenburg. "Speak a great deal of my inclination for them, advance nothing positive, make all to hope and all to fear . . . tell them the conduct of the English king will be the thermometer of our union."

Two problems arose in those early days. One concerned the Elector of Mainz's claim to a piece of territory belonging to Hesse. The elector had moved troops to the Hesse-Hanau border. Frederick informed him that as *Erbverbrüderter,* or traditional friend, of the House of Hesse Prussia would not fail to support it in case of war. The matter shou be settled peacefully, however — and with the Prussian king's help, it w The second problem centered on Herstal, a barony near Liège nota for having been the home of Pepin, Charlemagne's father, and later a base for Charlemagne's army. King Frederick William had inheri the holding in 1732, only to discover that its inhabitants preferred live under the Bishop of Liège's suzerainty. Since they ostracized Pr sian officials, at times even threatening them with physical atta Frederick William had been inclined to sell his rights for a small s but negotiations had come to nothing when he died.

When the good people of Herstal refused to pay homage to Fre ick, he asked his ministers for an opinion. They replied that there were two means available: force or renewed negotiation of a sale. Force would involve sending in two or three thousand troops, which could easily lead to war, because the Bishop of Liège was backed by France and Austria. The ministers preferred negotiation. Frederick shot back: "The ministers are clever when they discuss politics, but when they discuss war it is like an Iroquois Indian talking about astronomy. I shall be in Cleves this year, I shall try the soft line, and if it is turned down one will be treated as one deserves. The emperor is the mere phantom of a once powerful idol but presently is nothing."

Frederick's initial diplomacy had not solved very much by the time he returned from Prussia in August. The Austrian court seemed as reluctant as ever to act on Prussian claims; his ministers reported the same old vapid replies, pretty words and no more.

Nor was the Russian court willing to become directly involved in Empire affairs, although it was not unwilling to negotiate a treaty by which Frederick's back, Prussia and Pomerania, would be protected from Saxony, Sweden, or Poland if he went to war over the Juliers and Berg succession. But it was in no hurry to act.

Camas was reporting negatively from Versailles. Cardinal Fleury was reluctant to go any further than the existing treaty in support of Prussia claims; to do so would cost France the friendship of the Catholic electors, which would be needed in case of war or of an Imperial election.

Truchsess had fared no better at Hanover. Lord Harrington had written Frederick "in such loose and general terms," as he complained to Guy Dickens, as to be nearly meaningless.[1] He had planned to visit Hanover on his way to Cleves, but now he would go by way of Bayreuth. If the English king had something concrete to offer, he could return by way of Hanover or meet his Uncle George at Wesel.

After a short and strained visit with Wilhelmina, followed by the frolic across the Rhine, the king arrived in Wesel in late August and almost at once came to grips with the Herstal problem. He had already advertised his grievances to foreign courts. The Herstalians

> have not only committed several enormous outrages against the legitimate authority of their seigneur and master, but have also maltreated my officers of justice, imprisoned with no legitimate cause some of my officers and soldiers, disregarded my ordinances, refused to pay what they have always freely given formerly and what they should contribute to their legitimate seigneur, overthrown the order and the police, and finally raised in all ways, for more than two years, the standard of rebellion. . . . I see myself obliged, although to my great regret, finally to employ force, and to march a sufficient number of infantry and cavalry to bring these rebellious people to reason.*

In early September the Prussian king gave the Bishop of Liège two days to state whether he was still resolved to support his claimed sovereignty over Herstal, and whether he intended to protect the seditious subjects of this barony in their disorder. When that worthy failed to reply, Major General von Borcke occupied Maaseyk with two thousand troops. He moved in rapidly and expensively, demanding fifty gold louis a day for troop maintenance, in addition to a "contribution"

---

* Frederick later published a formal statement of justification which emphasized that this was not an affair of Empire but rather one "of Prince to Prince." The publication was variously received. "That is strong language," one ambassador complained to Podewils; "that is the language of Louis XIV." (Koser, *Geschichte*, Volume I.)

of 20,000 thalers. The bishop screamed his head off, but neither France nor Austria listened and the poor man was forced to negotiate. After an occupation of several weeks, he bought Herstal for 200,000 thalers instead of the 100,000 that Frederick William had earlier asked.

In the middle of the Herstal crisis Frederick came down with a severe fever. Instead of proceeding to Brussels to meet Voltaire, he invited the writer to the castle of Moyland, where he was being looked after by Algarotti, Keyserling, and Maupertuis. Voltaire found him sweating out a violent attack, "a small man in a dressing gown of coarse blue cloth . . . sweating and shivering under a miserable blanket." Once the fit passed, Frederick joined the company for supper and a discussion of "the immortality of the soul, liberty, fate, the Androgynes of Plato [*Symposium*], and other small topics of that nature." The visit lasted for three days, with the talk more cultural than political. Voltaire read his new tragedy, *Mahomet*, to the group. The two principals hit it off well. Voltaire described Frederick as extremely cultured and amiable, "a philosopher without austerity, full of gentleness and consideration, forgetting his rank when he is with friends. . . . It needed effort to remember that the man sitting at the foot of my bed was a sovereign with an army of 100,000 men." Probably at Fleury's suggestion, Voltaire hastened to express his support of Frederick's seizure of Herstal. General Borcke, he said, had gone to Herstal to engage the bishop in theological debate and had taken "two thousand good arguments with him."[2]

Frederick used his fever as an excuse to call off the proposed meeting with King George. Instead, he returned to Berlin by way of Wolfenbüttel, where he presided over the betrothal of his brother William to his own wife's sister, Princess Louise Emily.

Back at Rheinsberg, where physicians filled him with Pyrmont water against the persistent fever, Frederick had good reason to be pleased with his trip. He was being noticed and then some by European sovereigns. His *Anti-Macchiavel* had appeared in September and its "anonymous" author had fooled no one. Its controversial content raised many a royal and ministerial eyebrow. Who was this new king? How to explain his unprecedented foray into Strasbourg? How dare he defy Emperor Charles and hold Herstal to ransom? Why did simple fever prevent him from meeting with the King of England? What was he up to?

On the debit side, force had accomplished more than diplomacy and had brought an Imperial decree condemning Prussian action in Herstal and ending any chance of agreement with the Vienna court. Although a treaty of sorts was being worked out with the Russians, Frederick seemed no nearer to forging a profitable alliance with either France or

England, no nearer to securing vital guarantees of his claim to Juliers and Berg.

But at this point Juliers and Berg suddenly became unimportant. In late October Emperor Charles caught cold, ate too many mushrooms, and became very ill. "A man of spirit is not affected by a small matter," he said — his last words before he died. "This plate of mushrooms changed the destiny of Europe," Voltaire wrote, and he was correct.

25

CHARLES VI died on October 20, 1740. Frederick said of "had been born with those qualities which make a good citizen but not a great man."[1] Charles was fifty-six, the last male descendant of five centuries of Habsburg rulers. The news reached Rheinsberg five days later. Although ill, Frederick subordinated fever to fervor to send couriers galloping: Field Marshal Count Kurt Christoph von Schwerin and Count Heinrich von Podewils would report immediately. The following day he wrote to Voltaire that the emperor's death "upsets all my pacific ideas and I believe that come June it will be a matter of gunpowder, soldiers, and sieges rather than actresses, ballets, and theater. . . . The time has come for a total change of the old political system."

His decision had already been made. Three years earlier he had written to Grumbkow that the emperor's death "would bring vast upheavals with each kingdom grabbing what it could." Saxon and Bavarian electors had been looking forward to it; so had King Louis of France. In his last talks with Frederick, Frederick William had dwelt on the political vistas it would open to Prussia. And now Frederick wrote to Algarotti: "I shall not go to Berlin. A trifle such as the emperor's death does not require great changes. Everything was foreseen, everything arranged. Thus, it is a matter only of carrying out designs that I have long had in mind."

He at once made these designs known to Schwerin and Podewils. The matter of Juliers and Berg, he explained, was presently a dead end. Not only would outright seizure be clearly illegal while the Elector Palatine was still alive; it would infuriate Catholic electors, as well as Holland, and would probably bring Austria into alliance with France. Indeed, it might even precipitate a war against France, which Prussia could ill afford. Prussian territorial claims, he went on, were not limited to the west, to the Rhine, East Frisia, and Mecklenburg. They embraced parts of Silesia, claims traced to 1611 and, though steadfastly denied by Vienna, never relinquished by Prussia. Far better now to let the Vienna court worry about Bavarian and French ambitions in central Germany while he struck in a different direction. Like his great-grandfather the Great Elector, Frederick had long had his eye on Silesia.

Here was something to fight for, a big country, some two hundred miles long and from twenty to a hundred miles wide, with over fifteen thousand square miles of rich farmlands, prosperous cloth manufactures, untold mineral wealth. He had concerned himself nine years earlier with its obstruction to Prussian trade. It had cropped up from time to time in political discussions with the late king. Curiously, it had come up only the previous month, when the Vienna court wished to borrow money from Prussia. Frederick was willing to lend it, provided that Vienna would pledge in return the part of Silesia adjacent to his states. He now informed his startled auditors that he planned to seize and occupy the entire province, a project, as he later wrote, that would fulfill all of his political designs: "This would be a means of acquiring a reputation, of increasing the power of the state, and of ending the Berg litigation."[2]

Although Frederick spoke eloquently of Prussia's "incontestable claims" to large parts of Silesia, these claims were shaky enough, as he later admitted. But his claims to Juliers and Berg were legally valid, and the Austrian court was legally and morally wrong in contravening them. He realized that seizure of Silesia would mean war with Austria. But as he stressed to Schwerin and Podewils, the Vienna court would be hard put to react effectively.

Maria Theresa, the late emperor's twenty-three-year-old daughter who became Archduchess of Austria and Queen of Hungary and Bohemia, now ruled in her father's place. Maria Theresa — spirited, ambitious, stubborn. Forceful even at eighteen, convinced she would rule; "a princess of the highest spirit," reported the British envoy in Vienna, Sir Thomas Robinson. "Her father's losses are her own. She admires his virtues, but then she condemns his mismanagement, and is of a temper so formed for rule and ambitious as to look upon him as little more than her administrator." Deeply in love with her husband, almost obsessed with sex, she also loved dancing and gambling. An accomplished pianist and vocalist, careless in dress, pious in the extreme, boisterous on occasion, she had been poorly educated by Jesuit religious fanatics, and was almost totally ignorant of politics and government; she was armed "with nothing but her character," as her recent biographer, Edward Crankshaw, wrote, "her good nature, her religious faith, and the sense of the sacred nature of her imperial inheritance."[3]

Politically, she was badly off balance. Despite the Pragmatic Sanction so laboriously forged by her father, she almost had to beg recognition from both major and minor powers. Like her father, she would frantically cast about for new alliances, even with Prussia. The emperor's crown was forbidden to women, yet its possession was vital to the House of Habsburg's interest and pride. The crown would have to go to her consort and co-regent, Francis, Grand Duke of Lorraine. This meant winning the votes of the German electors, the three ecclesiastical and the five secular princes who would elect the new emperor, and of whom Frederick and George II of England were the most important. But other rulers lurked in the wings to claim either the Imperial crown or Imperial lands — or both. Spain and Piedmont wanted Austrian possessions in Italy. August III of Saxony and Poland desired territory in Silesia and Bohemia as well as the crown. Elector Charles Albert of Bavaria, who had refused to accept the Pragmatic Sanction, also wanted the Imperial crown. Indeed, Old Dessauer even urged Frederick to claim it.

The situation was as traditional as it was confused, the stuff of all the wars of succession during the earlier centuries. To Frederick, the main feature was Maria Theresa's temporary political paralysis. A faction of her court had realistically accepted the situation. Grand Duke Francis had told Borcke that once the emperor died, Austria could depend only on Prussia for support. Chancellor Sinzendorf was even rethinking the Berg question, Borcke added. Maria Theresa, Frederick argued, could not call German princes to arms, because the emperor was dead. In any event these minor rulers would be reluctant to sacrifice themselves for a crown too weak to support them effectively and too arrogant and tightfisted to repay them for their efforts. Prussia would be making war not against the Empire, but only against a *member* of the Empire (as in the recent case of Herstal) and then only to *save* the Empire and, with it, "the equilibrium of Europe and the liberty of Germany."

Nor could Maria Theresa effectively call on allies, Frederick argued. Spain was at war with England and was in no position to help Austria; on the contrary, Spain would welcome her debasement and gain new territories in Italy by it. France was quarreling with England in the New World, and, with war seemingly inevitable, would hesitate to respect her treaty with Austria. The Versailles court had accepted the Pragmatic Sanction with tongue in cheek; Cardinal Fleury had recently told Frederick's envoy, Colonel Camas, that Prussia was sufficiently powerful to act unilaterally concerning legitimate territorial claims, that such actions were justified. Given Fleury's secret diplomacy, his overtures to Cologne and Bavaria, and his troop concentrations near the Spanish Netherlands, this implied that the Versailles court would welcome Habsburg humiliation and would secretly support Elector Charles

Albert's claim to the Imperial crown, a situation that could easily lead to war against Austria.

If by some mischance France intervened against Prussia, Frederick could ally with England. England would not rush to Austria's aid. She already had her hands full with the Spanish war and the French threat and had recently proposed a new and favorable alliance with Prussia. She would be hard put to send an army to help Austria, particularly since such a move would expose Hanover to attack by Prussia and France. If, however, England proved awkward, Frederick could count on France. Holland had all it could do to meet treaty commitments to England; it also held large mortgages in Silesia and would probably be relieved to have Prussia guarantee them. Russia and Prussia had been negotiating a new alliance when the emperor died, but Russia in any event could not rush into action on Vienna's behalf; if she acted at all she would be threatened on one side by Sweden, on the other by the Ottoman Porte.

Maria Theresa was thus temporarily on her own. She lacked administrative, political, and military experience. Many people despised her husband, Grand Duke Francis. Numerous Viennese, provincial nobles, and peasants made no secret of their preference to be ruled by Elector Charles Albert of Bavaria. Her realm was in a condition close to crisis. Her ministers were all old men, timid, confused, and frightened, fit only to be embalmed, imagining, as the English envoy reported, the Turks in Hungary, Hungary in rebellion, the Saxons in Bohemia, the Bavarians before the gates of Vienna, and France responsible for it all. Dissent ruled, bankruptcy hovered. The royal treasury, which supported no fewer than forty thousand bureaucrats, contained a mere 100,000 florins. Royal revenues were mortgaged for years ahead. The army was shattered from its recent disastrous war with Turkey, which, in addition to draining the treasury, had cost nearly all the Balkan territories won by Prince Eugene in 1718. Generals Count von Seckendorff, Count Wilhelm Reinhard von Neipperg, and Count Franz Wenzel Wallis were still in jail, their reward for respective failures against the Turks. Silesia's common border with Brandenburg was undefended. No more than three thousand troops occupied the entire province, and most of these were stationed in small city-fortresses like Glogau and Neisse. There was no provincial force of importance. The various estates were frequently at loggerheads with Vienna and with each other. The Catholic province contained a strong, dissident Protestant population that presumably would welcome Prussian rule. The Prussian army was superior to the armies of its neighbors; it could march immediately. The seizure of Silesia would prevent Saxony from exercising its claims by force. The overall political situation favored the move. Finally, the Austrian court would never expect a winter invasion: the harvest had been poor throughout Europe, so the horses lacked fodder. Besides, gentlemen did not fight in winter.

The king and his two confidants discussed the pros and cons of Frederick's plan for four days. Schwerin and Podewils then retired to prepare a formal paper of their views "according to our feeble abilities." They did not agree with the king that Prussian forces must occupy Silesia in order to negotiate from strength of physical possession, but they did agree that he must act at once if Saxony showed signs of moving into the province. How to make the aggression possible was the real issue. As finally presented by Podewils, there were two political courses of action. The first was to offer Prussian support to the Vienna court, which would pay for it by ceding Silesia to Prussia: Frederick would guarantee *all* possessions; he would support the nomination of Grand Duke Francis for the Imperial crown; he would cede to Austria his rights to Juliers and Berg; and he would do everything possible to ensure future political stability by a treaty between Prussia, Austria, Russia, and the maritime powers. Should the Vienna court refuse this proposal, then Prussia must support Bavarian and Saxon territorial claims on Austria, and in return Bavarian and Saxon electors would guarantee him possession of Silesia in a formal treaty of partition to be guaranteed by France. France would be brought around by Prussia's support of the Bavarian elector's claim to the Imperial crown and by its ceding claims to Juliers and Berg to France for transfer either to the House of Palatine or to Bavaria. Frederick would hold Russia in check, if necessary, by treaties with Sweden, Denmark, and the Ottoman Porte.

Podewils and Schwerin favored the first course of action, because if it worked, it would re-establish the traditional balance of power, in which Austria stood as the bulwark against French domination of Europe. The second course, though feasible and perhaps necessary, might start a dangerous game of power politics that could end in great inconvenience and reversals of fortune to Prussia.

After further discussion, Frederick agreed to try the first plan and soon explained, ingeniously, to the skeptical English, Dutch, French, and Russian courts that it was for everybody's good, that Austria's salvation was vital "to conserve the peace of Germany, the system of the Empire, and the true welfare of the Germanic body." He personally held little hope for success, considering the overwhelming arrogance of the Vienna court. Francis had recently written to him asking for his friendship and support in these difficult times. Frederick, who knew and liked Francis, now promised Prussian support in a war that seemed imminent, but with a somewhat cryptic suggestion that he would have to be rewarded for the risk involved. Schwerin and Podewils returned to Berlin to set the machinery in motion.

Podewils was rapidly coming into his own. A civil servant since 1720, in the ministry of foreign affairs, he had increasingly earned King Frederick William's favor — even after his father-in-law, Grumbkow, had lost it — to the extent that the king had called him to his deathbed to witness his final instructions to the crown prince. Contrary to biographical legend, Podewils thenceforth began playing an important, even vital role in foreign affairs, though he frequently served as a whipping boy when Frederick was in a volatile mood. In the present important juncture, he continued to present to his monarch the potentially awkward results of such naked aggression. War is a nasty business, he warned; see what it had cost the Kings of Sweden and France. Prussia was neither as strong nor as united as these kingdoms had been. Her scattered dominions lay open to invasion; she had no allies. Also contrary to biographical legend, Frederick listened willingly enough and even encouraged the civil minister to play devil's advocate. But like Caesar the Prussian king could say:

> I could be well mov'd if I were as you;
> If I could pray to move, prayers would move me;
> But I am constant as the northern star,
> Of whose true-fix'd and resting quality
> There is no fellow in the firmament.[4]

He patiently answered objection after objection. To delay, he argued, would allow Saxony and Bavaria to act before him; he would gain allies — either France or England; his army was combat ready. Finally: "I give you a problem to solve. When one has the advantage, shouldn't one exploit it? I am ready with my troops and everything else. If I do not use them, then I possess what I do not know how to use. But if I do use them, they will say that I am competent to use the superiority that I have over my neighbors."

26

EVENTS continued to favor Frederick's arguments for an invasion of Silesia. The Elector of Bavaria, Charles Albert, made it clear that he was going to pursue ancient claims to the Imperial crown and to Austrian territories, ambitions secretly encouraged by Frederick. The English court continued to press for an alliance with Prussia. Reports from Vienna spoke of general confusion and fear among court councilors and a strong anti-Habsburg feeling. A courier from Saint Petersburg brought news of Czarina Anna's death. For a time it seemed as if a palace revolution would remove the "German party" that had surrounded her. All was confusion. The crown had gone to her niece's two-month-old son, who became Czar Ivan VI. Only with difficulty did her lover, the Duke of Kurland, make himself regent. But a few weeks later Marshal Münnich overthrew the duke and installed the Princess of Brunswick, mother of Ivan VI, as regent, with himself as strongman. This pleased King Frederick. His own Major Hans Karl von Winterfeldt was Münnich's son-in-law. Winterfeldt, armed with generous bribes, now left for Moscow, in the hope of persuading the Russian court to join Prussia in a defensive alliance.

Frederick was keeping a low profile at Rheinsberg, his genuine excuse being persistent fever. He was as isolated there as if he were on the moon, at times ebullient, at times pensive, at times sad, as when he learned of Suhm's untimely death. Most foreign envoys were not allowed near the place. To Cardinal Fleury's persistent questions of what the young king was up to, first Valory and then the special envoy, Marquis Louis Charles Anton de Beauveau,* could give little information. "The king works from eight to ten hours a day with Podewils and Schwerin," Valory reported. "They dine together and see no one."[1] In desperation Fleury hit on the foolhardy expedient of recruiting Voltaire as a spy and sending him to Rheinsberg, where he had so often been invited.

Voltaire arrived in late November to find about as pacific a scene as one could imagine. The queen was present; so were Wilhelmina and her family, along with the king's cronies. Judging from the usual round of dinners, plays, musicales, and solo flute performances by the king, he might again have been the carefree crown prince of Ruppin days, remote from problems of state, immersed only in books, culture, and quiet society.

Except that he spent most of his time in his private apartments.

Except that he already had convinced an envoy from the Elector of Mainz that he was "the most zealous [German] patriot with the best intentions in the world," providing Austria chose to ally with Prussia.[2]

Except that he already had written to Podewils that he would soon begin the "boldest, greatest, and most unexpected enterprise ever undertaken by a prince of this House."

---

* Beauveau had brought King Louis's condolences to Frederick on the death of his father. Two years older than Frederick, he had been commissioned in 1725 and had served in several campaigns. A brigadier at the time of his mission, he went on to play an active role in the First and Second Silesian Wars. He was mortally wounded at the siege of Ypres in 1744. When his men tried to help him, he said, "Go do your duty, my lads, I am doing mine." In December 1740, the Danish envoy reported that Beauveau was annoyed at the way he had been treated but when finally invited to a royal reception he, like others before him, found King Frederick to be irresistible once he set out to charm someone.

Except that old Chancellor Johann Peter von Ludewig had been summoned to Berlin, where he was secretly twisting history to justify a rape of Silesia.

Except that Prussian envoys in foreign courts were opening diplomatic offensives to pave the way for the Prussian move. Bribery and deceit were the watchwords: "Be active and vigilant; have the eyes of a lynx."

Except that for several weeks royal orders had caused unit commanders to buy horses and supplies while scurrying to prepare regiments and companies for a march falsely ordered to Hallenstadt.

Except that outside Berlin, near the Silesian border, supply officers were setting up bake ovens and filling enormous magazines with food and fodder to support a march into Silesia.

Except that foreign envoys in Berlin were reporting intense military activities and frantically speculating as to their purpose. "We wish that this young prince's great reading," Guy Dickens nervously reported in secret code, "and in particular Rollin's *Ancient History,* which is his favorite study, may not have filled his head with notions of imitating a Cyrus or an Alexander."[3]

Except that Frederick's envoy in Vienna, von Borcke, had presented to Grand Duke Francis his master's offer of alliance and protection in return for Silesia, a thinly disguised ultimatum accompanied by Borcke's demand for prompt action *"sans détour et sans finesse."*

Except that while the court ate, drank, and played, Frederick worked on a dispatch that would notify King George of his move, his defense of a crime about to be committed: "My only goal is the true good and conservation of the House of Austria. . . . The expedition that I am about to undertake is lively enough, but it is the sole means of saving Germany from destruction by the new engagements that the court of Vienna is ready to enter into with France."

Voltaire's coincidental presence at Rheinsberg neither fooled nor alarmed Frederick. "Voltaire has arrived," he wrote to Algarotti, "all tinseled with new beauties and much more sociable than at Cleves. He is in excellent humor, complaining less than usual of illness." Voltaire had some explaining to do. Frederick had recently written to him that he was very displeased with the first two editions of *L'Anti-Macchiavel,* which Voltaire had too freely edited. Voltaire, for example, had deleted an interesting passage about the Platonic tradition that emphasized the gulf between philosophical idealism and political reality. Frederick had illustrated this by saying that a philosopher makes an imaginary map of a country, but a traveler, guided by "analogy and working from experience," finds a much different country.[4] The king planted a story in the gazettes that the "anonymous" author disavowed either work.

Voltaire's humor dissipated even more when his political questions were treated with amused contempt. Frederick found his guest too bumptious and expensive. "The king does not like [Voltaire's] free and easy ways," Valory reported to Versailles. "He has changed his tone too quickly from that of adoration to one that is scarcely respectful."[5] Frederick, who paid him three thousand thalers for a six-day visit, wrote to Charles Jordan: "That is paying dear for a jester; never had a court fool such wages before." Voltaire treated the king in kind, angrily calling him "the respectable, singular, and amiable whore" in a letter to Maupertuis.[6]

Voltaire's verbose reports only further confused the French court. It was his opinion (gained from Valory in Berlin) that Frederick and Grand Duke Francis in Vienna had agreed on plans hostile to France. As for the military preparations in Berlin, he found it surprising that *le loi des lisières* — "the border king," as he contemptuously designated Frederick — should suppose himself capable of acting alone, in view of his limited resources. Yet he also told Valory of a confidential letter that Algarotti had received from the king, written as if "the demon of war were gripping him."

Frederick arrived in bustling Berlin in early December. The townsfolk by now knew something important was stirring, and they enthusiastically greeted their monarch. "The crowds were most unusual," reported one paper, "as if no one ever had the fortune to see Your Majesty."[7]

Troops were everywhere, the splendidly accoutered regiments lining the beautiful Unter den Linden, an impressive artillery train with sixteen hundred horses making up in front of the arsenal, large boats on the Spree being loaded with corn, hay, rations, heavy artillery.

The new envoy from Vienna, Marquis Anton Otto Botta d'Adorno, was appalled by the scene; he reported that "the city looked like a camp on the point of breaking up."[8] The "shrewd and discerning" Botta, in Frederick's later words, had brought proposals from Maria Theresa, but since they offered no territory, the king turned a deaf ear. Having correctly divined Frederick's intentions, Botta remarked that on his journey to Berlin he had found Silesian roads so muddy as to be nearly impassable. Frederick replied that those who wished could make the journey even if they might arrive dirty.

Frederick immediately ordered Borcke to offer large bribes to two Austrian officials — 200,000 thalers to the corrupt Sinzendorf, 100,000 to the secretary to Grand Duke Francis — to persuade their court to accept his proposals, and a day later he ordered the marshal of his court and former ambassador to Austria, Count Gustav Adolf von Gotter, to depart at once for Vienna to take over the critical negotiations.

In a final audience he informed Botta what Gotter was to offer. "You will ruin the House of Austria, sire," the envoy responded, "and hurt yourself at the same time." "The queen has only to accept the offers that are being made," Frederick told him.[9]

Frederick had already told the British envoy, Guy Dickens, that he had no intention of supporting the Pragmatic Sanction, and he implied that he would invade not only Silesia but Bohemia as well if it was necessary for "the publick good." "If the King your Master disapproves my Views, and enters into any Measures to prevent my taking whatever suits my Convenience, I am ready to go to War with him, as well as with the House of Austria."[10]

He called Valory to audience, praised Fleury — "a great man" endowed with "many remarkable qualities" — and suggested that he would ally with France if Versailles wished to seize the Imperial crown and give it to the Bavarian elector.[11] He ordered Joachim Wilhelm von Klinggraeffen, envoy to the Bavarian court, secretly and discreetly to encourage Elector Charles Albert "to pursue vigorously his claim to the Austrian succession and to commence raising an army." He ordered Count Truchsess, envoy to the British court then residing in Hanover, to explain Austrian perfidy and justify Prussian claims to Silesia. If Uncle George agreed, Frederick would support Hanoverian claims elsewhere. He ordered Count Karl Wilhelm Finck von Finckenstein, son of Frederick's old tutor and envoy to Saxony, to assess the situation and if necessary to buy information and assistance from Father Guarini, the powerful spiritual adviser to the Polish king.

General suspense continued for another week. Although Frederick struck most observers as singularly at ease, he faced certain pressure from such critics as Old Dessauer, who was miffed at not having been consulted or invited to join the expedition, the more so since his hated rival, Field Marshal von Schwerin, was to command one of the corps. Frederick replied politely that he had plans to use him, but he could not march with the king: "I reserve this campaign to myself alone so that the world will not believe that the King of Prussia marches to war with a tutor." To counter Old Dessauer's disruptive pessimism and fears, which he broadcast to the officer corps, Frederick told some departing officers: "I am undertaking a war, gentlemen, in which I have no other ally than your courage and good will. . . . Remember always the immortal glory that your ancestors won at Varsovie and Fehrbellin. Your fate is in your hands. Sterling deeds will bring promotions and rewards. . . . Farewell. I shall soon follow you to our rendezvous with glory."[12]

On December 13, 1740, foreign envoys received formal notification of Frederick's intentions to seize Silesia. That night the king appeared at a court ball, appropriately a masquerade. At midnight he strolled to a carriage, bade family, officials, and envoys goodbye, and with an escort of five hundred cavalry was driven to Frankfurt-on-Oder and on to headquarters at Crossen.

Here Field Marshal Schwerin had assembled the army, some twenty-eight thousand troops, of whom about eight thousand were cavalry, and a small artillery train of twenty 3-pounders, four 12-pounders, four howitzers, and six large mortars. A reserve force of twelve thousand would march from Berlin in two days. In the interim Frederick inspected battalions and squadrons and held impromptu court. Among the visitors were two Silesian noblemen, who, on orders from Breslau, the capital of Silesia, delivered a protest against Prussian invasion, a halfhearted gesture, seeing that each emissary invited the king to his castle should the march come nearby.

The Prussian army marched early on December 16 and soon crossed the undefended border into Silesia. In camp that night at Schweidnitz, Frederick wrote to Count Podewils: "I have crossed the Rubicon with flags flying and drums beating. My troops are very willing, the officers ambitious, our generals starved for glory; all will go according to our wishes, and I have reason to anticipate all possible good from this enterprise."

27

SILESIAN PEASANTS had never seen anything like it. First came Prussian hussars, riding mounts far too large and awkward. The eyes of the army — in theory, trained, tough horsemen — they were little more than inexperienced farmhands gaudily dressed in shell jackets, leather trousers, and boots, their heads covered with elaborately embroidered wolfskin busbys, their profession proclaimed by open fur-lined pelisses, short carbines, and wicked sabers with curved blades three and a half feet long.

They were supposed to learn what lay ahead, what villages, farms, enemy, terrain, roads, bridges. The point rode in single file, three men only followed by a platoon — honey for lurking enemy bear. An advance guard of several hundred followed the point, and behind that the main body of squadrons, which fanned out parties to probe suspicious copses and heights, prowl through farms and villages, question people, learn the best march routes, test bridges, plumb streams and rivers, and choose suitable cantonments for the night, the weather being too cold for tent camps.

An advance guard of infantry marched a thousand yards to their rear. The army followed several miles behind. Infantry claimed the roads — companies, battalions, and regiments marching in long columns, self-sufficient units with their own baggage and supply wagons and a small 3- and 6-pounder artillery train. The troops wore garrison clothing — coarse linen shirts, waistcoats of various colors (depending on the regiment), coarse wool breeches, short coats of Prussian blue, wool stockings dipped in tallow, which stank to high heaven, square-toed black leather shoes, and buttoned gaiters of white ticking. Each musketeer wore a three-cornered cloth hat; each grenadier the famous miter, a high peaked hat with brass front. A bayonet and sword hung in scabbards from a white leather belt. White leather bandoliers held tin canteens, linen bread bags, and cartridge pouches for the heavy flintlocks, with their awkward three-and-a-half-foot barrels and heavy iron ramrods. Extra clothes, bandages, cleaning gear for muskets, and odds and ends filled leather knapsacks to which tent pegs were tied — altogether some sixty pounds of gear per man.

Noncommissioned officers dressed similarly to the men but as a sign of authority wore gloves, a distinctive sword knot, and braided, cocked hat. Each carried a stick and a *Kurzgewehr*, or pike, that was used in a variety of disciplinary ways, usually brutal. A company counted fourteen NCOs, who ranged in rank from sergeant major to lance corporal.

Officers rode splendidly accoutered horses. Under long dark blue coats, the skirts pulled up and fastened behind them, they wore elaborately embroidered waistcoats and trousers tucked into knee-length boots and thick sashes embossed with silver thread. Their hats were also three-cornered but larger and stitched expensively with gold and silver thread. They wore no rank insignia as such, but their coats were adorned variously with finely worked gold thread, the famous *Brandenbourgs,* which resembled lightning flashes. Lapels and cuffs of variously colored velvet identified individual regiments, as did richly ornamented and securely guarded regimental standards carried by young ensigns. Officers also sported a protective gorget of silver, and those who had fought in the War of the Spanish Succession were allowed a sprig of oak leaves on their caps. Field marshals and generals were given coaches pulled by six horses; colonels and lieutenant colonels, coaches pulled by two horses. Senior officers were authorized to have from six to two supply wagons and an ample number of packhorse and riding horses; a captain could have one supply wagon and two riding horses; a lieutenant one packhorse and one riding horse.

Tucked between the long regimental columns were artillery and baggage trains, which consisted of hundreds of horses pulling the "battery pieces," immensely heavy bronze guns and their ancillary ammunition, powder and supply wagons (not to mention pontoons, entrenching tools, and extra ammunition for the infantry). Artillery consisted of 3-, 6-, 12-, and 24-pounder cannon (the designation based on the weight of the ball fired), 18-pounder howitzers, 10-, 25-, and 50-pounder mortars. The heavy, ornately tooled pieces rode on gaudy flat carriages of Prussian blue wood and black iron topped off by gray accessories, such as elevation wedges, ramrods, and cleaning sponges. Gun carriages and munition carts, each pulled by three to eight horses, carried a variety of ammunition. Iron and stone roundshot or cannonballs were the most widely used, the round iron balls doubling as fireballs when heated red-hot in brick kilns. The army carried two types of caseshot. One was grapeshot; it consisted of iron or lead balls spaced around a wooden spindle held by a cotton bag that the powder burned away, scattering the half-ounce lead balls into enemy ranks. A 3-pounder scattered fifty balls; a 24-pounder, three hundred balls. The other type was the more primitive canister shot, a metal can full of balls or simply scrap metal that burst to scatter the shrapnel. Mortars fired bombs, grenades, fireballs, and illumination shells. Bombs and grenades were hollow iron projectiles filled with explosive and fitted with a fuse. The illumination ball was an unsatisfactory affair consisting of a round linen sack holding the illuminating material along with several grenades and balls; it was supposed to burn on the ground and the exploding ammunition was supposed to keep the enemy from extinguishing it.

The carriages and wagons also carried barrels of powder, manufactured in the Jungfernheide mill after the Dutch fashion. A great deal of the black powder was required, the load varying from one fourth, one third, to one half of the ball weight, and this, taken with musket fire, explains the black acrid cloud that inevitably covered a battlefield. Most cannon were fired by cartridges filled with loose powder and ignited through a touchhole by a slow match (a piece of cord that burned like punk).

Cavalry squadrons flanked both forward units and the trains. These were cuirassiers, or heavy cavalry, who wore elegantly burnished iron breastplates and rode large and powerful horses. They were complemented by dragoons, or mounted infantry trained to fight on horse or foot. A rearguard formed of infantry and cavalry units followed the army, its primary purpose being to intercept stragglers and deserters; special units of provos, or bailiffs, probably the most hated men in the army (next to NCOs and officers), backed up the rearguard.

Quartering and feeding the army, including several thousand horses, posed immense problems. In decent weather heavy canvas tents were carried on supply wagons, but in cold weather tents were left in depots and the troops summarily quartered in houses and barns of luckless villages that got in the way of war; when houses and barns were lacking, the troops quartered in the field, their cloaks serving as blankets.

Horses were fed hay and oats carried in wagons and supplemented by local forage where possible. The staple troop ration seemed simple enough: two pounds of bread per day, free in wartime. In reality it called for quite a complex organization. When possible each man carried a three-to-six-day bread ration, and company bread wagons carried rations for another six days. They were supplemented by commissariat wagons, each carrying enough flour to keep a company in bread for ten days. A field bakery column carried portable bakeries, field ovens of wrought iron and brick that turned out about a thousand six-pound loaves every twenty-four hours.

Flesh supplemented the basic ration — two pounds of beef a week when possible, also free in wartime. Columns often included large herds of cattle. Beef, pork, chicken, and eggs were bought locally or perhaps more often stolen. Farmers brought vegetables and eggs directly into camp, where soldiers, wives and camp followers often presided over communal cookfires. Sutlers, semiofficial men and women, rode their own carts, which carried brandy, beer, tobacco, and more sophisticated foodstuffs. In camp they set up large canteen tents; these served as combination bars and stores and were closed promptly at eight P.M., when drummers beat tattoo to send the men to quarters.

The system of supply was organized on the French basis, with an intendant and four assistants reponsible for it. A commissariat traveled with each army and perforce held extensive local authority, which invariably gave rise to corruption and concomitant inefficiency, further heightened by the need to recruit civilian teamsters, normally peasants who were wont to run off during battle, and to hire or requisition local transport.

Supply columns also included a medical section of regimental surgeons who had graduated from the College of Medical Surgeons in Berlin. Company surgeons were little more than semiskilled men, usually barbers, able to give rudimentary first aid; they were hired and fired by regimental surgeons. The field surgery was carried in nine large hospital wagons supplemented by twelve supply wagons. In action these were formed into a *Wagenburg* dressing station (which a century later would become familiar in the American West) to receive wagons of wounded from field dressing stations. The state of the art was very primitive. One of the major medical practices was bleeding a soldier twice a year; he was also bled when ill or wounded. Regimental surgeons were nearly autonomous in the army, paying for their medicines, hospitals, and company barber-surgeons out of special allowances, part of which too often went into their own pockets.

Such an army would have caused congestion even if it traveled on good and plentiful roads. There weren't many roads, however, and most of them were unimproved, so special squads of *Zimmerleute,* or

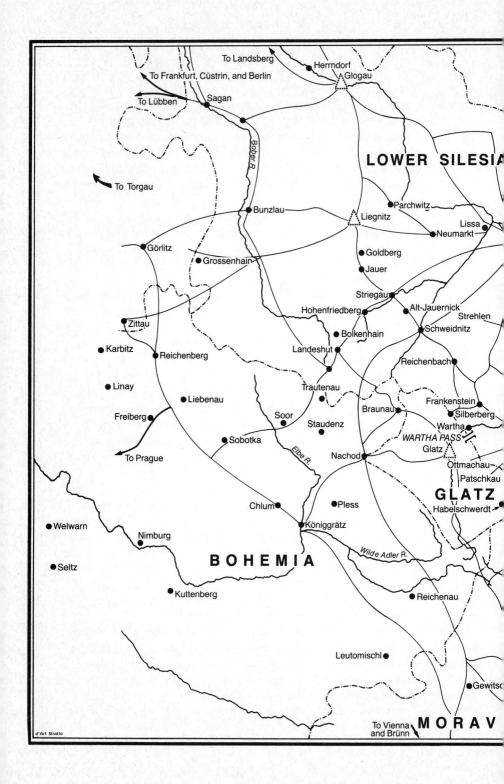

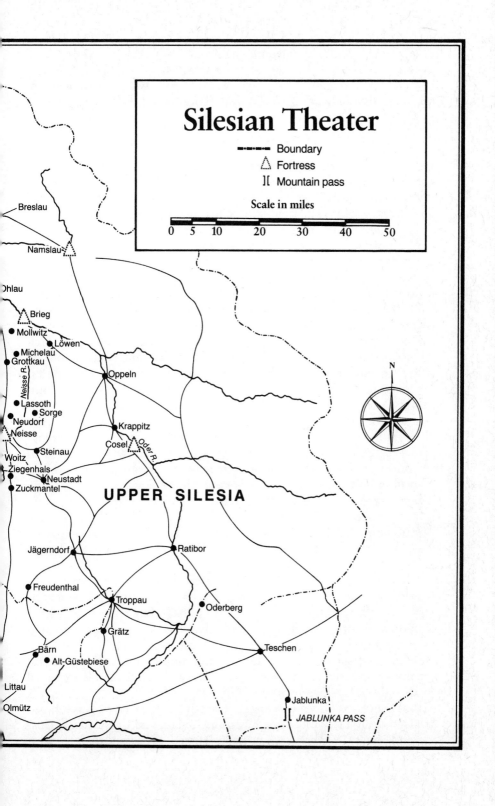

Silesian Theater

Boundary
△ Fortress
Ⅱ Mountain pass

Scale in miles

0 5 10 20 30 40 50

N

Breslau

Namslau

Ohlau

Brieg

Mollwitz

Löwen

Michelau

Grottkau

Neisse R.

Oppeln

Lassoth

Sorge

Neudorf

Neisse

Krappitz

Woitz

Cosel

Oder R.

Steinau

Ziegenhals

Neustadt

Zuckmantel

UPPER SILESIA

Jägerndorf

Ratibor

Freudenthal

Troppau

Oderberg

Grätz

Teschen

Bärn

Alt-Güstebiese

Littau

Olmütz

Jablunka

Ⅱ *JABLUNKA PASS*

carpenters, sometimes aided by engineers and pioneers, accompanied the advance guard to repair the worst sections and the bridges. Bottlenecks were frequent and a corps depth of twenty-five miles was not unusual, although the accordion operation could reduce it to fifteen and even ten miles.

Corps I, commanded by King Frederick, marched southeast on fortress Glogau, its left flank hugging the banks of the River Oder. Some miles to the south Corps II, commanded by Field Marshal Schwerin, marched on fortress Liegnitz, its right flank nudging the Bober River.

The columns moved swiftly and efficiently. By nightfall of the first day, a Friday, vanguard units were cantoned twenty-five miles inside the province. They marched again on Saturday, rested on Sunday, marched on Monday. Despite heavy rains and poor roads, the units continued to make good time. This was Lower Silesia, a gentle rich land of undulating fields, forests, and lakes, terrain contested by no enemy. As squadrons and companies passed through villages and towns, special details nailed printed copies of a royal proclamation on church and town hall doors. This Patent, of which a thousand copies had been secretly printed a month earlier, explained that Frederick had found it necessary to invade Silesia in order to prevent its being seized by a third power (Saxony), which would in turn threaten Prussian borders, as well as "for other cogent and important reasons."[1] I come not to conquer but to protect — so ran the gist of Frederick's cunning psychological message. There was something to it. Officers who tolerated ill treatment of civilians or theft or destruction of private property would be dishonorably discharged; soldiers would be flogged. Commanding officers were to pay village landlords and farmers for troop billets and local produce, and these orders in general seem to have been obeyed. The predominantly Protestant population accepted and even welcomed the newcomers. Local officials amicably discussed supply needs and helpfully advised on routes.

The king had every reason to be pleased, as he wrote to Prince William on the third day of the march. He had visited neighboring regiments to talk with the men and reward outstanding companies with a cash douceur of fifteen thalers, an effective leadership device he would use time and again. The soldiers were receiving sufficient rations and were in good spirits, despite the rain and muddy roads. Discipline on the march and in camp was excellent. Resistance was nil. He expected to seize fortress Glogau without difficulty.

Less than a week after crossing the Silesian border, Corps I was camped at Herrndorf, a few miles northwest of Glogau, and Corps II was closing on Liegnitz. A week after he had marched, Frederick wrote to Voltaire:

I am too tired to respond to your charming verses and too frozen to savor them properly, but this will pass. . . . We march from seven to four. Then I eat and work, receiving tiresome deputations; then comes boring business. These are men difficult to reform, men too hotheaded to restrain, lazy men to urge on, forever impatient men to calm, rapacious men to hold in check, garrulous men to listen to, silent men to entertain; then I must drink with those who are thirsty, eat with those who are hungry; I must be a Jew with Jews, pagan with pagans. Such are my occupations, which I would gladly give to another person if it were not that I aspire to glory.

He sent orders to Hereditary Prince Leopold, Dessauer's eldest son, to bring up the reserve for the blockade of fortress Glogau. Meanwhile he surrounded Glogau and continued to receive official deputations and answer mail sent on by Podewils from Berlin.

Frederick and his advisers had been partially correct in regarding the confusion that reigned in the Vienna court as an asset for Prussian strategy, and they were also correct about the weakened state of the Austrian army and the empty treasury. "Who would believe that no regulations existed for my troops?" Maria Theresa later wrote. "Each [regiment] had its own way of marching and maneuvering. . . . Some men fired fast, some at long intervals, and commands were expressed by different words in each unit. . . . In short, the conditions discovered were beyond description."[2] The first alert to the pending Prussian invasion had reached Vienna in early December to fall "like a thunderbolt from a cloudless sky," in Ranke's words. Maria Theresa later wrote that she found herself "all at once without money, without troops, and without advice."[3] As reports confirmed the catastrophic news, divided councilors hotly argued courses of action, and perhaps if the conservative faction headed by Grand Duke Francis and the Bohemian Chancellor, Count Philipp Kinsky, had won the day, some sort of compromise would have resulted.

But they did not prevail.

Despite the immense confusion caused by the emperor's death, Maria Theresa acted with the same energy shown a few months earlier by Frederick. "The queen gains the hearts of everybody," the British ambassador, Thomas Robinson, reported from Vienna; "she shows an uncommon quietness in talking, a like judgment in digesting, and a no less resolution in supporting the weightiest affairs of state."[4] She slashed court expenses, ordered army reforms, released imprisoned generals, sent Field Marshal Count Johann Pálffy to Hungary to win support of landowning nobles, appointed her husband as co-regent and member of the Secret Council. While doddering ministers wrung gnarled hands in impotent despair, the young queen turned from necessity more than

Maria Theresa, the indomitable Archduchess of Austria and Queen of Hungary and Bohemia. She was Frederick's nemesis for decades, "always weeping—and always annexing."

Below: The Prussian grenadiers. "We have totally beaten the Austrians. . . . Our troops performed miracles," wrote Frederick to Wilhelmina from Mollwitz in April 1741.

choice to Johann Bartenstein, a relatively junior official. He had served the emperor as confidential secretary and was in part responsible for the Pragmatic Sanction and for Austrian rapprochement with France following the War of the Polish Succession. "An Alsatian from a humble family," Frederick later sniffed, "but hard-working."[5] A Catholic convert, the secretary of the Secret Council was fifty years old, "rude, arrogant, overbearing, clever, but blinded by prejudice."[6] Nonetheless he was the only strong adviser she had — and he loved France as much as he loathed Prussia and King Frederick.

Bartenstein refused to share the general despair. He argued forcefully that the situation was not as perilous as some believed it to be. Peasant unrest was superficial and would soon quiet; the estates would quickly enough pledge fealty to the new queen; most important, France had accepted the terms of the Pragmatic Sanction and would never support the claims of the Bavarian elector to Austrian territory or to the Imperial crown. Maria Theresa accepted his argument that Prussia, not France, was the real enemy, and the rest of her ministers, some grudgingly, agreed.

The court having resolved to meet force with force, the queen ordered her military commander in Silesia to defend the province to the best of his ability. Considering the circumstances, it was a brave decision. Lieutenant General Count Maximilian Ulysses von Browne, a tall and forceful thirty-five-year-old Irish Jacobite and skilled veteran of Italian and Turkish campaigns, had arrived in Silesia only in early December. His total command amounted to about six thousand troops, of whom four thousand were tied to the fortresses at Glogau, Ohlau, Brieg, Neisse, and Glatz. This left about two thousand men to defend a province of over fifteen thousand square miles — just over twice the size of New Jersey — against a Prussian force reportedly twenty-five thousand strong. His early reports to Grand Duke Francis, written when Prussian intentions had become crystal clear, understandably stressed the need for immediate reinforcements; until help arrived he could fight only a delaying action. In mid-December he learned that he could expect no more than a few dragoon companies and one infantry battalion; additional units would not be available for several months. Meanwhile he was to defend Silesia to the best of his ability, using his own judgment at all times.

Browne had planned to hold the capital, Breslau, an open or neutral city that was, in his opinion, the key to the entire province. Abandoning this plan when the magistrates refused to allow Austrian troops in the city, he ordered the fortress commanders at Glogau and Brieg to hold out as long as possible while he fell back behind fortress Neisse to wait for reinforcements.[7]

The day after Frederick invaded Silesia his envoy in Vienna, von Borcke, delivered the ambitious five-point Prussian proposal. Frederick offered to guarantee Maria Theresa the accession and all of her German territories, and he would ally with Russia, England, and Holland for this purpose; he would vote for Grand Duke Francis as next emperor and would persuade other electors to do the same; he would cede his claims to Juliers and Berg to the Habsburgs; and he would pay the hard-pressed queen an indemnity of two million gulden. In return for effort and risk involved, the Austrian court was to cede all of Silesia to him.

Queen Maria Theresa, heavy with child, refused to see Borcke but waited behind a door to ensure that Francis forcefully rejected the Prussian demands. The queen, Borcke was haughtily told, would see the Turks before Vienna and would grant the territorial demands of Bavaria and Saxony rather than give Silesia to Prussia. King Frederick, Francis went on, would be very wise to remove his troops at once. The Austrian treaty with France concerning Juliers and Berg would terminate in less than two weeks, and the Prussian court would find the Austrian court amenable to a new and favorable agreement concerning these Rhenish provinces.

Count Gotter, Frederick's special emissary, arrived that evening. Gotter was liked in Vienna, where he had been the Prussian ambassador, but Maria Theresa refused to see him. Instead, Francis received him the next day. "I found the prince highly excited, simultaneously filled with pain, resentment, and anger that he had been deceived in his certain trust [of Frederick]," Gotter reported.[8] Francis turned a deaf ear to his reasoned arguments, and when Gotter asked whether the court wished him to remain in Vienna, Francis bade him "a good journey; he could leave when he desired." Gotter further reported a hostile political climate. The British envoy told him that Frederick's invasion of Silesia would cause him to be politically excommunicated from the community of all rulers; other ambassadors spoke of the "indefensible seizure of Silesia." Robinson begged him to persuade the Prussian king to withdraw his troops; otherwise, Austria would be thrown into the arms of France, completely upsetting the balance of European power and bringing on a general war. The Vienna court, Gotter reported, was receiving exact intelligence from Saxony on Frederick's movements and would fight: "Here the alarm is sounded, the cry of 'Fire' rings out, all allies are summoned, immediate help is expected, within a few months one hopes to raise a mighty army in order to repel force with force." Borcke joined Gotter in imploring the Prussian king to remove his army from Silesia.

Borcke's report of the earlier audience had reached Frederick on December 20. He was not surprised, as he told Borcke; he had foreseen that the Vienna court would be "but slightly edified" by his move. He expected Gotter's subsequent diplomacy to improve matters.

Gotter's pessimistic report reached him six days later at Herrndorf, near Glogau. Prince Leopold was on his way with a blockading force, Frederick was ready to march on Breslau, Schwerin would follow, Browne had fallen back on fortress Neisse, and Frederick was not in the least alarmed by the news from Vienna (although surprised that his propositions had been received with "so much acerbity and harshness"). It did not appear that the Vienna court would come around, he wrote to Gotter, but Gotter was to keep at the task and inform that court that whereas Frederick had demanded the entire province, he would now use moderation "and be content with a good part of it." In his own hand he added, "If despite my good intentions the duke wishes to ruin himself, then let him ruin himself."

Gotter and Borcke found Francis more inclined to reason in their next audience. If the Prussian king would say how much of Silesia he wanted, perhaps they could come to terms. The duke agreed with Gotter that some sort of long-term "mortgage" might be worked out, a plan favored by elder ministers and by Field Marshal von Neipperg, who dreaded the thought of a campaign in Silesia. Bartenstein, however, would have none of it. The Elector of Brandenburg's function in the Empire, he pointed out, was to hold the emperor's silver wash basin, not to invade his domains; the sentiment was shared by Count Kinsky.

Maria Theresa vigorously agreed. She had already ordered Neipperg to form a large field army, join Browne, and throw the Prussians out of Silesia. She had been promised English gold, and she was more determined than ever to fight. When she next learned that both the Saxon court and Poland promised full support, the issue was decided.

Gotter and Borcke received their walking papers. Their representations had been drawn up in a formal (and falsified) "Protocol," and this, along with Maria Theresa's blistering reply, was published in newspapers throughout Europe.

28

GOTTER AND BORCKE were still valiantly arguing the implausible in Vienna when Prince Leopold's blockading force began relieving Frederick's corps at Glogau. Leaving Marshal Schwerin to bring up the main army, Frederick marched on Breslau the next day with a small force of only ten grenadier companies and six squadrons of horse headed by fiery Major Hans Ernst von Zieten's hussars. Despite mud and some snow, the king was in excellent spirits. "All is going well and you will shortly see Silesia counted among our provinces," he wrote to Charles Jordan.

A day later Frederick learned that Neipperg had been ordered to form an army to come to Browne's support somewhere in the Neisse area. He now changed his march plan and ordered Schwerin to march with just over six thousand men directly on fortress Neisse. The field marshal was also to reconnoiter the Glatz area in strength and attempt to block important roads from Bohemia and Moravia. Frederick continued his own march to Neumarkt, where ten grenadier regiments joined him from Corps II. He marched at once on Breslau and on the first day of 1741 stood before the Silesian capital, a town of forty thousand, which quickly surrendered. In return for officials' taking the oath of allegiance to Prussia, agreeing to pay taxes and levies, and pledging to receive no foreign troops, Frederick promised full protection and a limited occupation, with a supply magazine and hospital set up in the environs. But this neutrality, he cautioned, could change if the fortunes of war so dictated. "Breslau is mine as of today," he jubilantly wrote to Podewils; "my troops are cheerful and in a good frame of mind. Our next task is to seize the line of the Neisse [River], Neisse itself, and fortress Glatz."

Frederick lingered at Breslau for four days, immersed in military and civil affairs and in answering correspondence that came from Berlin by special couriers. He went to considerable trouble and expense to appease the local nobility, not that he trusted them, but Breslau, neutral or not, would be an important base for supply magazines, commissariats, hospitals, and a field post office. The night before his departure he invited two hundred locals to a magnificent masquerade ball and gallantly danced with some of the noble ladies.

While Frederick waltzed, Zieten's hussars were trotting southeast along the southern bank of the Oder River, and other hussar squadrons, backed by dragoons, were prowling as far south as Strehlen. Schwerin's force had reached the Schweidnitz area, and a special detail under Colonel Tilio von Camas (who had returned to the army after completing his mission in Versailles) was probing the Frankenstein area before moving on Glatz. Schwerin would continue southeast to Ottmachau, where he hoped to cross the Neisse and bring Browne to battle.

At Breslau meanwhile Frederick had been reinforced by a few heavy cannon and mortars and 15,600 six-pound loaves of bread baked by seventy-eight local bakers working around the clock. Early on January 6 he marched on the small and weakly held fortress Ohlau. A day later he learned that Browne was falling back south of fortress Neisse. He ordered Schwerin to capture the fortress as soon as possible, sent him some cavalry units, and promised more infantry and artillery once Ohlau fell. His spirits remained high; he wrote the first "Letter of a Prussian Officer" and sent it to Podewils for anonymous publication in the *Journal de Berlin.**

Ohlau surrendered almost immediately, and Frederick marched to join Schwerin at Ottmachau.† He was still on the march when he learned that first blood had been spilled there, where a small garrison was valiantly defending the castle. Schwerin's field guns, small 3-pounders, were not powerful enough to demolish the castle door. Frederick sent cannon and mortars ahead with *Jägers,* or sharpshooters, armed with rifled carbines to fire at castle windows. He sent Schwerin a congratulatory message that ended, "Protect your person if you love me; it is worth more to me than ten thousand men. . . . I am waiting impatiently to see my beloved soldiers again. . . . For God's sake take care of them and yourself."[1] He ordered the field marshal to distribute meat, wine, and brandy to the troops. Three days later he arrived, and the garrison, seeing his mortars and 12-pounders, sensibly surrendered. Frederick showed his pleasure by distributing a large sum of money to the troops.

There was still work to do. Although Leopold had blockaded fortress Glogau so that "not even a cat could slip in or out," General Count Franz Wenzel Wallis showed no sign of surrender. General Prince Octavio Piccolomini at fortress Brieg had refused to surrender. Nor had the defended town of Namslau capitulated. Colonel Camas returned from Glatz to report that the fortress had been reinforced and was too strong to take by surprise attack, especially in winter; artillery was needed. He had lost eight men dead and wounded; the enemy had destroyed bridges and was defending mountain passes between Silesia and Glatz.‡ Browne's army, even if small, was still intact and awaiting reinforcements. Believing Browne to be at Neustadt (he was at Jägerndorf), Frederick ordered Schwerin to go after him with a special task force while he attacked fortress Neisse.

Neisse was the most important fortress in Silesia, and it was also the strongest, having been built in the Vauban style and maintained better than the others. Colonel Baron Wilhelm Moritz von Roth, its comman-

---

* The king wrote twenty-three of these during the First Silesian War. They are surprisingly straightforward, reporting victories to be sure, but also admitting checks, casualties, various difficulties. They are quite generous to enemy arms and commanders and also report on such matters as the numbers and condition of Prussian sick and wounded.

† I was recently in Ottmachau (Ottmichów today), an extremely attractive town. The bell clock tower flanking the main road is dated 1733, and the onion-domed church close by is from 1693. What better place for a lunch of cold chicken, bread, and beer than in the sloping garden before the church — and, as one ate, Schwerin's corps marching in with drums beating and trumpets blowing.

‡ Frederick blamed Camas for not having better organized his expedition. Camas was soon to die from fever. (*Oeuvres,* Volume 2, *Histoire de mon temps.*)

dant, was a brave and determined soldier who had no intention of yielding without a fight. He commanded a garrison of five battalions, perhaps sixteen hundred effectives, who had been working feverishly, along with the townspeople, to strengthen existing defenses. Learning of the Prussian approach, he had closed the gates to country traders, burned the suburbs on the southeast bank, poured water over the walls to coat them with ice, and kept ice from forming in the moats.

After reconnaissance, which drew several salvos from Roth's 24-pounders, Frederick realized that he could not storm the fortress; it was too strong. He ruled out a formal siege because of harsh weather and supply problems. There remained bombardment, as he informed Old Dessauer, of what he pejoratively referred to as "this nest of priests."

Screening Neisse in the south, Frederick deployed his army west and north of the fortress and began the immense task of emplacing cannon and mortars. This took nearly a week. He had only a few pieces with him. The bulk of his artillery, a train of eighteen heavy cannon and mortars and over 150 wagons pulled by 844 horses, was worming its way in convoy from Grottkau, a ponderous train struggling over frozen winding roads. Roads and bridges were frequently impassable, which meant forcing unwilling villagers to make repairs. It also meant delay. Eight days were required to travel fifteen miles.

Once the heavy guns arrived, earthworks had to be built; that meant hacking through frozen ground to level sites, then fitting them with beamed powder chambers, protective breastworks, wooden fascines, and gabions, the gaps plugged by supporting sandbags and woolen bags. Kilns had to be built to convert iron cannonballs into red-hot fireballs; then the heavy guns had to be pulled into position at night. A day before the first battery opened fire, a Prussian colonel sounded a trumpet outside the south gates and invited Colonel von Roth to surrender.* Roth discourteously replied with a salvo of fire. Prussian cannon opened fire the next morning, and a day later Frederick reported to Schwerin that sixteen fires had broken out in the town.

But Roth had foreseen this threat, and special crews easily extinguished them. Frederick moved the batteries forward — again an immense effort — but further bombardment brought no visible results. On the fourth day he abandoned the effort. His guns had fired over seventeen hundred projectiles, killed five soldiers and a few civilians;

---

* The trumpet, often used with the drum, as invitation to parley and for other signals is one of the oldest devices of warfare. The earliest trumpeters used animal horns. Later, wooden horns and conch shells were used. In Moses' time horns were made from silver, later copper. The Roman commander-in-chief always had next to him a trumpeter equipped with a giant instrument, the *buccina,* whose signals were relayed by trumpeters at the head of each legion. (Jeney, *Der Partheygänger.*) The interested reader will find a remarkable collection of military trumpets in the Cairo Museum.

Austrian cannon had fired over five hundred shells and killed five Prussians.*

Schwerin meanwhile was dragging his heels, the inevitable result of an active enemy fighting an effective rearguard action. Supply and transport shortages added to Schwerin's problems. He was already complaining that his soldiers were not receiving daily bread rations or their occasional chunks of meat, and that the supply intendants sent to him were totally incompetent. He was in a land "of ditches, mountains, valleys, and woods," as one enemy report put it;[2] he lacked vital maps;† he could get no information from hostile peasants. Small bands of hussars, irregulars, and armed peasants fell on struggling convoys and isolated outposts. Schwerin himself narrowly missed capture during a raid on Jägerndorf. Frederick managed to get some heavy cannon to him, and he moved once again on Browne, but always with caution far in excess of that warranted by enemy strength.

Outnumbered and outgunned, Browne slowly fell back toward the Moravian border, carefully avoiding main-force contact with the enemy, to whom he remained an x factor, a source of worry to Schwerin. Browne had already received orders from the newly appointed commander, General Count von Neipperg, to preserve his force at all costs while defending the Glatz–Upper Silesia–Moravia border area. Browne now met Count von Neipperg's protégé and deputy, Major General Baron Joseph Caesar Lentulus, at Jägerndorf, along with representatives of the pro-Austrian estates. The decision was to evacuate valuable supply magazines at Jägerndorf, Troppau, and Ratibor, then set up a sixty-mile cordon along the border by barricading major mountain passes and roads with abattis, or roadblocks of sharpened logs, trenches with earthworks, and even a few observation posts and blockhouses, all to be defended by two thousand local militia working in conjunction with Browne's force. Before Browne could begin to carry out this cordon defense plan (for which he had little use), he was forced to move into winter quarters south of Freudenthal. Extremely cold weather and heavy snow prevented further operations. General Lentulus returned to Olmütz, made further arrangements for the defense of Moravia, and then took command of fortress Glatz, where two regiments of Hungarian horse had arrived.

That effectively ended the campaign. By late January Prussian troops held most of Silesia, with small enemy garrisons locked inside three fortresses. (Namslau surrendered at the end of January.) Schwerin's force was variously deployed in screening major mountain passes that

---

* A handsome woodcut of the 1741 bombardment hangs in Neisse tower today.
† On December 28 Frederick had sent to Berlin for whatever maps of Silesia were available. (Preuss, *Friedrich . . . eine Lebensgeschichte, Volume 1.*)

stretched southeast from Silberberg and Wartha on the Glatz border to Jablunka on the Hungarian border. The estates in Lower Silesia were in general cooperating in the occupation, despite Frederick's insistence that in large part they had to support his army in Silesia, at a cost of about 2.5 million thalers a year, as well as provide recruits.

⟨▦⟩

Frederick's blitzkrieg had failed to bring the Vienna court to its knees. The Oder River would not belong to him until Glogau and Brieg had fallen, nor could he rest secure with fortresses Glatz and Neisse still in enemy hands. Browne had skillfully withdrawn his small corps into virtually inaccessible Moravian terrain, where it would soon be reinforced. Hope of a quick peace had vanished. Count von Gotter had arrived in mid-January from Vienna and left no doubt that Austria would fight Prussia to the end.

But all was scarcely lost.

Frederick's aggression had set European chancelleries into motion. The emperor's death had opened political vistas to rulers other than Frederick. If his invasion had replaced subtlety with steel, it paled beside the secret, highly ambitious intentions of King Louis XV, his chancellor Cardinal Fleury, and three bellicose advisers, Antoine Pecquet and the brothers Belle-Isle: Field Marshal Count Charles Louis and Lieutenant General Louis Charles, who was nine years younger and always called Chevalier de Belle-Isle. They read the situation as a new passport to French primacy on the European continent, invariably at Austria's expense.

King Louis and Cardinal Fleury were horrified by Frederick's invasion — the act of a madman, Louis called it. Less than a year earlier Valory had informed his court that "great things" were expected from Crown Prince Frederick when he took the throne: "He could soon win the love of his subjects and the admiration of his neighbors." Now his aggression dismantled Fleury's delicate cobweb diplomacy, designed to disguise an aggressive French policy. Fleury might still have held back but for the fire-eating advisers, in particular Field Marshal Count de Belle-Isle.

A tall, gaunt man of fifty-six who would soon become intimately involved with the Prussian king, Belle-Isle was described by Ranke as "dexterous, indefatigable, and ambitious." The Marquis Renatus Louis d'Argenson noted that "he ate little, slept little, and thought a great deal, qualities rare in France." On the other hand, he had "more ideas than judgment, and more fire than force." Belle-Isle, as well as his able brother, the chevalier, believed the time had come to crush Austria — first, by placing the Imperial crown on the head of Elector Charles Albert; second, by partitioning Austria's hereditary dominions so that

Maria Theresa would retain only Austria and Hungary. To accomplish this he foresaw a grand alliance of France, Prussia, Sweden, Spain, Sardinia, and Bavaria. Prussia was vital to the project. The special envoy, the Marquis de Beauveau, had recently reported that Frederick was no ordinary prince, that his alliance once lost could never be regained. Prussia, the newborn power, was in a position to change the entire traditional political system of Europe: "We must win her over because we can not afford to lose her."[3]

Not without some doubts, King Louis and Fleury (who did not trust Frederick for a moment) approved this ambitious plan. About the same time that Frederick's ultimatum was delivered to the Vienna court, the French ambassador in Munich had informed Elector Charles Albert that Versailles would support his claim to the Imperial crown and would subsidize a Bavarian army of twenty thousand, supporting its operations with a French army. Belle-Isle, appointed to represent France at the Frankfurt Diet, departed for Germany, where he would try to form a new and vigorous *Rheinbund* of electoral princes — to each of whom he would offer generous bribes — to support the Bavarian elector's claim.

The first item on the French shopping list was Prussia. Frederick had only just returned to Berlin when Valory delivered a letter from Cardinal Fleury, who argued for an immediate alliance between France and Prussia. Frederick's excursion into Silesia was of no concern to the Versailles court, Fleury explained, and if Frederick would back the Bavarian elector's claim to the Imperial crown, King Louis would sign a mutual defense treaty with him.

Fleury's timing was excellent. "I incline very much toward France, in case she wants me," Frederick had informed Podewils in early January. England's lack of response to Prussian overtures for alliance, and Count Ostermann's animosity in the Russian court, confirmed his preference. "We must accommodate to France and tune our flutes with theirs," he soon advised Podewils.

But several things slowed his hand. He did not altogether trust France, and he also knew the weakness of her major ally, Bavaria. Podewils once again played devil's advocate. Although an alliance with France held considerable advantages, he conceded, it would unleash general war and bring about an opposition coalition formed by England, Holland, Russia, Austria, and Saxony. If this happened, Prussia would be hard put to survive, let alone prosper. The Saxon and Vienna courts were about to sign a secret treaty. The Russian court under Ostermann's influence was leaning toward Austria. The situation was extremely dangerous. Would it not be more realistic, he asked, to shade Prussian claims to Lower Silesia and Breslau and ask England and Russia to persuade Vienna to accept peace?

Events did seem to make this plan more sensible, and Frederick began to agree with it. The Russian court suddenly warmed to a defensive alliance with Prussia, the harvest of 100,000 thalers in bribes tossed about by Mardefeld and Winterfeldt. Frederick did not rule out an alliance with England and Holland, either. By mid-January he had cooled toward an alliance with France and her allies. "I have always regarded a liaison with these powers as a last resource," he told Podewils. He would infinitely prefer to win a large chunk of Silesia by the mediation of England and Russia (each power to be rewarded). But if these powers joined Austria and attacked Prussia, then "there will be no other resource than to throw ourselves into the arms of France." Podewils was to keep Valory happy in Berlin but was to delay negotiations with France while Frederick secretly tried to win over England and Russia. At the same time he would keep after Versailles to strengthen Bavaria while persuading Bavaria to press her claims to the Imperial crown.

Frederick returned to Berlin in late January and at once arranged for more battalions, squadrons, and guns to be sent to Silesia. Old Dessauer was summoned for military talks, which predominantly concerned the security of Brandenburg against attack from either Saxony or Hanover. Frederick had earlier charged the field marshal to come up with a plan for positioning a corps of twenty-four thousand troops close to the Saxon border, a force that the prince would command. Dessauer was not pleased with Schwerin's present deployment and warned Frederick that detachments which stretched well over a hundred miles from Reichenbach to the Jablunka Pass would be vulnerable to hussar attacks from Moravia, just as Glogau was vulnerable to strikes from Poland. Frederick agreed and in turn charged him with forming new hussar squadrons from horsemen recently recruited in Poland. Young François Chasot, formerly in the French army, was already busy organizing a special *Jägerkorps* of mounted and unmounted huntsmen and foresters to serve with the royal bodyguard and undertake reconnaissance and courier missions.

The turbulent political picture seemed suddenly brighter. King George of England had written a letter that seemed to accept both the seizure of Silesia and an alliance with Prussia. Frederick happily accepted the olive branch, replying that he did not want to upset the peace of Europe. He had "seized all of Silesia . . . chased Browne into Moravia. . . . If I had the least intention of debasing the house of Austria, I need only have driven on to Vienna; but having only the rights to a part of Silesia, I have halted where its frontiers end." Uncle George as a Protestant prince would realize the barbarity of Catholic rule in Silesia and would help Frederick put an end to it. Now was the time for alliance: "Our interests, our religion, our blood, are the same, and it would be regrettable to see us act in a contrary fashion to each other, from which other jealous neighbors would not fail to profit. It would be still more regrettable to force me to concur in the great plans of France, which, however, I have no intention of doing unless forced to it." Similar sentiments were circulated to the Russian court and even to Vienna. Frederick would be content to gain Lower Silesia; he would even pay cash and otherwise accommodate Vienna with territorial guarantees. Although he would not immediately ally with France, that possibility should be held open to dampen any sinister plans held either by Saxony or Hanover. If either King August or King George became frisky, then Old Dessauer would be ready to march with an appropriate force to check him.

Of course he had to keep France thinking an alliance was possible. In a series of audiences with Valory, he did his best to hide true intentions while keeping the door open for further negotiations. So much for diplomacy.

If Frederick could conquer Silesia — if he could overwhelm those stubborn fortresses — then he could negotiate from the strength of possession. Because of this passionate desire for military victory, he cut short his Berlin stay and returned to Silesia in late February. Neither he nor Podewils yet realized that the English and Russian courts were playing a double game as involved as his own and were secretly negotiating alliances with Austria, Saxony, and Holland that were designed to invade, conquer, and partition Prussia.

29

ALTHOUGH envoys Gotter and Borcke had reported that the Vienna court was in no mood to negotiate over Silesia, King Frederick still did not realize the force of Queen Maria Theresa's fury. The queen may have been young and inexperienced, living in "profound melancholy," as one diplomat reported, but she was a determined woman. She *knew* that God was on her side, and she held no intention of allowing an inferior and bumptious heathen upstart to steal one of her richest provinces. Frederick had fallen into a cardinal sin of war: he had underestimated his opponent.

A lesser monarch than Maria Theresa, or perhaps a more intelligent one, might have gained time by territorial settlement and then struck back; this was often the way of European politics. Instead, Maria Theresa used the time gained by Browne's defense of Silesia, meager though it was. If he could not maintain his tiny force in that province, he nonetheless had slowed the Prussian advance and prevented it from spilling into Moravia and beyond. Tactical dexterity had given the queen breathing space.

She badly needed it. To mobilize a moribund Empire, to try to win alliance with the Versailles court, to gear her own lands for war, were immense tasks at once compounded by conflicting counsel and lack of money. Although she never solved the problem of internal discord, she would soon be given a loan by England (as Frederick might have foreseen, in view of European power politics). With that, she turned to raising a new army, and here she had two assets.

The first was a military tradition of several centuries. Despite Austria's recent defeat by Turkey, the army still contained proud regiments, proud commanders who would defend such fortresses as Glogau, Neisse, and Glatz for as long as possible, men who would continue to fight against heavy odds under able commanders like Browne. Veteran regiments were on hand in Italy. Austrian territories, particularly Bohemia, contained many well-trained soldiers to provide the nuclei of new regiments.

Her second asset was a partisan tradition of border irregulars, the famous *Grenzerer* (border people), *Parteigänger* or *Partisanen,* who seventy years later would be called guerrillas.* They came from Moravia, the Balkans, and Hungary. Many were Serbs of Greek Orthodox faith who had been pushed into Croatia and Slavonia by the great Turkish offensives of the fifteenth and sixteenth centuries. They had learned guerrilla warfare from the Turks, who used it not so much as a complement to conventional battlefield tactics than as a psychological tactic, the idea being that constant raids into new territories so sapped the power and will of local defenders that their feudal lords finally accepted Turkish rule in return for an end of the destructive raids. Once Turkey occupied Croatia, Slavonia, and central Hungary, the Habsburgs who ruled adjacent lands faced a situation similar to that of the Romans in later years of the Empire. As the Romans had done, the Habsburgs built "a chain of fortified villages, blockhouses, watch towers, and entanglements, guarded by a small cadre of experienced mercenary troops, and settled by military colonists."[1] These military settlements eventually stretched a thousand miles along Croatian and Slavonian borders, and it was their inhabitants who became known as *Grenzerer.* Since the common soldier was paid by booty taken from raids on the Turks, he soon became as adept as the enemy in swift, destructive raids.

---

* "What is meant by a partisan? By 'party' one means a corps of cavalry or infantry which goes to reconnoiter the enemy; and by 'partisan' is meant a man of war who knows the theater of war, who knows how to lead ambushes and to lead a party." (Saint-Geniés, *L'Officier Partisan.*) See also Hron, *Der Parteigänger-Krieg,* which offers the derivation of *Parteigänger,* one who goes to war with a special group.

Other factors added to the growth of a guerrilla tradition. Local feudal estates often had to defend themselves; serfs in the field always carried weapons and kept horses ready on which either to flee or to fight if a Turkish force appeared. When in time the Turkish menace somewhat subsided, a new conflict developed from rivalry between Hungarian-Croatian estates and the Habsburgs. The *Grenzerer* were a sore point with feudal lords, since they belonged to the Austrian military establishment and were thus immune from feudal obligations, and were neither Catholic nor Protestant. Moreover, they were not always on hand to defend the estates from the Turks. As a result, feudal lords developed a sort of general *Landsturm* formed of local militias commonly called Insurrectios and comprising nobles, serfs, and free farmers under a system called Portal Insurrection. These militias continued to exist in Hungary even after a regular army had developed.

This mélange of Turk, Habsburg, *Grenzerer,* and local Insurrectios bubbled for several centuries to produce a unique guerrilla product. In 1740 the kingdom of Hungary could put only three regular infantry regiments and some dragoon and hussar regiments in the field, but in time Moravia, Hungary, and the Balkan lands would supply thousands of irregulars — twenty thousand in Silesia alone in 1741. "The fierce Croatian and the wild Hussar," Dr. Johnson would call them: Karlstadters, Warasdiners, Hannaks, Teschenken, Heydukes, pandours — bands sharing a very old tradition of irregular warfare. Only the Warasdiners were uniformed, in square-cut green coats, tight red breeches, and black felt caps. The rest "dressed in their national costumes, with dirty white linen trousers tied at the ankle, sashes bristling with daggers and pistols, long Turkish muskets, and hooded red cloaks."* Strangely dressed, wild and undisciplined, mounted and on foot, often drunk and rapacious, and tending to desert whenever they wished, they posed numerous problems for their commanders, but they also performed a host of valuable missions, and they would cause Frederick and his army untold sorrows in the months and years ahead.

Prussian troops had not been long in Silesia when Maria Theresa began putting together her military assets. To her plea for help, Hungarian aristocratic landowners early sent a regiment of dragoons and a regiment of hussars, hard-riding horsemen far superior to any in Frederick's army. In late December she gave orders to mobilize an army of fourteen infantry regiments, five cavalry, and three hussar regiments — something over fifteen thousand foot and horse — that would assemble in the Olmütz area in Moravia. Browne's small force, complemented by General Lentulus's corps in Glatz, would screen the borders while this regular army assembled. Count Pálffy would continue to

---

* The Heeresgeschichtliches Museum in Vienna has a spectacular series of colored prints showing these various troops.

rouse Hungarian nobility to the danger in hope of recruiting irregular bands for service in Silesia.

Maria Theresa was not so lucky in commanders. Browne had already proven his ability, and the army's fortunes undoubtedly would have risen had he been allowed a free hand. Instead, at the insistence of Grand Duke Francis and Count Kinsky, the Silesian command went to General Count von Neipperg, a fifty-six-year-old veteran, soon to be promoted to field marshal, who had just been released from jail, where he had been sent after negotiating the unfavorable Peace of Belgrade with the Turks.

Neipperg was no ball of fire. A military ultraconservative, slow and cautious, like so many of his fellow generals in the Hofkriegsrath, or Supreme War Council, Neipperg was content to remain in Vienna while his new army assembled under Browne in Moravia. Neipperg did not want to fight a war in Silesia. He knew the state of the army and knew, too, that the court always promised more than it could deliver. On being guaranteed fifty thousand troops for Silesia, he remarked that no more than thirty thousand were available and that these were "badly clothed, badly paid, badly armed, and badly fed." [2]

Despite Browne's proven tactical ability and the army's growing strength, Neipperg insisted that he avoid any dangerous operations. Browne sharply disagreed. The cordon defense insisted on by the Hofkriegsrath and Lentulus was virtually useless, because the enemy could easily by-pass the frequently undefended obstructions. The Prussian army, he pointed out, not large to start with, now stretched from Liegnitz to the Jablunka Pass, a length of over two hundred miles in a depth of up to thirty-six miles; in other words, it was dangerously overextended. Schwerin's force, seven battalions and eleven squadrons, was deployed in a dotlike defense from the border of Glatz southeast to the border of Hungary. Prussian outposts were weak and isolated. The predominantly Catholic population was strongly anti-Prussian. The terrain was ideal for partisan warfare. Browne had kept a bridge to fortress Neisse by leaving a small garrison in Freudenthal; and as reinforcements, including bands of irregulars — small, voluntary units of Hungarian hussars and insurgents — reached him, he wanted to fight an active "small war" and perhaps even drive the enemy from Upper Silesia. In his own words: "The enemy quarters in Silesia are scattered to such an extent that it would not be costly to destroy them one after the other, but as my hands are so tightly bound, and General Neipperg insists so emphatically every day on the conservation of the troops without incurring any risk, there is no possibility of gaining an advantage, and I dare to undertake nothing." [3] Although Browne violated Neipperg's orders to a certain degree, he dared not fully exploit what, judging from results of his limited operations, was a heaven-sent opportunity to make life hell for Schwerin's people in the border country.

Curiously and contrarily, Neipperg ordered Lentulus, commanding in Glatz, to use the newly arrived Hungarian dragoons and hussars to move against Prussian border outposts.

Neipperg did not appear in Olmütz until March 10. Lentulus had already sent him a plan calling for invasion of Silesia either from Glatz or Moravia and continuing on to Brieg and Breslau to wedge between Frederick's and Schwerin's forces and destroy each in detail. Primarily to preserve security, Neipperg decided to march due north and cross the border in the Freudenthal area while Lentulus's cavalry marched east from Glatz directly on Neisse.

But the army was in no condition to march. Some battalions had not arrived, others were understrength, and most were not properly equipped, owing to a lack of funds. Magazines fell far short of requirements. The commissariat service was poorly organized and understaffed; the army lacked artillery, pontoons, and most of the twenty-five hundred supply wagons demanded by Neipperg.

Only in late March did the Austrians move out. Neipperg sent General Baron Johann Baranyay with a force of German cavalry, Hungarian hussars, and irregulars to cover his right flank and screen the Moravian border against Prussian raids. The main army followed. It consisted of twelve battalions, nine cavalry and two hussar regiments, sixteen cannon, and a pontoon train. Units carried four days of rations for men and horses. Supply wagons followed with another six days' worth of provisions.

It had been a winter of discontent for the Prussian army. Had Browne been free to operate as he had wished, it might have been a winter of disaster. The troops were not clothed for snow and bitter cold. Their undershirts, for example, lacked sleeves and backs. A disorganized commissariat system forced them to live largely off the land, but Browne's retreating corps had taken most of the ready provisions. Cold and hunger brought sickness and many desertions.

The enemy also had been difficult. Despite operational restrictions placed on Browne, a brisk little border war had been going on against isolated Prussian units and patrols. Few places in the world could have been more suitable for guerrilla warfare.* It was fought along the en-

---

* And is today. The entire Nachod border area between Czechoslovakia and Poland (yesterday's Bohemia and Silesia) is heavily timbered, mountainous, and very beautiful. I climbed slowly, stopping often to admire the views, and after a few kilometers began a descent. The terrain opens to wooded, rolling farmlands that lead to Glatz. North of Glatz the Neisse River comes as a surprise, since it is no more than ten yards wide in some places. Frankenstein is a pleasant little village in the middle of a large tableland spotted by copses, larger woods, and orchards. From Frankenstein I followed Schwerin's route, a picturesque open road flanked by border mountains to the south and southwest and plains to the east.

tire border, in part by enemy hussars operating out of Moravia and Glatz, in part by enemy irregulars, whom Frederick always termed "rabble" and Schwerin "bandits," operating out of fortress Neisse and remote border areas, in part by Silesian peasants urged to defiance by local Roman Catholic priests. The need for forage increased unit exposure, and nasty skirmishes were frequent. Convoys had been attacked and sometimes captured or destroyed; communications on occasion were cut. The Prussian effort to recruit in Teschen had backfired. Ungrateful Moravian peasants had even attacked Prussian patrols and captured one; in return the Prussians often sacked and sometimes burned hastily evacuated villages — a portent of things to come. The Prussian army was operating in enemy land. Enemy hussars are "ever more insolent," Schwerin complained; "everyone between the Neisse and the Oder is Your Majesty's sworn enemy." In Lower Silesia enemy hussars performed another function by terrorizing local villagers who were working for the Prussians (often under duress). From Ottmachau one officer reported that scarcely twenty of a hundred peasants reported for work on fortifications and that he was not receiving "one inch" of material for sandbags.

If the invaders often gave as good as they got in various encounters, the attacks were still unnerving. They kept tired units on the move, active when they should have been resting and reforming. They repeatedly interrupted supply convoys. Had it not been for grain captured south of Jägerndorf, Schwerin would have been in "dire straits"; as it was, "I have no more wine and am entirely dependent on miserable beer" — if Frederick would send him a cask of Rhine wine, he and his officers would drink the king's health!

Spies soon began to report an enemy buildup to the south, and the enemy daily grew more aggressive. Schwerin was in Jägerndorf when enemy hussars burst nearly into town in an attempt to capture him. "The enemy is well informed of our slightest movement, because all the locals are on his side," he reported to the king.[4] "Men and horses are packed together like herrings," one disgruntled cavalry commander reported to Schulenburg, "and because of the Imperial hussars they dare not leave their equipment and arms day or night; we are thus not in a position to make any repairs. . . . The hussars are located about four and a half miles away and because of their partisan group the roads are so unsafe that a small patrol dares not venture forth."[5] So serious was the situation that on February 20 Schwerin issued a long order alerting generals to possible enemy attack.

Frederick left Berlin on February 19. He stopped at Glogau, where he ordered Prince Leopold to turn the blockade into a siege. Once more mines and troops arrived, he was to storm the fortress. Frederick rode on to Schweidnitz headquarters, where, in his later words, he inspected various units "in order to reconnoiter the terrain, make changes where necessary, and inspect the condition of the troops."[6] He was not entirely satisfied. He found the officers zealous enough, but they were careless and lacked sangfroid, shortcomings already reported by Schwerin, particularly in the junior officers. He had already received Schwerin's nervous report of an enemy buildup, and now he learned of a serious clash on the Glatz border: an enemy surprise attack had killed twenty-one grenadiers and wounded thirteen. This seemed to him a particularly vulnerable area. With only a small mounted escort, he rode on to Frankenstein, from where he planned to inspect the Silberberg and Wartha defenses of the mountain passes against incursions from Glatz.

Frederick's concern for this area was not misplaced. Lentulus had made a lengthy reconnaissance of the border and had planned a series of raids, but before he could act, General Derschau had strengthened Prussian defenses, mainly by constructing strong roadblocks of sharpened wooden palisades defended by mutually supporting outposts. Shortly after Schwerin's alert order, Lentulus reported to Neipperg that "since the Prussians are so alert, there is nothing to try."[7]

Maria Theresa and Neipperg persuaded Lentulus to change his mind, but before he could arrange a large-scale attack, two reliable sources, one in Vienna (Frederick's old enemy, Field Marshal Count von Seckendorff) and one in Silesia (a Catholic prelate), informed him of Frederick's return to Silesia and subsequent movements. Learning that Frederick was to visit the Glatz border area, Lentulus set an ambush in the Wartha Valley. It almost succeeded. It probably would have succeeded, but the Hungarian hussar commander mistook a party of Prussian dragoons for the royal party and fell on them. The king was lunching at a nearby village when he heard musket fire and learned of the attack. At once leading his small escort of fifty gendarmes to the scene, he chased off enemy hussars and found that his own dragoons had fled, with a loss of eleven killed, fifteen taken prisoner, a standard, two kettledrums, and thirty-five horses.

Frederick was understandably furious. "I always told you those Schulenburg dragoons were good for nothing," he wrote to Old Dessauer. The aged Schulenburg received a scorching letter that described the breakdown of discipline and the squadron's wild flight. But Frederick was also reflective. He told Valory that the "adventure" would make him "more circumspect."[8] And to Podewils in Berlin he wrote:

> If it is my misfortune to be taken alive I order you unconditionally and at the price of your head that in my absence you will not follow my orders, that you will act as my brother [William, his heir as the Prince of Prussia] directs you, and that the state will take no unworthy action for my liberty. . . . I am king only when I am free. . . . If I am killed I want my body cremated in the Roman style, and the urn interred at Rheinsberg. Knobelsdorff in this case should fashion a monument like that of Horace at Tusculum.

Shaking off these morbid if dramatic thoughts, Frederick hastened to exploit the matter. Podewils was to protest to all envoys and newspapers this unheard-of attempt by the Vienna court to kidnap him.

The word quickly spread. *The Gentlemen's Magazine* informed English readers of the plot "for carrying off the Person of his Prussian Majesty," and reported in its April issue that "the king of Prussia's minister at Mentz [Mainz] has published a Memorial, setting forth, that notwithstanding the Moderation He [King Frederick] has long shown toward the Court of Vienna, yet that Court has been far from behaving so to him and has had Recourse to the detestable Expedients of employing Emissaries, Spies and Banditti to beset him, and even attempt his Life." [9] In denying such accusations, Maria Theresa for the first time used what would become her favorite description of the Prussian king: *le méchant homme*, the wicked man.

Frederick's near capture considerably strained already taut nerves. Things were not going well. More hussars were needed, and he was sending officers to Poland to recruit nine hundred men, from whom Dessauer would form six new squadrons — but that would take time. A few days after the border incident he moved on to fortress Brieg to see what could be done there. He established headquarters near the village of Mollwitz, which he identified as "close to Brieg" and, in a letter to Jordan, as "a village whose shape and name I don't know." In only a few weeks, it would be famous throughout Europe.

Unable to speed the siege, Frederick returned to Schweidnitz to supervise the Glatz border defenses, which continued to worry him. He was also upset with Schwerin, especially with the field marshal's decision to remove the garrison from Zuckmantel, which allowed Browne to reinforce the Neisse garrison. Schwerin should use more spies, Frederick grumbled to Dessauer. There were entirely too many enemy attacks on outposts and convoys, and as long as Browne had communication with Neisse, there was a real danger that an enemy attack could cut Schwerin's communications with Frederick.

The king's main problem was nothing new to a military commander. Despite the reinforcements arriving from Brandenburg, he was overextended, a fault that could be at least partly repaired by use of the regiments now tied up in the siege of Glogau. He sent orders to Prince Leopold to take the fortress by a surprise night attack. Leopold did so, a forty-five-minute assault that cost nine dead and forty-two wounded Prussians and made him a hero — with a cash reward of twenty thousand gulden. Frederick wrote to Old Dessauer that his son Leopold had achieved "the most beautiful act of this century" — which probably caused the Duke of Marlborough to turn in his grave.

Leopold's success helped to calm royal nerves. "I am in an advantageous position here," the king wrote to Jordan in mid-March, "and our affairs, thank heavens, are going marvelously." With the arrival of

Leopold and the Glogau regiments, he told one of his generals that he felt "no more uneasiness" at commencing the siege of fortress Neisse.

This halcyon mood was short-lived. Mardefeld, in Saint Petersburg, reported that Count Ostermann had won the power struggle in the Russian court and that Marshal Münnich, who had been Frederick's supporter, had resigned his offices and would soon leave Saint Petersburg. Meanwhile, Austrian, English, and Saxon ambassadors had proposed to the all-too-willing Russian court a plan to defeat Prussia and partition her territories. Here, suddenly, was "the blackest plot . . . the most detestable alliance in the world against me," as Frederick informed Truchsess in London. "I confess that this is a treacherous blow. . . ." he wrote to Podewils. "If subsequent news corresponds with what I have received, it will be necessary to conclude an alliance soonest with France, and it will no longer be I but Russia and England who will upset Europe."

30

PODEWILS AND BORCKE wanted nothing to do with a French alliance, which would mean only the sword. Podewils repeated his former arguments, though with little hope of success. "We are involved in the worst crisis ever faced by the House of Brandenburg," he told Borcke.[1] A Prussian alliance with France would mean a long and bloody war, he warned the king, and would prevent Prussia from making any agreement with Austria.

Perhaps so, Frederick replied, but the hostile powers were forcing his hand. He now ordered Old Dessauer to deploy his army at Göttin, near the Saxon border. If the hostile coalition materialized and the Russians attacked him in Prussia, he would go on the defensive in Silesia, march to join Dessauer, conquer Saxony, and then move on the Russians. If necessary, Dessauer would transfer the royal family and treasury to Stettin. Meanwhile he would ally with France. Valory, who was in Schweidnitz, was received at dinner and told of Frederick's desire for an alliance, providing that France would cause Sweden to make war on Russia if she moved against Prussia. Valory was to meet with Podewils in great secrecy and draw up a draft treaty.

Frederick was not running scared. Valory reported to friends in Berlin that His Prussian Majesty "was never in better humor or in better health than at present; full of spirits, and talking of nothing less than marching to Vienna."[2]

Such optimism was in part justified. No sooner had Saxony agreed to the invasion of Prussia when the prime minister, Count Heinrich von Brühl, began to have second thoughts, provoked by Old Dessauer's deployment at Göttin of a force larger than the entire Saxon army. Russian regiments marched from the Ukraine to Smolensk, but then halted. Ostermann was well aware of the shaky condition of the Russian army and was also worried by reports of a Swedish army assembling in Finland. So favorable were Mardefeld's dispatches from Saint Petersburg that on the first day of April Podewils informed Frederick "that the storm which began to form against us begins little by little to dissipate." The participants were in serious disagreement. Russia distrusted Saxony. "If the maritime powers [England and Holland]," Podewils continued, "can be detached, as I hope will be brought about in some way at least, the famous plot will go up in smoke and the mountain will give birth to a mouse." [3]

Such was the state of affairs when Frederick again took up the sword. The threat of an Austrian offensive was mounting, he wrote to Schwerin. He had received secret information, probably from Field Marshal Baron Samuel von Schmettau, who had left Austrian service and would soon join the Prussian army, that Neipperg with an army of about twenty-three thousand, would march on Jägerndorf while Lentulus from Glatz would make a diversionary attack on Breslau. Frederick wanted Schwerin to compress his command, as Dessauer was urgently advising, between Jägerndorf, Neustadt, and Zuckmantel (which had to be cleared of enemy) before joining Frederick's force at Neisse.

Schwerin disagreed with the change in deployment. He liked the present arrangement, which he incorrectly insisted was blocking all mountain passes from Moravia and Bohemia. Jägerndorf, he argued, was a key position, a "treasure," and to hold it he had to retain supply magazines at Troppau and Ratibor. He could easily hold this shortened line until mid-April; that would allow Frederick time to capture Neisse — and permit Schwerin to retain his independent command.

Frederick reluctantly agreed to leave things largely as they were — that is, his force spread north and west of Neisse, Schwerin's south and east of the fortress — at least until enemy intentions became more clear. Schwerin did agree to evacuate the Jablunka defense and the most distant Moravian outposts, and he also sent a force to take Zuckmantel. But the influx of enemy irregulars, compounded by supply shortages, brought him to a terrible state of nerves, and the upshot was that he now came around to the king's earlier way of thinking. But then the promise of reinforcements, along with new information that the Austrians were ready to march, caused Schwerin once again to change his mind and remain where he was.

Frederick had already decided against this. Leaving General Christoph Wilhelm von Kalkstein at Grottkau to prepare the siege of Neisse, he personally led the promised reinforcements, five infantry and four grenadier battalions, to Neustadt, where he met Schwerin. His intention was made clear in a letter to Dessauer: Schwerin was to fall back on Neisse and take up the siege from the south. But Schwerin presented new arguments against this move in a discussion that continued in Jägerndorf. Although the field marshal knew almost nothing of enemy intentions or movements, he doubted that, in view of the recent snowfall and consequent lack of forage, the enemy would cross the mountains until spring.

He was wrong.

Determined to reinforce the Neisse garrison, Neipperg had marched four days before Frederick and Schwerin met. Progress was maddeningly slow. A sudden thaw turned the roads to seas of mud, and peasant teamsters frequently rode off on horses, leaving wagons to stand idle. Then the weather again turned cold, and as the Prussian commanders conferred at Jägerndorf, Austrian columns were braving snow and cold to struggle up narrow treacherous roads leading to mountain passes at Zuckmantel and Freudenthal, a movement shielded by Baránthe yay's light horse and irregulars, who fanned out from front and flank to reconnoiter the land.

Having spent the night at Jägerndorf, Frederick was about to return to his command when Austrian deserters reported the imminent arrival of Neipperg's army, news underscored by the sudden sound of musket fire. Patrols next reported that Prussian outposts were skirmishing with enemy irregulars, and that Neipperg's vanguard was marching on Freudenthal, some thirteen miles south, evidently unaware of the Prussian presence.

Frederick was in serious tactical trouble. If Neipperg could wedge between his and Schwerin's commands, he could possibly destroy each force. That was indeed the Austrian plan. Even if the Prussians withdrew, Neipperg could still march down the Neisse Valley on Ohlau and its lightly defended ammunition magazine, and then to Breslau to cut the Oder River lifeline.

To retrieve the situation, Frederick sent aides galloping to General Duke Friedrich Wilhelm von Holstein-Beck at Frankenstein, to Kalkstein at Grottkau, to Fouqué in the east: forget the siege of Neisse, forget everything but immediate withdrawal north, to join with Frederick and Schwerin on the western bank of the Neisse River across from Sorge, where a boat bridge would be built. Schwerin at once called in scattered outposts, marches observed and harassed by Baránnyay's hussars and irregulars, who covered the area like locusts. To worsen matters, Lentulus's dragoons and hussars began cutting communications west of Neisse. General Holstein-Beck, commanding some eight thousand troops at Frankenstein, did not receive Frederick's orders and remained there, oblivious of the gathering storm until much too late.

Austrian and Prussian armies were moving in the dark, moving to unknown fates. Dogged by long supply columns, poor transport horses, and roads sometimes icy and sometimes mud, Neipperg marched more slowly, first to Ziegenhals, then to fortress Neisse, short marches of only five miles a day through compartmented country of streams and roads, country easy to lose a small army in, yet country whose flatlands were ideal for battle.

Frederick moved faster. He had begun to smell battle and he used a new marching order of two columns, each of six battalions, one column under his and one under Schwerin's command. On April 4, when Neipperg struggled to march five miles, the Prussians logged eighteen miles from Jägerndorf to Neustadt and on to Steinau, despite almost constant skirmishing with Lentulus's hussars. The smell of battle grew ever stronger. An aide rode off to Kleist at fortress Brieg: raise the blockade, march south to join the main army. Other aides carried orders to local commanders: all units to strip baggage to essentials, the ponderous baggage trains to move to Krappitz and take boats to Ohlau. That evening fire broke out in the village. "It was only good luck that saved the cannon and powder," Frederick later wrote.[4] It was snowing and cold; the troops were visibly suffering. Wrapped in a cloak, the king prowled among the bivouac fires, talking to the men, snatching an hour's sleep here and there. At daybreak the march continued through deep snow to Sorge, where the king hoped to cross the Neisse and join Holstein-Beck's force of seven battalions and six squadrons. Instead, he found Prince Leopold's advance guard facing several thousand enemy west of Lassoth. This was Neipperg's advance guard, General Baron Johann Friedrich Berlichingen's and General Baron Karl Joachim Römer's cavalry — six regiments of cuirassiers, five of dragoons — with infantry slogging up from behind, although Frederick did not yet know of that. The Prussians perforce stayed on the east bank. Leopold burned the village, crossed the Neisse, and joined the march, this time in command of the rearguard — a neat piece of work for which he was promoted to general.

The two armies were on collision course without either commander's realizing it. Frederick's columns continued the march north and on April 8 crossed the Neisse around Michelau and Löwen, the idea being to reach Grottkau and base on Ohlau in order to block any Austrian move against Breslau.* On the west side of the Neisse the Austrian army was also marching north, and on that same morning its

* Today the Neisse, now called Nyasa, is about sixty to seventy yards wide at Löwen, a small village. The Catholic church at Michelau, now Michatow, carries the date 1613, which kindly local people assured me was correct. So if it had not been snowing, Frederick could easily have seen the Austrian army, or at least large portions of it, from the bell tower. Incidentally, if the reader ever reaches these parts, he should eat at the only restaurant there is in Niemodlin — the only good meal I had in Poland.

advance guard had occupied Grottkau, Neipperg's idea being to seize the Prussian magazine at Ohlau, a fact Frederick learned that afternoon from captured enemy hussars. Neipperg did not realize that he was practically on top of the Prussian army; he wrote to Grand Duke Francis from Grottkau that he knew "neither where the King of Prussia had gone, nor the location of Field Marshal Schwerin, nor what had become of General Schulenburg and the regiments from Troppau, Ratibor, etc."[5] He intended to march early the next day without really knowing where. He and his generals supposed that the Prussian army numbered seven to eight thousand.

The fog of war had cleared a little in the Prussian camp. After learning that Austrian dragoons were in Grottkau, thus barring the way to Ohlau and Breslau, Frederick began deploying by wheeling columns to the right. That night the army sheltered in and around four villages a few miles southeast of Mollwitz, with headquarters at Algenau and Pogarell. His total force amounted to thirty-one battalions and thirty-four squadrons, some twenty-four thousand troops, along with sixty cannon of assorted caliber. He was still in difficulty, his force split, rations nearly exhausted. He now sent officers to Ohlau to report his arrival and to summon two regiments of cuirassiers — none of the messengers would make it through the screen of irregulars that infested the area. Nor did he know that Holstein-Beck, blissfully unaware of the crisis, was closing on Strehlen to the north.

The Prussian king did not sleep. To Jordan in Breslau he wrote that "we shall fight tomorrow. You know the fortunes of war, which respect the life of a king no more than that of a commoner. I don't know what will happen to me. If my time is up, remember a friend who loves you tenderly; if I am spared, I will write you tomorrow and you will learn of our victory." To Prince William: "We are just over a quarter of a mile [slightly over one English mile] from the enemy. Tomorrow must decide our fate. If I die, do not forget a brother who has always loved you tenderly. . . . I will govern forever my actions by the glory of Prussian arms and the honor of my House."

3 1

Sunday, April 9, 1741. It is overcast and snowing. Thick heavy flakes; you can't see twenty feet; blizzard weather, not good for battle, particularly when you don't know where the enemy is or his strength or what he wants to do. Frederick decides not to march. The exhausted troops

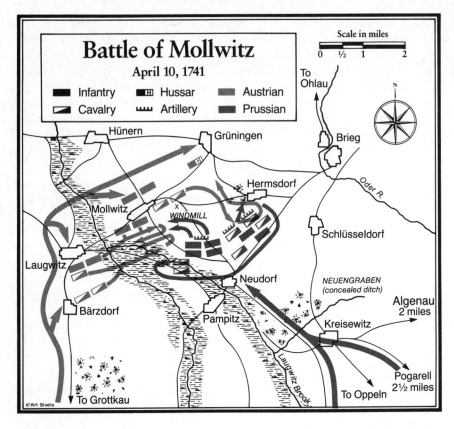

Battle of Mollwitz
April 10, 1741

Infantry   Hussar   Austrian
Cavalry   Artillery   Prussian

Scale in miles
0 ½ 1   2

To Ohlau

N

Hünern   Grüningen   Brieg

Hermsdorf

Oder R.

Mollwitz   WINDMILL

Schlüsseldorf

Laugwitz

Neudorf

NEUENGRABEN
(concealed ditch)

Algenau
2 miles

Bärzdorf   Pampitz   Kreisewitz

Pogarell
2½ miles

To Oppeln

To Grottkau

Laugwitz Brook

d'Art Studio

need rest, and perhaps, despite the snow, the cuirassier regiments will ride in from Ohlau. The snow eases in the afternoon. Aides ride through drifts to deliver orders to unit commanders: the army will march in five battle-ready columns in the morning; destination, Ohlau.

In the enemy camp Field Marshal Neipperg uses the day to consolidate his tired army. He is short of supplies, uncertain of the enemy's location, ignorant of the enemy's strength and intention, devoid of information, kept from him by hostile Lutheran farmers. His troops, the bulk of them poorly trained peasant boys, are very tired. The safest step, he believes, is to base on Brieg, which can supply needed rations. The decision means that his army will point in the wrong direction for battle. Hussars move out first, poke into Mollwitz for a look, move on to Grüningen. General von Römer's six cavalry regiments, the army's right wing in case of battle deployment, tread snow-covered roads and fields into Mollwitz village, which will be Neipperg's headquarters. General von Göldy's infantry, sixteen battalions and fourteen grenadier companies, straggle into Laugwitz village, a mile and a half southwest of Mollwitz. General von Berlichingen's five cavalry regiments, the left wing in case of deployment, canton in Bärzdorf village, about two and a half miles southwest of Mollwitz.

The visitation rudely surprises the locals. Three hundred hussars suddenly appear in Mollwitz. They find no enemy, steal what they can, move on to more loot up the road. Cavalry regiments follow like black clouds. Squadrons canton in houses and barns; swearing, sweating troops chop up neat wooden boundary railings to feed cookfires that spring like magic lanterns from the snow-covered ground; other parties empty barns of carefully hoarded hay, straw, barley, oats; they raid hen-houses, slaughter pigs and cows.

Mollwitz is in the way of war.

Neipperg confers with his staff in one of the houses. The conference solves nothing. He writes to Grand Duke Francis that the situation is puzzling "because the greater part of the enemy force is now believed to be between Löwen and Michelau on the Neisse [River] and the re-mainder at Ohlau. I am situated between them trying to decide on the best course of action — how to further my advance, considering the terrain here and the enemy movements, or what the enemy will do in view of his present situation." [1]

Poor old Neipperg. He had never seen very far in his military career, a professional myopia now compounded by snow and blizzard. Mon-day will be a rest day — or so he believed.

Monday, April 10, 1741. Frederick has worked fitfully through the night, impatient for dawn, impatient to reach Ohlau, with its vital trea-sures of food and ammunition. Dawn comes clear and cold but with sun. Two feet of crisp snow covers the flat ground, but the weather is fit for fighting. Drums beat at five A.M.; sergeants curse soldiers to their tasks. Half-frozen, hungry men grumble, slip from vile-smelling barns, relieve themselves, revive dormant fires, cook breakfast. Scouts ride to survey the flat white land ahead. This is Colonel Count Friedrich Ru-dolf Rothenburg's advance guard, four squadrons of horse, three squadrons of hussars, a sizable force that seems infinitely small in the vastness of a snow-covered Silesian plain.*

Meanwhile the army forms on the mill outside Pogarell. It will march west on Kreisewitz in five columns. The artillery train and essential baggage wagons claim the rude road; one infantry and one cavalry column march on either side of the road, cavalry outboard, infantry inboard, with ample intervals in case they are deployed into line. Car-penters march in front of columns to clear obstructions. Other cavalry regiments form the wings, with hussars lurking in reserve. Company wagons haul knapsacks and bread sacks. The men carry only muskets

---

* The battle site is today a part of a large military base.

and bandoliers, thirty cartridges per man. They march quietly. Officers are ordered to shoot summarily anyone who talks, anyone who fires a musket without orders.

The army marches at ten A.M.

All is quiet. Rothenburg's people round up a couple of peasants, chase some hussars out of Neudorf, continue forward on the white flatland now glistening in late morning sun. Austrian lookouts in the church steeple at Brieg spot the intruders and fire rockets to alert Neipperg in Mollwitz. Neipperg cannot imagine what the excitement is all about but sends some hussars to investigate. The patrol clashes with Rothenburg's squadrons, loses a few troopers; the rest break off action to report back to headquarters. About this time an officer arrives from Brieg with the disquieting news of the Prussian advance.

Neipperg is at dinner. Though surprised, he acts calmly and quickly. Drums call soldiers to arms, aides scurry hither and yon with orders to form battle lines. But the units are all pointed the wrong way, in anticipation of deploying into line *northwest* of Mollwitz. Now they must quickly about-face and deploy *southeast* of Mollwitz; that is, units designated for the right center and right wing must now become left center and left wing, a tactical adjustment that, as one participant drily noted, caused a great deal of confusion. No matter — troops excitedly muster, units form, men march. A group of them tells a landlord that they will "chase this cheeky snow king and his dandy soldiers back where they came from and cut strips from his hide."[2] Officers hurrying from Laugwitz tell an innkeeper to keep the soup hot: they will thrash the Brandenburgers and soon return. Neipperg is confident of victory; he remarks to an aide that he will send the Prussian king back to Apollo and his muses.

But neither Berlichingen nor Göldy is moving fast enough. Neipperg rides to the right wing to prod infantry and cavalry into action. On the Austrian left Römer deploys thirty squadrons of horse around a windmill that looms from the suddenly busy land. Artillery comes from Laugwitz like poky snails. Göldy slowly feeds infantry battalions into a center line. The Austrian deployment is ragged and full of gaps.

The Prussians meanwhile are marching. Their pace, too, is slow. There is the snow, then a hidden ditch, the Neuengraben (not shown on their map); then the columns must side-slip to the road to funnel through Kreisewitz Forest before resuming formation. It all takes time. The vanguard closes on the Neudorf-Brieg road about noon. Frederick talks to captured hussars, learns that Neipperg has occupied Mollwitz, Hünern, and Grüningen. Neipperg is thus in his way. He orders his commanders to deploy into battle lines.

At first it goes like Potsdam drill transferred to Silesia. Frederick designates army boundaries, the stream northwest of Neudorf on the left, the woods near Hermsdorf on the right. The army deploys in two lines, cavalry on the extreme right, infantry in the center, cavalry on the extreme left, baggage wagons to the rear with a two-battalion guard. Small 3-pounder cannon front each infantry battalion. Struggling teams, eight horses to a gun, pull the larger cannon a few hundred paces in front of the front line, eighteen of them in the center, ten on the right — bronze sentries that will fire when the enemy is in range. Engineers stand by the guns, squinting in the bright light as they try to estimate target distances.

But the snow-covered land is deceiving; it mocks space and perspective. General Count Adolf Friedrich Schulenburg's cavalry deploy too far west of the woods; they squeeze the land; the deployment area is not wide enough; alterations are necessary. Battalions designated for the first line must fall back and bend in clumsy flank defenses. Battalions coming to form the second line run into them. Confusion! Delay! On the left no room for cavalry; they are shunted across the brook. More confusion, more delay. Schwerin and Kalkstein sort things out on the left, Frederick and Schulenburg on the right. Here the king makes a special and unique adjustment, interweaving two grenadier battalions into Schulenburg's squadrons.* Frederick and Schwerin are finally satisfied. Neither seems to notice that Schulenburg's squadrons have deployed too far left.

It is about one P.M. Frederick orders the army to advance. Battalions and squadrons move out "with stirring music and flags flying, in a proper order," an officer later writes, "that I have never seen at the grand review in Berlin or Magdeburg."[3]

The "proper order" does not last long. Battalions and squadrons on the left flank are still being shuffled about. They lag behind center and right. Matters are better on the right, where heavy cannon unlimber within range of Römer's cavalry. But Schulenburg finally notices his mistake in deployment. To rectify it, to extend the battle line and cover his vulnerable right flank, he moves his ten squadrons of horse not toward Römer's cavalry but north toward Hermsdorf, from where he plans to wheel into attack.

From the windmill General Römer watches the Prussian movement. He and his troopers see Prussian gunners open fire. The first salvos scatter Austrian hussars, killing five men and forty-five horses. Prussian roundballs, each of six, twelve, or twenty-four pounds of black iron, begin to plough snow to Römer's front. The fire increases; the white ground turns to black trails. An Austrian witness later writes that the

---

* Frederick later attributed this new tactic to the lesson offered by Gustavus Adolphus at the battle of Lützen. More likely it was due to the advice of Field Marshal von Schmettau to the effect that Austrians relied particularly on their cavalry and in case of battle would charge with it.

cannon fired almost as fast as Austrian infantry — "ninety rounds fired while the troopers said one Lord's Prayer."[4] The Austrians watch Prussian gunners furiously swinging sledgehammers against elevation wedges. The balls come closer, they come home, horse and man are falling, their screams piercing the thunder of Prussian guns.

The fire suddenly ceases; the guns move forward; infantry and cavalry follow. The cannon again open fire. Römer waits for Neipperg's orders, but Neipperg is busy on the right and Römer waits in vain. His men are restless; "they begin to grumble and swear," an Austrian officer notes.[5] Men and horses are dying. Römer is an experienced general. He sees that Göldy's infantry are not fully deployed on his right, their few cannon have not even come up. He sees Prussian infantry advancing to strike Göldy's exposed left flank. Now he sees Prussian horse moving — and he cannot believe his eyes. He does not know Schulenburg's plan; all he knows is that the enemy is offering him an exposed flank.

It is about one-thirty P.M.

Römer's sword slashes air; squadrons move out, trot briefly northeast to evade cannon fire, wheel sharply right. These are veteran troopers, the best in Europe. Thirty squadrons of cuirassiers and dragoons, some three thousand horse keeping almost perfect formation in the approach, trot over treacherous snow. Prussian gunners see them come, realign the heavy cannon, switch some guns to caseshot, to shells holding anywhere from fifty to three hundred half-ounce lead balls, fearful cannonades that tear holes in enemy ranks. The Austrians seem oblivious, intent only on striking the exposed flank of Prussian horse.

The pace quickens; trumpets sound the charge.

Schulenburg realizes too late what is happening. In vain he tries to turn unwieldy lines. Enemy horse thunder in at full gallop to hit his ranks with lance and saber. His lines break like so many toothpicks. To most of his men, anywhere is better than here, and desperately they run to anywhere. Römer's people follow, push them to the woods, push them into the fire of their own infantry, close on exposed cannon, slash gunners to death, turn loaded guns to fire into Prussian lines, spike some, take others away.

Frederick is with Winterfeldt's grenadier battalion on the extreme right.* Riding into the melee, trying to rally the cavalry "as one would a pack of stags," he collects a few squadrons and turns on the enemy. Though split by the infantry battalions, Römer's troopers hurl themselves forward to smash the counterattack. Römer is shot dead; Len-

---

* Winterfeldt had only recently returned from his successful diplomatic mission to Saint Petersburg.

tulus is wounded. But the attack continues; it sweeps Prussian squadrons across the battlefront to the Prussian left. Frederick and Schulenburg extricate themselves with difficulty. They struggle back to the right, where the infantry are holding, though firing now to front and rear. Smoke covers the battlefield, a black curtain hanging all the way to the outskirts of Ohlau.

Schulenburg will not suffer his disgrace. An inept commander but a big man and brave, his life is the honor of his regiment. He has been wounded, and now, standing in the saddle, sword in hand, he furiously wheels his foaming horse to curse confused squadrons into attack formation. The enemy hits hard, a saber slashes Schulenberg's face, an eye falls from its socket. He holds his cheek together with one hand, remains mounted, continues forward. An Austrian bullet finds his body, kills him. His fall is the fall of his troops. Once again Austrians chase Prussian horse from the field.

Schwerin reaches the right wing. He finds an appalling tactical mess. Torn bodies cover red snow, a ground of distorted faces and twitching limbs, the once pure air acrid with powder smoke, filled with screams of dying men and horses, of commanders bawling confused commands, of trumpet blasts, musket and cannon fire. Everywhere is confusion and fear, laced with noble acts and valiant deeds. The situation is more than critical. Prussian horse have vanished, heavy cannon are knocked out, infantry are fighting for their lives, soldiers firing frantically, often uselessly, Austrian infantry forming in line but not yet advancing, Austrian cannon finally in position.

Schwerin finds the king in the middle of this tactical nightmare. Frederick is leading by example, exposing himself to almost certain death in trying to rally stragglers into cohesion. A few feet away a cannonball tears an aide's head from his body. It is the king's young cousin Prince Frederick of Brandenburg-Schwedt. There is no time to grieve. Enemy horse press in. François Chasot intercepts a blow intended for Frederick; blood spills over him from a deep cut in the head.[*] Schwerin suggests that Frederick turn the command over to him and leave the battlefield. He argues that the kingdom is more important than a battle lost, that the king can go to Oppeln, where the army will follow if defeated. Frederick refuses. A new cavalry attack interrupts the argument. It is beaten off with difficulty. Schwerin becomes more upset when he sees infantry of the second line firing in panic, without command. He appeals to Prince Leopold and to the king's adjutants. It is a matter of the crown, they all agree, the preservation of Prussia. Frederick is confused. He is the product of a week and more of march and

---

[*] Voltaire later put the deed in verse: "Where this illustrious Chasot, this formidable warrior, / By his valor saved the greatest of our kings. . . ." (Schlözer, *General Graf Chasot*.)

countermarch, of worry over the enemy, over rations and ammunition, over Holstein-Beck's absence, of two sleepless nights, of long hours of writing orders, of deployment and battle, of young Prince Frederick's death, of Römer's frantic charge, of Schulenburg's death, of soldiers spilling guts and puking blood as they scream, cry, and die. Frederick is human, no bigger than his shadow. He yields.

It is about four P.M.

Schwerin takes command. The Austrians are winning; no doubt about it. But Römer's cavalry have suffered more than Prussian commanders suppose. His once compact squadrons are scattered, with many of them now on the Austrian right, many to the rear, *hors de combat*. Nowhere on the Prussian right has Prussian infantry broken. Battered in places, terrible casualties, yes, but not broken. Schwerin rides to them; he wants ranks put right, fire discipline restored. His generals ask whether he will retreat. "Over enemy bodies," he spits back.[6] Officers respond, units shape up, firing commences on order — front rank first, then the front rank kneeling to reload while the second and third ranks fire, a steady, often effective fire backed by bayonets plunging into soft underbellies of intrusive Austrian horses.

Schwerin senses a change of tempo. Battle always has a pulse, and now it quickens and Schwerin's finger is on it. He has taken heavy losses; he is short of powder, ammunition, and daylight. He is twice wounded. He orders live men to strip dead men of ammunition. He joins battered battalions together to extend his first line. He and General Heinrich Karl von der Marwitz ride to the front of the extreme right wing, to the bleeding first battalion of guards. Schwerin talks briefly to officers and men. He wants one more effort. Aides race to the left wing to order General von Kalkstein forward. Drummers beat commands, trumpets blow, battalions unfurl banners, gunners fire what cannon are left, tired men breathe deeply, an army moves forward.

An Austrian officer watches. He later wrote, "I have never seen anything so superb; they marched with the greatest composure, straight as a die, as if on parade; their weapons glittering in the sun produced the most splendid effect, and their fire was a steady peal of thunder."[7]

But the enemy is not yet beaten. Austrian cavalry check Kalkstein's advance. They are driven off, and Zieten's hussars pursue while Rothenburg's dragoons push against enemy infantry. A final enemy attack on the Prussian right is splintered by Prince Leopold's second line. When enemy horse cut behind him, he turns his third rank, and bayonets and musket fire break the attack. Neipperg — hat and jacket pierced by bullets, one horse shot from under him, two more wounded — tired Neipperg sees the Prussians advancing, does what he should have done earlier: he orders Göldy's infantry forward, brings cavalry from right to left. But the battalions refuse to budge. Göldy falls — soon to die — and the advance falters.

The Prussian left continues forward. The enemy watches in horrified fascination. "They advanced step by step in amazing formation," an Austrian officer later wrote. "Their artillery fired ball and canister without interruption, and once they were in range their musket fire never stopped a moment."[8]

It is about six P.M.

Neipperg loses control. Römer's cavalry are long since gone from the field. Berlichingen's cavalry on the right are exhausted; in fury, the general attacks his own troopers who are leaving the field, but this does no good. In the center, the infantry refuses to advance. Men shuffle sideways like cattle seeking shelter from a storm. Men fire aimlessly. Lines turn to columns thirty to forty men deep. Gaps wide enough to accommodate a regiment of horse open in the line. Neipperg is looking at defeat in detail. He orders a general retreat south on Grottkau. Prussian hussars follow for two miles, but it is dark now, the Prussians are tired, leery of lurking enemy hussars. Schwerin calls off the pursuit. The main job is done.*

It is about seven-fifteen P.M.

The battle is won.

Frederick leaves the battlefield with a small escort, stops at the baggage dump to pick up the money chest and important papers. He sends an aide with a report of events to Old Dessauer — the battle is lost, he warns; Dessauer must act accordingly. The party rides fifteen miles to Löwen, rests briefly, crosses the Neisse at twilight, continues on to Oppeln, eighteen miles east. It is dark when they reach the town gates. A summons to open is greeted with fire from an enemy sentry. Barányay's irregulars are occupying Oppeln. Frederick's flight across the Oder River is blocked. Only one option remains. He turns back to Löwen. What will he find? A beaten army, Austrians, captivity?

The party follows the king. Hussars capture some members of it, including the mathematician Maupertuis. The king reaches the outskirts of Löwen in early morning to learn of the victory. He has ridden nearly seventy miles. He returns to the battlefield.

The battlefield is not pretty. Enormous fires are already consuming carcasses of once splendid cavalry mounts; troops are gorging on the welcome meat. Harnesses, reins, stirrups, saddles, many of them bloodstained, lie in careless heaps. Burial parties of soldiers and peas-

---

* The fourteen Prussian squadrons from Ohlau arrived toward the end of the battle. Schwerin wanted to send them after the retreating enemy, but Prince Leopold objected so vigorously — presumably because of the disorganized state of the army and especially the cavalry — that Schwerin put the decision to Colonel Count Hans Christoph Friedrich von Hacke, one of Frederick's adjutant aides. Hacke sided with Leopold, and Schwerin backed down, an interesting example of the influence of an adjutant aide at this time. (Orlich, *Geschichte*, Volume 1.)

ants are hacking huge graves from nearly frozen ground. This is the victor's task. He must bury perhaps a thousand of his own, another thousand of the enemy. Bodies are stripped of clothing, shoes, boots, and accouterment before the rude interment. Few records are kept, most names forgotten.

Then there are the wounded. Neipperg has taken the walking wounded with him, but several thousand Austrians and several thousand Prussians remain. They are the charge of the provos, who must clean the battlefield. They kill the hopelessly wounded, strip them of clothes, boots, weapons, toss them into graves. The rest go to field hospitals for treatment by exhausted surgeons, who have been awash in blood the night through. For four days the wounded are treated and evacuated, some going to Ohlau, where churches are serving as hospitals, some by boat to larger towns. Six hundred seriously wounded enemy are sent to villages near Brieg, whose commandant is charged to look after them; others are treated locally; those who can travel are sent to Breslau.

Treatment is rudimentary. Burly orderlies hold men down and dose them with brandy and opium, or "Chinese pills"; surgeons saw off splintered limbs, sew arteries and veins, cauterize the mess. Skulls are trepanned, in some cases cut away. Surgeons use long primitive probes to locate musketballs and pieces of shrapnel; cuts are sewn together; the wounds are dressed with lint cloth covered with generally useless ointments, in the tradition of the famous sixteenth-century military surgeon Ambroise Paré. The patient is bled of twelve to fifteen ounces of blood *before* treatment; if he survives, he is bled again and again. More often than not a seriously wounded man does not survive. Gangrene, putrid fever, lockjaw, and dysentery are the usual killers. There is no relief from these except death.

32

WHILE TE DEUMS were sung in the Prussian camp, Frederick sent couriers racing to friends and foreign courts with news of the victory. "We have totally beaten the Austrians," he wrote Wilhelmina two days after battle. "They have lost more than five thousand men, as many dead as wounded and prisoners. We have lost Prince Frederick . . . General Schulenburg . . . and plenty of other officers. Our troops performed miracles." In sending Podewils an exact report to be printed and distributed to all courts, he proudly wrote of the four-hour "spirited battle" and the Austrian flight, "notwithstanding that this army

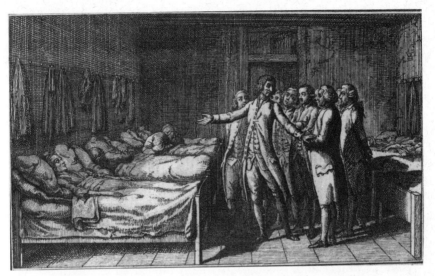

More often than not, a seriously wounded soldier does not survive. Gangrene, putrid fever, lockjaw, and dysentery are the usual killers. There is no relief from these except death.

Working parties of peasants and Prussian soldiers dig communal graves. "Few records are kept, most names forgotten."

was at least 6000 men stronger and had almost three times as much cavalry."

But as Frederick tabulated the price of victory, jubilation turned to remorse, then reflection. He later admitted to a loss of twenty-five hundred dead and three thousand missing and wounded of his own troops. A week after battle he told his brother William that "we have beaten the enemy, but everyone mourns, the one for a brother, the other for a friend; in short, we are the most distressed victors that you can imagine. God preserve us from such another bloody and murderous affair."

Frederick was not sure who had made the most mistakes, he later wrote, he or Neipperg. Neipperg had hit on an excellent operations plan but had not carried it out very well. He could easily have ended the war by attacking the Prussians at Jägerndorf. Instead, he had allowed himself to be surprised at Mollwitz — the fault of his hussars — and was thereby beaten.

On the other hand, Frederick, wrongly influenced by Schwerin, had made the first and cardinal error of dispersing forces instead of concentrating them at Neisse and maintaining communication with General Holstein-Beck at Frankenstein. As a result he had had to fight a battle from which there would have been no retreat in case of defeat. He had erred again at Mollwitz by wasting time in prematurely deploying the army instead of marching directly on separated Austrian cantonments, which would have yielded an immense victory, comparable with that of Blenheim. It was his own fault. Lacking experience and skill, he had been overcautious. He should have allowed Rothenburg more freedom; then he could have attacked and probably dispersed Römer's cavalry before they formed. His officers, he wrote, needed more and better training. They were too involved with petty details, with parade ground formalities; they were too cautious in the advance. Schwerin alone was an experienced and capable tactician. Holstein-Beck was lacking imagination and was so unaggressive that the day after battle he had allowed the beaten Austrians to slink by his position without attacking their exposed flank. (He was nonetheless soon promoted to field marshal.) "The grace of God and the bravery of my infantry" alone had saved the day, the king wrote to Podewils; the battalions "stood like walls and fought like lions."

The cavalry were something else again, "not worth sending to the devil," as Frederick wrote to Old Dessauer. He did except one meritorious action on the left, but in general he was disgusted with their performance. Nor was he satisfied with the mobility of the artillery, whose rate of fire, in any case, was too slow for his liking.

All these shortcomings must be corrected. "Mollwitz was the school of the king and his army," Frederick later wrote, and it is to his credit that he, unlike other European rulers, immediately set about making the needed changes.[1]

It is not to his credit that he failed to recognize other obvious shortcomings. It is perhaps understandable but still regrettable that he never publicly mentioned his own flight from the battlefield, never openly attempted to explain it or justify it or condemn it. He had not made proper preparations for a campaign in difficult country nor had he obtained available maps, but he probably did not have time to secure them and saw no real necessity for them, in view of enemy weakness. And he did not prepare adequately for siege warfare, a failure that would affect future campaigns. He failed to recognize either the advantages in or dangers from irregular warfare and because of tactical blindness very nearly lost a kingdom before fighting a battle. Together these failures spelled a dangerous disregard of enemy strength, and that is a major violation of the rules of warfare, particularly when the violator is by nature an aggressive and impulsive commander.

Field Marshal Neipperg fell back to an almost unassailable position by fortress Neisse. He had nothing to celebrate and much to regret. He placed his own losses at about eight hundred dead and thirty-eight hundred wounded, missing and prisoner, with some seventeen hundred horses killed. Although he insisted that the Prussians had suffered far higher casualties, he had to admit that those Prussians had beaten him, and he had to explain why.

Neipperg chose to blame a dead man — not the first or last time such an expedient has proven convenient to a man in trouble. His generals and staff officers supported him, not surprisingly, seeing that it was also their defeat. Berlichingen, Browne, and Lentulus each read and approved the special "Relation" submitted to Grand Duke Francis. The primary cause of defeat, Neipperg explained, was General Römer's "unfortunate, unexpected, and precipitate" opening attack, made "without my orders," on the Prussian right wing. The secondary cause was untrained infantry, which refused to advance at the critical moment.* (He passed over his own and other staff and command failures almost without comment, nor did he explain what Römer was supposed to have done when cannonballs smashed through his squadrons while Prussian infantry advanced toward Göldy's vulnerable flank.) If the war were to continue, he advised, the court would have to recruit a professional foreign army of twelve to fifteen thousand troops,

* The Austrian historian A. Arneth wrote that the majority of Neipperg's troops had served in the recent war against Turkey and thus were "well-tested and reliable." (Arneth, *Geschichte*, Volume 1.) He also noted that the defeat demoralized Austrian troops and that even some generals refused to serve under Neipperg in the future. (Volume 2.)

"through whose good example our own troops perhaps could be put right." The court should either make peace or ally with a great power imbued with offensive spirit.[2]

The queen wrote comfortingly that she did not blame Neipperg in the slightest; indeed, his preparations had been "zealous, wise, and careful."[3] Obviously the Prussians had been badly hurt, to judge from the number of deserters and their failure to follow Neipperg's retreat. Even his rival within the Austrian military command, Field Marshal Count Ludwig Andreas von Khevenhüller, replied that this was what had to be expected from a winter campaign undertaken by a weak and untrained army. If the Prussians had been able to maneuver, he added maliciously but accurately, "you would have been completely annihilated." He advised Neipperg to retire into Bohemia, where he could keep an eye on Bavaria and also join the Saxons if they allied with Austria. The task now was to build a new army. Since the infantry could not be depended on, "we must make small [guerrilla] warfare and not presume to win battles."[4]

Neipperg had already decided on this course of action. A few days after the battle he ordered General Barányay to strike up the left bank of the Neisse with a hussary-cavalry force some thirteen hundred strong; his mission was to attack Prussian outposts and convoys and cut communications.

The blood had scarcely dried on the Mollwitz field when Frederick turned to the siege of fortress Brieg. "Our affairs go well, and I believe that in a few days we shall be masters of Brieg," he wrote to Jordan. Brieg was still under siege when he moved the bulk of the army to a camp north of Mollwitz for training. But now detachments of Barányay's corps appeared at Mollwitz and along the Ohlau-Breslau road, even at the gates of Breslau and Brieg. Frederick responded by setting up outposts along the roads and tying them together with infantry and cavalry patrols, usually of 120 men under a captain. After surrounding the new camp with outposts backed by fortifications, he set about training infantry, cavalry, and artillery along tactical lines worked out in lengthy correspondence with Old Dessauer.

Frederick was mainly concerned with reforming his cavalry in the tradition of King Charles XII of Sweden, a master of hard-hitting cavalry tactics. Prussian cavalry had never been much good, a force largely for show, big men riding big horses. This was largely King Frederick William's fault; he and Dessauer had always been more interested in improving the infantry, which earlier in the century was more important than cavalry for siege and defense of fortresses, and also much cheaper — cavalry cost three times as much to keep in the field. As early as 1725 Seckendorff in a report to Vienna wondered whether "the terribly large [Prussian] horses, some of them nineteen hands," could support the infantry in long and tiring campaigns.[5] During the Rhine campaign in 1734, Crown Prince Frederick was struck by the difference between the bulky Prussian horses and the lighter Austrian units. He later wrote that Prussian horses "were the size of elephants and could neither maneuver nor fight. There was not a review but that some cavaliers fell from awkwardness. They were not masters of their mounts, and their officers had no notion of cavalry, no idea of war, no knowledge of terrain, neither theory nor practice of maneuver essential to cavalry in combat."[6] In 1739 the Prussian army of eighty-one thousand had fewer than eighteen thousand horses, or about 22.5 percent of total strength.

The first fault was not human; it was horse. Regimental commanders were now authorized to begin buying smaller, more nimble horses. The second fault was human. Most cavalry officers and hussar officers lacked any real knowledge of their profession; they were "more farmers than officers," Frederick grumbled to Dessauer. Mollwitz had shattered cavalry morale. To mend this serious casualty, to give soul to tired, dispirited men, the king started a training program from bottom up. His formula was simple and effective, valid today: discipline plus drill equals soul equals pride equals confidence equals excellence. Men and horses were trained singly, then in small groups. Once self-confidence and spirit began to return, they worked in sections. Frederick's training hallmark was swiftness and mobility, tactical adroitness that could produce shock power. A month after the battle, cavalry majors were reporting to the king's tent at seven A.M. for personal instructions. Units remained on semi-alert; on the king's order, they could saddle up and move out in fifteen minutes. Hussar training was in the hands of fiery Major von Zieten, who had trained under Count Barányay.

To gain a more offensive spirit the cavalry henceforth was to depend on the *arme blanche;* as a rule only the sword would be used in the attack, with the carbine reserved for defense against enemy hussar and irregular attacks. In discussing the merit of firearm or sword, the king told one general, "Kill your enemy with the one or the other; I will never bring you to an account with which you did it."[7] In the attack the traditional "evolutions" would be replaced by a few preliminary movements; then the squadrons would move out at a trot until they were a hundred paces from enemy lines, when they would break into a gallop. How best to employ them? Frederick leaned toward mass deployment on the army's wing, the embryo of a concept that he would bring to powerful maturity in time.

Artillery posed another problem, one more mechanical than human. At Mollwitz a large number of cannon had been lost because the guns were deployed too far in front of the infantry. Henceforth gunners would unlimber only fifty paces ahead of the first line and would open fire at a thousand paces. When Dessauer pointed out that this did not solve the problem of coordinated fire, Frederick suggested that a few 12-pounders be put on the wings to serve as assault artillery. He also wanted battalions to have their own 3-pounders. He was not pleased with the artillery performance at the siege of Brieg. Siege batteries had not been built quickly enough; the guns had fired too high. Field and siege artillery would continue to bother him; he never would be fully satisfied with this arm.

The cause was partly the state of the art. Cast-bronze guns were heavy and awkward, aiming devices primitive, powder generally of poor quality and powder loads consequently unreliable, projectiles often badly cast. These defects would be overcome only by technological advances. But it was in part the king's fault, one he had in common with other sovereigns. Artillerymen and engineers were not traditionally of the nobility and thus were second-class officers. By not making artillery a proper branch of the service, he failed to provide an encouraging environment where these defects in time might have been overcome.

He did substantially increase the artillery by adding a second battalion of field artillery. Further changes and increases would be made under the chief of the artillery, the recently promoted Lieutenant General Christian von Linger. A major change would soon be made in the 3-pounder, which would be cast with a conical chamber to make it lighter. This was the invention of Captain Johann Holtzmann, who also designed a new limber built to carry a hundred rounds exclusive of munition wagons.

Frederick made no radical changes in infantry training, which continued to concentrate on rapidity of fire and march and fire discipline. Mollwitz convinced him that the musketeer's allotment of thirty cartridges must be doubled, the additional cartridges to be carried in company wagons and distributed just before deployment.

Impatient as always, Frederick longed to bolster diplomacy by the sword. Two days after Mollwitz he was suggesting to Dessauer the possibility of a preventive war against Saxony. Shortly after Brieg surrendered, he wrote to the prince that he was considering a push into Glatz. Dessauer did not like the idea. The operation, he replied, would encounter numerous obstacles, both because of supply difficulties, and because "mountain warfare must be fought quite differently from war in the plains."[8] He advised Frederick instead to establish magazines at Brieg and cross the Neisse there or at Löwen, which should force Neipperg to withdraw to Zuckmantel and even into Moravia, thus leaving Frederick free to besiege fortress Neisse. The king agreed but then discovered that Neipperg was too strongly entrenched for this move, though in an attempt to bring him to battle and also to ease supply problems, he moved camps, first to nearby Grottkau and then to Strehlen.

Neipperg meanwhile was slowly being reinforced. His orders were to remain on the defensive until British, Russian, and Saxon armies marched to Austria's aid. Until then he would continue to fight a "small war." Newly arrived units were sent to join those operating along the Ohlau-Breslau road, and some were sent to the right bank of the Oder to interdict the road from Poland to Breslau. The fresh units were commanded by names soon to become famous to some, infamous to others: General Count Franz von Nádasdy, General Count Sandor Károlyi, Major Baron Franz von der Trenck, General Baron Joseph von Festetics, Colonel Count Adam Dessewffy, Major Friedrich Wilhelm von Menzel, and a score of other hard-riding commanders whose small parties raised a dozen kinds of hell with the Prussian enemy. "Bandits," Frederick contemptuously called them, and in part Neipperg agreed. He had already issued sharp warnings to the free-booting armed peasants of Wallachia, who happily plundered and killed their own people, particularly Protestants, and now he came to grips with von Trenck and his pandour corps of some thousand savages. Trenck, "a man of the extreme," as a biographer termed him,[9] was bold, greedy, foolhardy, but tactically shrewd. A daring raid on Schweidnitz failed not because of Prussian countermeasures but because of the revolting behavior of his pandours against the civil population. Such were the excesses that Neipperg relieved him of command and, when he refused to go, arrested him and sent him to Vienna for trial. Major Menzel took over and the small war continued through summer and autumn, as first one side and then the other scored small but often bloody tactical victories. In early July, Dickens's replacement as British envoy, John Carmichael, the Earl of Hyndford, reported from Breslau that

> the Austrian Hussars are daily hovering about this Town to pillage the provisions and Baggage Wagons, which go between this Place and the Camp, and make it very unsafe for any body to stir abroad, so that people are little better than Prisoners at large. This morning the Hussars have carried off 500 head of cattle . . . 300 of which belonged to the King and 200 to Breslau.

A week later he wrote:

> The Imperial Hussars, and particularly the Croats and Warasdiners, have committed such outrages and cruelties in some parts of the upper Silesia towards Bohemia and Moravia that they have revolted the minds of the people and even those that are Catholicks, to such a degree, that they give the Prussians immediate notice whenever they appear in the Country.[10]

The main advantage of the small war to the Prussians was the training provided to hussar and cavalry units. In late July the French envoy, the Marquis de Valory, wrote to Cardinal Fleury of his astonishment at the improvement in these units. Lord Hyndford attended one review in which men and horses "appeared very well" and were observed by Austrian hussars from a distance. A month later Frederick informed Dessauer that "my cavalry is now complete and in the condition that I expect it to be."

33

VICTORY AT MOLLWITZ made Frederick the most sought-after monarch in Europe, and foreign envoys from Berlin were soon pouring into Breslau. But the diplomats scarcely solved Frederick's political dilemma. Military stalemate spelled political stalemate, with a great danger of isolation. There were three ways to put matters right. One was to win total military victory in Silesia, impossible at the moment, because Neipperg occupied a virtually unassailable position by Neisse. Another was to forge an alliance with France, with all the potential pitfalls that entailed. A third was to reach a compromise settlement with the Austrian court, which England now as earlier offered her good offices to achieve.

France was still crucial. Valory had been pressing for a treaty, and Frederick guardedly agreed but did not rush matters. He was aware of the danger to Prussia from radical change in Europe's balance of power, especially if France gained ascendancy at Austrian expense. Today's ally could prove tomorrow's enemy, a truism hammered home by Podewils, who again played devil's advocate in lengthy correspondence with his master. Open alliance with France, he argued, would represent an abrupt departure from Prussia's traditional relationship with Austria and the German princes. Though on occasion this had been strained and broken, it invariably healed. Far better, Podewils concluded — and Frederick agreed in part — if Prussia could reach a satisfactory understanding with the Vienna court.

They were still arguing the issue of alliance when King George told Parliament that England was bound by treaty to aid Austria in her war against Prussia. Parliament voted what he wanted, including a £300,000 subsidy to Maria Theresa and another £200,000 to subsidize auxiliary troops for Hanover's protection.

Field Marshal Charles Louis de Belle-Isle reached Silesia in late April. The gaunt French nobleman arrived in Breslau with his usual regal entourage, only to be kept cooling his heels, the unwilling victim of royal oneupmanship. When finally given an audience in headquarters at Ohlau, he again argued for Prussia to join what would become the League of Nymphenburg. France would guarantee his conquest of Silesia in return for alliance; French, Bavarian, Prussian, and, it was hoped, Saxon armies would defeat Austria, partition the Habsburg empire, and make the Elector of Bavaria the new Holy Roman Emperor.

Frederick was tempted, but only if France would take an operational role. Pointing to the coalition rapidly forming against him — Austria, England and Hanover, Saxony, Holland, and Russia — he wanted Belle-Isle's promise of concerted military action: first, against Austria by France and Bavaria (and by Sardinia, Spain, and the Kingdom of the Two Sicilies against Austrian forces in Italy), second, against Russia by France and Sweden. Then he would sign a formal treaty. Desultory action, he emphasized, could easily open him to attack from three sides and bring about his defeat. Russia already was mobilizing; he showed Belle-Isle a recent alarming report from his envoy Mardefeld in Saint Petersburg. In view of Prussia's extensive and open frontiers, this was an inevitable fear, and Belle-Isle apparently accepted its validity.

The two hit it off well and soon became good friends. Frederick found Belle-Isle "charming beyond imagination," and Belle-Isle was full of admiration for Frederick's army and campaign plans. He was struck by the simplicity of the camp, by the plain uniforms of the king and his generals, who wore jackets so short that they might have been vests. Although champagne was served at dinner, it accompanied only three courses — boiled meat, roast meat, and vegetables — served to a table of twelve in the sleeping area of the king's tent.

Frederick's attention to detail amazed the Frenchman. He rose at four A.M., mounted, and inspected every post and outpost of the camp, concerning himself with details that in the French army were left to mere quartermasters. He personally issued all orders, read all reports. Belle-Isle watched him interrogate deserters and spies, even a couple of prisoners. He personally drilled a battalion for his guest's benefit.

> The weather was terrible [Belle-Isle reported to the French minister Jean Jacques Amelot de Chaillou] and snow fell in thick flakes, which however did not prevent the battalion from drilling as if it had been the most beautiful weather. Aside from the magnificent appearance of this unit, which is extraordinarily well trained, it marched and carried out its movement with indescribable precision. But what distinguished it the most is the rate of fire . . . carried out by sections and divisions in every possible way, but always with the same confidence despite the snowfall; they fired *en détail* up to twelve rounds a minute,* and at least six rounds

* Later commentators have unfortunately translated *en détail* as "individually," which is patently impossible, since a veteran rifleman would have been taxed to fire three rounds a minute. Belle-Isle undoubtedly meant *Hackenfeuer*, or salvos by divisions. (Generalstab, *Kriegsgeschichtliche Einzelschriften*, Numbers 28–30.)

a minute in section and division fire, which seems unbelievable if one has not seen it.[1]

They spoke a similarly aggressive language, but each from the point of his own interests. Frederick found the field marshal obsessed with the partition of the Habsburg empire, as if all of Maria Theresa's provinces "were up for auction." Noting the envoy's preoccupation one day, he asked if anything was wrong. "Nothing, sire, except that I just don't know what to do with Moravia." "Give it to Saxony," Frederick replied, "and then the King of Poland [Elector of Saxony] will join our alliance."[2]

Belle-Isle left Breslau the day that Lord Hyndford, the British envoy, arrived. A Scot with no diplomatic experience but with a distinguished parliamentary career — "honest, candid, and sound," Ranke called him — Hyndford was to drive home the importance of Prussia's coming to terms with Vienna to end "a war, which, if continued, must in its consequences, inevitably destroy the Liberties of the Empire, the Protestant religion, and the Balance of Power in Europe."[3]

After some delay Hyndford was taken to Frederick's camp outside Brieg. His reception was frosty. It was plain from King George's recent speech to Parliament, not to mention the anti-Prussian diplomacy being practiced by British envoys in Dresden, the Hague, and Saint Petersburg, Frederick told him, that England was supporting Austria, so there was nothing to discuss. Hyndford patiently countered the accusations. King George's speech was directed against France and her allies, not Prussia. England sincerely wanted to arrange an accommodation between Prussia and Austria. In the end Frederick grudgingly agreed that Hyndford should open negotiations with the Vienna court through the British ambassador there, Sir Thomas Robinson. Frederick had considerably warmed to Hyndford during the audience and asked him to dine. In this and further meetings, Hyndford did not attempt to gloss over patent difficulties. Frederick's insistence on Lower Silesia and Breslau, he told Podewils, was unacceptable to Vienna, which regarded this area as the truly valuable part of Silesia. Hyndford urged Frederick to scale down his demands. He refused, but did agree to negotiate further along lines already presented to the Vienna court by Count Gotter; he also raised his cash offer to three million thalers and agreed to an armistice if it was for a minimum six months.

Hyndford sent the terms to Vienna, confident that agreement would result, that Frederick would lower his territorial demands, that Maria Theresa would happily end the war.

His Lordship had reckoned without a queen's fury fired by political ignorance. Maria Theresa was not to be placated. Frederick had no right to steal one of her richest provinces. Moreover, her father had signed a treaty with France that she believed Cardinal Fleury would respect. She also believed that she could buy off the Bavarian elector's pretensions to the Imperial crown with some territory in the Spanish Netherlands. Fears of renewed Turkish aggression were allayed by the Porte's ratification of the Treaty of Belgrade. Finally, she had been invited to Pressburg to be crowned Queen of Hungary, which could mean additional military aid from the all-powerful Hungarian nobility.

Maria Theresa accordingly received Lord Hyndford's mediatory proposals with disdain. In late May, Robinson informed Hyndford that Maria Theresa would consider a "just and reasonable" treaty with the King of Prussia but refused Prussian claims to Silesia (although she would probably cede the duchy of Glogau). She insisted on the validity of the Pragmatic Sanction and "would make no proposals, but would await them."[4]

This was scarcely the stuff of concession, and when she also turned down the English proposal for a truce, Hyndford's mission had failed — at least for the time being.

Before Maria Theresa's rebuff, Valory had reported that France was attempting to persuade Sweden to renew war with Russia, which she would probably do in return for an alliance with Prussia. The Versailles court stood ready to subsidize a Swedish force of twenty thousand. It was already paying for a Bavarian army that would be ready to march on Austria in July, an effort to be supported by two French armies. The news excited Frederick. Convinced of British duplicity, insulted by Austrian intransigence, he was turning increasingly toward France. "Valory is right," he wrote to Podewils. "There now, my friend, there now, how much longer shall we wait in order to become the dupes of London and Vienna?"

When Podewils still cautioned against rushing into the arms of the French, Frederick scornfully replied, "You believe what you wish but without examining facts, and you would convince yourself that a mistress who is a whore is faithful to you." England was "playing" with Prussia to keep her isolated and thus avoid general European war. The time had come for action: "If we have allies, we will be respected; if we have none, we will be laughed at." Podewils and Valory were to draw up a treaty in greatest secrecy. Podewils was to give Hyndford the impression that an arrangement with Vienna could still be made. "Deceive the deceivers!" the king thundered.

As with most treaties of that day, that of Breslau consisted of two parts, one whose general content was made known to other courts, another, usually the more important, that theoretically would remain secret. The first part called for a fifteen-year defensive alliance; each party would guarantee the other's European possessions and promise military aid in case of attack by another power. The secret portion was more complex. Should Frederick succeed in retaining Lower Silesia and Breslau, he would yield forever his claim to Juliers and Berg, which would revert to the Elector Palatine (and thus remain under French influence). He would also vote for the Elector of Bavaria, Charles Albert, when it came to electing a new Holy Roman Emperor. In return, King Louis would guarantee Frederick's claim to Silesia, foment war between Sweden and Russia, and also send troops to the Elector of Bavaria "to put him in condition to act with vigor" against Austria. The Versailles court not only would subsidize a Bavarian army but if necessary it would support Charles Albert with a strong French army.

Podewils and Valory signed the document in early June. "I argue now, Monsieur le Cardinal, whether you are a better Frenchman than I," Frederick jubilantly wrote to Fleury. And to Belle-Isle: "I am counting on seeing in two months from now your standards deployed on the hithermost banks of the Rhine."

The king's euphoria did not last very long. Within a week he was pushing his new ally for action. "Don't forget the promises you have made me," he reminded Belle-Isle. "I await their accomplishment with all ardor and impatience." By mid-June he was protesting to Valory that Sweden was not yet acting against Russia:

> I declare to you then that the whole of your treaty is void if Sweden does not act for France and if the Bavarian elector does not act and if Belle-Isle does not enter Germany to act this autumn in Bohemia and Austria. Do not believe that I am allied to the king your master on any other conditions, and do not count any longer on me if you do not fulfill your engagements, as I am resolved religiously to fulfill mine. Tell this to the Cardinal [Fleury] and to Monsieur de Belle-Isle, for if France thinks it can deceive me France is mistaken.

Maria Theresa's fortunes were meanwhile improving. By late June she had made a secret treaty with England that called for combined operations against Prussia, and she had formally requested support of the Saxon and Russian courts. Hanover and England and Holland had demanded that Frederick evacuate Silesia. She was reinforcing Neipperg's army and wanted him to cross the Neisse and advance northwest, either to fight the Prussians if opportunity occurred or move on Schweidnitz in an effort to capture its important magazines. Neipperg was not too optimistic; he wrote to Grand Duke Francis that if his march prospered, he could think of retaking fortresses Brieg and Glogau, but that if he were beaten in battle, he could not guarantee to hold Neisse and cover Bohemia and Moravia. In view of these "ticklish circumstances," he requested "a clear and firm answer."[5] He was advised that much depended on the hoped-for march of the Saxons and Hanoverians; in any event, Francis wrote, he should think more in terms of "a small movement" that would impress everyone with Austria's offensive intentions and would cause more Prussians to desert. Maria Theresa, however, urged positive forward action.

She and Francis meanwhile had traveled to Pressburg, where she was crowned Queen of Hungary. Her address in Latin to the Diet was well received, and the coronation went smoothly enough.

Sharp reverses followed. The young queen was still in Pressburg when she learned that France and Prussia had signed a treaty. The ministers "fell back in their chairs like dead men," Robinson reported.[6] The queen refused to believe French duplicity, but when Cardinal Fleury admitted that a new coalition did exist, panic swept the Vienna court. Neipperg was still shadow-boxing with Frederick in Silesia. Western borders were weakly defended. The rest of the army was in Italy. Nothing could be expected from Hungary for some time. Nor could anything now come from England. Admiral Edward Vernon's naval disaster at Cartagena had shocked king and country, and "fear was suffocating the court," one diplomat reported. Continental allies — Hanover, Saxony, Denmark, and Hesse — suddenly cooled. King George, fearing for Hanover's safety, was again pressing the Vienna court to make peace with Prussia.

Preservation of the balance of European power now became more important to the Habsburgs than the destruction of Prussia. Maria Theresa reluctantly agreed to offer Frederick two small provinces in the Netherlands plus two million thalers if he would evacuate Silesia and make peace. When Ambassador Robinson told her he doubted that the Prussian king would accept, she angrily replied, "I wish he would reject it."[7]

She needn't have worried. By the time Robinson reached Prussian headquarters, Elector Charles Albert of Bavaria had managed to field an army of twenty thousand and had seized Passau. France was actively equipping her armies. Frederick once again was writing friendly letters to Valory, Fleury, and Belle-Isle, the last having been made commander-in-chief of French armies in Germany. "I have given orders to my ministers at Frankfort and to my generals to act completely in accordance with Monsieur de Belle-Isle's wishes," Frederick informed Valory at the end of July.

Frederick had already treated Lord Hyndford's overtures with disdain and now in early August he rudely spurned Robinson's opening offer of a cash settlement to leave Silesia. The envoy upped the ante, first with one, then both of the Netherlands provinces. "Beggarly offers," Frederick sniffed before pointing out that the queen could not legally give away these lands, which were guaranteed by the Barrier Treaty of 1713. If she wanted peace, he said, she must give him what

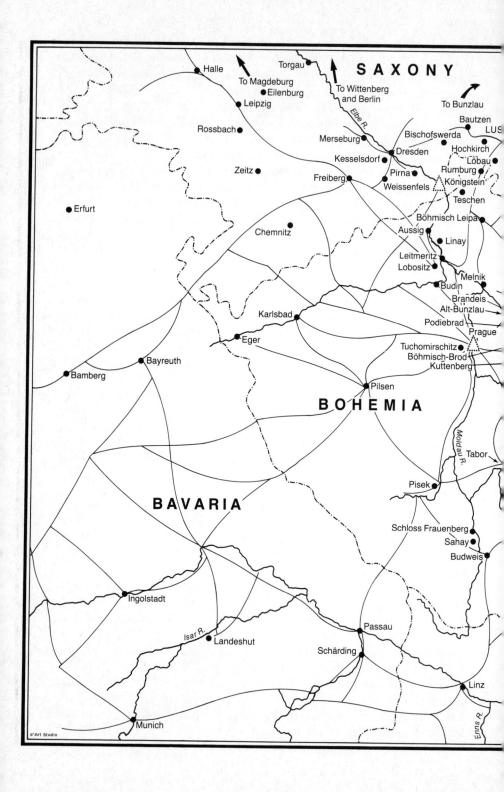

he desired. Robinson heatedly pointed out that to preserve the balance
of power, a coalition of England, Russia, Saxony, and Austria might
be necessary. "No threats, sir!" the king warned. "If you please, no
threats!"[8] Prussia had the means to handle Russia and the King of
Poland. As for the King of England, "if he does not attack me, I shall
not attack him, and if he attacks me, then the Prince of Anhalt [Old
Dessauer] will treat with him." Frederick replied to Robinson's and
Hyndford's further entreaties by stating that he would retain Silesia
come what may. With that, he abruptly broke off the audience.

The dispirited ambassadors returned to Breslau in time to witness
the sudden military occupation of the Silesian capital. This was Frederick's punishment for the treacherous behavior of Catholic nobility
and clergy, and also a precaution in case Neipperg intended to march
on the place. A few days later, Robinson left for Pressburg, his mission
a failure.

34

THE WAR expanded.

In early August Sweden declared war on Russia. In mid-August, Field
Marshal Count François Marie de Broglie led a large French force,
thirty-two thousand foot and ten thousand horse, across the Rhine. At
Donauwörth he joined the Bavarian army in which the French would
ostensibly serve as auxiliaries under Elector Charles Albert's supreme
command. A second French army, commanded by the Marquis Jean
Baptiste François Maillebois, marched on Meuse, occupied Liège and
Dinant, and camped opposite Düsseldorf, where it was joined by small
auxiliary forces belonging to the Electors of Cologne and the Palatinate, each of whom received French subsidies. This was a shielding action to prevent interference from England and Holland and also to
pave the way for possible later incursions into the Spanish Netherlands
and Hanover. The Elector of Saxony (King of Poland) apparently intended to join the anti-Austrian coalition in return for Moravia and
Upper Silesia once victory resulted, and to send an army to strengthen
the Bavarian-French effort against Austria.

By early September one Bavarian-French force was in camp at
Schärding, from where, as Frederick had proposed, it would march on
Linz and down the Danube Valley to Vienna. A second French force
was assembling in the Upper Palatinate, from where it would march
into Bohemia to cut off General Prince Christian Lobkowitz's small
corps.

These preparations greatly excited Frederick, who had for some time seen a chance to end the war quickly and favorably. Two months earlier he had urged Elector Charles Albert to strike while the enemy was weak: "To make a master stroke [you] must take Passau, Linz, and then, hugging the Danube, march straight on Vienna." In late July he sent his newly recruited Master General of Artillery, Baron Samuel von Schmettau, formerly a field marshal in the Austrian service, to Munich as personal military representative. Schmettau was to persuade Charles Albert to march immediately; the French contingent could catch him up by water. Schmettau was also to steer Charles away from useless — indeed, dangerous — operations in Bohemia. Instead, Charles was to invade Austria, "march on Vienna," and put a quick end to the war. Schmettau soon reported that the elector was in complete agreement with Frederick's thinking but that his army was not ready to march.

Prompt allied action was vital if Frederick was to enjoy military success in Silesia. Neipperg had marched in late July, a leisurely nine-day effort that brought him to the Neisse, some fourteen miles from the Prussians. In due course he crossed the river, camped at Baumgarten, and in mid-August marched northwest toward Reichenbach.

Frederick's intelligence was worse than ever, the result of difficult terrain, poor weather, and the usual swarms of light troops that screened the main army. He at first believed that Neipperg was only changing camps, perhaps in order to send cavalry units to Bohemia, but then he learned that General Festetics was marching northwest toward Schweidnitz with a large force of light troops. To counter this threat, he marched on Reichenbach, a move that forced Neipperg to turn around and camp in the Frankenstein area.

Although Frederick was pleased with the new camp, his position was not a good one. Enemy irregulars were keeping him tactically blind. They prowled everywhere, striking convoys, attacking patrols and outposts. Supply was difficult, morale low, desertions were increasing. He wanted desperately to attack, but Cardinal Fleury pointed out that once the Franco-Bavarian army entered Bohemia, Neipperg would be forced to leave Silesia; it would be better to avoid the risk of losing a major battle and instead follow the enemy into Moravia.

The Prussian king now decided on a new plan. He would make a surprise march southeast to Neisse, cross at Ottmachau and Woitz, and put his army between the fortress and Neipperg's army. If Neipperg chose to attack, fine; if he withdrew, then Frederick could besiege the fortress that he desperately needed for the winter. A few days later he notified Podewils of his intentions, adding that the House of Austria was on the verge of destruction — "We will shortly hear the lamentations of Jeremiah."

It was not to be. Neipperg's light troops erased any hope of surprise. Their stinging attacks, coupled with rain and fog, slowed and even

halted the march. "You could scarcely see three paces ahead," Prince
Dietrich of Anhalt-Dessau noted in his diary.[1] Kalkstein, who commanded the vanguard, had to stop frequently to clear passes of hussars.
In the darkness he got lost and marched in circles. By the time he reached
the Neisse River, the main army had arrived, only to find Neipperg,
who for once marched rapidly, occupying the opposite heights. In camp
at Woitz, Frederick impatiently awaited arrival of his artillery and baggage train, a ponderous convoy of two thousand wagons that had been
constantly harassed by irregulars, who on one occasion had to be beaten
off by bayonet attack.

There would be no decisive battle now, a failure the king blamed on
Kalkstein. Instead, he moved to a new position closer to Neisse. Neipperg set up camp not far distant. The two armies were "like two furious lions," Frederick wrote to Jordan, "lying tranquilly each in their
lair."

The appearance of French and Bavarian armies had brought near panic
in the Vienna court. Even Minister Bartenstein, who had repeatedly
assured Maria Theresa that the King of France would never take arms
against Austria, now argued for a new alliance with England and Prussia. But, although neither the queen nor her ministers were yet willing
to meet Frederick's demands, the king did not burn all his bridges to
the Vienna court. Lord Hyndford, still in Breslau, made no bones about
England's fears for the safety of Hanover, not to mention the destruction of Austria. Nor was Maria Theresa's apparent desire for peace to
be lightly dismissed, in view of Frederick's somewhat precarious tactical situation and his suspicion of allied intentions. Hyndford proposed
in great secrecy to General von der Marwitz, now the governor of Breslau, that Frederick be given Lower Silesia, including Breslau, for withdrawing from the war.

Frederick was quietly interested. It would not hurt to let the Vienna
court know that he was still willing to deal, albeit on his terms. These
were Byzantine in the extreme and they well illustrate his love of the
bizarre. A trusted aide, Colonel Baron Georg Konrad von der Goltz,
explained them to Hyndford. In return for all of Lower Silesia and the
city-fortresses of Neisse and Glatz, the Prussians would conduct a mock
siege of Neisse, whose garrison would duly "surrender" and be allowed safe conduct to Moravia. Meanwhile Neipperg's army, vital to
the defense of Bohemia and Lower Austria, could safely retire into Moravia — and "all this was to be accomplished in twelve days."

Maria Theresa was not ready to go this far, but she decided to trust
Neipperg and Hyndford with further negotiations. She would give Lower
Silesia to King Frederick if he would fight on Austria's side and vote

for Grand Duke Francis as emperor. Frederick informed Hyndford that he was "to reply to the court of Vienna that the Elector of Bavaria will be emperor, and that my engagements with the Most Christian King [Louis XV] and the Elector of Bavaria are so solemn, so indissoluble, and so inviolable that I will not abandon these loyal allies in order to enter a liaison with a court that can only and forever be irreconciled with me." The letter made such good reading that he sent the Bavarian elector a copy.

On the surface, his loyalty to the alliance seemed wise. He and the Bavarian elector were about to sign a formal treaty of alliance. The Saxons were ready to join the anti-Austrian forces. The Bavarians had finally marched. As Frederick had predicted, they met almost no opposition and were soon in Linz, whose estates readily paid homage. Panic again prevailed in Vienna, where Khevenhüller was frantically trying to repair neglected defenses with the aid of six thousand hastily impressed civilians. Thousands of Viennese had fled the capital, taking what valuables they could; the court had fled, some members to Pressburg, some to Graz. Frederick had already decided to cross the Neisse "and chase the wretched Austrians into Hungary" when a new offer came from Pressburg via the Neipperg-Hyndford-Goltz secret channel. In return for peace, Frederick could have Lower Silesia but not fortress Neisse. He spurned this offer, crossed the river, and in early October had forced Neipperg to withdraw and was wondering whether he could attack the Austrian army without too much loss.

His answer was that he could not, but he based it on more than immediate tactical considerations. Maria Theresa would soon be reinforced by troops from Hungary and Italy. The Swedes had been badly beaten by the Russians at Willmanstrand; perhaps the latter would now send troops to help Austria, perhaps the Saxons would back off from the anti-Austrian alliance. From Linz, General Samuel von Schmettau, Frederick's military adviser to the Bavarian elector, reported allied dilatoriness, which possibly stemmed from secret peace talks with the Vienna court. The elector was caught up in the pomp of homage. Troops were neglected, morale was low, no magazines were established, marches were disorganized and slow, baggage trains delayed, there were hard feelings between French and Bavarian contingents, the Bavarian treasury was empty. Only reluctantly did the army march from Linz to cross the Enns River. Between Krems and Saint Pölten, it halted and began preparing to march into Bohemia.

This was contrary to Frederick's entire strategy, which the elector had enthusiastically endorsed. It came as a shock both to Frederick and Schmettau, but they had reckoned without French influence. France was willing to shatter the Habsburg empire, Schmettau wrote, but not replace it with a strong Bavarian empire. Rather, Versailles wanted to establish a number of secondary European powers, Bavaria and Saxony among them, through which it could control central Germany. It did not want the Bavarian elector to make a triumphal entry into Vienna.

The elector had been adversely influenced by a shrewd French diplomat familiar to Frederick from Berlin days, the Marquis de Beauveau. Following Belle-Isle's orders, Beauveau argued convincingly that if the Saxons were left alone in Bohemia, they would conquer and keep that kingdom. When Schmettau privately forced him to admit the validity of Frederician strategy, he allegedly replied, "But then this man [Elector Charles Albert] would no longer want us, and that would be against our interest."[2]

Elector Charles insisted that he wanted to do as Frederick advised, but that his army was too small to go it alone. France was paying for the Bavarian frolic; Prussia was not. He was indeed worried about Saxon ambitions concerning Bohemia, and instead of marching on Vienna he would push into Bohemia to seize Prague.

Such machinations were precisely what Podewils and other anti-French advisers had warned against. Their words gained further weight when Frederick learned that Marshal Belle-Isle had promised the slippery Saxons the moon and a piece of cheese to come into the war. "Is it necessary then to be the enemy of France to be her most favored?" Frederick plaintively asked Belle-Isle in a letter that strongly defended Bavarian claims to Bohemia over those of Saxony. Then he learned, quite by chance, that neither the Versailles nor the Bavarian court wanted him to have Glatz and Upper Silesia (which he demanded in return for any Saxon territorial gains). He also learned of more secret dealings between Vienna and Versailles, and thought that Fleury would abandon the alliance if the Austrians offered him Luxembourg and a part of the Brabant. Fleury further irritated him by signing a treaty of neutrality with Hanover without using Frederick's good offices, as promised, thus depriving the Prussian king of any credit with Hanover and England.

If Frederick harbored suspicions, real or imagined, justified or not, about his allies, Maria Theresa harbored a deep fear of those allies. If Bavaria and France refused her offers, a march either on Vienna or Prague would be deeply embarrassing — perhaps disastrous — while her main army was tied down in Silesia. She desperately needed time, time for the promised Hungarian levies to arrive, time for her regiments in Italy to reach the Tyrol. During September and early October, directives flew to Neipperg, each yielding more and more to Frederick's "ultimatum," each giving the field marshal broader powers of negotiation as the Prussian king remained adamant in his demands and as Neipperg stressed the hopelessness of his position and his desire to be relieved of command. The queen surrendered in early October; she ordered Neipperg to meet with Hyndford and Goltz to arrange a secret peace on Prussian terms.

The capitulation found willing ears. Inactivity and accompanying desertions were hurting the Prussians as much as the Austrians. Despite entreaties and downright threats, the allies were still moving like glue, their future plans unclear. Instead of commanding the armies in the field, Belle-Isle remained in Frankfurt. When the Bavarian elector should have been on the outskirts of Vienna, he had still not moved beyond the Enns River. The siege of Prague was an unnecessary accessory to the main strategy. The upshot would be that during the winter the Austrians would be reinforced by troops from Hungary and Italy, and that could mean only a prolonged and costly campaign in 1742.*

At Hyndford's suggestion, Frederick met secretly with him, Goltz, Neipperg, and Lentulus at the remote château of Klein-Schnellendorf, located midway between the two armies. With Hyndford adjudicating, the principals agreed to Frederick's original terms, that is, Neipperg to withdraw into Moravia while the Prussians carried out a mock siege of fortress Neisse. Once the garrison "surrendered," it would follow the main army. The Prussians would then take up winter quarters in Upper Silesia and possibly Bohemia and would not act offensively against Austria, her allies, or Hanover. From Moravia, Neipperg would send small parties of hussars to "attack" Prussian convoys and posts in order to deceive Frederick's allies. An effort would be made to write a formal treaty by late December, according to which Austria would cede Lower Silesia, Breslau, and Neisse to Prussia. Frederick stressed that the agreement, which he refused to sign, must be an "inviolable secret," that if it became known, he would be instantly absolved from its terms. Hyndford's protocol guaranteed this important condition. Once various details were settled, Frederick and Neipperg discussed earlier campaigns, and Frederick went so far, if Hyndford is to be believed, as to advise him on future operations against the Bavarians and French.

Frederick was playing a dangerous game with the Klein-Schnellendorf agreement. It could easily destroy what credibility he still possessed in

---

* Elector Charles Albert noted in his diary, "I also received a letter from the King of Prussia in which he informed me that he believed I was already in the suburbs of Vienna, and urged me extremely to advance and cross the Danube at once. Lacking artillery, I had no reason to advance toward Vienna, where without being able to begin the siege I could accomplish nothing, having no intention to go there only to return. Nonetheless, I yielded to the lively representations of the Prussian king, and, with no other design than to please him and not risk losing his friendship, I moved on Vienna unwillingly and totally contrary to the objective that I had of going to Prague." (Heigel, ed., *Das Tagebuch Kaiser Karls VII.*)

foreign courts. If it proved fraudulent, if the Vienna court failed to arrange a formal treaty, he could not protest too loudly. On the other hand, he was certain that the Vienna court would never keep the secret, and he probably valued uncertainty over credibility. In this sense it was a more important replay of his earlier foray into Strasbourg. Who was this King of Prussia? What would he do next? He was determined to make himself equal in recognition to the Kings of France and England, to the Czarina of Russia, to the Queen of Hungary. As he later told Valory, "I do not want to make war as a subaltern; I want to act as I choose."[3] In so doing he was also accomplishing his primary strategic goal, the conquest of Silesia, while allowing his army to go comfortably into winter quarters.

But there was a further consideration. By withdrawing from the action, he would create a new military situation, one that he could subsequently influence in a number of ways. With that, he moved a step closer to his long-term goal of becoming a third power capable of influencing the destiny of Germany and perhaps even of Europe.

35

THE HOAX of Klein-Schnellendorf was played with all the intensity of a theatrical performance at Rheinsberg. To Podewils, who supposedly knew nothing of it, Frederick wrote that he was marching in an effort to cut enemy communications with Moravia; if he failed, he would besiege Neisse. *Podewils was to notify all foreign ministers at Breslau of this plan.* Frederick informed the Bavarian elector that he would shortly move against Neipperg, either to give battle or to force him into fortress Neisse or back to Moravia.

So far, so good. But now Podewils reported that rumors of an agreement between Prussia and Austria were circulating "in rather exact terms" in Breslau. Dowager Empress Emily in Vienna had written her son-in-law, the Bavarian elector, of the agreement; the envoy Thomas Robinson and Field Marshal Count Khevenhüller informed their respective colleagues in Dresden of it. Other leaks followed. The news spread like wildfire. "The king is in a terrible temper," Goltz wrote to Hyndford, and "has ordered me to notify you, that if the court of Pressburg does not put this right, and if the secret is not better preserved in the future, he will not be bound to the treaty."[1] Frederick wanted no less than an official denial from Khevenhüller to be announced by Austrian diplomats throughout Europe.

While this demand was traveling to Pressburg (where it would be ignored), Frederick continued to treat his allies as if nothing untoward had happened. "Neipperg, having been deceived by demonstrations of my moving into Moravia, has decided to protect this province, which has caused me very promptly to begin the siege of Neisse" — this to the Bavarian elector — "at the same time as I have sent twenty-two squadrons of cavalry on the heels of Monsieur de Neipperg." The siege was difficult, he explained to one and all, since the defenders had flooded the area, but once it was accomplished he would march into Bohemia, blockade Glatz, and establish communication with the French, who were marching on Prague. A week or so later he announced the capture of Neisse to the Bavarian elector: "To my great regret the bombs have caused frightful damage." The elector was not to worry about rumors of a Prussian peace with Austria: "I can positively assure him on my honor that I have not made peace with the Austrians, and that I will make it only when Your Electoral Highness will be satisfied." Frederick ordered all Prussian envoys to deny that a peace treaty had been made, and he created more smoke by signing the partition treaty with Bavaria and Saxony by which he guaranteed Upper Austria, Tyrol, Bresgau, and Bohemia to Bavaria, and promised his vote to Charles Albert at the Imperial election. The Bavarian elector in turn guaranteed Silesia to Prussia and promised to sell Glatz to Prussia for 400,000 thalers. Frederick now put his troops in winter quarters and left the war to others.

That war looked black to Maria Theresa. In those early November days no less than three armies, French, Bavarian, and Saxon, were poised in Upper Austria and Bohemia, ready to march where they wished. The main Austrian army, under Neipperg, was slowly struggling back to Neuhaus, its ponderous columns fighting tortuous mountain roads, its already meager ranks slimmed further by sickness and desertions. Reinforcements were only slowly assembling. Vienna still lay open to the enemy.

Maria Theresa was saved by that enemy's ineptness. Having ignored Frederick's advice to march on Vienna, Elector Charles Albert moved into Bohemia to establish bases before besieging Prague. On learning in mid-November that Belle-Isle had finally lashed the Saxons into marching into Bohemia, he decided to advance directly on the capital, join the Saxons, and begin the siege.

Neipperg's army meanwhile had been joined by Grand Duke Francis, who personally took command for the march to Neuhaus. Various fragments that had been driven back by the Franco-Bavarian advance were added to the main body, along with reserves from Vienna, hastily

mobilized Hungarian units (mostly irregulars), and Browne's and Lobkowitz's corps. After securing his Moravian-Bohemian base with Hungarian irregulars, Francis marched with thirty-six thousand troops to
break the siege of Prague. But Francis was no soldier, and his command
was not auspicious. His army strolled rather than marched, enjoying
frequent rest days while its commander and generals went hunting.

The French and Saxons before Prague seemed equally feckless. Finally, with the Austrians approaching and with thunderous messages
from Belle-Isle, who was sick with sciatica in Dresden — "Take Prague!
Days and hours are precious!" — the allies moved.[2] In late November
they stormed thinly held walls, the governor surrendered, the estates
paid homage to a new master, and Charles Albert was crowned King
of Bohemia.

But Maria Theresa's position was not as black as it appeared. Francis's army now held the line Budweis-Wittingau-Neuhaus-Tabor, which
meant that the victors of Prague were cut from their brethren holding
the fortified Linz area in Upper Austria. And now Austrian regiments
from Italy — nearly fourteen thousand fresh troops — along with contingents of Hungarian irregulars, joined Khevenhüller's new command
at Waidhofen in the Tyrol.

Count Khevenhüller was a bright star in a drab military firmament.
Fifty-eight years old, he was a veteran of the Wars of the Spanish and
Polish Successions and the Turkish wars. He had written voluminously
on infantry and cavalry operations. His most famous work, *Maxims of
War,* offered ten rules of warfare, of which the first is possibly the
soundest: "Call on God." This he proceeded to do in the Tyrol. Further
inspired by a portrait of Maria Theresa and ten-month-old Joseph, which
accompanied a fulsome letter giving him operational carte blanche (including authority to arm local peasants), he put together an army that
was unusually effective, considering its disparate elements. All told, he
commanded nearly fourteen thousand infantry, forty-three hundred
horse, a thousand hussars, two thousand Warasdiners, three hundred
pandours, and other Hungarian irregulars commanded by Major General Baron Johann von Bernklau, Lieutenant Colonel Menzel, and Major Trenck.*

In late December Khevenhüller crossed the Enns and began attacking
French outposts. He used irregulars, both independently and in combination with infantry, as shock troops, whose small horses galloped
straight toward the enemy, their riders bent to shield themselves, then
suddenly rising with slashing sabers to cut through anything in the
way.

---

* A few months later Khevenhüller would write Maria Theresa that Bernklau had the correct
blend of daring and caution for special operations. He also admired Menzel and Trenck for
courage, but they lacked Bernklau's military education. (Arneth, *Geschichte*, Volume 2.)

Outpost after outpost gave way; garrisons threw down arms to run in panic. By the new year Khevenhüller had forced Count Henri François Ségur to withdraw behind the walls of Linz, which he surrounded, first to blockade, then besiege. "The world learned with astonishment," Frederick later wrote, "that 15,000 Austrians were holding 15,000 French at Linz."* A week later a force of regulars and irregulars under Bernklau seized the enemy's main magazine at Schärding. Corps Bernklau flooded into Bavaria, the road to Munich lay open, the Bavarian government was panic-stricken.

In less than three months, then, Maria Theresa's military situation was almost completely reversed, the result mainly of the Klein-Schnellendorf agreement. But as the Prussian king had formerly held the balance position of military strength, so did he still — and now Elector Charles Albert frantically sought his aid.

The change for the better in Austrian military fortunes did not please Frederick. It was becoming more obvious that the Vienna court did not intend to make a formal treaty. Although a draft treaty reached Breslau after his departure for Berlin in early November, it would have pledged him to help delay the Imperial election and given his support eventually to Grand Duke Francis; none of this had been discussed at Klein-Schnellendorf.† The Vienna court also continued to publicize the agreement, which reinforced Frederick's belief that Maria Theresa's real intention was to settle with France and Bavaria, then turn on Prussia. Schmettau was reporting pessimistically from the elector's headquarters, where French and Bavarian generals squabbled away the days and the only man capable of putting things right, Marshal Belle-Isle, remained in Dresden, a sick man. If matters did not soon improve, Frederick wrote in mid-November, he believed that the Austrians would bring the allies to the peace table.

He had already begun tying himself into allied operations, albeit cautiously. In late October he had sent Prince Leopold with a sizable force to Bohemia to camp between Königgrätz and Saxony, a position, he explained to the elector, "that by itself makes a kind of diversion and

---

* Frederick's figures (as usual) were incorrect. The Linz garrison had about ten thousand. (Hillbrand, *Die Einschliessung von Linz 1741/42.*)

† On October 27, 1741, Hyndford reported to Lord Harrington in London: "I am afraid My Lord they [the Vienna court] carry their views and expectations too far, for they don't seem yet to have lost sight of the Imperial dignity, and they have the King of Prussia before the Treaty is concluded, disoblige publicly his new Allies, which he will not do. . . . I will inform the King of Prussia of part of the contents of this Memorial, for I must take the liberty to castrate it, for if given entire it would do more harm than good." In Hyndford's opinion, Frederick's motivation in wanting the treaty could well have been "an honest design of preventing the utter ruin of the House of Austria by France and its Allies." (British Foreign Office, 90/51.)

covers the Saxon march." He refused, however, to allow Leopold to join the Saxons, as Charles had requested; they were too far away, and he would not expose Lower Silesia. But Schwerin would move a large force into Moravia and seize Troppau and Olmütz as bases for further operations with the allies.

On the political level he censured England's continuing aid to Austria, a violation of her treaty of neutrality. Prussian and French envoys would soon deliver a thinly veiled warning that if it was not stopped, Hanover would be endangered. He congratulated Elector Charles Albert on becoming King of Bohemia and repeatedly assured him and other allied leaders that he was doing everything possible to expedite the Imperial election. He continued to deny to all concerned that he had made peace with Austria.

Despite the lofty sentiments of *L'Anti-Macchiavel,* Frederick was rapidly coming to trust no one and no thing. When in Silesia he had written to Voltaire that "men are not made for the truth. I regard them as a herd of stags in the park of a grand nobleman, with no other function than to breed and fill up the park." When the Spanish court continued to press for a treaty with Prussia, Frederick turned it down. "What astonishes me," he wrote to Podewils, "is that the world never becomes wiser, and that after one sees so obviously the frivolity of guarantees, principally in regard to the Pragmatic Sanction, one still allows oneself to be taken in by guarantee treaties. All men are fools; that is what Solomon said, and what experience proves."

Frederick believed he had been foolish to ally with France, who had let him down; he had been foolish to deal with Austria, who was obviously insincere. Circumstances now compelled him to deal again with the allies. He would do so, but very carefully. Although he ordered Leopold to support the allied advance with both cavalry and infantry, the prince was to operate only on the allied left so as not to be cut from the Silesian border. He was to take no chances and was not to advance very far, "since through this move I wish only to show the world that rumors of a peace with Austria are groundless and that I have not detached myself from my allies." Prussian cooperation would depend on the allies' determination to occupy as much of Bohemia as possible before going into winter quarters. Frederick was not willing to offer more help, because he believed that Schwerin's corps would have its hands full with a small war.

But events moved him closer to the allies. In early December he learned of a palace revolution in Saint Petersburg. With the aid of the regiment of guards, Elizabeth, Peter the Great's daughter, stole the crown from the regent, Anne, and the young Ivan, and banished Marshal Münnich.

Although Frederick regretted the loss of Münnich's support, he believed that the upheaval removed "the last resource" counted on by Austria and England, since it did not seem likely that Elizabeth would uphold earlier promises to Austria.

It was also obvious that the Austrian court had no intention of formally ceding Silesia to Prussia. When Hyndford informed him in late November that the draft treaty had arrived from Vienna, Frederick did not even ask to see it. In mid-December he told Hyndford that he no longer felt bound to the Klein-Schnellendorf agreement, because Vienna had repeatedly violated its terms. He was sorry — had Maria Theresa respected it, he could have saved Moravia and the two Austrias for her. As it was, she was bound to lose everything. Hyndford's counterarguments fell on deaf ears. "Upon the whole," he grumpily reported, "there is nothing to be done with this prince while his affairs go on so successfully."[3]

A few days later Frederick wrote to Marshal Belle-Isle that in the coming year he would lead the Prussian army through Moravia to strike the Austrian flank if the French simultaneously would attack the Austrian army's front. As much as he would like to see Belle-Isle in Berlin, he would prefer to meet him at the gates of Vienna. Belle-Isle responded enthusiastically: there was no reason that allied forces could not march directly on Vienna and end the war.

None of this signified Frederick's renewed faith in the allies. He was not pleased with their tactical dispositions in Bohemia, and he hoped that Belle-Isle would cause them to advance deeper into the country before taking up winter quarters, for only this could force the enemy back into Austria. When Belle-Isle instead spoke of moving the Saxons to the rear and the French behind the Moldau, Frederick replied that he would then move Prince Leopold's corps behind the Elbe. The threat worked: the Saxons advanced, and Frederick's other wishes were respected. Another irritant was that, he suspected, the Bavarian and French courts were secretly working toward a separate peace with Austria, and he believed that Belle-Isle's failure to take field command resulted more from this than from illness. He also suspected, correctly, that the Saxon court was dealing secretly with Versailles in order to obtain a large chunk of Bohemia.

These suspicions were in large part confirmed when the French king summarily transferred Belle-Isle to Frankfurt to supervise the Imperial election and put Marshal Broglie in field command. Broglie was old and decrepit, his body and mind maimed by attacks of apoplexy, yet arrogant and unbending, willing to ally with no one. Here the allies were on the point of attacking Budweis in order to extend their position as deep into Bohemia as possible, as Frederick had urged, and do-nothing Broglie was going to sit idly by in Pisek. Belle-Isle's presence was vital to future operations. "Under your command the French troops are heroic," he wrote to the marshal; "under Broglie they are only cunts." He went so far as to petition Fleury, "For God and your glory, deliver us from Marshal Broglie, and for the honor of the French troops, return Marshal Belle-Isle to us." *

At this crucial point Schmettau and Valory brought the Bavarian elector's pressing appeals for help to Frederick at Potsdam. Despite Belle-Isle's recall, the king had been reasonably sanguine about the military situation. Schwerin had dexterously pushed through mountain passes without losing a man or horse, bad weather notwithstanding, to occupy fortress Olmütz, the gateway to the great Bohemian plain. The town of Glatz had surrendered, and Leopold was investing its fortress, whose hoped-for surrender would help to ensure the security of Lower Silesia. Allied forces perhaps twenty-five thousand strong were safely in winter quarters behind the Sazawa River. Austria, on the other hand, was allegedly in such difficult straits that, Frederick now believed, a combined allied demand could force her to the peace table. It would seem, he concluded, that he had retained the "balance position": each side needed him.

It was time for a break from public affairs. A few weeks earlier he had written excitedly to Voltaire that the famed mathematician Leonhard Euler and lesser fry had arrived in Berlin and that the Academy was flourishing: "You can see that war has not deadened my taste for the arts." But in early January, at the height of the Berlin carnival, he complained to Voltaire:

> I find myself so occupied by the great affairs which the philosophers call nonsense that I am not able to think of my pleasure — the one solid blessing in life. I fancy that God has made asses, Doric columns, and kings to carry the burdens of the world, where so many other beings are made to enjoy the blessings that it produces. Just now I am here [Berlin] arguing with a score of Machiavels more or less dangerous. Pleasant poetry waits at the door, unable to have an audience. One speaks to me of boundaries; another of rights; still another of indemnity; these of auxiliaries, of marriage contracts, of debts to pay, of recommendations, dispositions, and so forth.

Now he was looking forward to several weeks of idyllic life at Rheinsberg.

Schmettau's graphic description of the elector's woes changed idyll to fantasy. Frederick learned that the allies in Pisek were inactive and

---

* Frederick later wrote: "This century was sterile in great men for France; that of Louis XIV produced them in droves. A priest's [Fleury's] administration ruined the military. Under Mazarin this consisted of heros; under Fleury, sybaritic courtesans." *(Oeuvres,* Volume 2, *Histoire de mon temps.)*

quarreling; the troops were in shocking condition; the main French-Bavarian army was penned up in Linz; Khevenhüller's and Bernklau's irregulars were rapidly turning the Bavarian border into a wasteland before driving on to Passau and Munich; Elector Charles Albert was at panic station in Munich, sending meaningless orders to Marshal Broglie and to the Saxon general, Count Johann Baptista Polastron, to attack in Bohemia to take the pressure off Bavaria — orders that neither commander could or would obey; the main Austrian army was "very sensibly placed" in winter quarters, its back against the Danube, its right covered by the Wittingau marshes, its front at Tabor, its left on Budweis, another force under Lobkowitz at Iglau.

He had not realized the seriousness of the situation. It was suddenly clear that if he did not intervene, the war would be lost, his allies would sign a separate peace with Austria, and in no time a large Austrian army bought with English gold would be pounding on Silesian gates. But there was another consideration. France was proving to be a broken reed despite her vast armies. If Frederick could intervene to save the situation, if he could join with Bavaria and Saxony to force Austria to a peace, might this not be the beginning of a counteralliance, a *German* alliance, that would attract England and Russia, push France back across the Rhine, and at the same time keep Austria in line?

He saw two possible courses of action. Schwerin's corps could march south, join the Saxons and French, and march on Wittingau while Broglie simultaneously moved from Pisek to strike the Austrian left at Budweis. There were two difficulties. By the time the allies reached Wittingau, the Luschnitz River, a major obstacle, would have thawed, and the crossing would have to be made by boat bridge, in face of a strong defense. Further, forward magazines would have to be arranged, since the land between the Luschnitz and the Sazawa had been denuded by visiting armies.

A far more favorable plan, Frederick decided, was to march with the Saxons and French to force Prince Lobkowitz from Iglau, then advance to the Thaya River, from where he would threaten Hungary and Lower Austria. This move would force Khevenhüller to abandon the siege of Linz or cause Francis to abandon his present line and enable Broglie to march to the relief of Linz.

This was the plan that he sent to the Bavarian elector in mid-January. He personally would lead the Prussian army in the new campaign, but he insisted on command of the Saxon and French contingents. He would not expose his troops to ruin by "those gentlemen who understand their profession so badly and who blunder so rashly that it is difficult to believe." Convinced that the Bavarians, Saxons, and French had no other choice than to accept, Frederick sent Valory to Dresden to explain the new plan. He himself followed a day or two later.

36

KING FREDERICK'S PARTY included his brother Prince Henry and assorted senior generals, who were treated with every honor at Dresden. Armed with a map of Moravia, Frederick presented what can only be called a strategically sound operations plan. Once Khevenhüller and Neipperg withdrew from Bavaria and Bohemia to Lower Austria, Broglie could relieve Linz. Come spring, the allies would move on Vienna and force Maria Theresa to either come to terms or face total defeat.

But a plan is only as good as its operational components. From the beginning, the Saxon and French components ensured ultimate failure. Prime Minister Brühl and two Saxon commanders, General Count Maurice and General Count Friedrich August Rutowsky, objected that a campaign in Moravia would expose Prague and the left flank of the French army to Neipperg's main Austrian force, now quartered around Neuhaus, southeast of Prague. If the campaign failed, Saxony would be open to invasion. The Saxon army was short of supply, and no provisions existed for the proposed march.

Frederick responded that without this operation Saxony would be in even greater danger of invasion, that he was leaving behind Old Dessauer with thirty thousand troops to protect Saxony. He would arrange to provision the Saxon corps. And if, once in Iglau, the Saxons felt themselves unable to advance to the Thaya, he would go it alone while they covered his right flank. At this point King August joined the conference. Frederick repeated the briefing "like some sort of Oriental vendor displaying his merchandise as best as possible," stressing that the Polish king would never have Moravia "if he would not go to the trouble of taking it." "August answered yes to everything," Frederick later wrote, "with an air of conviction mixed with a look of boredom." Count Brühl did not like the way things were going and broke off the meeting so that the king would not miss the overture of a favorite opera. "Ten kingdoms to conquer would not keep the King of Poland one minute longer," Frederick noted.[1]

The following morning he used the influence of the Polish king's confessor, Father Guarini, to win provisional agreement to the plan, including his command of allied troops. What seems clear from the records is that the Saxons agreed, on condition that they were provisioned, to march on Iglau, which they would garrison while the rest of their army took up winter quarters. They did *not* agree to advance with the Prussians to the Thaya River.

With these inconclusive conferences behind them, the Prussians traveled on to Prague. The plot thickened at Aussig, where one of Broglie's adjutants, Major Marsilly, who was on his way to Dresden, informed the Prussian king that once Broglie was assured of the allied march on Iglau, he would advance on Budweis and Tabor, as Frederick desired, and would do all possible to drive out Neipperg or at least keep him occupied. But when Frederick explained that after taking Iglau he would march to the Thaya, Marsilly objected that this would expose the left and rear of the French to attack. Although upset, Frederick invited him to stop by his new headquarters at Alt-Bunzlau on his return from Dresden.

In Prague, General Moreau de Séchelles, the French supply chief, confirmed to Frederick that he would supply the Saxons. "I shall make the impossible possible," he promised with appropriate Gallic drama.[2] Prince Leopold joined the party for the journey to Alt-Bunzlau, and Marsilly arrived there from Dresden. According to this officer's reports to Broglie, the Prussian king promised that once Iglau was taken, the Prussians would follow the enemy to wherever he fell back, be it in Moravia, be it in Bohemia; Frederick asked Broglie only to hold his army together, undertake nothing against the enemy, and be ready to fall back on Prague if necessary.* The party then rode to Glatz to reconnoiter the weakly held fortress.

Field Marshal Schwerin, who was not well — he had a nervous condition manifested in part by severe migraine headaches — met the party at Landskron, where the allied field commanders, the Knight of Saxony (King August's half brother) and Count Polastron joined them. The Saxon commander announced that he was against the operation. His army was already falling back on Prague; it badly needed supplies; a winter operation would accomplish nothing. However, if it was undertaken, then the Saxons must not remain in Iglau but must advance to the Thaya — which Frederick wanted but which was contrary to the Dresden agreement. Polastron, who commanded the small French contingent, added more complications. Originally ordered by Broglie to place himself under Frederick's command, he had since received counterorders from the French marshal. Broglie had learned of the Dresden conference and was furious that he had not been consulted. He had ordered Séchelles in Prague not to supply the Saxons, and Polastron was to participate only in the capture of Iglau, after which Broglie wanted the entire allied army to march on Neuhaus, a move refused by Frederick because the area was devastated and could feed neither man nor horse. To add to the confusion, Schwerin wanted to march on fortress Brünn, known to be in poor repair, storm it, then march on

* It seems doubtful that Frederick would have said any such thing, but perhaps he did with the thought that once the operation was a success, Broglie would come around to the Prussian strategy. It is more likely that Marsilly misunderstood him or even purposely obfuscated matters.

Pressburg — a plan angrily rejected by the king. The Prussians were not strong enough in troops or artillery to assault Brünn, and Frederick hoped that the Hungarian nobles, especially the northern Protestants, would turn on Vienna and actively rebel or at least stay out of the war.

King Frederick seemed dangerously oblivious of these contradictory operational concepts. Perhaps his attitude resulted from the conviction that his strategy was correct — and in theory it was. Perhaps it stemmed from his belief that the allies would be defeated without his aid — which was probable. Perhaps it was from professional disdain of the dilatory allied rulers, commanders, and armies — with good reason. Perhaps from natural impatience compounded by a long and tiring trip in cold weather — which was understandable. Perhaps from a belief that his mere presence in southern Moravia would bring the Austrian queen to the peace table — which was doubtful. Whatever the reasons, he now calmly informed all present that the armies would assemble on the stated departure lines in early February.

Probably overawed by the royal presence, neither the Saxon nor French commander offered serious resistance, at least to the march on Iglau. But this did not mean they accepted the total plan, as Frederick supposed was the case. For he now informed King August that he and the allied commanders had agreed to march to the Thaya and that Broglie should be informed!

At Schwerin's headquarters in Olmütz the Prussian king learned that the Elector of Bavaria had been elected Emperor Charles VII on January 24, Frederick's thirtieth birthday. Countering this good news was the discovery that Schwerin had not carried out orders to build extensive magazines to support the march south. This led to another quarrel so serious that Schwerin divorced himself from the entire operation on grounds of illness. Schwerin had turned over the supply problem to Colonel Count Karl Christoph von Schmettau, who, like his older brother, had left the Austrian army for Prussian service. The king apparently believed either that the supply problem would be solved in due course or that he could squeak by for what he was certain would be a short campaign.

Disturbing news also arrived from the allies. Törring's Bavarians had suffered severe defeat at Schärding and General Ségur had "beaten the chamade" to surrender some ten thousand French-Bavarian troops at Linz. A courier brought an ambiguous letter from Marshal Broglie, who expressed complete agreement with Frederick's plan while fundamentally changing it to suit his own designs. Broglie explained that Khevenhüller, having taken Linz, would advance on Pilsen and Eger to cut his communications. Accordingly, after seizing Iglau, Frederick and the Saxons must march not to the Thaya, but to Neuhaus and Pilgram while Broglie crossed the Moldau to come up on the allied right.

The king angrily refuted the French marshal's reasoning by return letter. When the Dresden court took fright and suggested a fallback on Prague, he replied that if Saxon troops withdrew to Prague, he would return to Silesia, and Saxony would forfeit any chance of obtaining Moravia. He complained vigorously to the newly elected Emperor Charles of allied ill will and weak command: "After having obtained everything at Dresden, I am refused everything in Moravia." His annoyance spilled over in a letter to Voltaire. He longed for the arts but he had only war. What could one make of a brain filled "with hay, oats, and chaff"? His sanity, he wrote, was saved only by draft chapters of Voltaire's new work, *Le Siècle de Louis XIV*, "my sole consolation, my relaxation, and my recreation."

He still fancied himself on top of the situation. When a special envoy arrived from Grand Duke Francis, who sincerely wanted peace and eventual alliance with Prussia, Frederick, although politely receiving him, was brutally and, by his later admission, stupidly frank: Francis must not believe that the King of Prussia would desert a powerful alliance to join a queen *"sans amis, sans allies, et sans ressources."* Her British subsidy was spent. Hessian and Danish auxiliaries promised by England would not arrive. France was bent on her isolation and ultimate destruction. He had tried to prevent this by the agreement of Klein-Schnellendorf. Now Maria Theresa must make peace. She must guarantee him Silesia and Glatz, cede most of Moravia to Saxony and Bohemia to Bavaria. He did not want Austria for a neighbor, but neither did he wish for her total destruction, since she was a necessary counterbalance to the House of Bavaria. As for a meeting with Francis, the time was inappropriate. He agreed, however, to maintain contact with another envoy sent from Vienna, a priest named Count Franz Giannini. He did not reply to a new and extremely generous proposal from Lord Hyndford on Maria Theresa's behalf. Peace could result only from military success. Confident that the forthcoming operation would soon bring Austria around, he ordered Podewils to come to Olmütz to handle future negotiations.

In early February Frederick led a Prussian force of nineteen infantry battalions, thirty cavalry squadrons, fourteen hussar and uhlan squadrons — about fifteen thousand troops and thirty-two pieces of artillery — south from Olmütz in a march to join Saxon and French corps at Gross-Bitesch. The ponderous corps, some nine miles wide and eighteen miles deep, moved slowly, the officers, including Frederick, walking beside their horses because of icy roads. Enemy hussars operating out of fortress Brünn, and hidden by fog, plagued the columns; on one occasion they captured a dragoon officer only a thousand yards from the royal train. But in four days the task force seized a number of Austrian outposts before joining nearly sixteen thousand Saxons under Rutowsky and another three thousand French under Polastron. A few days later the allied army moved on Iglau, which, as Frederick had forecast, Lobkowitz left without a fight but with empty supply magazines. Step one of the Prussian king's plan had been achieved.

But all was scarcely roses. At Gross-Bitesch, Count Maurice and Rutowsky were using all the old arguments to persuade the Prussian king to join Broglie's army, which of course he refused to consider. Maurice had brought Broglie's reply to Frederick's last letter, and the king now learned that Polastron's corps was to rejoin the French army immediately. Polastron interpreted his orders so as to allow him to march on Iglau, where Frederick had to let him depart. Rutowsky had also received orders from Dresden to join Broglie and declared himself free of Prussian command, now that Iglau had been taken. In response, Frederick wrote to King August that he still intended to march to the Thaya; if August withdrew Rutowsky's troops, he would suffer "the most regretful consequences," a barely veiled threat that the Prussians would leave Moravia.

In short, things were not going the way the king had hoped. His mood was evident in a letter to Polastron: "The weather is becoming horrible, the French leave me, the Saxons are weary of Moravian huts and long for Prague palaces; deserted on all sides, I must seriously think of winter quarters." *

At this dismal point there was a favorable shift. The Imperial election having resolved a good many of Cardinal Fleury's fears, the old prelate swung once again to Belle-Isle's war party. Additional subsidies were promised to the new emperor to rebuild his shattered army. In the spring, a French army thirty thousand strong would cross the Rhine to bolster sagging allied forces. Both King Louis and Emperor Charles now made it clear that the Saxons meanwhile were to remain under Frederick's command wherever he marched.

With Saxon outposts stretching south and east from Iglau to cover his right flank, Frederick pushed forward to the Thaya. From headquarters at Znaim he set up a series of posts that reached across the Imperial highway leading from Brünn to Vienna. Small task forces moved into Lower Austria to levy food requisitions and cash contributions. One order alone called for the prelates, estates, and officials of a small area to send to Znaim, within thirty-six hours, 400,000 thalers in cash,

---

* Polastron replied, "I take the liberty to assure your Majesty that I, my generals, officers, and men would have found it an honor to serve under your command in any weather and in any land, and that at your side we would have preferred Moravian huts to Prague palaces." (Generalstab, *Die Kriege Friedrichs des Grossen. Erster Theil: Der Erste Schlesische Krieg, 1740–1742*, Volume 3. Hereafter Generalstab I followed by volume number.)

twenty thousand pecks of oats, twenty thousand pecks of corn, and sixty tons of hay. If the deliveries were not made, the force was to sack monasteries and abbeys and take priests and nobles as hostages. With his left wing just over thirty miles from Vienna, with Zieten's hussars probing up to the Danube bridges, Frederick triumphantly wrote to Fleury: "Regarding my operations, they are having the total effect I hoped for. Monsieur de Broglie is completely out of danger, Prague secure, the dismayed and discouraged enemy retiring on Lower and Upper Austria, Lower Austria inundated with our troops, who are able to fight and win when the enemy has the audacity to stand. Heaven be praised that our superiority is re-established." He expressed similar optimism a few days later to the emperor and to Belle-Isle.

That letter marked a significant change in his thinking. Only a few weeks earlier he had believed that his march would bring Austria scurrying to the peace table. He was wrong. Maria Theresa's court not only had remained oblivious of his overtures but had showed every sign of continuing military resistance. Even as he wrote, one of his corps was sparring with Austrian cavalry, the vanguard of the main army, which Frederick had reason to believe was bent on attacking him. Too weak to carry on alone, he now had to bring his allies, especially France, back into the picture. Thus his letter to Fleury, thus similar letters to other allied commanders, to whom he sent a detailed plan for the forthcoming spring campaign, a combined operation that would begin in May and, as he informed Emperor Charles, needed only "good plans well concerted and then vigorously carried out" to bring a favorable peace by July.

But Frederick had not yet realized that the more grand a strategy, particularly one involving envious, ambitious, and greedy allies, the more difficult it would be of accomplishment. He was reckoning without several important factors. What had begun as a logical strategy was rapidly turning into impulsive tactics. As a result, he was about to suffer a frustrating and dismal winter before admitting to strategic and tactical failure.

37

IT WAS A WINTER of small war, and the enemy was daily winning. Irregulars kept the Prussians tactically blind and off balance. On at least three occasions in late February, Frederick thought battle was imminent, only to discover the opposite. The uncertain situation caused him to send for six battalions and twenty squadrons from Olmütz, which meant more mouths to feed. He wanted battle but, as General Schmettau repeatedly pointed out, he would be better off to hold what he had until the promised French armies reached Bavaria and until Saxon heavy cannon arrived for the siege of Brünn. Frederick's small corps would be up against at least thirty thousand Austrians, Schmettau argued, and he could expect no immediate reinforcements from either Glatz or Olmütz, which were too far away. Better to avoid battle and position units to prevent the enemy from remaining north of the Danube while keeping close track of that enemy.

Frederick for once agreed with a subordinate's advice and shifted units accordingly. But information on the enemy was not easy to come by. Patrols combed local areas with but scant result. "I beg you to have more spies in the country than there are chickens in Poland," he wrote to Count Rutowsky. But spies were also in short supply. Unlike parts of Silesia this was hostile land of "cunning and ill-disposed" peasants, as August Friedrich Eichel, the king's forty-four-year-old private secretary, early complained. The Vienna court had armed peasants and persuaded them to strip fields, bury produce, and leave farmsteads, taking horses and livestock to the woods and mountains. The Prussians found only "deserted huts," Frederick complained, and "almost no horses." Partisans operating from fortress Brünn had almost entirely cut allied communications. And now Schwerin reported that twelve thousand Hungarians — "the most horrible breed that God has created," the king wrote to Fleury — were moving on Skalitz, from where they would reinforce the Brünn garrison, already over six thousand strong. Another ten thousand reportedly were pushing north, intending to march through the Jablunka Pass and cut off Upper Silesia.

Partly to counter the Hungarian threat and partly to ease supply shortages, Frederick in early March began shifting the two armies. The Prussians moved east down the Thaya River and then north on the far side of the Sazawa River in order to screen Brünn from the Hungarians. He ordered the Knight of Saxony, who had replaced Rutowsky, to pull in southern outposts, occupy Znaim, and work his way toward a blockade of Brünn. He also sent Prince Dietrich, with a task force of eight thousand foot and horse, to chase the enemy from Skalitz and Ungarisch-Brod, a fast-moving mission in which Zieten's hussars played a major role and which was so successful that some of the irregular force fled back to their homelands. He next ordered Leopold to lead a task force from Glatz to push the Hungarians from Upper Silesia and "scour the whole area." Old Dessauer was summoned to march from Brandenburg with a fresh corps of twenty-three battalions and thirty squadrons. In mid-March the king took headquarters outside Selowitz, where he prepared for the "decisive battle" certain to be fought. The new 3-pounder cannon had arrived, lighter, more maneuverable, and with increased accuracy. In battle they would deploy in front of first-line battalions, two per battalion, with some distributed to the second line. "Dispositions" and "Instructions" for infantry, cavalry, and hussars flowed from his headquarters. "It is quite certain that we shall have a battle," he excitedly notified Jordan on March 19. Four days later he informed Voltaire that he would soon be in battle with the principal Austrian army.

Marshal Khevenhüller's recovery of Linz had greatly encouraged Maria Theresa, as had further gains in Bavaria. On the day Charles Albert was crowned Emperor Charles VII, Menzel's irregulars plundered their way into Munich to leave the luckless emperor in Frankfurt without a capital and precious little kingdom. Armed with the promise of another half million pounds sterling from England, where Sir Robert Walpole's fall in favor of Lord Carteret was to her favor, Maria Theresa was not ready to meet Frederick's humiliating terms. A fresh appeal to Hungarian nobles brought a promise of forty thousand more recruits, over half of which Pálffy almost at once put into the field. Vienna kept anti-Prussian propaganda flowing to other courts in an attempt to break the hostile alliance against Austria. England was rumored to be sending an expeditionary force of sixteen thousand to Flanders, where it would be joined by a Dutch army and by various auxiliary corps to free Austrian regiments there or perhaps go to war against France.

Vienna's long-awaited reply to Frederick's peace overtures reflected the changed situation. Count Giannini delivered it in early March. Although Vienna was willing to make concessions to Prussia, it would offer nothing to Prussia's allies. Alliance with Prussia would be welcome enough, Maria Theresa wrote, but Austria would fight on until suitable terms could be worked out.

Just how Austria could best fight on had been a subject of great concern in the Hofkriegsrath and in the field armies. A few weeks earlier Maria Theresa had persuaded her husband, Francis, to turn over command of the army to his brother, Prince Charles, and return to Vienna. She hoped that Charles would drive the French from Bohemia and then turn on her other enemies, a strategy favored by her powerful adviser Bartenstein.

She chose the wrong man for the job — a frequent error of hers. Charles was a courtier, a heavy drinker, a gambler, and womanizer, who surrounded himself with generally unsavory friends. Empty-eyed and heavy-jowled, his face scarred by smallpox, he lacked confidence and resolution, and was fit to cope successfully neither with the tactical challenges of a difficult campaign nor with the command feuds that raged incessantly in the Austrian army. But Charles was the queen's favorite (he would in time marry her sister), and she gave him full authority to act as he would.

Authority upset rather than pleased the young nobleman. It wasn't so much that he refused to attack the French; Charles refused to attack *anyone*. Charles refused to *move*. Charles saw danger everywhere — a weak army, delayed reinforcements, generals with no desire for war, a growing sicklist, no money to pay officers and men. Once the army was fit to march, what then? Should he attack Saxons, Prussians, or French? A war council in early March finally agreed to attack Saxons and Prussians in order to protect Lower Austria and Vienna. Charles submitted this plan to General Maximilian Browne, who had been absent on account of illness, for a written opinion. Browne tore it to shreds. The only logical target, he insisted, was Broglie's small French corps at Pisek. If he was defeated, the Saxons would retreat and the Prussians would think hard about advancing any farther on their own. The strategic key was Bohemia, "the bride" for which Austria should be fighting. To march east to attack the Saxons and Prussians in Moravia was to open Bohemia to the French. This would force Khevenhüller to abandon his offensive in Bavaria, which was exactly what the Prussian king wanted. Once Bohemia was lost, Browne warned, it would not be easy to regain.

Browne's blunt advice only confused Charles, who again asked the court for a specific target. But dissension ruled there, too. Bartenstein agreed with Browne, but Marshal Count Lothar Königsegg held for an attack of the Prussians and Saxons, and so now did the queen, who ordered Charles to the task. His further delay brought a plaintive compromise: he could attack *any* of her enemies, but he must *move,* since inaction only played into enemy hands. When this produced no result by late March, she ordered him to move against the Prussians and Saxons.

King Frederick's position had continued to deteriorate. Hostile locals not only deprived invaders of subsistence and information, but soon caused serious tactical setbacks. Working with hussars and irregulars, armed peasants repeatedly sneaked in under darkness to burn villages held by Prussian troops. "Not a day passes," Frederick complained to Jordan, "but what two or three villages are burned" by *Bauerngesindel* — peasant rabble. The few peasants who remained in the area lied about Austrian positions and of course informed on Prussian movements. Reprisals followed. The Prussians burned villages, tortured and executed peasants — to no avail. A force under General von Truchsess was attacked by three thousand enemy and had to fight a five-hour "backs-to-the-wall" battle in which Truchsess was wounded before being extricated by a relief force.* Schwerin was increasingly plagued by enemy parties, which struck outposts and convoys, even raiding Olmütz to capture magazines and the recently arrived royal baggage. Tighter security measures and forced marches in cold weather tired the troops and resulted in long sicklists; in late March Prince Dietrich had to evacuate two hundred men, and the Saxons estimated that over five thousand of their soldiers were sick, mainly as the result of insufficient rations.

The communications problem also grew worse. With Leopold at Glatz and then Upper Silesia, Schwerin at Olmütz, Broglie at Pisek, Rutowsky at Iglau, the emperor and Belle-Isle at Frankfurt, couriers at best would have been hard put to do their job. But couriers were frequently captured, along with dispatches that were not always written in cipher. To avoid capture, they had to travel circuitous routes. Trips normally requiring a day or two sometimes took two weeks. Irregulars long since had cut direct communications with Olmütz, and dispatches had to go via Prague. "I thirst for news of our army and allies," Schwerin wrote in early March, and other commanders agreed. The result was frequently confusion and consequent loss of tactical cohesion.

The most serious problem, however, was chronic lack of food and forage. This had been a problem from the beginning, solved only in part by food and forage requisitioned from Lower Austria. When that was eaten, it had to be replaced from local sources. Moravia was austere country, and it was winter. There were no rivers for boat convoys to bring food from Silesian depots. Peasant carts and horses had vanished. Already in late February, Rutowsky was complaining of short rations and increasing numbers of sick men and horses. Frederick had no forage to give him: "As for bread, I will be able to furnish it to you in some way, although I have only just started my magazines, having subsisted until now from one day to the next." Austrian troops had earlier eaten out the operational areas. Prussians and Saxons were soon dependent on supplies from rear area magazines. But Colonel Schmettau, in trying to build sufficient magazines at Olmütz, had been plagued by command confusion, lack of money, general area shortages, and enemy interdiction. In mid-March, when Frederick was preparing to fight a "decisive" battle, he discovered that in all of Moravia there were magazines for only about four weeks of operations instead of for several months, as he supposed. A week or so later he realized that his own army had supplies for only four days! He blamed Schwerin entirely for this monumental foul-up, which caused him "great chagrin."

---

* Frederick rewarded Truchsess with an annual pension of two thousand thalers, commissioned a noncommissioned officer for bravery, replaced the men's personal clothing and packs, and promised life pensions to the permanently disabled.

"You have not followed the least of my commands in Moravia . . ." he stormed, "and now you have spoiled everything." *

"This light cavalry is everywhere," the king informed Fleury; "it cuts our communications, as do the armed peasants, so that I have not yet seen to subsistence." A day later he wrote to Emperor Charles, "We will be nearly destitute in Moravia; we are surrounded by hussars, who prevent us from making magazines; the country is ruined by Neipperg's requisitions made during the last campaign."

Frederick now received reports that the main Austrian army was marching from Krems into Bohemia to attack Marshal Broglie's army. Lacking proper intelligence, Frederick could not know that this was "smoke" purposely generated to fool him, that Charles would march on Moravia, not Bohemia. It did not much matter, because, what with his lack of food and relatively weak numbers, he could not risk battle, whether in Moravia or in Bohemia; he could not risk being cut from the Elbe and Lower Silesia.

A major change of plan was necessary.

In early April he announced his new strategy. The Saxons would fall back on Prague. The Prussians would also fall back to the Chrudim area, east of Prague, to screen the Saxon withdrawal and wait for Old Dessauer's reinforcements. Prince Dietrich would command an "army of observation" stretching from Olmütz to Upper Silesia. Some three thousand Saxon sick would be carted to Olmütz for evacuation to Silesia. Broglie meanwhile would fall back on Prague, where if necessary he could be joined by the Prussians to support him and the Saxons against any Austrian attack.

The armies marched in early April, a confused, slow, and hazardous business. Mixed corps of hussars and peasants led by the famed partisan commanders Barányay and Nádasdy dogged the columns, with irregulars and armed peasants falling on isolated units and convoys. Dietrich's force was so hotly pursued that a subordinate commander, Fouqué, had to march his people in a defensive square. Saxon troops had the worst of it. After a successful attack by Warasdiner irregulars at Austup, villagers fell on Saxon wounded, stripping and killing them. A relief force burned the guilty village, along with some fifty peasants, including women and children. The columns were plagued by lack of food and transport. Sick and wounded died like flies. They did not reach the Bohemian border until mid-April. The Prussians marched more rapidly, closing on Leutomischl in mid-April and a few days later

---

* The reprimand, not altogether justified, infuriated Schwerin, and when the king added insult to injury by giving Old Dessauer command in Upper Silesia, Schwerin asked for extended sick leave. Instead, the king sent him to Neisse to head a border commission. From here he went on to take the waters at Karlsbad, and finally retired to his estate.

on Chrudim.* This was a remarkable march of 110 miles over diffi-cult — in part mountainous — terrain in thirteen days of generally bad weather.

But now King Frederick was in good country, where the army could rest and refit. Once Old Dessauer's people arrived he would count some twenty-eight thousand troops. Meanwhile he would screen Lower Si-lesia while keeping an eye on Prague and waiting for further develop-ments.

38

THE DISMAL SITUATION in Moravia had earlier caused Frederick to make an estimate of the situation in the form of two documents, one listing reasons for him to remain in the present alliance, one for making a separate peace with Austria. Although he believed that it was "poor policy" to break his word by leaving the alliance, this was his least concern: "Conjunctures make alliance and not alliance conjunctures," he instructed Cardinal Fleury. If he could see the present campaign through and win just one battle, he should be able to arbitrate the peace and gain the loyalty of much of the Empire.

On the other hand, the French could be defeated in detail by the Austrians (because of sloppy methods); or the French could be forced to transfer their army to fight the British and Dutch (and thus leave Frederick naked before his enemy); or the French could become an all-powerful victor (owing to Prussian arms). In each case Frederick would be the loser; indeed, he might easily forfeit all he had gained.

He was in a proper quandary. "If the French prosper in Bavaria," he wrote to Podewils in late April, "we shall perhaps attain our goal, al-though with difficulty; if the war flares up in Flanders, we shall have more trouble. In a word, the entire political structure is in such a con-fused and problematical state that whichever way one turns, one risks taking a poor role." One thing was certain: there would be no quick end to the war. As he drily wrote to Voltaire concerning a plan for perpetual peace sent to him by a French prelate, "The plan is very practicable; it lacks only the consent of all Europe to make it succeed."

---

* Leutomischl (today's Litomýsl) is a beautiful town with a wide main street and castle and churches on the hills to the east. Northwest of the town the land becomes undulating, mildly hilly. Chrudim is a very hilly, not unattractive town whose cobblestones were undoubtedly trod upon by Prussian troops.

It is not clear when Frederick first began to think of a separate peace. Probably it was never far from his mind. Although he had hotly spurned earlier Austrian offers, as his tactical position deteriorated his tone altered and he became nervous and less sure of himself. In late March Count Giannini, secretly summoned to the Selowitz headquarters, was told that Lord Hyndford had been called to Breslau, where a peace would be negotiated within six weeks. In the interim Frederick would remain on the defensive unless he was attacked, and the Vienna court should not take alarm from Old Dessauer's march. His instructions to Podewils regarding the talks with Hyndford show his state of mind. If England wanted to win him, then "you will be able to extract much more than we hope for"; if not, "we must water our wine" and get what could be had. But under no circumstances would a peace involve him in another war; he would not accept the dethronement of Emperor Charles VII; he would not guarantee Austria's territories. But the more he thought about it, "the more I regard it as necessary to gain a prompt peace." He would consider joining a defensive alliance with England and Holland once he was at peace with Austria. In fact, he would even consider an alliance with the Vienna court. But if Hyndford spoke in a "superior way," Podewils was to reply in kind. Frederick was not asking for peace but was willing to accept it, providing the main terms of his earlier "ultimatum" were met. Hyndford's delay in leaving Berlin was very upsetting, and Frederick's impatience increased when Valory turned up in Chrudim with new French demands for military action, which he curtly refused to consider.

Hyndford and Podewils met at Breslau in late April. The British envoy made it clear that the Austrian position had changed radically since February. Maria Theresa saw no reason to accept the earlier Prussian demands. Although willing to cede Lower Silesia and either the county of Glatz or a portion of Upper Silesia, she would not hear of Frederick acquiring the county of Königgrätz and she would not hear of "reasonable satisfaction" for his allies. Moreover, if peace was to result, Frederick must guarantee all Austrian territories and actively aid her against all enemies.

Frederick replied in a stream of directives that changed from indignation to pledges of loyalty to threats, compromise, and philosophical resignation. Podewils was to stress the Hungarian queen's "dilemma." If she could not defeat the French and Saxons without Frederick's help, what would happen if he remained in alliance with them? If she was strong enough to resist French, Saxons, and Prussians, then would she not be able to defeat the French and Saxons if Prussia stayed neutral? (Hyndford replied, with a laugh, "I find this dilemma as accurate as a demonstration of Newton. I wish only that one thought so at Vienna.")[1] Frederick furnished Podewils with numerous arguments in favor of a separate peace. Khevenhüller and his Hungarian irregulars — "of use for little else than bandits" — had fallen back to Landeshut; the French had seized Eger to reopen communications with Bohemia; fortress Glatz had surrendered; Frederick was daily growing more powerful — "I can fight, besiege, defend, or attack, whatever I regard as necessary," he boasted. His greatly increased army would soon be ready to join with Broglie; the Russians now wished to ally with Prussia.

Podewils was to introduce these arguments one by one. He would dispute territorial demands "foot by foot" but also give way when necessary "so that we may have the peace." Significantly, the king no longer demanded territorial concessions for his allies — but neither would he go to war against them. Finally, Podewils was to offer Hyndford 100,000 thalers to bring it off. Hyndford was no magician. All he could do was send the Prussian reply to Vienna and wait for its answer.

For three weeks Frederick alternated between hope and despair. The Vienna court had every reason to make peace with him, but such was its "conceit and braggadocio" that he doubted it would see the light.

And yet he needed peace. He had been wrong about Austrian plans. Prince Charles had not moved on Broglie's army, but rather into Moravia, which forced him to send reinforcements to Prince Dietrich's corps of observation. "Hunger and the admirable work of Monsieur de Schwerin," as he bitterly put it, had caused Dietrich to retreat from Olmütz, leaving a large number of cannon and quantities of munitions, powder, and provisions to the enemy. Dietrich had suffered further losses during the long march to Silesia, where he took quarters between Troppau and Jägerndorf. Once again Austria held all of Moravia.

The Saxons, contrary to promises, had retreated to Leitmeritz, north of Prague, where they could do no tactical good and a great deal of harm by eating up the area. Marshal Belle-Isle had taken field command once again and was arguing for immediate Franco-Prussian operations both in Bohemia and Flanders. Frederick was appalled. He could not send troops to Flanders, he told Belle-Isle; he was heavily committed along the Moravian border and would soon have to support another large force in Upper Silesia. The country between Chrudim and Budweis was barren, with no rivers to carry supply boats. He would need five hundred wagons to haul enough flour for three weeks. In addition he had to feed twelve thousand cavalry and three thousand artillery horses and would have no forage until spring. Allied armies were nowhere near ready to move down the Danube, which he continued to insist was the only proper strategy by which to end the war.

Despite Maria Theresa's blunt orders of late March, Prince Charles had moved cautiously, in the manner encouraged by his new military mentor, Marshal Königsegg. The field marshal had soldiered for half a century and was a man of vast experience and knowledge. But he was also slow and irresolute, which had earned him the name of General Rasttag — General Restday.

The army had begun assembling in Znaim only in early April. It did not leave until April 12, when it slowly followed Prince Dietrich's retreat north to Olmütz. Shrugging off the pleas of his generals at Brünn, Charles made no move to attack either the retreating Saxons or Dietrich's force. Although partisan operations badly hurt both Saxons and Prussians, the former escaped into Bohemia and the latter to Olmütz. The Austrians held all of Moravia, but it did them little good, since their enemies were now comfortably in Silesia and Bohemia.

Maria Theresa as usual called the next move. The Vienna court had learned that Frederick had built large magazines in Pardubitz and Königgrätz, where he planned to reinforce his army. Charles would therefore march over the mountains to Leutomischl and Königgrätz and attack the Prussians before they received reinforcements.

Königsegg was horrified. The retreating Prussians and Saxons would have taken what limited food and forage could be found in the mountains, and the army's supply system could not be counted on. Each wagon and gun would need eight horses, not four, for mountain roads; the difficult march would take a terrible toll of men. The Prussians could easily attack the tired and scattered columns as they debouched from the mountains. The army instead should fall back on Brünn and then march, not on Königgrätz, but on Prague, before Broglie could reinforce the garrison. The Prussians, Königsegg argued, were obviously too weak to give battle; otherwise, Frederick would have come to Dietrich's aid at Olmütz. Charles agreed. Leaving a corps of irregulars under Festetics to cover northern Moravia, he fell back on Wischau. Here he received a letter from Grand Duke Francis that totally rejected his new plan. While Königsegg prepared to march to Brünn and then west to Saar, he hurried to Vienna to plead his case. Nádasdy meanwhile would reconnoiter the Deutsch-Brod area in Bohemia.

Prince Charles arrived at Saar on May 10. He reported that Maria Theresa and her advisers, particularly Francis, had left no doubt that they wanted him to move against the Prussians instead of marching on Prague. The queen nonetheless left the final decision to him and Königsegg and to Prince Lobkowitz, who was now summoned. The three commanders decided to march on Prague via Czaslau and give battle if necessary. Lobkowitz was to divert Broglie by a march on Pisek before attacking the French garrison at Schloss Frauenberg. The main army would cross the Bohemian border on May 12.

The abortive campaign and subsequent uncertain situation had meanwhile told on the Prussian king. "He was in a frightful state," Valory later wrote. "His eyes were wild. All his remarks were harsh, his laughter forced and sardonic, his jokes full of bitterness."[2] And now Hyndford and Breslau received an answer from the Vienna court. Maria Theresa would make peace only if Prussia joined her war against France.

"I nearly fainted on receiving your letter," Frederick informed Podewils. "I now see clearly that we have nothing to hope for from the Hyndford negotiation and must renounce entirely a separate peace." New reports confirmed that Prince Charles was marching on Prague with the intention of fighting the Prussians if they got in the way.

Here at last was "an act of Providence." Gone now was hesitation, vanished any doubt. Frederick's blood was up. He had a rendezvous with his favorite whore, battle. "He breathes only revenge," Eichel noted to Podewils as the army marched. "It is said the enemy marches on me," Frederick wrote to Cardinal Fleury. "Pray say some masses so that this may happen and so that we can finish in a thunderclap a war it is not in our interest to continue."

39

Tuesday, May 15, 1742. King Frederick learns from patrols and deserters that enemy hussars are holding the bridge at Neu-Kolin and are in Kuttenberg and Czaslau. He thinks that the Austrians intend to seize his principal magazines at Nimburg, Pardubitz, and Podiebrad, then wheel west to march on Prague. To counter this plan, he moves out early with ten battalions, ten cavalry and ten hussar squadrons, an advance guard of about ten thousand. Prince Leopold is to follow with the bulk of the army, about eighteen thousand, once bread wagons arrive from Königgrätz.

Frederick's corps marches due west and reaches the heights of Podhorzan about noon. Cautious for once, the king takes up a defensive position. Reconnaissance reveals an enemy force several miles south along the heights of Wilimow.* He believes that this is part of Lobkowitz's army, possibly seven to eight thousand strong, which will rein-

---

* Podhorzan (today's Podhörozany) offers a splendid view of the entire Prague plain. The Prussian army subsequently marched through wooded rolling country interspersed with open fields, fox-hunting country like much of southern Ireland and western Virginia.

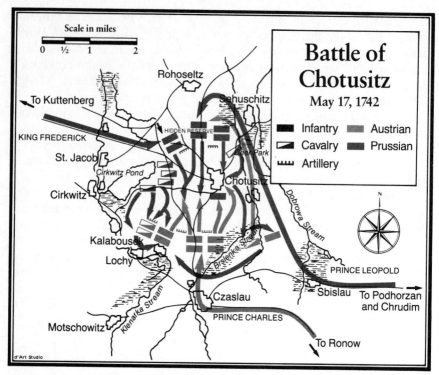

Scale in miles
0 ½ 1 2

Battle of Chotusitz
May 17, 1742

Infantry   Austrian
Cavalry   Prussian
Artillery

Rohoseltz

To Kuttenberg

Sehuschitz

KING FREDERICK

HIDDEN RESERVE

Deer Park

St. Jacob

Cirkwitz Pond

Chotusitz

Cirkwitz

Dobrowa Stream

Kalabousek

Brsjenka Stream

Lochy

PRINCE LEOPOLD

Czaslau

Sbislau

To Podhorzan and Chrudim

Klenarka Stream

PRINCE CHARLES

Motschowitz

To Ronow

d'Art Studio

force the main Austrian army that he supposes is still miles away to the
east. He sends Colonel Winterfeldt to Leopold with orders to march
on Czaslau at daybreak. New patrols ride south and west as security
outposts ring the camp. The troops remain dressed, under arms, their
horses saddled. There is no bread. They bake tasteless flour cakes.

What Frederick has seen is the Austrian advance guard. Prince Charles
is marching this day to Wilimow. He meets Nádasdy's hussars there to
learn that Frederick's force is marching from Chrudim to Podhorzan.
Charles rides to the heights north of Wilimow and observes the enemy
camp. He cannot tell whether it is a whole army or only a part. Whatever the case, he wants battle. The army will march early on Ronow.

Wednesday, May 16, 1742. Prussian patrols report that the enemy camp
at Wilimow has disappeared. Frederick rides to the heights to confirm
this. He reasons that Lobkowitz, wanting to avoid battle, is marching
east to join the main Austrian army. He sends Colonel von Schmettau
with new orders to Leopold. His own force marches shortly after five
A.M., destination Kuttenberg.

Leopold, still without bread, marches at four A.M. The day is hot,
the road dusty, terrain tiring. At some point Colonel Schmettau delivers the new orders. Leopold is to march west of Czaslau and take po-

sition astride the Czaslau-Kuttenberg road behind Brslenka Stream. Here he will be close to Frederick's camp in the Kuttenberg area; here they will wait for supplies and bake ovens from the Elbe magazines before going after the Austrians.

Leopold's columns soon close on the heights of Podhorzan. They are held by enemy light troops, who vanish when fired on by cannon. But from the heights the prince sees a large camp a few miles south. From the number of tents, he estimates that it is large enough for twenty-eight to thirty thousand men, that is, the main Austrian army. And now deserters report that this very army is advancing from Wilimow. Charles must be planning to move on Czaslau, Leopold decides; perhaps he already holds it. He changes march direction to the northwest. Aides ride to inform the king of the Austrian presence and ask him to fall back from Kuttenberg to join the main army.

Leopold's march is delayed by enemy hussars and irregulars guarding the Dobrowa Stream. By the time they are beaten off and the heavy guns pulled across the single wooden bridge at Sbislau, it is late afternoon. The march continues. He learns that enemy troops are in Czaslau. His own troops are filthy from dust and exhausted from hunger and the up-and-down terrain through country plagued by enemy hussars and Warasdiners operating out of Czaslau. The columns close late on Chotusitz village. They can march no farther this day.

Regiment Schwerin arrives about midnight to occupy Chotusitz. It is a typical elongated village with a main street forty-five yards wide running north to south and flanked by small stone farmsteads with thatched roofs. A church stands in the center. Troops move to its sanctified shelter. The main army camps north and northwest of the village. Tents are thrown up, horses unsaddled. Exhausted men eat gruel made of flour and water.

There is no word from the king.

About ten P.M. Leopold sends Captain Johann Albrecht von Bülow with a new message to Frederick. The enemy is very close, he warns. He begs His Majesty to join him; he desperately needs bread.

In the afternoon of this same day Frederick with a small party reaches Kuttenberg. He chases off a flock of enemy irregulars, captures a large quantity of bread fresh from local bake ovens. Deserters report that Charles's army will not reach Czaslau for another two days. The rest of his troops arrive and are billeted in surrounding villages. He hears nothing from Leopold (enemy hussars having prevented couriers from reaching him). Captain von Bülow finds the royal headquarters around midnight. Frederick is not impressed with Leopold's urgency. He is certain that the enemy is two days distant. He sends Leopold two thousand loaves of bread. He himself will march before daybreak and bring more bread. There will be battle, all right, but it will be after a day of rest, and it will be the Prussians who march: "Then we must attack the enemy immediately, whoever he is. . . . I promise, unless Providence should be against us, that the enemy will be ours."

The Austrian army marches early on Wednesday for Ronow. The men move on narrow, low roads with overhanging wooded heights. They are soon hot, thirsty, dirty, hungry, and tired. At Ronow in late afternoon Charles and Königsegg learn from General Nádasdy of Leopold's advance to Podhorzan. The two commanders watch the Prussians stumbling from the heights. There is still time to attack. But they do not like the marshy terrain; they worry about enemy strength. They believe that the Prussian advance guard is in the Kuttenberg area. Clearly this force intends to march there. Better for the hussars to harass Leopold's columns. Better to wait for favorable terrain. Then they will surprise the enemy, win a great victory, erase forever the stain of Mollwitz.

But their orders to Nádasdy are not clear. He rides that evening with his hussars, not north toward Leopold's columns but northwest toward Frederick's advance guard at Kuttenberg, about twelve miles distant. They ride at night over unfamiliar terrain. They learn from peasants that the enemy is dispersed in cantonments. It is dark, impossible to obtain details. Nádasdy bivouacs and sends a courier to inform Charles that the enemy army is at Kuttenberg.

Charles meanwhile orders a night march to Czaslau, a little over seven miles away. They army moves west in three columns. Heavy baggage remains in camp, where tents are left standing and fires burning to deceive Prussian patrols.

Thursday, May 17, 1742. The Austrians march all night. It is a beautiful spring night with full moon, but the land is difficult, cut by streams; the air is heavy; the going on narrow winding roads is slow. Columns close south of Czaslau only about four A.M. Nádasdy's messenger arrives to report that the enemy army is camped around Kuttenberg. So Charles and Königsegg are right. They will surprise those damned Prussians.

Charles's advance guard marches from Czaslau about five A.M. Cavalry leads the columns. The troopers cross Brslenka Stream by two stone bridges just outside Czaslau. Suddenly they spot enemy outposts. They halt. Patrols confirm that Leopold with the main Prussian army is camped behind Chotusitz, scarcely more than two miles to the north. The news is disturbing. But never mind. Their plan changes. They will attack here.

But units are delayed in marching up and in crossing Brslenka Stream, which girdles Czaslau to the north. Infantry must funnel through two narrow bridges. Cavalry must ford streams. Commanders take three hours to deploy twenty-eight thousand troops into battle lines. Charles stands on a hill one kilometer northwest of Czaslau. Most of Leopold's army is hidden from his view.

Captain von Bülow delivers Frederick's reply to Prince Leopold around two A.M. Bread wagons roll in under escort shortly before daybreak. While the six-pound loaves are distributed to ravenous troops, Leopold rides to a height on his right wing. He sees enemy cavalry deploying on the heights east of Cirkwitz Pond. He watches for an hour. It is clear that the enemy is forming to attack.

It is about six A.M.

Leopold rides to his commanders. He orders General Wilhelm von Buddenbrock's cavalry to deploy behind the heights on the right with the flank anchored on Cirkwitz pond. His heavy artillery — only four guns — is moved to a hill fronting Buddenbrock's position. Kalkstein's infantry will deploy on Buddenbrock's left to carry the line to Chotusitz. Leopold rides east, picks up Lieutenant General Adam Friedrich von Jeetze and canters to the flatland north of Druhanitz. Jeetze is to deploy his infantry here, the right resting on Chotusitz, the left tied in with General von Waldow's cavalry, which will carry the line to the deer park by Sehuschitz. Once deployment is carried out, the heavy guns on the right will open fire, Buddenbrock's cavalry will attack, the infantry will follow. Leopold returns to the right wing, sends the king a report of his deployments and intentions.

It is about seven A.M.

The troops are tearing into thick loaves of bread when Leopold's orders reach subordinate commanders. The men are still tired, unfamiliar with the land; there is confusion. Troops grudgingly shuffle into formation. Tents are left standing. Matters go well on the right, where heavy guns are brought up and unlimbered, where Buddenbrock's squadrons deploy in defilade, almost completely hidden by undulating terrain to their front. But matters are not so prosperous with the infantry. Kalkstein's battalions are slow in forming lines on Buddenbrock's left. Jeetze apparently misunderstands his orders. Leopold wants four infantry battalions in line east of Chotusitz. Jeetze places only one battalion here and three battalions on the heights south of the village. Marshy terrain slows the deployment of men and horses. More delay. Dangerous gaps open east of Chotusitz. Kalkstein's battalions move slowly. Another dangerous gap opens west of Chotusitz.

Frederick's camp stands early to arms. A 3-pounder cannon fires to signal march alert to distant detachments. Guard battalions march at five A.M. They are joined by other units at Neuhof. Colonel Johann von Bronikowsky's hussars do not hear the cannon; they sleep blissfully on. Frederick soon receives Leopold's message. He sends word that he is on the way and will deploy his squadrons and battalions into the second line. He sends Rothenburg's dragoons forward, orders a fast march for the infantry. "We arrived as much cavalry as infantry at full trot," he recalled.[1]

It is about seven-thirty A.M.. The four heavy cannon are firing from Leopold's right when Frederick trots in with eight battalions, which he pushes into the second line, a defilade position hidden from enemy view. Someone gallops off to fetch Bronikowsky's sleeping hussars. Leopold canters up to report the situation. No time remains to ride the lines.

It is a sunny, hot day.

King Frederick on horse studies the scene from a hill on the Prussian right. Some twenty-eight thousand Prussian troops are struggling to form a line two miles or so from left to right. Dust covers much of the effort. Dust also rises from the south as Austrian soldiers march to the attack, two lines of infantry with horse on either flank, a front of about two and a quarter miles stretching from east of Cirkwitz Pond to the east of Brslenka Stream. Frederick watches carefully. From what he can make out, the enemy looks a little ragged. In crossing Brslenka Stream, flanks begin to outspace center, a dangerous concave formation noted by the blue-gray eyes.

Austrian horse probe from the right, east of Cirkwitz Pond. Prussian 3-pounders join the fire of their bigger brothers. Iron cannonballs fly a thousand yards to smack into men and horses of General Count Karl Batthyányi's waiting squadrons. The Austrians fall back. There is confusion.

Frederick watches. Batthyányi's squadrons are disorganized. A gap opens on the Austrian left. Colonel Schmettau carries a brief order to Buddenbrock: Attack at once.

Buddenbrock's cuirassiers move to battle line. The seventy-year-old general leads them forward, a very compact advance, a formation that moves "first at a trot, then a gallop," a mass of armed horsepower, a shock unit of thundering hooves, of flags held high, of flashing sabers and terrifying cries.

Shock they do.

Buddenbrock is a first-class general, brave as they come, and bold. He moves fast, tears into the first line of Austrian horse to send the squadrons reeling back to the Czaslau bridges. Rothenburg's dragoons thunder in from close behind, tear through the second line of enemy horse.

So far, so good.

But now trouble. The dust is blinding. Before Buddenbrock's people are reorganized, three enemy regiments strike his dispersed squadrons in front and flank. The battle loses cohesion; men strike blindly — "*à la hussarde,*" it is called. Rothenburg's dragoons are also in trouble. He attacks too far to the left, runs into flank infantry regiments. The dragoons fight furiously, but the infantry holds. Enemy cavalry suddenly charge from out of the dust and cut the dragoons to ribbons. Rothenburg is slashed across arm and breast. Bronikowsky's hussars finally arrive and charge to battle, proudly garbed in new green uniforms. Some Prussian troopers take them for enemy. Cries of being cut off bounce from man to man.

Frederick sits on his horse, watching. He sees only immense clouds of dust. It is eight A.M.

Slaughter rules the Prussian left. Jeetze is weak east of Chotusitz, where Brslenka Stream divides the lines. Part of the force is defending in front of the village, part between village and brook, part between brook and the extreme left. It is swampy ground, the worst possible for cavalry. But General von Waldow, desperately wanting to repair the stained performance at Mollwitz a year ago, leaves his sickbed to lead three cuirassier regiments to the attack.

The horses pick their way through rutted land, cross the stream, and move to the south. Austrian cuirassiers gallop to the attack and cut up the two lead regiments. Regiment Prince William picks up the survivors, smashes Austrian ranks, hacks through a large reserve force of Warasdiners, then gallops southwest to strike the Austrian left wing from the rear — a wild three-mile ride that costs the regiment half its men and horses. Survivors join the melee to mix with Buddenbrock's, Rothenburg's, and Bronikowsky's squadrons. Waldow is wounded; officers and men are dying all around him.

Meanwhile Jeetze is in trouble on the left. The Austrian cavalry have regrouped. Prussian dragoons of the second line ride to the attack. The Austrians fall on them, send them reeling from the field. The Prussian left is now exposed. Jeetze feeds in three battalions to extend Regiment Schwerin's left, another battalion to try to plug the hole on the right.

Charles and Königsegg are watching this action with their principal commanders. All agree that the Prussian left is disorganized. Charles will attack at once. Lieutenant General Count Leopold von Daun protests that artillery fire must precede any attack over open ground. Charles yields. Foaming horses pull heavy guns to the Austrian right. Sweating gunners unlimber, load, and fire. Battalions of three infantry regiments move to the attack. Two more regiments will follow. These are not the hungry, confused, halfhearted, and ill-trained men of Mollwitz. They approach with shouldered arms. On command they halt, unshoulder arms, load, and fire. They continue the advance with fixed bayonets. An immense fight quickly develops.

King Frederick and aides hear new sounds of heavy battle on the left.

Frederick's own position is tenuous. He cannot leave the right wing as long as the cavalry action continues to his front. He sends Prince Leopold to take command of the left.

Leopold finds battalions and squadrons locked in full battle south, east, and west of Chotusitz, with enemy units snaking in to attack the village from east and north. There is still a gap on the right of Regiment Schwerin. He plugs this with three battalions from the second line and sends his final battalion from the second line to hold the village with the help of General Ernst Friedrich von Werdeck's dragoons.

Leopold is facing the enemy's major attack. Charles feeds in more battalions. The Prussians are fighting superbly but are falling back. The Lutheran chaplain Seegebart appears and, with bullets whizzing about him "like swarms of gnats," exhorts his sheep of Regiment Leopold to hold "in the name of God and the king." [2] They hold for an hour; most of them die. The Prussian line gives way in places. Austrian cavalry appear east of Chotusitz. Nothing is in their way. Werdeck sees the danger, leads some dragoons against them. He and his horse are killed; the survivors limp back to Chotusitz. They are soon joined by tired soldiers falling back from the southern heights, many clutching torn heads, bellies, arms, legs. They take cover in rude cottages and barns, fire from upper windows. The Austrians press in from front and flank. Tactical integrity vanishes. Small unit fights small unit, man fights man, the bayonet rules. "Thus the massacre began," an Austrian commander later wrote. [3] The Prussians fight very hard. Unit commanders are everywhere, imploring, exhorting, threatening — many fall. The Austrians set the village on fire. Thatched roofs instantly flame to thick smoke.

Meanwhile, five regiments of enemy cavalry sneak around the Prussian left flank. This is a master stroke. But now they reach the tents — and stop. Booty is better than battle. Furious officers scream threats. No one pays attention. They take what they can and retreat.

The village of Chotusitz is burning. Heavy smoke adds to powder smoke and dust to obscure confused battle actions. The burning village divides an already compartmented terrain. Prussian defenders stumble, burned and coughing, to the north of the village. The enemy follows and pushes them to the fields. Leopold collects retreating remnants to form a new defensive line. He bolsters this with units from the second line on his right. These people have not yet fought. They are eager and fresh, standing "like lions" to halt further enemy advance. The Austrians attack. Salvos of musket fire and 3-pounder caseshot shatter their ranks. But now the Prussian line wavers. A battalion begins to give way. Its commander, Major Karl Erhard von Kalnein, takes the standard to lead it forward. The troops give way again. Again he raises the gold-embroidered bullet-whipped standard. His men rally and hold.

Charles feeds in his last battalions. Only three regiments are guarding the Austrian left flank. But here Austrian horse win the confused cavalry battle. Rothenburg and Waldow are badly wounded, their squadrons as dispersed as those of Buddenbrock and Bronikowsky. Bruised and beaten, they fall back and disappear toward Kuttenberg. Austrian cavalry follow. The dust settles. It is about nine-thirty A.M.

A short, stocky king hunched on horseback is watching from the Prussian right. Hard-riding aides bring reports from along the line. Chotusitz is lost. Enemy cavalry are plundering the Prussian camp. His own cavalry are fleeing toward Kuttenberg. But enemy horse also leave the field; there will be no devastating charge from them as at Mollwitz — and that is crucial. Frederick watches the smoke and dust of battle far to the left, where Charles and Königsegg are looking for a victory.

With the Prussian left absorbing Austrian fury, with the Prussian right intact, Frederick orders twenty-one fresh battalions to attack. They come from behind him. Heavy guns pave the way as these troops march out rapidly in precise lines. They advance several hundred yards to the heights, wheel left. Now battalion 3-pounders fire from front and from intervals between battalions. It is total surprise. The Prussians, marching like automatons, strike the Austrian left, shatter the protecting regiments, hurl them back on center and right. Leopold on the left exploits the surprise, orders a fresh attack. Prussian bayonets drive an astounded enemy from Chotusitz. Frederick's oncoming battalions loom like an anvil against which Leopold can hammer the enemy. Charles and his generals recognize the danger. Their attack has failed. They are in terrible trouble. They retreat.

The Austrians move out about noon. A few battalions with some artillery and cavalry cover the vital stone bridges across Brslenka Stream. Austrian commanders later report an orderly retreat, and this is true in part. According to Frederick, they retreat in great confusion, and this is also true in part. Certainly they leave several thousand dead and wounded men and horses on the field; they leave seventeen cannon and ten munition wagons, the terrified teamsters having cut the traces and ridden off to anywhere; they leave mounds of knapsacks and six hundred wounded men in Czaslau, which Prussian units now occupy.

Frederick watches them go. A small force of infantry and cavalry will follow, but only for a few miles. The rest of the army is in no condition to march, much less to fight. Some Austrian cavalry regiments are unaccounted for, and thus remain a threat. The troops are exhausted and hungry, supplies are short, casualties heavy. Leopold, who is wounded, joins the king on a height south of Brslenka Stream. Frederick embraces the prince, promotes him to field marshal.

Austrian columns shuffle back through Czaslau, spirits low, guns abandoned, a cavalry rearguard skirmishing with Prussian hussars. They dig in for the night at the village of Habern, from where they will continue the retreat to Deutsch-Brod on the Sazawa River.

Fires light the morbid scene of recent battle. Busy surgeons, aprons long since soaked with blood, will work the night through — will work for several days and nights — their efforts always accompanied by pleading cries of wounded and dying men. Working parties are already digging enormous graves south of Chotusitz while fires consume carcasses of once-splendid horses.

It is dark now. The troops eat horsemeat.

The battle of Chotusitz is over.

40

CHOTUSITZ was a major Prussian victory, and Frederick hastened to spread the news. Black smoke still hovered over a field of dead and dying as he scribbled his signature on dispatches that senior commanders would carry to European courts.

Wartensleben carried one to King August: "I am writing to report a complete victory over the enemy. I have no time to tell you more."

General Samuel von Schmettau carried news of "the complete and signal victory" to Emperor Charles: "My satisfaction is so much the greater since by it I hope Your Imperial Majesty will see himself master of Bohemia."

Borcke rode with a message to King Louis at Versailles: "Prince Charles has attacked me and I have beaten him." Other officers carried the word to the Berlin court, to Old Dessauer, Jordan, Podewils, Broglie, Belle-Isle, and Valory.

Despite fatigue, the king at once composed a lengthy "Relation" of the battle. "It is by me and in no way lies," he wrote to Dessauer. Podewils was to publish it in Breslau and Berlin and in "German, French, Dutch, and English newspapers," with copies sent to all Prussian envoys abroad for widest circulation. He was tired as a bird's neck but proud of himself and his army. In *his* mind it was *his* victory, one "greater and more complete than that of Mollwitz," he wrote to Queen Elizabeth. Dessauer was miles away in Silesia; Schwerin was sulking in fortress Neisse. "Our cavalry in part has been very brave and acted heroically. The infantry was superb," he wrote Dessauer, whose army was to hear a solemn Te Deum "sung under the fire of cannon and small arms."

At a religious service the following Sunday, his chaplains thanked God for the victory. Three salvos fired from enemy cannon honored the dead of both sides. Promotions followed for officers and men who had distinguished themselves. When the brave chaplain Seegebart refused a captain's rank, he was otherwise rewarded; Chasot, who had saved the king's personal baggage, was given the Order of Merit and a valuable holding.

Jubilation soon turned to remorse and reflection — the Mollwitz syndrome. There was no escaping the heavy casualties. Dead lay everywhere — some two thousand Prussians and a thousand Austrians, over twenty-five hundred horses. Naked bodies still covered the field four days after battle. Surgeons worked on over two thousand Prussian wounded and a similar number of enemy. A great many of these must have died. The king leased no less than nine acres of fields south of Chotusitz as a communal cemetery for twenty-five years.

Yet many men survived. A week after the battle the king wrote to Podewils that "our losses diminish the more one checks them. . . . I will canton my army in order to care for it and refit it; a few months will repair our losses." Over three thousand Austrians and four to five thousand Prussians were missing, either prisoners, deserters, or fatalities. The Prussians had lost twenty-five hundred horses to the enemy in addition to those killed, but a reinforcement of six thousand infantry and cavalry that arrived five days after the battle greatly helped to repair these gaps.

Frederick's jubilant dispatches served a dual purpose. Besides informing all Europe that Prussians had beaten Austrians for a second time running, they were designed to force his allies to action. Maria Theresa, he believed, would have to make peace with him to avoid total ruin. His neutrality could still be bought, but he wanted Königgrätz and Pardubitz in addition to Silesia, and he refused to guarantee the queen's lands. The deal must be made within fifteen days.

The allies could help. By encouraging them to act, he could lighten the onus that invariably would result from his making a separate peace. If they refused to move, or if they moved maladroitly, they would cause him to forfeit his favorable political position, and no one then could blame him for abandoning the alliance. If they moved quickly and intelligently, they could force Maria Theresa to make peace on terms favorable to them, and Frederick could take much of the credit. The main Austrian army, he pointed out, was in shambles, shorn of a third of its strength, the commanders confused, officers despondent, troops discouraged; over six hundred deserters had come to the Prussian camp within a few days after the battle. Only Lobkowitz's small corps, some seven thousand, was fit for battle. He was besieging Schloss Frauenberg, an easy target for Broglie's force at Pisek. After reporting his victory to Broglie, Frederick wrote: "It is extremely important to the common cause that you do not allow the enemy time to get his bearings; considering the important blow that I have struck the enemy, it is out of the question that your army would do nothing." The Marquis de Maillebois, an able French general, had closed on Eger with a sizable force. He could easily join Broglie. Lobkowitz must be attacked and beaten before Khevenhüller crossed the Danube to reinforce Charles. General von Schmettau repeated this analysis to Emperor Charles and traveled on to Prague to persuade Belle-Isle to take field command and try to bring the Saxons back into the war.

Broglie marched on Frauenberg in late May. At Sahay his army ran into some Austrian cavalry and beat them, a skirmish that the French treated as a great victory, sending more couriers to foreign courts than there were enemy dead, Frederick said in one of those remarks which so endeared him to allied commanders. Greatly outnumbered, Lobkowitz made a night withdrawal to Budweis. Broglie occupied Schloss Frauenberg and stood still, believing that nothing more could be done until he received reinforcements.

In early June the Belle-Isle brothers visited Frederick and found him in sour humor. The Saxons were refusing to march, and the French were up to old tricks, delaying military action while jockeying for political gain. Neither of the Belle-Isles nor the senior generals in their entourage seemed impressed with the Prussian victory at Chotusitz; to Frederick's annoyance they did not even wish to visit the battlefield. He also had it on good authority that Fleury was offering to sell out Prussia to both Vienna and Saint Petersburg, and Marshal Belle-Isle's honeyed words only strengthened that suspicion. When the marshal urged him to march to the Moldau, he hotly refused. He had fought a major battle, his troops were exhausted, supplies short, lines of communications under frequent attack by enemy irregulars and peasants. Hussars had recently ridden into Glatz to strip Prussian wounded of clothing and belongings.* Sickness, hunger, and enemy irregulars were slowly pushing Dessauer out of Upper Silesia.† It was high time his allies took up the burden. For the record they agreed that the Saxons must join the French, the war should be as short as possible, and the

---

* On May 25 the king ordered a major to hang a few citizens and priests of Glatz who were suspected of treachery. In addition, "You shall erect a large gallows and inscribe on it: 'Punishment of those faithless, perfidious and treacherous subjects.' " (Generalstab I, Volume 3.)
† In late May, Dessauer asked to be transferred and when this was refused he proposed leaving a few light cavalry regiments and several battalions in Upper Silesia and bringing the rest of his force to Bohemia. Frederick would not hear of it. Instead, Dessauer should send "commandos" of infantry, cavalry, and small cannon against the insurgents. "I know from experience, if the Hungarian people are allowed to have their own way and are able to attack here and there, they become only more daring, but if one attacks and pursues them with suitable preparations and precautions, they will then soon respect one."

allies should seize as much territory as they could. *Beati possidentes* (The blessed possess), as Frederick put it.

He was scarcely surprised when the allied situation began to worsen. While Broglie at Frauenberg waited in vain for reinforcements, Prince Charles advanced from Deutsch-Brod with the main Austrian army to join Lobkowitz. Khevenhüller meanwhile crossed the Danube with a strong detachment and was marching to join them. Frederick correctly believed that Broglie would soon be in trouble. "It is impossible to count all the faults that these [French] generals have made," he complained to Jordan.

His worst fears were realized when the reinforced Austrian army marched on Frauenberg. Broglie retreated in great confusion, and with considerable loss of men and baggage, to Pisek, from where he explained his retreat to the Prussian king. "I am very annoyed about it," Frederick unsympathetically replied, "but I hope that you will be able to support your position there." Broglie instead retreated almost immediately on Pilsen and from there on Prague. Enemy hussars, Croats, and peasants had a field day, striking long slow columns and throwing them into confusion and rout. Ill and demoralized, soldiers slipped off to nearby woods, only to be killed by lurking enemy. Broglie also lost all his personal baggage, an immense quantity of silver plate, and forty thousand livres in cash. Simultaneously, Austrian irregulars increased their activity in the Prussian area, even attacking the Pardubitz magazine.

Fearful that French reverses would cause Maria Theresa to cancel Lord Hyndford's negotiating authority, fearful also that a new battle for Prague was forming, one in which his army would have to play a major role, Frederick instructed Podewils to make "a solid and stable" peace as soon as possible. While final conditions were being worked out with Hyndford in Breslau, the Prussian king began giving his allies not-so-subtle hints, since he wanted neither to "surprise" nor "disorient" them. He told Valory that thanks to Marshal Broglie "there is no longer a French army," so Prussia must make the best peace possible.[1] To Fleury he wrote of the bad state of affairs "for which I scarcely see a remedy. . . . I believe that in these such critical circumstances there remains scarcely any other remedy than to get out by a peace, which must be made with conditions as favorable as possible." A similar assessment went to Emperor Charles. After reciting the latest reverses to Marshal Belle-Isle, including the Saxons' refusal to march, Frederick concluded: "I regard this affair as a voyage undertaken by several [rulers] to the same destination, but which, upset by a shipwreck, places each voyager in the right of providing for his particular security, of saving himself by swimming and landing where he is able."

By mid-June Podewils and Hyndford had agreed on all but minor points. The Vienna court would cede nothing to Bavaria or France but was willing to make peace with Saxony, providing her troops at once evacuated Bohemia. Frederick also agreed to leave Bohemia within sixteen days; he dropped demands for Königgrätz and Pardubitz; and he agreed to assume four million thalers' worth of Silesian mortgages held by British and Dutch merchants. A major row developed over the issue of Silesian boundaries, but too much was at stake for either court to break off negotiations. Frederick finally yielded and, to his great relief, peace preliminaries were signed at Breslau.

"Although in time we might have had a better peace," he wrote to Podewils in congratulating him, "we could also have had a worse one. . . . For the good of the people whom I govern, I could not have done otherwise. In short, it is a great and fortunate event that puts my House in possession of one of the most flourishing provinces of Germany."

The king suppressed news of the treaty for as long as possible, but troops had to march, magazines had to be sold. The secret was out before the last Prussian troops retired into Silesia in late June. The allies reacted predictably. "No puppet can imitate Valory's contortions," Frederick told Podewils. "His eyes were zigzagged, his mouth widened, he fluttered about in a strange way, and all this without having anything good to say to me. His greatest anxiety rested on the part that I should take after the peace." At Versailles the news caused some Cabinet members to faint; Cardinal Fleury burst into tears. To Emperor Charles it was one more murderous blow. The Saxon court acted with restraint and soon began its own peace negotiations with Vienna.

BOOK FOUR

Peace — and War

1742–1746

The war, then, that is appropriate for the king of Prussia to make is compulsory in order to antici-pate the evil design of his enemies.

— *Frederick the Great, 1744*

FREDERICK'S personal letters from Moravia leave no doubt of how much he had missed the artistic and intellectual life. In March, when preparing for an Austrian attack, he had asked Jordan to send works by Cicero, Caesar, and Boileau. In early April, when preparing to evacuate Moravia, he asked Knobelsdorff to report on the royal estates and gardens and on the progress of the new opera house. He repeatedly pressed Jordan for personal news, activities of old friends, Berlin gossip, the arrival of musicians, singers, dancers. In May he wrote to Algarotti, "As soon as the war is over you will see me a philosopher more than ever attached to studies." In June he excitedly reported his purchase of Cardinal de Polignac's rich collection of antiques. He spoke longingly of basking under the superb lime trees in Charlottenburg and of enjoying the soft solitude of Rheinsberg.

It was not to be.

Cannon may have ceased firing and bells may have sounded from a hundred Silesian steeples, but he was still king. Peace brought little surcease from labor. "Listen, dear friend Jordan," he wrote from Glatz, "I have too much to do here — fortifications, law, economy, military — to write at length." It was worse at Neisse: "I am having great projects done here; this place should become the barrier of the state, the guarantee of my new conquests. From here I am directing the new arrangements of the province; I am regulating legal affairs, and am arranging the economy." Finally, from Breslau: "I have finished all my affairs and return to my country with the consolation of having no reproach to make against myself." *

Frederick returned to Berlin as king in every sense. He was thirty years old. He had added nearly sixteen thousand square miles of rich

---

* The task would be left largely to Count von Münchow. Frederick judged it so immense and important that he refused to allow his friend to marry until his affairs were completely settled.

lands and well over a million subjects to his small kingdom, not to mention an annual income of four and a half million thalers. Just as important, Brandenburg-Prussia was no longer a blustering joke in European courts. "You are the arbiter of Europe," no less a statesman than Cardinal Fleury told him, and if the good man exaggerated, it was undeniably true that by the sword Frederick had made Prussia an important power that henceforth would play a vital role in European politics.

But promotion had not come cheaply, nor would it be easily retained. Valory found the king to be extremely restless, not feeling well, and in grim humor — all of which he blamed on the royal conscience (upset by having abandoned his allies). More likely the king was bordering on physical and mental exhaustion. His always weak stomach had been causing trouble, as had hemorrhoids, and for the first time he seems to have been bothered by rheumatism and gout. He had perforce neglected internal affairs; administration and finances were disarranged. The war chest was virtually empty; the army needed recruits, arms, cannon, horses, and equipment; expensive fortifications had to be built in Silesia. The treasury held a meager three million thalers; salaries had to be paid and large Silesian mortgages were owing to merchants in England and Holland. Only time and hard work could revive Prussian fortunes. Above all he must keep Silesia and avoid a new war — at least until he was ready to fight one.

These needs were paramount. Before leaving Bohemia Frederick had written to Podewils that "for some years the foundation of our politics should be a happy quietism." He was not so naïve as to believe that saying was obtaining. He knew far too much about hatred and revenge to think that either Austria or his recent allies would forgive and forget his brand of *Realpolitik*. "Happy quietism," in reality armed neutrality, depended on "a good and large army, a good treasury, redoubtable fortresses, and ostentatious but undemanding alliances."

Back in Potsdam the king committed himself to a daily routine that began at four in the morning and continued until eleven at night. Awakened by a servant, who placed a cold towel on his face, he was shaved and had his hair powdered. He dressed quickly, in plain blue military jacket with yellow waistcoat and breeches and knee boots. Servants brought the morning mail in large baskets, as in his father's day. He drank coffee while reading scores of letters, reports, and dispatches that concerned every facet, internal and external, of the sprawling kingdom. He dictated replies to secretaries until nine, when military aides arrived to report and receive orders, usually an hour's business. The rest of the morning went to military inspections (he frequently drilled a battalion of the Potsdam Guards), to private correspondence, and sometimes to special audiences with commoners who had petitioned for royal justice.* Dinner was at noon, usually with about twenty-four people, mostly generals talking military business. They were served generously and well — hot, spicy dishes washed down with champagne and followed by fresh fruit. Dinner normally lasted two hours. After a promenade on foot or horse, the king signed the day's correspondence and retired to writing, reading, and composing poetry and music. An evening concert commenced at six and included several flute solos composed and played by the king. The court sat to supper at ten. Frederick was usually in bed an hour later.

This daily routine was broken by the rare visit to Rheinsberg and by occasional visits to Berlin. But companionship was lacking. Keyserling and Rothenburg were ill; his friend the intellectual rebel Marquis Jean Baptiste d'Argens and Charles Étienne Jordan were both busy in Berlin; Algarotti was in Dresden, from where he refused a pension and residence in the Prussian court. Time was precious, taken up by spring and autumn military reviews, by numerous inspection trips to other provinces — scarcely relaxing, because he traveled with a minimum of equipage and comfort, and so much work had to be done during the visits.

It was a disciplined existence unknown to monarchs of the day, and it resulted in an administrative output of almost inconceivable proportions. Leaving aside hundreds of personal letters and various private writings, leaving aside hundreds of political dispatches, many of them long and complex, it accounts for stacks of civil edicts, many of them the famous Cabinet orders that are found in the *Acta Borussica,* the multivolume collection of official Prussian documents. Probably thousands more have been lost. These extant documents show his deep involvement in civil administration, on both the national and provincial levels: selecting provincial officials, awarding civil pensions, organizing new departments, founding new industries and expanding old ones, financing land reclamation and colonization, procuring foreign artisans and tradesmen, constructing new canals and improving old ones, dredging new harbors, reorganizing Berlin police, improving postal services and roads, refining customs and excise procedures, regulating forests and mines, investigating new crops, and encouraging maritime trade.

He was not yet sufficiently experienced to move rapidly and decisively in all civil spheres, nor did a depleted treasury allow reforms that in any event would conflict with traditional privileges of the provinces, not to mention their ponderous and confused administrative systems. His first steps were tentative, cautious, sometimes awkward, but as he

---

* Under a traditional right known as the Gravamina, commoners, including serfs, could write directly to the king for redress of wrongs.

gained confidence and funds became available, he began to spread his administrative wings. His aim was clear enough. He wanted a strong central government that, by improving the welfare and thus the output of his subjects, would bring funds to increase the army and, with that, the security of the kingdom.

He was more at home in military affairs and was soon repairing losses in men and mounts. As early as mid-August the British envoy, Lord Hyndford, reported that "he is augmenting his army every day." In early December he wrote that the new battalions

> will be very soon formed, for every Regiment of Foot is to give Five Men per Company, and the King of Prussia has recruiting Officers in almost every province of Germany and He takes the Opportunity of the Empire's being without a Head, of drawing Numbers of Recruits from all parts, either by Menaces or good words; He supports the little Princes and Counts of the Empire against the great Ones, upon Condition they find Recruits for his officers.[1]

It was not all work. Shortly after his return, royal physicians sent the king to take the baths at Aix-la-Chapelle. With his brother Henry in tow, he stayed for two weeks of bleedings; he imbibed large quantities of foul-tasting mineral waters and suffered hours of hot mud and mineral baths. "We see many foreigners here," he wrote to his brother William, who had managed to evade the trip, "a number of Dutch officers, but very little distinguished company."

Voltaire briefly visited him. "I have seen him as one seldom sees kings," he wrote to a friend, "much at my ease, in my own room, in the chimney nook, whither the same man who has gained two battles would come and talk familiarly, as Scipio did with Terence. You will tell me I am not Terence; true, but neither is he altogether Scipio." * Voltaire described the king as treating two famous physicians, Cappel and Gotzweiler, "as he treated other powers" — that is, arbitrarily. Frederick did not hesitate to lecture them on the finer points of diagnosis nor to scoff at prescribed regimens. Nevertheless, the stern routine — he was to write no poetry; he was not even to *think* — seems to have relaxed him. Although he complained of vertigo, he put on weight and left the spa tan and refreshed, a convert forever to medicinal baths.

---

* Terence (c. 184–159 B.C.) was brought to Rome as a slave and was eventually freed; he became a famous writer of comedies. Scipio the Younger (c. 185–129 B.C.) was the conqueror of Carthage. Frederick on this occasion offered Voltaire a house in Berlin, a country house, and a generous pension if he would reside in Prussia. "I prefer a second story in the house of Madame de Châtelet," Voltaire wrote to a friend, "and I hasten to Paris, to my slavery and persecution, like a little Athenian who had refused the bounties of the King of Prussia." (Parton, *Life of Voltaire*.)

Field Marshal Count Leopold von Traun of Austria, who pushed the Prussian army from Bohemia in 1744. Frederick regarded this campaign as his education in warfare, with Traun the teacher.

Frederick returned to Berlin in 1742 to be declared "the arbiter of Europe" by Cardinal Fleury.

A model of its kind, the Berlin opera house had over two thousand seats, parking for a thousand carriages, and a rich interior décor with elegantly appointed boxes.

Contact with Voltaire as usual had proven intellectually stimulating. "You have given me such a strong taste for work," he wrote in mid-November, "that I have written an epistle in verse, a play, and some very curious memoirs. . . . I am still working on the last and do not believe that I will finish the work until next year." *

Other pleasant activities marked the months. Cardinal de Polignac's antiques arrived and were installed at Charlottenburg palace.† In December the new opera house opened in Berlin. A contemporary described it in detail: a model of its kind, over two thousand seats, parking for a thousand carriages, enormous entrances, spacious lobbies, rich interior décor with elegantly appointed boxes, perfect acoustics, special ventilation, expensive precautions against fire, advanced stage techniques. Frederick described the opening performance, a mediocre work by Karl Heinrich Graun called *Cléopatra et César,* to Wilhelmina: "I have never seen a spectacle more elegant and magnificent. Our voices are very superior to those of last year, and the dancers are as good as there are in Europe." He continued to spend large sums to attract the finest performers, including Barbarina,‡ and he remained in Berlin for Fasching, the winter carnival, with its endless round of festivities, elegant dinners, magnificent balls, masquerades, theatricals, and sleigh rides. But though the court frequently enjoyed all-night parties, its king retired early to awaken to affairs of state. Frederick could never long ignore a war that he had helped foment — particularly when its shifting tides began to threaten his new frontiers.

42

BEING the "arbiter of Europe" while avoiding anything more than "ostentatious but undemanding alliances" meant a clever and prolonged juggling act by the Prussian king.

---

* It would become the *Histoire de mon temps,* which he did not finish until late 1746.
† The collection included statues, vases, urns, marble tables, and sculptures, one of which was Bernini's bust of Cardinal Richelieu.
‡ Tiny Barbarina Campanini was a famous Venetian dancer who contracted to come to Berlin. Her English lover protested, and she canceled the contract. When neither doge nor senate would intervene, Frederick arrested a passing Venetian ambassador and announced that he would be held until Barbarina arrived. She reached Berlin in the spring of 1744. To soften the procedure, Frederick allowed her to name her own salary, which she did — five thousand thalers a year, considerably more than the average general or minister. Preuss wrote of the king's infatuation with her beautiful eyes, and he apparently did have a brief affair with her. Voltaire held that her legs were the attraction, because they resembled those of a boy.

Austria, he realized, remained the major threat, and it was important to appease her. He had earlier accepted an olive branch from Grand Duke Francis, to whom he wrote a flattering letter that welcomed peace and promised friendship. In late October he sent a new ambassador to Vienna. Lieutenant General Count Friedrich Ludwig von Dohna was to do everything possible "to cultivate and make even closer the friendship, union, and good harmony'" between the two kingdoms. Frederick would further Austrian interests where possible and would be "charmed" to lend his good offices to bring about general peace, above all in Germany.* Maria Theresa reciprocated, in part. She received Dohna with every courtesy, told him she was delighted to have Prussian officers in her army as observers,† praised Prussian arms in general, and welcomed the idea of a negotiated peace with the emperor, albeit on terms unacceptable to Frederick.

Caution also applied at the Saint Petersburg court, where Prussia had come into some disrepute, thanks to French and Austrian gold. The Prussian envoy, Mardefeld, was nonetheless working toward a defensive treaty that would guarantee Prussia's and Russia's European states against all powers except the Ottoman Porte, Persia, or other Eastern states. "I know that fundamentally an alliance with Russia is only an ostentation . . ." the king wrote to Podewils, "but it is certain that those who are in alliance with us will not be against us, that by it we protect our back, that this alliance will gain the respect of all Europe, that we will appear more formidable than we are, and will achieve by a stroke of the pen what we have been unable to gain by other means." Czarina Elizabeth was delighted when Frederick accepted the Order of Saint Andreas and in return sent her the coveted Order of the Black Eagle.‡

England was a different matter. The Prussian king generally welcomed British proposals for a defensive alliance as well as apparent willingness to negotiate a guarantee of Prussian rights to Mecklenburg and East Frisia. In return he would guarantee English and Hanoverian lands "without reserve and without condition." "If we remove the thorn

* Dohna was also to try to fathom Austrian intentions vis-à-vis Prussia and report in detail on the Austrian army, economy and finances.

† Frederick had sent twenty-six officers under Colonel Bernhard Heinrich von Bornstedt to serve as observers. They reported on Austrian quartermaster techniques, new cavalry formations, and hussar tactics. Colonel Bornstedt was also recruiting Austrian soldiers for Prussian service, and Maria Theresa demanded his recall, which was granted. Instead of a reprimand, he was given a regiment.

‡ Mardefeld reported that the czarina much admired the Prussian king, who was held in general high esteem by the court, but that she feared his power, the more so because of his connections to the ousted rulers. Frederick instructed Mardefeld: "If the curious would know the value of the diamonds in the Order [of the Black Eagle] . . . you can firmly say that you are told they cost nearly 30,000 thalers."

of succession from our side," he wrote to Podewils, "nothing will ever be able to alter the good harmony between the two nations. . . . Without that, we should only postpone a quarrel which on the first occasion would not fail to break out."

He was delighted that England was trying to bring peace between Austria and Bavaria. He did not, however, agree with the desire of Lord Stair, leader of British forces in Flanders, to fight an imperial war against France. "I understand that he [Stair] is a wild man," Frederick told Otto Podewils, his envoy to the Hague and nephew of his minister, "and he must be mad, for it is inconceivable that a man of good sense would be able to have ideas parallel to his own."*

As he made clear to London and the Hague, he would never join an offensive war against France. In common with the British, he wished to destroy or at least limit French influence in Germany. The way to do that, however, was to bring about an honorable peace between Austria and Bavaria, then check French (and Austrian) pretensions by an alliance of German states, including Prussia, with England and Holland. Toward this end he reluctantly signed the Treaty of Westminster with England in November.

Although determined to keep France in check, Frederick agreed in large part with Ambassador Valory, who bluntly told him "that his fall would be an inevitable result of French humiliation." He regretted that France had suffered such severe military reverses, for which he blamed Broglie: "Does one hold me responsible that Marshal Broglie is not a Turenne?" he asked Fleury, referring to the brilliant seventeenth-century military leader. "I am not able to make a screech owl into an eagle." Prussia had every reason, he explained, for wanting to be friends with France. "I am convinced that the House of Austria will not forget, as long as it continues to exist, either [the loss of] Lorraine or Silesia, and that in consequence our interests will always be the same." If France went to war with England, Prussia would remain neutral.

In truth Frederick was becoming ever more disillusioned with France. Fleury's constant intriguing against him at Saint Petersburg and other courts was as annoying as the French army's ineptness was dangerous. A possibility of French defeat could not be discounted, Frederick pointed out to the elder Podewils in September 1742, and if that happened Austria would soon pounce on Silesia. Frederick continued (in drawing a blueprint for what would happen in 1756): "One will put forward as an objection the alliance [of Prussia] with England and its guarantee, but I reply that England, occupied in Flanders as she is, and as she will

---

* Otto Podewils reported to his uncle in Berlin, "I replied that in other matters he [Stair] did not lack good sense, nor even genius; but that when one touched this chord, he was no longer the same man."

be even more so if the Queen [of Hungary] makes peace with France — I say that England in this case will be of no use to us and that perhaps the Saxons will be very glad to join the Austrians in order to cut us from all sides, and that perhaps at Vienna they flatter themselves that they will be able to enroll the Russians in this plan." It was far-fetched, the king continued, "but in a century so extraordinary as ours, no event should appear impossible, and it is better to be prepared than taken by surprise. Tell me what you think of all this, and tell me candidly your feeling about it. It is always good to be on the alert in order not to lose by indolence what one has earned by activity." *

"Happy quietism" could go only so far. As French military fortunes waned, as Austria scored impressive victories in Bohemia, Bavaria, and Italy, as England grew increasingly bellicose and aggressive in Imperial affairs, as Emperor Charles continued to lose effectiveness, and, not least, as the Prussian army and treasury improved, Frederick began shifting to another role, that of ardent protector of emperor and Holy Roman Empire. His goal was to create a third force that would prevent either Austria from toppling the emperor to regain hegemony in the Empire or England from winning undue influence there. In mid-February 1743, Frederick wrote to Podewils and Borcke: "You do not consider the consequences of the march of the English into Germany. They will go into Swabia, will attract to themselves all the princes of the Empire, and will compel them to join their troops to those of the English. They will force the French to leave the Empire, will give the law to Germany, will make the Grand Duke [Francis] King of the Romans, and will then care nothing for all the declarations that they have made to me." †

That month, Frederick welcomed peace proposals secretly submitted by Emperor Charles to him and to the British king, and ordered his envoys at the Imperial Diet "to make every effort in the world and use every resort to conserve the neutrality of Germany so that at least a Neutral Army of the Empire can be created" — to which he would furnish a powerful troop contingent. Podewils and Borcke continued to argue that because of the apathy of German princes, "there are very slight expectations for the formation of a neutral army by the emperor." This brought a biting reply to the "chicken-hearted ones [who]

---

* Nothing can better illustrate the relationship between the king and Podewils than the correspondence of this period. On several occasions Podewils (and Borcke) offered gratuitous advice and were thanked for solid and helpful opinions; on occasion the king rudely rejected their opinions. His occasional suggestion that Podewils was bribed was probably unjustified.
† "King of the Romans" was the title given to the man next in line for the title of Holy Roman Emperor.

have inherited, I believe, the exalted cautiousness of d'Ilgen [former minister of foreign affairs], of timid memory." The ministers replied that whether Frederick liked it or not, they had spoken the truth. Frederick then tried unsuccessfully to prevent Lord Stair's forces — the so-called Pragmatic Army of some forty-three thousand British, Hanoverian, Saxon, and Austrian troops that had marched into Juliers-Berg the previous February — from advancing into the Palatinate. He subsequently objected to the harsh occupation of Juliers and Berg, and foreign courts were warned that Prussia would prevent any pretender, such as Saxony, from seizing these small duchies. When Emperor Charles complained of the "violent proceedings" of Lord Stair, Frederick replied that he had made "the most serious representations" to the English court, which then promised only a brief occupation and indeed reprimanded Stair. As a member of the Empire he could do no more, he wrote, "without the agreement of all the other members." It was a similar story when the emperor withdrew from the war and tried to form an army to protect the Empire. As Podewils and Borcke had warned all along, the majority of German princes were not interested as long as the emperor remained irresolute and France militarily unreliable.

France was still central to Frederick's diplomacy. Frederick had hoped that Cardinal Fleury's death in late January would open the way for more aggressive military operations against Austria and for stronger support of the emperor, but he was soon commenting acerbically on the Count d'Argenson, the new minister of war, and on King Louis himself — a good man, Frederick called him, whose only fault was that he was king. (He wrote of Fleury, "Too much good was said of him during his life, but too much blame was given to him after his death.") He bluntly advised Louis that his one resource was all-out battle against Austria and England "on land and sea." The Versailles court must not only subsidize an Imperial army of neutrality, Frederick insisted, it must also field large French armies.

The French surrender of Prague and continuing French military failures drew scornful remarks. Marshal Broglie had been given command of the allied army in Bavaria, bringing with him what Valory called "the spirit of disorder familiar to his Bohemian command." Instead of compressing French and Imperial forces into a limited, strong defense, as Seckendorff urged, he spread them in a long, weak line that invited attack.

In the spring of 1743, Prince Charles, served by Khevenhüller, Browne, and von Daun, began nibbling at these succulent targets. Broglie's subsequent retreat "surpassed all that I was able to imagine of his cowardice and ineptness," Frederick railed. The defeat of Marshal Duke Adrien Maurice de Noailles by King George's Pragmatic Army at Dettingen in late June 1743 was the last straw. "No, I no longer want to hear the name French," Frederick informed Rothenburg. "No, I no longer want you to speak to me of their troops and generals. Noailles is beaten. By whom? By some people who don't know how to make a deployment, and who have made none. I speak no more of it." When Voltaire turned up at Potsdam in September, his mission once again to learn Prussian intentions, Frederick treated him kindly but was openly derisive when it came to discussing politics. In despair, Voltaire submitted a list of questions, which Frederick rudely annotated. Concerning the wisdom of France: "I admire the wisdom of France, but God preserve me from ever imitating it." To a plea for commitment: "I have no connection with France; I have nothing to fear nor to hope from France. . . . That monarchy is a body with much strength, but without soul or energy."[1]

Such talk was not to be taken too seriously. Frederick was aware of Voltaire's mission, which, in his words, "became a game, a mere jest." French defeat at Dettingen had terrified the Prussian king, who foresaw a new alliance of England, Austria, Saxony, Denmark, and Russia that would be hostile to Prussia. He was overreacting, however, and soon enough realized that neither England nor Austria knew how to use the victory. Nonetheless he hurriedly dispatched young Count Karl Wilhelm Finck von Finckenstein — "the little evil spirit," Hyndford called him — to plead the emperor's case to King George and Lord Carteret and to insist that "no peace can be made with the emperor with my exclusion."

Frederick's initial indifference to the proposed treaty with Russia changed to enthusiasm when the Saint Petersburg court discovered a plot to replace Czarina Elizabeth with the infant Ivan and the regent, Anne. Largely the work of the Austrian envoy, Botta, the coup rebounded sharply on the Austrian, Saxon, and British courts. Relations between Saint Petersburg and Vienna would soon reach an all-time low. Meanwhile, Prussia's hand was greatly strengthened. "Strike while the iron is hot," Frederick ordered his envoy Mardefeld. Now was the time to tie "our interests with Russia as strongly as possible. . . . It is necessary that our interests and those of the Empress be absolutely the same." If the czarina would furnish Prussia with a small troop contingent, only five or six thousand men, "she would have her share of the glory of having given peace to Germany." Mardefeld could spend another forty thousand thalers "to make the liaisons between me and the Russian court so perfect that I alone, to the exclusion of the others, would be the most favored." To Podewils he wrote, "If according to all appearances the attentions of Mardefeld are not in vain, I will see myself in a position to play a magnificent role in Germany."

Thus inspired, Frederick again called for a militant league of German princes to support the emperor. But when he personally tried to sell this idea in September, he found apathetic listeners at Bayreuth and Ansbach, downright hostility from the powerful, pro-Austrian Duchess of Württemberg — "a woman of fickle, violent and capricious temper," Ranke noted — and nothing from the Bishop of Bamberg, who refused a meeting on grounds of old age and church duties. The reason was clear: Austria was in the ascent; the Empire in the descent. Although Seckendorff, sent by the emperor to Ansbach, assured Frederick that Imperial princes would commit troops if Prussia would head an Imperial association, Frederick was unimpressed. The Imperial army, which he inspected in company with its commander, Marshal Count von Seckendorff, needed eight thousand recruits, Frederick informed the emperor; its officers were old and infirm and, even worse, of low station. "The ways of negotiation have failed up to the present," he wrote to Podewils in late September, "and negotiations without arms make as little impression as notes without instruments. It is a matter then of giving weight and value to the propositions of mediation that one makes, and it is a matter of putting an army in the field cloaked in the name of the Empire." A year hence, the king went on, he would be willing to provide an army of thirty-six thousand on the emperor's behalf.

This was the basis for the secret Act of Association, which called for German princes to pledge military contingents to the emperor. As became clear during winter of 1743–1744, it could not prosper. Most of these rulers were under the Habsburg thumb, either because of religion or Austrian (that is, British) gold. The French army had been beaten and driven from Germany; remnants of the Imperial army were huddling impotently under a neutral flag. The Austrian and Pragmatic armies were close by.

Nor was Prussia's role realistic. Frederick refused to come forward as leader of these German princes, insisting this was the emperor's role. His pose as the defender of the Empire had so far proved a dud. Numerous German princes were as frightened of Prussia as they were of Austria. Frederick's power politics had won him few friends, and his suggestions to secularize monasteries and seize bishoprics had further alienated spiritual rulers.

Frederick's failure was a setback but not a defeat. At Saint Petersburg, Mardefeld's generosity with Prussian gold was having the desired effect. Anti-Austrian sentiments of court advisers were heightened, and the long-delayed treaty was signed in November. Among other things, it confirmed the Treaty of Breslau, thus indirectly gaining the Russian guarantee of Silesia.

More important in the long run was Czarina Elizabeth's request to Frederick to recommend a suitable bride, preferably one of his sisters, for her nephew and successor, Grand Duke Peter.* Not wanting to

---

* Karl Peter Ulrich of Holstein-Gottorp was a royal orphan brought to Russia by Elizabeth. He converted to the Greek Orthodox Church as Peter Federowitz and was named grand duke and her successor — an unfortunate choice, as it turned out, for everyone but Frederick.

expose a sister to the dynastic upheavals of the Russian court, Frederick asked Podewils to shop around. Their choice was fourteen-year-old Princess Sophia Frederika, daughter of the Prince of Anhalt-Zerbst, a Prussian general who commanded the Stettin fortress and was married to the sister of the Crown Prince of Sweden. Sophia was "beautiful, large for her age, and fully matured," so Elizabeth was informed.

Frederick arranged for the immediate departure of mother and daughter, who received a warm welcome at Saint Petersburg. Elizabeth soon approved of the young princess and in due course she converted to the Greek faith as Catherine Alexievna — and in time became Catherine the Great.

Elizabeth wanted another bride, preferably a Hohenzollern, for Sophia's uncle, the thirty-three-year-old Adolph Frederick, a Holstein-Gottorp prince who had been named successor to the old Swedish king. This time Frederick agreed to name a sister and eventually decided on twenty-three-year-old Ulrica, who later became Queen of Sweden.

43

EXACTLY WHEN the King of Prussia decided to return to war is anyone's guess. Despite his insistence on "happy quietism," the occasional martial thunder, encouraged by such hawks as Schmettau and Rothenburg, had sounded long before the repair of army and treasury was completed. But he was not to be pushed. When Count Samuel von Schmettau, now holding the titular rank of field marshal, argued for war in the spring of 1743, he was firmly squelched; and to a later argument that Prussia must act before Austria invaded Silesia, the king replied, "Whoever lets a limb be amputated before it is gangrenous is meeting one evil with a worse evil."

Foreign envoys could find few clues. Those who gained audiences, those who observed His Majesty, found him calm and relaxed, as sharp and witty as ever. "The King of Prussia seems to be more occupied with preparations for Operas and Balls," Hyndford wrote in October 1743.[1]

He did not share his political thoughts with his friends. The letters to Jordan were crammed with verses, frivolous and pleasant remarks, a request for fruit vines and for the latest developments of the opera. Nor did he confide in generals and ministers. Old Dessauer was suspected of unhealthful ambition. Field Marshal Schwerin was languishing on his estates in partial disgrace and would be rehabilitated only in early 1744. The royal family remained in the dark. The king's letters to Wilhelmina were generally affectionate, at least until the spring of 1744, when she foolishly arranged a marriage of one of her ladies in waiting that embarrassed the king politically and led to a quarrel lasting nearly two years. His letters to his mother, the Dowager Queen Sophia, and to William, the Prince of Prussia, are short and of little interest. There was an unpleasant moment over William's romantic "indiscretions" in the winter of 1743 and a poor showing of his regiment at a later review, but his evident contrition soon put things right. In early 1744 the king confirmed him as heir, warning him not "to mix in intrigues and hatch plots in the state" but rather study the administration of the country that he would one day govern: "Our country requires a ruler who keeps his eyes open and rules by himself. . . . Only through very hard work and constant attention [to] masses of details will great things be accomplished for our House." He was delighted to learn that William's wife, Princess Louise, was pregnant, and after the baby's birth the following September he pressed his brother to have more children for the good of the Hohenzollerns. He gave similar advice to Prince Henry and in June presented him with the Rheinsberg estate.

But the thunder never completely ceased, and as the treasury and army grew stronger and as Austria and England became more openly villainous, it slowly turned to a storm. An Austrian treaty with Saxony formed one thunderhead; Russia's treaty with Saxony, another. Then in early 1744 Frederick received a copy of a treaty he had heard mentioned the previous autumn. This was the Treaty of Worms, brought about by England with Austria and Sardinia and soon joined by Saxony.

The treaty called for King Charles Emmanuel of Sardinia, in return for certain Italian territories, to support an army of forty-eight thousand to fight in Italy until peace was concluded, not only in Germany but also between England and Spain. France and Spain had been on the verge of concluding a treaty with Sardinia, so this was a considerable victory for England. Two articles particularly upset King Frederick. The second article, which confirmed previous treaties, did not mention that of Breslau (by which Prussia had gained Silesia). The thirteenth article called for Sardinia to replace Austrian arms in Italy once the Spanish had been driven out, thus enabling Maria Theresa to transfer a large army back to Germany. To Frederick's suspicious mind, this suggested that Austria, backed by England, was trying to invalidate the Treaty of Breslau as a prelude to attacking Silesia. This would explain why the Vienna court had begun a military buildup in Moravia and Bohemia, he reasoned, and why Saxony had allied with Austria, thus forming another threat to Prussian borders.* Podewils and Borcke did not share the king's pessimism, and an argument ensued in which they made a number of sensible countersuggestions not accepted by the king.†

The Treaty of Worms prompted a lengthy and remarkable analysis in which Frederick postulated his principal enemies as England and Austria: "The question follows: What precautions must be taken against these dangers that menace the King of Prussia?" There followed a lengthy discussion that listed Prussian and enemy resources, courses of action, risks involved — what today would be called an estimate of the situation. Prussia's major resource was "to have a strong and capable standing army, and sufficient finances for it." Next, "to make an alliance with Sweden and Russia, defensive and, if possible, offensive." Then, "a conditional alliance with France in order to recover Bohemia from the Queen of Hungary and partition it among the emperor, Prussia, and even Saxony, lacking which the Queen of Hungary remains always too powerful." Prussian delay in taking positive action would only strengthen Austria; therefore "it would be necessary to attack [the Austrians] during 1744." In conclusion, and by way of anticipating 1756, the king wrote, "The war, then, that is appropriate for the King of Prussia to make is compulsory in order to anticipate the evil design of his enemies."

Timing depended largely on French, Russian, and Imperial courts. In mid-February Frederick sent Count Rothenburg, whose ulcerating arm was still shedding bone splinters from wounds received at Chotusitz, to work on a new and secret treaty with Versailles. Rothenburg carried a list of Prussian demands; the main one called for positive and powerful military action before Prussia broke her peace with Austria.‡

As finally worked out with the emperor and the Versailles court, in August of 1744 Prussian columns eighty thousand strong, in the guise of Imperial auxiliaries, would invade Bohemia, occupy Prague, and then take winter quarters to the south and southwest. A French army commanded by Marshal Duke François de Coigny and an Imperial army

---

* A spy in the Dresden court had been reporting the negotiations to the Prussian envoy for some time.

† Frederick later cited this treaty "as one of the principal causes of the war that the [Prussian] king subsequently declared against the Queen of Hungary." (*Oeuvres*, Volume 2, *Histoire de mon temps.*) Reinhold Koser pointed out that Podewils constantly fought the desire of such hawks as Schmettau and Rothenburg to go to war, and in this respect was supported by Old Dessauer, Marshal Schwerin, and General Goltz. (Koser, *Geschichte*, Volume 1.)

‡ This was secret diplomacy. Rothenburg was sent to Paris ostensibly for specialized medical treatment. In carrying out his mission he was to by-pass the Prussian envoy and French foreign minister to negotiate directly with King Louis. Frederick apparently did not inform Podewils of the mission. (Koser, *Geschichte*, Volume 1.) Frederick found in Rothenburg "a union of French grace and German judgment, which appeared to him to constitute a model of perfection." (Ranke, *Memoirs*, Volume 3.)

commanded by Marshal Count von Seckendorff would force the Austrians from Bavaria, take winter quarters, and commence a combined offensive in early 1745. A second French army would concentrate in Flanders to tie down the Pragmatic Army and threaten Hanover.

In early March the king ordered regimental commanders to put their trains in order so that they could march within fourteen days if necessary. A month later he was working daily on his operations plan: "I see by experience," he wrote to Major General von der Goltz, who was charged with arranging for supplies, "that it is not the matter of a day to set 100,000 men in action." His biggest problem was logistics, the transport of flour and heavy cannon from Magdeburg to Bohemia. New cannon were not even on hand yet, nor would cavalry find forage in Bohemia until the harvest. Nonetheless, he hoped to be ready by end of July, but, as he repeatedly stressed to Versailles and Frankfurt, this depended on a treaty with Russia and Sweden and on vigorous French action. He also worried about Saxon intentions: "I would take a terrible risk," he told Rothenburg, "to commence operations in Bohemia and leave an enemy such as the Saxons behind me."

These factors scarcely halted steady progress toward a new war. In May Frederick signed the Treaty of Frankfurt, a secret alliance with Emperor Charles, Charles Theodor, the Elector Palatine, and Landgrave William of Hesse-Cassel. France had thrown off her fragile cloak of Imperial auxiliary to declare war on England in March and on Austria a month later, which meant that the main theater of war would again shift from Italy to Germany. Coigny commanded one army on the Upper Rhine. Noailles commanded a much larger army in Flanders that, once joined by King Louis, would march on the Spanish Netherlands. The Versailles court was preparing to send Prince Charles Edward, son of the Old Pretender, James Stuart, with an expeditionary force of nine thousand troops across the Channel to lead a rebellion and force the Hanoverians from the English throne.* To meet this threat, the English court retrieved twelve thousand troops from the Pragmatic Army, declared war on France in early April, and asked Prussia for military support, as specified in the Treaty of Westminster. Frederick replied that if Britain were attacked, he would at once march to her defense, but that her aggressive naval actions had brought war with France, and therefore Prussia was not bound to furnish the troops called for in a defensive treaty. When Hyndford tried to pursue the matter, Frederick refused him an audience.

The Imperial army, augmented by Hessian and Palatine auxiliaries, was well entrenched at Philippsburg under Seckendorff's command; from there it would march in accordance with Coigny's plans. From

---

* The expedition was forced to turn back in early March because of contrary winds.

Russia, Mardefeld reported favorable treaty negotiations with Sweden and Russia. After a slow start, Rothenburg's mission at Versailles was prospering, thanks in part to King Louis's mistress, the Duchess of Châteauroux, who admired King Frederick.

Frederick was now virtually committed to a new war, with the final objective, as he wrote in early May, of "nothing else than the weakening of the House of Austria and the preservation and restoration [of the territories] of the emperor." Although he could not march until August, he told Rothenburg, "nothing will prevent the operations of this year in which I have engaged myself . . . 80,000 men at Prague on the first of September." By mid-May a revision of the Franco-Prussian Treaty of 1741 had been agreed and would allow France to join the Union of Frankfurt.* Obese King Louis, having forsaken the pleasures of the chase, both in the field and in bed, had toddled off to war with an equipage that included a theater company. His Majesty's presence graced Noailles's army, which was attacking the barrier forts with almost no resistance from the Pragmatic Army.

All well and good, but Frederick would have profited from information concerning the main Austrian army. His officers had reported favorably the previous autumn on the operations of Prince Charles and Marshal Khevenhüller, and on the daring and eminently successful, if often cruel, operations by irregulars. Khevenhüller had died during the winter but had been replaced by an extremely competent and shrewd tactician, Field Marshal Count Otto Ferdinand von Traun. Traun subsequently had retrained the army of the Rhine in anticipation of the 1744 campaign. In April Maria Theresa had ordered Charles to advance toward the Rhine. To Traun's expressed concern about a Prussian reaction, she wrote: "Do not worry about the Prussian king."[2]

This was the situation when Frederick, more troubled than ever with "violent colicks," traveled to Pyrmont to take the waters, which did him little good and which he resented for taking up so much time. Although momentarily diverted by the death of the Prince of East Frisia,† he continued to worry about the possibility of revolution in Russia and French-Imperial lethargy. Nonetheless, in early July he in-

---

* The Union of Frankfurt was a diluted version of the association of German princes that Frederick originally hoped to form. It was more what the nineteenth-century German historian Alfred Dove called "a princely conspiracy in foreign pay," albeit legitimate enough from the constitutional standpoint. (Koser, *Geschichte*, Volume 1; Berney, *Friedrich der Grosse*.)
† Frederick at once ordered a corps to march into the territory and take possession in his name, and he announced that he would fight any country disputing his claim. None did. An easy occupation followed. Estates and magistrats paid homage, Imperial and Dutch garrisons eventually marched off, and the king had a new piece of kingdom.

formed Podewils of his decision to go to war. Podewils strongly disapproved, sagaciously pointing out that success would depend on French honor and determination and on Russian friendship and neutrality. The failure of either court in these respects could cost the king more than even the loss of Silesia. Podewils refused to accept Frederick's argument that the war was forced on Prussia by evil designs of his enemies. Once Prussia went to war, Podewils countered, France would behave as it had earlier, and Prussia would soon bear the entire burden. He agreed that it was in Prussia's interest to support the emperor, but it was nevertheless unnatural to save a drowning man at the expense of one's own life. Further, the situation could probably be resolved by an accommodation with England and Austria.

Frederick had scarcely brushed aside these eminently sensible objections when he learned of a new crisis in Russia. Chétardie, the French envoy in Saint Petersburg, had been arrested and expelled from the country on grounds of maligning the czarina, an event that greatly strengthened the already strong hand of the chancellor, Count Alexei Bestushev.* This was outweighed, however, by favorable reports from Mardefeld. Mikhail Vorontsov, who was in Prussian pay, had been named vice-chancellor on Bestushev's promotion, and Czarina Elizabeth seemed to favor an eventual alliance with Prussia and Sweden. But next came the alarming news that the French had failed to prevent the Austrian army from crossing the Rhine, an operation brilliantly spearheaded by Nádasdy's irregulars and one that allowed Prince Charles to put an army of sixty thousand in Alsace with scarcely any losses. "This is sufficient for me to determine my operations," Frederick informed King Louis. "I will march at the head of my army [on] August 13, and [will be] before Prague at the end of the same month. I am, it is true, overlooking some considerations, and am perhaps pledging myself to a perilous enough move, but I wish to give Your Majesty proofs of the affection and friendship that I have for him." He went on to offer the French king, now at fortress Metz, some positive warnings, though in flattering and courteous language. Without decisive action by the French, all would be lost. Also, French success would depend in large part on choice of generals, and Marshal Belle-Isle should command in Bavaria. He continued with a lengthy homily on offensive operations. A more blunt letter went to Marshal Noailles; it pointed out that Coigny's recent failure to prevent the Austrians from crossing the Rhine was due entirely to poor defensive strategy. In late July he sent Field Marshal Schmettau to join the French king and encourage him to offensive operations at all times.

---

* Bestushev had broken the French cipher and presented candid excerpts from Chétardie's reports on Elizabeth's lurid life style.

That month the British envoy reported from Berlin that "the preparations for Warr go on here, Night and Day, without interruption."[3]

44

IT WAS NOT FRANCE that in the end decided matters for Prussia, nor was it the emperor or Empire. It was not England or Austria, certainly not Russia. In the end it was the Prussian army and the money necessary to support it in the field.

In the spring of 1743 Frederick had decided to increase the army by eighteen thousand men in case he had to send a corps to East Prussia to counter a Russian invasion. The men came from home and abroad. Scores of Prussian officers variously disguised scoured the Empire. "The swiftness of recruiting is unbelievable," a Dutch diplomat reported.[1]

Hussar officers and troopers were signed on in Hungary and Poland when possible, and Frederick even wondered whether Maria Theresa would sell him a complete hussar regiment once she had made peace with the emperor.* He unsuccessfully tried to obtain Cossacks, Tartars, and Kalmuks from Russia.† Mardefeld was to recruit Russian cavalry officers without worrying about their courage or ability, since, as Frederick put it, he merely wanted "the name of Russia associated with my army in order to awe other powers."

Operations and training presented the next problem. In a series of orders for generals issued in July and August 1744, just before he reentered the war, Frederick stressed the need to increase mobility. Generals were not to take costly equipages into the field, and they were forbidden to use silverware. Younger officers were restricted to one packhorse and one riding horse. Troops were to deploy with as little personal gear as possible. Infantry and cavalry swords were even shortened to reduce weight.

Cavalry had to deploy rapidly and in good order with ten paces between squadrons in the first line. The second line would deploy three

---

* Hungarian horses were better than Hungarian hussars. In August 1744, General von der Marwitz, commanding in Upper Silesia, commented on the excellent horses recently received from Hungary, but added, "Desertion also increases and indeed native Hungarians go off with horses and full tack." (Lippe-Weissenfeld, *Husaren-Buch*.)

† The king apparently hoped to establish a Cossack breeding colony, writing to Mardefeld, "I would certainly like to have two to three hundred [Cossacks], especially if I can have them as families, that is with wives and children, in order to settle them in my country." Mardefeld advised against pursuing this since Russia was underpopulated and the czarina would never agree.

hundred paces to the rear, with forty to sixty paces between squadrons. Hussars were to cover cavalry flanks and rear. The cavalry commander would attack either on order from the king or on his own volition if he observed enemy movement. Any commander allowing himself to be attacked would be discharged with infamy: "The Prussians shall always attack the enemy."[2] Speed and shock power were vital to the opening attack, which would not cease until it had smashed both lines of enemy horse. During the charge, troopers were to rise from their saddles to increase saber slashing power, and stirrups were buckled short for this reason. Hussars and twenty or thirty troopers from each squadron would pursue the enemy while the second cavalry line attacked the infantry flank. If the initial charge failed, flanking hussars had to turn on enemy horse to give cavalry squadrons time to re-form. Once the enemy was in retreat, hussars were to dog him as much as possible during the night.

Enemy partisans in the last war had left their mark. The king emphasized the importance of properly located and alert outposts that could support one another if attacked and in turn could be supported by the main army. He also called for careful disposition of baggage on the march and during battle. Hussars were to play an important role as the army's eyes. Dragoons and cuirassiers, he realized, could carry out security and reconnaissance functions only in the immediate camp area, say within four or five hundred meters, in addition to providing cover for supply convoys. Hussars, however, would set up distant outposts so that the enemy could never take the army by surprise. For this purpose "commandos," groups of two to four hundred hussars, would be sent out to conduct themselves like "a spider in her web, which cannot be touched without [her] sensing it."[3] Hussar training was particularly rigorous. Squadrons rode daily, with and without saddles, except in heavy frost. A trooper was trained to snatch a small object from the ground at full gallop; he had to be able "to wheel and turn on a space of a thaler." The ten best men of each squadron were equipped with rifled muskets, mounted on the best horses, and specially instructed in marksmanship and scouting.

A new *Feldjäger* corps would, it was hoped, improve communications. Initially consisting of sixty mounted huntsmen commanded by Colonel Count Hans von Hacke, the corps was stationed in Berlin and was responsible for delivering letters and dispatches to Potsdam. In spring of 1744 the king formed a foot *Jägerkorps* that was to consist of units of two hundred men armed with rifles for increased accuracy and range. The corps grew very slowly owing to lack of skilled hunters and woodsmen.

Earlier introduction of new 3-pounder cannon, two per infantry battalion, with the Holtzmann limber chest, which made the gun initially independent from its munition wagon, had improved artillery mobility. The state of the art was such that effective ranges remained about the same, but General Christian von Linger and Colonel Ernst von Holtzmann continued to make improvements. Cannon were now being cast with cylindrical rather than conical chambers, and new and lighter metals had been used to cast Linger's 12-pounder, which was to replace the 6-pounder. Holtzmann had invented a 10-pounder howitzer, along with a new saddle limber for it and other cannon, and had also invented a gun carriage for the 50-pounder mortar, as well as a crimped canister shell for 24-pounder cannon that improved killing power within a small radius. Both Linger and Holtzmann had been promoted and decorated. "I have tested the new cannon and they are excellent," Frederick told Old Dessauer in early 1743.

Just before marching, in August 1744, the king issued a "Disposition" for artillery. The new 3-pounders would unlimber in front of the first infantry line, three men to a gun, a lieutenant commanding the guns of each brigade. Reserve cannon would remain with harnessed limbers in front of the second line, two men to a gun. A lieutenant and thirty gunners would be in reserve on each flank and in the center to replace casualties. Four howitzers would unlimber in the center of the first line and four on each flank, each served by two men. Ten 12-pounders and six 24-pounders, each with a crew of four, would cover either flank and maintain steady fire on enemy cavalry with nine-ball canister shells and, at short range, smaller ball canister shot. Once Prussian cavalry attacked, all cannon would shift fire to enemy infantry and would use solid balls. This was to be rolling fire, moving to the rear as Prussian cavalry attacked the first lines. At six hundred yards heavy guns would change to canister shot, as would 3-pounders at three hundred yards.

The king also introduced a major innovation in supply arrangements. By the spring of 1744 his food wagons had increased to over thirteen hundred, a quarter of which were to be pulled by horses, four to a wagon, the rest by oxen. Oxen were not only much cheaper (eighteen thalers each), but they ate only hay or straw, were believed to be more suitable for mountainous and swampy terrain, and could be slaughtered for fresh meat. New ammunition wagons were also being built, as were a substantial number of pontoons.

Frederick's orders covered what he called "the preservation and order" of troops: "The one is inseparable from the other."[4] When taking quarters in villages, commanders were to provide their men with sufficient bread and provisions, including fresh beef and a supply of beer or brandy. Generals and other officers were not to take all the houses in a village, but were to give the troops a fair share.

The health of his troops was of constant concern to the king, as was proper care of sick and wounded. At Potsdam adjutants daily brought him medical reports, and he frequently conferred with doctors as to the proper treatment of the sick. He made weekly inspections of the infirmary in Potsdam. During inspection trips and reviews, he emphasized the importance of proper medical care. A commander must be "father and nurse to the sick, and they would love him for it." In preparing for the new war, he ordered Count Rothenburg in Paris to contract for twelve French surgeons.* When the army marched in 1744, General von der Marwitz was left in Upper Silesia with twenty-two thousand troops. His *Feldlazareth* included six surgeons, six hospital administrators, two pharmacists, eight nurses, and four kitchen women.

Commanders were to stress religious devotion. Catholic as well as Protestant chaplains were provided. The king required attendance at Sunday services. He permitted women to live with soldiers in garrison and field. When the army marched in 1744, only a limited number of wives were allowed to accompany it. The remainder had to stay in garrison but were paid *Brotgeld,* or basic subsistence money. To care for the wounded from the last war, the king built the Berlin invalid home, and he also set up a special section in the Potsdam orphanage for officers' orphans who were too young to enter the Berlin cadet corps.

The king used the Potsdam Guards to experiment with new formations and tactics, including night attacks. Officers from distant regiments were brought to Potsdam for training, and Potsdam cadres were sent to field regiments to spread the new word. The king held spring and autumn reviews at Tempelhof and Bornstedt, Stettin, Magdeburg, Halberstadt, Cüstrin, Frankfurt, Glogau, Breslau, Ratibor, Neisse, and Glatz to check on training progress. In early August he wrote to the Prince of Prussia from Neisse: "I found all regiments improved in appearance and in better condition than I had hoped, fortress construction almost finished, and the entire country now completely organized according to Prussian standards. Within a year no one will realize that the Austrians once lived here, and all my measures will have been carried out."

In autumn of 1743 the king had held the first field exercise with combined arms — a radical innovation. A cuirassier regiment and twelve companies of grenadiers marching from Berlin to Potsdam were attacked by five hussar squadrons, which forced the grenadiers to defend themselves in a small village. In coming to their assistance, the cavalry were ambushed and forced to fight their way back to Berlin — a ma-

---

* They arrived in Berlin in July 1744. The two master surgeons were each paid a thousand thalers a year, the ten apprentice surgeons three hundred thalers a year. We hear of them again in Prague during the Second Silesian War, but unfortunately they did not work out very well and probably returned to Paris. (Richter, *Geschichte des Medizinal-Wesens.*)

neuver, the Dutch envoy reported, that was carried out "to the great satisfaction of His Majesty and to the admiration of a large number of spectators."[5]

In August a member of the royal party, Prince Ferdinand of Brunswick, noted that they had traveled seven hundred miles and that the king had personally inspected eighty-five battalions and 153 squadrons! In September, Lord Hyndford reported that the King of Prussia "keeps his Troops in continual Exercise, and they are indeed in extreme good order. . . . Next week a body of foot are to entrench themselves and are to be attacked on all sides by the horse and hussars."[6] That winter lectures on attack and defense of fortified camps became daily fare for officers of the Berlin garrison. At Potsdam in the spring of 1744 the king experimented with the advance of large infantry units.

Rebuilding Silesian fortresses was an immense task. Those at Glatz, Neisse, and Cosel were to cover border crossings from Bohemia, Moravia, and Hungary; those at Brieg, Breslau, and Glogau to secure the line of the Oder. Prince Ferdinand wrote ecstatically of concealed glacis and water-filled ditches, strong outer forts and mined approaches. At Neisse the chief engineer, General Gerhard Cornelius von Walrave, abandoned some traditional procedures to emphasize "offensive" defenses by construction that allowed easier sallies from the main fortress. This was slow and expensive work. Seven thousand civilians were employed at Neisse alone. Ranke wrote that the masons were paid eight groschen a day. In theory Silesian revenues were to pay the costs. In fact in early 1744 Frederick suddenly had to find a half million thalers to carry on the work. In late March 1744, Ferdinand wrote from Neisse that its fortifications "are of an infinite beauty and already so far advanced that by July all will be finished."

The expensive effort helps to explain why civil projects were put on the back burner. It also accounts for extraordinary economies, such as deferring a promised pension to the Marquis d'Argens for a year because of "my disturbed finances."

Whatever draconian measures were employed, they seemed to have worked. The *Kriegscasse*, or war chest, amounted to 1.3 million thalers at the end of the last war. By autumn of 1744 it had risen to six million thalers, which, if used "with prudence," was strong enough for two campaigns. The army now numbered 140,000 men, with field units ready to march.

45

SHORTLY BEFORE the Prussian army marched, foreign envoys in Berlin were handed an "Exposé," a lengthy statement of reasons that obliged the King of Prussia to furnish Emperor Charles with auxiliary troops. This document was simultaneously published in newspapers at home and abroad and distributed to all foreign courts. It was essentially an exercise in pan-Germanism: Vienna was the chief culprit in the disruption of the German empire, and England and Holland were supporting her. The Empire must be saved. The declaration concluded: "In a word, the king asks nothing, and he does not act in his personal interests; His Majesty has recourse to arms only to restore liberty to the Empire, dignity to the emperor, and peace to Europe." Lieutenant General Count Dohna read a less spirited statement to Austrian ministers in Vienna, after which he dexterously avoided angry mobs and left the capital.

A week earlier, the envoy Johann von Wallenrodt had called on the King of Poland in Warsaw to present Imperial directives that authorized Prussian auxiliary troops to march through Saxony. This upset Count Brühl considerably but brought little more than a shrug from King August, Wallenrodt reported. In Dresden, Colonel Winterfeldt presented copies of these documents to officials and demanded that they appoint local commissars to assist Prussian columns, a fait accompli accepted only after the liberal application of "threats, pleas, scolding, and soft words" — followed by Prussian troops crossing the border. Winterfeldt and Marshall Schmettau engaged a contractor to build bridges at Pirna for the Elbe crossing. The old Duke of Weissenfels, who commanded the Saxon army, proved surprisingly helpful. When there was no money to pay for bridge construction, he volunteered a generous loan. He also transferred Saxon forces away from Pirna and turned over army bake ovens and a large supply of flour to the Prussians.

While a French army in Westphalia threatened Hanover to keep Britain quiet, another French army, along with the Bavarians, was supposed to push the Austrians back across the Rhine and dog their retreat through Bavaria.

Meanwhile, two Prussian corps would march through Saxony into Bohemia to Prague, where a third corps from Silesia would join them. Prague, known to be weakly held, would be stormed or invested. The bulk of the army would then march south and winter at enemy expense. Simultaneously General von der Marwitz, commanding a corps twenty-two thousand strong in Upper Silesia, would conduct a spoiling operation into Moravia to deprive the enemy of subsistence from this area. Old Dessauer would command a corps of seventeen thousand in Brandenburg to keep the Hanoverians and Saxons quiet. Come spring, French and Bavarian armies would continue to march down the Danube, and the Austrians, caught between two fires, would have to make peace.

King Frederick commanded the major force, some twenty-seven thousand foot and 12,500 horse divided into four independent corps. This army would march to Pirna, cross the Elbe, and continue down the west bank. Hereditary Prince Leopold, commanding a corps of about thirteen thousand foot and three thousand horse, was to march through Lusatia to Zittau, occupy Leitmeritz, and move down the east bank of the Elbe to Alt-Bunzlau and Brandeis. Marshal Schwerin, who had been restored to favor, would bring a third corps of about ten thousand foot and fifty-six hundred horse from Silesia to cross the Elbe at Königgrätz, take up a defensive position at Pardubitz, and send an advance guard to Alt-Bunzlau.* A fleet of some five hundred river boats carrying heavy artillery — eighty field and sixty siege cannon plus thirty mortars — and a three-month supply of bulk provisions was loading at Magdeburg, its voyage to Dresden-Pirna-Leitmeritz to be secured by a strong ground escort under Lieutenant General Casimir von Bonin.

All went well to start with. Units crossed the Saxon border on schedule and without opposition. The king had ordered strict march discipline. Troops were to pay for everything, either with cash or official vouchers. Untoward incidents seem to have been at a minimum, despite the obvious hostility of Saxon ministers. Local officials for the most part cooperated in arranging for the purchase of provisions and advising on march routes and quarters. Troops were well fed and housed, and Lord Hyndford's reports from Berlin of massive desertions seem to have been great exaggerations. The country was rich; peasants were eager to sell produce. Frederick's own detachment, which included his brothers William and Henry, bought an eight-day supply of brandy and enough live cattle for ten days of meat (a pound per man per day) in Bohemia. Leopold's columns, marching through Lusatia, closed on schedule at Zittau, a major achievement, considering that there was a train of seven hundred wagons carrying flour and fodder, each pulled by four oxen, with another six hundred of the beasts to be slaughtered for meat.

By late August all the columns had crossed the Bohemian border.

---

* An alert foreign observer would have been impressed by Schwerin's rehabilitation. It began in mid-1743 when the king invited him to Berlin, probably to discuss new army regulations. It continued during the 1743–44 carnival, when he was shown every honor. The following summer he was honored by receiving Princess Louise Ulrica, who was traveling to Sweden to marry the Swedish crown prince. (Varnhagen, *Schwerin,* and Schwerin, *Feldmarschall Schwerin.*)

River boats at Pirna were off-loading heavy artillery to lighter ships for the run upstream to Leitmeritz. The first phase of the campaign was nearly over. An envoy from King August complimented the Prussian king on the behavior of his troops: "They passed through Saxony like Capuchins, but with this difference, that whereas the monks got everything gratis, the Prussians on the contrary paid for everything." [1]

Despite reports of active military preparations in Prussia over the past months, neither Maria Theresa nor her councilors expected Frederick to march. Maria Theresa quickly recovered from surprise. Such, after all, was to be expected from "the monster," as Grand Duke Francis exclaimed when learning the news. But could Frederick, she wondered, have made a serious error? Could this be an opportunity not only to defeat him militarily, but to recover Silesia and deliver her subjects from heretical rule? "We could gain a great deal if we could crush this devil with a battle," Francis wrote to his brother Charles. [2]

While Bartenstein poured forth a flood of political invective against the deceitful Prussian king, Maria Theresa hastened to Pressburg, where Hungarian aristocrats, in return for further political concessions, promised another sixty thousand troops. (The envoy Dohna soon reported long rows of wagons filled with recruits coming through Vienna on the way to Bavaria.) She then invoked her treaty with Saxony to ask for twenty thousand auxiliaries, persuaded the English court to grant her a special subsidy of £150,000 (of which a third would go to the Saxon elector), and for good measure asked the Russian court to send an army to Kurland to threaten Prussia. She also ordered Prince Charles — more than ever her favorite since his marriage to her sister — in Alsace to recross the Rhine and march on Bohemia as fast as possible. While the Prussians were crossing the Elbe, the Austrians were recrossing the Rhine, a particularly hazardous operation because of nearby French and Bavarian armies. These, however, did not interfere, and in early September the army was safely in Cannstatt, near Stuttgart, from where Charles would shortly march northeast to meet the new threat.

Charles had left the able General Batthyányi with a corps of about twenty thousand hussars and irregulars in Bavaria. The general had already been ordered to move closer to Saxony and had marched to Amberg in the Upper Palatinate. He had also sent a force of irregulars under Lieutenant General Festetics to support the weak Prague garrison, and he was now ordered to march into Bohemia.

By the time the Prussians were crossing the Bohemian border, Batthyányi had closed on Pless and was preparing to march on Pilsen. He had sent a battalion of Dalmatian irregulars to screen the Erz Mountains and harass enemy columns debouching onto narrow mountain roads. Another irregular unit, under Colonel Szapáry, was covering the Eger-Saaz-Prague road. Festetics was already operating in hilly country north of Prague, with orders to raise local militias and fight the Prussians as opportunity arose.*

The Prussian king was not totally unaware of these developments. He knew that Prince Charles was falling back in Alsace and showed signs of recrossing the Rhine. On August 20 he informed the King of France that Batthyányi had marched from the Palatinate to defend Prague. But a few days later he received several overdue dispatches from Marshal Samuel von Schmettau at Metz. The first reported that King Louis was about to die from an incurable abscess of the brain. The second reported that he would live but would require lengthy convalescence. Belle-Isle was staying with the king while Noailles marched with the army.†

Frederick would have preferred it the other way around, he told Schmettau, but he was still convinced that the French army could not fail to slow the Austrian retreat and cause large losses "so that I have ample time to take Prague, Budweis, Tabor, and Frauenberg, and perhaps Eger, before the enemy can arrive on the Bohemian frontiers."

Disturbing rumors also reached him that the Saxons planned to send an auxiliary force to join the Austrians in Bohemia. Frederick believed that King August would stay out of the war in return for territory promised by Emperor Charles and because Old Dessauer commanded a hefty Prussian corps not far from the Saxon border. Nevertheless, he wrote conciliatory letters to August and the Duke of Weissenfels, promising to return horses that had been improperly commandeered and to take care of remaining expenses incurred by the army.

Schmettau next reported that Charles had recrossed the Rhine with no hindrance from Noailles or Seckendorff. This was frightening news. "I believe it superfluous," Frederick at once wrote to King Louis, "to say to Your Majesty how much this unexpected event upsets my plans." It was more vital than ever for the French and Bavarians to slow the

---

* Batthyányi circulated the queen's Patent, which offered peasants and farmers two ducats per Prussian deserter plus one ducat to the deserter, two if he accepted Austrian service. Maria Theresa seems to have believed that new battalions could be formed from enemy deserters. Her notion may have resulted from the Austrian envoy's inflated reports from Berlin of Prussian desertion. (Oesterreich Kriegsarchiv, *Oesterreichischer Erbfolge-Krieg, 1740–1748*, Volume 7. Hereafter *Erbfolge-Krieg* followed by volume number.)

† King Louis became ill on August 8 and a week later was believed to be near death. The Bishop of Soissons ("a fanatic imbecile," in Frederick's words) insisted that the king disown his mistress, the Duchess of Châteauroux, before receiving last rites, so she was sent packing. A humble surgeon, correctly convinced that his king ate and drank too much, administered a strong emetic, which quickly cured him. He was soon writing impassioned letters to his banished duchess, who herself died soon afterward.

Austrian march, and Schmettau was to stress this at Louis's headquarters. "I swear that I no longer know what I can expect from France," the king dejectedly added. His pessimism was not misplaced. Instead of pursuing the Austrian army into Bavaria and Bohemia, the French army turned to the siege of Freiburg while Seckendorff with the Bavarians languished beyond the Neckar River.

The enemy had already appeared in the Prague area, though in no great strength. Shortly after crossing the Bohemian border, the advance guard of Karl von Schmettau (now a general) captured a hussar officer who reported a large increase of irregulars in the area (Batthyányi's Dalmatians). A few days later a serious clash occurred when Zieten with thirteen hundred hussars attacked one of Festetics's detachments, killed sixty, and took some forty prisoners and a number of horses, with very light losses.

This welcome news reached the king at Budin, together with General Schmettau's assurance that the country up to Prague was now nearly free of enemy. Despite contrary rumors, Schmettau reported, Batthyányi was still on the Bohemian border. The king also learned that Prince Leopold had chased the enemy from Teschen and used local peasants to clear the Elbe of boulders, trees, and sunken boats. The first skiffs had reached Leitmeritz to off-load heavy cannon for the difficult road trip to Prague. Marshal Schwerin's columns had closed on Prague ahead of schedule, a solid achievement, given the rugged terrain and lurking enemy, and were soon joined by Leopold's corps. In early September the king tied in to Schwerin's right to complete a difficult and complicated march, "but," as he wrote, "what are fatigues, difficulties, and danger in comparison with glory?" *

The problem now was the capture of Prague.

Prague's neglected defenses had recently been repaired in part, and some of them were naturally strong. Frederick and his generals soon decided against a direct assault until siege guns arrived from Leitmeritz.

This would not be overnight. Partisan attacks on narrow mountain roads made almost impassable by heavy rains either halted or slowed convoys to a crawl. Supply trains had been delayed on the march from Saxony. Oxen, unable to pull the heavily loaded wagons through mud, were mishandled by teamsters and died by the hundreds. Stranded wagons in Upper Bohemia offered rich booty to hostile peasants. Frederick had only one road to the Leitmeritz magazine with its inadequate

---

* I recently traced the king's march from Pirna to Prague. The Elbe Valley is still beautiful in part, with an occasional castle perched on a hill, like the one outside Aussig. Unfortunately much of the landscape is marred by factory and port complexes, but one can still see why it used to be called Saxon Switzerland.

bake ovens. Only a few days after closing on Prague he could not issue bread to his men.

Hungry troops hammered out fascines and other siege necessities while General Walrave, aided by two French engineers familiar with the defenses, planned the siege. He opened the first trenches in front of the Ziskaberg, in a large area of five sectors backed by four artillery batteries. The guns arrived on September 8. They opened fire three days later. The fire was effective, and an infantry assault the next day captured two outer works at small loss. A French observer, though impressed with the splendidly disciplined infantry, did not think much of Prussian engineers and their siege techniques. The troops, he noted, were poorly trained for siege warfare; in firing on the enemy, they killed more of their own soldiers than did enemy fire![3]

Further breaches in the walls — some two thousand shells were fired in three days — brought surrender a few days later. When the Prussian king refused to allow the garrison free passage, the fight continued. On September 14 a diarist noted that "at least a thousand shells and fire bombs fell in the city."[4] Many citizens fled and those who remained petitioned Harrach to surrender, which he did two days later.

Couriers carried the word to courts everywhere. "Prague is taken," Frederick joyfully informed Marshal Holstein-Beck in Breslau. "We have sixteen thousand prisoners of war. Fire some cannon from the ramparts in celebration and sing the Te Deum." *

46

SCARCELY had Prague surrendered when Frederick issued new orders. General Baron Gottfried Emanuel von Einsiedel was to hold the city with five thousand troops. General Count Christoph Ernst von Nassau with a large task force — ten battalions and thirty squadrons, including Zieten's hussars — was to march south, seize Tabor, Budweis, and Frauenberg, establish magazines, build bakeries, and choose a camp site for the main army.

---

* The garrison numbered about eleven thousand, of which over half were invalids and local militia. Six thousand of the latter were discharged, fifteen hundred troops were sent to Silesian fortresses, and twenty-five hundred were recruited for Prussian garrison duty (of whom half soon deserted). (Generalstab, *Die Kriege Friedrichs des Grossen.* Zweiten Theil: *Der Zweite Schlesische Krieg, 1744–1745,* Volume 1. Hereafter Generalstab II followed by volume number.) Some regular Austrian troops swam the Moldau and escaped. Furious citizens, claiming Jewish deceit and treachery, sacked the Jewish quarter. (*Erbfolge-Krieg,* Volume 7.)

The first columns moved out only three days after Prague had fallen. "We are currently marching on Tabor and Budweis," the king wrote to Podewils, "in order to become master of these parts and to oblige Prince Charles and Batthyányi to fall back on Upper Austria. If they do not do so, they will be beaten."

The fall of Prague caused General Batthyányi to send cavalry reinforcements to garrisons at Pisek, Tabor, and Budweis. With his remaining force of irregulars, he withdrew southwest to Cerkowitz, from where he could harass enemy operations across the Moldau and maintain communication with the main Austrian army approaching from the southwest and, ultimately, the Saxons, who would march from the north.

Maria Theresa meanwhile had been urging Prince Charles to move as fast as he could to Bohemia.* By the time Prague fell, the Austrians were still a fair distance from the Bohemian border. Charles was in Vienna making supply arrangements; the army was under command of Field Marshal Count Otto Ferdinand von Traun.

The sixty-seven-year-old Traun had replaced Khevenhüller, who had died the previous winter. A distinguished veteran of the War of the Spanish Succession and a field marshal since 1740, he had recently fought well in Italy, from where he had been sent to command in Moravia. He had gone to the Bavarian command in April with orders to attack Seckendorff. Fearing Prussian intervention, he had delayed too long, and Seckendorff had taken up a strong defensive position in Philippsburg. Prince Charles meanwhile had unsuccessfully tried to stir local British, Dutch, and Austrian forces to action against the French. Charles joined Traun's main army at Heilbronn in mid-May and soon crossed the Rhine under the noses of two armies. This opening push into Alsace was undoubtedly Traun's doing. He was smart, shrewd, and cautious. Like Khevenhüller, he also knew how to use irregular forces.

Now, while his army slogged through the beautiful if rugged terrain of northern Bavaria, he fanned out his light troops: General von Nádasdy with three hussar regiments and some pandours to reinforce the Amberg garrison; General von Minsky and a thousand Warasdiners to Budweis to spy out and report on the coming enemy.

Despite poor roads, vile weather and enemy harassment, General Nassau's task force advanced on schedule and captured Tabor after slight

* Not the least of Maria Theresa's reasons was to keep Francis, whom she now called "der Alte" — the old man — in Vienna. She had constantly to fight against his desire to rejoin the army, frequently resorting to tears. "But," as she complained to her sister Marianne, "what can they [tears] accomplish with a husband after nine years of marriage?" (Erbfolge-Krieg, Volume 7.)

skirmishes, in which Zieten's hussars once again shone. After setting up a magazine and bakery and forcing locals to swear allegiance to Emperor Charles, Nassau continued southwest. Budweis and Frauenberg were strongly held, he reported, and all bridges over the Moldau had been demolished. Nassau next attacked Budweis, which Minsky surrendered in return for free passage of his meager garrison, some eighteen hundred Croatian irregulars who marched off "with flags flying and music playing." The general now moved on Frauenberg, which also quickly surrendered. Nassau garrisoned both places, opened supply magazines, and repaired defenses with the aid of two thousand impressed peasants. But contrary to expectations, he found few munitions. His musketeers had only sixty rounds each, and he was too far from Prague to easily repair this and other shortages.

Marshal Schwerin's and Prince Leopold's contingents duly reached Tabor, but Major General Count Karl Posadowsky's long supply train, which followed Leopold's wing, lost a thousand oxen and perforce abandoned two hundred and fifty wagons that carried a vital fifteen-day supply of flour — "the beginning of all the misfortunes that afterward arrived," Frederick later wrote.[1] The army remained at Tabor until a five-day supply of bread was baked, then marched to a camp about five miles east of Thein on the Moldau. Hans Winterfeldt's task force found the Thein bridges torn up and enemy irregulars nearby. He reported that Count Batthyányi, with a force of twenty thousand light troops, was in the area and that Charles was marching on Pilsen with the main Austrian army. Other reports received in the king's headquarters put Charles already east of Pilsen, marching on Budweis, and still other reports had the Saxons moving on Eger.

As in Moravia two years earlier, Frederick's strategy had backfired; his allies had let him down. King Louis was at Metz, impatient with the fumbling French siege of Freiburg, wanting only to return to Versailles and the Duchess of Châteauroux. Noailles's arguments to send a corps to threaten Hanover had been countered by the antiwar party, which pointed to new dangers from military setbacks in Italy. Despite Frederick's urgings, French diplomacy had remained feckless in Warsaw and Moscow, thanks to what Ranke called "the golden showers of England." Now the Austrians would be reinforced by a Saxon corps of twenty thousand under the Duke of Weissenfels.

Marshal Seckendorff had delayed his march for over three weeks, which gave the Austrians ample time to fortify Ingolstadt and Passau. As the king wrote to Marshal Schmettau in early October: "The goal of the operations of the King of Prussia has been to make a diversion into Bohemia in order that Seckendorff can march into Bavaria. Once Seckendorff does not do this, the diversion of the King of Prussia becomes useless."

The king was already overextended. He was a hundred miles from the Elbe magazines, and his nearest base was Prague, fifty miles distant, with no defensible strongpoints along the way. Prague itself was weakly held, supplied only with difficulty from the Leitmeritz magazines. Not only were the roads often impassable, they were always dangerous. His teamsters did not know how to handle oxen; in early October four hundred beasts could no longer work and were put up for sale. General Einsiedel in Prague was feuding with his generals, particularly Walrave, who was building outer fortifications that could not be manned for lack of troops. Major Jakob Cogniazzo's irregulars frequently raided *inside* the city. Einsiedel's reports to the king were carried by three couriers, in the hope that one would get through. Wounded and sick soldiers filled hospitals. In early November over two thousand casualties arrived in bread wagons and were put in monasteries, convents, and finally palaces. The meager field hospital, manned by two Prussian and two French surgeons with only a few assistants, could not possibly cope with the wounded. Soldiers died, morale plunged, desertions increased.

Prussian martial law and widespread looting enraged the citizenry. In late September, Prussian officers began sacking private palaces and mansions so thoroughly "that scarcely a nail remained on the wall." In early November a Prussian officer noted that "the plundered goods are packed in casks as if they were flour; many of them, however, have been bought by the Jews, who stand on the best terms with the Prussians and help them in all possible ways." * All of the citizens had been disarmed. When an alarm was sounded, civilians had to enter the nearest house. All windows had to be lighted at night, and residents could not go out after dark. Such a policy naturally caused citizens to sabotage the occupation whenever possible.

The Prussian army was operating in a land of hatred, controlling only the ground it walked on. Despite strict orders from the king, the excesses continued, most notably the savage behavior of Lieutenant Colonel von Schütz, commanding the White Hussars, who frequently forced local peasants to act as guides and, once their usefulness ended, killed them. "His route was marked by such murders," wrote Varnhagen von Ense, who was serving under Schütz as a captain. It was also marked by rape and torture, by plundered and burned villages. Peasants needed little encouragement from local bailiffs and priests to scorch the earth. They filled wells with earth and stones, emptied barns and stables, buried corn, hustled livestock to the wooded hills. "Thus the army found only desolation and empty villages," Frederick later wrote.

* General Walrave was one of the biggest offenders. Locals called him *"General Voleur,"* General Thief. He made no secret about it, requesting permission in one report to the king to take "the beautiful Prague furniture" to his Magdeburg house. (*Erbfolge-Krieg*, Volume 7).

"No one appeared at camp to sell food, and the people, fearing harsh Austrian punishment, could not be persuaded to sell anything at any price."[2]

Communications rapidly became impossible. Dispatches from Berlin, Frankfurt, Metz, and even Prague took eight days; later, they took a month if they arrived at all. "For four weeks I was without news, without letters, unable to find good spies, not knowing if Prince Charles, Batthyányi, and the Saxons were in Bohemia or Peking," the king complained to a friend. He learned only in early October that the Saxons were about to march against him, that the French were still at Freiburg, that Seckendorff was west of Munich instead of approaching the Braunau area, as had been planned.*

He was also tactically blind. As in Silesia in 1741 and Moravia in 1742–1743, hordes of irregulars were screening the main army's movements, and the Prussians could not penetrate the screen. Local peasants could not be relied on, spies could not be trusted, captured hussars and pandours knew no more than the Prussians. The enemy, however, knew the exact location of Prussian units, the exact strength, the exact direction of marches. "The least maneuver, the least movement" was instantly reported, Frederick later wrote despairingly.[3]

Guesswork in warfare is a dangerous proposition.

Not knowing what to believe, Frederick believed what best suited his hopes. He believed that the Saxons were marching on Eger (true) and that the Austrians were marching on Budweis (false). The Prussians would soon depart for Thein, Eichel informed Podewils in late September, "there to cross the Moldau and go straight on the enemy to give battle where he finds him. . . . His Majesty anticipates a happy result and hopes by this to chase the enemy from Bohemia." In early October engineers built a boat bridge across the Moldau, and the troops crossed without difficulty. Frederick sent the information to the King of France, adding, "The Austrians having been cut from Vienna, it is expected that they will hasten to recover their country."

The Prussian king was now determined to fight a big war. His enemy was content with the little one.

Marshal Traun and Prince Charles meanwhile had marched on Pilsen. While the two commanders were in Pilsen, wondering what to do next, and while Frederick was in Tabor, wondering what to do next, Bat-

---

* The Saxon march came as a terrible blow. As late as September 10, Frederick wrote to his envoy at Frankfurt, "I am working vigorously at present to bring the Saxons to our side, and I hope very much to succeed." Saxony's action was the more worrisome because she could not have come into the war without Russia's guarantee of protection for her exposed country. Thus Frederick's Russian diplomacy, for which he had held such high hopes, had suffered a severe setback.

thyányi's hussars captured a Prussian courier. He carried dispatches from Marshal Schmettau at Metz and from the envoy Klinggraeffen at Frankfurt, which confirmed that the Prussians planned to march up the Moldau to Budweis, and that only a weak garrison remained in Prague. In late September the prince informed Maria Theresa that he was crossing the Moldau to march on Tabor, his purpose being to cut the enemy from rear area supplies while irregulars deprived him of local supply, thus forcing him to evacuate Bohemia. Weissenfels, with twenty thousand Saxon troops, would soon close on Eger and could be employed as the situation warranted.

It was a sound plan, probably Traun's work, and it is particularly interesting because of its employment of irregular forces. Thanks to Batthyányi (shortly to take command in Bavaria) and his irregulars, the Austrians were in a tactically superior position. They were solidly based, with ample supplies, and were informed instantly of any enemy movement. Traun and Charles realized that the enemy was tactically blind. They intended to keep him that way and let hunger do the rest. "In truth I believe that the good Lord has blinded him [Frederick]," Charles wrote to Grand Duke Francis on October 6, "for his movements are those of a fool."[4]

47

THE MAIN PRUSSIAN ARMY crossed the Moldau with no difficulty. While Frederick reconnoitered westward, the Austrian army was at Mirotitz, twenty-five miles north. He did not know this, nor did he know that the Austrian plan was predicated on his movement to Budweis.

He did know that he was being closely observed. A detachment under Colonel Janus that was trying to collect food north of Tabor was jumped by five hundred of Colonel Dessewffy's shrieking, saber-wielding hussars, who had been alerted by peasants. Janus fought furiously but lost over half of his detachment — and his own life.

More irregulars showed north of Zirnau. Frederick thought they were the advance guard of the Austrian army and put his own army in battle order. He was wrong. They were an enemy detachment of irregulars operating out of Pisek. The Austrian army had marched east, where it would soon be joined by the Saxons.

Only three days after crossing the Moldau, the Prussian king realized that he would have no battle. There were no more provisions in Thein, no flour, no fodder, no help from the countryside. Men were hungry; morale was low; Schwerin and Leopold were quarreling so much that the king had to intervene. On October 8 the diarist of Regiment Kalkstein noted, "Hunger, sickness, and a terrible desertion have appeared in the army."[1] A report stated that the Austrian army was north of Pisek, that Nádasdy had crossed the Moldau and was probably advancing on Tabor, which was full of sick soldiers (including Prince Henry) and was held by only one battalion. If Charles marched east, he would cut Frederick's army from Prague.

The only answer was retreat. A force under Nassau marched to reinforce Tabor, whose magazine still held an eight-day supply of flour. A large convoy of wagons was to go to Budweis to pick up bread but in the confusion never left Thein. On October 8 the army recrossed the Moldau and marched north. A rearguard of two grenadier battalions and Zieten's hussars was to hold Thein until bread barges arrived from Budweis. Some six thousand irregulars under General Johann von Ghilányi easily forded the Moldau and attacked Zieten's people; there was a prolonged and nasty fracas that left several hundred dead and wounded on each side before the Prussians, outnumbered and short of ammunition, rode off.* Prince Maurice's infantry meanwhile had met the bread barges but after the loss of Thein was forced to scuttle the precious cargo.

Food now was very short. The army marched toward the smell of bread, to a camp a few miles northwest of the Tabor bakeries. But reports that the Austrian and Saxon armies had crossed the Moldau revived the king's hope for battle. "In crossing the Moldau Prince Charles could have no other plan than of coming to fight me," he later wrote to Seckendorff. When the reports proved false, the army was again running out of bread and could continue the march only to Beneschau, where the enemy reportedly had built a large magazine and from where Frederick could protect communications between Prague and Pardubitz. This meant leaving the garrisons at Budweis, Frauenberg, and Tabor on their own.†

The new camp stretched behind a chain of lakes in front of Beneschau and solved very few problems. Although communication with Prague was easier, wagons and horses were in short supply. Soon after the army's arrival, a convoy delivered nearly seventy-five thousand four-

---

* King Frederick personally met and congratulated the survivors, giving special praise to Zieten, whom he had recently promoted to major general. (Lippe-Weisenfeld, *Husaren-Buch.*) Frederick later noted that the Romans had used such demonstrations to inspire the other troops to valiant deeds. (*Oeuvres*, Volume 2, *Histoire de mon temps.*)

† Frederick made this decision because he did not want to abandon the sick and wounded. He was also convinced that he would defeat the Austrians in battle and the garrisons would thus interdict an enemy retreat.

pound loaves of bread, enough for two days. The supply intendant in Prague could have furnished more but lacked transport and money. The king sent Colonel Winterfeldt with a strong detachment to the Leitmeritz area, where he soon rounded up six hundred wagons and ninety-six hundred bushels of flour.

But time was running out. For weeks there had been no meat, no brandy, no beer, often no bread. The men were reduced to mixing flour with water to cook a tasteless gruel. This diet, combined with poor water from stagnant ponds and a great deal of hard marching over muddy roads in foul weather, was exacting a terrible toll. Dysentery and debilitating fevers swept the ranks; three fourths of the infantry were sick. There were no hospitals, no medicines, no satisfactory treatment. Autumn suddenly turned cold, troops already ill shivered on straw-covered tent floors soaked with excrement. Hastily built *Feuerhütten,* or small shelters, could not be adequately heated. Desertions jumped to fifty and sixty a day. Morale became so low that officers had to tell their men that they would soon move to winter quarters.

And now the king received Marshal Schmettau's overdue reports — delayed nearly a month — only to learn that he could expect no helpful allied action. Discouraging reports arrived from General von der Marwitz in Upper Silesia. His incursion into Moravia had not been successful; fortress Olmütz remained Austrian.

Thus stymied, Frederick sent a force to evacuate garrison and stores at Neuhaus. Couriers carried orders to garrison commanders at Budweis and Frauenberg: Evacuate the garrison and fight a "partisan" withdrawal to the main army.

When the Prussians recrossed the Moldau, the Austrian army was impatiently waiting for its Saxon allies. Prince Charles and Marshal Traun had been kept accurately informed of Frederick's movements by commanders of the irregulars.

The situation was fairly evident, they believed. An Austrian-Saxon march to the northeast would force Frederick to march either back to Prague or to the Elbe magazines. If he returned to Prague, Charles would cross the Elbe to the east and cut Prussian communications between Prague and the magazines in Königgrätz and Pardubitz. This would force Frederick to leave Prague, but he would have to strengthen its garrison at the expense of his army, which the Austrians could then attack. If Frederick moved to the Elbe, Charles could seize Pardubitz, send light troops into Silesia to force the king to march reinforcements there, and then attack the weakened Prussian army when it marched.

Meanwhile some tactical fruit could be plucked. Colonel Trenck with eighteen hundred pandours, reinforced by infantry and hussars, marched south to attack Budweis and Frauenberg. Trenck cut the water supply to Frauenberg, left a screening force there, and went on to make a spirited night attack at Budweis, which at first failed. He had lost several hundred dead and wounded and was about to abandon the attack when the commandant, nearly out of ammunition, surrendered. The tiny Frauenberg garrison soon gave in. Another Austrian corps had isolated the Tabor garrison, which yielded a day after Budweis fell.

Having ensured communications with Austria and Moravia, Charles crossed the Moldau and edged north until a few miles from the enemy. Several days later the Saxons, wearing green twigs in their hats in the Austrian manner, crossed the Moldau to join their ally.

The total force was about ten thousand stronger than the Prussians. Hoping to lure Frederick into an attack, Charles took up a strong defensive position, his right at Janowitz covered by a series of ponds, his center and left on well-defended heights, with the Saxons extending the line west.

On learning that the Austrian and Saxon armies had camped but six miles away, Frederick hoped that Charles would attack, that he finally would have that "decisive battle" which would put matters right. But Austrian failure to move put the shoe on the Prussian foot. The troops received a two-day ration of bread and on October 23 marched in eight columns. Charles immediately sounded the call to arms while he watched what one of his staff officers called "a bold and beautiful maneuver."[2] Bold and beautiful — but useless. After Prussian soldiers spent a hideous night of cold under arms, the Prussian king and his generals surveyed the strong enemy position and abandoned any idea of attack. Watching the withdrawing enemy, disconsolate Austrian generals urged Charles to attack, but Traun persuaded him not to; the terrain was not favorable. Besides, hunger was doing a better job.

Traun was correct. Frederick's position was hopeless. Not sure what to do, he crossed the Sazawa and camped south of Pischely. General Nassau with a large corps proceeded east toward Kuttenberg and Neu-Kolin to ensure communications with Pardubitz and Silesia. Ghilányi's hussars and irregulars merely retired eastward and continued to harass his columns, which nonetheless reached Neu-Kolin at month's end.

Nádasdy meanwhile had tied in with Cogniazzo south of Prague. A hussar unit captured two hundred bread wagons coming from Prague. Cogniazzo's people jumped a courier carrying Marshal Schmettau's highly critical reports of French and Bavarian operations — an indiscretion that led to Schmettau's loss of royal favor.* To counter partisan operations, Frederick stationed battalions in villages on the road to Prague, but a major attack from Prague against Cogniazzo accomplished nothing. Once again the king was tactically blind; communica-

---

* Schmettau was never again employed in diplomatic or military affairs. He died in Berlin in 1751.

tions were delayed and broken. He had no idea of Nassau's location. Schwerin, moreover, had become disgruntled and, now ill, asked for and received extended sick leave.*

The king had not yet decided whether to occupy Prague or retreat across the Elbe (he had only one day's supply of bread left) when he learned that Charles was marching east. Frederick knew this country well: it was that of Chotusitz and glorious victory. Here was a possible threat to communications with Pardubitz and Silesia, but here also battle was possible. Frederick marched east, hoping either to intercept the enemy or to reach Kuttenberg before him. Lack of bread delayed departure by a day, and now he learned that Charles had crossed the Sazawa to gain a day's march on the Prussians. The king perforce turned north to Böhmisch-Brod and ordered Leopold to join him. There he learned that Nassau was safely camped at Neu-Kolin. With his left flank secure, he decided on another attempt to bring Charles to battle. But a heavy storm forced him to pitch tents at Gross-Gbel while the enemy dug in at Kuttenberg.

With the two armies camped not far from each other, irregular warfare ruled. Communications with Prague were cut. At Neu-Kolin Nassau beat off an attack only with difficulty. Provisions soon ran short in the Prussian camp, forage was entirely consumed, water contaminated, the weather cold and rainy, desertion rife, dysentery raging. Worse, the army was being devastated by the dreaded *Fleckfieber,* or typhus, usually fatal and spread by louse-ridden troops.† Frederick had little choice. North of the Elbe were villages with warm houses for sick men; north of the Elbe were farmsteads with food and fresh water, forage for horses. Wagons lumbered across a pontoon bridge on November 8, the army following in two columns.

Frederick held important and well-defended bridgeheads at Neu-Kolin (under Nassau) and Pardubitz (under du Moulin) south of the Elbe, which he believed would ensure communications with Prague and the Elbe magazines and would block the enemy from Silesia. With four infantry battalions and forty hussar squadrons, Prince Leopold commanded a chain of posts along the Elbe, which was especially vulnerable because of its narrowness and numerous fords. The king held the bulk of the army at Bohdanetsch, north of Pardubitz.

Frederick did not expect further enemy activity except for the usual small war, with which he could cope. When he learned that Charles

---

* Frederick later told Valory that there was no braver man in the world than Schwerin, who was invaluable on the battlefield, but was also careless in planning, obstinate, and divisive. Leopold, though a *poule mouillé,* or milksop, on the battlefield, was excellent in the general management of an army and in procuring supplies.

† Soldiers were issued a mercury compound for louse prevention. To make it easier to rub into long hair, they mixed it with butter. Taken with the pork fat that they used on their socks, the odor must have been overwhelming.

had sent nine thousand troops to Bavaria to check Seckendorff, he wrote to Prince Leopold, "The Austrian campaign is probably at an end for this year." In his opinion, peace negotiations would soon begin, possibly with Russia, Holland, and Sweden as mediators, and he sent Podewils a considerably scaled-down set of conditions for consideration.

48

PRINCE CHARLES would happily have ended the campaign for the year, since his wife in Brussels was about to give birth. But Maria Theresa paid no attention to his objections that the army was weakened and tired. Charles was to chase the Prussians completely from Bohemia.

This was scarcely a simple matter. An opening attack on Neu-Kolin by Baron von Trenck failed (he was badly wounded in both feet). A partisan effort to seize a guarded bridge failed, as did a more sophisticated attempt to bridge the Elbe; a pontoon train took a wrong turn and bogged down in a marsh, and its unfortunate captain had to be restrained from committing suicide. A second effort would fare better.

Enemy movements had caused King Frederick to place the army on general alert and take appropriate countermeasures. He strengthened the Pardubitz and Prague garrisons. But, as he wrote to Leopold, he did not believe "that the enemy's true intention was to cross the Elbe because of the difficulties he would find in so doing."

He was rudely awakened by cannon fire on November 19. During the night Austrian and Saxon grenadiers had paddled small boats soundlessly across the river. Only in daylight did sentries fire on enemy parties to alert Lieutenant Colonel Georg von Wedell. Wedell's battalion, supported by Zieten's hussars, rushed to the scene and were met by heavy infantry and artillery fire. For three hours they fought magnificently against two thousand grenadiers supported by cannon.* Heavy casualties — a hundred dead and nearly as many wounded — finally forced the battalion back to Wischenjowitz Wood, where another battalion joined. By nine A.M. infantry and artillery were crossing the nar-

---

* The King was loud in praise of Wedell, whom he thereafter called Leonidas, after the King of Sparta who was killed while defending the pass of Thermopylae. Prince Charles was also impressed with the defense. He told his officers that "these Prussians are lions. The queen would be invincible if she had such as these who with a handful of people held back my entire army for many hours." (Generalstab II, Volume 1; Erbfolge-Krieg, Volume 7.)

row river on five pontoon bridges; the cavalry used several nearby fords.

Wedell had sent no fewer than three couriers to the king asking for help, but they had been intercepted by Ghilányi's irregulars. Not until noon did Frederick learn the horrible truth — that almost all of the enemy army had crossed the Elbe. This was more than a tactical setback. Considering his dispersed forces, it could easily turn to tactical disaster.

Aides now galloped to distant commands with orders to march at once on Wischenjowitz Wood. Frederick had already decided to retreat into Silesia because of lack of food. Nassau was ordered to evacuate Neu-Kolin and withdraw as best he could, and similar orders went to Einsiedel in Prague. By early December the main army of half-frozen, half-starved, sick, and exhausted men had crossed into Silesia.

⬤═══⬤

Queen Maria Theresa was still not satisfied. Undeterred by the advice of her commanders — "To continue the war now means to ruin your army which you will need next year," Charles warned her [1] — she ordered an invasion of Silesia in which the regular army would be joined by a newly raised Hungarian levy commanded by Field Marshal Count Franz Esterhazy.

In early December Colonel Buccow's hussars and irregulars pressed into Glatz, which Colonel Fouqué was defending with only a small force. Other light units under Nádasdy, Ghilányi, and Count Lucchesi followed. Austrians soon held most of Glatz, with Buccow's hussars pushing out to Wartha, Frankenstein, Neisse, and Neustadt, the troopers tacking up copies of a royal "Manifest" that claimed all of Silesia for Maria Theresa.

The enemy had already moved into Upper Silesia, which General Marwitz was defending with only about twenty-two thousand troops. General von Wartenburg had evacuated Oppeln in late November. In early December an enemy hussar force some five hundred strong crossed the border to enter Pless; it was a short-lived success, bloodily terminated by Wartenburg's cavalry attack on December 12, which killed and captured several hundred Hungarians and sent the rest running.

King Frederick meanwhile had arrived in Schweidnitz, where he was met by Old Dessauer, summoned from Brandenburg. In late November the king had sent Count Münchow the plan for winter quarters. Despite the queen's "Manifest," Frederick did not believe that the Vienna court would break the Treaty of Breslau by a formal invasion of Silesia, particularly so late in the year. Annoyed with Fouqué for having fallen back in Glatz, he reinforced Lieutenant General Hans von Lehwaldt's corps and ordered him to retake the principality. He severely reprimanded Marwitz for not having prevented the hussar incursion, but he did reinforce the Ratibor area. Enemy troops in Moravia, he informed Marwitz, were of no significance and were only moving into winter quarters. After a few days in Schweidnitz he turned over the command to Dessauer and on December 12 was in Berlin.

Ominous reports chased him. The enemy was obviously invading in strength. Lehwaldt had been unable to retake Glatz. In Upper Silesia, Jägerndorf, Troppau, even fortress Cosel were in danger. At Troppau, Marwitz and his generals wanted to call in the Jägerndorf garrison and retire on Ratibor. Commanders were demoralized and confused. Münchow, charged with supplying the army, could not keep up with tactical changes. Where supplies failed, regiments scoured the land.

> The behavior of our army is such [Münchow complained] that citizen and peasant are already running away and even the best-disposed citizens are entirely alienated. . . . In a word it is as if there were no longer a king. Those who above all should check this disorder answer all remonstrances, reflections, and complaints only with a contemptuous smile. . . . More than half the land has grievances against us. . . . We no longer have an army; what we have is a bunch of people held together through custom and the authority of officers who themselves are all discontented.[2]

Supply commissars in Schweidnitz similarly complained. Dessauer judged the overall situation so serious that he asked the king to return.

Frederick at first refused. He was mentally and physically exhausted. Valory reported to Versailles that he was drinking himself into oblivion every night. His field marshals, the king wrote to Dessauer, could easily manage if they had the will: "Do not tolerate the enemy in Silesia but expel him immediately." As for Marwitz's proposed retreat: "I am tired of evacuating. . . . Do not allow the enemy time, but force him by active measures to renounce his designs." Further pessimistic reports from Marwitz and from Prince Leopold, who was ill with gout, brought a change of mind. Only eight days after reaching Berlin, the king left for Silesia and a meeting with Old Dessauer at Liegnitz.

The Prussian position had deteriorated. Marwitz had withdrawn to Ratibor and died of a heart attack. Prince Dietrich assumed command, and almost completely out of fodder, retired on Cosel. General Károlyi's hussars and Count Esterhazy's irregulars followed. The main Austrian army converged on Neustadt. Hussars and irregulars flooded the land; fortress Neisse was surrounded by raiding parties; a major attack by Lehwaldt on Patschkau had failed.

The king brushed off these setbacks. Wartenburg's earlier "massacre" at Pless had increased his contempt for the Hungarian partisans, a bunch of rabble worth no more worry than other irregulars. The main Austrian army was in winter quarters and would attempt nothing. The Saxons were in winter quarters as well. From Crossen the king informed Podewils that the "formidable invasion" consisted of a corps of at most four thousand horse.

So what was the tactical answer?

Attack! After hurling blunt and concise orders at Dessauer, the king left again for Berlin, from where he continued to barrage the field marshal with aggressive demands.

And he was correct.

The recent Hungarian levy had never really gotten off the ground. Only about eight thousand recruits appeared — less than half of what was expected — and they were ill trained, ill armed, and ill supplied. Their friendly reception by sympathetic Silesians was soon forfeited by their rapacious requisitions of food and money. The troops were poorly dressed and cold. Desertion soon began and increased after Wartenburg's victory at Pless. Neither Charles nor Traun wanted the new campaign. The army had made ninety-seven marches since early in the year; it lacked supplies and money; the sicklist was high; snow covered the land. On December 15, the day before his twenty-six-year-old wife died in labor in Brussels, Charles wrote to his brother Francis: "In conformity with orders we are marching and will continue to march into Silesia, but I repeat — this undertaking does not please me." Having gained Neustadt, the Austrian commanders looked forward to a quiet winter. By the time Dessauer was ready to march, Charles, brokenhearted by the news of his wife's death, had returned to Vienna, and Traun was commanding.[3]

The Prussians crossed the Neisse on January 9 and continued south toward Neustadt. Traun could not believe the early reports. His army was not battle ready. When the reports proved accurate, he sent Ghilányi and Nádasdy forward to shield withdrawal to Jägerndorf. Despite weather so cold that many soldiers suffered frozen hands and feet — a few were even frozen to death — and delay caused by supply problems, the Prussian advance continued to Neustadt and on toward Jägerndorf while Nassau moved on Troppau. In less than two weeks Traun's army, ranks sharply thinned by desertions, had been forced into Moravia, where it again took up winter quarters.

There remained the irregulars. Traun's withdrawal caused Esterhazy to shift his main force to Moravia with detachments at Ratibor and Oderberg. These fell victim to a two-pronged attack by Nassau and Zieten in early February. Now in possession of Upper Silesia, the king replaced ailing Prince Leopold with Margrave Charles, whose headquarters were at Troppau. In mid-February he wrote: "Good results coincide with your arrival. You have only to shake the enemy powerfully here, where he becomes cheeky, or in the country drive him away, where it is to my advantage."

While Nassau marched in Upper Silesia, Lehwaldt moved into Glatz.

His orders were to evict the enemy, burn his large magazine at Nachod (in Bohemia), and reoccupy Glatz. Prodded by the king, who sent Nassau's report on the capture of Ratibor to Fouqué so that he and Lehwaldt could match it, the Prussians attacked Habelschwerdt. It was a bloody victory won in knee-high snow and one that caused the Austrians to evacuate all of Glatz.

Only in mid-February did the exhausted, sick, and decimated Prussian army take up winter quarters.

49

THE KING OF PRUSSIA was not a modest man, so it is the more refreshing to read his scathing critique of the Bohemian campaign: "No general ever committed more faults than the king in this campaign."[1] His first fault, he went on in admirable candor, was failure to provide supplies for at least six months of operations. "One who wishes to build an army," he quoted Homer's *Iliad,* "should take the stomach for foundation." He knew that Saxony was allied with Austria, so he should have either forced her to change allegiance or conquered her before he entered Bohemia. He had made the supreme error of marching on Tabor and Budweis instead of chasing the wily Batthyányi from the country and seizing the Pilsen magazine, which would have prevented Charles from entering Bohemia. He had left too weak a garrison at Prague, and after its capture he should have sent his heavy cannon back to Silesia. While Traun played the role of Sertorius, he concluded, he had played that of Pompey. Traun's generalship was a model of perfection and should be forever studied. Frederick regarded the campaign as his education in warfare, with Traun the teacher.

But as usual he failed to tell the entire story. His was as much a political as a military failure, which Podewils clearly recognized. The siren of military success sounded too loudly; the picture of pageantry was painted too brightly in the royal mind. Significant signs were not heeded; cautionary voices not heard. Why did he think he could win over the Russian court (and thus control Saxony), given Chancellor Count Bestushev's immense power harnessed by British and Austrian gold? Why did he flatter the French king, only to denigrate French arms in unnecessarily insulting notes to Valory and Seckendorff?

Frederick later wrote that the delay in taking Prague, coupled with Charles's march on Bohemia, caused him to consider a major change in plan. Influenced, however, by the wishes of Emperor Charles, King

Louis, and, above all, Marshal Belle-Isle, he wrote, each of whom stressed the importance of ensuring Prussian communications with Bavaria, he had adhered to his earlier plan of advancing to Tabor and Budweis for the winter.

A host of historians have accepted these royal words, which tend to shift blame for the Bohemian debacle to the allies. But neither Frederick's temperament nor his correspondence of the time supports them. On the day Prague fell, he wrote to Emperor Charles, "I congratulate Your Imperial Majesty on this acquisition. . . . I will march the 20th to Budweis with all the army." Three days later he wrote to Podewils: "We are currently marching on Tabor and Budweis in order to render ourselves master of those parts and to oblige Prince Charles and Batthyányi to fall back on Upper Austria. If they do not do so, they will be beaten. . . . One battle won and the politics will turn as strongly to our advantage. . . . I am convinced that I am not mistaken in this affair." A few days later he repeated to Podewils his strategy of forcing the Austrian army either to retire to Upper Austria or face being cut off (and presumably destroyed). Far from going on the defensive, a course contrary to his nature, he was running with bit in teeth, convinced that the seizure of Prague would hold the Saxons in check, convinced that he could meet and beat the Austrian army in battle without outside help.

The king also blamed an inadequate supply service and poor intelligence for much of his difficulty. But this was his own fault. He had faced similar supply problems in 1741–1742. Why hadn't at least some of them been solved? Why had he not increased the number of field bake ovens? Why had oxen not been tested before they were taken into the field? Why had teamsters not been trained to the beasts' peculiar needs, so different from those of horses? The king crossed the Moldau because a spy told him the Austrians were marching on Budweis. Why had he made this critical decision without confirming the spy's report — which was false?

The disastrous campaign was a terrible blow to his prestige at home and abroad. But it was also a salutary lesson. Valory noted the change. He found the king much less arrogant, his language less intemperate and biting. As Frederick himself later wrote, "Good fortune is often more fatal to princes than adversity: the former intoxicates them with presumption; the latter renders them circumspect and modest."[2]

The Prussian army was in trouble. It had lost millions of thalers' worth of soldiers, horses, muskets, cannon, pontoons, equipment, wagons, and personal baggage. Although enemy claims of thirty thousand deserters were inflated, a third or even more of that figure seems justified.

Desertions continued, especially in remote garrisons, where food was lacking and quarters insufficient. Many officers were dispirited; the supply service was in a mess; sicklists were running high.

It was up to Old Dessauer to start the rebuilding process, and he did so. A sick army, a disorganized army, even a demoralized army, is not necessarily a beaten army. Units remained intact and were organized receptacles for new bodies. Many of the new bodies were old ones: deserters returning to the flag. In late December the Prussian king not only issued a general pardon for any deserters returning within six months but promised each man a six-thaler bonus! He also sent fifty teams of officers and NCOs abroad to recruit, and he signed secret treaties with a number of smaller rulers to furnish contingents. He accepted twenty-seven hundred Austrian prisoners into his service, and sent most of them to garrisons to free Prussians for field duty. Unit commanders in Silesia received replacements from local cantons. Commanders forcefully conscripted throughout Silesia and Glatz — "married and unmarried, rich and poor, even fifteen-year-olds," an Austrian general reported.[3] By March the army in Silesia was still short about eight thousand infantry, but no cavalry and only seven hundred hussars. The shortages were repaired in the next few weeks.

Horses and wagons were scarcer than recruits. Losses had been enormous. Frederick did not try for full replacements, since he planned to fight the next campaign on interior lines in his own country, where peasants would furnish wagons and teams. Replacement mounts for cavalry and hussars began arriving in December. By March units were still short twelve hundred horses, with another sixteen hundred down sick.

Most of the baggage had been lost during the retreat, and utensils were in short supply. Owing mainly to lack of funds, these shortages were only slowly repaired. To meet a serious need of food, oats, and hay, the king lifted tolls on corn and fodder from Mecklenburg and Poland.

Despite such problems, Dessauer rang up some outstanding tactical successes. Nassau and Winterfeldt gave the Hungarians a severe beating at Ratibor, and Lehwaldt defeated the Austrians at Habelschwerdt and forced them from Glatz. Nassau could not sufficiently praise the bravery of his hussars. "And the infantry," he reported to the king, "has been in such good spirit that they forget all fatigues they have endured and display the greatest zeal for battle."[4]

But Dessauer was old, tired, and grieving. His wife of forty years had died in January, his three sons were seriously ill, and in late February a serious typhus epidemic broke out in his command. For some time he had been wanting to leave Silesia, and in mid-March the king agreed to return to take command.

While Old Dessauer was rebuilding the army in Silesia, the king had turned to waning political and financial fortunes (leavened by intimate suppers with the enticing dancer Barbarina Campanini in Count Rothenburg's house). The Prussian failure in Bohemia had greatly weakened his diplomatic hand, but he still had treaties with France, England, and Russia and he was secretly approaching Turkey, who he hoped would threaten Austria and Russia. And he still had an army, which he intended to employ against Austria and, if necessary, Saxony in the spring — a firm martial sentiment bluntly expressed to all foreign courts.

Not long after reaching Berlin, he had sent the King of France a twelve-page report of his campaign, a remarkably objective document, and accompanied it with praise for the French capture of Freiburg. He followed this by reporting the Austrian invasion of Silesia and invoking his treaty with France, begging Louis to "take the most vigorous measures" and to "redouble his efforts" to prevent the Vienna court from achieving its goal.

He wrote similarly to the King of England, who would have been impressed neither by his nephew's protest of the terrible consequences to the Empire if people like Maria Theresa went around breaking treaties, nor by his invoking aid under the Treaty of Westminster. But George's hand had been strengthened by a change in the ministry, which saw the fiery Lord Carteret replaced by the more conservative Lord Harrington, "a worthy and able man," in Frederick's words, who allowed hope for a reasonable peace. Lord Chesterfield, a professed admirer of the Prussian king, would soon leave for the Hague as ambassador, which added to Frederick's optimism. His envoy to London, Johann Heinrich Andrié, was to appeal covertly to Parliament and the public to support the true defender of the Protestant faith while also pointing out that Prussia could not pay interest, much less redeem Silesian mortgages held by British merchants, until there was peace.

Frederick also asked Czarina Elizabeth for help under their existing treaty. He expected little result as long as British gold ruled Chancellor Bestushev, but he would have been satisfied if Saint Petersburg remonstrated with the Vienna and Saxon courts and used its good offices to bring peace in Germany — a mediation that he privately regarded "as the last string in my bow." Mardefeld was to continue bribing various ministers — he was authorized to pay Bestushev 100,000 thalers in return for support of Prussian territorial claims. If Mardefeld believed that a splendid carriage would really please the czarina, Frederick would have one built, but if not absolutely necessary he would like to avoid the expense.*

---

* The czarina was very pleased indeed. The carriage was made and sent by sea transport in early 1746.

He had reason for concern. To refit the army and support the next year's campaign would cost about 5.5 million thalers. He had 1.2 million on hand. To raise the rest meant mortgaging or selling various territories or borrowing in one form or another. This would not be easy, because his recent disaster in Bohemia had suddenly turned Prussia into a poor risk in European money markets. (In the end he would borrow a substantial sum from Brandenburg estates.)

˙ It was almost uncanny how Frederick made light of these problems. It was as if the army had suffered a minor tactical setback. He wrote to Emperor Charles not to worry, but only to take precautions against a winter attack. Come spring, Marshal Maillebois's French army on the Rhine would be ready to march, and so would the Prussian army. Marshal Belle-Isle even then was on his way to Potsdam to coordinate plans for the spring.

Belle-Isle never reached Potsdam. In late December Frederick learned that the marshal had been arrested in Hanover and would be taken to England as prisoner of war. This was another blow. The spark plug of the Versailles war party, Belle-Isle was Frederick's chief supporter. His absence, taken with the sinister death in early December of King Louis's mistress and King Frederick's supporter, the Duchess of Châteauroux, opened the way for the peace party to approach Austria.

Frederick nonetheless carried on as if nothing adverse had happened. For the next several weeks, in letters to King Louis and Marshal Noailles, he hammered home the danger of an Austrian attack on the emperor's scattered forces and the need to reinforce Imperial troops in Bavaria and the Upper Palatinate, as well as Maillebois's weak corps on the Rhine. The French king meanwhile should send another representative to discuss operational plans.

Andrié, in London, was getting closer to Lord Harrington, who Frederick hoped could bring a peace between Prussia and Austria. In a superb example of diplomatic poker, Andrié was to explain that the King of Prussia at present was "in the most beautiful situation in the world," having chased the Austrians from all of Silesia; that he would be able to begin the coming campaign with every hope of great success but nonetheless would sacrifice his interests in order to achieve peace (providing, of course, that he received territorial reimbursement).

The king had just finished dictating his dispatch to Andrié when he learned that Emperor Charles had died. Only forty-eight, but broken in mind and body, he had been attacked by gout in the foot. The evil humors soon spread to the chest and killed one of the least effectual if most tragic rulers of the century. His heir, Maximilian Joseph, was neither old enough nor capable enough to pick up the Imperial torch. "A pious child," Seckendorff called him, weaker by far than his father, captive of ministers corrupted by Vienna. Here was a "terrible crisis,"

Frederick wrote to King Louis, one that could easily dissolve the Union of Frankfurt and put a Habsburg back on the Imperial throne: "It is certain that the emperor could not have died at a worse time for all our interests, and that this event upsets all our measures."

The French answer was to propose the King of Poland (Elector of Saxony) for the Imperial crown. Valory and the Chevalier de Courten (Belle-Isle's replacement) were sent to explain the plan to Frederick at Potsdam. Since this might cause a rupture between Saxony and Austria, Frederick agreed to swallow his resentment of King August's perfidy for "the good of the common cause." But he warned that Count Brühl, who had been bought by bribes from London and Vienna, would sabotage Valory's mission in Dresden.

When this happened, when diplomacy failed, the situation required military action. But here the situation had become equally unfavorable. In northern Bavaria, Bernklau's irregulars had pushed the Imperial army and the French back to the Danube. An Austrian-British-Hanoverian corps had occupied the Lower Palatinate with no interference from Maillebois, who retreated across the Main, a success that caused the ruler of Hesse to pull out of the war, thus dissolving the Union of Frankfurt. Maillebois's retreat, Frederick told Louis, was "an event as disadvantageous in these circumstances as the loss of a battle." He agreed in large part with the plan of military operations brought by Courten. Frederick called for operations "only as they complement the political scene and relate to present circumstances." He supposed that the intention of France and her allies was still to humble the House of Austria or at least to prevent its attaining the Imperial dignity. To reduce the Vienna court's influence in the electoral college at Frankfurt, Maillebois had to advance vigorously to cut communication between the ecclesiastical (pro-Austrian) electors and Hanover and fight whatever force got in the way. The recently reinforced Bavarian army, commanded now by the ineffectual Field Marshal Count Ignaz Törring, needed a bold and aggressive general such as Prince Louis de Conti to lead the march on Vienna while the Prussians advanced into Moravia or, at the very least, contained a large Austrian force on the frontiers of Bohemia and Moravia.

This plan received only lukewarm attention at Versailles, where the antiwar party was growing more powerful. Maillebois remained inactive. Neither Conti nor any other general was sent to command the Bavarian army. In mid-March Batthyányi attacked the Bavarian winter quarters (as Frederick had warned) and pushed that army back on Munich. He then struck General Ségur's French-Palatine corps to send it into wild retreat to Swabia. The young elector fled Munich for Augsburg; the Austrians again occupied the capital; the Hessians declared neutrality; and the Bavarian court opened peace talks with Vienna.

Meanwhile the Prussian king learned that in January the Vienna court had fashioned a quadruple alliance — an extension of the Treaty of Worms — with Saxony, England, and Holland. He suspected that a secret clause in what was called the Treaty of Warsaw called for further British subsidies to Austria and for Austrian-Saxon military operations against Prussia.

He was correct.

50

THE KING returned to Silesia in mid-March 1745. From his head-quarters in fortress Neisse, he looked on four separate army corps. Their condition varied considerably. Only a few units were up to scratch. Sickness was widespread. Even normal dysentery is not easy to cure under ideal conditions. Inadequate food and crowded, unsanitary, and cold quarters only prolonged misery as bleedings and purgatives only further weakened already weak men. Typhus spread through Upper Silesia and into fortress Neisse. It was a particularly virulent type, with black spots followed by large boils that resembled plague blisters and resulted in death a few days later.

Fearing that peasants would call it the plague and stop food deliveries, the king officially termed it putrid fever. It struck at random — officers, doctors, soldiers, wives, children, Prince Maurice of Anhalt (who survived). The patient was first bled, then given white wine or, failing that, water mixed with lemon juice or vinegar. Clothing and bed linen of the dead were buried, infected units isolated as much as possible. Overall figures are lacking, but in Upper Silesia at the end of March eighty-five hundred infantry and eleven hundred cavalry were sick; during the month seven officers, fifty-one NCOs, and 820 men died. Münchow was reprimanded for the "hard, unkind, and thoughtless proceedings" of civil officials toward sick soldiers, who often lacked beds and were forced to lie on barely covered floors. The disease continued to take a heavy toll, and the king refused to allow either Prince William or Prince Henry to leave Berlin. Frederick finally agreed that William could join him in a few weeks but urged him to impregnate his wife before departure from Berlin.

Sickness was only part of the morale problem. Some commanders were slack, felt sorry for themselves, resented the recent disastrous campaign, were tired, and wanted leave. Their requests were abruptly refused, without exception. Instead, the king imposed a heavy training program and called for frequent reports on combat readiness. "It is astonishing how quickly bravery or fear communicates to the multitude," he later wrote. Training followed by successful, small-scale operations would restore confidence and morale (as it had to the cavalry after Mollwitz): "Punishments, rewards, blame, and praise, employed as appropriate, change the make-up of men and inspire them with feelings foreign to what one would believe from their natural sodden states." If offered examples of uncommon valor, they will attempt to emulate: "Ordinary men become heroes. Talents are often numbed by a type of lethargy: some strong jolts awaken them, and they exert and develop themselves." Commanders were to send out frequent combat patrols, and caution drew sharp warning: "Conduct yourself at all times as a man of courage. I will have no timid officers; he who is not bold and brave does not deserve to serve in the Prussian army." [1]

Neither Maria Theresa nor her close advisers had the slightest intention of making peace. With Prussian popularity at a low in the Empire, the Bavarian court talking peace, Marshall Maillebois's French army retreating, the treasury repaired by British gold, Saxony committed to supplying thirty thousand troops, Russia making friendly overtures, and, not least, the Prussian army obviously on the ropes, the reconquest of Silesia was not only axiomatic in the queen's mind, it was an obsession.

The only question was how to achieve it.

Bavaria first had to be removed from the war. This was done by bribing Count Seckendorff, who coerced the young and inexperienced Bavarian elector into signing the Peace of Füssen, which guaranteed his territories in return for peace and his vote in the Imperial election. Then Silesia had to be taken, a task for young and grieving Prince Charles and the old and ailing Duke of Weissenfels. Cautious Marshal Traun had been transferred to the Bavarian command, a gross error on the queen's part. After acrimonious argument, Charles and Weissenfels, neither of whom trusted the other, agreed to open the campaign with Esterhazy's Hungarians, reinforced by infantry and hussars, moving up the Oder to draw the Prussian army to Upper Silesia. The main Austrian army would advance from Königgrätz to Braunau and, joined by the Saxons, continue through the mountains to Schweidnitz and Breslau.

It would have been a satisfactory plan had the Prussian army been as weak or the Austrian army as strong as supposed. Neither was the case. While Dessauer and Frederick had been rebuilding their army in Silesia, Charles had been in Vienna and his senior commanders were enjoying life in the capital or on their estates. Money was short, supply difficult. In early May at Königgrätz, Charles found serious shortages of men, food and raw fodder. Decrepit supply wagons could scarcely be used. He seems to have done little to repair these and other deficiencies. Instead, the troops were told that the Prussians were weak and exhausted; they would not fight. It would be a matter of walking into Silesia and picking up rich booty.

Suspecting what his enemy had in mind, the king in early April ordered Old Dessauer — now rested from his recent ordeal in Silesia — to set up a corps in Magdeburg. "If they [his enemies] come here," he wrote to Podewils, "I will let them peacefully pass through the mountains, then smash them, and if the Saxons are involved, the Magdeburg corps will be instantly ordered to enter Saxony and put everything to fire and sword."

Spies continued to report an Austrian-Saxon buildup in Moravia. Frederick correctly regarded the small war as a diversion designed to attract him there while the enemy invaded Lower Silesia. But where would they strike? Reports from envoys, border troops, and spies greatly differed. Only one fact was certain: he did not have sufficient force to guard three hundred miles of border, much of it in mountainous and difficult terrain.

His dilemma was eased in mid-April, when a discontented Austrian officer, Captain von Krummenau, arrived in Prussian headquarters to receive a colonel's commission — and to tell the king about the Austrian order of battle and plan of operations. According to Krummenau, Charles and Weissenfels pictured their armies marching through the mountains to debouch without hindrance onto the inner flatlands of Lower Silesia, where they would meet and defeat the Prussian army.

Frederick at once informed Podewils of this development and described his own plans. If England failed to intervene and the enemy attacked, Podewils was to move the royal family, treasury, and archives to Stettin and was to request military and financial aid from the French. Frederick left no doubt that a crisis was at hand: "The game I play is so considerable that it is impossible to take a calm view of the outcome."

A few days later he transferred his headquarters to Patschkau in order to concentrate his army between there and Frankenstein. This would put him on the flank of any enemy march, either from Olmütz on Neisse or from Glatz on Schweidnitz. To keep an eye on both Saxons and Austrians, he sent Colonel Winterfeldt with a task force to the Landeshut area; Colonel du Moulin commanded an observation corps around Schweidnitz.

It was at this crucial point that he learned of the Bavarian elector's decision to make a private peace with Austria. It was another major blow, but there was nothing to do for the moment other than wait. For this, he chose the somewhat incongruous surroundings of a Cistercian monastery near Kamenz, where he was guest of an ardent admirer, Abbot Tobias Stusche, with whom he had earlier corresponded. He continued to send evacuation instructions to Podewils. Hacke would command a small garrison in Berlin to prevent incursions, but there was no hope of a real defense with fewer than twenty thousand troops, and he could not spare them. Warned by Lord Chesterfield that England could not restrain Vienna and Dresden from aggressive action, the king again stressed his plight to King Louis and begged him to send Prince Conti's army into the heart of Hanover; he also hoped France would persuade Turkey to attack Hungary.

He continued to deal with a host of public and private affairs, sending his portrait to Czarina Elizabeth (at her request), reminding the envoy Baron Johann Chambrier to send some designs of French chairs. Life in the monastery was extremely pleasant. "We dine every day in the garden, where our prelate gives us beautiful music," Prince Albert of Brunswick noted.[2] "I believe that you are astonished to see me so tranquil in the most violent crisis of my life," the king wrote to Podewils. "This is a matter of rolling with events that one can't change."

The royal temper flared when Frederick received a lengthy letter from the King of France that tried to justify his position. In annotations prepared only for Podewils, Frederick emphasized what he regarded as French perfidy and outright lies. France was entirely responsible for Bavaria's defection; Louis's claimed services "cost the late emperor his country twice and the present emperor his country once." As for the valor of Count Ségur's troops in a recent combat with Batthyányi, "The troops of the king, with all due deference to them, acted like cunts. . . . French valor is an invention." The French king's so-called measures on behalf of Prussia drew particular scorn: "If France makes diversions as favorable to the King of Prussia as those of Bavaria, she is entreated to save herself the trouble." Once again he concluded that he had nothing to hope for from France. Rather unwisely, considering the French king's sensitive nature, he wrote to Louis that the Flanders campaign would not help Prussia any more than the Spaniards descending on the Canary Islands or the King of France taking Tournai or Kublai Khan besieging Babylon.

Frederick was still not convinced that the Austrians and Saxons would attack. But on May 19 he learned that they were marching from Königgrätz. Podewils was to send the King of France a letter prepared some time ago; it asked for a large money subsidy and diversionary military operations. Frederick's own march would begin shortly: "We thus finally come to the dénouement."

It was time to draw in his forces. Zieten rode with orders for Margrave Charles at Jägerndorf in Upper Silesia to join the main army, leaving Major General Heinrich von Hautcharmoy with a small corps to counter Esterhazy's raids. The margrave, with only six thousand troops, had to make a fighting withdrawal against some twenty thousand enemy, a costly but very successful operation that won the king's particular praise.* Near Landeshut, Colonel Winterfeldt's corps beat off a vicious attack by Nádasdy and Franquini. Taken with the great French victory at Fontenoy, where British and Dutch troops suffered heavy losses from a brilliant defense by Maurice of Saxony (for some time a field marshal in the French army), these victories caused Frederick to believe that the Austrians would postpone a move on Silesia for several weeks. "Fortune changes suddenly to our advantage," he wrote to Podewils, instructing him to exploit the victories in newspapers and diplomatic channels.

But three days later he informed Podewils that the enemy armies were assembling at Schönberg on the border: "We will form our camp tomorrow, and as these people have neither food nor forage in these mountains, they will come to Schweidnitz to procure them. I have indeed foreseen this, and this is the place where I am resolved to attack them."

5 1

Sunday, May 30, 1745. The main Prussian army is at Frankenstein. It is about fifty-nine thousand strong, with fifty-four heavy cannon. "I do not tell you of my dispositions," the king writes to Podewils, "but I can assure you that I would submit them without concern to the criticism of Condé and other great generals" — referring to the Prince of Condé, a French marshal whose victories in and after the Thirty Years' War won him the name "The Great Condé."

Frederick learns that the Austrians are marching northeast toward Landeshut. Winterfeldt at Landeshut estimates Austrian-Saxon strength at about seventy thousand. Du Moulin reports his hussars skirmishing with enemy hussars in the Schweidnitz area.

The Prussian army marches north toward Reichenbach. The king tells Podewils that the "army is striking and filled with the best will in the world, and with an unparalleled hatred of the Saxons."

· · ·

* Frederick openly praised Zieten's performance and that of the cavalry commander, Colonel Reimar von Schwerin. "Embrace Schwerin a thousand times for me," he wrote to Charles, "and tell him that I shall never forget his bravery or his conduct. . . . Praise the soldiers a thousand times and tell them I am pleased beyond expression." He gave Schwerin a bailiwick as reward. Winterfeldt was promoted to major general.

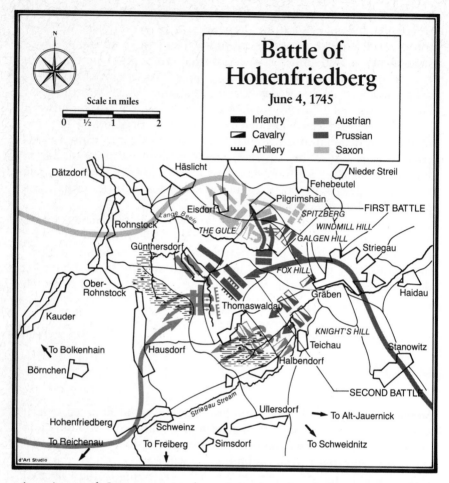

Austrian and Saxon armies have joined at Landeshut — some fifty thousand Austrians, nearly twenty thousand Saxons, and several thousand irregulars. Their approach marches have been slow; supply has been difficult because of poor weather, bad roads, and hostile peasants paid by Prussians to deliver enemy hussars and horses, the former preferably dead, the latter alive. "The country is one of the most difficult that I have seen," Charles reports to Grand Duke Francis.[1] But the troops are in good condition, and discipline is excellent, possibly because of the bodies of deserters that dangle from gallows along the march roads.

The old Duke of Weissenfels is confident. Once the Prussians are beaten, he tells a local priest, "a strong corps will immediately invade the Mark and march on Berlin."[2] Prince Charles is also buoyant. He learns that Cosel has been captured, that most of Upper Silesia is Austrian controlled. He hopes to debouch in the Bolkenhain-Hohenfriedberg area, cut Prussian communications, and force the enemy either to battle or retreat across the Oder. Two days earlier he reported to Maria Theresa that the enemy had retired on Schweidnitz "and would not be of a mind to maintain a defense there very long." But the previous day he somewhat ominously informed Francis that "I know nothing of the enemy."[3]

Monday, May 31, 1745. The Prussian army marches to a new camp between Alt-Jauernick and Schweidnitz. Frederick sends two grenadier battalions to du Moulin, who occupies Striegau, and establishes hussar posts on hills northwest of Striegau and Gräben, outposts so far forward, he reports, "that the enemy will have difficulty surprising us."[4]

Army headquarters are at Alt-Jauernick. Frederick places an observation post on top of the Ritterberg — Knight's Hill — from where he scans mountain exits to the south. He visits it several times this day, intently studying the silent land through a spyglass.* There is no sign of the enemy.

Prince Charles learns that the Prussian army is between Frankenstein and Reichenbach. Although Weissenfels had planned to spend several days in Landeshut, he now agrees that he and Charles can reach the plains at Striegau before the Prussians can block mountain exits.

Tuesday, June 1, 1745. By evening the Austrians are in camp east of Freiberg and Alt-Reichenau, with the right wing on the Hohenfried-berg road. The Saxons are on their left, not far from Bolkenhain.

Nádasdy reports from Freiberg that Prussians are in the Schweidnitz area. Charles rides to a height and spots the enemy camp.

He will march for Bolkenhain in the morning. Wallis will occupy Hohenfriedberg.

Wednesday, June 2, 1745. Frederick learns that fortress Cosel has fallen; a Prussian subaltern deserted and informed the enemy of its weak spots.

Reports of small enemy detachments marching on Hohenfriedberg arrive. More reports by evening: an enemy camp of approximately seven thousand troops is west of Freiberg; another large camp is in mountain defiles west of Hohenfriedberg; a few tents are in the town itself.

The king smells battle. "The enemy descends today from the mountains," he writes to Podewils, "and tomorrow we shall attack him."

·   ·   ·

---

* I recently visited this area, which is in today's Poland. Essential terrain features appeared but slightly changed. Villages have undoubtedly grown, but gray stone, red tile roofs, and green onion domes are as they were in 1745. Windmill Hill is even complete with an ancient windmill, but I could not locate the commemorative monument described by earlier writers.

The main Austrian army camps west of Hohenfriedberg with Saxons on the left. Wallis's advance guard reaches the western heights. Charles and Weissenfels survey the scene. There is no sign of the Prussian camp. Although Nádasdy has reported no enemy movement this day, they suppose that the Prussians are now in Striegau. They tentatively agree to advance to the plains in the morning, but will meet again before so doing.

Late this night Charles writes to his brother Francis "to report that the entire army is together and that tomorrow I descend to the plains. I have made my preparations in such a manner that I believe the enemy will find it difficult to prevent us from doing this. He is on the point of changing his locations, toward which direction is still uncertain. It is midnight."[5]

Thursday, June 3, 1745. Charles and Weissenfels ride to their observation point. It is seven A.M. A spy has reported that the Prussians are still in camp at Schweidnitz, that the Prussian king is entirely confused, that his army is already beginning to retire on Breslau. The information suits their wishes. They have no idea that their spy has received a great deal of money from the Prussian king for reporting such.

They agree that it is time to march. Troops strike tents, leave packs behind. The advance guard moves out before noon: General Ernst Georg von Kalckreuth's cavalry to Thomaswaldau, General von Wallis's infantry to Halbendorf and Ullersdorf. The main army follows, eight columns, infantry in the center, cavalry on the wings. With waving flags and ringing music, they debouch from four passes onto the plain. Charles and Weissenfels are at lunch, greatly enjoying the splendid scene. By late afternoon camps are laid out. Only the left wing is delayed. When it finally comes up, the line stretches over four miles, units occupying hastily staked-out camps, troops weary, looking forward to bread and sleep, never dreaming of battle.

Charles is in headquarters at Hausdorf, Weissenfels at Rohnstock. There is no sign of the enemy. But on this day Prince Louis of Brunswick writes to his brother, "I doubt strongly that he [Frederick] will allow us to debouch quietly under his nose."[6]

King Frederick rides early this same morning to Knight's Hill. Enemy fires are plainly visible in mountain camps — a sure sign, he tells his officers, that the enemy will soon march. Austrian soldiers, he explains, *always* cook early on the day of march. He returns to headquarters, summons generals, reviews his orders. The army is placed on alert.

Back on the hill in late afternoon, the king and his generals watch eight clouds of dust swirl from the plain. They see staff officers hastily marking out camps. Dust settles to reveal troop columns. They are in march order. This is no deployment for battle.

The French envoy, the Marquis de Valory, arrives with news of the French capture of Tournai. Frederick congratulates him: "I hope I shall have good news to report to your king. The enemy are where I want them and I shall attack tomorrow."[7]

Du Moulin advances at eight P.M. to hussar posts on heights north of Striegau and Gräben. The main army follows, but leaves tents standing, watchfires burning. It marches in two columns on Striegau. Du Moulin's cavalry meanwhile run into some Saxon uhlans north of Gräben. They avoid a skirmish. His infantry occupy Mühlenberg — Windmill Hill. Saxon uhlans and infantry move up to the Spitzberg, not far from du Moulin's posts. Du Moulin wisely chooses not to attack. The Saxon commander believes that he is facing only a weak detachment that can be sent running in the morning.

By nine P.M. the main Prussian army is marching in silence, crossing streams with water up to the knees.* Marquis de Valory, his bulk closeted in a wagon, watches. He is astonished by the "prodigious discipline" and lack of stragglers.

A report reaches Prince Charles an hour later that enemy troops are approaching the Saxon left wing. It is passed to the Duke of Weissenfels.

Nádasdy reports that some Prussians are advancing. The troops are ordered to remain alert and under arms, but no one believes that this is more than a detachment of cavalry.

Friday, June 4, 1745. Prussian columns close on Gräben after midnight. By two A.M. the army is deployed fronting Teichau, its right on Gräben, its left on Stanowitz. Troops remain under arms but gain a two-hour rest. Their king strolls through the lines, talking to the tired men. It is a beautiful night, fresh, the sky filled with stars. The king wraps himself in a cloak for a brief nap on open ground. He awakens before daybreak. Aides summon the principal generals: the army will march to the right, cross Striegau Stream. Buddenbrock's cavalry on the right will advance on Pilgrimshain and join du Moulin's attack north of the Gule, a narrow lowland running through the plain, with Nassau's infantry in support. Left-wing cavalry will cover infantry of the left in their march to a line between Thomaswaldau and Teichau. Infantry to attack only with bayonet if possible; if fire is necessary, the infantry is not to open until 150 paces from the enemy. Cavalry to attack with sabers in hand, no quarter given, the face the target. Once

---

* Frederick later wrote: "When it is a matter of an important operation, it does not matter if the soldier wets his feet a trifle." (Preuss, *Friedrich . . . eine Lebensgeschichte,* Urkundenbuch.)

enemy cavalry are beaten, they will strike enemy infantry in flank and rear.

Troops are falling into formation when cannon fire sounds from the north. This is from Saxon guns on Spitzberg. Du Moulin at once moves to the attack. Surprised Saxons fall back from the hill. Du Moulin deploys fifteen cannon on its slopes as his infantry and cavalry move on Pilgrimshain. Frederick orders six 24-pounders to deploy on Fox Hill. He will command from Windmill Hill.

The Duke of Weissenfels arises early and rides to his troops. It is a clear and beautiful spring morning. At about four A.M. he hears cannon fire and learns of the Prussian advance. He orders the advance guard to fall back on Pilgraimshain. He places his infantry on the right; the cavalry will attack south of Pilgrimshain.

Saxon cavalry ride proudly to the field. They see enemy horse and charge. They hit Count Rothenburg's first line, twenty-four squadrons of cuirassiers. They scatter a few squadrons but now meet General Christoph von Stille's second line, twenty squadrons of dragoons. General von der Goltz moves in on the left, charges two Austrian regiments, presses them back. On the right Bredow is outflanked by some Saxon squadrons, but du Moulin's hussars send them running. Stille's dragoons clean up isolated Saxon horse. Stille will later write to a friend, "If you had been present you would have admired the union of steadiness and courage displayed by our troops."[8]

Weissenfels is not pleased. He orders the cavalry to re-form and attack again. It is not any better. Squadrons are caught in cross fire. Prussian cavalry have re-formed and are waiting. Squadrons fight squadrons. The Saxons give way. Von der Goltz is in the middle of it. So is Saxon General von Schlichting. The former general single-handedly captures the latter general to add to military lore. Prussian reserve cavalry now attack. At six A.M. Saxon horse give way and retire from battle.

Weissenfels deploys his infantry in two lines from the Gule to the village of Eisdorf. The first line of sixteen battalions deploys behind a series of small dams. They are backed by a second line of fourteen battalions stretching hooklike to Eisdorf. But the first line lacks their cannon, victims of marshland encountered on the approach march.

Prussian lines move forward, twenty-one battalions regally commanded by such as the Prince of Prussia, Prince Leopold, Prince Dietrich, Prince Maurice, the Prince of Bevern, Count Truchsess. Flags are flying, drums and trumpets play "The March of the Grenadiers" while overhead cannonballs from heavy guns on Fox Hill smash into Saxon lines.

The Saxon cannon finally arrive. Batteries fire deadly canister shot

and punch holes in approaching Prussian lines. At two hundred paces
the Saxons open musket fire. Flanking Prussian regiments answer with
fire while marching, an ineffectual reply scorned by Prince Leopold,
whose proud regiment marches with shouldered weapons.

It is about six-thirty A.M., a hot morning already clouded by powder
smoke and dust, by suffering and death. The smoke helps the Prussians, because an east wind blows it into enemy lines. Half-blinded,
thirsty soldiers are no contest for the Prussian assault. They fall back
on the second line. On the left Truchsess with six battalions presses in.
He is killed by a cannonball. In the center eleven battalions wade through
ditches and ponds. On the right du Moulin, reinforced by four battalions, presses into Pilgrimshain and Eisdorf to threaten the enemy's left.
The Saxons are in general retreat. Prussian cavalry come onto the field
to strike their left. Five companies attacked by dragoons refuse to surrender. The Prussians, having learned of a Saxon order to give no quarter,
reciprocate: four hundred men are killed, including the colonel; the
others are taken prisoner.

The Saxons are in full retreat to Häslicht and beyond. The first battle
is over.

Prince Charles early hears cannon fire but assumes the Saxons are attacking Striegau. A report from Weissenfels rudely corrects this impression. He leaves his headquarters at seven A.M. and rides forward to find
an immense battlefield. Thirty-three battalions of Austrian infantry are
deployed in two lines just east of Günthersdorf, with cavalry still negotiating swampy ground north of Halbendorf.

King Frederick moves to Fox Hill to watch the deployment. His own
people are delayed by tight terrain. Aides, including his brother Henry,
scurry to push them on. The left-wing cavalry is stopped by a broken
bridge. Major General Baron Friedrich Wilhelm von Kyau on the far
side with ten cuirassier squadrons is attacked by fifty-six squadrons
under General Baron Johann Friedrich von Berlichingen. Prince Ferdinand with five battalions is isolated on the left. The king runs out of
aides. Valory is present and admires "the steadiness, activity, and discipline displayed by the infantry."[9] His thoughts are shaken when the
king sends him forward to find the absent cavalry. He stumbles on
Major General Friedrich Leopold Gessler's reserve squadrons, who are
not what the king has in mind but who will do until Nassau and Zieten
finally charge to Kyau's aid. Forty-five Prussian squadrons fight sixty-
six Austrian squadrons and win.

Half an hour later, sixteen Prussian battalions are sorted out and
march in line against the enemy between Thomaswaldau and Günthersdorf. It is the Gule repeated. It is flags flying and drums beating; it
is Austrian canister shot and musket fire; it is an awesome, inexorable

body of marching Prussians who refuse to disintegrate. Then it is assault by bayonet. The enemy falls back; the villages are seized. The king lowers his spyglass and turns to a French observer. "The battle is won," he states.[10] He returns to Windmill Hill.

But hard fighting continues in the center, where Count von Daun's infantry, firing from ditches, takes a terrible toll. Regiment Hacke loses half its men; Regiment Brunswick-Bevern counts two hundred killed, five hundred wounded. Frederick orders Gessler's dragoons, fifteen hundred troopers, to the attack. They come as "saviors," a survivor will write, "at full gallop through our ranks."[11] They hit hard, take twenty-five hundred prisoners, sixty-six standards. Daun is wounded. The enemy falters.

Prince Charles is watching. His center is in great trouble. His cavalry is gone, his right flank exposed. The Saxons have vanished to open his left flank.

At nine, Charles orders a general retreat on Reichenau. Nádasdy's horse and Wallis's corps are standing by, not committed to battle. They cover the march back to the mountains.

They leave a field of ghastly carnage, thousands of dead and dying men and horses. As dust settles, as smoke clears, a victorious King Frederick orders brandy given to all wounded — Prussians, Saxons, and Austrians.

52

THE KING'S dispatches written immediately after battle were brief and to the point in reporting "a complete victory over the enemy." To Old Dessauer he wrote, "The army, cavalry, infantry, and hussars have never so distinguished themselves. . . . This is the best I have seen and the army has surpassed itself." To King Louis, basking in the victory at Fontenoy and the capture of Tournai: "You will have seen that I have not long delayed in following your example. Now it is Prince Conti's turn." To Podewils: "You know the use that you should and can make of this news; I have kept my word. Everyone and my brothers have fought like lions for the country; never have the ancient Romans done anything more striking. Adieu. May heaven let me be as content with politics as with arms."

The king's reports leave no doubt of his immense satisfaction with the army. Praise flowed over deeds by units and individuals. Gessler and Karl von Schmettau's final cavalry charge, which chopped up six enemy regiments and took twenty-five hundred prisoners, was "an action unheard of in history." The battle was unusual in another way: every Prussian unit participated. The king had brought combined arms to the battlefield, a masterly tactical accomplishment, considering the difficult communication and movement in awkward terrain. He recognized this. "What is certain," he wrote, "is that the battle of Friedberg is one of the greatest actions in history, because all the corps have fought and not one failed to make its attack." He later wrote that at this battle the cavalry had finally become "what it should be and now is."

It was an expensive victory. Frederick numbered his losses at twelve hundred dead and wounded, but later accounts suggest forty-seven hundred. The Austrians suffered over five thousand casualties, the Saxons thirty-four hundred. One authority calculated that about four thousand were buried on the battlefield. The Prussians captured an additional fifty-five hundred Austrians and fifteen hundred Saxons, including four generals. Deserters flowed in for several days, so many that Frederick counted total Austrian losses at twenty-five thousand.

Here was the true significance of Hohenfriedberg. It was a tactical not a strategic victory. Frederick later described it as a fleeting victory that gained him only time. He was mistaken. It was a victory that promoted him to the top rank of military commanders and shattered enemy morale. Never again would Prince Charles willingly move against this colossus; never again would Charles's officers fully trust him; never again would Austrian and Saxon soldiers willingly fight under his command.

King Frederick at first hoped for decisive political results from his victory. Two days after the battle he wrote to Podewils, "This will bring us a good peace and a long rest. . . . I am at present busy crowning the work." He was referring to a pursuit by a strong corps led by du Moulin and Winterfeldt with Zieten in the van. Later critics have pointed to a lackluster follow-up and an attempt to annihilate the Austrians or Saxons. The king never considered such an action. The enemy's retreat was covered by a rearguard of fresh troops. The Prussians were tired. Provisions and munitions had to come from Schweidnitz; wagons and teams were in short supply. Von der Goltz went so far as to warn the king that he could not logistically support even a *slow* march into Bohemia. Thousands of wounded had to be tended and evacuated; Valory wrote that the king cared for enemy wounded as if they were his own.

Nor did the king believe pursuit was necessary to attain his political goal. Maria Theresa had suffered severe defeats in Italy, Flanders was lost, the Prussians would soon approach Bohemia, a French army covered Frankfurt, Holland was tired of war, the Russians inactive. "We will pursue to Königgrätz," he wrote to Podewils on June 7, "where we shall halt. Profit from this news and exploit it hugely in the Empire, at Hanover, and in Russia; I believe that this will bring a good peace, and that it is certain that we will get something or other out of it."

The action continued favorably. "Tomorrow the advance guard marches on Königgrätz," Frederick notified Podewils on June 18, "and this is my ne plus ultra. . . . I am not making the mistakes the enemy wishes me to. . . . It is a matter only of waiting to see the outcome of your diplomacy."

By late June the two armies were not far distant, the Austrians and Saxons south of Königgrätz in a strong defensive position stretching east from the confluence of the Elbe and Adler Rivers, the Prussians northeast of the city in an equally strong position. "To see these two armies ranged around Königgrätz," Frederick later wrote, "one would have said that it was one army besieging the place."[1]

This static situation suited him. His fragile supply lines to Silesia were momentarily safe, even though a shortage of wagons and teams continued to plague him. General Nassau had been sent to Upper Silesia with a sizable corps to join Fouqué and Hautcharmoy in cleaning the Hungarians from the land. Old Dessauer, close to the Saxon border, was making various marches to worry the Saxon court. Frederick likewise was feinting here and there to annoy Prince Charles. The army was living off the land, which meant that Charles would not be able to use it for winter quarters — one more reason, the king believed, for the enemy to make peace.

Spring and summer passed pleasantly enough, although it was marred by Charles Étienne Jordan's death from tuberculosis in late May. Pierre Louis Moreau de Maupertuis had accepted the king's invitation to move to Berlin and become president of the Academy of Sciences, which would provide some solace for the loss of Jordan's intellectual companionship. "We amuse ourselves here as best we can," Frederick wrote to Rothenburg, stationed not far away. "In addition to my ordinary occupations, I read a great deal, and I can assure you that, excepting some light skirmishes, one would believe it a peacetime camp." He was delighted that Rothenburg's agent in Paris had purchased on his behalf "a beautiful table" and "5 protretis von Wato" — as the king wrote to his confidential treasurer, Fredersdorff[2] — for 2550 thalers and was negotiating for a chandelier of rock crystal. He also wanted "two beautiful groups of huge marble to decorate a garden. The subject doesn't matter, providing that it be beautiful. If they cost five to six thousand thalers, I will pay. Perhaps he could also find some beautiful marble vases, decorated with gilt, to place in a garden — all to beautify Potsdam."

By mid-July the Prussian supply problem was growing acute, and fresh land was needed. Frederick crossed the Elbe to Chlum, his left on the river, his right on Sadowa on the Bistritz River. From here he could block any enemy corps coming from Bavaria through Saxony. He also had an eye on the Saxon army, which could make no movement "that I can't see from my tent," as he wrote to Dessauer. If the Saxons shifted units to the homeland, he would reinforce Dessauer: "I see myself as nothing more than an observation army that must cover your operations." The new camp was "beautiful, almost like a garden." Local peasants were friendly. "Everything is brought to us in abundance: above six hundred carts laden with fruit and all other provisions come to the camp daily."[3]

To Frederick's discomfiture, however, the small war quickly heated up, with the Austrians as usual scoring more successes than Prussians. Prince Ferdinand of Brunswick perhaps unwittingly expressed Prussian disdain for this type of warfare: "They have wounded two of our people with their muskets while hiding like thieves and robbers behind trees and not showing themselves in the open as becomes proper soldiers."[4]

The battle of Hohenfriedberg was a bitter disappointment to Prince Charles and the Vienna court. On the night of the defeat, Charles wrote to Grand Duke Francis, who was about to command the Austrian army of the Rhine, "The misfortune is all the more painful to me in that our troops have behaved like idiots. Forgive this expression, but I am furious."[5] Worse was to come during the retreat. Not only were plundering and extortion of money commonplace; so were the most vile sexual excesses, torture, and execution of innocents, a performance that, as Frederick's confidential secretary, Eichel, wrote to Podewils, has made "the Austrian name so foul that almost no Silesian can hear it without indignation."*

Maria Theresa could repair this embarrassing defeat only by aggressive political and military action. Fending off British attempts to arrange a peace with Prussia, she appealed to European courts to help her confine the King of Prussia to his own lands. Minister Count Joseph Khevenhüller went to Dresden to infuse the Duke of Weissenfels with new fire and draw the Saxon court from any move toward an alliance with France or Prussia. Khevenhüller visited Charles en route and reported that, despite the lesson of Hohenfriedberg, he still surrounded himself with people "whose incompetence, arrogance, and boorishness" should render them "unworthy of his trust."[6] This report

---

* King Frederick exploited this at length in a published brochure that cited specific instances of rape, torture and murder. (Droysen, *Geschichte*, Volume 5-(2).)

apparently washed over the queen's head. Prussia must be defeated! She sent her "dear prince" new recruits, another ten battalions of infantry, a cavalry corps, and two senior commanders, the terrible-tempered Prince Lobkowitz and the old and ailing Duke of Arenberg. Saxon replacements brought Charles to a strength of over sixty thousand. He agreed that an offensive was called for and thought he saw his chance when his opponent crossed the Elbe to camp in the Chlum area, surely the first move in withdrawing to Silesia. If the allied army crossed the Adler River to cut Prussian communication with the Glatz magazine, then the enemy would have to retreat — without Charles's having to chance a new battle.

It was a good enough plan, but neither Austrian nor Saxon generals liked it. Neither army trusted the other; not a few Austrian commanders wanted peace with Prussia. Although the Saxon army had been substantially reinforced, the defeat at Hohenfriedberg had embittered old Weissenfels and his subordinates, who understandably blamed Charles for having left them in the lurch. Weissenfels steadily rejected Charles's plans while arranging for part of the army to return to Saxony.

Stymied by the Saxons but spurred by Maria Theresa, Charles began crossing the Adler "by bits and pieces" to build a new camp opposite the Prussians. He was confident that he would soon force them back to Silesia — all without battle.

53

VICTORY at Hohenfriedberg did not bring peace. Frederick soon learned that there was no hope of a French diversion in Bohemia or Hanover. His blunt letter demanding a large subsidy had angered King Louis. Although he wrote fulsomely to the French monarch — he went so far as to compare him with Louis XIV (no doubt choking on his words) — the damage had been done.

Nor had Lord Harrington lived up to the Berlin court's expectations, a disappointment that Frederick blamed on Uncle George, who was sulking after his defeat at Fontenoy. Harrington all along had spoken encouragingly of mediation to gain what Frederick liked to term "a just and reasonable accommodation," but by early July he was convinced that England was playing a double game.

Nor could he expect much from the dissolute Czarina Elizabeth and her corrupt ministers: "I ask nothing more than that Russia remains at rest." Rumors that the Bavarian elector was being coerced by Vienna into sending troops to the Austrian army were worrisome, but the envoy Klinggraeffen was doing his best to persuade him to remain neutral, as he had promised.

Saxon obstinacy was a final problem. Frederick wanted to separate Saxony from Austria and cause King August to withdraw his army from Bohemia. Toward this end, he promised the French court to support its effort in electing August to the Imperial throne, and he also hoped to frighten Saxony into neutrality by keeping Old Dessauer's corps close to the border. If that court did not come around, he warned Podewils in mid-July, Dessauer would invade Saxony; indeed details of this were already being worked out. A few days later he sent a lengthy "Manifest" that justified such a move; it was to be secretly printed in French and German and held ready for distribution.

The "Manifest" leaves no doubt of how deeply the Saxon ulcer had inflamed the king's thinking. Treacherous Saxony had cost him the previous year's disaster in Bohemia. He was convinced that the Saxon elector would continue to fight with the Austrians for his destruction. And now he learned that Prince Conti had recrossed the Rhine, leaving Bavaria to the enemy — "and as by that I see myself abandoned by the French, and all Empire affairs at the mercy of our common enemies, I fear extremely for the results produced by this unfortunate event."

The king was drawing closer to a preventive war against Saxony, not alone to avenge the "cruel insults" of the court and to bring about peace. "It is necessary at the same time," he informed Podewils, "that Saxony and all our neighbors learn that one will not offend us with impunity, and that they understand that they must not so lightly ally themselves with our enemies."

Prince Conti's withdrawal across the Rhine offered the necessary justification. Dessauer was reinforced and ordered to be ready to march. The king replied to Podewils's repeated protestations, "I have procured superiority in this country [Bohemia] and even if the Saxons were compelled to detach [their auxiliary corps in Bohemia], I will detach proportionately and will go on the defensive in Bohemia, where I can subsist better with 35,000 than with 80,000 men, and where I will draw out the campaign at length." No matter what Podewils's doubts, a preventive war was necessary: "Hard times demand hard measures."

Frederick declared war on Saxony in mid-August, but the winds of doubt, many blown by Podewils, caused him to hold up orders for Dessauer's march. France had not confirmed a subsidy; Harrington was talking again of negotiation on Prussia's behalf; there was a new rumor that France would land the Young Pretender in the British Isles (which would force a large part of the British army to leave the continent); Bavarian troops had not yet marched to Saxony's aid; the Prussian army was more than holding its own in Bohemia.

For the moment he could do little more than accept events. He was comfortably enough situated at Chlum, writing to Dessauer of his superiority over enemy irregulars. But Charles's move almost opposite his camp surprised him, and he marched immediately to protect his northern routes. From new headquarters at Semonitz he looked east to the Elbe, his left anchored on Jaromirz, his right on Hohlolaw opposite the Austrian right wing. The move was defensive, in keeping with his role as observer. When a few days later a Saxon contingent marched to the home country, Frederick sent a corps to reinforce Dessauer further.

At Semonitz the king learned that his secret "Manifest" had been published in a Hamburg newspaper, an embarrassment compounded by rumors of a new Austrian-Saxon treaty dedicated to Prussia's demise. Then Valory informed him that the French court was willing to pay a subsidy of only 500,000 livres a month, a sum scarcely sufficient to support four battalions of infantry and three regiments of hussars. Frederick angrily turned down the offer, "suitable only for a minor prince," and for a time refused to speak to Valory. He was still smarting under this blow when he learned of Count Keyserling's sudden death in Berlin. Only two months earlier he had lost his beloved Jordan and now "dear Césarion," bon vivant of carefree Rheinsberg days, was gone. "In less than three months I have lost my two most faithful friends," he wrote to his old friend the widow Camas. "It is difficult for a heart as sensitive as mine to extinguish my profound sadness."

Relief of sorts arrived when Roman Catholic Prince Charles Edward — Bonnie Prince Charlie — landed in Scotland to draw Highland bands to his banner of rebellion. Two weeks later he proclaimed his father James VIII, king of Scotland. The frantic English Parliament demanded the recall of the British army from Flanders. Despite a major victory in the New World — the capture of fortress Louisburg and all of Cape Breton — Harrington judged England's position to be "melancholy and hopeless." Desperately needing another continental ally, the government reopened peace talks earlier requested by Prussia. They hoped to return, as the British historian Sir Richard Lodge put it, "from the ambitious schemes of 1743 to the sounder policy of 1742."

Frederick jumped at the offer, even yielding his demands for Prussian territorial gains. The result was the Convention of Hanover, the prelude to a definitive treaty of peace that the British would present to Vienna and Dresden for signature. Based on the Treaty of Breslau, it guaranteed Prussian possession of Silesia. In return, the Prussian king guaranteed Austrian holdings and promised his vote for Grand Duke

Francis at the coming Imperial election. The convention was signed in Hanover in early September. "I believe I have escaped from a labyrinth," he wrote to Mardefeld, "which in the long run could have caused me in many respects a thousand difficulties."

The king was being overly optimistic. The Saxon court saw its promised rewards slipping away and would not commit itself without Vienna's concurrence. The Vienna court had no intention of having such a treaty shoved down its throat. Maria Theresa ignored the British envoy's entreaties, and Frederick's secret overtures to Prince Charles for a cease-fire brought only negative replies. Grand Duke Francis was elected Holy Roman Emperor *without* the Elector of Brandenburg's vote.

Doubt replaced hope. The king was in a vile temper, plainly discouraged, abandoned by France, threatened by Russia, suspicious of being a pawn to British interests. "After having been cheated, we will be mocked," he warned Podewils. To Rothenburg, ill with a kidney disorder, he glumly quoted Blaise Pascal that "the earth is a frightful prison peopled by miserable rascals, all without faith and without honor." The loss of his close friends — "his family" — weighed heavily. He felt widowed and orphaned, he wrote to Duhan, his old tutor, "a heart-rending grief more gloomy and grave than mourning clothes." His military situation was slowly turning sour. He had eaten out the area, and supplies from Silesia were slow and uncertain. He had already decided to withdraw north to Trautenau. "It is not I who command an army," he wrote Podewils, "but flour and forage are the masters."

The army marched on September 19. Fog shrouded the columns, but early morning sun soon appeared to help Franquini's irregulars successfully ambush some Prussian hussars. Harassed and tired units closed on the Staudenz area late in the evening.*

On the premise that Prince Charles would march via Nachod to Eipel to cut Prussian communications with Glatz, Frederick took up a position with his right wing north of Staudenz, the army stretching behind the village east to Eipel and the River Aupa. The army fronted marshlands, and single battalions and hussar squadrons east and south of Burkersdorf guarded the right flank. But the dominant terrain feature, Graner Koppe — Graner Hill — northwest of Burkersdorf was not occupied.

It was a poor campsite. There were too many copses and woods, the terrain was restricted, good neither for infantry nor cavalry, for offense or defense. Enemy irregulars virtually surrounded the position to make

---

* I recently toured this area, whose hills, woods, and tight defiles make excellent terrain for guerrilla warfare. Nearly two and a half centuries later it is not difficult to see why the Austrians were able to surprise King Frederick nor why Prince Charles later had so many problems in deploying and controlling his army at Soor.

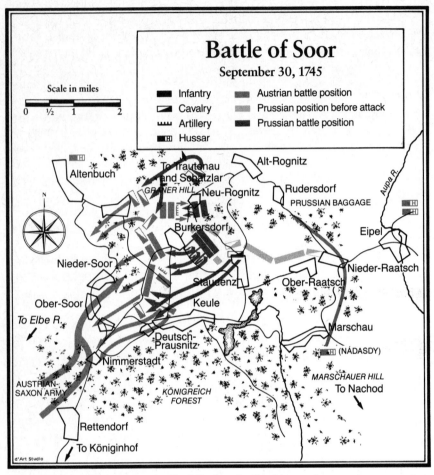

Battle of Soor
September 30, 1745

Scale in miles

0   ½   1   2

■ Infantry   ■ Austrian battle position
▭ Cavalry   ■ Prussian position before attack
〰 Artillery   ■ Prussian battle position
⊞ Hussar

Altenbuch

To Trautenau and Schatzlar

GRÄNER HILL   Neu-Rognitz

Alt-Rognitz

Rudersdorf

PRUSSIAN BAGGAGE

Burkersdorf

Eipel

Nieder-Soor

Staudenz

Ober-Raatsch

Nieder-Raatsch

Ober-Soor   Keule

To Elbe R.

Marschau

Deutsch-Prausnitz

(NÁDASDY)

Nimmerstadt

MARSCHAUER HILL

AUSTRIAN-SAXON ARMY

KÖNIGREICH FOREST

To Nachod

Rettendorf

To Königinhof

d'Art Studio

the Prussian king as tactically blind as he had been the previous year in
Bohemia. Irregulars threatened and sometimes cut communication not
only with the Trautenau bakery but with vital retreat routes to
Schweidnitz and Landeshut. Foraging parties with large escorts — up
to three thousand horse and eight thousand infantry — were frequently attacked. "Each bundle of straw was bought with blood," the
king wrote.[1] Night after night drummers called tired men to arms. Light
troops struck convoy after convoy. Dessewffy fell on a flour convoy
north of Trautenau, and the ensuing battle cost the Prussians ninety-
three dead and wounded. The partisan leader went on to burn most of
Trautenau.

It was obvious that the army must withdraw farther (as Prince Charles
had foreseen). Frederick farmed out corps under du Moulin, Winterfeldt, and Lehwaldt to ensure lines of retreat to the north. He had
already sent two contingents to Dessauer. This left him dangerously

weak at Staudenz. On September 29 his army counted thirty-one battalions and fifty-one squadrons, scarcely over twenty thousand troops.

Although Charles commanded an Austrian army of over forty-one thousand, in addition to about ten thousand hussars and irregulars, he had refused to consider the "solid operation" so vigorously demanded by Maria Theresa. The Saxons had transferred more regiments to Saxony; he could not trust the remaining Saxon units; Nassau had recaptured fortress Cosel in Upper Silesia and was clearly in ascendancy over Esterhazy's Hungarians; his own commanders — Lobkowitz and Arenberg — advised against outright attack; his supply system was shaky; and besides he planned to accomplish his goal with the small war.

Certainly his irregulars were performing yeoman service. Franquini, in King Frederick's words *der böse Geist* — the evil spirit — successfully raided Jaromirz with the idea of capturing Valory and his papers.* Baron Friedrich Daniel Saint-André and Baron Franz von der Trenck attacked Neustadt in early September and were chased off only with difficulty by Lehwaldt's and du Moulin's relief corps.

These minor successes did not satisfy Maria Theresa. In acrimonious letters to her "dear prince," she made it clear that she wanted the Prussians chased out of Bohemia. On learning of the Prussian march to Staudenz, Charles decided to follow the right wing. Two days after crossing the Elbe, he learned from Nádasdy that this wing seemed vulnerable to attack. Lobkowitz agreed. Charles was less certain than they, but tentatively decided to march on September 29 in the direction of Soor, from where he would make a surprise attack.

Charles was never a resolute commander. Having decided to attack, he now discovered any number of reasons not to. One was his army, another the terrain, a third the lack of enthusiasm felt by his commanders. "I don't see that anyone much desires a battle," he wrote his brother, the new emperor. "If the thing were possible, I would gladly venture something, but the enemy lies in impassable mountains and can be reached only through narrow passes." And to Maria Theresa: "The enemy is still located where one can hardly attack him."[2]

Another reconnaissance in company with Lobkowitz and Arenberg changed his mind. The army would attack as planned.

---

* Valory's secretary, Darget, passed himself off as the envoy and was captured but turned over only unimportant papers. The Croats stole most of Valory's valuables. He was furious because Frederick, who had been treating him shabbily in any event, thought the episode was very funny and publicized it. Poor Valory — not long afterward his house in Trautenau was burned down by Dessewffy's raid.

54

Wednesday, September 29, 1745. At noon a deserter appears in the Prussian camp. The enemy, he says, is at Königinhof, and troops have received three days of bread rations.

King Frederick instantly and incorrectly divines the enemy plan: Charles will cross the Elbe and put himself between Trautenau and Schatzlar to block the main Prussian route to Silesia. Frederick sends a force to spy out the enemy. It runs into Dessewffy's light troops and returns to camp. Prussian hussars enjoy a peaceful if brief chat with Austrian hussars. Prince Charles, they say, is planning a great blow.

The king pays scant attention to these reports. He is convinced that Charles will not attack. And Charles will not gain a march on him, since the Prussian army is to march on Trautenau the following day. He does not think it necessary to occupy Graner Hill.

Charles and Field Marshal Prince Lobkowitz ride early to view the Prussian camp. Nothing there is changed. Lobkowitz now argues against the attack: the ground is not suitable for cavalry; the Prussians are strong in infantry and will counterattack. Charles is aware of these difficulties but nonetheless orders the army to march.

The advance guard commanded by Count Königsegg moves out at eleven A.M. Packs and baggage remain in camp. Infantry cross the Elbe on pontoon bridges, cavalry ford the river. Königsegg is to occupy heights east of Ober-Soor and await further orders. A reserve of three dragoon regiments follows, then the main army. The troops march through Königreich Forest. They neither smoke nor talk. The march is not easy. Commanders make wrong turns; they get lost. It grows dark. More confusion. It is midnight. Deployment is far from complete.

Thursday, September 30, 1745. Prince Lobkowitz, commanding the left wing, occupies Graner Hill overlooking the Prussian right. This is the key position: sixteen heavy cannon fronting infantry that reach out hooklike on the farther flank; cavalry behind and to the left. The main army is still struggling into position along the chain of hills south of Graner Hill. It forms two lines: the first, of ten battalions fronted by a battery of heavy cannon; the second, much longer line snaking south to reach nearly to Deutsch-Prausnitz, which is covered by cavalry. Nádasdy's irregulars position to the east, ready to strike the Prussian rear and flank. Other irregulars under Saint-André and Trenck close on Eipel to block enemy retreat. Franquini and Dessewffy to the north are to prevent Lehwaldt's corps from reinforcing the trapped Prussian army.

The troops deploy quietly. A Prussian battalion in woods south of Burkersdorf is only five hundred yards from the enemy but is not alerted.

It is four A.M., close to daybreak, but Charles is still not satisfied. He shifts more units to Graner Hill. Battalions are still deploying.

It is daylight and Charles is still not satisfied. Sun floods the hills; fog shrouds the enemy below. Charles wants the fog to thin, wants the rest of his army in position. He can wait no longer. The attack is to come from the left. Lobkowitz orders the cavalry to move out.

At five A.M. Frederick is in his tent, giving march orders to generals. He is interrupted by an adjutant, who reports that the Austrian army is in battle order on heights west of Burkersdorf.

The king hurries from his tent, sees that the enemy has gained his right flank, orders a solitary drummer to beat the call to arms, orders hussars to reconnoiter north. Sleepy soldiers spill from tents to fall into battle formation. Troopers saddle horses; squadrons form. Gunners limber up cannon; the acrid smell of slow matches permeates heavy morning air.

Frederick and Prince Leopold gallop over fog-blanketed land to right-wing outposts. They hear enemy cannon fire. It comes from Graner Hill and is directed against his hussars.

But why doesn't Charles attack?

Frederick sweeps sun-lighted hills with his glass, sees lateral movements along a two-mile front. So the enemy is still deploying! He scans Graner Hill, notes heavy artillery flanked by infantry, sees enemy cavalry standing motionless on the crest.

He does not have many options. He can attack, defend, or retreat. One is as bad as another, but he has to do *something* before the enemy comes hurtling down on his fragile flank. He returns to army center, mind made up. He will attack the Austrian left on Graner Hill. But first he must shift his lines to parallel those of the enemy. Assault regiments must move to the Neu-Rognitz area, where there is enough open ground for an envelopment maneuver. Then, while left and center hold, he will attack from the right to seize Graner Hill and open an exit to the north.

His army is ready for battle by six A.M., but the enemy is still not advancing. Regiments wheel right, cavalry on each flank, parade ground maneuvers practiced a million times. General Samuel von Schlichting with infantry and hussars position west of Staudenz to cover the rear. Regiment Kalkstein will hold Burkersdorf. The regiments that will assault Graner Hill begin a flanking march across the mouths of angry cannon. Cavalry move out first, infantry follow. There are eleven battalions in all. Lead units must march seven hundred yards, final units twelve hundred yards. At first it goes well. Fog covers the hollows; sun hurts enemy vision. But the fog lifts, cannon fire, grenades cascade into trotting columns, iron balls tear holes in infantry ranks. Then it is over.

The dead lie still; the survivors reorganize, ready to attack; a few cannon arrive and open fire.

Frederick is mounted; near him are his brothers William and Henry. He canters to the right wing, orders cavalry on the far right to wheel about and attack the enemy flank. Buddenbrock and Goltz lead the attack, Posadowsky and Katzler bring up the second line. Rothenburg is critically ill from gallstones but has himself brought to the battlefield in a sedan chair to watch the varicolored squadrons, standards snapping in the breeze, trot over undulating land, negotiate a deep ravine, begin what every cavalryman dreads: an uphill attack.

Austrian troopers are watching. They regard the hill as unscalable. But what is this? The mad Prussians are attacking *uphill*, up a steep hill against the most furious fire that Buddenbrock can remember. Suddenly it is too late for carbine and pistol. The enemy is on them, a furious and confused melee, with no one the winner. But now, as the Prussian second line storms into the fight, the Austrians begin to break. Lobkowitz orders them to hold. He personally kills three officers for cowardice but is jostled into a ditch by his own men. Twenty-seven of forty-five Austrian squadrons run from the field and get in the way of approaching infantry.

A few Prussian squadrons chase them; the rest are exposed to counterfire. Squadrons ride to protective cover of woods. They are hurt. Two colonels are killed. Buddenbrock storms the rest back to order. They are still in the fight.

Frederick meanwhile orders his infantry to seize the cannon on Graner Hill. Generals Adam von Jeetze and Peter von Blanckensee lead six battalions to the attack. They are to march seven hundred yards up a gentle slope with no cover. Gunners manhandle 3-pounder cannon forward, open fire. Prussian infantry march with shouldered weapons to the cadenced beat of drum. Austrian gunners stare in disbelief. But only for a moment. Sweat-sodden gunners hastily switch to canister, swab barrels, ram home charges. Protective infantry open musket fire. Cannon roar to rip vast holes in the approaching lines. The lines do not falter. A ball tears into Prince Albert, the twenty-year-old brother of the Queen of Prussia, marching at the head of a grenadier battalion. He joins the dead. The survivors are about 150 yards from their goal. They halt, open salvo musket fire. They are not many now; their fire is not effective.

Colonel Baron Anton Beneda, watching from the Austrian side, sees their weakness. He leads five grenadier companies down the slope. His troops are eager; they run to the attack shouting "Long live Maria Theresa!" The Prussians stop, begin to fall back. Brigade Blanckensee fights furiously, yields foot by foot. Blanckensee is killed; his son and adjutant dies at his side. Lieutenant Colonel Georg von Wedell's battalion is left with only a quarter of its strength. Now the brave colonel, the man Frederick called Leonidas of the Elbe, falls dead.

Frederick watches. He is waiting for Fouqué's and Bonin's five battalions of the second line. If the Austrians press the counterattack, it is all over. But the earlier cavalry defeat has confused the enemy. Neither infantry nor cavalry reinforce Beneda until too late.

The Prussian second line moves out, also with shouldered weapons, also to the beat of drums. Their advance is easier, because Austrian reinforcements, five grenadier companies, storm down the slope and prevent their own cannon from firing. Prince Leopold sees the second line advancing, orders first-line survivors to strip cartridges from dead and wounded, then re-form. He orders a bayonet attack. Beneda's exhausted men fall back, the Prussians move forward, gunners desert cannon, Graner Hill is taken.

But there is confusion in the Prussian center, where Burkersdorf is burning. The heavy enemy battery south of Burkersdorf has found its target. Part of the Prussian line moves out but is stopped. Prince Ferdinand of Brunswick takes command.* He leaps from his horse, stops the aimless firing, orders a bayonet attack. He leads a Guards battalion forward; other units join. Enemy fire cannot stop the momentum. Prussians close to force fourteen enemy battalions from the heights southwest of Burkersdorf.

It is about eleven A.M. The Austrian left and center are in retreat, but there is still fighting as units fall back to woods north of Soor.

The Prussian left wing is dangerously quiet. Thirty-six Austrian squadrons are peering down on Rochow's twenty squadrons. But they do not attack. The king reinforces Rochow, who does attack. Austrian cavalry leave the field without a fight! Rochow turns on the Austrian right-wing infantry jammed into three and four lines in tight terrain. There is almost no battle. A single cuirassier regiment takes over eight hundred prisoners.

The enemy line is in full retreat to Nieder-Soor. Prussians follow to heights between Deutsch-Prausnitz and Nieder-Soor.

What of Nádasdy's irregulars? Perhaps Schlichting's strong force west of Staudenz frightens them off. Perhaps the smell of booty — the Prussian camp and a baggage train moving slowly a mile or so to the north — is too strong. Hussars and irregulars fall on camp and convoy. The small Prussian escort is quickly hacked to pieces. Civilians, including Eichel and Dr. Lesser, are taken prisoner, along with royal servants. All royal baggage, horses, snuffboxes, silver, books, flutes, and official papers are also taken. In addition to eighty-five thousand thalers in

---

* Ferdinand was wounded in the leg. His brother Prince Louis commanded the *Austrian* center. Prince Albert, the third brother, had already been killed on the Prussian right.

cash, immensely valuable silver, fine clothes, and linen, the trunks contain wine. Soon there is an orgy. In the confusion Eichel manages to destroy the most important papers and the cipher key. Drunken hussars throw more papers into a fire. Prussian wounded are dragged from bread carts, killed, and stripped. Women are raped; sutlers sodomized, then roasted to death. The orgy ends with the approach of a detachment from Lehwaldt's corps. The Hungarians ride off with booty and prisoners, including the king's favorite whippet, Biche (Darling).

"We have totally beaten Prince Charles. . . ." Frederick wrote Podewils on the evening of victory. "The battle has been terrible but very glorious. I was near being surprised, but God be praised all is well." And on the following day: "Of the four battles that I have seen, this was the most fierce. I was in a sense surprised but this was repaired by prompt and sudden resolution, although the fault was not mine but that of Natzmer's hussars."

The king placed Prussian casualties as at least five hundred dead and perhaps fifteen hundred wounded. The toll was much higher: nine hundred dead, over twenty-seven hundred wounded. One out of four infantrymen was a casualty — a total of nearly thirty-eight hundred — and six hundred horses. He wrote that enemy losses, including over three thousand prisoners, exceeded six thousand, and this was fairly accurate. He regretted losing his baggage, the fault of an "idiot of an officer" charged with looking after it, but at least it prevented an attack by eight thousand light troops. Wedell's death was tragic, Frederick wrote to his valet-cum-treasurer, Fredersdorff; Prince Albert's less so. "I deplore the death of your brother Prince Albert," Frederick wrote to his wife, "but he died bravely although of his own free will and necessarily. Some time ago I informed the duke [Albert's father] of what would happen and I often told this to the victim, but he would not listen and I am astonished that he was not killed long before." While criticizing himself for poor judgment — he remarked that he had fought at Hohenfriedberg for Silesia, at Soor for his life — Frederick did not stress his failure in misjudging Austrian intentions, his lack of reconnaissance, his neglect in occupying Graner Hill. Yet such thoughts perhaps contributed to a migraine headache two days later so severe that he could not write a proper report. But neither did he emphasize his own very great act of generalship by pulling off a victory though surprised (and outflanked) by an enemy twice his strength. One thing was certain in his mind: Austria would now make peace. "If our negotiations don't prosper today, they never will," he assured Podewils.

On the fatal day of Soor, Prince Charles fell back on Königinhof, sent baggage and wagons to the rear, and the next day followed with the army to his old camp south of the Elbe. He was a shattered man, "with tears cascading from his eyes," as he informed Emperor Francis that he had been "totally beaten." Aside from the absurd performance of Nádasdy's irregulars, the principal fault lay with the cavalry, which "were taken by such fear that they could not be counted on against the Prussian cavalry." [1] Charles did not mention that he had forfeited almost certain victory by dilatory command performance.

The defeat somewhat dampened the Imperial coronation a few days later, but it left Maria Theresa more determined than ever to bring Prussia to its knees. Charles was to carry on the war. If the army was not up to it, then he must use light troops. Only a few days after the battle, the partisan commanders Nádasdy, Dessewffy, Franquini, Saint-André, and Trenck set out on the Prussian trail. But Charles soon learned that more was expected of him. An Austrian-Saxon treaty of late August called for full prosecution of the war, nothing less than a combined attack against Prussian home territories.

Charles wanted no part of it. He had lost a great many officers and men; he lacked provisions and equipment; he had no money; an invasion of Silesia was madness; the army was not up to a winter campaign; Nassau supported by armed Silesian peasants had pushed Esterhazy's abortive effort from Upper Silesia and nearly a thousand irregulars had summarily returned home; the Prussians were about to invade Moravia. Finally, he did not trust the Saxons.

Maria Theresa and the Saxon court brushed off these objections as fleas of fear. Once the Prussians withdrew into Silesia, the Austrians and Saxons would attack as planned. Charles was to work out operational details with the Duke of Weissenfels and Counts Brühl and Rutowsky.

55

THE PRUSSIANS remained at Soor only a few days. There were the dead to bury, the wounded to evacuate to Landeshut. Fredersdorff sent his master a new secretary, a bed, medicines, money, a new cipher, and a flute made by Quantz — "not a very good one," Frederick grumbled. By Sunday all was in order and a Te Deum was sung. But provisions were short, enemy light troops active. The army marched to Trautenau accompanied by the usual swarm of enemy partisans. This nuisance was more than made up for by reports of Nassau's victories in Upper Silesia and by optimistic dispatches about the envoy Andrié's negotiations with the English. Frederick not only believed that peace was imminent but that it was time for a change in his diplomacy. France had been tried and found wanting. "Our system henceforth," he wrote to Podewils, "is to tie ourselves the most tightly possible to [the English] . . . and to think in what way we can unite our interests so that the English will believe themselves obliged to support us in any eventuality." Then came word that England had ratified the peace preliminaries, "the first good news that I have received in fifteen months." This could not only end a war he was thoroughly tired of; it could lead to a new alliance of Prussia, England, Holland, Denmark, Sweden, and Russia. He was even willing to send six battalions to England to fight against the Young Pretender in Scotland, but only after Austria made peace. Convinced that the Vienna court *must* come to this, he ordered Old Dessauer to take up winter quarters.

Despite the rigors of small war, the king's optimism continued as the army moved toward Silesia. It was not a pleasant march, although nineteen-year-old Prince Henry won the king's praise for his defensive tactics. The columns were constantly harassed and several times attacked by Nádasdy's people. Nevertheless the king wrote to Podewils that he expected peace any day. The military situation was quiet; the Austrians were said to be going into winter quarters shortly; the frontier area fifty miles into Bohemia had been eaten out; and the retreating Prussians by royal command had smashed doors, windows, and ovens in every house in every village along the way: "Not a soul can subsist there." Just before turning over command to Prince Leopold, he told Podewils, "I have succeeded in everything that I had hoped for in the campaign this year, and I return with tranquil mind." Nevertheless it was vital for him to gain a foreign subsidy, from England or from France. The war chest held only a few thousand thalers: "I do not know what will become of us if we do not soon find foreign help."

The secret Austrian-Saxon plan that was to put the King of Prussia "in horrible embarrassment" was ready by mid-October. A corps under General Count Nikolaus Grünne would march from Bavaria to join the Saxons near Leipzig. This army would make a surprise attack on Old Dessauer, whose troops were dispersed in winter quarters; throw him back to Magdeburg; cross the Elbe to cut Prussian communications between Silesia and Brandenburg; then strike as opportunity presented. Unwilling Charles was to contain the Prussians in Silesia, giving battle if necessary, while the operation unfolded. He optimistically interpreted this as a screening mission. In late October his army marched northwest, its goal Görlitz in Lusatia, from where it would protect the Saxon rear.

Frederick's hope for peace began to wane even before he reached Berlin. If England were intent on producing peace, why would Hanoverian troops suddenly replace Austrian troops in the Pragmatic Army, thus allowing the Austrians to march to Bohemia? At Potsdam he learned that Czarina Elizabeth, far from respecting his request for aid against Saxony, suggested that Prussia was the aggressor and that Saxony deserved aid. If Prussia invaded Saxony, she would send troops to the King of Poland.* Then he learned that an Austrian corps was marching to Lusatia, and that Prince Henry, ill with smallpox at Crossen, was in critical condition. "Tranquil spirit" had changed to "great inquietudes." This was not living, he complained to Podewils, but, rather, dying a thousand times daily.

Prince Leopold next reported that Nádasdy, with fourteen thousand light troops plus many cannon, had reached Friedland; he subsequently wrote that Charles was marching on Reichenberg and that Nádasdy and the Saxons were building bread ovens in Friedland.

These enemy movements formed one of the king's "great inquietudes." What was the enemy up to? Hastily dispatched spies to Saxony had not yet reported when the answer came from an unexpected source. The Swedish envoy in Dresden learned of the intended attack and the plan to defeat and partition Prussia. He was a great admirer of Frederick's and at once passed the word to the Swedish ambassador in Berlin, another admirer, who passed it to the king.

Old Dessauer was ordered to assemble his sleeping army at Halle and prepare to march. Neither Dessauer nor Podewils believed that the Saxons would strike and argued hotly against the move. Frederick overrode them. Dessauer returned to his army, and in mid-November the king departed for Silesia, "leaving Berlin," as he later wrote, "in consternation, the Saxons in expectation, and all of Europe attentive to the forthcoming winter campaign."[1]

His plan was simple enough. Once the Austrians entered Saxon territory, Dessauer was to march on Leipzig, for then Frederick would be justified, in Russian eyes, in taking appropriate countermeasures. If that city was too strongly defended, he was to continue to Torgau and force the Saxons to retire on Dresden. Should Grünne invade Brandenburg, Dessauer was to defeat the Saxons and attack Grünne's rear. Frederick meanwhile would march on Lusatia to fall on Charles's army and drive the Austrians back to Bohemia. Hacke, with a corps of five thousand,

---

* Envoy Mardefeld reported that Russia was in no position to send an army anywhere: "A barking dog does not bite." Frederick was not so sanguine but realized that it would take a Russian corps several months to reach Saxony.

was left at Berlin to discourage an incursion there by Grünne. In case of emergency, the court, treasure, and archives would be moved to Stettin.

Frederick rejoined the army southwest of Liegnitz. He used a ruse earlier employed to trap the enemy at Hohenfriedberg. In this case he circulated orders that no Prussian unit would violate Saxon frontiers. The Prussian army's mission was to move on Crossen, and active preparations for the move were ostentatiously taking place. At the same time he quietly recalled Nassau from Upper Silesia and charged him with defense of Lower Silesia and the vital Schweidnitz magazine.

Screened by a large advance guard, the army marched to the Bober River on November 20. All told, it counted something over thirty thousand. Two days later, Winterfeldt, who had moved nearer the Queis River, reported that the Austrians had entered Lusatia and were billeted between Lauban and Görlitz. Prussian deception had paid off: Charles did not suspect that the main Prussian army was close by.

Having confirmed the Austrian presence, Frederick ordered Dessauer to march at once. He himself was marching on Naumburg only a few miles behind his advance guard and would cross the Queis on November 23.

Charles had been told that the Queis was as formidable an obstacle as the Danube; in fact, it was little more than a stream. He learned of Prussian intentions only on November 23 and turned his army to north-south, his left on Hohkirch, his right on Schönberg.

At Naumburg the Prussians waited for heavy fog to lift, made an easy crossing, and on a sunny day marched west on Görlitz. Aside from a brush between hussars and Saxon uhlans, the march met no resistance, at least until the advance guard reached Katholisch-Hennersdorf, defended by one Saxon infantry and three cavalry regiments. Zieten's hussars at once attacked, and grenadiers followed. Greatly outnumbered, the Saxons retired with a loss of over nine hundred prisoners. The Prussians suffered a hundred casualties, including Zieten, who was shot in the leg.

Some nine miles distant, Charles had heard the firing but learned of the attack only in late afternoon. Neither he nor Lobkowitz deemed it advisable to send reinforcements, which would risk "being defeated in detail."[2] Instead, Lobkowitz retired south to Schönberg, and on the following day the entire army retreated southwest after a futile effort to save the vital Görlitz magazine.

Undeterred by very cold weather, which had come suddenly and for which the troops were not dressed, the Prussians pressed on to Görlitz. The meager garrison at once surrendered riches of bread, flour, rye, oats, hay, and straw; the city fathers, to save their heads, paid a war tax of 100,000 gulden. The Prussians turned southeast, hoping to catch the Austrians at Schönberg. In a characteristic display of leadership, the Prussian king told his troops that great exertions and forced marches lay ahead, but he promised to avoid murderous battles and guaranteed comfortable winter quarters.

Prince Charles spotted the Prussian army marching through the morning fog. He estimated enemy strength at forty thousand compared with his own eighteen thousand. His generals were quarreling and issuing contradictory orders. His officers were despondent, his units ragged. The men had had no hot food for days; they lacked baggage and tents; they were cold and sick and were deserting in hundreds. A march over the mountains to join the Saxon army was out of the question. Retreat was the only answer. Charles fell back southwest of Zittau, the Prussians closely pursuing. In darkness the Austrians continued on to Gabel in Bohemia, sacrificing hundreds of wagons filled with valuable provisions.

Frederick did not pursue. In a brief but almost bloodless campaign that cost Charles some five thousand men, magazines, and most of his baggage train, he had accomplished his mission. "We have done the impossible in moving so swiftly," he wrote to Podewils. Pointing to his own casualties, thirty dead and seventy wounded, he added, "I have done everything that a general can do with the least spilling of blood and with the greatest results."

The king established headquarters at Görlitz and, as promised, put the troops in warm quarters. He increased daily rations to one pound of meat, one pound of vegetables, two pounds of bread, and two quarts of beer per man. He described peasants and villagers as anti-Austrian, the result of heavy requisitions and harsh treatment. "All the country is for us," he told Podewils. Feeling completely secure, he sent Winterfeldt with a task force of infantry and dragoons to join Nassau in chasing enemy irregulars from the Hirschberg Valley, a swift and successful operation and the prelude to reclaiming Upper Silesia.

Frederick hoped to make the enemy split final. On his behalf the British envoy in Dresden, Thomas Villiers, offered the Saxons a moderate peace based on the Convention of Hanover. Giving teeth to his words, he sent Lehwaldt with a large corps to Bautzen. Lehwaldt discovered that Grünne's corps, only thirty miles from Berlin, had turned around to recross the Elbe and join the Saxon army. The Saxon court, instead of responding favorably to his peace offer, packed up and moved to Prague. Frederick prepared to march west in support of Old Dessauer, who over a week earlier had been ordered "to fall on the Saxons."

56

OLD DESSAUER held the key to the Prussian plan, but he was very slow in turning it. The field marshal, now sixty-nine years old, did not believe in the present campaign. His normal ill humor vented itself in all directions, here levying heavy requisitions, there hanging a legitimate but luckless Jewish peddler who he decided was a spy. Dessauer received the king's orders to march on November 22 but refused to leave Halle until food and cannon had arrived. Still at Halle five days later, he read Frederick's report of victory at Katholisch-Hennersdorf, which concluded, "In these circumstances there is nothing else for you to do than to attack the enemy army at Leipzig, and I do not doubt with good success."

The king's letters grew increasingly exhortative. Still, two more days passed before Dessauer marched. He found only weak forces at Leipzig. Count Rutowsky had learned of Charles's retreat and had fallen back behind Dresden with the main Saxon army. The garrison at Leipzig surrendered the following day, thus opening the road to Meissen, but Dessauer waited another two days for heavy artillery and bake ovens. The march resumed with little opposition — but for Torgau, not for Meissen. The forces at Torgau surrendered, and Dessauer halted to wait for bread.

In anticipation of joining Dessauer at Meissen, Frederick had moved Lehwaldt to Kamenz and his own headquarters to Bautzen. He had heard nothing from Dessauer, who he supposed was on the way to Meissen. He had learned that Prince Charles was marching from Gabel to Leitmeritz, from where he would enter Saxony to join Rutowsky. Saxon ministers meanwhile had begun peace negotiations, and Podewils had been summoned from Berlin, but it soon became obvious that the Saxons were stalling in order to permit the Austrians to reach Dresden. Frederick was not deceived. He ordered Dessauer to demand a "contribution" from Leipzig — "the more cash the better" — and, after explaining the overall situation, "vigorously to pursue" operations. Lehwaldt would be waiting for him at Meissen and they would advance on Dresden: "Your Highness has cause to hurry before other factors make the project more difficult."

"Other factors" included both the Russians, who were said to be sending a corps to Saxony's aid, and the Austrians in Leitmeritz. Frederick judged that Prince Charles would need six marches to close on Dresden; thus, it was vital to settle with the Saxons before December 12.

Frederick might as well have sent orders to Mars, for he now learned that Dessauer was still at Torgau, sixty miles north of the target. Even worse, he had summarily decided to cross the Elbe there and join with Lehwaldt on the *eastern* bank — but he had to wait a few days for a fresh bread supply.

Even a saint would have exchanged crucifix for dagger. The king was no saint. He had not been well; he had no appetite and could not sleep, he reported to Fredersdorff. He was like "pregnant women with flighty appetites." Dessauer's outright disobedience of orders changed exhortation to fury. His reply was carried by a young aide, Captain Wilhelm von der Oelsnitz, who handed one of the most prestigious warriors of the century a sharp reprimand: unless Dessauer changed his ways and followed orders, "I will be forced to extreme steps which I would prefer to avoid." Oelsnitz also, in accordance with orders, personally had to read him the riot act. The combined effect, as the captain reported, placed the prince "in the most grievous chagrin." It was obvious, Dessauer wrote, that the king had always hated him and always would — but at least he agreed to march as ordered, though in his own time.

It was not good enough. The Austrians were moving on Dresden; Charles had already arrived to confer with Rutowsky. Dessauer was moved neither by fact nor threat. Only on December 10 did he march, but at last the royal reprimands seemed to penetrate. Perhaps the old soldier realized that infamous conduct could undo a heroic past and bury the ancient and august title of Anhalt-Dessau in a dungheap of infamy. Now he moved rapidly to Meissen, where Lehwaldt was waiting to join him.

Dessauer's surge of activity was all too brief. Chastened by a Saxon ambush in which ailing General Roell of the dragoons, also sixty-nine years old, was pulled from his coach and killed, Dessauer halted at Meissen and wrote to the king for "positive orders" as to where and how far he should march on the following day. The king replied, "Your Highness knows that it is my intention that he is to chase the Saxons from the country. Therefore, I repeat that this is my positive order."

Dessauer met the Saxons on December 15 near Kesselsdorf, about six miles southwest of Dresden. The battle did not start until the afternoon of a cold and short winter day. The main Prussian assault failed with heavy losses. The battle probably would have been a draw had the Saxon wing not sprung from defended positions to attack the attackers — thereby blocking their own artillery fire. A counterattack sent them running, pushed into the left flank, and turned it, and another attack pushed in the center shortly before dark. Retreat became general. The Austrian corps on the extreme right played no part in the battle but joined the retreat, which fell back on Prince Charles's approaching columns. Charles quickly wheeled about — and the battle was over.

It was another expensive victory. Over seventeen hundred Prussians were killed, over three thousand wounded, most of them infantrymen. The Saxons counted thirty-eight hundred dead and wounded besides a loss of some six thousand prisoners. "I feel infinitely sorry for the dead and wounded," the king wrote to Fredersdorff, "but still it is better [to have them] at Dresden than at Berlin."

And all for naught. At Meissen on the day of battle, King Frederick received a dispatch from the British envoy, Villiers, who had accompanied the Saxon court to Prague. He reported that King August wished to make peace on the proposed terms. Villiers had been given full authorization to negotiate a peace and it was said that the Austrian court also wished peace on the same terms.

Frederick learned of Dessauer's victory shortly after reading this document. On the next day, he shifted headquarters to Wilsdruff, where Dessauer's full report arrived. He replied that he was delighted at "the particular dexterity with which my dear prince has executed my orders"; he would like to tour the battlefield.

Burial parties were still hacking into frozen ground, frozen surgeons were still hacking into mutilated bodies, when the king reached the battlefield. He saw the tactical problem at a glance; later he wrote that he would have attacked much farther right. Still, Dessauer had pulled victory from defeat. Gratitude replaced anger. He rode to the field, dismounted, removed his hat, walked over to the old and tired field marshal, whose jacket showed three bullet holes, openly embraced him, and thanked him and the surrounding generals for the victory. For four hours he toured the field, listening carefully to individual accounts of the confused action; he was the center of attention for scores of curious Dresden citizens attracted to the scene. The troops received a royal order of thanks with two unusual rewards. All infantry regiments that had fought and Dragoon Regiment Bonin could henceforth play "The March of the Grenadiers"; regimental commanders were authorized to fill vacant spaces by promotions as they saw fit. Dessauer's leadership was particularly praised in Frederick's published report of the victory.

The rest was mere formality. The Saxon army was shattered. At a war council on the night of defeat, Prince Charles offered to attack the following day if the Saxons would support him. Rutowsky turned him down cold, and so probably did Count Friedrich Harrach, chancellor of Bohemia, sent by Maria Theresa to negotiate a peace. On the same night, Harrach reported to Vienna that Charles should never again be entrusted with command of any army that would fight the Prussian king. Both armies now retreated to Pirna, where Rutowsky refused another such proposal by Charles. The small Dresden garrison quickly surrendered to the Prussians, who occupied the city.

Peace negotiations pushed ahead mainly because the principals were virtually bankrupt. Villiers, the Saxon minister Ferdinand von Saul, and Harrach arrived in Dresden to join Podewils in working out a treaty that included the Palatine and Hesse-Cassel. Although Harrach would have liked to tear out his eyes as he saw himself about "to forge chains of perpetual bondage for our august empress,"[1] there was little argument: when Saxon ministers became obdurate, Frederick threatened to return to Berlin and leave his army in Saxony. On Christmas day the Peace of Dresden ended the war with Prussia, but not with France. Frederick generously rewarded the negotiators, giving Harrach a valuable diamond ring and Villiers his portrait set with diamonds to the "supposed value" of eight thousand thalers. King August gave Podewils ten thousand thalers in cash and twenty thousand in treasury notes. Maria Theresa gave Villiers a large gold snuffbox set with diamonds. The Duke of Weissenfels gave him a diamond ring, diamond cuff links, and a diamond shirt stud.[2]

The terms were those of the Treaty of Hanover, what might be called a status quo peace based on the Treaty of Breslau. King August had to pay Prussia a million thalers in war damages. Maria Theresa confirmed the Treaty of Breslau, which acknowledged Prussian sovereignty over Silesia, and guaranteed Prussian territories. Frederick guaranteed her lands and agreed to the election of Francis as Holy Roman Emperor.

He remained aloof from negotiations, but was so busily occupied with petty affairs that, as he complained to Maupertuis, he had not had time for three days to read Cicero and was forced to divorce himself from the muses. He paid courtesy calls on the royal Saxon children, ordered Te Deums sung in local Protestant churches, and saw to it that the wounded Saxon officers and soldiers received care. He also took informal afternoon promenades, to the delight of the citizens, attended the opera, recruited oboe and bassoon players for Berlin, gave small dinner parties, and wrote poetry when not playing the flute. He also sent priceless Meissen porcelain to a few friends as "emblems of the fragility of human fortunes," as he wrote to Maupertuis, selected sixteen hundred recruits from surrendered Saxon militia, bought several hundred pack mules at inflated prices — and seized more than enough cash and porcelain to make up for the loss of baggage at Soor.

On learning that the treaty had been signed, he told Podewils: "Thank heavens for the good news. . . . I flatter myself with the hope that the work will be lasting."

It was time to go home. Escorted by cavalry, the royal carriage stopped at Wusterhausen, where the king ate a noon dinner with his brothers William and Ferdinand, who joined him for the final leg of the trip. A few miles from Berlin he was greeted by a mounted party of young subjects shouting *"Vivat Friedrich der Grosse!"* The cry was repeated when the procession trundled through the city gates. Cannon boomed and bells rang as carriages drove through crowded streets to the palace. Citizens there chanted the new refrain: Long live Frederick the Great!

The king left his carriage and turned to the crowd. "I see that my subjects love me," he muttered. "They did not greet me thus on my accession."[3] For a moment he studied the scene. Then he saluted the throng, removed his hat, and disappeared into the palace.

Frederick the Great was thirty-three years old.

BOOK FIVE

The King Rules
1746–1756

It was Sparta in the morning, Athens in the afternoon.

— *Voltaire*

57

AS IS THE WAY with soldiers, the King of Prussia returned from war a different man. Physically, there was no great change. The French ambassador, the Marquis de Valory, wrote at this time of his pleasant face with "an attractive and witty smile, but often mocking and bitter." Valory was struck by his beautiful if slightly protuberant blue eyes, "wild when he was displeased but otherwise none more gentle, affectionate, and alive when he wished to please."

For five years the king had driven himself hard, and it showed. He was still fit enough for tough campaigning, but a rich diet of hotly spiced foods and too much Hungarian wine and French champagne had made him heavy. He was already a little stooped, which caused him to look even shorter than his five and a half feet. "His health is precarious," Valory wrote, "his constitution is fiery, and his routine contributes not a little to heating of his blood." He suffered from colic (indigestion), gout, hemorrhoids, and, not surprisingly, insomnia. "The King of Prussia's Physicians think he will never attain to a great Age," the British envoy reported shortly after the king's return, "being often troubled with the Cholick and having now and then some Attacks of the Gravel and Stone, when his Majesty drinks much Champagne Wine and does not take care of His Health." [1] He was also becoming a hypochondriac, imposing a score of imaginary diseases on intimidated and frightened doctors, and trying home remedies that varied from drinking water laced with fennel or coffee spiced with white mustard to applying hot mustard poultices to his feet; these were supposed to draw the evil humors of gout from the upper body. He had become nervous; his pudgy ring-decorated fingers darted frequently to an elaborate porcelain snuffbox in his jacket, one of dozens available in the Charlottenburg and Potsdam palaces — their total worth was well over a million thalers.

He was becoming careless in person and dress. Spanish snuff, imported at considerable cost, often stained his upper lip, and he bathed infrequently (though this was not unusual for the times). Except on gala occasions, he wore faded military breeches, a blue jacket, stained high boots, and a three-cornered felt hat. Surrounded by favorite hounds, which were allowed on couches and chairs in the royal apartments, he often tossed them bits of food, wiping his soiled fingers on his snuff-stained jacket.

Such eccentricity was common to royalty. But allied to it and compounding it was a mild logorrhea — he talked almost incessantly during audiences and meals, often to the exclusion of others. Gone was the salutary effect of the disastrous Bohemian campaign that Valory had earlier noted. "This prince speaks much and very well," the envoy now wrote, "but he scarcely listens and he ridicules any objections that one puts to him." His particular defect, Valory went on, was a general contempt for mankind. He placed too much emphasis on intelligence and not enough on common sense.

Nor was he content. He had been looking forward to peace, but when cannon slept and bells rang it was requiem, not joy. Jordan and Keyserling were gone. "I am a stranger in Berlin, without ties, acquaintances, or true friends," he wrote to Podewils. He still had Duhan, but the former tutor was a sick man, and he died a few days after the king's return from war. Frederick was alone now, frightened of Berlin, Potsdam, Charlottenburg, "all the places that recall memories of my friends, whom I have lost forever."

War had hardened him to a dangerous degree. The golden days of Rheinsberg had clouded over. Too distant for practical use, the estate had been given to Prince Henry. Enlightenment had yielded to reality. No longer was Frederick a young and frivolous king out to make his mark. War had threatened house and kingdom with extinction. Where once he spoke of fame and glory, now it was of duty, honor, country.

And with good reason.

The treasury was almost empty, internal affairs had badly deteriorated, the army was understrength, most of Europe was at war, Prussia lacked allies — and Prussian borders remained vulnerable.

Frederick had inherited an extraordinary administrative machine largely built by his father to further an absolutist concept of rule.

In the lexicon of kings, effective government was royal rule with no questions asked. To perpetuate this in Brandenburg-Prussia, where the monarchy had seized most of the administrative control of the kingdom from the nobility, King Frederick William early in his reign had established the General Directory in Berlin. It consisted of four ministerial departments charged with the collection of taxes, the administration of crown lands, cities, towns, counties, and provinces and such ancillary responsibilities as maintenance of posts and roads, police, and schools, land reclamation, colonization, and major construction projects. Separate ministries handled foreign affairs and justice, and from time to time the king established commissions and agencies for special tasks. The army remained his own bailiwick.

The king ruled the Directory, which reported to him from Berlin and which in turn received royal directives, or *Cabinetordres*, for implementation throughout the kingdom. Provinces were administered through *Kriegs- und Domänenkammer* — War and Domain Chambers, like the one in which Crown Prince Frederick ate humble pie in the grim Cüstrin days. Provincial chambers dealt with two subordinate administrations, the *Landräte* — land officials — in the villages and countryside, and the *Steuerräte* — tax officials in towns and cities. Land and city officials reported to their respective chambers, the chambers reported to the Directory, and the Directory reported to the king. In theory the Directory served as buffer between the crown and provincial administrations, but the king on inspection trips dealt directly with the chambers and with subordinate officials.

This form of central administration contained a great many flaws, not least because it was still a feudal day: the *Junker*, the landowning aristocrats, were still powerful and very protective of their traditional authority; sprawling and diverse provinces each had traditional rights and needs, as did towns and cities. The *Landräte* were aristocratic representatives of groups of local estate owners. They were appointed by the king and were responsible for collecting the *Contribution*, or land tax, from farmers and peasants (noblemen were exempt); for overseeing the canton system of recruiting; and for carrying out provincial directives that concerned landed estates. This naturally caused a good deal of conflict and dilution of local administrative efficiency. The *Steuerräte*, on the other hand, were bureaucrats, whether retired officers or civilians, who were responsible for carrying out royal directives in cities and towns and for collecting the all-important excise taxes. These duties involved frequent collision with the chambers and also with army garrison commanders who were more powerful than civil officials.

It was an absolutist concept of government. Frederick William wanted to strengthen this rule. Toward this end he intentionally held the Directory and provincial chambers in rigorous thralldom, infiltrating them with secret agents called the *Fiscal* — "rather ominous men," a modern historian has described them, "[who] aside from being state attorneys, functioned as professional in-service spies in every branch of the central and provincial administration."[2] Their reports allowed the king to play one minister against the other and to frighten lesser fry half to death; he frequently annotated reports with crude drawings of gallows and on occasion hanged a corrupt official *"pour encourager les autres."*

Not unnaturally, ministers and officials, the targets of abuse from the king and from aristocratic *Landräte,* often joined forces in order to survive, juggling accounts here and there, circumventing awkward royal directives where possible, trying to cover themselves by delayed reports and shifted responsibilities — all to the intense frustration of the fat little King Frederick William at Potsdam.

The system nonetheless survived by a combination of bluster and threat tempered with royal rewards. The king allowed his ministers and senior officials comfortable salaries, perquisites, and generous pensions, and often overlooked peculation and bribery, partly because they were difficult to prove, partly because he indulged in similar practices to gratify his manic desire for big men to fill the ranks of the Potsdam Guards.

The result was predictable. Frederick William, by creating the Directory, founded a powerful bureaucracy that functioned according to its own unwritten rules. By 1740, it could not easily respond to new circumstances and situations. The same could be said of provincial chambers and the Ministry of Justice.

King Frederick did not altogether approve of the administrative system that he inherited. From the beginning he correctly identified it as a bureaucratic machine whose ministers and officials were far too restrictive and unimaginative, bogged down in minutiae, caring only for personal comforts and advancement, dissolute and corrupt, frequently no more than indolent, careless "idiots" whose irresponsible actions daily alienated subjects, who formed the true wealth of the kingdom.

He had made his displeasure known almost immediately after acceding to the crown. In addition to a series of warning ukases to the Directory and provincial chambers, he canceled the weekly meetings of the Directory that the late king had held and, instead, summoned individual ministers to Potsdam, though not often. He created Department V, which was responsible for increasing trade. After seizing Silesia, he placed its administration in a ministry separate from the Directory. The two wars prevented major reforms, although he continued to denigrate the civil administration, frequently warning officials to do away with "intrigue" and "chicanery" and to improve performance.

Early in 1746 he again took the civil administration to task. Reports from spies — he had retained the dreaded *Fiscal* used by his father to infiltrate various bodies — and complaints from subjects left little doubt that royal directives were too often being ignored or sabotaged. Provincial officials lacked the "zeal, industry, and integrity" demanded by "duty and honor." Construction projects suffered from "stupidity, laziness, and malice," which resulted from poor management. "Bad, inexperienced, and disloyal people" working in supply departments were to be replaced by those who were "energetic, honest, and vigilant." In February he sent a minister to investigate the Cüstrin chamber, whose president was severely reprimanded and transferred to Minden. In May and June he reprimanded a ranking Königsberg official for unsatisfactory reports and finally sacked him. So unsatisfactory were reports from the Königsberg chamber that he resolved to travel there and make his own investigation during the coming year.

He early began chipping away at ministerial perquisites. Ministers were to make fewer inspection trips, which Frederick deemed to be too often administrative boondoggles, and when a minister did travel, his entourage was to consist of no more than two carriages, each pulled by four horses, in contrast to "substantial equipages and trains of clerks, toadies and servants." When the new president of the Cüstrin chamber asked for twenty-four horses, he was rudely informed that a chamber president was not that important; he could have eight horses only.

Zurechtweisungen, or royal reprimands, continued to flow to various chambers and to the Directory. Not satisfied with the handling of army quartermaster affairs, he transferred them to the new Department VI, under Minister Heinrich Christoph von Katte. In October he was shocked when a prominent official was caught selling state secrets to the Russian envoy's secretary. All departments were ordered to review security arrangements and make necessary corrections. The request of the Pomeranian chamber to increase pensions of minor tax employees to two thalers a month drew a stinging negative: "You gentlemen think too actively of my expenditures without sufficient reflection on income."

In 1748 a major case of fraud in Pomerania brought a royal explosion. The episode caused the king to revise the 1722 "Instructions" to the General Directory to eliminate three major weaknesses that "must be absolutely changed and replaced in the future." Tax revenues and the status of colonization were henceforth to be reported honestly and accurately; ministerial intrigues had to cease; ministers had to examine minutely the financial machinery of all boards and chambers. "It was all the same whether the estates or the peasants were cheated. The interests of the country were the interests of the king. Accounts must be wound up and strictly balanced at the end of every year."[3] The new "Instructions," issued during the summer of 1748, called for a certain duplication of effort in an attempt to gain better and more honest reports, and also for efficiency reports on subordinates.

But nothing much changed in the following years. Many of the documents published in the *Acta Borussica* bear marginal notes in the king's inimitable style — *"ist recht"* (good); *"ist ganz recht"* (quite right) — but many more are marked *"ist zu vague"* (too vague); *"ist nicht recht"* (not right). Senior and junior officials and ministers continued to receive sharp reprimands. The Cleves chamber was accepting too many apprentice councilors. "You take on more apprentices than there are stars in heaven," the king scribbled on one request. Provincial authorities were remiss in allowing young nobles to leave the country without the king's permission. Henceforth all subjects who were qualified for higher education would be educated in home universities; that is, if they desired employment after completing their university education.

The Directory was neglecting such important matters as promotion of trade and commerce and the renewal of Jewish restriction laws. A revised edict governing Jews was published in 1750. A wealthy Jew could leave his "protected" status to only one child. Only a Jew with a capital of ten thousand thalers could apply to the king for permission to live in the kingdom. Certain categories of Jews were not allowed to marry and could not own rural property, but some dispensations were probably granted if sufficient money was donated to the recruiting fund. Rabbis and cantors were merely "to be put up with." The edict made it very clear that the king did not want the Jewish population to increase.[4]

The problem of security leaks again arose. In April 1750, the king issued a lengthy fourteen-point operational directive to govern the security of secret archives. The matter would come up again, as would the problem of young nobles going abroad, as would censorship of offensive newspapers and a dozen other subjects that would appear in still another two volumes of the *Acta Borussica* before the peace ended.

58

ADMINISTRATIVE REFORM was an uphill task. Such were the country's needs that a skilled and efficient bureaucracy would have had difficulty in realizing them. Unfortunately the kingdom lacked that, nor did machinery exist to provide the needed experts.

The king's apologists have said that he inherited an administrative system impossible to reform, but this statement is contradicted by some major reforms that he did accomplish. The king's antagonists have said that he did not want an efficient civil service, since it would threaten royal absolutism, but this statement is contradicted by hundreds of *Cabinetordres* designed to produce more efficient bureaucratic performance, which was necessary to increase the crown's income.

Neither his failures nor his achievements lend themselves to simple explanation. The conflict that had been going on between ruler and aristocracy in Brandenburg-Prussia for centuries was still very real. King Frederick William's famous statement "I shall ruin the authority of the Junkers; I shall achieve my purpose and stabilize the sovereignty like a rock of bronze" is one of those catch-all declarations that fade under subsequent scrutiny.

The relationship was not one way. If the Junkers supported crown, then the crown must support the Junkers. In return for yielding political authority, the Junkers retained virtually all manorial authority with unquestioned social and economic superiority. Sons not needed on the latifundia were very nearly guaranteed army commissions or satisfactory civil service positions. The situation produced a static, stagnant, highly compartmentalized society in which the peasants — little more than serfs — were totally subservient to the nobility and would remain so despite later semi-emancipatory reforms attempted by the king.

This was what Frederick inherited — and he embraced it. If the crown was a rock of bronze, then it rested on the glacial base of the nobility — "the foundations and pillars of the state," as he wrote in 1752 — whose preservation was vital to the kingdom. Considering his background, the influence of his mother and her court, his tutoring and reading, his francophilia, his artistic sensibilities, and the excellent performance of aristocratic officers in his two wars, this attitude is not too surprising. Within the context of the man and his time, it would even have been permissible had ample qualified nobles been available for public service.

Frederick had some excellent ministers, envoys, and senior officials, educated aristocrats who performed well (and in turn were generously praised and rewarded). But these were a hallowed few, and not easily replaced. Even mediocre men were difficult to find. Where he needed many, he found few, and this was the great drawback to the system.

His attitude seems almost incomprehensible. He knew that most of the nobility were rudely educated. He frequently dealt with Junkers on inspection trips, harsh landlords for the most part, many of them former army officers, boorish, beer-swilling types familiar from Frederick William's Tabagie. He had earlier complained about the poor education of his officers. Yet he did little to encourage their civil education and a great deal to discourage it. No aristocrat (much less commoner) could leave the kingdom or be educated abroad without the king's permission, which was rarely given. In many ways they were as confined as the citizens of towns and cities. They were not allowed to sell land to commoners, nor were they allowed to go into trade. They were intended first for the army, second for civil service. Those who remained on the land or retired to the land were to increase production of food and subjects, collect the land tax from the peasants, and provide a sufficient number of recruits to the army.

Frederick wanted no part of social mobility. His father early in his reign had established a crude elementary school system. Frederick in later writings spoke of the need for schools, but other than bringing in some fugitive Jesuits for teachers, he seemed content to leave the problem to provinces and counties. The serf tills the land, the farmer farms, the shoemaker sticks to his last, the artisan to his trade, the merchant to commerce, the preacher to prayers (and rural schools). The middle class and peasantry could never equal the nobility in competence, ability, loyalty, and honor — and that was that.

It is all the more maddening in that he early admitted to the problem. In 1746 a Cabinet order called for all officials to give their sons a good education and put them on the right path, thus earning royal grace and ensuring for each lad a good position.

A *good* position?

If that son was well educated — and many sons were educated well by private tutors, some going on to universities at Halle and Königsberg — and did enter public service, he was already imbued with the parochial conventions of his father, who was more concerned with covering his back than with suggesting administrative improvements. He was assured of a minuscule salary, which encouraged indolence and corruption; he knew that errors would rarely be forgiven and that there would be no argument — in this sense the civil service was run like the army. And he knew that no matter how hard and efficiently he worked — this was the crowning blow — his career would be sharply limited because of the common blood in his veins.

Nor could he win a commission in the army except under extraordinary circumstances. (If he had studied mathematics he possibly could become an artillery or engineer officer.) The Great Elector and King Frederick William had promoted commoners to commissioned rank as a matter of course, and Frederick William had installed them in the civil service as foils to the nobility. Not so King Frederick, himself a total aristocrat.

Frederick's failure to encourage natural talent, indeed this denial of natural talent, was his greatest weakness. Can it be explained altogether by early influences? Or could it not in part unconsciously have stemmed from fear of his own inadequacies?

Whatever the deficiencies of the Prussian administrative system, the merits were sufficient for it to play a large role in some positive accomplishments of these peacetime years.

The Second Silesian War had brought Frederick close to financial ruin — not surprising, since it cost around twelve million thalers. During 1745 he had spent not only the last of the "old treasury" left by his father but over another million of current income. By October 1745, the treasury held just under twenty-three hundred thalers. Financial disaster was averted by a special property tax, which raised well over a million thalers. This was quickly spent, and the king managed to squeak through only by "contributions" levied in Saxony and by a Saxon war indemnification of a million thalers.

Neither an empty treasury nor a deficit government was acceptable to the king. "If the country is to be prosperous," he later wrote, "if the prince would like to be respected, he must keep his finances in order; an impoverished government has never won esteem."

No sacrifice was too great to restore the kingdom's financial health. Civil and military expenses were pared to the bone until a surplus was built from land taxes, taxes on imports, income from the royal domains, the salt monopoly, postal fees, and road and river tolls. In light of the normal operating expenses, particularly the military, and the kingdom's relatively inefficient financial system, the recovery was little short of miraculous. The amount of cash on hand grew steadily from 1746, not only for the "old treasury" and the "large treasury," but for several subtreasuries that were to cover the cost of mobilization, remounts, uniforms, and the like in case of war. By 1748 the army was again combat ready, and in 1749 the king was able to resume interest payments on the Silesian mortgages and even project full payment by 1752.* In 1749 the large treasury — barrels of gold and silver stored in basement vaults in the Berlin palace — approached four million thalers. The king wanted more, and ordered the mathematician Euler "to examine the accuracy of the algebraic calculations for the lottery according to examples of lotteries in the Italian cities." A year later it was close to five million, but that did not include subtreasuries, which held over a million and a half thalers.

By 1752 the large treasury had grown to six and a half million, but this still was not satisfactory. The same year the king called for an annual surplus of five million thalers, which in time would build the large treasury to twenty million! He grew very excited in 1753, when Fredersdorff sent him a recipe to make gold. For several months he enthusiastically supported his personal treasurer's alchemy and was very disappointed when it did not succeed.

Nevertheless, by the spring of 1756, just before the outbreak of the Seven Years' War, the total treasury contained nearly twenty million thalers.

Once the treasury and army had been repaired, King Frederick resumed a number of delayed land reclamation projects along the Oder and Netze Rivers. The program began close to Stettin with the building of dikes and draining of marshes. Not nearly enough workers were

---

* A nasty complication delayed this time schedule. British privateers seized some ships belonging to Prussian merchants. The king insisted on full restitution if he was to settle the Silesian debts, about his only weapon short of invading Hanover. The matter was satisfactorily settled by the Convention of Westminster in 1756.

available. Soldiers and military engineers were used; some areas resembled military camps. In other areas force was necessary to obtain boats from local peasants. By 1753 some four thousand colonists from abroad were settled on the reclaimed land. Between Freienwalde and Cüstrin the king opened canal construction that would shorten the course of the Oder by eighteen miles. It would in time provide sufficient land for six thousand colonists. He drained marshes around Netze and settled Polish families there in small farmsteads. He found sufficient fallow land in the Old Mark and in Pomerania to support over twenty new villages. He persuaded Priegnitz nobility — only with great difficulty — to open unused land to colonists, which resulted in twelve new villages by 1753. A year earlier he proudly noted that he had established 122 new villages (many of them named for outstanding officials and officers). He would continue to drain marshlands in Pomerania and along the Oder, where in time he hoped to settle 100,000 colonists; the Warthe marshes around Cüstrin, once drained, could support another twelve hundred families.

These colonists were quite reasonably subsidized as part of an overall agrarian policy designed to make the kingdom largely self-sufficient in foodstuffs. The king's edict of 1743, which encouraged the cultivation of hops, had eliminated the need to import that staple of beer brewing, and he now introduced the potato, which won only a slow acceptance, and encouraged cultivation of fruit trees and forage crops. Peasant farmers were taught improved cattle-breeding methods, a subject of particular interest to the king. Unfortunately he could do nothing about perennial crop damage from hailstones, locusts, and drought, but increased potato cultivation and full corn magazines more than once saved parts of the kingdom from famine.

Frederick built three major canals, one to expedite the export of wood from the New Mark; one that joined the Oder to the Havel; and one that had been begun earlier, the Plauen, which joined the Havel to the Elbe and greatly facilitated commerce between Magdeburg and Berlin.

He had inherited a primitive mercantile trade system and an adverse balance of trade, with imports exceeding exports by over a million thalers a year. It was to tip the scale in his favor that he had established a fifth department in the General Directory to handle industry and trade and eventually colonization. He was not pleased with its progress, and when its director died, in 1749, the king personally assumed responsibility for it.

The director was probably glad to escape this earth. To gain a favorable balance of trade in an agricultural country of limited crop production, almost no industry, no banks, and very little capital was a herculean task, particularly with His Majesty constantly on one's back, insisting that it could be done. There was no reason, for example, that the kingdom could not become a leading manufacturer of silk as fine as that produced in France or Italy. The large number of mulberry trees that the Great Elector had planted throughout the Mark had survived vicious winters. If the trees survived, so ran royal reasoning, then silkworms would have plenty to eat, and if silkworms had plenty to eat, they would make a great deal of silk. More trees were obviously needed, and the king granted prizes to villages that planted the most. By 1752 he counted over 400,000 trees and was dreaming of manufacturing forty to fifty thousand pounds of silk a year that would be worth some 250,000 thalers. The trees would not be worth harvesting for another six years, but meanwhile culturists could be trained for the great day. Silk manufacture could also proceed despite the lack of skilled labor, which would be made up by recruitment abroad and training at home, at royal expense, until two thousand artisans could supply the material. In time he hoped to see an important silk industry with large sales at home and abroad — a costly ambition never realized.

He was on safer ground with wool. His father had subsidized wool manufacture by building a central factory in Berlin that also produced French cloths, including serge and cotton. Frederick added a number of wool magazines in the country from which artisans could borrow raw material and pay for it once the manufactured cloths were sold. He also imported Merino rams from Spain to breed a special long-haired sheep that improved the quality of wool. He wanted merchants involved in the industry not only to peddle the final product but to advise on what products were wanted in and out of the kingdom. Proper quality was ensured by traveling inspectors. Linen production grew steadily, thanks to Silesian mills, which exported so profitably that Frederick called them his "Spanish Peru." The manufacture of chintz and calico, forbidden by Frederick William as too frivolous, was started and grew slowly; it was the province largely of skilled Huguenot immigrants.

To attract spinners from Poland, Saxony, and Mecklenburg, he offered each family a house, a small garden, and a meadow large enough to feed two cows. It cost the crown sixty thalers to settle a family of five. Frederick hoped to settle a thousand families a year for twelve years, because a survey showed that the trade could support sixty thousand spinners. By 1752 he had established manufacturing colonies in the Old and New Marks and in Pomerania.

Prussia's population had grown to 5.3 million by 1756.* "Since this axiom is certain," Frederick wrote in 1752, "that the number of sub-

---

* Koser gives a figure of 4.1 million, less than one third of Austria's, one quarter of France's, and one half of Britain's populations. Berlin had grown to over 100,000. Paris and London counted over half a million each. (Koser, *Geschichte*, Volume 1.)

jects makes the wealth of the state, Prussia was now able to consider herself twice as powerful as she had been in the last year of [King] Frederick William."

Merchants generally found hard going, but some prospered. In 1749 David Splitgerber and G. A. Daum, who owned one of the most successful trading houses in the kingdom — Frederick frequently utilized them as court bankers — opened sugar refineries in Berlin and Potsdam. There were small textile factories in the capital and elsewhere. A dimity mill made the city of Brandenburg prosperous. Leather goods were manufactured at Frankfurt-on-Oder, stockings and handkerchiefs in Berlin, Magdeburg, and Potsdam. Ironworks were opened in heavily wooded areas and soon supplied arsenals with cannon, bullets, bombs, and other army needs. Salt refineries were opened at Minden and expanded at Halle.

But the king was not satisfied. A tremendous potential existed that was not being fully exploited. The knife and scissor industry at Neustadt could have been tripled. The kingdom needed more homemade needles. It lacked good paper, buttons, handkerchiefs, silk ribbons. To keep money from going abroad and to attract capital, he wished to manufacture everything that was now imported. Prussia had natural markets to the East: Poland and Russia had no factories. But such commerce would have to be carefully regulated with an eye on Jewish traders, "because nothing is more contrary to commercial trade than the illegal [smuggling] trade made by the Jews." He also hoped that a small trading company at Embden, to which he granted a royal charter, would be able to bring medicines and spices from the Indies at cheaper prices than the Dutch.*

The major drawback to all these projects was lack of capital. Private funds were in short supply, and the average merchant had no chance of borrowing from abroad. Capital to establish new companies and new factories had to come from the crown, and there was only so much money available. "I have just emerged from a difficult war," the king wrote in 1752. "I have been forced to use state revenues for the most pressing matters, as much to rehabilitate the army as to build fortresses, replenish the treasury, increase and equip the artillery, and pay the English debts." It would be up to his successor to carry on the work: "As life is short and my health poor, I do not assume that I shall be able to perfect any of my projects; but I should give an account of them to posterity because I have examined all of these things [and] I can show him the way and indicate to him the means of making the state one of the most populated and flourishing in Europe."

---

* This trade was carried on by only two ships and was interrupted by war in 1756.

59

FREDERICK'S outstanding administrative success of this period was a complicated legal reform whose history fills most of the pertinent volumes of the *Acta Borussica*.

His father had inherited an archaic, hopelessly confused, and very dishonest judicial system: "The miserable justice cries aloud to high heavens!" he exclaimed soon after his coronation in 1714.[1] A subsequent investigation produced a catalogue of such judicial abuses as ignorant and corrupt judges and lawyers, prolonged trials, exorbitant court costs and legal fees, and an almost unbelievable tangle of courts and jurisdictions.

The system certainly needed reform, but Frederick William, possibly foreseeing the consequences to himself, did not push the process. Although he forced lawyers to wear a demeaning black cape and habitually called them "clowns," "imbeciles," "scoundrels," "dogs," and coarser names, he substituted bluster and threat for more positive action. Only in 1737, in a fit of pique, did he appoint a commission from the Ministry of Justice to draw up a reform plan.

The three-man commission included two field marshals, whose knowledge of law was questionable, but it also included Samuel von Cocceji, a fifty-nine-year-old scholar, professor of law, author of legal texts, veteran judge, and judicial investigator. He was not a brilliant legal theorist, but he was a hard-working, conscientious, and capable administrator, well suited to create and implement a reform "such as no other German prince yet possessed."[2]

Cocceji's plan was scarcely to Frederick William's liking. It meant abandoning *Kabinettsjustiz,* or arbitrary interference by use of *Machtsprüche,* the right of the king to decide a case or appoint a commission to do so. Cocceji wanted an independent judiciary in which no one, including the king, was above the law. He asked for qualified, adequately paid judges, a reform that would have cost a great deal of money and would have ended the royal appointment of a judgeship to anyone who donated large sums — five hundred to two thousand thalers — needed by the king to buy big men for the Potsdam Guards. Frederick William nevertheless paid lip service to the report and the following year appointed Cocceji chief minister of justice.

The report rubbed conservative ministers the wrong way, particularly the justice minister, Field Marshal Georg Detlof von Arnim, a well-educated, worldly, and capable Junker who saw inherent dangers to landowning nobles in *any* judicial reform. He sabotaged Cocceji's position to such an extent that the king formed another commission,

Count Heinrich von Podewils, minister of foreign affairs, often mocked as "monsieur of the timid politics" but also greatly respected by the king

Grand Chancellor Samuel von Cocceji, father of Prussian legal reform

By 1746 Spanish snuff and elaborate snuffboxes had become a major expenditure for Frederick. The 130 snuffboxes he kept at the Charlottenburg and Potsdam palaces were valued at about a million and a half thalers.

this one headed by von Arnim, whose machinations forced Cocceji into semiretirement (where he quite happily wrote lengthy legal treatises). The second commission was preparing an indictment of Cocceji when the king died.

The new king correctly divined that a centralized judicial system was vital to royal absolutism and that fair judicial processes were vital if the kingdom was to prosper. Yet he moved slowly. Though he reinstated Cocceji as chief minister of justice, he did not altogether trust him. But Cocceji almost immediately won royal favor with a legal brief that justified the rape of Silesia. In 1742 he did good work as minister of justice in Silesia, and the king consulted him more and more. In 1743 Cocceji argued the need for "a solid plan" of legal reform, and Frederick agreed: "But I hope that you will draw this in such a basic way so as not to get to the bark of the wicked tree but rather the root. For the guilt in my opinion does not lie so much in the salaries of minor officials and on the advocates and their lot as on entirely other causes."

Cocceji bravely reported that "there will never be a hope of good justice in your lands if learned, experienced, and honorable [court] presidents and councilors are not appointed and sufficiently paid." Present laws were confused; they were based in part on obsolete laws taken from Latin and Saxon codes. What was needed instead, he said, was "a specific, universal common law . . . in the German language [and] including a universal legal proceeding." Courts had to be inspected every three years by ministry officials empowered to settle abuses on the spot. Only "honorable, learned, and experienced lawyers" were to be allowed to practice, and the hated black cloak was to be done away with.

Cocceji in effect was calling for a new legal system. Frederick responded cautiously. Although impressed by the jurist's "good and praiseworthy intention," he found many "unsoluble difficulties" at the present time and would have to defer action. One problem was lack of money; another, Cocceji's abrasive relationship with von Arnim. "If His Excellency," Cocceji wrote to Podewils, whom Frederick had appointed peacemaker, "knew all the tricks Monsieur von Arnim has played on me in the eyes of both kings, he would be surprised at my patience, and he would agree with me that this very revered lord hides beneath a pleasant appearance the Jesuit and the Italian, two extremely dangerous animals."[3]

After Frederick's return to Berlin in January 1746, he complained to Cocceji of "a wholly rotten state of justice." He later wrote, "The public had accustomed itself to evading the laws. The attorneys made a shameful corruption of the good faith; it sufficed to be rich to win one's case, and to be poor to lose it."[4]

Cocceji responded in May with still another reform plan, which he wanted to introduce in Berlin courts, an effort blocked by Arnim. The king meanwhile had ended one major abuse by forbidding provincial courts to send cases either to foreign or domestic law faculties for decision, and he ordered that a counsel's final plea must eliminate polemics and harangues and stick to fact.*

A few months later the king sent Cocceji to Stettin to investigate alleged judicial abuses. Cocceji confirmed their existence and asked leave to try his reform plan there. When Frederick agreed, the minister wrote his own lengthy instructions and early in 1747 left for Stettin with six assistants (three of whom would later become grand chancellors), his major mission being to streamline existing procedures: "that all trials, including appeals, should be concluded within one year; that only well-trained and competent judges be appointed; that the courts be reorganized in a logical and coherent system of appeals; and that the oral procedure replace the written one wherever possible."⁵ Cocceji was to set up a small claims court to adjudicate claims under twenty-five thalers and was to experiment with a common fund, financed by court fees, from which judicial salaries could be increased.

Cocceji worked in Pomerania for five months. It was an amazing performance and must have included the knocking together of a great many official heads. In May he informed the king that he had settled one lawsuit that had lasted two hundred years and filled more than seventy volumes! At year's end he reported "that all of the 1600 old trials that were pending before the courts in Stettin . . . have been settled; of the 684 new trials, only 183 are left."⁶ His commission expanded its work in 1748 by amalgamating various tribunals and courts into a single body, with ancillary courts for particular cases such as inheritance and the property of minors. The reforms placed Pomeranian justice in the hands of twenty-eight officials instead of forty-five, and salaries for the twenty-eight were substantially increased. In addition the minister wrote a unified code of trial procedures, which soon became mandatory throughout the kingdom.

As documents in the *Acta Borussica* demonstrate, the king maintained the liveliest interest in this reform program, on occasion offering such legal snippets to his ministers as orders to eliminate the death sentence for sodomy. (It was perhaps at this time that a cavalryman was found guilty of sodomy. "Will he be hanged?" the king was asked. "No," he replied, "transfer him to the infantry.")

Cocceji meanwhile had transferred the reform program to Berlin,

---

*During the Dresden peace negotiations the king managed to have a privilege called *non appellando* applied to most of the kingdom. Henceforth Prussian dominions were free from jurisdiction of Imperial law courts; thus no case could be prolonged by appeal to the Imperial court, a vital reform undoubtedly instigated by Cocceji.

where he again collided with von Arnim. This time the king backed Cocceji, and Arnim resigned.* Frederick had already given Cocceji the title of grand chancellor, the Order of the Black Eagle, and had enno-bled him. He now gave him an estate and a gold copy of a commem-orative medal that showed the king balancing the scales of justice with his scepter.

Cocceji continued to implement reforms throughout the kingdom and to reorganize Prussian courts to establish "a clear and coherent course of appeals from the lowest to the highest courts."[7] The old jurist finished his days by writing what he hoped would be his major contribution, the *Corpus juris fridericiani (The Frederician Law Code),* which attempted to relate Roman, Saxon, and canon law to the partic-ular conditions of Prussia. Unfortunately he was not a great legal the-orist, and this final work soon faded into oblivion.

His influence was nevertheless enormous, and his reforms were em-ulated in a good many kingdoms. Frederick never tired of the Sisy-phean task of trying to reform further the Prussian legal system. Un-fortunately the conduct of judges and lawyers frequently did not live up to Cocceji's standards, and legal abuse remained a major problem in the kingdom.

60

SHORTLY AFTER RETURNING to Berlin in 1746, the king resumed work on what would become the *Histoire de mon temps,* a lengthy political-military treatment of the first five years of his rule, which he had started writing in 1742. He finished it late in 1746, worked it over for a month or two, then consigned it to secret archives, from where he would retrieve it thirty years later for rewriting (and posthumous publication).

It is a curious work of fourteen long chapters, written in French, under the stylistic influence of Xenophon, Thucydides, Polybius, Cicero, and Caesar. Neither memoir nor commentary, as he explained to Vol-taire, it was rather a large-scale portrait "of the European convulsion," with emphasis on the contradictory nonsense of those who govern (thus explaining its suppression): "I have touched on some of the most im-portant [political] negotiations and some of the most remarkable facts of war; and I have leavened such with reflections on the causes of events

---

* Arnim retired to his estates until the king, who respected his talents, called him back to Berlin in 1750 and appointed him postmaster general. He died in 1753.

and on the different effects that a single factor produces when it occurs at a different time or in other nations." In a lengthy foreword, he explained that he wrote nothing but the truth: "The archives are my guarantees. The reports of my ministers, the letters of the king, of [other] sovereigns, and of some important men who have written me are my proofs."[1]

It was an ambitious project that did not altogether match its author's pretensions, but it offers invaluable insights into his thinking. While not denying the importance of politics to war, he places war on a higher plane of importance, perhaps an inevitable judgment, in view of his aggressive temperament, recent military successes, excellent army, exposed borders, lack of allies, and the fierce nature of European politics. He also leaves no doubt as to the importance of offensive warfare in gaining a political objective. The work glorifies the Prussian army and praises individual deeds of valor while often denigrating foreign rulers, armies, and generals. On occasion Frederick criticized his own campaigns and deeds (but he left convenient lacunae for such events as the ignoble flight from the Mollwitz battlefield). The narrative sometimes drags; there are errors in names, places, and dates; there is superficial reasoning and that curious fatalistic strain which permeates all his writings. But the work is also interesting, instructive, and often amusing.

After completing the history of his brief reign, the king turned to his forefathers. The final result would be *Mémoires pour servir à l'histoire de la maison de Brandebourg (A Dissertation on the History of the House of Brandenburg)*, which was first published as a complete work in 1751. Frederick finished the first part, which brought the House to 1640, the time of the Great Elector, in early 1747. His new "reader" (more appropriately, listener) was Claude Étienne Darget, former secretary to the envoy Valory. He read the work to a special session of the Academy of Sciences "before the princes and princesses of the royal House and the highest functionaries of the state." Frederick next completed the history of his father's reign, which, perhaps significantly, was not read to the Academy, then the histories of the Great Elector and King Frederick I, which were read in 1748.

The *Mémoires* are not as lively as *Histoire de mon temps*, but they do show the king's deepening awareness of the traditions of the House of Hohenzollern. The writing is formal and pedestrian, with only flashes of the royal wit. He is exceedingly kind to his father, all things considered, but his real praise is reserved for the Great Elector and his expansionist policy. Only fifteen years earlier his tutor in Cüstrin had sourly noted that "the crown prince did not know whether his forefathers had won Magdeburg in a card game or otherwise."

This was no longer the case.

Histoire de mon temps should not be read in isolation, a fact that has escaped a good many commentators. Its military bias is more than coincidental. While Frederick was writing it, the unstable condition of European politics, with real or imagined threats to Prussia, was very much on his mind. It was written at Potsdam, a military beehive where he was surrounded by such bold and aggressive commanders as Winterfeldt and Rothenburg.

Frederick was never far removed from his army. He frequently drilled the Potsdam Guards, not only in close order but in battalion maneuvers, and he continued to study military history, particularly the works of Vegetius, Caesar, Folard, Turenne, Santa Cruz, de Quincy, and Feuquières.

All the while, he was writing, in secret, another work, which was finished in rough draft in late 1746. It would be expanded and printed in 1748 under the short (and famous) title, *Les principes généraux de la guerre (The General Principles of War),* thirty-nine quarto pages in the king's hand with ten colored plans to illustrate some of the thirty-one "articles," or sections.[2]

"The wars that I have waged," so reads the introduction, "have made me reflect profoundly on the principles of this great art which has made and overturned so many empires. The Roman discipline now exists only with us; in following their example we must regard war as a meditation, peace as a rehearsal."

The strategic and tactical meat of *The General Principles* is Prussia's place in European politics, her open borders, hostile neighbors, limited human and financial resources, her disciplined and mobile army — and King Frederick's personal experiences in both Silesian wars, where Prussian arms had won five major battles against numerically superior opponents.

These factors, taken with the king's aggressive, ambitious, and impetuous temperament, argued against several types of war. He did not want to fight long wars or winter wars or siege wars. He did not want to fight prolonged campaigns in hostile lands, like Bohemia and Moravia. He did not want to fight more than one enemy at a time, and then only where he chose to do so. If forced into war, he would opt for a strategic offensive, which at times might call for a tactical defensive. If he met with severe reverses, he would change to a strategic defensive, which at times might call for a tactical offensive. The book leaves little doubt that he foresaw fighting the next war in enemy territory, undoubtedly Austrian, but with secure lines of communication to his kingdom.

The thirty-one articles, some lengthy, some brief, range from general maxims to specific strategic and tactical principles for offensive and defensive war at home and abroad in different types of terrain. A variety of camps and marches are defined in detail, along with special sections on supply, communications, fighting against light troops, and the like. The sections are in no particular order, and there is some repetition and contradiction. The work nonetheless is unique for its time. It offers excellent insights into eighteenth-century warfare, and it emphasizes the king's preference for offensive battles with highly trained and disciplined troops.

The General Principles begins with a section on the defects and virtues of Prussian troops. The major defect is the tendency of foreign mercenaries to desert. This must be prevented at all cost, and Frederick lays down fourteen rules for doing so. Aside from maintaining normal tight camp security — strengthened hussar patrols and chasseurs hidden in grain fields at night, for example — commanders are to avoid marching at night and camping close to large woods. But a good general, on the other hand, must see that the troops do not lack any necessity, "be it bread, meat, bedstraw, brandy."

It is no less vital to preserve discipline, "the foundation of the glory and conservation of the state." This can be done by a combination of reward and punishment. The commander must be popular, chatting with troops in tents or on the march, seeing to their proper diet, sparing them useless work, exposing them to danger only when necessary: "Be their father, not their executioner." But he must swiftly and severely punish troublemakers, mutineers, looters, and deserters.

One lengthy section is devoted to the talents needed by a great general: "A perfect captain is a man of reason. . . . I suppose, above all, that he be a worthy man and a good citizen." He must be secretive, a quality "indispensable to anyone who conducts great affairs." He must always disguise preparations for attack and tell his plans to no one until just before their execution. He must forever dissimulate, never showing discouragement when news is bad. He must praise junior officers who perform well. On occasion he should ask advice from a subordinate general and praise him if the plan works — even though he may have previously decided on the same move. "He is the sentinel of his army; he should . . . foresee and prevent all the harm that can possibly happen to it." He must always use reason: "What plan would I make if I were the enemy?" * After deciding on one or more such, he must rapidly alter position, camp, depots, and detachments to meet foreseeable dangers. Although he should carefully think out plans beforehand, once in battle he must act decisively: "It is better to make a

---

* The good general, Frederick wrote to Prince Maurice of Saxony, must be adaptable: "Fabius can always be a Hannibal, but I do not believe that a Hannibal would be capable of following Fabius' conduct." Maurice's future success, the king wrote, was certain: "You foresee events too closely to misjudge their outcome. The book of events is vast; but foresight and ability can correct chance."

bad decision and execute it on the spot than to make no decision." He must be prepared for anything: "Be active and indefatigable; cast off all sluggishness of body and mind. Otherwise, you will never equal the great captains who serve us as examples."

No matter how able the general, he is subject to human weakness — fatigue, illness, poor judgment — and to fortunes of war, and he will be condemned for something that is not his fault but rather that of a subordinate: the commander of an advance guard who lost his way, a courier who failed to deliver a vital command, a spy who revealed the order of battle, an ineffective patrol, a traitor within a fortress. Fortune though can work both ways, and the able general must not fail to exploit a favorable if unexpected event. Should, however, an "accident" or defeat occur, he must minimize the loss and do all possible to repair troop morale while carrying out a retreat for which he has already prepared.

A closely related section is called "Knowledge of the Country." A commander can learn a great deal from a map: the nature of the area — hilly or flat — its cities, villages, roads, rivers, marshes. In mountainous country it is particularly necessary to reconnoiter, map in hand, in order to discover essential terrain features, such as land suitable for camps, hidden defiles, and unknown roads. A section called "Du Coup d'Oeil" — which in this context may be translated as "Terrain Appreciation" — comes next. It calls for two talents, one for judging on the battlefield the number of troops that the field can hold; this may be acquired by experience. But the other and completely superior talent, for judging instantly all the advantages that can be taken from the terrain, can be acquired only by one born with a happy genius for warfare.

Subsequent sections analyze the terrain in operational detail, pointing not only to advantages that can be gained from proper exploitation but to pitfalls that await the unwary. The entire work is spotted with references to famous military actions of the past and to the author's personal experiences in the Silesian wars.

Frederick did not pretend to cover all points: "I have learned from my slight experience of warfare that this art is inexhaustible and that, in pursuing it, one constantly discovers new things." The work was treated as a state secret, shown only to the Prince of Prussia, to whom it was dedicated, before being placed in the archives.

6 1

The General Principles should not be confused with various "Instructions" or regulations that the king continued to hurl at infantry and cavalry generals. Translated into German by Eichel, they repeated many of the precepts contained in *The General Principles* but went into more unit detail.[1]

They changed very little. An infantry or cavalry sergeant in 1740 would have felt at home in the 1756 army. Regulations continued to stress the need for highly disciplined units trained for offensive warfare. Those for the infantry concerned basic formations, manual of arms, loading and firing, and various deployments, particularly from column into line and back again. The king wanted all movements carried out in virtual silence to avoid confusion caused by shouting — a point stressed in several orders and in later maneuvers.

Cavalry and hussar regulations called for increased shock power by modified attack formations, and specified exact distances for trot and gallop.* Horses were not to be overfed: they were to have guts, not bellies, in the king's words. Units were to train rigorously at all times in all weathers. Many of the regulations were petty, changing the distance between men in close-order formation a few inches or altering unit intervals and various rates of march, the sort of thing that subsequent generations of military men would dote on. A wise Prussian officer did the same: in 1747 the king ordered all officers to read them four times a year "in order not to forget what was in them." A year later he published new regulations and ordered generals and staff officers to read them twice a year, captains five times, and lieutenants once a month!

Annual reviews were to ensure that the regulations were providing a homogeneous body of troops trained to a high state of discipline. A great deal of time was spent on minutiae, on single regimental reviews in which the king inspected uniforms, equipment and weapons, recruits (who were generally asked questions as to their welfare, a gambit initiated by Frederick's father), and cavalry remounts before observing close-order drill, including manual of arms followed by unit exercises. The general reviews were quite grand affairs, involving numerous reg-

---

* Immediately after the war the king appointed Major General Hans von Winterfeldt as a sort of inspector general of hussars to oversee their considerable expansion and increased integration into battle tactics. In battle the hussar first line was to approach the enemy at a trot, saber hanging loosely from the waist. At thirty paces the saber was taken in hand, the horse spurred to gallop, and the attack carried out with shrill cries.

iments of infantry and cavalry prancing around to the tune of cannon fire, the whole designed to impress foreign observers as much as to test the troops.

Just as *The General Principles* should not be confused with army "Instructions," military reviews should not be confused with maneuvers. Field maneuvers were made as realistic as possible. Infantry marched long distances, slept in tents or on the ground, cooked combat rations, and often ate cold food. Cavalry and hussars rode fast and hard; Valory was surprised by the number of horses lost on a single maneuver and the countless broken arms, legs, and ribs of the troopers. Maneuvers were designed first to ensure that units had learned standard tactical movements and formations. "The infantry practiced various deployments, formations, attacks in open country, attacks of outposts, defense of villages and entrenchments, river crossings . . . retreats and finally all those maneuvers necessary before the enemy," the king later wrote. "The cavalry practiced different attacks with closed and open ranks, reconnaissances, green and dry foraging, various formations, and forming prescribed alignments."[2]

They were also to test tactical precepts that the king was secretly working out. As explained in *The General Principles,* he favored offensive warfare, and in view of his numerical inferiority, he wanted not only to attack with the greatest possible mass of infantry and cavalry (and presumably artillery) but to maintain the momentum of attack for as long as was necessary to score a decisive victory. To accomplish this, the army had to fight *as a unit,* with infantry, cavalry, artillery, and hussars supporting each other, a combined arms effort that had proven so successful at Hohenfriedberg.

Frederick hoped to achieve this by the *Schrägangriff,* or oblique attack. He is supposed to have come on the basic idea in studying the ancient tactics of the Greek general Epaminondas, but it more likely stemmed from the melding of formal study with lessons learned from the Silesian wars.

The general idea was to maneuver the enemy to terrain suitable for battle, preferably compartmented land in hilly country that offered protection to one's own flanks and rear. The main army was then deployed so as to threaten enemy lines and thus hold them in place while a concealed corps of cavalry and foot leaped forth to strike a vulnerable flank with shock tactics. With cavalry and infantry pushing in the flank, with hussars charging in from the rear, the luckless enemy retreated while they could. Then, with artillery and cavalry harassing the retreat, the Prussian commander would reorganize his army into columns and pursue in an attempt to either cut off the enemy or destroy their magazines.

By 1746 the *Schrägangriff* was a fundamental weapon in the king's tactical arsenal. It would be repeatedly tested, examined, and altered during the next ten years. Magnificent in its simplicity, it boldly exploited the best features of the Prussian army — discipline and mobility — to overcome numerical superiority: "An army of 100,000 men," the king wrote in The General Principles, "if taken in the flank can be beaten by 30,000 men, for the battle will be decided quickly."

This was all very well — but how was the commander to bring it off? By having perfectly disciplined troops. Frederick cited Vegetius, who centuries earlier had written in his famous work, Epitoma rei militaris, "Roman discipline triumphed over the size of the Germans, the might of the Gauls, the cunning of the Greeks, the masses of the barbarians; and it subjugated all the known world." Keeping even disciplined and highly trained troops in attack formation posed an immense problem, particularly when it came to fire and movement. So awkward was the long and heavy musket, so prolonged its loading and inaccurate its fire, that earlier theoreticians like Jean Charles de Folard suggested replacing it with the pike, a heresy not altogether rejected by Maurice of Saxony, Marshal Khevenhüller in his time — or the Prussian king.

In 1742 Frederick had ordered his generals to retain mass formation in the attack, to press against the enemy, as opposed to engaging in a fire fight that, by disrupting the formation and prolonging the attack, cost more men than a swift advance. He repeated the order two years later. Prince Leopold at Hohenfriedberg marched his attack battalions with shouldered weapons into Saxon lines, which he broke with bayonet attack. Mass formations advancing without musket fire proved decisive at Soor. In 1746 Frederick wrote that he preferred attack by shouldered weapons because firing only holds up the attack. In short, "Infantry fire is for the defensive, the bayonet for the offensive."

He did not discuss the disadvantages. Although the oblique attack could be prepared for in part by normal artillery fire and cavalry charges, it was still vulnerable to enemy artillery firing deadly canister shot and, finally, to lines of troops firing musket salvos. What Frederick had was only horse- and manpower. What he needed was the power of the modern tank. Without such a thing, the attack could be costly indeed, and losses could not easily be replaced by experienced soldiers necessary to the tactic. Add to this that it was designed primarily for use against Austrian armies of the Silesian wars, armies that were rarely well commanded, did not adjust rapidly to tactical necessity, were not well disciplined, and had neither effective cavalry nor artillery. He may have recognized some of these shortcomings, which would explain his orders to commit inferior troops, such as battalions of irregulars, to the initial assault whenever possible.

Frederick started testing the tactic in 1746. In August of the following year he personally led a corps of five battalions and eight cannon out of a wood to attack a like-sized force commanded by Prince Henry. A month later similar maneuvers were practiced following the Breslau review (a massive display, with cannon firing thousands of shots to signal formations and movements).

In 1748 Frederick invited the eighty-year-old French military theorist Folard to Potsdam to help with tactical experiments, an invitation Folard declined because of fragile health. Continued experiments convinced Frederick more and more that the oblique attack would be the decisive tactic in the next war and that it could be used more generally than he had supposed. He modified it in a 1748 "Instruction" to infantry generals by allowing the attacking infantry to halt and fire when they were within close range of the enemy, then go after them with bayonets and not fire again until they were at the enemy's back.

Variations continued to be tested. In 1748 Prince Maurice of Anhalt advanced all his troops without firing, and that autumn William, the Prince of Prussia, led his men to within fifty paces of the "enemy" before opening fire. At maneuvers in 1750 on the Templehof plain outside Berlin, the attacking infantry first fired after the "enemy" had turned in retreat. In exercises from 1753 to 1756 dozens of units attacked without firing muskets. No doubt inspired by Folard's pike tactics, the king experimented with the noncommissioned officer's *Kurzgewehr,* or staff, trying lengths that varied from seven and a half to thirteen feet, finally settling on ten.

This did not mean that he rejected musket firepower. Units continued to master swift loading and firing. In 1753 troops in one exercise attempted to load during the advance in order to attain a greater rate of fire, a notion that was impractical because of the intricate process of loading. In 1755 some units tried volley fire without the first line kneeling, and this failed because of the length of the muskets and the compactness of the ranks. The king also increased the powder load of the musket in order to fire a heavier ball, and he cunningly changed from the walnut stock (at fifteen groschen per weapon) to maple (at four groschen).[3] Frederick kept an open mind on this point and after the Seven Years' War would emphasize the importance of musket firepower, but only because of improved Austrian defensive tactics. The point was to achieve the speed and precision required for the tactic. An observer of maneuvers at Potsdam in 1754 was astonished to see infantry columns deploy into line *during* the approach march. After watching a maneuver at Stargard, he described how thirty battalions, approaching in columns, formed into two lines "in nine or ten minutes," a movement "that appeared to me completely new."[4]

Coordinated cavalry attack was vital to the tactic. Infantry and cavalry generals had earlier been ordered to study each other's regulations.

Maneuvers in which seventy and more squadrons carried out mass attacks were not uncommon. As with infantry, the operative words were speed and precision. In 1752 the king wrote, "The end purpose of these maneuvers is to overthrow the enemy by the furious shock of the cavalry attack."

Artillery was vital to the concept but does not play a major role in extant records, probably because technological shortcomings greatly restricted tactical use. Frederick constantly encouraged artillery experts — old General Christian von Linger, General Bauvraye, Colonel von Holtzmann, and Lieutenant Colonel von Dieskau — who were trying to improve weapon performance. He studied all project reports with great interest and always attended final trials of new pieces. The experts continued to experiment but with no outstanding success. Frederick probably realized that he was technically stymied, which would explain his calling heavy artillery "a necessary evil."

Frederick also improved the medical service. The 1748 "Instructions" called for prompt evacuation of wounded by detachments from regiments that had taken the most casualties (probably to keep other units intact in case of need). At Frederick's insistence Surgeon-General Cothenius organized the field medical service with stationary general hospitals at Breslau, Glogau, Stettin, Dresden, Torgau, and Wittenberg, field (or mobile) hospitals within call, and dressing stations, to be protected from enemy fire in locating them behind some convenient hillock or in a ditch.

Frederick realized that terrain and technological shortcomings would often call for more conventional tactics. He offered a variety of general and specialized tactics in *The General Principles* — for attacking heights, crossing rivers, countering light troops, and the like. Maneuvers frequently tested such tactics. In 1748 Prince William led an attack by seven battalions, four squadrons, and seven cannon against a smaller corps commanded by Prince Henry, the idea being to show the advantage of possessing heights both during attack and retreat. This maneuver included "enemy" guerrilla units commanded by two aides. In the autumn of 1749 the king led a field exercise in bridging and crossing a stream.

After the grand review at Spandau in the autumn of 1753, somewhere around forty thousand troops, including an artillery corps of fifty-one cannon, carried out involved maneuvers concealed behind a strong security screen. This was a twelve-day field effort quite unusual for the time. Combat conditions were simulated, the men ate bread cooked in field ovens, lived in tents with straw floors, and were provided with wood for cookfires. A detailed record estimated an overall supply expense of twenty-eight thousand thalers. Smaller and shorter maneuvers were held at Spandau in the autumn of 1754 and 1755.

62

THE EUROPEAN WAR continued while the Prussian king was repairing his kingdom, treasury, and army. Frederick was delighted to have
escaped from it with his realm intact. He seems to have believed, at
least initially, that he could remain a pacific spectator. To his reader
Darget's warning that Austria would never respect the Peace of Dresden, Frederick replied that he was not worried about the Vienna court,
which feared his army and would remain quiet for the dozen or so
years of life left to him. He had eliminated debt-ridden Saxony as a
threat. He could now rest easy. "I would not henceforth attack a cat,
except to defend myself," he told Valory. Back in Berlin he expressed
similar sentiments to Podewils, adding that Russia would play little
part in German affairs. The "happy quietism" of 1742–1743 had
changed to "my peaceful system." Let others fight while neutral Prussia
regained strength.

This was scarcely realistic, and the king must have realized it. Only
six months before the peace, he had written to Podewils that "although
any particular peace can be regarded only as a poor palliative, one can
still regard it as a truce, made under the guarantee of the maritime
powers [England and Holland] and the Empire, that will allow us the
time to breathe and that delays for some years the storm that was about
to smash over us."

He had not been back a month before potential enemies again invaded his turbulent mind. "I wish the Empress [Maria Theresa], the
King of Poland, Count Harrach [of Austria], and Count Brühl [of Sax-
ony] could better conceal their Enmity to His Prussian Majesty," Thomas
Villiers reported to England in late January. "It cannot long remain
secret, and may at last give Jealousies very prejudicial to the Affairs of
Europe, but particularly to the Austrian and Saxon dominions."[1] Mardefeld in Saint Petersburg reported active military preparations, which
suggested an attack on Prussia in the spring. Though Frederick could
not imagine "the pretext or the goal," he was plainly worried. By late
February he was also concerned about British duplicity. A visit by Villiers, who spoke in "plenty of sophisms," together with the failure of
the Stuart rebellion and a short-lived ministerial change in favor of
Frederick's old antagonist Carteret ("Lord Firebrand" — now the Earl
of Granville), made him doubt the sincerity of the Treaty of Hanover.
By mid-March he was convinced that Carteret was negotiating with
Russia, Saxony, and Austria to Prussia's disadvantage, a suspicion that
did not altogether die when Lord Harrington shortly replaced Carteret.

Within a few months, then, diplomatic aloofness had given way to political exigency. Frederick obviously needed friends. Envoys Johann Andrié in London and Christoph von Ammon in Amsterdam were to improve relations with those governments. Frederick offered to mediate a peace with France and England, even going so far as to suggest conditions. Baron Johann Chambrier was to make the same offer to Versailles. At the same time he warned the Austrian court not to involve the neutral German empire in a new war against France, a warning repeated to the Imperial Diet.

Russia remained his major concern. Her military buildup continued in Livonia. Artillery trains were marching on Riga in late April. If the Vienna court made peace with France, Frederick wrote to Mardefeld, then Austria, in conjunction with Saxony and Russia, and probably Denmark and Hanover, could attack him in Silesia. His fears were somewhat allayed when Saxony signed a subsidy treaty with France and when Mardefeld insisted that Russia would undertake *nothing* for at least a year. This was fortunate, the king wrote, in view of "the very great expenses" that mobilization would have required. Nevertheless, extreme vigilance was the watchword, and Mardefeld was to demand a categorical statement from Chancellor Bestushev on Russian intentions. "If these people attack us this year," he wrote to Podewils in mid-June, "my situation will be perilous. . . . The army still lacks tents and many other necessities, [and] resources are exhausted." Thus it was necessary to walk a diplomatic tightrope — to change from lion to fox as he put it — in order to gain time. *Chi a tempo a vita* (Who has time has life) was a maxim that had appealed to him originally in the Cüstrin cell.

But rumors of a new treaty between Russia and Austria soon stirred the pot of fear. Otto Podewils, who had replaced the ailing Dohna in Vienna, was charged with a detailed intelligence mission that gave priority to military affairs. He was to try to recruit a spy in the Hofkriegsrath. Although Frederick did not doubt the evil intentions of the Austrian court, he did doubt that it could finance its many projects. Yet he was relieved to learn in midsummer from "reliable sources" that the Austrian treaty with Russia was essentially defensive, designed only to prevent Prussian military intervention in Bavaria on behalf of France. This was a dangerous misconception that Otto Podewils would shortly attempt, not very successfully, to correct.* Royal optimism rose higher when Villiers assured him that Great Britain did not want new troubles in the north and that England was ready to guarantee formally his possession of Silesia, a guarantee that would also be a condition of any general peace.

---

* The king was mistaken when he regarded Austria as the leader and Russia as the follower. A secret article called for return of Silesia to Austria, and, as Koser remarked, the treaty placed Russia in the Austrian camp for the rest of Elizabeth's reign. (Koser, *Geschichte*, Volume 1.)

By midsummer, then, the king was confident that he was out of danger for at least a year, since it was too late for Russia to act against him even if she wished and even if she could find necessary funds. Now it was time to win the guarantee of German courts to the Peace of Dresden, a task he set about fervently.

Frederick continued to wear the skin of the fox. He told Chambrier to assure the Versailles court of his high regard for France. He would do all possible to keep Empire princes neutral. He followed Maurice of Saxony's campaign in Flanders "step by step," congratulating the field marshal and King Louis on the former's brilliant victory at Rocroix and on the "wise mixture of prudence and audacity" of Maurice's operations. He favored a subsidy treaty between France and Sweden but did not wish to involve Prussia directly, nor did he hold much hope that France would come up with the cash; to ask that court for money, he wrote, is like asking "a Catholic priest to say a mass [merely] for the love of God."

He continued to woo the English court, praising Villiers, a man of as much heart as intelligence and, as he wrote to Andrié, a man who would make a splendid replacement for Laurence, the British envoy in Berlin, a Hanoverian whom he did not trust.

Austria had meanwhile replaced Russia as his biggest worry. He did not believe that a proposed peace congress would result in a general peace, but he feared that once peace did come, Austria would move against him and try to persuade Russia to do the same. Otto Podewils was to recruit agents for this contingency, Austrians of high rank who would be paid several thousand thalers a year. He was also to submit biographical studies — "portraits" was the king's word — of everybody from Emperor Francis downward and attempt to divine each one's thinking. More than ever, Frederick wrote, "it is necessary to act as if Hannibal were at the gates and to remember that vigilance is the mother of security."

The king's diplomacy continued its impulsive and uneven course in 1747. Lord Chesterfield, who had replaced Harrington, was sending Villiers to Berlin as British ambassador and was also trying to influence the Vienna court favorably toward Prussia. But Chesterfield's heavy-handed efforts to enlist Prussia on Austria's behalf in the war against France brought an angry outburst that all too clearly emphasized Prussia's increasing isolation. "I am astonished by English politics," the king wrote to his minister Podewils. "They see all Europe as one large republic created to serve them; they never enter into the interests of others and use only guineas as persuasive arguments." Prussia and Austria could never be friends, "because friendship is never the fruit of hatred." Everything must be reciprocal, and above all there must be some degree of common interests. European politics are forever ruled by prejudices abandoned only with greatest difficulty:

> One strays methodically from supposition to supposition; the conclusions are just but one is often deceived concerning the principles. At Vienna I am believed to be the implacable enemy of their house; in London I am believed to be more ambitious, restless and rich than I am; Bestushev thinks that I am vindictive; at Versailles I am believed to be blinded by my interests. They all deceive themselves, but what is annoying is that these errors can cause dangerous consequences.

The task was to try to anticipate them and move Europe from a prejudiced view of Prussia.

Meanwhile, it was necessary to win the Empire's approval of the Treaty of Dresden and with it the guarantee of Silesia. The king appreciated that this guarantee was fundamentally a chimera, because if he broke with Austria, the Empire would never help him militarily. Nonetheless, it would serve as a psychological deterrent to Austria, particularly in conjunction with England's guarantee to Prussia. Similarly, a defensive treaty with Saxony would help to check Vienna. An "unostentatious" treaty with Sweden could do no harm and could even bring about rapprochement with Denmark.

Yet nothing seemed to work out. By mid-1747 Frederick was again convinced of British duplicity both in Saint Petersburg and Vienna. The Austrian court was as arrogant as ever, treating Ambassador Podewils with calculated rudeness and moving ever closer to Russia. The Russian court had forced Mardefeld's recall — the eighty-three-year-old envoy would die the following year — and had arbitrarily imposed a new envoy, Count Karl Hermann Keyserling, on Prussia.* The proposed treaty with Saxony came to nothing, and it was increasingly obvious that the treaty with Sweden would not extend to Denmark. On the other hand, the war continued, which meant that Austria could take no action against Prussia.

But now a new and ominous note appeared in the king's correspondence. Because of information from an Austrian spy recruited by Otto Podewils in Vienna, the king wrote to his envoys Joachim Wilhelm von Klinggräffen and Baron von Chambrier two lengthy letters that foretold, perhaps unconsciously, the breakup of the "old system" of the European balance of power: "The Vienna court, seeing that it is impossible to detach me from the interests of France, is now taking the opposite point of view and has decided to do everything to detach France

---

* Keyserling was apparently a distant relative of "Césarion" but is not identified in any of the standard biographical dictionaries. Frederick did not want him but perforce yielded to the appointment and planned to win him by bribery. In the end he came to like and respect him.

from me." Vienna at the same time was moving Saxony from French influence into an alliance with Austria and Russia. The Vienna court was everywhere spreading falsehoods and insinuations to the effect that France could never rely on Prussia, which would always be indifferent to French interests; it was inflaming Saxony's hatred and jealousy of Prussia; it was turning England against Prussia by reports of a secret treaty between Prussia and France with concomitant danger to Hanover; it was doing everything possible to persuade Empire estates to abandon neutrality and join the war against France; it had turned Russia into an enemy of France. Chambrier was to relay these charges to the minister of state, Marquis Louis de Puyzieulx, and stress the necessity of France and Prussia remaining united to check Austria's pernicious and destructive designs.

The French court did not pick up the gauntlet. It was, as usual, financially *in extremis*. There was little Frederick could do except remind Puyzieulx that he had always spurned Austrian efforts to turn Prussia against France. Meanwhile he had been heartened by reports from Count Finck von Finckenstein, who had replaced Mardefeld as envoy to Saint Petersburg, of the pacific disposition of the Russian court, which should continue as long as it was subsidized by British gold. As for the peace conference that opened at Aix-la-Chapelle in late October, Frederick believed "it would come to nothing"; the war would continue and Prussia would do its best to keep the Empire princes neutral.

The war did continue and at year's end gained a new ingredient. The Russian court, prompted by British subsidies, agreed to march a corps of thirty thousand troops to the Low Countries to join the Austrians and their allies. The news did not upset Frederick, but he was furious with Valory for spreading rumors in Berlin that Prussia was going to move on Austria in order to force her to keep troops at home — a canard that he vigorously denied to all foreign ambassadors while continuing to proclaim his policy of total neutrality unless attacked.

Despite Chambrier's repeated representations to Versailles, Prussia was, in fact, moving slowly away from France toward England. It was scarcely a sudden move; there were hurdles to overcome. English privateers had seized Prussian ships, which brought strong protests from Potsdam and a threat to cease interest payments to British merchants who held Silesian mortgages. But this was a relatively minor irritation in view of Frederick's political needs, and was in part assuaged by the arrival in the spring of 1748 of Chevalier Henry Bilson Legge, the new British envoy, who reported England's desire to move closer to Prussia once the war ended. The overture was welcomed by Frederick in Legge's first audience. "His Majesty's answer was as gracious as possible . . ." Legge reported. "The King of Prussia's heart is still German, notwithstanding the French embroidery which appears upon the surface."[2] In a further audience, Frederick informed Legge that he was willing to conclude a defensive alliance with England but could not abandon his present neutrality.

The long war ended in spring of 1748, when France, England, and Holland signed peace preliminaries at Aix-la-Chapelle. At the insistence of the British, the preliminaries included a guarantee of Prussian possession of Silesia. Frederick was ecstatic. For the moment British piracy could be forgotten; Russian policy became unimportant. As he prematurely but presciently informed Otto Podewils in early June, "The European system is already effectively altered in its essentials."

63

FREDERICK'S friendly feelings toward England did not last long. He was soon disillusioned with the pro-Hanoverian secretary of state, the Duke of Newcastle, who quickly backed away from a new alliance. By late August he had returned to neutral ground, in no hurry to ally with England or any other power. "The entire art of politics," he advised his sister Ulrica at this time, "consists in bending one's plans to contingencies, to prevail by force at one time and to temporize at another." But he also suggested to her that the only constant powers were France and the Ottoman Porte. The English envoy, Henry Legge, that autumn judged his usefulness at an end and asked to be recalled. "The Fear of Losing and the Desire of Gaining are Principles which have the most Operation at this Court," he reported to London in November.[1] At the end of 1748 Frederick was slowly turning back toward France.

The rapprochement continued early in 1749, when an alleged treaty of aggression between England, Austria, and Russia presented Frederick with several nightmarish situations, including the possibility of a Russian attack on Prussia in conjunction with a Danish corps, an English fleet in the Baltic, and an Austrian land corps. "I must confess that all these circumstances taken together present a chaos that I am unable to unravel without further clarifications from you," the disturbed king informed Klinggräffen, his new ambassador to England, in late February.

Further ominous reports convinced him that war in the spring was inevitable. He countered by moving closer to France, continuing to withhold payments to British merchants on the Silesian debts — and preparing his army for the field. But England did not want a northern war, and since Russia could not go to war without British subsidies, the situation cooled. By April Frederick was convinced the crisis had passed. It left him isolated in anxiety, fearful of British, Russian, and Austrian plans. Though grateful for French support and eager to bring about an alliance with France and Turkey, he doubted that France could be relied on in the crunch.

Rumors of Russian intentions against Sweden continued to circulate throughout summer and autumn, but by mid-October the king was assured that Russia had waited too long and that peace was certain for the rest of the year. "In all things there is a favorable or auspicious moment," he wrote to General von der Goltz. "If grasped when presented, it offers a hope of success, but if it is allowed to pass by, it can scarcely be regained, and all the good reasons that one has had for the project come to naught."

But though Russia had missed the boat this year, Bestushev undoubtedly would continue to make trouble. As for Austria, Frederick wrote to Chambrier, "You can definitely reckon that if within five years the Vienna court does not involve itself in some incident and keeps its freedom of action, it will undoubtedly provoke me and try to start a new war, as is without question guaranteed by the arrangements she currently makes."

Frederick moved closer to France during 1750 while outwardly maintaining a policy of strict neutrality. Without French influence, Prussia could not hold Bestushev in check in the north, could not prevent England and Hanover from gaining undue influence in Empire affairs, and could not delay Vienna from having the infant Joseph elected King of the Romans, the prelude to his one day becoming emperor.

When France checked a flare-up in the north early in the year, Frederick not only secretly thanked Puyzieulx but promised that if Russia attacked Sweden, he would honor his alliance with Sweden and send troops. He also agreed to negotiate subsidy treaties with Cassel and Saxe-Gotha on France's behalf. He was sorry to lose Valory, who was royally seen off with a warm letter, the king's portrait, and three thousand thalers in cash. He showed every courtesy to the new French envoy, an Irish Jacobite, Robert Francis Talbot, Lord Tyrconnell, with whom he would soon develop a confidential relationship.

Tyrconnell's mission was to reinforce the French alliance with Prussia in order to counter the northern league that was forming against Prussia and Sweden. He succeeded admirably, in part through diplomatic ability, in part because of external events. That summer the Prussian court was surprised by a formal visit from one Mustapha Aga, who announced himself to be the personal envoy of the Khan of the Crimean Tartars. Though mocking him privately, Frederick made an ostentatious show of entertaining him, mainly to upset the Saint Petersburg, Saxon, and Vienna courts, which quailed at the thought of the khan's fifty thousand troops at the Prussian king's disposal. Tyrconnell added to their discomfiture by giving the visitor a splendid dinner party.

Frederick's hand was also strengthened by the arrival of a new British envoy. England had long since backed away from its proposed alliance. Legge was replaced with Sir Charles Hanbury-Williams, a versifying, egotistical, pompous, and irascible diplomat. Sir Charles never forgave King Frederick for limiting his initial audience to "exactly five and a half minutes," a coolness also exhibited by Count Podewils, who on all social occasions made "me a Bow without speaking to me." [2] Sir Charles was soon sent to represent King George at the Warsaw Diet, a calculated rudeness that Frederick resented and countered by ordering his envoy at Hanover not to return to London with the English court.

Frederick already had instructed his envoy in Warsaw, a perceptive diplomat named Ernst Johann von Voss, to work closely with his French opposite in sabotaging the Polish Diet to frustrate the designs of Austria and England concerning that country. French and German gold, along with dexterous diplomacy, did the job. The Versailles court followed this achievement with a proposed treaty of commerce to which Frederick favorably responded by sending Heinrich von Ammon as special envoy to the French court. During this entire period Frederick was feeding Tyrconnell in Berlin a great deal of secret information pertaining to the maritime powers, Austria, and Russia.

Tyrconnell continued to grow in favor, at Hanbury-Williams's expense. Back in Berlin, Sir Charles fell into extreme disfavor by openly mocking and criticizing the king in Berlin society. Frederick all but had him socially ostracized before his recall in early 1751.*

Count Bestushev's machinations in the north, which Frederick believed were encouraged by England and Austria, also influenced matters. When Bestushev suffered a severe attack of colic in October, the Prussian king hoped it would kill him: "But since generally good people die too soon and wicked people too late, it must be feared that the same thing will happen in this case." Positive diplomacy was at a standstill. Czarina Elizabeth was torn between bottle and bed, temporarily uninterested in affairs, often refusing to sign important papers, sometimes threatening overzealous ministers with permanent residence in Siberia. The Prussian resident secretary, Konrad Heinrich Warendorff, could report little more than diplomatic gossip. Frederick did not like the situation and in late November wrote, "Put your most secret papers in a safe place and burn those that could compromise my

---

* Hanbury-Williams's reports of this period were more gossip than fact and in part were dangerously inaccurate. He was upset by his treatment and complained to Podewils, who offered no advice. The king continued to ignore him, and the princes would not speak to him.

interests, in particular the anecdotes that the late Baron von Mardefeld has written for Count Finckenstein's instruction, and the general report that the latter made on his departure from Russia." Frederick all but ignored the Russian envoy in Berlin, a rudeness that terminated in his abrupt recall in December. He was ordered to depart without taking formal leave. Frederick recalled Warendorff and diplomatic relations were broken.

Austria remained the archenemy, a haughty and arrogant queen and court that, despite the Treaty of Dresden, refused Empire guarantee of Prussia's possession of Silesia, refused to treat honorably with Imperial electors in the election of a King of the Romans, stirred up trouble in Poland and the north, strengthened fortresses in Bohemia and Moravia — and was clearly eager for a future war with Prussia.*

Thus France remained not so much a natural as a necessary ally of the moment. But a few clouds hovered over Prussian relations with Versailles. Puyzieulx had warned Tyrconnell of the Prussian king's capricious behavior. Tyrconnell enlarged on the subject in a very perceptive report in September:

> It is very true that His Prussian Majesty often passes very rapidly from fear to tranquillity. I confess to you that I have often attributed these changes to the confusion of the moment. . . . I believe he is more frightened than tranquil because his timorous nature always makes him see the dark side of things and as a result he is afraid of committing himself. I do not believe him very well-intentioned but am persuaded that in the present circumstances we can count on him, because it is in his interest, he knows it, and is convinced that he would be crushed the moment that we abandoned him. I will try to hold him always to this belief.

Further reports spoke of the king's frequent "timidity" and subsequent repentance, which tended to explain his changeable ways.[3]

Frederick had considerable reason to be timid. French lethargy, in part explained by perilous finances, was already working on his fears. He wrote to Chambrier in October that for some time he had been amazed at French indifference to British intentions and actions that openly opposed France in Europe. He repeated this complaint in December and further objected to *French* changeability, doubting that the Versailles court intended to carry out the proposed subsidy treaties that Frederick had been negotiating. He was astonished by Madame de Pompadour's influence on King Louis and asked Chambrier whether she was equally influential in political and foreign affairs. Indeed she was, Chambrier replied, and Frederick ordered him to move closer to her.

Another cloud was not so easily discernible. In late November

---

* Otto Podewils had been ill for some time and was recalled in January 1751. The main result of his embassy had been to secure new plans of Moravian and Bohemian fortresses, along with a model of a new mortar, which he brought back in his official luggage.

Chambrier reported the warm reception of Count Wenzel von Kaunitz, the new Austrian envoy, by the French ministry, which hoped that he would respond by maintaining a good relationship "and that this system could suit the two powers."

Here was a very serious warning that Frederick should have respected. Instead, he rejected it out of hand. Vienna would never be close to Versailles, Frederick scornfully informed Chambrier, if only because of English influence on the Austrian court.

Frederick was greatly underestimating Austrian diplomacy. Prompted by Johann Bartenstein, Maria Theresa had already decided on establishing good relations with France. Her instrument was Count von Kaunitz, a relatively young diplomat who had made his mark in Turin and Brussels and had gone on to distinguish himself as Austrian ambassador at the Congress of Aix-la-Chapelle. The forty-one-year-old Kaunitz was described as having "the frivolity of a Frenchman, the astuteness of an Italian, and the profundity of an Austrian."[4] He detested all things Prussian and was sent to Paris to lay the foundation for a new alliance, an effort strongly encouraged by Madame de Pompadour.

Maria Theresa meanwhile was continuing a series of reforms begun shortly after the war ended. She was putting her finances in an order "unknown to her ancestors" and would soon enjoy an annual income of twenty-four million thalers. She pulled the army from lethargy by pensioning off elderly officers, tightening discipline, visiting army cantonments to boost morale, rewarding younger officers for excellent performance of duty. She opened a military academy in Vienna and founded a school of artillery under the Prince of Liechtenstein. He enlarged this branch to six battalions, spending 100,000 thalers of his own money to buy new cannon. Maria Theresa's reforms, all new to the Austrian government, later won King Frederick's admiration; she was, he wrote, "a woman executing plans worthy of a great man."[5]

Matters did not change greatly in the new year of 1751, when European politics entered one of those pleasant if all too rare quiet periods. There was nothing to report from Potsdam, Frederick informed his sister Wilhelmina in April, "where I lead a quiet and blissful life."

It was true that Frederick, Prince of Wales, had died at end of March.* King Frederick was sorry, but felt it fortunate that the prince died before the old King of Sweden, since his replacement, Prince George, was only thirteen and King George so old and infirm that England should now logically want to preserve the peace. The King of Sweden did die

---

* "Poor Fred" was the forty-four-year-old heir whose marriage to Wilhelmina had been so greatly desired by Queen Sophia Dorothea years earlier.

a few days later, and the accession was smooth enough. Frederick advised his sister Ulrica and his brother-in-law, Adolf Frederick, now King of Sweden, to do all possible to bring together various conflicting internal parties.

The Versailles court had also shaken off some lethargy. Louis was building up his navy, and he granted a subsidy to Sweden sufficient to send troops to Finland. Frederick met Chambrier at Wesel in June. He was shocked by the old ambassador's "sickly and extremely feeble" state, and indeed it was their last meeting; Chambrier died a week later. Frederick replaced him with George Keith, the former Jacobite lord marshal of Scotland. The king had invited Keith to Potsdam in 1746 and found him, as he wrote to Prince William, "very charming, his appearance as serious as his conversation is open," and had made him a member of the court with a pension of two thousand thalers a year. Now Keith arrived in Paris accompanied by an adviser, Baron Dodo Heinrich von Knyphausen, the second son of King Frederick William's minister. Keith's instructions from the king touched on three principal areas: tranquillity in the north, the election of the King of the Romans, and an alliance between Prussia and Denmark. Keith was not to interfere with the treaty of commerce, which special envoy Ammon was still patiently negotiating.

Franco-Prussian relations suffered two setbacks shortly after Keith's arrival. Puyzieulx, who was pro-Prussian, was forced to retire because of poor health, and his office went to Marquis François de Saint-Contest. Then a few weeks later Tyrconnell suffered a violent vomiting of blood and was in severe danger, a great blow to Frederick, who had grown immensely fond of him, of "his judicious dealings, honest and upright, which have won him all my esteem."

Tyrconnell lived for another half year, however, and Saint-Contest soon struck Keith as an excellent minister, "a man of very good sense, very devoted to affairs and instructing himself on them with care, possessing a good memory, and speaking clearly and precisely." He highly valued and very much wanted an alliance with Prussia, Keith reported early in 1752; moreover, he was the only minister who kept Keith informed of la Pompadour's activities. Although the king continued to grumble at French indolence, he had to admit that France was his only possible ally in opposing future Austrian aspirations in regard to Germany.

64

KING FREDERICK conducted his orchestra of state from the Potsdam palace, an imposing but ugly structure that the architect Georg Wenzel von Knobelsdorff had tried to beautify by raising the wings and breaking the frontal monotony with stairs leading to a columned portico. The structure's innate austerity evoked unpleasant memories of earlier days and was never to the king's liking. "I amuse myself with study, music, architecture, gardening, and all sorts of agreeable occupations," he wrote to Wilhelmina in late 1746. The reference to architecture and gardening concerned a project begun during the war and now nearing completion — a summer palace on the Weinberg, just outside Potsdam gates.

Sans-Souci was completed in the spring of 1747, an event marked by a magnificent dinner for the entire court. It was a relatively simple but beautiful one-story palace built to Frederick's own plans, which were contrary to Knobelsdorff's ideas and led to a serious quarrel. The building was surrounded by gorgeous gardens, and the land sloped down to the river in six glass-covered garden terraces that eventually provided out-of-season grapes, cherries, figs, and pineapples for the royal table and a few fortunate friends. It was exquisitely decorated inside (if perhaps somewhat overdone) and the grounds were filled with walks flanked by imposing statuary. It was a perfect retreat.* "The house, the garden, the furniture, the statues," the courtier and diarist Count Ernst von Lehndorff rhapsodized, "in short, everything is enchanting and delightful."[1]

It was the king's favorite residence, and he never tired of adding to it. In time he would build a Greek temple, an orangery, a Chinese pavilion, and a magnificent gallery for his growing and immensely valuable collection of paintings. He continued to buy Watteau's work, became devoted to Lancret, shifted to Correggio, Veronese, and Tintoretto, and went on to buy twelve Rubenses and eleven Van Dycks as a starter.†

* Sans-Souci can easily be visited today and is well worth the effort, as is Potsdam (Russian soldiers and all). Refurbishing, however, moves slowly. When I first went through the palace, Voltaire's bedroom was closed for redecoration. On a second visit five years later I found it still closed but bribed a custodian to have a look. It was still not finished.

† When Rothenburg was in Paris in 1744 he bought two tableaux by Watteau for eight thousand thalers, a price that the king criticized as exorbitant. He also found a tableau by Lancret "that represents the Italian theater with all sorts of agreeable and well-executed figures"; the price was twelve hundred livres. He noted that Watteau's paintings were getting hard to find. The Sans-Souci gallery was completed in late 1755. Frederick wrote to Wilhelmina that he had a hundred paintings on hand (including the above) and was waiting for another fifty from Italy and Flanders.

He engaged actors, dancers, and singers for its theater, entertained lavishly yet, considering the time, in an unusually informal style. It is probably fair to say that, with the exception of the time at Rheinsberg, Frederick's happiest days were spent at Sans-Souci.

There were some shadows in these years. In addition to suffering from chronic ill health, the king was becoming increasingly isolated, a man who lacked those personal relationships which help to erase fatigue and ease physical discomforts. Although he bemoaned the deaths of his intellectual friends, it is doubtful that those friendships would have altered matters. Real friendships require time, confidence, and trust. He had little time; he wished to confide in no one; and he was suspicious of the world.

His family relationships were often stormy, as could be expected when emotions are stifled by duty and ambitions fed by envy.

We can pass over most of them quickly. The dowager queen resembled a porcelain caricature in her comfortable court at Monbijou, where she frequently entertained her children. Frederick had come to dislike this court and its vacuous society but generally dined with his mother when he was in Berlin. He always treated her with the greatest respect, referred to her as the queen, celebrated her birthdays with extravagant fêtes, gave her costly gifts, wrote her polite little notes — but never discussed with her anything more serious than Berlin society. He concerned himself with her health, which was unstable, and in 1756, on leaving for the Seven Years' War, said goodbye by letter so as not to upset her.

His wife, Elizabeth, did not much concern him. Known as the "reigning queen," she was comfortably quarantined in Schönhausen palace, and he saw as little as possible of her. In the spring of 1746 William asked whether she should be included in a family outing to Charlottenburg. "If my prudish sourpuss takes part," Frederick replied, "she will, I fear, ruin the whole thing."

Two sisters, Sophia and Louise, had made bad marriages and never tired of complaining about their husbands or of asking the king for money. His correspondence with Ulrica while she was crown princess remained innocuous for several years, although he did warn her and her husband not to antagonize the Swedish senate, a warning frequently repeated after she became queen in 1751. As Frederick feared, the autocratic behavior of the pair led to a serious rebellion in 1756, from which he dissociated himself, explaining to the British envoy that Ulrica had repeatedly ignored his warnings and advice. He remained on excellent terms with Charlotte, who was happily married to the Duke of Brunswick, and he enjoyed the company of Emily in Berlin, though this relationship suffered a setback when he imprisoned her alleged lover for life and she became mentally unstable.

An earlier quarrel with Wilhelmina had been compounded when she stupidly paid her respects to Queen Maria Theresa, who had come to Frankfurt for her husband's coronation as Holy Roman Emperor. The long storm finally subsided but emotional débris remained. She would visit Potsdam, they would exchange small gifts and correspond frequently, but the letters are dominated by discourses on singers, operas, plays, family comings and goings, philosophical ramblings, and lengthy reports on each other's myriad illnesses. In 1757, not long before Wilhelmina's death, a lost battle, a lost mother, and an errant brother combined to renew the vigorous friendship of earlier years — but this was on paper, and war prevented a meeting.

The king's brothers were of more concern. Ferdinand was still too young to cause serious problems. Prince Henry was another story. He and William, the Prince of Prussia, had accompanied Frederick in the last campaign. Similar to the king in many respects, Henry had proven himself an adroit commander in the retreat from Bohemia and at the battle of Soor. A combat-seasoned major general at the age of twenty, he felt that he had earned a place in the sun. Instead, he had Rheinsberg, a regiment, and neither enough money nor sufficient freedom to support his desired way of life. To the king he was *le petit Henri,* and little Henry was forced to live most of the time at Potsdam with the king.

They quarreled in 1746, probably because Henry was sulking. If he wished to remain cold and distant, the king wrote, that was up to him: "It is only my intervention in your love affairs that sometimes softens your attitude toward me, when you have need of it. Moreover, the slight friendship that you show me on all occasions does not impel me to make new efforts of love to a brother who gives so little in return." Another letter complained of Henry's "constant aloofness . . . and total indifference." A letter from Henry, not extant, asked what he had done to incur such royal displeasure. The reply was reminiscent of Frederick William's letter to the crown prince eighteen years earlier: The king reviewed Henry's transgressions (not least of which was a host of disastrous love affairs), but to make peace sent him some plans, presumably military, that he had requested. After a six-month silence Henry requested permission to go abroad to study various armies. It was out of the question, the king replied. He would learn nothing, since foreign armies were so different from the Prussian army; he could not go to France or Austria without causing political difficulties; his life was not to be jeopardized "except for the safety of the fatherland."

There is a three-year gap in their extant correspondence but relations do not seem to have improved in the interim. Henry's regiment did not please the king in the spring review of 1749, and he placed one of his colonels in actual command: "Sir [not *Mon cher frère,* as in other letters], I have found it appropriate to put your regiment in order because it was destroying itself. . . . If I have made changes it is because they are appropriate. You will need to make plenty in your own conduct." Henry persuaded William to intervene and when that gambit failed — as they should have known it would — Henry asked for another regiment. The king's refusal led to an ugly scene and another scolding letter: until Henry developed a solid character and learned how to behave himself, he was not to be let out of sight, much less given the mansion that the king was building for him in Berlin. Henry bowed to this decision, and another crisis was over.

His surrender was virtually complete. He continued to live under the royal eye, probably thankful when he escaped to his detested regiment at Spandau or to his mother's tiresome court at Monbijou. He accompanied the king on inspection trips to Silesia and Prussia. When the king decided he should marry Princess Wilhelmina of Hesse-Cassel, he seems to have made no real protest; it was the only way to gain liberty, and he could pay his debts from the bride's dowry. Frederick returned from Silesia in the autumn of 1751 to find Henry "infinitely changed to his advantage," as he told Wilhelmina; "more gentle and well-behaved than he has been." It was an act. Henry did not hide his unhappiness from his friends. When Wilhelmina questioned the king about Henry's attitude, he replied that they had not discussed it, "but I believe, in any event, the woman will be good for him."

The wedding took place in late June of 1752. Although the court was impressed by the bride's wit and beauty, Henry's "gloomy countenance" did not change as he made his responses with "grave and serious air." It was a disastrous marriage. Count Lehndorff reported that only four months later Henry was having an affair with the intelligent but intriguing Countess Bentinck, and there would be more affairs, until the marriage became a mockery — one more reason for Henry to resent the king's domination of his life.

Frederick's relationship with William, the Prince of Prussia, who was ten years younger than the king, was less stormy — at least for a while. Lacking Henry's intellect and natural talents, William was less assertive and sometimes sycophantic in his letters and no doubt in the king's presence. Much of their correspondence was sunny, but there were shadows enough to suggest hard times ahead — indeed, to suggest the final terrible tragedy only a decade away.

One shadow was the king's paternalistic attitude toward his brothers, perhaps understandable in view of the Hohenzollern ethos and age differences. Even as crown prince he had chastened William for indiscreet political statements, a scolding repeated in 1743 and 1744: "It becomes you ill to participate in intrigues and hatch plots in the kingdom." A dynastic marriage to Princess Louise Emily, Queen Elizabeth's younger sister, did little to improve William's happiness but did bring him official recognition as heir to the throne, his own establishment in Berlin, an infantry regiment (in addition to his cavalry regiment), and subsequently an heir, Prince Frederick William. Although promoted to lieutenant general in 1745, William was not allowed to join the army in Silesia, despite repeated pleadings that he be allowed to prove himself militarily. His only function, he complained, was to produce children. If that was true, the king shot back, why had he produced only one wretched child when the future of the House demanded more? He was finally allowed to come to Silesia, but was given no command in the final campaign.

And he was not given a significant command in peacetime. Although he was in Frederick's earlier position as crown prince, he lacked his older brother's intellectual and cultural independence and had to rely on Berlin society for amusement. In essence, this was court society centered on Monbijou, an environment, as Count Lehndorff's diary indicates, not so much immoral as vacuous. Dinners, suppers, dances, masquerades, amateur theater, opera, plays, games of blindman's buff, cards, drinking bouts, gossip, and of course marital intrigues and affairs. On occasion William escaped to his Oranienburg estate or to his cavalry regiment at Kyritz, but only with the king's express permission. He was not overly interested in the estate or in either of his regiments. He seems not to have been overly interested in *anything* other than women — "The Prince of Prussia likes every woman better than his wife," an ambassador later reported[2] — and in avoiding the king's trenchant criticism.

At first this was relatively simple. When pushed to produce another heir, William pointed out that "children do not come on command," a fact unwillingly accepted by the king. Frederick was delighted when a second son, Henry, arrived in late 1747. He was pleased when William wanted to improve himself by reading, and recommended books on history, politics, and criticism while offering philosophical homilies on honor, duty, and truth. But if Frederick was suffering from "hemorrhoid-colic," then he replied with dark thoughts on the general degradation of mankind.

William occasionally was invited to Potsdam and sometimes on inspection trips. The king sent him *The General Principles of War*, which was dedicated to him. No great discussion ensued, but perhaps the correspondence has been lost. The relationship continued on an even keel until the spring of 1749, when William's cavalry regiment showed poorly at the Spandau review and when William chose to defend Henry, who was in hot water for the poor showing of his infantry regiment. William eventually backed down, only to get in trouble because of his own infantry regiment the following spring. After some acrimonious correspondence, the king abruptly ended the discussion, but he also gave William and Henry a blunt warning:

> Only in military questions do I know no forbearance. If my brothers set a good example, I will be infinitely pleased. If they do not, I shall instantly forget any relationship and do only my duty, namely, to maintain everything in proper order during my lifetime. After my death you may do as you will, and if you wish to deviate from the basic principles and from the system which my father has introduced, you will soon experience the consequences. That in a few words is all I can say to you.

The next two years were serene enough. In August 1751 William's wife bore a daughter, Wilhelmina. That disappointed the king — "but one must take things as they are," he wrote to the father. He also sent him an "Instruction" for the upbringing of the eldest son, seven-year-old Frederick William. This was in the Hohenzollern mode, and William meekly accepted it. Ulrica, now Queen of Sweden, asked William to visit in spring of 1752. The king was sorry, but he had to refuse permission because of the delicate political situation; he was sure William would understand.

It is doubtful that he expected understanding from either brother by then. In *The Political Testament* of 1752, written expressly for William, who would succeed him, there is a brief section on princes of the blood — difficult, arrogant people who refuse to accept obedience or any form of subjection and who support any intrigue or cabal. The best way to treat them is "to put down briskly the first who raises the standard of independence, to treat them with all the distinction that belongs to their station, to cover them with all exterior honors, but keep them away from [serious] affairs and trust them with command of troops only deservedly, when they are known to have [sufficient] talent and character."

65

THE SAME FACTORS that inhibited a close family relationship — lack of time and insistence on secrecy — prevented the king from developing intimate friendships. Although he sometimes used the people closest to him as sounding boards (rarely accepting their advice), they were essentially on hand for relaxed badinage. This was on two levels. Senior officers, including princes of the blood, generally attended noon dinner, where the talk was largely military and there was some horseplay. Supper was more informal and intellectual, with lively verbal exchanges. Wine in each case flowed freely. In spring of 1747 Frederick wrote to Fredersdorff that 200 *antals* of Hungarian wine — 11,000 bottles — had been delivered to the Potsdam cellar at a cost of 12,598 thalers — and the king wanted another such delivery in the autumn!

Military favorites were men of action, aggressive commanders like Rothenburg, von der Goltz, Winterfeldt, Lentulus, Chasot, and Stille. They were complemented by such intellectuals as the scientist Pierre Louis de Maupertuis; the chief of protocol and court jester, Baron Karl von Pöllnitz; the architect Georg von Knobelsdorff; the physician Jules de La Mettrie; the philosopher Marquis Jean d'Argens; and the reader Claude Darget. Later came the poet François Thomas d'Arnaud, who spoke only in verse; the military writer Count Lancelot de Turpin; Abbé Jean de Prades, who replaced Darget as reader; and numerous visiting luminaries such as Johann Sebastian Bach, who arrived in cantor's robe to compose a fugue dedicated on the spot to the admiring king.

Prince Maurice of Anhalt-Dessau visited in autumn of 1746. "He bores me to death," Frederick wrote to Prince William, "and I shall get rid of him as soon as possible." He was no more gracious when Old Dessauer died in 1747, a non-event so far as Frederick was concerned. The old favorite Count Francesco Algarotti turned up in early 1747, "more restrained and reasonable than formerly," Frederick noted. The king made him a chamberlain at three thousand thalers a year, but the rapport was gone and he soon moved on. Dowager Queen Sophia visited that autumn, as did Wilhelmina. Jacob Keith, George's brother, who had won military fame in the Russian army before falling victim to court intrigues, arrived to take up service as a field marshal. Frederick found him "gentle, intelligent, clever, [a man] of charming manners."

The painter Amédée Vanloo also arrived in early 1748 to bolster Frederick's newly founded Academy of Art. His first commission was to paint the ceiling in the Sans-Souci theater with Apollo and the nine muses; the dancer Barbarina Campanini emerged as Terpsichore. General Asmus von Bredow, a member of the Academy of Sciences, visited "and did his bit for sociability." Father Bastiani, a friend of the king's from Silesia, dropped by to tell salacious stories about Pope Benedict XIV. Frederick did not believe most of them and was convinced that the good priest had read more of Ovid's *Art of Love* than of his breviary.

Count Finckenstein returned from his Russian embassy in early 1749 to tell the king "wonderful things" about the Russian court. Field Marshal Count Maurice of Saxony turned up that summer in a pedantic and loquacious mood. "I am being instructed . . . on the art of war," Frederick wrote to Voltaire. "This marshal would appear to be the professor of all the generals of Europe."

Nothing about this social scene was very exciting, and it is not surprising that Frederick in private letters sometimes complained of boredom. Only in July 1750, with the arrival of Voltaire, did Frederick's spirits lift.

Voltaire's disapproval of Frederick's military adventures had brought their correspondence almost to a halt. It began to revive after Frederick's return from the wars. Despite his predilection for things military, he remained intensely interested in arts and sciences.

The Academy of Sciences usually met every week, and its papers were published annually. They covered a wide field, all the way from Professor Samuel Formey's thoughts on dreams to Dr. Eller's writings on the body's formation and new experiments with human blood to one Monsieur Gleditsch's contribution on the growth of mushrooms to the king's own histories of the House of Hohenzollern. Frederick almost never attended the sessions, but he was proud of the Academy, and he had made Voltaire an early honorary member. Voltaire continued to correct Frederick's own contributions, which included essays on superstition, religion, and manners, verse elegies, funeral orations, and writings on ancient and modern government. In 1749 Frederick again urged the famous writer to take residence at his court.

As Frederick had changed, so had Voltaire. The "divine Emily," the Marquise du Châtelet, had begun to grow tiresome as early as 1744, when she complained about Voltaire's frequent illnesses and resultant lack of libido. She was thirty-eight and Voltaire fifty. For some years he had been in love with his young niece, Marie Louise Denis, who now, at the age of twenty-six, was suddenly widowed. Consolation led to consummation. Voltaire's wavering libido revived, and the affair prospered.

Voltaire and Emily remained together for a few more rather grim years. To complicate matters, Emily fell in love with Marquis Jean François de Saint-Lambert, a thirty-one-year-old courtier at King Stanislaus's court in Lunéville. Their affair continued at Cirey. In mid-1748 Emily was sleeping with her new lover while Voltaire was writing to his niece, "I press a thousand kisses on your round breasts, on your ravishing bottom, on all your person which has so often given me erections and plunged me in a flood of delight." At which point the divine Emily at age forty-two became pregnant!

Voltaire behaved quite well. When asked by Emily and Saint-Lambert how she should explain the father's identity to her husband, Voltaire replied, "As to that, we will put it among the miscellaneous works of Madame du Châtelet." That winter they visited Paris, from where Emily wrote passionate letters to her lover and Voltaire conducted anatomical researches on his niece.

Frederick continued to urge Voltaire to come to Sans-Souci. He had written an epic poem of about four thousand verses; he was working on essays and plays; he sent Voltaire an epistle on Darget; he was correcting dozens of other poems, elegies, and epistles for inclusion in his

Oeuvres. He was only too aware of numerous faults in his writings, and he had the leisure now to study with Voltaire: "God knows if I shall have another such [year]."

Voltaire might never have responded but for an unfortunate event. In early September he wrote to a friend: "This evening Madame du Châtelet, being at her desk, according to her laudable custom, said, *'But I feel something!'* That something was a little girl, who came into the world forthwith. It was placed upon a volume of geometry." Emily became very ill — presumably a victim of puerperal fever — and died, as did the baby. Voltaire took the loss to heart. "I have lost a friend of twenty-five years," he wrote to Frederick, "a great person whose only defect was to be a woman." He soon recovered and moved to Paris, where Marie Louise lived with him. Here he published an anticlerical work. The Vatican banned it, and the proclerical court faction in Paris set about disgracing its author.

Frederick, meanwhile, had brought Voltaire's protégé, the poet d'Arnaud, to Sans-Souci at a good salary, the implication being that he could become Voltaire's replacement as literary favorite. With his position now threatened at home and abroad, Voltaire agreed to make the trip, providing he was paid sixteen thousand francs, in addition to salary, to cover travel costs (among them the medicines for his myriad illnesses) for himself and his secretary, Como Alessandro Collini.

It worked well — at first.

Voltaire was rapturous. Elegantly housed in apartments recently occupied by Maurice of Saxony, he wrote to his intimate friend Count Charles d'Argental about operas, plays, philosophy, and poetry, of "grandeur and graces, grenadiers and muses, trumpets and violins, a meal of Plato, society, and liberty. Who would believe it? Nevertheless it is all true and of it all nothing is more precious than our intimate suppers."[1]

Two weeks later he wrote that the king was showering him with attention and kindnesses. Frederick concerned himself with affairs of state from five A.M. through midday dinner, then devoted the rest of the day to belles lettres, including three hours of work with Voltaire. A week later Voltaire wrote to his niece that he had been appointed a court chamberlain with key, decorated with the Order of Merit, and given an annual pension of twenty thousand francs, plus *all* expenses. The king would provide a house in Berlin and would pay Marie Louise four thousand francs a year if she would come there. But Madame Denis wanted no part of Prussia or its king and thought that Voltaire was very foolish to consider permanent residence. "The King of Prussia will be the death of you," she wrote — and she was nearly correct, but not for the reasons she cited.

Voltaire's enthusiasm grew. Wilhelmina appeared and made a great fuss over him, as did all members of the royal family. Then came a great *carousel* in Berlin. After fireworks, plays, and operas, it ended with a military pageant in the palace courtyard, which had been transformed into an amphitheater. Three thousand troops formed an honor guard. Streets and amphitheater were lighted with forty-six thousand lanterns. As Voltaire walked to his box, people called his name. The performance followed. Four quadrilles, or groups of mounted knights, equipped and armed as Persians, Greeks, Romans, and Carthaginians, each led by a Hohenzollern prince, performed the most intricate mounted maneuvers. "Not the least confusion," Voltaire wrote to d'Argental, "no noise, all the assembly seated at ease, and silently attentive." [2] A joust followed, after which Princess Emily awarded first prize to the Prince of Prussia. Voltaire was enchanted and scribbled a verse that turned her into Venus awarding the apple.

Voltaire was practically groveling in admiration of his host, who resembled Marcus Aurelius except that he wrote excellent verses when he took trouble to correct them. His prose was admirable, but he wrote too quickly. His *Histoire de Brandebourg* would be a major work, providing it was carefully corrected. In early October he wrote to his patron, "I prostrate myself before your scepter, your pen, your sword, your imagination, your justness of understanding, and your universality."

Voltaire was allowed to do about what he wanted, to come to the king's table or be served in his apartments. On one occasion the king sent him an invitation to supper in the form of a cryptogram:

$$\underline{P} \quad \text{à} \quad \underline{ci}$$
$$\text{viens} \quad \text{100}$$

(viens souper à Sans-Souci).

Voltaire replied: Ga *(J'ai grand appétit).* By late October he was working only an hour or two a day with the king and was otherwise busy with his own writings including his work, begun years earlier, on Louis XIV. His time with Frederick was giving him new strengths. "I learn in correcting him to correct myself," he wrote to d'Argental. "It seems that nature has made him expressly for me; all my hours are delightful. I have not found the least prick of a thorn among my roses." [3]

He soon stopped going to midday dinners, where there were "too many generals and too many princes." He greatly enjoyed their suppers, where only French was spoken. "German is for soldiers and horses," he wrote to a friend, "necessary only for the march." [4] Conversation was "often instructive and nourished the soul." Count Francesco Algarotti was always amusing.* Prince Henry turned up to act in *The Death of Caesar;* he proved a good actor who spoke faultless French

---

* Algarotti was living in Berlin but sometimes came to court. He returned in 1754 to Italy, where he died ten years later.

Voltaire and Frederick at Sans-Souci. "It seems that nature has made him expressly for me; all my hours are delightful," wrote Voltaire to Count d'Argental in 1750.

Completed in 1747, Sans-Souci was Frederick's summer palace and retreat. The terraced glass-covered gardens supplied out-of-season grapes, cherries, and figs for the royal table and favored friends.

The famous "round table" of Sans-Souci. Voltaire, on the king's right, wrote to a friend that he was in "the paradise of philosophers."

Barbarina Campanini, the beautiful Venetian danseuse with whom Frederick was briefly enamored. Voltaire held that her legs were the attraction, because they resembled those of a boy.

and was very pleasant. Pierre Louis de Maupertuis was not very exciting, but La Mettrie, with his explosive ideas — he was a physician expelled from France for his atheistic writings — was great fun for short periods. All in all, he was in "the paradise of philosophers."

66

VOLTAIRE found only one thing wrong with paradise. It was boring. He soon missed the excitement of Paris and the intellectual stimulus of the d'Argentals, not to mention Marie Louise's pretty little bottom. A monastic society generally has a pecking order, and the king's court was no exception. People were envious of Voltaire's position, and he was never one to hide his exalted intelligence. D'Arnaud particularly resented him. In an ugly scene, fomented by the king, Voltaire taxed the young poet with ingratitude toward his niece, Madame Denis, who had been so kind to him. D'Arnaud replied that that was why he had slept with her! Voltaire furiously demanded that d'Arnaud be banished from the court, and Frederick reluctantly agreed.

Voltaire had been planning for some time to return to France but continued to postpone his departure on the grounds of poor health. Though regally housed in the Berlin palace for the carnival, he hated the cold, and his illness lingered. "I am so sick that I no longer feel my afflictions," he told Darget. "My soul is dead and my body dying." [1]

Money revived him.

For some years affluent Prussians had been making large profits by redeeming discounted Saxon notes at full value, a traffic that Frederick had finally forbidden to save Saxony from bankruptcy. Such a transaction held immediate appeal to Voltaire, an experienced and greedy speculator. Ignoring the king's edict, he gave a broker ten thousand thalers to buy Saxon notes at discount in Dresden and bring them to Berlin for redemption. This luckless man, a Berlin Jew named Abraham Hirschel, gave Voltaire some diamonds as security. When Hirschel produced no quick profit, Voltaire decided he had been swindled and stupidly brought a lawsuit. The ensuing publicity in European courts annoyed Frederick. "It is a matter of a rogue cheating a swindler," he wrote to Wilhelmina, but he nonetheless appointed the grand chancellor, Cocceji, to adjudicate. Hirschel was found guilty and sentenced to several years of hard labor. Voltaire paid a small fine, but his image suffered; he was the laughingstock of Europe. He had also acquired scurvy and lost two front teeth. And he had angered his royal patron, who had shown him every kindness and consideration during his lengthy illness. His abject letters brought candid replies. "I kept the peace in my house until your arrival," Frederick wrote to him, "and I inform you that if you have a passion for intrigue and cabal, you have come to the wrong man. . . . If you can make up your mind to live like a philosopher, I shall be very glad to see you here; but if you abandon yourself to all the transports of your passions, and if you wish to be at odds with everybody, you will give me no pleasure by coming, and you may as well remain in Berlin." Voltaire hastened to eat crow and soon returned to Potsdam.

Frederick was not being altogether altruistic. He still wanted Voltaire's tutelage. In early April he had been sent a copy of Count Maurice of Saxony's *Les Rêveries*. The rambling work so amused him that he decided to write a long poem on the art of war, "as Ovid had put the art of love in verse form," he wrote to William. As was his way, he was soon churning out reams of rhyme for Voltaire's perusal. Voltaire not only corrected the work, some sixteen hundred lines, but added three hundred lines of his own. He also objected to the vague and languid style, incorrect choice of words, and imprecise imagery.[2] Frederick slavishly respected his objections. The final work, *L'Art de la Guerre,* was completed in August and published the following year. It owes a great deal to Boileau and Voltaire and it would be pleasant to praise it. Alas, it is a dreadful piece of work, a paean to German arms extolled and frequently quoted by generations of German historians.

Ironically it brought a sort of peace to Potsdam during a particularly exciting time for the *beaux esprits*. In late June the first volume of Diderot and d'Alembert's *Encyclopédie* was published. It has been called "the most famous of all experiments in the popularization of knowledge," and it must have been the subject of lively debate in the Sans-Souci dining hall.[3] Voltaire had suddenly become much more attractive. Like many writers, he was at his best when creating. He was eating three meals a day and growing stronger. "I have lived six consecutive months with my king," he wrote to a friend, "eating like a devil and taking, like him, a little powdered rhubarb every other day. Imagine an admirable château, the master of which leaves me entire liberty, beautiful gardens, good cheer, a little employment, society, and delicious suppers with a philosopher-king who forgets his five victories and his greatness."[4] At the end of August he wrote to the Duke of Richelieu that he had been entirely seduced by "the large blue eyes of the king, by his gentle smile and charming voice," not to mention his devotion to work, his many kindnesses, and the gift of delicious liberty that he had never enjoyed in France.[5]

But snakes were at work in paradise.

Voltaire wrote to Marie Louise in early September that the physician La Mettrie often spoke privately with the king and that they had discussed Voltaire's position at court and the jealousy it caused. According to La Mettrie, the king said, "I shall have need of him for another year at the very most; one squeezes the orange and throws away the peel." Voltaire was stunned. He brooded over the matter for the next few months and probably would have continued to quiz La Mettrie had that wórthy gentleman not suddenly died.

Enter Pierre Louis Moreau de Maupertuis, president of the Academy of Sciences and Letters, highly regarded by the king, given a magnificent house near the royal park outside Berlin. Here he maintained a botanical garden and experimented with breeding of various animals, including humans. He was the guiding genius of the Academy, as shown by his extensive and intimate correspondence with the king; he had corrected many of Frederick's literary works; he had recruited some excellent talent; he had expanded the anatomical college and opened a school for midwives; he was about to open a school of astronomy; and he had other projects in mind. But Maupertuis was claimed by what Frederick called an "uneasy spirit." He was irritable and given to jealousy — and he drank far too much brandy, which in part accounted for his perpetual poor health.

Maupertuis did not appreciate Voltaire's royal reception, which carried with it a salary larger than his own. He resented Voltaire's fame and showed it. Voltaire in turn complained of Maupertuis's "tyrannical" running of the Academy and, according to the king, wanted to replace him as its president. "I suffer Maupertuis," he wrote to Marie Louise in autumn of 1751, "not having been able to pacify him."[6]

That might have been the end of it, except for a quarrel in the Academy. A rift had been developing there for some years between one school of thought, headed by Maupertuis and the mathematician Euler, and another, headed by Formey, the Academy's secretary, who favored the philosophical school of Gottfried Leibniz and Christian Wolff. In 1752 Maupertuis and one of his protégés, Samuel Koenig, fell out over this same question, and Koenig wrote a paper that accused Maupertuis of being a scientific fraud. Koenig could not produce cited evidence — a letter from Leibniz — and was expelled from the Academy; he subsequently published an account of the affair. Voltaire leaped to Koenig's aid and anonymously published a paper in his defense. Frederick did not want Maupertuis or the Academy humiliated, so *he* anonymously published a not very satisfactory reply to Voltaire's work. Everyone knew the king had written it, and Voltaire unwisely demolished its arguments in a published letter to Koenig.

As the nineteenth-century biographer James Parton wrote, the affair should have ended there, with no one very happy and no one really harmed. But Maupertuis, who was very upset and was drinking heavily, sought to repair his reputation by publishing a book of twenty-three *Letters,* in which, among other projects, he proposed to dig an enormous hole in the earth in order to see what was there; to blow up an Egyptian pyramid to see why it had been built; to found a Latin-speaking city and thereby improve the language; to refuse payment to a doctor until the patient was cured. "Maupertuis has become entirely mad," Voltaire wrote to his niece in early October.[7] He followed with a work, *Diatribe of Doctor Akakia,* that satirized the *Letters* and tore Maupertuis to pieces: "If these imaginary letters were really written by a president, it could only be a president of Bedlam."[8] This was published under a false license and widely distributed.

Frederick had warned Voltaire not to publish this work, because it ridiculed the Prussian monarchy and nobility. Voltaire was already skating on thin ice; at the start of the quarrel Lord Marshal Keith had warned him that "someday, some big Prussian will box your ears," and Maupertuis had told the king that his guest was openly criticizing the royal verses, which he described as "dirty laundry" for him to wash. Voltaire agreed to burn the manuscript, but instead persuaded the king's own printer to produce the work. Frederick wrote him a strong letter — "If your works entitle you to statues, your conduct deserves chains" — and put him under apartment arrest until he agreed to behave himself. "I have frightened him on the side of the purse" (with a large fine), Frederick told Maupertuis, "and it has had all the effect I expected. I have declared that my house is to be a sanctuary, and not a retreat for brigands and scoundrels to distill poisons in."

The court had moved to Berlin for the Christmas carnival when copies of *Doctor Akakia* appeared in local bookstores. Frederick had them publicly burned in three places and on Christmas Eve wrote to Maupertuis, seriously ill with fever, a charming letter that enclosed the ashes "as a cooling powder."

Voltaire already had decided to leave Prussia. "I see plainly that the orange has been squeezed," he wrote to Marie Louise. "It is necessary now to think of saving the rind." On New Year's Day of 1753, he sent the king his Order of Merit and chamberlain's key and announced his return to France in a self-pitying letter. Frederick returned the trinkets, a shaky peace was restored, and Voltaire finally departed in late March, ostensibly to take the waters at Plombières. He took not only the trinkets with him but also a volume of the king's own poetry that in part defamed royal contemporaries. At Leipzig, Voltaire received a threatening letter from Maupertuis and replied by publishing a new, even more insulting *Doktor Akakia,* which was immensely popular. After a leisurely journey through Gotha, where he and his secretary, Collini, were guests of the ducal family, he reached Frankfurt in late May.

"I laugh at your impotent wrath . . ." the king wrote to him. "Confess that you were born to be the prime minister of Cesar Borgia."[9] The king wrote to Wilhelmina that Voltaire "has behaved like the greatest scoundrel in the universe. . . . It is indeed a pity that the great talents of that man should be tarnished by the blackest and most perfidious soul, which embitters and spoils his whole existence." He had already ordered his representative in Frankfurt, Franz von Freytag, to intercept the famous man of letters and retrieve the medal, key, and all writings in the king's hand, including the volume of poetry. If Voltaire resisted, he was to be arrested.

Freytag carried out his mission with what Frederick termed "a brutal exactitude," which included an initial interrogation of eight hours! Although Voltaire surrendered the medal and key, he could not locate the volume of poetry. Freytag put him under house arrest at the Golden Lion Inn. Voltaire wrote indignant letters to the Holy Roman Emperor — Frankfurt was an imperial or "free" city* — and to Minister d'Argenson, one of his supporters in France. But Marie Louise turned up before the missing volume. "I come here to conduct my uncle to the waters of Plombières," she wrote to King Frederick. "I find him dying, and, as a climax of evils, under arrest, by Your Majesty's orders, in an inn, without being able to breathe the open air."[10] After three weeks of quasi-imprisonment, Voltaire and Collini tried to escape, were caught, and, if Collini is to be believed, roughed up and had money and jewels taken. They and Marie Louise were put in separate rooms under guard in the scruffy Goat Inn. (The Golden Lion refused to have them back because of Voltaire's "incredible parsimony.") The missing volume finally turned up, and two weeks later Frederick ordered their release.

Voltaire and his niece never forgave the king. Marie Louise later took vengeance by telling Madame de Pompadour of Frederick's disdain for her (which had serious political repercussions). Voltaire took vengeance by writing his secret memoirs, in which he accused Frederick of homosexuality. The work was not published until after Voltaire's death.† Frederick himself was relieved that the affair was over: "You

---

* Voltaire was being held illegally, but Prussian influence in Frankfurt was so strong that the city fathers did not dare interfere.

† In late 1752 an anonymous and scurrilous volume of Frederick's alleged homosexual affairs was published in Paris. Voltaire broke an eight-month silence to write to the king, disclaiming authorship. Frederick replied, "I never believed you were the author of these libels; I know your style too well. Even if you were, I would gladly forgive you." (Friedrich der Grosse, Briefwechsel . . . mit Voltaire, Volume 3.) Frederick wrote to Lord Marshal Keith that the volume did not in the least upset him. No ruler yet had escaped poisonous treatment — and he did not want to be an exception to the rule. (Gooch, Frederick the Great.) Frederick wrote to Maupertuis in late 1753 that Voltaire was the author of the libels, which he wrote in a disguised style. Voltaire's further letters to the king for some time were formally and coldly answered by Frederick's reader.

won't catch me that way again," he wrote to Lord Marshal Keith in Paris.

Time would repair some of the damage. The poet and the king would eventually resume a pleasant correspondence. But they would never again meet.

67

IN THE SUMMER OF 1752 Frederick informed Maupertuis that he was writing a serious work. Like the history of his early reign, it would have to remain a state secret. He was in a particularly pensive mood: "I have lost almost all my friends and old acquaintances and I find consolation only in study and work." He finished the project in late August: "My thoughts are so somber that I am ashamed; I am making a political testament."

Written from April to August — written, that is, at a time of extreme political tension in the north, of the largest military maneuvers ever held in Prussia, of a nasty attack of gout, of a disruptive quarrel with Voltaire, of Prince Henry's reluctant marriage, and of the many daily tasks of running a kingdom — *The Political Testament* remained totally secret until it was read by Frederick's successor, thirty-four years later. It is a lengthy work that reviews Prussia's administrative, legal, and financial machinery, the king's activities, taxes, treasury, internal improvements, industrial and agricultural production, army — the state of the kingdom in general; where it has been and where it is going. Of particular interest is the diplomatic portion, which tells us more about the king's thinking than many later works by learned men.

Prussia was surrounded by powerful and jealous powers, the king wrote. Austria was the most ambitious. Maria Theresa, who had inherited her father's arrogance, wanted only to enslave Germany while expanding her territory: "Her current policy is to re-establish her army, put her finances in order and maintain the peace until her arrangements are completed, to strengthen [her] alliances, as she has done in uniting the most closely in a short time with Russia, England, and Saxony."

England was a similar evil. King George II, Frederick's uncle, hated Prussia because of her quarrels with Hanover and increase in power. For this reason he supported Austria. But that support would end with his death. His successor would not allow Hanover to influence British diplomacy to such a dangerous degree.

Russia was not a real enemy but rather an "accidental enemy"; the enmity was the work of Bestushev, whose rude withdrawal of the Russian envoy from Berlin in 1750 had caused the present diplomatic stalemate. This would change with Bestushev's death. But Russia would continue to keep her hold on Poland, to work with Austria in defending against the Turkish threat, and to maintain as best she could an influence in northern affairs. Fortunately the Russian empire was ruled "by a sensual woman who abandons the care of her affairs to a minister corrupted by other powers. . . . Her successor [Grand Duke Peter] is a prince without intelligence, without descendants, and, more, hated by the Russians."

Saxon enmity stemmed in large part from Count Brühl, a corrupt man whose stupid politics resulted in an alliance with Russia and Austria "that exposed the royal family to all the hazards of war without giving them the least hope of profiting from the advantages."

Holland was another fringe enemy without the regents' knowing why. Holland hated France and had abandoned itself to England, who had ruined its maritime commerce. It suspected that France and Prussia would like to seize the republic: "Distrustful, uncertain, envious, totally feeble, and without money."

Of the friendly powers, France was the most powerful in Europe, dedicated to reducing the power of Austria, supporting the rights of Imperial princes, diminishing England's maritime commerce, supporting her ally, Spain, maintaining her influence in the north, and playing a major role in all the affairs of Europe while moving her borders to the Rhine. Unfortunately, she was ruled by a feeble prince whose authority was divided among his ministers. Thanks to an avaricious mistress, la Pompadour, and venal courtiers, the treasury was empty and the kingdom labored under debts. In a country where "pleasure is the god," affairs must naturally suffer. France was not a good ally. Her treaties were designed to put the entire burden on the partner so that she remained free to act as she pleased.

Sweden's prime concern was Russia: "Her animosity against Muscovy incites her to revenge herself for her last unfortunate war . . . but if her hatred animates her, her impotence holds her back." As an ally, she was a burden, able only to call for help, not render it.

Denmark was intent on seizing Holstein and holding down Sweden. Basically a sea power, she was not much of an aggressive threat but would be able to defend herself from land attack.

Feudal Poland remained divided and weak, of danger to no one.

The Empire was more divided than ever: "A King of England crosses the Channel with a bag of guineas, and some moderate sums serve to corrupt the most powerful of the Corps Germanique. They have become merchants; they deal in the blood of their subjects [that is, by leasing out soldiers]; they sell their votes in the College of Princes and that of the Electors. I believe that they would sell themselves if someone could be found to buy them." Their loyalties were various. Allied to Vienna were the Electors of Hanover, Saxony, Bavaria, Mainz, Trèves, and the eccelsiastical princes. Allied to France and Prussia were the Elector Palatine, the Elector of Cologne, and the Dukes of Württenberg and Brunswick. Those still up for auction were Hesse and Saxe-Gotha.

Powers of lesser interest to Prussia were Spain and Portugal. Spain was inseparable from France for reasons of maritime commerce and her pretensions against Austria in Italy. Portugal and Sardinia were not very important, nor was the Papacy with its moribund pope, content to keep his job and say quiet masses at Saint Peter's.

The Turkish empire was ruled by a feeble man, Sultan Mahmud I. His advisers were profoundly ignorant of European affairs, his army obsolete; but thanks to Persian civil wars, he was free to attack Russia or Austria.

The Prussian king regarded Europe "as a republic of sovereigns divided into two powerful parties," France and England. Power was balanced between them. "This policy, once established in Europe, prevents large conquests and renders wars fruitless, unless they are conducted with a large superiority and unvarying [good] fortune."

What was Prussia's position? Such was the current situation

> that Prussia will never lack allies. In order to select them it is necessary to cast off all personal hatred and prejudice, be it contrary, be it favorable. The interest of the state is the sole motive that should rule in the council of Princes. Our present interests, particularly after the acquisition of Silesia, are to remain united with France, likewise with all the enemies of the House of Austria. Silesia and Lorraine are two sisters of whom Prussia has married the elder and France the younger. This alliance obliges them to follow the same policy.

Neither could afford to see the loss of the other's territory with the concomitant strengthening of Austrian power. The alliance also extended in the other direction, with France contesting England, Prussia contesting Hanover: "This is the same thing, and the interests of two courts find themselves on common ground. . . . You see that this alliance is natural, that all the interests of the two crowns are mutual, and that, accordingly, the particular circumstances of Europe have formed these bonds rather than the ability of negotiators." There was a final reason. Prussia could expect territorial rewards from an alliance with France but none from an alliance with Austria or England.

Although King Frederick expected war, his present policy was to prolong peace for as long as possible. It was necessary for France to repair her finances and escape from "total lethargy." For a war to succeed, Bestushev had to be toppled, his successor won over; the King of

England had to die; Turkey had to have a new ruler; France had to find an ambitious and powerful premier. Even if these conditions were met, Prussia should act cautiously, allowing others to wear themselves out in fighting if possible. His successor was to remember Cardinal Fleury's maxim: "The one who remains the master of his adversary is the one who has the last penny in his pocket."

Meanwhile the King of Prussia had to be many things to many people. An invariable conduct, an unchangeable character, allowed an enemy to predict one's reactions. "The great art is to hide one's plans, and for this it is necessary to cloak one's character and give only a hint of a strength measured and tempered by justice." It was vital to remember that "each circumstance, each time, each person, demands a different treatment."

Negotiations were, of course, important to successful policy. Qualified and incorruptible ambassadors were vital to the process, which is why he had founded a school for ambassadors in Berlin, where twelve young gentlemen were being trained for foreign service. Spies were also vital. Since 1747 the Austrian ambassador's secretary in Berlin had reported regularly, and since early 1752 a chancery clerk in Dresden, Friedrich Menzel, had reported secrets of the Saxon Cabinet, particularly its correspondence with Saint Petersburg and Vienna: "These types of wretches are useful; they are like compasses that guide navigators while the somber clouds of politics leave them in the dark." On the other hand, the ruler must take extraordinary precautions to see that his own officials are not corrupted.

What of the future? The House of Brandenburg held incontestable rights over Bayreuth, Ansbach, and Mecklenburg (the last contested by Hanover). Legality aside, nothing could benefit Prussia more than acquiring Saxony, Prussian Poland, and Swedish Pomerania. Saxony would be the most useful acquisition, since it would provide Prussia with a fortified frontier against Austria.

How were these territories to be acquired?

> One must dissemble and hide one's plan, profit from events, patiently await those which are favorable and when they have arrived act with vigor. What would facilitate this conquest would be if Saxony were in alliance with the Queen of Hungary, and that this Princess or her descendants broke with Prussia. Here would be a pretext to invade Saxony in order to disarm her troops and entrench oneself in the country.

Frederick found this idea so appealing that he offered his successor a rough operations plan. For it to succeed, the Ottoman Porte would have to keep Russia busy; Prussia would have to raise as many enemies as possible against Austria to cause a division of forces.

Once Saxony was subjugated, Prussia would carry the war to Moravia: "A decisive battle won in this province would open the gates of Olmütz and Brünn and the war would approach [Vienna]." This effort would be helped by an auxiliary force of forty thousand troops raised in Saxony, auxiliaries hired from Imperial princes, and twenty thousand troops recruited in Hungary. Part of this force would easily conquer Bohemia. If England objected, France would threaten Hanover. Peace would give France all of Flanders, Moravia would be returned to Austria, the Polish king would receive Bohemia — and Prussia would keep Saxony. It was an ambitious plan, Frederick admitted, but even if all of Saxony were not conquered, Prussia could seize at least a part.

The next most desirable province was Polish Prussia, whose possession would further consolidate the kingdom and largely eliminate the Russian threat to East Prussia. But the preferred means for the acquisition of this country would be political, not military: "Acquisitions made by the pen are always preferable to those made by the sword. Less chance is incurred, and neither treasury nor army is ruined." The acquisition of Polish Prussia brought to mind, Frederick wrote, what King Victor Amadeus of Sardinia had told Charles Emmanuel: "My son, it is necessary to devour the Milanese as one eats an artichoke, leaf by leaf." A factious and corrupt elective monarchy, it was to be acquired by city and district. The length of the Vistula, including Thorn, Elbing, and Marienwerder, would be fortified. Danzig would be reserved as "the last morsel," since it would make all of Poland subject to Prussian whim.

The third most desirable acquisition was Swedish Pomerania, but this could be gained only by treaty, which Frederick regarded as unlikely but possible under certain circumstances.

These few pages left no doubt to his successor that he recommended a vigorous and bold policy of expansion:

> If this House produces great princes, if the army is kept in its present discipline, if the sovereigns economize in time of peace to provide the costs of war, if they know [how] to profit from events with ability and sagacity, finally if they have come to an agreement themselves, I do not doubt that the state will increase and aggrandize itself, and that in time Prussia will become one of the most important powers of Europe.

68

ALTHOUGH *The Political Testament* discounted the value of France as an ally — "to be her ally was to be her slave," as Frederick earlier had put it — he continued to cultivate this court for the rest of 1752. In early October he sent King Louis an extraordinary letter "with all the candor and trust that I owe to such a good ally." He began by complimenting the French king for maintaining the tranquillity of the north and protecting Charles Theodor, Elector Palatine, against Anglo-Austrian evils.

But his main point was how to maintain the present fragile peace in Europe. Having condemned Machiavelli, he now proposed a simple Machiavellian solution. France was to persuade the Ottoman Porte to make war on Austria! Sultan Mahmud I would protect himself by sending his Janissaries off to war, thus preventing their plotting against him. Such a war would exhaust Austrian finances and ruin her army, because it would be fought in the pestilential climate of Hungary. Russia would join in, but she was short of money and had no decent generals: "These troops can be regarded as a strong body with no head." England could not support her allies financially. If Austria defeated Turkey, she would gain only Serbia and could not threaten European peace for another ten years. "Our interests and intentions are the same," he concluded; "we want peace, and I believe that what I propose is the most certain way to maintain it." He did not add that Austrian impotence would open the way for his own expansionist dreams in Saxony, Poland, and Pomerania.

Frederick wrote to King Louis again in December, this time about Polish affairs. If Austria succeeded in placing Prince Charles on the Polish throne, that would upset the balance of power and would mean the enslavement of Germany and wars for France more violent than any since the reign of Charles V.* Frederick called for an alliance between France, Sweden, and Prussia to support Poland, but the only real guarantee of peace was his earlier plan to persuade the Porte to go to war against Austria and Russia.

The Prussian envoy in Paris, Lord Marshal Keith, warned that France was in no position to act on this proposal. Nor would it be an easy matter to win Madame de Pompadour's favor. King Louis's negative reply confirmed Keith's warning, and for the moment there seemed nothing more for Frederick to do other than observe events.

---

*Emperor Charles V, 1500–1558. His conflict with Francis I of France led to four bloody wars.

Frederick's diplomatic position did not essentially change in 1753. To the Prince of Prussia's optimistic suggestion that the peace would continue, the king replied: "Do you not imagine, my dear brother, there are a hundred envious and a hundred opportunities that can stir up things, and, unless one is deprived of reason and foresight, one can not be too much on one's guard and cannot consolidate too much the arrangements necessary to resist the large number of enemies that we have."

Nor was he exaggerating. His new spy in Dresden was supplying copies of secret diplomatic dispatches to and from Dresden, Saint Petersburg, and Vienna. Saxony seemed ready to sign the Treaty of Saint Petersburg and thus join the anti-Prussian alliance of England, Russia, and Austria. That summer England proposed a subsidy treaty with Russia, whereby a corps of Russian troops would march to Hanover's defense if necessary. The Vienna court continued its anti-Prussian propaganda campaign in the Empire and elsewhere. Taken together, these formed a "base conspiracy" (in the king's words) against Prussia.

He found it difficult to counter politically. France was nudging bankruptcy and behaving more lethargically than ever. At this dismal point Frederick's main ally was his army. That September he held the enormous Spandau review and maneuvers, which he strengthened psychologically by refusing to allow foreign observers. He was also successful in sabotaging Russian-Austrian plans at the Polish Diet, again in conjunction with French diplomacy.

There was a similar political story in 1754. He continued to try to arouse Versailles from inactivity, but his frustration is clear from his dispatches. Politically impotent, he turned to lighter matters. Marshal Keith was to find "a really good cook who has a very delicate taste and who can make these light and subtle sauces which are so popular at present." He received Belle-Isle's son, Count Gisors, that spring and allowed him to witness otherwise secret military reviews — presumably so that his reports would rouse France from its sleep. In late May he inspected Pomerania and Magdeburg and in late June spent a few days in Bayreuth before taking the waters at Sans-Souci. Lord Marshal Keith returned from Paris because of ill health. He was replaced by Baron von Knyphausen, who was soon being threatened with dismissal if he did not start behaving like a diplomat rather than a simple gazetteer.

Sterile diplomacy is often dangerous diplomacy in that it allows problems to develop that are later difficult if not impossible to solve. If 1753 and 1754 were inactive years politically, they nevertheless saw the continuation of the dangerous if undeclared war between England and France. Although quiescent and confined largely to the sea, it would evolve into a war for possession of North America and the Indies, a war that, ironically, would be fought mainly in Europe and mainly by powers not remotely interested in overseas possessions.

(🔮)

The Turkish sultan died early in 1755. Despairing of French action in Constantinople, Frederick sent his own man, a young lieutenant named Hande, to see whether a treaty of alliance was possible, to determine who could be bribed for how much, and to procure all possible information on the new sultan, Osman Ibrahim. Hande traveled as one Karl Adolf von Rexin, privy commercial counsel and chargé d'affaires, and was provided with 300,000 thalers in letters of credit.

England and France meanwhile had begun a naval race that Frederick believed would lead to war at sea and, in a year or so, to war in Europe. In early April he regarded this war as inevitable and directed Knyphausen to suggest "very adroitly" to the new foreign minister, Count Anton Ludwig Rouillé, that France should at once seize Hanover and then ask England whether she would like to make peace.

Rouillé welcomed the suggestion and wondered whether Prussia would undertake this operation on behalf of its ally. Knyphausen was to explain that this was easier to suggest than to execute, since sixty thousand Russian troops were in Kurland, Saxony was allied with England, eighty thousand Austrians were ready to attack Prussia, and both Denmark and the Porte were question marks. Frederick's major concern was the threat from Russia, which France could scarcely neutralize. He saw no urgent need at this time to renew his treaty with France; it would not expire for another year. He agreed with Podewils that Versailles should state the terms of renewal, particularly since France was faced with what could well be a ruinous war.

Frederick did not like the way the war was going for France. If France had won the upper hand in the Ohio Valley, it was suffering heavy losses at sea. Part of the problem, Knyphausen reported, was Madame de Pompadour, who insisted on a naval war, because a land war would mean separation from King Louis!

Convinced that the undeclared war was going to involve Germany, Frederick announced his willingness in Paris, London, and Vienna to mediate a peace between France and England. The French court was now thoroughly alarmed. At Frederick's request, Rouillé proposed to send a special envoy, Duke Louis Jules Nivernois, "to confer with [Frederick] on the measures that it would be appropriate to take relative to the act of hostility that England had just committed." Frederick was willing to receive Nivernois, but not to commit himself. He was appalled by French weakness. If it keeps up, he wrote to Knyphausen, the French will have no allies and will have lost all the respect they had in Europe. One course only could retrieve their fortunes: seizing Hanover immediately. Once lost, time and opportunity can never be regained.

British diplomacy gained while French diplomacy faltered. Lord Robert d'Arcy Holdernesse stressed to the Duke of Brunswick that the peace of Germany was dependent on the Prussian king. England wanted no less than a "formal promise" that Prussia would undertake nothing against Hanover nor would she aid France in any such attack. Frederick, not surprisingly, refused to commit himself but did point out that the present quarrel was stupid, that "the game was not worth the candle." The Canadian territories that England and France were fighting over were not worth the cost of what he later called "the codfish war." He wanted immediate mediation by Austria, Holland, Spain, and Denmark; he would employ his good offices with France. There was no reason that satisfactory peace preliminaries could not be reached by spring. Brunswick could also inform Holdernesse that once Prussia's treaty with France expired, Frederick would be amenable to English propositions concerning the neutrality of Hanover. Holdernesse replied that England would like to ally with Prussia. All very well, Frederick said, but there were problems, such as Britain's refusal to pay reparations for ships illegally seized. For what reason, he continued, should he abandon an alliance with France? He would have to have "a much more clear and direct" proposal before deciding anything. Affairs thus remained in limbo.

From Vienna, the Prussian envoy, Klinggraeffen, reported the disturbing news that increased military preparations pointed to "some design": enforced recruitment, the purchase of cavalry horses, the refurbishing of artillery, the building of magazines in Bohemia. From Russia came reports of more troops assembled in Kurland and Livonia, where trains of artillery and large magazines were being prepared while troop galleys were being sent to Reval. The two courts, Vienna and Saint Petersburg, were said to be holding secret conversations, from which the king feared the worst.

The British approach thus found a willing ear at Potsdam. In late November, Abraham Michell, the Prussian resident secretary in London, reported that Henry Fox, a Cabinet minister, had stated his devotion to King Frederick. Lord Holdernesse had stressed to Michell the defensive nature of the subsidy treaty with Russia. He read the treaty to Michell and added that King George, who wished to unite closely with Frederick, would renew all previous guarantees to Prussia, "that, in the brilliant position of Your Majesty, you can prevent the fire from starting in Germany and can conserve the peace there, that Your Majesty held the olive branch in one hand and the sword in the other, that thus it was up to him to consider which one he would like to use." Holdernesse promised to settle the ship reparations question, provided that Prussia paid off the Silesian mortgages. Michell was taken to Lord Newcastle, who confirmed everything Holdernesse had said.

Here was a diplomatic offensive; here were words with meat — and Frederick relished them. He replied through Michell that he intended to do all possible to maintain the peace in Europe, and that a treaty of neutrality between England and Prussia for Germany would help him reconcile England and France. He appreciated the new guarantees. He regarded the reparations question as a "bagatelle," but since it caused trouble, it should be done away with. He would also like England to offer freedom of commerce for Prussian ships during the present war or at least to define "contraband cargo."

At year's end he had not decided whether he should ally with France or England — or either. He would have liked peace. Lacking that, however, there was no doubt that he was moving closer to his uncle's island kingdom.

69

RAPPROCHEMENT with England continued into the new year, 1756. Frederick's warm reply to British proposals drew an enthusiastic response from Whitehall. England agreed to pay Prussia £20,000 in reparations for seized cargoes, and Frederick agreed to pay off the Silesian mortgages. Those formalities out of the way, the two powers signed what the Prussian king called "a convention of neutrality," an agreement to keep Germany neutral for as long as France and England were at war.

The Convention of Westminster upset the French court. Baron von Knyphausen had warned that it was not necessary, since France had no intention of invading Hanover. Versailles would view a treaty with England as a great insult; it was a matter of *amour propre*. The king's best policy, Knyphausen sagely advised, was to remain neutral and persuade France to guarantee Germany's neutrality.

By the time Frederick received these dispatches, the Duke of Nivernois, Versailles's special envoy, had arrived in Berlin. Although Frederick appreciated Knyphausen's analysis, he wrote, he could not understand what all the fuss was about. French diplomacy had been virtually stagnant. Nivernois was supposed to have come in September but did not appear until January. He had been well received; Podewils had been completely open with him; there was no conflict of interest between the new treaty and the present treaty with France. Frederick did not have to ask Versailles for permission to treat with anyone, and he wanted to renew the present alliance with France despite its hostile statements.

The king assumed this innocent posture in other courts. Privately he regarded the treaty as a diplomatic coup, not so much because it would help prevent war but because it drove a wedge into what he regarded as the anti-Prussian alliance of England, Russia, Austria, and Saxony — "a formidable league under which sooner or later the State would have to succumb," as he described it to the Prince of Prussia. "This is how the Romans divided their enemies, and in fighting them one by one, conquered all of them." He continued:

> This year [of peace] that I believe to have gained is worth more to me than the five preceding ones, and if subsequently I can serve as mediator to the belligerent powers, I will have made the greatest role possible for Prussia in peacetime; and don't underestimate the pleasure of seeing the Queen of Hungary checked, to humiliate or rather annihilate Saxony, to drive Bestushev to despair. Here are the results that will come from a small stroke of the pen.

The treaty also produced a bad effect in Vienna, whose court was amazed that two electors of the Empire had dared to make a treaty without even telling the emperor, much less asking his permission. But Count Kaunitz, now Maria Theresa's first minister, regarded it as "the decisive event to Austria's salvation," by which he meant that it would wean the French court from its present pusillanimous negotiations in favor of an aggressive treaty devoted to Prussia's demise.[1] Frederick was aware of the possibility of an alliance between France and Austria, but it would probably involve no more than the neutrality of the Low Countries, and he doubted that it would be directed against him: French and Austrian interests were diametrically opposed and France would never dream of aggrandizing its former enemy. He repeatedly emphasized to concerned envoys that France would never contribute to Austria's welfare and that Austria would never forsake her alliance with Britain — a bold and totally inaccurate analysis shared by the British court.

Adding to his optimism were Nivernois's favorable reports to Versailles. Frederick had opened the ratified treaty from England in Nivernois's presence and allowed him to read it, including the secret articles. Both Frederick and Podewils liked the envoy, "who appears to me of a very estimable character," Frederick told Maupertuis, "with much intelligence and knowledge; he is without pretentions, his simple manners bespeak the sincerity of his soul." The envoy responded in kind. But Knyphausen reported from Paris that the copy of the treaty sent by Nivernois had caused "the greatest consternation" in the French court.

Frederick regarded this as momentary pique, which would vanish once Nivernois returned to France and explained the Prussian king's desire to bring peace between France and England. Frederick sent England's preliminary offers to the French court in late February. England was willing to make some minor boundary adjustments in Nova Scotia and to return some captured French warships. Frederick apologized for not having obtained a better offer, but at least King Louis would see that "I never lose sight of his interests or his glory."

This confused and volatile situation continued for another two months. France spurned British offers and demanded the return of her warships before talks could proceed. Frederick continued to pour oil on troubled waters but at the same time was upset by the negotiations between France and Austria. He learned that the Russian court had not yet ratified the subsidy treaty with England. On the favorable side, Versailles dispatched the Marquis de Valory to Berlin for the forthcoming treaty negotiations between France and Prussia. England was also going to send a new ambassador to Berlin. At Versailles, Nivernois stressed Frederick's desire for peace. Knyphausen suggested that the Prussian king write directly to Madame de Pompadour, in view of her increasing power. Frederick replied that if she wished to make him some offers, perhaps he would respond, but otherwise it would only be a crass gesture.*

Knyphausen next reported that Austrian rapprochement with France was what Count Kaunitz had been assiduously cultivating since 1749. Although the French foreign minister Rouillé denied that negotiations with Vienna were under way, Frederick warned the English court that the two powers could conceivably conclude a treaty that would allow France to invade Hanover or Holland while Austria struck Prussia, with the Empire remaining neutral. In that case the key would be Russia: "As long as England would be certain of Russia," he wrote to his envoy Michell, "the Austrians would not dare to undertake to change allies and the [European] system."

The English court agreed. Lord Holdernesse continued to assure the Prussian king that "the Petersburg court would always remain attached to English interests, and of that there was not the least doubt," a sentiment repeatedly expressed in the months ahead. Frederick was not so sure. Intercepted dispatches spoke of a strong anti-English faction, headed by the current favorite, Count Ivan Shuvalov, which had been undermining English influence. Czarina Elizabeth reportedly had ratified the subsidy treaty with England, only to regret her action when she learned of England's alliance with Prussia. By mid-April the king seemed to

---

* Empress Maria Theresa had been personally corresponding with Madame de Pompadour for some time. It is also probable that Madame Denis and Voltaire had spread word of Frederick's mocking remarks to antagonize her further.

regard war as inevitable. "It is a matter of having patience," he wrote
to the Prince of Prussia, "and seeing what comes."

The situation began heating up in May with reports that Austria and
France had signed a treaty of neutrality. Then came news of a French
landing at Port Mahon and the seizure of the British-held island of
Minorca. Meanwhile the new British envoy, Andrew Mitchell, arrived
in Berlin. Minister Podewils found the forty-eight-year-old minister "open
and sincere . . . full of good will. He speaks [French] well enough, but
with a very strong English accent." Frederick soon received him warmly
at Potsdam, where he kept him overnight so as to continue the important audience. The son of a Scottish minister, Mitchell was a well-educated and well-traveled lawyer who had become close friends with
Montesquieu when he was in Paris in 1735. His interests went far beyond the law; they included Cicero's philosophical works, the history
of England, Germany, and France, religious orders, morals, Roman
coins, antiquities, epic poetry, statues, engravings, and many other subjects — all of which delighted Frederick.[2]

Mitchell's highly secret reports give us excellent insight into the royal
mind at this crucial period. The king more than once emphatically declared "that He did not think that the Peace of Germany would be
disturbed this Year" (a sharp change from his April thinking). The
French landing on Minorca was unfortunate, because France might
trade Minorca to Spain in return for an alliance against Britain.* Otherwise, Britain had little to fear from France and its weak and irresolute
ministry. He himself had no intention of renewing his present treaty
with France or of guaranteeing French possessions in America, though
as for *that* war, "he could not help wondering at the Absurdity of both
Nations, to exhaust their Strength, and Wealth, for an Object that did
not appear to him to be worth the while." Should France and Austria
form an alliance, Prussia would make common cause with Britain and
would fight both France and Austria. The king was still concerned,
however, about Russia's attitude, which Mitchell assured him was believed in London to be pro-British.[3]

The long and remarkable relationship between the King of Prussia
and the British ambassador was faithfully recorded by Mitchell in several volumes of dispatches and in a personal journal. The two men
struck it off so well that the Prussian envoy in London, Abraham Michell, was instructed to thank Lord Holdernesse for sending "a person
who, although not of the first rank, was worthy of [the king's] esteem
and confidence."

---

* The English court rejected this notion, sensibly arguing that Spain would not commit herself
for such a small return as Minorca.

Sir Andrew Mitchell, British ambassador to Prussia. In 1758 Frederick ordered his new reader, Henri de Catt, to see Mitchell as often as possible. "He is sincerely attached to me, and is a man of very solid and wide education. He is integrity itself."

The battle of Lobositz, October 1756. "I have never seen such prodigies of valor, cavalry as well as infantry," wrote Frederick to Field Marshal Schwerin.

The various themes struck in the initial audience were replayed throughout the month as the danger of war steadily grew. Frederick now saw little hope of reconciling the French and British courts. He was certain that France and Austria had signed a treaty. Austria refused to explain her intentions to England. England intended to declare war on France. All this made the Russian question ever more important, as Frederick repeatedly warned Holdernesse, who insisted that Saint Petersburg remained firmly for England and its alliance with Prussia.

Formal announcement of the Franco-Austrian treaty in early June was anticlimactic, as was Kaunitz's intentionally muddled explanation of the treaty to England. Frederick thought that Kaunitz was mad. He told Mitchell "that this Alliance between the Courts of Vienna and Versailles was unnatural, and could not last." But at the same time Austria would never have signed such a treaty if it did not believe that it could win over Russia. He warned Mitchell "that France was stretching every nerve to gain Russia, that the court of Vienna joined with France in endeavouring to seduce Russia into their cabals, that no pains or expence might be spared to preserve our interests there."[4]

Russia had taken priority in the king's thinking. Should England fail to hold on to this court, then she must win the Ottoman Porte and persuade the sultan to warn Russia and Austria against beginning a war. She must also reinforce her troops in Hanover by subsidizing a host of minor German princes to replace troops that had been withdrawn to England against the threat of a French landing. Frederick also wanted to know whether England would send a fleet into the Baltic to prevent Russian landings in Pomerania in case Russia attacked him. The question was the genesis of what would become a very sore point in Frederick's future relations with Britain. Holdernesse assured the king that, despite extensive naval commitments, King George would use "his utmost efforts" to provide such a fleet when necessary. Holdernesse qualified this commitment in July, because he had been advised by experts that such a fleet would probably be of little use against galleys and vessels that draw little water. But in August he reaffirmed the commitment. Contrary to Frederick's later writing, the convention of Westminster did not promise such a fleet, and it was specifically refused in the renewal treaty of 1758. None of this, however, excused the breaking of a solid pledge to an ally.

Ominous reports kept arriving at Potsdam. Klinggraeffen told of continuing Austrian preparations in Moravia and Bohemia. The Vienna court was planning to establish a large "corps of observation" in Bohemia that would include cavalry regiments presently stationed in Hungary. Ernst von Schlabrendorff, the new Prussian minister in Silesia, confirmed this activity: two thousand peasants working day and night on the Olmütz fortifications, large magazines of grain being assembled, Field Marshal Maximilian Browne and a party of engineers reconnoitering the entire border area as prelude to establishing a corps of thirty thousand troops at Königgrätz, ammunition wagons being constructed at Königgrätz, Pardubitz, and Chrudim, and, finally, cavalry regiments in Hungary alerted for the march to Moravia — a key indicator, in the king's mind, of Austrian offensive intentions.

Frederick responded by reinforcing Silesian regiments and ordering Schlabrendorff to have all magazines ready by autumn. He next received reports of Russian troop concentrations in Livonia and Kurland and of another corps around Smolensk. Count von Finckenstein informed Mitchell that the king "is very desirous to know immediately . . . what Assistance He may reckon upon from England in the present Juncture, in Case he should be attacked . . . and in what shape this assistance is to come, whether in Troops, Ships or Money."[5] Field Marshal Lehwaldt in East Prussia was alerted to the possibility of a Russian attack. In late June the king had "one foot in the stirrup and I believe the other will shortly follow," as he told Wilhelmina.

Marshals Schmettau and Keith and other officers taking the baths at Karlsbad were ordered to return to their posts. Commanders were to call in all furloughed troops. Certain regiments were alerted to move into Pomerania, from where they could march to join Lehwaldt's corps. Mitchell reported that "the Waggons, and other Carriages, are getting ready, everywhere; the Arsenals have been opened, and great quantities of Arms, and Ammunition given out."[6] Finckenstein was to prepare an eighty-page brochure in German and French, reviewing Austrian evils against the Protestant religion.

Frederick was convinced in late June that "a very difficult war" was inevitable. He summed up the situation in a lengthy *mémoire* written expressly for Mitchell and the British court.

> Germany is menaced by great calamities [he concluded]. Prussia momentarily expects to see war break out, but all these unfortunate circumstances do not daunt her; three things can re-establish the balance [of power] in Europe: the close and intimate relation of the two [British and Prussian] courts, some extraordinary efforts to form new alliances and thus thwart enemy goals, and the boldness to face up to the greatest dangers.[7]

70

FREDERICK was still uncertain of Austrian intentions. Vienna was continuing its military buildup, and it seemed likely that the French had agreed to make a diversion in case Austria invaded Silesia. He could march in fifteen days if necessary, he wrote to the Prince of Prussia.* Andrew Mitchell delivered the welcome information in early July that King George would do all possible to send a fleet into the Baltic in case it was needed. Frederick was duly appreciative — the correspondence of this period reads as if Prussia and England had been eternal allies — and replied that he would request it only if absolutely necessary. Mitchell reported that England was working hard to keep Russia within the fold, and recent dispatches confirmed that Saint Petersburg had stopped war preparations and was withdrawing forward regiments.

It was a confused situation, and the tension told on the king. "I am taking the waters to cleanse an old body," he wrote to William in early July, "and to condition it for exertion. I don't yet know what is going to come of all this; my reports are so contradictory that it is impossible to divine the future clearly." He continued to hope that peace would last out the year, but his hope faded as adverse reports reached Potsdam. Knyphausen warned from Paris that Frederick's credit was totally ruined at Versailles: "It has been reported to the king," Knyphausen wrote, "that Your Majesty has openly said that the French government was too weak for its allies to have any confidence in it and that this was a kingdom with many arms but no heads." Klinggraeffen in Vienna reported on Austrian preparations for war. Maria Theresa's strategy was to make Prussia appear the aggressor so that she could claim help from her allies.

Frederick's patience had been wearing thin, and now he acted. Klinggraeffen was ordered to inform Maria Theresa "in my name that, learning from several sources the movements that her troops are making in Bohemia and Moravia, and the number of regiments which have gone there, I ask the empress if this preparation is made for the purpose of attacking me."

Despite the calmness he mentioned in various letters, Frederick was growing more bellicose. Prompted by further reports from the Hague of Russian-Austrian intentions to attack him and, not least, by Lieutenant General Hans von Winterfeldt's aggressive advice, he had probably

---

* Princes William and Henry, who bitterly resented not being consulted on state affairs, were very much against war with France and blamed the situation on the "wicked" Winterfeldt.

decided on fighting a "preventive war" against Austria. In an audience at Potsdam he thanked Andrew Mitchell for his government's offer of support in case Prussia was attacked. If England could keep Russia quiet, Frederick would provide twenty thousand or even thirty thousand troops for Hanover's defense, although he did not believe that the French would attempt anything against Germany this year. But he warned that Russia was absolutely lost to England, that, in Mitchell's words,

> the Russians certainly intended to attack Him this year on one Side, while the Empress-Queen [Maria Theresa] was to have attacked on the other, but that the Russians were not ready, and have been prevented by divers accidents from executing their Part of the Plan; which however He is informed is only deferred till the next Spring. . . . The Intentions of the Court of Vienna have manifested themselves beyond all doubt by the great Preparations made in Bohemia and in Moravia, and by the unguarded Declarations that some of their ministers and generals have made.[1]

Count Podewils was also at Potsdam at this time and in a lengthy session with the king once again played devil's advocate, as he had done in both the First and Second Silesian Wars. He courageously implied that the king's analysis of enemy intentions was not founded on altogether authentic information. Aggressive action on the king's part could bring only terrible consequences and would drive Russia and France into respecting treaty guarantees with Austria. By not acting (although remaining on military alert), the king would gain ten months in which to recruit allies inside and outside the Empire, continue peace negotiations between France and England, and recruit auxiliary troops on England's behalf. The king reacted to this sage advice as Don Quixote did when Sancho Panza advised against the boat trip on the Ebro: "What are you afraid of, cowardly beast? What are you weeping at, butter-heart? Who is pursuing you, soul of a house mouse?"[2] On that Wednesday afternoon in the Potsdam palace, Podewils was abruptly dismissed with the words "Adieu, Monsieur of the timid politics."

Frederick again had "one foot in the stirrup." In late July he told Mitchell that he expected an evasive reply from Maria Theresa but that "if Her Imperial Majesty will give Him Assurances that She will not attack Him, neither this nor the next Year, He will be satisfied and will give reciprocal Assurances to Her Imperial Majesty on His part."[3]

Early on a Monday morning, the second day of August, Eichel hurried to the royal chambers with a dispatch from Klinggraeffen in Vienna. Such was Habsburg protocol, he reported, that several days were required to gain an audience with the empress-queen, but he had finally delivered the Prussian king's message. Never had mountain labored so mightily to bring forth mouse. Holding a little paper in her hand the plump empress read: "That, affairs in general being in crisis, she had judged it appropriate to take some measures for her own security and that of her allies, which would be held as detrimental to no one." According to an unknown officer diarist, the king summoned "Field Marshals Schwerin [and] Keith and the Prince of Prussia and held a long conversation with them. Much was spoken of war."

The king ordered Klinggraeffen by return courier to inform Maria Theresa that the King of Prussia knew of her plans with Russia and knew that the two powers had deferred their attack on Prussia only until the following spring. In view of this knowledge and the continuing Austrian military preparations, which included posting hussars and Croats along his frontiers,

> as if we were in full war, I believe myself to have the right to demand from the Empress a formal and categorical declaration, consisting in an assurance, either oral or in writing, that she has no intention of attacking me, not this year, nor the coming year. . . . It is necessary to know whether we are at war or at peace. I give it to the empress's arbitration. If her intentions are pure, now is the moment to bring them to light; but if I am given an oracle-like reply, uncertain or inconclusive, the Empress will have to blame herself for all the results of her tacit confirmation of the dangerous projects that she has formed with Russia against me.

If the empress-queen gave "a fair and favorable answer" to this demand, he told Mitchell a few days later, he thought that there would be peace in Germany for two years. Meanwhile, he would proceed with his own preparations.

There now occurred a diplomatic accident that in part was the king's fault. Klinggraeffen had not entirely satisfied Frederick as envoy. The king had reprimanded him so often for vacuous reports based on poor sources that poor Klinggraeffen was scared of his own shadow. On receiving the king's new orders, he asked Count Kaunitz to arrange an audience, but Kaunitz demanded a written *mémoire,* to which the empress-queen would reply also in writing. A confident envoy would immediately have complied. Klinggraeffen instead wrote to the king that he felt it was too important for him to undertake, and asked the king to send the necessary document himself.

Frederick received this thunderbolt on August 13. He was understandably furious. Numerous regiments had been alerted to march, and now came "this major blunder," as he wrote to Schwerin (who had taken command of the Silesian regiments and was at Neisse), "which upsets all my plans." A courier immediately took the necessary paper, along with a stinging reprimand, to Klinggraeffen. The king did not expect a satisfactory response, nor was he worried about being branded as "aggressor," he told Mitchell, since the real aggressor was the one who had made the first blow "necessary and unavoidable." Perhaps he recognized the absurdity of this dangerous reasoning, for in the same audience with Mitchell he said "that he wished for nothing so much as peace, he knew he could get nothing by war, and yet he was forced to it." Still, the possibility existed that the Vienna court would reply pacifically. "The Courier from Vienna is not yet returned," Mitchell informed his court on August 24; "the Impatience with which He is expected, is not to be described."[4] Marching orders, which had been sent to key commanders in Berlin, Magdeburg, and Halberstadt, were frantically postponed.

The courier returned the next day with Maria Theresa's reply — "if it could be called a reply," Frederick wrote. The empress-queen denied the existence of an offensive alliance with Russia against Prussia — and nothing more. "The response is impertinent, haughty, and contemptuous," the king wrote to the Prince of Prussia. It was what Frederick expected, and perhaps what he wanted. Klinggraeffen was to make a final attempt to demand the assurances of security that the king requested. This was merely for show. "As I no longer have security for the present or future," he wrote to the envoy, "there remains only the force of arms to confound the plots of my enemies; I march."

"This morning between four and five o'clock," Andrew Mitchell reported on August 28, "I took leave of the King of Prussia, mounted on Horseback. . . . After a very short Exercise of His Troops [He] put Himself at their Head, and marched directly for Belitz, whence, tomorrow, He will enter the Saxon Territory."[5]

BOOK SIX

The Seven Years' War

1756–1763

Hostilities should not be confused with aggression. The one who makes the first plan to attack his neighbor breaks the engagements that he has undertaken for the peace, he plots, he conspires; this is in what true aggression consists. The one who has learned of it and who does not take the initiative is a coward; the one who foresees [the plan of] his enemy commits the first hostilities, but he is not the aggressor.

— *Frederick the Great, August 1756*

THE KING OF PRUSSIA'S plan of operations had been theoretically touched on in *The Political Testament* of 1752. It had subsequently been modified, but his goal remained the defeat of Austria before Maria Theresa and her allies could invade and defeat Prussia.

The first task was to seize Saxony, not only to eliminate her as a threat to future operations but to use her army, treasury, and natural wealth to help fight whatever war developed. The second was to advance the army into Bohemia, there to quarter for the winter at Austria's expense. The third was to invade Moravia from Silesia, seize fortress Olmütz, and advance on Vienna in the hope of ending the war.

Frederick contemplated nothing more than the first two tasks in 1756. Field Marshal Count Kurt von Schwerin was to remain with a corps of twenty-five thousand in Silesia to prevent enemy incursions from Hungary and Moravia. Field Marshal Hans von Lehwaldt, with a corps of thirty thousand, was to guard East Prussia against any Russian move. The main army, which Frederick commanded, was to seize Saxony and proceed into Bohemia.

The main army marched in three corps in the general direction of Pirna. On the right, Prince Ferdinand of Brunswick, with nearly fifteen thousand troops, was to close on Chemnitz; his hussars probed the mountainous border country to the south. On the left, the Duke of Brunswick-Bevern, with nearly eighteen thousand men, would traverse Lusatia to close on Bautzen. In the center, King Frederick, accompanied by Field Marshal Jacob Keith and commanding a force of nearly thirty thousand, was to march toward Dresden. A fleet of three hundred river boats, carrying additional cannon, munitions, food, fodder, and medical supplies, simultaneously sailed from Magdeburg.

It was almost a peacetime exercise. "The Soldiers, flushed with the Memory of their former Successes, set out with a thorough Persuasion of Victory," Andrew Mitchell reported, "and indeed it is surprising to see with what Alacrity and Chearfulness they have returned from their

Harvest Work."[1] The columns crossed the Saxon border on August 29. Forward elements distributed printed proclamations, which were also sent to foreign courts, to justify the Prussian presence and promise good behavior. Companies carried their own bread; commanders requisitioned meat and vegetables by voucher and paid cash for horses. Looting was strictly prohibited, and from all reports incidents were at a minimum.

There was no resistance at first. The Saxon court had learned of Prussian plans and retired its small army to the Pirna defenses. On the day of invasion, Hans Dietrich von Maltzahn, the Prussian envoy to Saxony, met with King August and his prime minister, Count Brühl, to explain the reasons and guarantee the country's security, including that of August's estates, and the well-being of the royal family. August at first accepted the fait accompli but was soon persuaded by Brühl to join the Saxon army near Pirna. From here, he protested the invasion and asked Frederick to leave the country in return for a treaty of neutrality. The royal correspondence was extensive — as Frederick later sardonically wrote, "It was easier for the Saxons to write than to fight."[2] Frederick replied that he wanted the Saxon army disarmed and disbanded — and he occupied Dresden the next day. While August vociferously protested Prussian aggression to European courts, a Saxon council of war agreed to fight until help arrived from Austria.

The three corps meanwhile had closed on their objectives; Dresden yielded five hundred cannon and ten thousand muskets. Frederick confiscated the electoral treasury and income, a task that was delegated to a special War Ministry headed by Minister Friedrich von Borcke in Torgau. Of an estimated annual income of six million thalers, the king would be satisfied with five million (less costs of food and forage deliveries, requisitioned horses, and winter quarters, but supplemented by harsh "contributions" from towns and estates). The king also seized incriminating political documents in the Dresden palace, where Queen Maria Josepha remained in residence. These included the treaty of partition, which called for defeat and dismemberment of Brandenburg-Prussia by Austria, Russia, and Saxony. Frederick replied to a third rejection of his demands by the Vienna court by publishing a lengthy exposé, including incriminating correspondence, to justify his actions. "I have heard a Part of it read," Andrew Mitchell reported; "it is wrote with great Spirit."[3]

The Austrian reply sealed the fact of war. It was now a matter of the Prussians' getting to Bohemia as rapidly as possible. On September 10 the king moved his headquarters to Gross-Sedlitz, west of Pirna; his right extended south to the Duke of Brunswick's corps. Only a few kilometers away the Saxon army held a defensive triangle that ran from fortress Sonnenstein by Pirna, southeast nearly to Langen-Hennersdorf, then in a hook northeast to fortress Königstein, towering above the Elbe almost on the Bohemian border. Marshal Count Friedrich Rutowsky commanded only about twenty thousand troops, but what he lacked in men he made up for in terrain. The Pirna country was once called the Saxon Switzerland, a beautiful wild landscape that built on either side of the Elbe to a series of pine-covered sandstone hills sloping to deep boulder-strewn valleys and streams — twenty miles of torn nature reaching to Teschen.* Rutowsky's major weakness was a shortage of supply, which was aggravated by King August's arrival with a large entourage of courtiers and horses. But the marshal believed that he could hold out until relieved by the Austrians.

Frederick was plainly annoyed by the situation. Rutowsky's camp could pass "for one of the strongest fortresses of Europe." An attack would cost too many men, and he wanted the Saxon army for his own later use. Confident that the enemy could not hold out long for want of food, he demanded that King August capitulate. August offered to allow Prussian occupation of certain cities and even to furnish hostages as a guarantee of Saxon neutrality. Frederick rejected this proposal and sent Winterfeldt to the Saxon camp with a demand for an alliance. August refused — the Saxons would fight if attacked.

Frederick surrounded the camp as well as he could, a blockade designed to prevent a breakout and force surrender by hunger. To prevent the Austrians from relieving Rutowsky, he sent Keith south with a strong corps. Brunswick, commanding the advance guard, struck an Austrian corps commanded by Major General Count Karl von Wied at Nollendorf, pushed it back, and continued his march. Keith followed with the main force to camp just north of Aussig, from where he effectively blocked roads into Saxony. General Christoph Hermann von Manstein led a task force to seize Teschen and secure Elbe navigation.

The Austrian court's decision to defer the combined Austrian-Russian attack on Prussia until the spring of 1757 did not interrupt its military preparations, although these were not nearly as extensive as Klinggraeffen had been reporting. Despite reforms, begun in 1748, that had brought some improvements, the Austrian army was not in top condition. Severe shortages in men and matériel had been one reason to defer the attack.

Faced with the Prussian buildup, Maria Theresa in early August appointed Field Marshal Maximilian Browne to command about thirty-two thousand troops in Bohemia, and placed twenty-two thousand under General Prince Octavio Piccolomini in Moravia. By mid-August

---

* This area is still beautiful, and Königstein, which I recently visited, is magnificent. Standing 270 meters above the Elbe River, it is a breathtaking example of a sixteenth-century fortress. The walls are noble, the views without parallel, the armories fascinating.

Browne had decided that Frederick might well attack through Saxony. Desperately short of arms and supplies, he asked for reinforcements and permission to shift his corps northwest while bringing Piccolomini to Königgrätz. The court was frightened by Frederick's demands for a guaranteed armistice and quickly agreed. Browne was reinforced with a corps under Wied (which Brunswick encountered on his march into Bohemia), and other shortages were repaired at least in part. The court had ordered units in Hungary and Italy to march to Bohemia and had put its forces in the Spanish Netherlands on war footing.

Frederick's invasion of Saxony, and the Saxon court's decision to remain at Pirna rather than march to Poland or Bohemia, put Vienna in a dilemma. Browne wanted the Saxons in Bohemia. He hotly argued against taking his army into Saxony. He was not ready to march; he still lacked artillery, munitions, and magazines. Moreover, he needed a detachment from Piccolomini in Bohemia as cover against Schwerin in Silesia. Overruled by the Hofkriegsrath, which decided that the Saxon army must be saved, he sent Wied's corps to Aussig. He himself would march when Piccolomini's corps arrived at Königgrätz. He hoped that the Saxons could hold out for eight days, as he wrote to Emperor Francis, so as to win time to consolidate his forces.[4]

On September 20 Marshal Browne was at Budin, over twenty-five miles from the Saxon border, from where he was still trying to work out a relief operation to save the Saxon army. His general idea was to push north on the west bank of the Elbe while the Saxons broke out to the south and joined him. To Count Rutowsky's reply that this was hopeless, Browne agreed to advance on Lobositz as a deceptive measure to distract the Prussians. Detachments on the right bank of the Elbe nearly to Aussig would screen a separate corps marching inland to Schandau. The Saxons would cross the Elbe on a boat bridge on the evening of October 11 to join the Austrians.

It would be difficult to conceive of a more unlikely plan of operations. But on September 25 Browne sent Colonel Count Franz Moritz Lacy with a small force to Leitmeritz, from where, once reinforced, he would march to meet the Saxons at Schandau. Meanwhile Browne would move north to Lobositz with the main army.

Thursday, September 30, 1756. Browne marches from Budin about seven miles north to Lobositz, where Lacy, in a change of plan, joins him with two regiments. He deploys some thirty-five thousand troops in combat formation. His advance guard deploys northwest of Lobositz, its right on the Elbe. Croatian irregulars occupy a dominant hill, the Lobosch, which slopes down to walled vineyards and fruit orchards. His center behind a road leading from Lobositz to Tschischkowitz appears vulnerable, but a stream, the Modlbach, has turned the

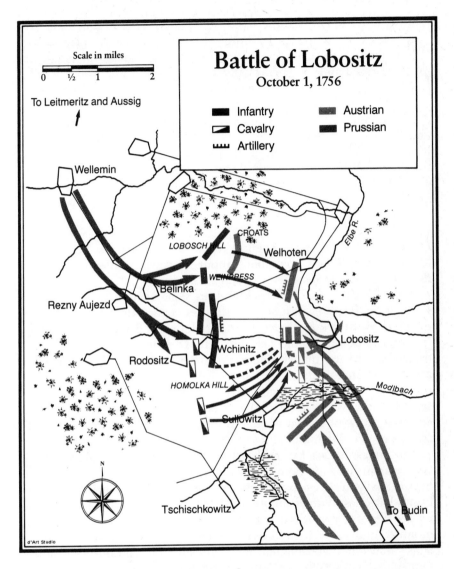

Battle of Lobositz

October 1, 1756

Infantry   Austrian
Cavalry   Prussian
Artillery

Scale in miles

0   ½   1   2

To Leitmeritz and Aussig

Wellemin

CROATS

LOBOSCH HILL

Welhoten

Elbe R.

WEINPRESS

Belinka

Rezny Aujezd

Wchinitz

Lobositz

Rodositz

HOMOLKA HILL

Modlbach

Sullowitz

N

Tschischkowitz

To Budin

d'Art Studio

land east of the road into marshes, a natural defense complemented by irregular troops hiding in bushes and ditches to the front. The main army deploys behind the stream with a large plain to its rear.

Spies report that Frederick and Keith are advancing south from Aussig, each with a corps of twenty thousand. That evening Browne describes the situation to Emperor Francis, adding, "Thus it is very probable that tomorrow or the day after we shall fall on each other."[5]

Frederick learns at daybreak that Browne has built bridges over the Eger at Budin and is improving the road to Lobositz. "It appears that tomorrow we shall have the honor of seeing the Austrian gentlemen face to face," he writes to the Prince of Prussia, who is with Keith.

Joined by Keith's columns, he marches south through thick fog. En route hussars report an enemy camp on the plain of Lobositz. He rides forward, dimly sees the camp, and brings the army to the heights west of Lobositz. It is dark; the terrain is difficult; some units are delayed; there is confusion. Men remain under arms, horses saddled. Brunswick and other commanders confer with the king in his military carriage. Major General von Schmettau suggests that Browne will fight only a rearguard action while his army crosses the Elbe. Frederick listens to other opinions but gives no orders for the next day. Brunswick comes away in full admiration of his "cheerfulness and coolness" in a confusing and dangerous situation.

Friday, October 1, 1756. The last troops and guns arrive before daybreak. The Prussians now count about 28,500, considerably weaker than the enemy opposite, but strong in cavalry.

It is five-thirty A.M. Frederick and his senior commanders ride forward to Schmettau's battalion. An officer reports an enemy army on the plain, but thick fog hides it. Frederick orders Brunswick to deploy forward battalions on the right and left. The move brings cannon fire from vineyards on the left. He returns to headquarters and orders the army to advance in attack formation. Infantry followed by artillery and cavalry deploy in line between Rezny Aujezd and Belinka. The right and center are to clear Wchinitz of enemy irregulars, then wheel left and press Browne's right wing into the Elbe. The Duke of Bevern will take Lobosch Hill and hold fast.

The attack begins favorably. Brunswick scatters irregulars with a few cannon shots and occupies Homolka Hill. Colonel Karl von Moller moves heavy artillery to its forward slopes and opens fire on the Lobositz batteries. A shell splinter kills Major General von Quadt. Lieutenant General von Kleist is badly wounded in the foot but remains mounted and active.* An observer will later write of Austrian cannonballs "sometimes plunging into the earth behind us and throwing stones and clods high into the air, sometimes falling among us and snatching men out of the ranks as if they were pieces of straw."[6] In the center the Prince of Prussia reaches the Weinpress, which is heavily defended by irregulars. On his left Bevern's people work slowly across the Lobosch slopes. Irregulars hidden in walled vineyards take a nasty toll. Bevern is reinforced and with great difficulty brings heavy guns forward.

At eight A.M., Frederick is on the right at Homolka Hill. Sun covers the hills, but fog hugs the great plain. He sees enemy cavalry in front

---

* Kleist died of his wounds early in 1757.

of Lobositz. Is there an army on the plain? Or, as Schmettau believes, is the main army crossing the Elbe below Lobositz? Patrols probe to the Modlbach to find crossings defended. Artillery fire continues from the town. Is the enemy waiting on the plain to attack his right? He cannot take the chance. He stops Brunswick's attack on the right, brings up reinforcements — and stands still.

It is not one of his brilliant moments. He is disturbed and indecisive. For want of anything better, he orders Generals Gessler and Kyau, two heroes of Hohenfriedberg, to attack enemy cavalry by Lobositz.

By eleven, the fog has begun to lift. Twenty squadrons of dragoons and cuirassiers filter through the infantry. Right-wing squadrons trot toward Sullowitz, which Kyau reports is defended by infantry backed by two lines of cavalry. Kyau takes some casualties. His cuirassiers accordingly move eastward, with the dragoons on their right but considerably to the rear. Austrian dragoons exploit the gap to hit Kyau's right. Prussian dragoons attack the attackers, and a general melee follows, a fighting mass that moves slowly toward Lobositz. And then — disaster. Prussian cavalry are suddenly fighting in land cut by wide ditches. Croats hiding in the brush fire from the flanks; Austrian cavalry attack their front. The Prussians give way and limp back to Homolka Hill.

Frederick sees that this is no rearguard action. He anticipates an enemy attack and orders the rest of his cavalry to form in front of the infantry. Gessler meanwhile sorts out returning squadrons. Someone gives an order to attack. The king is nonplussed. Fifty-nine squadrons, over ten thousand horse, are suddenly trotting forward. Men and horses are raked by musket and artillery fire from Sullowitz, then by guns behind the Modlbach, finally from irregular fire around Lobositz. But now the cavalry is pushing Austrian squadrons into Lobositz on the left and throwing other squadrons back into the funneled defile between the town and the Modlbach.

Browne sees the danger. He pulls two cavalry regiments from his left flank with others to follow. They hit the Prussian flank hard. The Prussians are hurt. Their attack stops; they turn to retreat. But horses are tired. Some are mired in marshy meadowlands, some surrender. The rest struggle back to Homolka Hill, "where I arranged them [behind the infantry] as if this were a maneuver," the king shortly informed Marshal Schwerin.

At noon the fog is gone and Frederick can see the enemy center and left. Enemy infantry advance from Sullowitz but are beaten back by Colonel Moller's guns. Bevern's people are fighting for their lives on Lobosch Hill, where Croats "send one salvo after the other" into the Prussian intruders. Prussian survivors strip the dead and wounded of ammunition. It is a new kind of war, a war of individual fire and movement, not the usual "regular or sustained fire," as Brunswick will later write, but rather each soldier firing at will.[7] Frederick watches fresh enemy units advance from Lobositz. He feeds Bevern more battalions. Cannonballs are falling on Homolka Hill. An aide wants him to move out of range. "I am not here to evade them," he answers.[8] He orders his own troops to send half of their ammunition ration, thirty cartridges each, to Bevern's people.

Frederick does not like his battle. Early in the afternoon he turns command over to Keith and moves his headquarters to Wchinitz as a preliminary to breaking off the action. Keith is not pleased, either. He sends still another battalion to Bevern. It arrives in time to face a new attack by Colonel Lacy's infantry. Inspired by an aide, Major von Oelsnitz, riding the line, the Prussians press down corpse-covered slopes to bring new heart to the survivors. Now the battle is hand to hand, with bayonets and musket butts. The enemy begins to break; the break becomes a rout; Lacy is wounded; his troops press back into Lobositz. Keith hurries to this decisive flank and orders an attack on Lobositz. Frederick is informed and returns to take command.

It is three P.M. Houses are burning in Lobositz when Prussian infantry push in. Furious troops move from house to house. No quarter is given. Regulars and irregulars jump into the Elbe to escape death by fire and bayonet, only to be drowned. Browne's main army is withdrawing to its earlier positions, covered by cavalry between Lobositz and Sullowitz. Frederick is in no position to attack. He halts the action. The Prussians camp under arms, a defense stretching from the Elbe to Homolka Hill.

At midnight Browne's army begins the march back to Budin.

The battle of Lobositz is over.

72

FREDERICK was forced by political necessity to advertise the battle of Lobositz as a Prussian victory. He was correct according to that day's definition, since the enemy had left the field. From headquarters in a magistrate's house in Wchinitz he sent word of his gratitude to all regiments for their "extraordinary valor." He described the battle in a long report to Field Marshal Schwerin, in which he boasted, inaccurately, that twenty-four thousand Prussians had defeated sixty thousand Austrians, but added that "the Austrians are more cunning than formerly and you can take it from me that if we cannot put much heavier cannon against them it would cost innumerable lives to beat them."

He could not sufficiently praise Bevern. Moller of the artillery had "done wonders and has aided me prodigiously. . . . I have never seen such prodigies of valor, cavalry as well as infantry." Heavy casualties brought tears to his eyes — he did not mention the figure, which has been officially estimated at over seven hundred killed and nearly nineteen hundred wounded. He rated Lobositz as a better victory than Soor, and he believed that it would bring Saxon surrender.

So confident was he that the Saxons were nearly starved that he had permitted a supply wagon of food to be sent to King August. Another indication of the Saxon plight was the French envoy's request for a passport. This was refused, and when Count Charles de Broglie tried to cross Prussian lines, he was arrested. This caused a political uproar in the Versailles court, which recalled Valory from his post at Berlin, thus virtually declaring war on Prussia.

Frederick was trying to turn Lobositz from a frog into a prince. It was true that Browne had left the field, but it was of his own volition and the withdrawal was in no way a rout. He had suffered about the same casualties as his enemy but was better able to stand them because of his superior numbers. More important, peacetime reforms had told. Infantry, cavalry, and especially artillery had performed better than in the Silesian wars, and the irregulars continued to perform invaluable services.

But neither were the Saxons rescued. King August had agreed to Browne's plan. The bulk of his army was to assemble in fortress Königstein and on the night of October 11 cross the Elbe on a pontoon bridge. They would then push through the Prussian defense of a rocky bluff. Cannon fire would signal their arrival to Browne's corps at Schandau, and the forces would meet to retire into Bohemia.

Browne's relief corps, about nine thousand strong, marched east from Budin, crossed the Elbe, and moved north, shielded by detachments on the right bank. En route, Browne received a message from Brühl that the Saxon crossing would be delayed for twenty-four hours. His own march continued almost on schedule.

Deserters meanwhile had informed the Prussians of Browne's presence. Prince Maurice and Lieutenant General Winterfeldt estimated his strength at about five thousand. No longer in doubt as to the enemy's intention, Margrave Charles of Schwedt began reinforcing Prussian units between Browne's position and the intended Saxon bridgehead.

The Saxons finished the pontoon bridge on the night of October 12. Throughout that cold and rainy day Saxon troops had been marching from Königstein, their rearguard skirmishing with Zieten's hussars. They were hungry to start with — they had immediately eaten the single bread ration that was issued — and by the time they reached the Elbe they were wet, cold, and exhausted. They began crossing late that night,

General Friedrich Wilhelm von Seydlitz. Cavalry generals senior to Seydlitz were displeased when he was put in command at Rossbach. He settled matters with a simple statement: "Gentlemen, I obey the king and you obey me."

Below: Frederick receiving the captives at Königstein, October 1756. Seventeen thousand Saxon troops were submitted to mass military baptism, Prussian style, to form twenty new battalions commanded by Prussian officers—a great idea that didn't work out.

and by morning the small bridgehead had expanded by seven grenadier battalions, but they had little artillery, no food or tents, and their ammunition pouches were wet and thus temporarily useless. Artillery fire from Königstein on the Prussian defenses proved ineffective because of limited vision. By late afternoon the bulk of the army was across the Elbe, infantry was probing eastward, but cavalry and most of the artillery were still at the bridgehead and, because of a clumsy bit of work, most of the pontoon bridge was floating swiftly down the Elbe.

Margrave Charles had learned of the crossing and was moving more troops to the threatened area. Frederick at Lobositz also learned of Browne's presence, turned command over to Keith, and marched north with fifteen squadrons of dragoons.

Browne was in camp about six miles from the bridgehead. He had heard cannon fire early that morning, but when it did not continue he stayed where he was. (These were the guns from Königstein.) In mid-morning he received a note from Brühl asking him to hold on until the following morning, when the Saxons would attack. Browne was short of food but replied that he would wait until nine the following morning in order to assist a breakthrough, though he doubted it would work.

His pessimism was justified. Rutowsky had already called a council of war which agreed that the only hope was surrender on favorable terms. King August, who had remained in Königstein, reluctantly accepted the inevitable. On the morning of October 14, Rutowsky arranged an armistice with Winterfeldt. By evening a draft of the Saxon surrender reached the Prussian king. Frederick was tired but delighted, convinced "that everything is going wonderfully well." He quickly altered the terms to ensure that the Saxons would enlist in the Prussian army. This stipulation was accepted, and for the next several days some seventeen thousand troops were submitted to mass military baptism, Prussian style, to form twenty new battalions commanded by Prussian officers. Saxon officers were excepted and given parole on condition that they not fight against the Prussians in this war. Frederick also returned all flags, standards, and drums to King August and decreed that Königstein would remain neutral. August, his two sons, and Count Brühl were given free passage to Warsaw, where August would make his court.

Browne had waited as promised. Hearing no fire, he nonetheless delayed his departure until afternoon. Except for a few skirmishes with enemy hussars, the return march was uneventful, "but we returned in the deepest depression," one observer wrote.[1] The relief corps was back at Budin on October 19.

Frederick had written to Prince Maurice over a week before the Saxon surrender that he could not remain at Lobositz much longer. The land was nearly bare of forage, winter would close the river to ships, and deteriorating roads and enemy irregulars would hinder convoys. The Lobositz area could not support an army through the winter, and with Browne holding Budin and the right bank of the Elbe, no other camp in the area was to be thought of. In late October the withdrawal north began.

There remained Schwerin's force, which earlier had marched into Bohemia to hold Prince Piccolomini's army at Königgrätz. During the Prussians' time there, they ate up as much of Bohemia as they could. But Schwerin was plagued by supply shortages and by hordes of irregulars, who posed a real threat to his lines of communication with Silesia. On Frederick's orders, he began a withdrawal in late October, a skillful maneuver that had his force back in Silesia by month's end with no serious loss.

Browne, also suffering from supply shortages, took up winter quarters shortly after the Prussian withdrawal into Saxony. Piccolomini followed suit, ending the year's campaign.

73

WINTER brought little rest to Frederick in his headquarters at Dresden. It was true that he could look at some positive achievements. His army had been tested and found not wanting. He had eliminated Saxony as a threat to future operations. Saxon surrender had provided him with enough soldiers to form ten new regiments for his army. Von Borcke's War Ministry in Torgau was already functioning well. In the coming months, indeed years, Saxony would contribute large quantities of men, money, matériel, and food to the Prussian army.

Yet his position was not entirely secure. Internal sedition was already at work. Saxony did not want to be occupied by Prussia, and Saxon soldiers did not want to be Prussian soldiers. It had been a great mistake to allow Saxon units to remain together under a new flag rather than integrating them into Prussian units. The new battalions were not only unreliable — one entire regiment escaped to Poland — but downright dangerous.* Saxon officers who had not fled to Poland or Austria were spying for King August. Queen Maria's court in Dresden was a hotbed of sedition, reporting Prussian strength and movements to Vienna, Versailles, and Warsaw. Alert Prussian sentries intercepted nu-

---

* The king disbanded two Saxon regiments in April 1757 because of "secret plots and conspiracies." He tried to avoid further trouble by shifting troops from one regiment to another, but this maneuver was only partially successful.

merous letters, including some found in a shipment of puddings, but others went to and fro.

A more serious problem came from outside Saxon borders. In January the Imperial Diet formally banned Prussia from the Empire and declared war on her. As Count Podewils had warned, Austria and the Empire would soon be joined by Russia and France. Frederick's alliance with England was still untested. He was trying desperately to alert the British government to a probable French attack on Hanover and to his own precarious position. He sent General Schmettau to Hanover to point out the extreme dangers and to offer military advice. Hanoverian ministers were obviously eager to remain neutral. English ministers were divided; progress was slow. There were only the beginnings of the allied army promised by King George. Frederick had no other allies (though he hoped to persuade Turkey to attack Austria); his army, even if excellent, was relatively small; his treasury and internal resources were limited.

His situation had darkened in December with a report that Russia had begun new preparations for war. Knyphausen, home from Paris, reported that Versailles was going to send an auxiliary corps to Bohemia after all, as well as an army of sixty thousand to the Lower Rhine. Late in the month Frederick believed that Austria would attack Saxony in the Elbe area and probably Lusatia (in order to march on Berlin), as opposed to invading Silesia with its strong forts. He had already decided, unless fresh intelligence radically changed matters, to remain on the defensive until green forage was available. It was all the same where the enemy attacked, he wrote to Schwerin, providing he was beaten: "The upshot of all this should be to move the war to Moravia." Once Austria suffered a severe defeat, he believed that France would not be so aggressive, and he also hoped that England meanwhile would have formed a respectable army in Hanover.

But also in late December Andrew Mitchell was informed by his colleague in Saint Petersburg that Czarina Elizabeth and her court regarded the Prussian withdrawal to Saxony as a retreat. Russia would shortly join the Treaty of Versailles and, in return for large subsidies from France and Austria, would send an army of eighty thousand, not counting Cossacks, for operations with Austria against Prussia.

> I have long expected what has now happened [Frederick said], and have told you [Mitchell] so several times. We must now make use of all resources and exert ourselves to the utmost. I will do my part and I hope you will do yours, but we lose time and nothing is yet settled; our enemies are making the greatest efforts, and we ought to do the same. Upon the success of the next campaign depends everything; if it is favorable, the war will not be long, and it is with this view that I spare no expense to make myself strong and to look my enemies in the face.[1]

A Russian attack was not of immediate concern, he wrote to Field Marshal Lehwaldt, since Marshal Count Stephen Apraxin could not appear in East Prussia before June and since he would probably divide his force to send a corps against Silesia. Mitchell reported that Apraxin was not pleased with the state of his army, which lacked officers, men, and horses. The marshal had secretly informed Grand Duchess Catherine that his orders were not to attack Memel or the Prussian army, but to march through Poland directly to Silesia. This was important information. Frederick brought Lehwaldt's strength to thirty thousand troops, a corps that, taken with the promised Baltic fleet from England, should form a reasonable defense of the province. If the information was correct, Lehwaldt was to follow Apraxin with the bulk of his force and attack him from the rear. If it proved false, he should attack as planned. If defeated, he was to abandon Prussia altogether, although this was a last resort.

Frederick told Wilhelmina in early January that he was going to Berlin, but only for a few days; there was so much to do in Saxony, "where my presence is the more necessary, especially as the coming year will decide my fate and that of the state as well as the liberty of Germany." His main purpose was to prepare secret instructions for Count Finckenstein in Berlin in case of military disaster. The royal family, government, garrison, treasury (including the crown jewels), and archives were to go to Cüstrin, Magdeburg, or Stettin. Silver and gold plate was to be taken from the palaces and melted down for coinage. If the king was killed, affairs were to continue "without the slightest alteration." If he was taken prisoner, he would cease to count as king, and his successor, William, was not to pay the slightest attention to anything that he wrote while a prisoner. No province or other ransom was to be offered for his release. The war would continue as if he had never existed.

Frederick would have been considerably relieved had he known of the indecision and wrangling that ruled secret councils in Vienna, Versailles, and Saint Petersburg. In theory these allies, with a combined strength of 250,000 troops, would attack Prussia from three directions and after her defeat take whatever of her territories they wished. In fact, conflicting objectives, compounded by jealousy, greed, fear, and ineptness, sabotaged the grand plan from the beginning. By late February it was clear that Marshal Apraxin (with a finger firmly on the czarina's pulse) was in no hurry to march and would not move until June at the earliest.

The French court was behaving typically, acting neither quickly nor decisively. King Louis objected to sending an auxiliary corps of twenty-four thousand to Bohemia; he had other commitments. Then in early January a wretch of unsound mind plunged the blade of a penknife into the monarch's corpulent body. The wound was superficial but the fright was great. The court did not easily recover, and a change of ministry further slowed matters. Not until early May was the second Treaty of Versailles signed. According to its provisions, France would send an army of 105,000 to the Lower Rhine, she would subsidize six thousand Württemberg and four thousand Bavarian auxiliaries for the Imperial army, and she would pay Austria an annual subsidy of twelve million gulden.

Austrian plans were also in disarray. Marshal Browne dangerously underrated the Prussian king as someone "who acts more from caprice than system and keeps everything to himself. He never has a fixed plan, and the least small maneuver is sufficient to throw him off and make him change his mind."[2] Browne argued for an offensive into Silesia. Neipperg, now the president of the Hofkriegsrath, wanted a small force left in Moravia and the main army to attack either Lusatia or Saxony, but only when good weather arrived. Count Kaunitz wished to attack early; Emperor Francis agreed: it was vital to crush the Prussian army and advance to the heart of the kingdom. Prince Charles, who took up the top field command in February, recommended an attack of Lusatia, with secondary operations along the Silesian border. Victory in Lusatia, he argued, would free the Elbe for shipping and greatly facilitate communication with the French and Russians. While a corps held Frederick's army on the Elbe, the main army could invade either the Prussian homelands or Lower Silesia. By mid-April two armies were to march, one, nearly ninety thousand strong under Charles, to move on Saxony and Lusatia; the other, about fifty-eight thousand under Count Daun, to march to the Bohemian-Silesian border. General Nádasdy's light troops and irregulars, some eleven thousand, would operate along the Moravian-Silesian border; Nádasdy would be under Daun's command.

The premise of this plan was that Frederick would remain on the defensive. Count Johann Baptista Serbelloni, commanding at Königgrätz, twice warned the Hofkriegsrath of a possible Prussian invasion of Bohemia. Neipperg replied that the enemy, now as earlier, would remain on the defensive.

Frederick's situation brightened considerably in mid-February, when an impassioned speech by the British minister William Pitt won parliamentary support for all-out war in alliance with Prussia. Hanoverian hopes for neutrality vanished overnight. Frederick could now anticipate an allied army protecting his right flank from French attack.*

---

*Hanoverian efforts to win neutrality nonetheless continued and developed into a minor crisis in March. King George resolved this by declaring the Duke of Cumberland commander-in-chief of the new army, to Frederick's enthusiastic approval. Relations continued to improve, and in April Frederick wrote to the British king about his plans for the new campaign.

The king held a fair idea of enemy intentions by mid-March. As he wrote to Schwerin and Winterfeldt in detailed operational analyses, he believed that spring would bring a two-pronged Austrian attack against Saxony and Lusatia, with a large French army, reinforced by Austrian and Imperial troops, moving into Germany. He intended to keep sixty thousand troops on the Elbe, thirty-five thousand in Lusatia, and fifteen thousand in Silesia. Once the Austrians were beaten or the French chased from Germany, he would take the offensive. If Russia remained quiet, he would transfer Schwerin's force to Saxony and replace it with Lehwaldt's corps from East Prussia. In case both Austria and France remained on the defensive, then he would move into Bohemia. He was taking the army out of cantonments and transferring his headquarters to Lockwitz.

Neither Winterfeldt nor Schwerin agreed with this passive plan. Each in his own way argued for an aggressive push, from Saxony or from Silesia, to destroy enemy magazines. *Audaces Fortuna juvat* (Fortune favors the bold), they reminded the king. Frederick had been thinking along the same lines for some time. No longer was a mere spoiling operation good enough; no longer was it a matter of temporarily weakening the enemy. Probably to their astonishment, Schwerin and Winterfeldt learned that in mid-April the entire army would invade Bohemia — "a *coup d'éclat* in order to give spirit and *fermeté* to his allies," as Andrew Mitchell reported the king's explanation.[3] Schwerin and Bevern would join forces at Jung-Bunzlau and continue on to Leitmeritz. Prince Maurice of Dessau would march via Komotau, make a feint against Eger, and clean that area of the enemy while the king moved south to rendezvous with Schwerin and the Duke of Bevern. If Browne remained at Budin, Schwerin would stay at Leitmeritz while Frederick crossed the Eger west of Browne's left flank, thus forcing him either to battle or to retreat to Prague. If he chose to retreat, Frederick would pursue and try to bring him to battle. The king also planned to send a newly raised *Freikorps,* or irregular force, under Lieutenant Colonel Johann von Mayr into Germany to raise contributions, "terrify the German princes," and slow the formation of an Imperial army. This plan, with march schedules, reached various commanders in early April. The king stressed that success depended on total secrecy in order to achieve surprise. Commanders were to correspond only in code; the original dispatch went by one route, a copy by another.

This bold plan upset Schwerin, who wrote that he could not possibly march to the king's schedule. But it was vital that he did march, Frederick replied: a delay of two or three days would probably forfeit surprise; the Austrians were about to occupy Jung-Bunzlau, which would ruin everything. Schmettau replied with further remonstrations and suggested alterations that implied a separate campaign on his part. Frederick had had enough:

Whether you beat the enemy [Serbelloni at Königgrätz] or do not beat
the enemy, I order you, after pursuing him, to march on the Elbe toward
Leitmeritz or Melnik, which is the decisive blow. This is the power of
our plan, and you will be responsible if you do not execute my orders to
the letter . . . [for otherwise] your expedition will be a pure loss. The
mortal blow against the enemy must be delivered behind the Eger. [Once
Browne is] beaten and driven from his magazine, all of Bohemia will
fall. . . . That then is my firm will to which I order you positively to
conform in every respect. . . . If you do not march to the Elbe . . . I
will have to withdraw to Saxony for want of food, and you will have
caused such nonsense. For the salvation of the state depends on your
expedition; if you do not carry it out according to my will, you will pay
with your head.

74

CONSIDERING such factors as time, space, enemy forces, mountainous terrain, poor roads, and difficult communications, the Prussian march
came off remarkably well.

Schwerin's corps moved out first, on April 18, four columns commanded by Manteuffel, Winterfeldt, Hautcharmoy, and Fouqué. Poor
mountain roads delayed supply trains, enemy irregulars dogged the
march but offered no serious problem, and Serbelloni made no move
with his corps from Königgrätz. A week after marching, Schwerin's
corps had reached Sobotka, not far from the intended rendezvous with
Bevern's corps, coming from Lusatia.

Bevern marched two days later than Schwerin, the theory being that
Marshal Königsegg, on learning of Schwerin's advance, would withdraw from the mountain country. Bevern was slowed by considerable
skirmishing but still made excellent time and arrived northwest of Reichenberg late on April 20 to find that Königsegg was defending the
town. He attacked at once, a brisk action that cost Königsegg some
nine hundred casualties — versus seven hundred of his own — and
forced him to order a general retreat. On April 28 Schwerin and Bevern
were in Jung-Bunzlau, whose magazines held food for forty thousand
men for three weeks.

King Frederick's advance guard, commanded by Prince Ferdinand of
Brunswick, marched before dawn on April 22 and pushed the Austrians from Linay the following day. Frederick followed with the main
army, which included thirty-nine hundred wagons carrying a ten-day
supply of food and fodder, with more coming by boat. Prince Maurice,
who had marched farther west, joined the king's army at Linay. Fred-

erick continued south. Brunswick's left flank, commanded by General Ludwig von Zastrow, ran into heavy fire from irregulars on the right bank of the Elbe. Zastrow was killed and his two battalions suffered over a hundred casualties. Major General Christoph von Manstein took over; the march continued. On April 25 Frederick reported his position north of Budin to Schwerin, who was ordered to march on Melnik to close the trap on Browne if he remained in Budin. The letter was intercepted by irregulars. On the following day Prince Maurice found a favorable crossing area on the Eger southwest of Budin. The army crossed on pontoon bridges two days later.

Field Marshal Maximilian Ulysses von Browne was in Prague on April 19 when he learned of Marshal Schwerin's march into Bohemia. Interpreting it as a "spoiling" operation, he wrote to Prince Charles, his commander-in-chief, the following day, "It is incredible how the King of Prussia inopportunely tires his troops by meaningless marches and countermarches."[1] He equally discounted a report from the west bank of the Elbe of threatening enemy movements. Two days later he learned of the Prussian march from Saxony, then of Königsegg's defeat at Reichenberg. It now occurred to him that Frederick was up to something more than tiring his troops with useless marches. Moving headquarters to Budin, he ordered the Duke of Arenberg's corps on the upper Eger to join him. On April 26 he informed Prince Charles that the Prussian king was opposite him with fifty thousand troops and that he would give battle between Eger and Prague.

Arenberg had not arrived by the time the Prussians crossed the Eger. Browne decided that he could not stand alone. He fell back behind Tuchomirschitz, northwest of Prague.

Frederick watched Browne's army in the form of a great dust cloud withdrawing south from Budin. General Hans von Zieten's hussars followed to seize some magazines — a welcome contribution — when Browne continued his retreat. Frederick meanwhile brought up the army south of Budin. Troops received a much needed day of rest while supply and artillery trains lumbered into camp. Frederick learned that Schwerin and Bevern were at Jung-Bunzlau and obviously had not received his orders to march on Melnik. He immediately wrote to Schwerin that within a few days he planned to attack Browne at Tuchomirschitz. Bevern was to bring a corps of infantry and cavalry to Melnik, and Schwerin would cross the Elbe and march east of Prague to block Browne's escape route. As the king wrote to Wilhelmina, he believed that Browne would retire on Tabor — "after which will follow the siege of Prague and Eger and the sending of a Prussian corps into the Empire to bring France and the princes to their senses."

Schwerin did as he was ordered, but not very willingly. The magazine at Jung-Bunzlau was his single supply source, and he wanted to protect it at all costs. On the first of May, Winterfeldt marched with the advance guard, crossed the Iser, and continued on toward Brandeis. General Wartenberg's hussars ran into Croatian irregulars outside of Brandeis and in a brisk action pushed them back to the Elbe bridges, capturing many prisoners, munition wagons, tents, and the personal baggage of two Austrian generals. A Croat bullet killed Wartenberg, whose men thenceforth cut down all Croats who tried to surrender. The irregulars had previously tarred the vital bridges, and survivors now set them on fire and destroyed them. Pontoon bridges had to be laid, a lengthy process that delayed the army's crossing for several days.

While Frederick was resting his army south of Budin, while Schwerin and Bevern were preparing to march from Jung-Bunzlau, while Königsegg was waiting nervously southwest of Brandeis, and while Browne was reorganizing his somewhat tattered army at Tuchomirschitz, a newcomer arrived on the scene. This was no less than Prince Charles of Lorraine, commander-in-chief of the Austrian army.

Charles had left Vienna in late April, intending to confer with Serbelloni at Königgrätz. But unfavorable reports caused him to proceed directly to Prague, which he found in a great state of confusion — defenses neglected, citizens fleeing the city. The next day he learned that Königsegg did not believe he could stand against Schwerin, whose strength he put at fifty thousand. Charles agreed, and Königsegg began withdrawing to the right bank of the Moldau at Prague, leaving hussars and irregulars on the Elbe. At Tuchomirschitz, Charles found Browne's and Arenberg's corps disorganized and confused, the officers and men plainly demoralized by the long retreat. Browne was "in a very sorry condition. The first thing he said to me was that he was in a state of utter misery, and wished he were dead. He thereupon burst into tears. . . . I was shocked to see the army in complete confusion: nobody had any orders or knew what he was supposed to do."[2] As was the Austrian custom, Charles called a council of war. Browne, apparently revived, argued for an offensive, but Charles and the assembled generals decided that the army should join Königsegg's corps on the other side of the Moldau by Prague. Charles had already ordered Serbelloni (who was soon to be relieved by Marshal Daun, marching from Moravia) to leave a garrison at Königgrätz and shift the bulk of his force westward.

Charles called another council of war at his new headquarters, southwest of Prague. He proposed to leave a garrison in Prague and withdraw the main army to join with Serbelloni. Browne argued that

Prague must be held at all costs. Other generals agreed that further withdrawal would completely demoralize the army. Charles unwillingly yielded, strengthened the garrison by thirteen thousand, and formed the rest of the army, just over sixty thousand, in two lines north of Maleschitz, its left resting on the Ziskaberg, its right hooking to Sterbohol to the south, irregulars screening the front.

As Browne's corps pulled out of Tuchomirschitz, Zieten's hussars moved in, and the main army quickly followed. Browne's retreat was now obvious, and Frederick hurried to bring him to battle — to "a decisive affair" — before Serbelloni could reinforce him. While an advance guard dogged Browne's force, Frederick divided his army. Keith, with thirty-two thousand, was ordered to cover the capital from the west and bridge the Moldau to the south.* Frederick, with about twenty-four thousand men and fifty heavy cannon, crossed the Moldau below Prague early on May 5. There was no sign of Schwerin, who was to join the king here. He was about nine miles to the north and had not received the king's most recent orders (the courier had been captured by enemy hussars), so he was standing still. He was jolted from his quiet when an aide delivered *"une lettre fort piquante"* — a very sharp letter ordering him to march that night.

Schwerin's columns began closing on the main army shortly after midnight.

75

Friday, May 6, 1757. Prince Charles in headquarters at Maleschitz greets the day calmly. His army holds a strong defensive position and he is expecting a reinforcement of nine thousand men from Serbelloni's corps. He knows the Prussians have crossed the Moldau, but he also believes that the bulk of Schwerin's army is at Brandeis.

The Prussians will certainly not attack this day.

But now disturbing news arrives. A few cannonballs drop through morning fog on the light horse to the front. Irregulars stalking the Elbe report strong enemy forces advancing from Brandeis. The advance guard of two enemy columns approaching from north and northwest push back outposts at Prossik.

It is about six A.M. Charles orders battle formation. He commands

---

* The task was given to Prince Maurice of Dessau, but the pontoon train bogged down and the bridge was completed only after the battle. Lieutenant Colonel Friedrich von Seydlitz's cavalry tried to ford the river during the battle, but in vain.

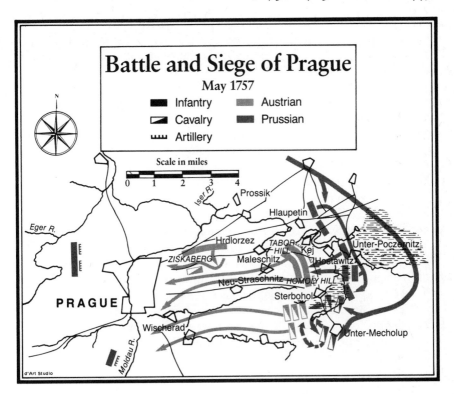

Battle and Siege of Prague

May 1757

Infantry ■■■   Austrian ▨

Cavalry ⊏▨   Prussian ■■■

Artillery ⊔⊔⊔

Scale in miles

0 1 2 3 4

the left wing, a strong force stretching from the Ziskaberg east to Kej. Browne commands the right wing, which hooks south to Sterbohol, with cavalry holding the extreme right flank. But Charles is short some five thousand cavalry, which are in Prague on fodder detail. His army counts about fifty-five thousand.

The troops are soon deployed, arms at the ready, heavy cannon moving up, horses saddled. There is no sign of the enemy. Units alternate between cooking breakfast and attending mass.

The Prussian army marches early. Schwerin's columns reach the heights of Prossik, chase off enemy outposts, and wait for the king's columns. They arrive shortly. At about six A.M., the Prussian army is joined, some sixty-four thousand troops.

It is not the king's finest hour. He is ill from colic, throwing up constantly. Still he rides with Schwerin, Winterfeldt, and some aides to the heights east of Prossik. The air is clear; enemy lines are plain to see. A few cannonballs greet them but fall far short. They study the enemy through brass spyglasses. Frederick makes it clear they will attack. But where? They reject the northern front out of hand. This leaves the enemy right wing in the area of Unter-Poczernitz and Sterbohol. Frederick is not up to further reconnaissance. This is for Schwerin and Winterfeldt. They report that an attack can be made between Sterbohol and Hostawitz, although marshy meadows will make it difficult, and the enemy can probably be outflanked on the right.

The king likes the report. He will command the center, Schwerin the left. Units are shifted accordingly. Winterfeldt's battalions move out as vanguard of the left, Prince Johann von Schönaich's cavalry and Hans Zieten's hussars will circle behind to come up on his left.

The marshes and narrow trails delay deployment. A series of carp ponds east of Unter-Poczernitz are bridged with difficulty. It is very hard going. Men sink in places to their waists; others pick their way over narrow dams. Battalion cannon cannot move over such terrain and are shifted to the single available road, which is already crowded with heavy guns, now delayed. The approach march, slow and awkward as it is, continues without enemy interference, thanks to the rolling terrain. Meanwhile Prussian cuirassiers of the first line deploy south of Sterbohol. The dragoons are still coming up. Winterfeldt's infantry finally debouches onto lowlands west of Unter-Poczernitz.

Browne suddenly spots the approaching infantry. He notifies Prince Charles, who sends him strong reinforcements from the left. Browne shifts his cavalry south between Sterbohol and Unter-Mecholup. General Hadik with two hussar regiments is on the extreme right, vanguard of another hundred squadrons of cavalry. Just north of the cavalry on Homoly Hill is a battery of heavy cannon. Infantry battalions reinforce the lines north to Kej, but some are delayed by a deep ravine at Hrdlorzez.

It is about ten A.M. Winterfeldt's infantry pushes southwest of Unter-Poczernitz, with Schwerin himself bringing up the main body. The going is very slow through the marshlands. Austrian guns from Homoly Hill open canister fire. The men struggle on. Units are disorganized, the troops soon exhausted. Winterfeldt sees the danger in delay. Without orders he leads eight battalions to the assault. They are joined by three flanking regiments.

The king rides up and complains to Schwerin that the isolated attack is premature. *"Frische Eier, gute Eier,"* the old field marshal responds before riding to join his cavalry in the assault.[1] Schwerin means that the early bird gets the worm. These are the last words he will speak to his king.

Schwerin rides to Prince von Schönaich, who, with only twenty cuirassier squadrons, is waiting for his dragoons. Schwerin orders him to attack and be damned. The Prussians charge Count Joseph Lucchesi's first line, send it reeling back, but the second line holds while Hadik's hussars move in from left and rear to send the Prussians in retreat. But now the delayed dragoons, twenty squadrons, arrive, and so do two hussar regiments sent by the king from his reserve. Thus supported, Schönaich attacks again. Zieten's hussars from the left outflank Hadik and wedge his hussars from the main body. But again Austrian numbers tell, and from a fearful dust cloud of men and horses the Prussians retire south of Sterbohol. The disorganized enemy does not pursue.

What of Winterfeldt's attack? Fourteen battalions move out with shouldered muskets, Schwerin's orders being not to fire but to use only the bayonet! Only a few battalion cannon are available; the others are stalled on that damned road, which is ruining everything. Heavy cannon fire from Homoly Hill tears through the lines; enemy light cannon shift to canister fire. Regiments Schwerin, Fouqué, and Kursell count fifty percent casualties. Generals Fouqué and Kursell themselves fall wounded. The survivors advance. They are three hundred paces from the enemy right, which begins to waver. Then Winterfeldt is shot through the throat and falls. The attack falters.

Schwerin is watching. He sees his regiment give way. This will never do. With an aide, Captain Alexander von Platen, he gallops to the ranks. Platen is shot dead. Schwerin seizes a battalion standard, leads his men forward. Five canister balls kill a seventy-three-year-old man. Panic-stricken soldiers stream from the field, a wild retreat stopped only by Zieten's hussars.

Meanwhile the king, still throwing up, is sending aides to hurry the march of the second infantry line and the heavy guns. Batteries move into position south of Hostawitz and northeast of Sterbohol while twelve battalions of the second line reinforce the vulnerable center.

It is about ten-thirty A.M. In the Austrian camp Browne wants to exploit his victories on the right by a general counterattack. He is giving these orders when a cannonball smashes his leg. He is badly hurt and is evacuated. The counterattack fizzles to a few isolated and fruitless advances.

But now twelve battalions of the Prussian second line reach the field. From west of Hostawitz, Generals Heinrich von Hautcharmoy and Joachim von Treskow lead eight battalions forward, an advance supported by fire from the new heavy battery on their left. Bevern follows with ten battalions.

It is too much for the Austrian line. Its right falls back to its old position by Homoly Hill. But Hautcharmoy wedges into the middle to force back both enemy flanks. With that, the heavy battery on Homoly Hill is uncovered and hastily withdraws.

Zieten meanwhile rounds up fleeing Prussians and, reinforced by twenty-five fresh squadrons, returns to the attack against the far Austrian right. It is a strong, bold move that sends enemy squadrons reeling. Those who stand are struck by following dragoons. Flight is survival. They run. They are beaten and will not appear again. Their flight exposes the Austrian right, which also retreats. Exhausted Prussian horse cannot follow very far.

The Austrians suffer another important casualty. Prince Charles collapses and is evacuated to Wischerad, where he is bled and finally regains consciousness — but he, too, is out of the battle.

It is about eleven A.M. Frederick calls up more reserves, orders Prince Ferdinand of Brunswick to attack at Kej. Count Königsegg commands the Austrian line here. It is vicious fighting, but Königsegg is outnumbered and a bayonet attack sends his shattered regiments back to Maleschitz and Tabor Hill. Hautcharmoy is wounded; Treskow takes over and with Bevern pushes after the enemy.

There is still the right flank. Major General Manstein commands the first line north of Kej Pond, Prince Henry the second line. Concerned with center and left, Frederick sends no orders to these commanders. Manstein grows increasingly frustrated by the sound of battle. He decides to attack the defended heights of Hlaupetin. Austrian irregulars quickly give way, the grenadiers pursuing toward Hrdlorzez. Henry is annoyed by the unauthorized attack but decides to support it. He sends Manstein one battalion and follows with a regiment. Enemy guns on Tabor Hill open fire. Henry sends Manstein an order to wait for the battalions coming up. Artillery fire is hurting Manstein's grenadiers. They escape to a protective valley north of Tabor Hill. Henry orders up his reserve regiment and some cannon and continues toward Hrdlorzez.

West of Hrdlorzez ravine is infantry commanded by Generals Clerici and Peroni, who are suddenly ordered to Maleschitz. This move opens their left flank to Henry's cannon and, suddenly, to attack by Manstein's people from the valley and by Brunswick's regiments from the front. Peroni is killed, Clerici badly wounded. Their troops fight hard but are driven from Tabor Hill. Henry with two regiments continues his advance on Hrdlorzez. Somewhat ingloriously, he leads the advance into a muddy brook and is almost drowned before musketeers pull him out. He recovers and is soon looking at Königsegg's left flank. The Austrians again retreat west.

Frederick is directing the action in the center. He feeds in reserve battalions as needed. His line stretches southeast from Hrdlorzez to Maleschitz and south to Neu-Straschnitz, his left flank covered by cavalry and infantry. He hopes that his left wing can reach the Moldau south of Wischerad to block enemy escape to the Sazawa River.

The Austrians are still not beaten. There are the fresh regiments anchored on the Ziskaberg; they now wheel to form a line facing east, the left still on the Ziskaberg. Tired and confused Prussians on the right see fresh Austrian units. They pause. Frederick orders a cavalry charge, but only one cuirassier regiment responds — to no effect. But the Prussian left does not pause. It is strong, and the enemy line begins to break.

On the far Prussian right Henry, sword in hand, rides from battalion to battalion to urge a final attack on the Austrian left. It is unnecessary. The enemy right has folded, and now the center and left are in full retreat.

The battle of Prague is over by three P.M.

Most of the enemy fled into Prague. Some escaped to the south, a few were captured, but there was no thought of major pursuit. Dead and dying men covered the long battlefield. Prussian battalions were so confused that they were not sorted out until the next day. Prussian casualties numbered four hundred officers and some fourteen thousand men, of whom over thirty-four hundred were killed. One field marshal and one general were dead, three other generals, including Hautcharmoy, would soon die from wounds, Winterfeldt and Fouqué were seriously wounded. "I have lost Marshal Schwerin, one of the greatest generals of this century," Frederick wrote to King George of England. Austrian casualties counted over four hundred officers and about thirteen thousand men, of whom nearly forty-three hundred were prisoners. Browne was mortally wounded and died a few weeks later — "a gallant man," Frederick wrote to Wilhelmina, "and I believe their best general." Numerous deserters from Prague and from Daun's army continued to come in for days.

"We have totally beaten the Austrian army," Frederick wrote to Wilhelmina that night. "They are entirely separated, a large part have escaped to Prague, and I hope to make all their generals and almost all their infantry prisoners of war." To his mother, the dowager queen, he jubilantly wrote, "The Austrians risk losing the entire campaign, and I find myself free with 150,000 men. . . . The Austrians are dispersed as straw in the wind. I shall send a part of my troops to compliment the French gentlemen, and I shall follow the Austrians with the rest of my army." Glowing accounts of the battle continued to be sent to relatives and friends. "My brother Henry has worked wonders," he informed the Prince of Prussia, not very tactfully, since William had not participated in the battle.

All this was for public consumption. The victory had certainly upset the Vienna court and put the city in great alarm. It also added weight to Lieutenant Colonel Mayr's rapacious campaign, which had caused several Catholic electors either to declare neutrality or look sourly on the "ban of the Empire" passed against Prussia. Nor was the French court favorably impressed with its ally's dismal show of arms. And in England the Prussian king's popularity was at an all-time high. Even women and children sang his praises, Lord Holdernesse informed Mitchell.

But Mitchell found the king "unflushed with Victory, and moderate in the midst of Success." Frederick privately admitted that his battle to destroy the Austrian army had failed. He blamed Prince Maurice of Dessau for not having constructed the vital bridge; he blamed the cavalry for feckless performance; he blamed General Manstein's premature and senseless attack on the far right.

In turn he was blamed by his brothers and some of his generals, not alone for undertaking a hopeless war that could end only in ignominious peace (if not total destruction of Prussia), but also for pushing on to Prague in too great a hurry.

Perhaps he also blamed himself, for he later wrote that "the pillars of the Prussian infantry" had fallen in this battle.

76

A DAY after the battle of Prague, Frederick informed Field Marshal Keith that their most urgent task was to force the enemy inside city walls to surrender — "and then I believe that the war will be finished." Assault was out of the question, but, because of the swollen garrison and limited provisions, a siege should soon bring surrender. An effective siege, however, demanded heavy guns. To bring the ponderous siege train from Pirna to Leitmeritz by boat and then overland to Prague would require several weeks.

Frederick saw nothing wrong with this. The capital could be blockaded until the guns arrived; there was no danger of it being relieved. He believed that Marshal Daun (who had replaced Serbelloni) was at Königgrätz with a mere twenty thousand troops. Daun reportedly was ruled by fear and confusion; he lacked forage and bread; he had no desire to attack anyone. Zieten upset this comfortable assumption by reporting that Daun was moving on Böhmisch-Brod with a considerable force. General Georg Puttkamer, whose hussars had pursued the Austrians retreating southward, reported that a large number had escaped across the Sazawa to join the Austrian rearguard, which now numbered about sixteen thousand. This unhappy situation caused the king to send a strong task force under the Duke of Bevern to observe the Austrians.

The Prussians meanwhile had cleaned the Prague battlefield, an immense task. "It is dreadful beyond conception to walk in a field of battle after a victory," a Prussian officer wrote, "to see friends and enemies, men and horses, the dead and dying, all heaped together . . . and almost floating in blood. . . . The stench of carnage fills the air with infection, and the groans of those that yet live rise as it were in

Battle of Kolin
June 18, 1757

Scale in miles
½ 1 2 3

Infantry   Austrian
Cavalry   Prussian
Artillery

N

To Nimburg

Elbe R.

To Prague
Wrbschan
Planjan
Novemiesto
SLATI SLUNCE
Brzistwi
Chosenitz
Krzeczhorz
Hradenin
Kolin
EICHENBUSCH
Radowesnitz
Kaurzim
Krychnow
Swojschitz
To Kuttenberg
Malotitz

d'Art Studio

union on every side." The peasants had fled in panic, and because the
ground was "hard and rocky, the interment of the dead went on more
slowly than usual."[1] There were not nearly enough Prussian surgeons,
so more had to be hastily brought in from Saxony and Brandenburg,
along with nurses, dressings, and medicines. The lightly wounded were
evacuated to Welwarn, from where they were transported in empty
flour wagons to Leitmeritz and further evacuation to Dresden.

Soldiers were also busy fortifying the area with mines and *chevaux
de frise* and preparing sites for siege guns coming from Saxony. Croatian irregulars were cleaned out from the Ziskaberg vineyards. Enemy
irregulars swarmed around the army, attacking supply convoys from
Leitmeritz and otherwise harassing the Prussians. The victors were also
under frequent cannon fire from Prague. In many places the Prussian
camp was only a thousand yards from the walls or within range of
enemy cannon, and the soldiers had to be on constant guard against
raiding parties. A large one was beaten off, with heavy Austrian casualties. Another one succeeded in capturing several cannon.

It was not a pleasant period for the king. He learned from the Duke of Brunswick that the Vienna and Versailles courts had signed a new treaty, which pledged France to take the field with 115,000 to 120,000 men and not lay down arms until Austria had seized all of Silesia. Podewils reported that Russian ships and galleys had entered the Baltic. A deserter testified that Prague held a two-month supply of provisions.

Frederick's main hope was to bombard the capital into submission. The siege train brought twelve 50-pounder mortars with six thousand bombs; twenty 12-pounder cannon with twenty thousand balls; ten 24-pounder cannon with ten thousand balls. Added to the army's own artillery, these formed siege batteries of fifty-eight heavy cannon and guns — not nearly enough for the task at hand.

A rocket flared over the Ziskaberg to open the bombardment on the night of May 29. Cloudbursts that night and the next day severely hampered operations, but on the third day fires sprang up in the old city. The bombardment continued to cause fires and some damage but failed to break the enemy's will. Munitions soon ran short. Only nine days after the bombardment had begun, Keith was ordered to begin dismantling his batteries. Only starvation would bring surrender. Bombardment had turned to blockade, which had to continue indefinitely.

Tactical failure never bothered Frederick for very long. The key now, he decided, was to push Daun into Moravia. With no hope of relief, Charles would surrender Prague, and Frederick would be free to march on the French.

The Duke of Bevern was at Kolin with nearly nineteen thousand men. Frederick reinforced him with another five thousand and pressed him to move against General Nádasdy at Gang. Marshal Daun was at Czaslau, showing no desire for battle, nor did the king believe that his army counted fifty thousand, as reported by Bevern.

Bevern easily pushed Nádasdy's light troops from Gang and Kuttenberg, and Daun began retirement on Deutsch-Brod. But Maria Theresa, leaning that Charles could hold out at Prague only until June 20, ordered Daun to relieve him. Early on June 13 Zieten's corps ran into Nádasdy south of Kuttenberg, and behind Nádasdy came Daun's entire army! Zieten's prompt covering action gave Bevern time to fall back on Kolin. Here he learned that King Frederick (who had no idea of recent events) was personally on the way with a reinforcement of four battalions, six squadrons, and fifteen heavy cannon.

After considerable confusion, Bevern and the king met at Malotitz. Frederick ordered Prince Maurice to join them with another corps. He then tried to outflank Daun, but was unsuccessful.

Daun was being his usual cautious self. On June 16 he marched northwest on Planjan in order to gain the Prussian left flank and secure his line of supply (and possibly retreat) by holding the Imperial highway. Late that evening the main Austrian army was deployed in two

lines facing west between Hradenin and Krychnow. General Beck's irregulars held Planjan, and Nádasdy's irregulars remained south of the
main army.

(◎▦◎)

Friday, June 17, 1757. With Nádasdy's irregulars squatting to his rear
and swampy ground on Daun's left, the Prussian king does not even
consider an attack. Instead, he screens his right and turns the march
northwest. Late that evening the army is safely camped between
Wrbschan and Kaurzim, a good position with protected flanks: thirty-
three thousand men and twenty-eight heavy cannon ready for battle.

The army is scarcely in the camp when outposts report a large dust
cloud from the direction of the Austrians. Frederick hurries to a nearby
height. The enemy is obviously in movement, but where and why he
does not know.

Friday–Saturday, June 17–18, 1757. Daun learns of the Prussian march
and receives false reports that Frederick this night will be reinforced to
a total strength of sixty thousand. Fearing for his right flank, he shifts
the army to face north, his left behind the marshlands of Swojschitz,
his right at Radowesnitz. The move will be complete by early morning:
fifty-four thousand men and sixty cannon ready for battle.

Saturday, June 18, 1757. A beautiful clear night turns to early morning
fog. Frederick is still ignorant of enemy plans. He sends General Joachim
Treskow with a task force to seize heights north of Planjan. They are
crowded with Croatian irregulars, who run at the sound of cannon.

The army marches at six A.M., Zieten leading the advance guard
through Planjan east on the Imperial highway. The first line follows
him, the second marches on the left, picks up Treskow's corps, and
continues east through fields of growing corn. At Planjan the king climbs
the church tower but fails to spot the enemy. The country is new to
him; he has no map. All he knows of the enemy and the terrain is what
he can see. His luck is better at Novemiesto, where, from the top story
of an inn, he sees enemy lines. Austrian infantry are standing under
arms, cavalrymen are mounted, cannon ready. Frederick judges this to
be Daun's right flank, which he believes to be vulnerable. He will attack here — not knowing that this is Daun's center, not knowing that
Nádasdy's corps forms the right flank.

The advance guard halts at Slati Slunce, the Golden Sun Inn. The
main army comes up. Zieten with a strong hussar force prowls eastward. The day is already hot, the troops already tired. They rest while
the king rides with Bevern and some aides to study land and enemy.
Back at the inn, the king issues orders. General Johann von Hülsen's
advance guard will attack Daun's right flank. The main army will fol-

low and, when west of Krzeczhorz, will wheel right to the attack. Prince Maurice will support Hülsen. Cavalry will remain behind each wing. Zieten will cover the left flank, Bevern the right.

Daun watches the enemy march and halt. With the bulk of the Prussian army here, Daun's left is safe. He moves his reserve behind the second line of the right wing.

It is nearly one P.M. Daun is puzzled at the enemy's long halt. What is he up to? Prussian bayonets suddenly glisten in the sun, answering his question. Dust rises as columns march eastward. Daun and his officers are momentarily fascinated by the spectacle. Then they realize that Frederick intends to attack. Orders are given, aides ride forth, drums call infantry to arms, troopers mount, gunners stand by cannon.

An hour later, flanked by Zieten's hussars, Hülsen's battalions march on Krzeczhorz. They brush off musket fire from Croatian irregulars, but canister shot and the fire of heavy cannon tear up their ranks as they push forward. Hülsen is reinforced, seizes Krzeczhorz and a large stand of oak trees — the Eichenbusch — storms the heavy battery to the south, and captures seven guns. Frederick sends more cavalry to join Zieten's sweep against Nádasdy's corps, which forms Daun's extreme right. Nádasdy is pushed back to Radowesnitz. Hülsen can turn safely to the attack.

Daun begins to reinforce Count Wied's infantry on the threatened right with two infantry regiments backed by four cavalry regiments.

Frederick in front of the left wing is watching Hülsen's attack. Enemy cannon increase fire — a ball careens not far from his horse. Canister fire is shredding Hülsen's battalions. The king orders Prince Maurice to march obliquely to his support. Maurice misunderstands and marches on Chosenitz. Even worse, part of Hülsen's force is moving west *across the enemy front*. The king gallops to Maurice, furiously orders him to turn his battalions. Now he hears an unwelcome sound of battle on his right. He gallops along the line and learns that Major General Manstein, against orders, is attacking Croat-infested corn fields. Unable to stop the attack, which leaves a dangerous gap in the line, Frederick fills it with four battalions from the second line. He returns to the left wing. Hülsen still needs help. In desperation, the king draws his sword and on horseback leads some units through the high corn. Hülsen sees them coming. His heavy cannon are in position. He attacks the enemy flank, overruns a heavy battery.

Meanwhile, Treskow's nine battalions are moving against the Austrian center. It is a good defense backed by heavy cannon. The attack falters, then presses on. But one division yields; the Austrian center is confused; the right is in trouble. Daun suddenly sees defeat instead of victory.

But the Prussian left and center begin to falter. Thanks to Manstein's private war on the right, the king has no reserve battalions.

And now it is the enemy's turn. If Daun did order retreat, as some observers say, his generals pay no attention. Wied receives reinforcements, drives the Prussians from the oak wood, occupies it to threaten Hülsen's left. Hülsen and Treskow, very weak now, are momentarily stymied. It is up to the cavalry. Frederick orders General Peter von Penavaire forward. The sixty-seven-year-old general hopes for surprise. He moves in west of Brzistwi. The surprise is a ravine and enemy cannon fire, followed by a clash with enemy horse. The attack stops; his troopers retreat to the Imperial highway.

Frederick sends in his cavalry reserve. General Christian Siegfried von Krosigk and Colonel Friedrich Wilhelm von Seydlitz approach with cuirassiers from the north, see the desperate situation, attack the Austrian right. Troopers with sabers gallop through corn fields, pass through Hülsen's thin ranks, smash into enemy horse, and send them reeling. But the enemy is strong; he counterattacks. The Prussians stand, attack again, are beaten off. Krosigk is killed, Seydlitz driven to retreat. Manstein is also losing his private war on the right. Outnumbered and with ammunition exhausted, the battered battalions begin retreat to the Imperial highway.

It is six P.M. Austrian cavalry attack the Prussian left from front, flank and rear. Units form squares in desperate efforts to hold ground. It is futile. Treskow is wounded and captured, along with scores of officers and men. Cavalry charges smash through the squares. Nineteen infantry battalions are shattered. Frederick orders Penavaire to provide cavalry cover for the retreating infantry. He no longer controls his squadrons, which are in retreat to the north. Nor can Zieten's people move their exhausted horses. The king momentarily loses his head. He summons a small troop to charge the battery south of Chosenitz. A cannonball smashes its ranks. The king rides almost alone. "Will His Majesty take the battery by himself?" an aide asks.[2]

Frederick stops. He is beaten. He sends Keith an order to lift the siege at Prague. He rides to his right flank, where Bevern commands six fresh battalions. Bevern's and Schönaich's cavalry will cover the retreat to Nimburg.

77

KOLIN was the king's first defeat, and it was a near disaster. The battle of Prague had cost over fourteen thousand casualties, and now

Kolin cost another fourteen thousand, including five thousand prisoners. Many wounded would in time return to service, and prisoners would be exchanged, but for the moment the once splendid army was seriously weakened.

Prompted by the specter of total defeat, Frederick moved rapidly. His first priority was tactical: to re-form the Kolin survivors and ensure that army's integrity while simultaneously quitting Prague before Daun's approach.

Frederick left the battlefield of Kolin late Saturday night. Sick and exhausted, he slept at Nimburg. In the morning he watched the survivors of the first battalion of Potsdam Guards file past, four hundred out of a thousand, and he wept. His emotion was brief. He turned command over to Prince Maurice of Dessau and rode to Prague, where Marshal Keith and Prince Ferdinand of Brunswick were already preparing a withdrawal.

The mood at Prague was grim, an atmosphere "of discouragement, discontent, and foreboding," Andrew Mitchell reported, with open and bitter criticism of the king's campaign.[1] He was referring to the Prince of Prussia and Prince Henry, and perhaps to Marshal Keith. An observer later wrote that when news of the defeat reached Prague, the assembled commanders "all stood silent, only the Prince of Prussia breaking out into loud lamentations and accusations."[2] Prince Henry wrote to William's wife, Princess Louise Emily: "So now Phaeton [Frederick] is fallen, and we do not know what will become of us. . . . Phaeton has looked after himself and retired before the loss of the battle was entirely decided."[3] Prince Ferdinand priggishly informed his sister Emily that "this is the consequence and the price paid for decisions taken in haste, without deference to the counsel of men of experience."[4]

How much of this reached the king's ears is not known, but he had too many favorites not to have learned what was happening. Yet his various letters and directives to William and Henry show no hostility. And no matter Henry's or Keith's grumbling, each was doing a good job: by late Sunday, most of the siege cannon and heavy baggage was moving north to Leitmeritz for water transport to Dresden. Frederick and Prince Ferdinand of Brunswick led the Ziskaberg contingent early the next day "with ringing music and the greatest pomp," in the king's words, to Alt-Lissa and finally to Leitmeritz.

Marshal Daun required considerable time to recover from the battle of Kolin. He had lost over eight thousand killed, wounded, and missing. It was the Austrians' turn to clean the battlefield and evacuate wounded and prisoners, and it all took time. There were also Te Deums to sing in celebration of that rare achievement, an Austrian victory.

Even news of the Prussian withdrawal from Prague failed to hurry the careful marshal. Several days passed before he joined Prince Charles, southeast of Prague. The two did not get on well and neither seemed intent on following the Prussians to deliver a coup de grâce. Lacking a real operations plan, they sent Lieutenant Colonel Baron Gideon von Loudon with two thousand irregulars down the left, or west, bank of the Elbe. General Nádasdy, with a larger corps, some thirteen thousand, followed Prince Maurice's army. The main Austrian army moved to Brandeis, northeast of Prague, and stood still. Caution was the watchword, it seemed, until Frederick again showed his hand.

Frederick was strictly on the defensive when he reached Leitmeritz on June 28. Lodged in the bishop's palace, he was at first "low spirited and saw nobody," Andrew Mitchell observed. Here he received a letter from Wilhelmina, reporting that, according to Chevalier Hubert Folard, the Versailles court was apprehensive lest Frederick make peace with Austria. She wondered whether she should query Folard and Marshal Belle-Isle as to what peace terms France wanted, and Frederick urged her to do so. A day or two later Mitchell found the king in reasonable spirits, talking "very reasonably and with great coolness upon the unhappy event" of Kolin: "What chiefly distresses him is the number of enemies and the attacks they are threatening in the different parts of his very extended dominions." He was strategically blocked and wished that England could make a peace. Barring that, he again asked for a small naval squadron to sail to the Baltic. In great embarrassment he told Mitchell it was possible that he might have to ask Britain for a subsidy, even though his "aversion to subsidies is now as strong as ever." Mitchell went on, "It is the first time I ever saw His Prussian Majesty abashed, and this was the only conversation I have had with him, which seemed to give him pain."[5]

There were also local problems. There were the wounded and the cannon to ship back to Dresden; prisoners to exchange with Daun; an enormous amount of back correspondence to answer; arrangements to be made for troop replacements from home cantons; the Austrian army to locate and attack if possible. Colonel Loudon's irregulars appeared and soon infested the main roads, falling on a Prussian party of two hundred that was escorting General Manstein to Dresden. Despite severe wounds, Manstein left his carriage, drew his sword, refused quarter, and was killed.* Nádasdy was harassing Prince Maurice, who fell back to Jung-Bunzlau, an unnecessary move that displeased the king. Frederick had already given this command to the Prince of Prussia. William had begged for an important appointment for years, but the king, though

---

* Frederick later described Manstein as "famous for having begun the battle of Prague and being responsible for the defeat of Kolin." (*Oeuvres*, Volumes 4 and 5, *Histoire de la Guerre de Sept Ans*.)

not derogating his military talents, believed that he lacked sufficient resolution. Now, perhaps because he had done a good job commanding Keith's rearguard during the retreat from Prague, perhaps also as result of his ill-judged criticisms of the king, he had one. He had not yet taken it up when Maurice compounded royal displeasure by announcing that he had to fall back on Zittau. This completely contradicted Frederick's tactical plan, and he refused to hear of it. William now relieved Maurice of command. It was scarcely a happy arrangement. William was surrounded by senior advisers, the Duke of Bevern, and four lieutenant generals — Schmettau (William's favorite), Winterfeldt (whom William and Schmettau detested), Fouqué, and Goltz, none of whom liked the other. Communicating with the king was also difficult because of enemy irregulars.

At this critical point a courier brought news that the dowager queen, seventy-year-old Sophia Dorothea, had died — a shock the greater since she reportedly had recovered completely from a recent illness. Her death was the final blow. "All misfortunes overwhelm me at the same time," the king wrote to Princess Emily. "I am more dead than alive." For two days he saw no one. Then he unburdened his grief to Andrew Mitchell and returned to the living. "I am forced to act," he told Wilhelmina, "and don't have time to give free course to my tears."

Wilhelmina had proposed still another move toward France. This was to send the lord chamberlain of her court, Chevalier Louis de Mirabeau, to meet with Madame de Pompadour and the Abbé Bernis (who had replaced Rouillé as foreign minister) on Wilhelmina's behalf. La Pompadour "is the sole cause of the bitterness against you," she informed her brother. "She has been told of some remarks, true or false, that you are said to have made against her and the king." Frederick authorized Mirabeau to offer Madame de Pompadour 500,000 thalers to arrange a peace and much more than that if, at the same time, "she can be enlisted to procure us some benefits." Count von Wied, a brother of a Prussian general, offered another entrée to the Versailles court. If Frederick sent an envoy to his house with a peace proposal, he would try to see that Belle-Isle presented it to the court. The king subsequently sent Colonel Johann Friedrich von Balbi, an engineer officer whom he knew, with a brief four-point plan and authorization to sign preliminaries.

He had reason to try anything. As victory at Prague had caused various enemies to hesitate, defeat at Kolin spurred them forward. Russia had invaded East Prussia. One army of eighteen thousand commanded by General Count Wilhelm von Fermor had closed on Memel, which was under siege and expected soon to fall. Field Marshal Count Stefan Apraxin with another seventy thousand troops was pushing back Marshal Lehwaldt's corps of thirty thousand. Sweden declared war and prepared to march on Pomerania with seventeen thousand. A French army seventy thousand strong under Marshal d'Estrées captured Embden and moved on the Duke of Cumberland's army, some forty-seven thousand men, which withdrew. The Imperial army, commanded by Field Marshal Joseph Friedrich von Sachsen-Hildburghausen, gained new life and was shortly reinforced by an Austrian contingent of eight thousand, bringing its total to thirty-three thousand. France sent a new force of thirty thousand under Prince Soubise to join the Prince of Hildburghausen in recovering Saxony. Prince Charles and Marshal Daun were at Brandeis with some seventy thousand troops, bent on gaining revenge against the hated Prussians. Frederick summed up his position to d'Argens: "Look at me as a battered wall breached by the misfortunes of two years."

The Austrians were his most pressing worry. Shortly after the Prince of Prussia assumed command at Jung-Bunzlau, he was instructed to retire northwest on Hirschberg to make it easier for the two armies to join in case of need. He was to eat out the country and protect the large magazine at Zittau. And he was to garrison Reichenberg, Grottau, and Gabel as he saw fit. Frederick approved William's further retirement on Neuschloss. His retirement on Böhmisch-Leipa drew a mild reprimand — he would soon be in the middle of Saxony without knowing it, Frederick cautioned. William nervously reported that he had only a ten-day supply of bread and almost no meat; enemy irregulars were preventing deliveries from the peasants. He wanted "positive orders" about his next move. After explaining the critical overall situation to his brother, the king wrote that he himself had two tasks: to cover Saxony from the south, and to fight the combined French and Imperial armies coming from the west. William would be reinforced and was to cover Lusatia and Silesia. "I am not able to prescribe to you the manner of execution," the king went on. "All this is very difficult, but consult your generals and take the best course as called for by circumstances." One thing was certain: William must stop retreating. That would always result in lack of bread and forage and loss by desertion as great as if one fought a battle. When William, plainly insecure and apprehensive, continued to argue, the king replied, "If you keep retiring, you will find yourself driven to Berlin within four weeks."

Prompted by Maria Theresa's frantic exhortations to do *something*, Prince Charles and Marshal Daun crossed the Elbe early on July 14 and marched on Gabel to outflank William's left. General Puttkamer on convoy duty was at the castle with four battalions. William heard lively cannon fire, called a council of war (from which Winterfeldt absented himself) — and did nothing. If Gabel was taken, he advised the king, he could march on Zittau only by a roundabout route through the mountains. A day later he reported that "we are in a very critical situation," but he still did not know whether Gabel had been taken. "You have lost your mind," the king responded. "Do you want to abandon your magazines, give up your cover of Lusatia? It would be better to give ten battles than to come to that. . . . You are following some timid counsel, which will ruin you, the state, and me. All these wretched maneuvers are coming from Schmettau's advice, who always sees black; I wish that the devil had sooner taken me than to have given him to you." On July 16 the prince reported, "Gabel is taken; I have only four days of bread; I march tomorrow via Kamnitz and Rumburg."

The replies were brutal. On July 18: "You are losing everything. Why did you not march with the army to aid Gabel on the fourteenth? After this it is impossible for me to trust you with command of an army." And on the next day: "You know neither what you want nor what you are doing. . . . You will always be a wretched general. . . . As long as I live I shall never trust you with the command of ten men."

It was too late for effective recrimination. Puttkamer held out against a corps of twenty thousand for three days before surrendering. William's difficult retreat on mountain roads often too narrow to accommodate wagons cost most of his baggage and supplies before the exhausted columns, further thinned by numerous desertions, closed on Zittau.* Here the Austrians had gained the dominant height and bombarded the town. Wooden huts blazed, fire devoured all magazines, and the trapped garrison had to surrender. William, now a sick man, continued the retreat to Bautzen in Lusatia.

His withdrawal had made the king's position untenable. Leaving Marshal Keith to evacuate magazines and Prince Maurice with a corps to screen the Pirna passes, Frederick marched north. On the way he learned from Andrew Mitchell that the British navy was overcommitted and could not send the promised squadron to the Baltic. "I was glad to find that he bore the disappointment with more temper and calmness than I expected," Mitchell reported. The envoy received another dispatch at Pirna; it reaffirmed Britain's alliance with Prussia, her intention to land a force on the French coast to draw the French from Germany, and her readiness to grant Frederick a subsidy. The hardpressed king received Mitchell's words "with a flow of gratitude not to be described," but he did not wish to negotiate a subsidy until his present situation was favorably resolved, for if it were not, he did not wish to become a useless burden to his allies. "I was pleased, but not surprised," Mitchell wrote, "with the noble dignity of this answer, for I

---

* I recently traced Prince William's retreat through this beautiful semimountainous land of enormous wooded hills and deep valleys, narrow roads, and tight turns — perfect guerrilla country that grows more difficult as one nears the border. What is surprising is that *any* of William's demoralized columns reached their destination.

have seen the King of Prussia great in prosperity, but greater still in adversity."[6]

Frederick almost immediately marched on to Bautzen, which he reached two days later than Prince William.

The king had ordered William and his generals to await his arrival outside Bautzen. He rode to the rendezvous in early morning. He scanned the waiting party, ignored his brother's salute, and dismounted. Flanked by Winterfeldt (who had been forgiven his sins*) and von der Goltz, he sat with his back to the others. A few uneasy minutes passed. Then General Goltz arose, approached William and his entourage, and in a firm voice announced the king's will: the prince and his generals deserved to be sentenced to death by court-martial, but William's position prevented this.

Few princes have suffered such humiliation; we can only sympathize with William, despite his costly errors. Very formally he replied to Goltz that he would welcome a court-martial. The following day he wrote to the king that he did not deserve the least reproach for his actions. Frederick replied that he and his generals were entirely responsible for the present "desperate situation. . . . Your ears are accustomed only to the language of flatterers; Daun has not flattered you, and you see the results." The consequences, he continued, could well prove disastrous to the kingdom: "You and your children will bear the consequences more than I. Despite this, be convinced that I have always loved you."

William must have greeted the final sentence with raised eyebrows. A few hours later he sent an aide to ask the king whether he could leave immediately for Dresden. Frederick coldly replied, "The prince may go where he will."

The brothers never again met.

78

THE PRUSSIAN move north solved almost nothing. Frederick wanted to bring the Austrians to battle, but he was forced to wait for flour from Saxony; he had only enough bread for three days and could not march until he had a nine-day supply. He now learned that the Duke

---

* The record is not clear, but apparently Winterfeldt was asleep during the crucial conference at which William and his generals decided to retire on Rumburg. This could well be true, since Winterfeldt was still recuperating from his throat wound and since William loathed him. Further, he was the most aggressive infantry general in the army and undoubtedly would have insisted on the relief of Gabel.

of Cumberland had finally stood against Marshal d'Estrées at Hastenbeck. Now, Cumberland was in retreat to Minden, not for strategic reasons but because his army's baggage had been sent there by mistake! No matter that the king was still hopeful for a separate peace with Versailles — that was far distant and very uncertain. No matter that the Hastenbeck fiasco had returned William Pitt to office. Pitt could not put an army in the way of either Duke d'Estrées or Prince Soubise. Hanover and Saxony stood open to attack from the west, and behind them, Brandenburg-Prussia.

More than ever it was urgent to seek out the Austrian enemy, as he explained in a letter to General Winterfeldt. Spies had reported accurately over enemy positions; only a secret conference with Marshal Daun could have told him more, he told Jacob Keith. It was now necessary "to strike while the iron was hot"; he intended to fight "a decisive battle" against Daun during a ten-day campaign, after which he and Keith would return to Dresden. But this depended on bread, and bread depended on flour, on the convoy "on which all my hopes are founded," indeed "on which I base the last hope of the state."

The vital convoy finally arrived and the army marched. The move caught the enemy off guard. The Duke of Bevern's hussars captured General Beck's baggage and forty pandours and almost got the general. They surprised General Nádasdy at dinner, and although he escaped, he lost some baggage and some secret correspondence from the Dresden court. But this was mere prelude to disappointment. The main Austrian army east of Zittau was so strongly entrenched on a dominant height that attack was out of the question. This left the king in an uncomfortable situation, since forage was in short supply. The cavalry "are eating you and me up," he complained to Bevern. To add to his problems, Austrian irregulars invaded Silesia and forced him to send a detachment there. Then he learned that Prince Maurice had fallen back from Cotta (against orders) because of Loudon, who commanded a mere twenty-five hundred irregulars: "I am not in the least satisfied with your conduct," he informed Maurice. "Go after the bastards. . . . Where is Prussian honor? . . . If your father [Old Dessauer] heard this he would turn in his grave." Peace overtures to France remained in limbo; both the French and the Swedes were reportedly marching against him. The French had overrun Hanover, and the Russians were carving up East Prussia, with the Cossacks committing terrible atrocities. His own bread supply was running out; he had tried without success every trick to lure Charles from his position. Obviously the brief campaign he had such hopes for was a failure.

In late August Frederick left Bevern and Winterfeldt with thirty-six thousand troops to screen Lusatia and Silesia and returned to Dresden.

His confidential secretary, August Eichel, found him amazingly "fresh and lively," as if he were in Potsdam during peacetime. Andrew Mitchell reported him "in as good spirits as if he had returned from a successful expedition." Peace with France, the king believed, would depend on a favorable outcome of the present campaign. He hoped to enlist the Ottoman Porte, where his envoy had £50,000 to work with. He was now forced to ask England for a subsidy of four million thalers — approximately £670,000 — for the next year. Mitchell pointed out that this would be the largest subsidy ever granted by England and that King George would have to satisfy Parliament as to how the money would be spent. King Frederick replied that he would not know that until the present campaign ended. He was not pleased to learn that Hanover was negotiating a treaty of neutrality with the enemy; it would be the "end of everything."

Having failed to bring Charles to battle, he turned westward. His small corps had been joined by Prince Maurice's corps, a total of only twenty thousand men, for a march on Erfurt "to thrash all the rabble that I shall find there" — by which he meant the French and Imperial armies. He hoped to find battle by mid-month: "September will decide our destiny during the winter."

More bad news arrived. Marshal Lehwaldt had attacked Marshal Apraxin's army of one hundred thousand Russians but was forced to retreat. The battle of Gross-Jägersdorf had cost the Russians dearly, but Lehwaldt had suffered over three thousand casualties. He was tired and sick and asked to be relieved, a request refused out of hand.

Frederick's earlier approaches to the French court had come to naught. Folard and Mirabeau failed to reach Madame de Pompadour, and Belle-Isle refused to become involved. Prompted by Wilhelmina and Voltaire, Frederick now turned to the Duke of Richelieu, a notoriously corrupt man who had replaced d'Estrées in command of the main French army. Frederick sent him a flattering letter and an undisclosed sum of money to gain his help in ending the war with Prussia. The effort failed before it began, with news that Richelieu and the Duke of Cumberland had signed the Convention of Kloster-Zeven, by which Hanover withdrew from the war and Cumberland's army became neutral, with each contingent taking quarter in its own land. This left Prussia alone to face the onslaught.

The strain was beginning to tell. Frederick and Keith were now so weak militarily that deceptive measures were necessary to keep the enemy at bay. Regiments were frequently transferred from one village to another and given new names so that spies would report an exaggerated order of battle. Prussia was nearly bereft of allies, the treasury almost empty, the enemy overwhelming. Winterfeldt in Lusatia had been mortally wounded in an attack by Nádasdy. The king originally had been informed that Winterfeldt's injuries were slight; indeed, Frederick wrote to him six days *after* his death. The shock of the general's death was all the greater. Frederick wrote to Wilhelmina that he was "so oppressed with grief that I would rather keep my sadness to myself." He was looking forward to dying sword in hand rather than suffering defeat followed by tyrannical rule of his enemies: "Sorrow is a century, death an instant." He had thought of suicide after the Kolin disaster and now proposed a mutual suicide pact with his sister. Wilhelmina pointed out that fortune has a way of changing: "A great genius like yours finds resources even when all is lost, and it is impossible for this frenzy to continue."

The frenzy did continue, and it is greatly to Frederick's credit that, aside from frequent lengthy jeremiads to Wilhelmina, Finckenstein, and on occasion his sister Emily, he conducted matters calmly and soundly. Mitchell was with him and reported that he "bears his Misfortunes with a great Magnanimity, and tho' They come very Thick, one upon Another, He never appears discouraged or disconcerted." [1]

Frederick's numerous letters to his commanders leave no doubt as to the extreme peril the army was facing — and no doubt of his determination to fight to the end. "In our situation," he wrote to Prince Ferdinand of Brunswick, "we must be convinced that one of us is worth four of them." But in late September he expressed doubts of survival to Finckenstein: "Some miracles are necessary or we are lost."

There had already been some miracles, albeit man-made. The first was the continuing dissension that reigned in the hostile alliance. In this autumn of 1757 the armies of Austria, France, Russia, and the Empire had virtually surrounded Prussia. A concerted effort could not but have overwhelmed him. But divergent goals compounded by fear, apathy, irresolution, jealousy, lack of money, and sheer political and military ineptness prevented such an effort. Marshal Apraxin's precipitate retreat was another miracle — he suddenly withdrew from East Prussia. The amazed Prussians thought that perhaps the czarina had died, which would have brought to the throne the pro-Prussian Grand Duke Peter, or that the Turks had invaded the Crimea. Neither was the case. A shortage of food had caused Apraxin to fall back on Tilsit. The march in cold, rainy weather had left his troops and horses exhausted and sick. Many of his wagons had to be burned. The disorganized and disheartened army made a further autumn offensive out of the question. More miracles were to come. Frederick performed a financial miracle by turning 400,000 thalers' worth of private silver into 800,000 thalers' worth of coins — a miracle brought off by simple alloy. He stopped all pensions, cut civil salaries in half, and then suspended them. Yet another miracle occurred when Ferdinand of Brunswick arranged an armistice with the Duke of Richelieu until the following spring, thus freeing some of Brunswick's troops for operations elsewhere.

Other miracles were needed, and Frederick set about, unknowingly, to receive them. In late September he withdrew his own small corps behind the Saale, where he hoped that Hildburghausen, "whom I regard as a fool, will follow me; then he marches on me and I fall on his back." From here he sent secret orders to Marshal Lehwaldt to retire on Marienwerder and Schwedt, from where he would either chase the Swedes back to Swedish Pomerania or go to the Duke of Bevern's aid in Silesia. Maurice was moved west of Leipzig in case Frederick needed help to fight the Imperial army. Bevern, who was falling back on Glogau, was sharply ordered to return to Breslau.

But all of this as yet solved nothing. On October 10 the king informed Count Finckenstein, "I regard our affairs as hopeless. . . . I no longer have resources and we should expect to see our misfortunes increase from one day to the next. Heaven is witness that this is not my fault." His mood darkened when he learned that an Austrian corps under Count Andreas Hadik was marching on Berlin. He ordered Prince Maurice to cross the Elbe at Torgau to block the Austrians at any cost — "to the last man" — while he and Brunswick hurried to the attack. But the enemy move was no more than a raid. Hadik's small corps reached Berlin on October 16, occupied only a part of the city, accepted a cash contribution of 200,000 thalers (and two dozen pairs of ladies' gloves), and departed before dawn the next day without doing any real damage. Frederick sent Maurice to follow him and Brunswick to shield the capital while he remained north of Torgau. On learning that General Baron Ernst Marschall with a corps of fifteen thousand was at Bautzen, Frederick decided to attack him there, push him back into Bohemia, and continue on to Schweidnitz to clean the enemy out of Silesia before the campaign ended.

But Keith suddenly reported from Leipzig that Soubise and Hildburghausen were in full march eastward; the French army was at Camburg; the Imperial army at Zeitz. "Things here have changed very much in one day," Frederick informed Maurice. No longer was Silesia the target. Soubise was marching on Leipzig and Hildburghausen on Halle, after which they would fall on Magdeburg and perhaps Berlin. "This is why I am waiting for them," Frederick told Finckenstein, "so as to engage them in a decisive battle, in order to free my hands here and then to protect my provinces in great distress elsewhere."

The trick now was not to frighten the enemy away. Frederick cautiously drew in his forces toward Keith in Leipzig — his own corps to Eilenburg, Maurice to villages west of the Elbe, Brunswick to Halle. It was a trap — providing the Imperial and French armies were serious in their advance.

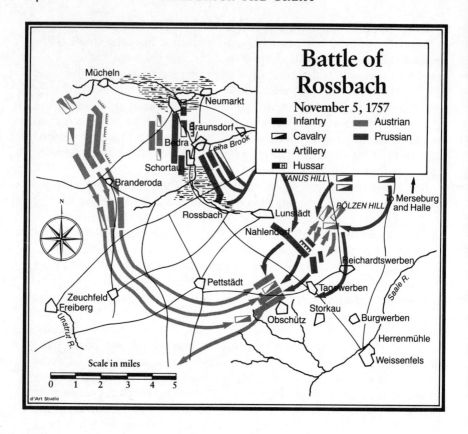

Battle of Rossbach
November 5, 1757

Mücheln

Neumarkt

Braunsdorf

Bedra

Leiha Brook

Schortau

Branderoda

VANUS HILL

To Merseburg and Halle

Rossbach

Lunstädt

PÖLZEN HILL

Nahlendorf

Reichardtswerben

Pettstädt

Zeuchfeld
Freiberg

Obschütz

Tagewerben

Storkau

Burgwerben

Saale R.

Unstrut R.

Herrenmühle

Weissenfels

Infantry
Cavalry
Artillery
Hussar
Austrian
Prussian

Scale in miles

0   1   2   3   4   5

d'Art Studio

79

THE FIFTY-FIVE-YEAR-OLD Prince of Hildburghausen was not a happy man. The contingents that made up the Imperial army lacked men, money, and matériel. A favorite of Madame de Pompadour, Prince Soubise, who commanded the French corps, showed little inclination to submit to Hildburghausen's command. Richelieu's reinforcement of twelve thousand troops arrived with no tents, no supply wagons, no reserve artillery, no munitions; indeed, most of the troops lacked shoes.

Soubise refused to cross the Saale river, much less attempt anything against the Prussians. Now, at the end of October, the Prussian army, commanded by its king, was at Weissenfels and Merseburg, obviously preparing to cross the river. Hildburghausen was at Storkau, worrying about his supply lines to Erfurt; Soubise was southwest of Merseburg. There was no agreed plan; neither commander would join the other.

Hildburghausen finally gave in and joined Soubise at Mücheln in early November. He was not pleased with the new camp, which is "so confused," he wrote to Emperor Francis, "that I have never seen the like in my life."[1] The French cavalry commander, Count Claude Louis de Saint-Germain, noted that the position opened the flank and rear to enemy attack: "The camp . . . was detestable in every respect," he later wrote, "and we would only have been beaten there or died from hunger."[2]

Thursday, November 3, 1757. King Frederick's corps crosses the Saale at Herrenmühle in early morning, the cavalry fording the river. Maurice and Keith cross at Merseburg. The king does not know that his enemies are at Mücheln. He reasons that they are probably falling back on the Unstrut River for supply reasons: "As for me, I shall act the pandour," he had informed Keith the previous day, "and as soon as I have crossed the Saale I shall try to cut their convoys from Freiberg." Nevertheless, Maurice and Keith are to join him in case the enemy is on hand: "One battle will decide everything," he tells Keith. He arrives at Braunsdorf in midafternoon to learn that the enemy is close by. He rides to some heights south of Bedra. It is nearly dark, but he makes out — and peasants confirm — that the enemy army *is facing north.* He decides to attack its right flank in the morning. He returns to headquarters in the Braunsdorf rectory. The rest of the army arrives that evening. He issues attack orders and goes to bed.

On this same day, Hildburghausen insists on a change of camp, because the Prussians undoubtedly will march from Weissenfels. Soubise is not interested. Soubise is showing a sudden desire for battle (hitherto absent); perhaps he sees another Kolin and a marshal's baton. The two commanders are still arguing in the afternoon when hussars report that the Prussians are marching from Weissenfels. Soubise agrees to change camp that night. The Imperial army shifts to heights south of Branderoda while the French move their front to the east. Prussian hussars disturb the camp during the night.

Friday, November 4, 1757. King Frederick early learns of the enemy move. At three A.M. he rides to heights west of Schortau, where a full moon shines on the new enemy position. He estimates their strength at fifty-five to sixty thousand. He will attack despite his number, twenty-one thousand. Three hours later he again examines the position. The enemy is well entrenched, heavy with cannon, too strong to attack. Besides, the men must be hungry and will have to make a move. Then Frederick can either attack or force them back to the Unstrut. He decides to withdraw behind Leiha Brook to wait for Hildburghausen's move. It is a splendid position. The Prussians can see the enemy; the enemy cannot see the Prussians.

Hildburghausen's desire to withdraw to the Unstrut is dampened by the Prussian presence. He and Soubise consider two possibilities: to maneuver the Prussian king out of his position or to attack him. The decision, largely Soubise's, is to march east on Tagewerben in order to outflank the Prussian left. By threatening Frederick's communications to Weissenfels, this will force him either to retire or to attack. Should he do neither, they will attack the day following. Hildburghausen is not pleased with the plan.

Saturday, November 5, 1757. Hildburghausen perhaps dreams of glory. He awakes inspired. He writes to Soubise at five A.M. that they should not lose a moment in attacking the Prussians! Soubise is interested. At daybreak Saint-Germain's cavalry and Loudon's irregulars push back Prussian outposts from the heights west of Schortau and remain there to cover the Prussian right. Hildburghausen and Soubise ride there and hold a brief council of war. They agree on an immediate attack.

Eight A.M. Drummers call men to arms; the army prepares to march. This is a slow process. Soubise insists on changing his order of battle. Then he waits for his professional pillagers to come in from outlying villages. Several hours pass before the army marches.

Frederick learns of considerable movement in the enemy camp. General Seydlitz and Colonel Mayr are sent out but are driven back by fire from Saint-Germain and Loudon. Frederick climbs to the roof of the manor house in Rossbach village. He studies the enemy through a spyglass. As he stands there, the point of the army appears. It is marching south, obviously to the Freiberg magazine. Frederick hands his glass to an aide, Captain Friedrich von Gaudi, and goes downstairs for dinner.

Eleven-thirty A.M. Hildburghausen cannot persuade Soubise to march. He moves out on his own. Soubise grudgingly follows. Just north of Zeuchfeld the columns, with cavalry and hussars in the lead, turn left toward Pettstädt. Five wide columns make for a ponderous march. Hildburghausen and Soubise are still arguing, the former for immediate attack, the latter for a day's delay. At two P.M. the army halts at a small farmstead.

Frederick is eating dinner when Gaudi reports an enemy turn toward Pettstädt. Gaudi suggests that the enemy is trying to outflank the Prussian left, and Mayr confirms this. Frederick receives the suggestion very ungraciously, because it is obvious that Hildburghausen is marching on Freiberg. Nonetheless he takes Keith, Brunswick, Henry, von Geist, and Seydlitz to his private eyrie. They see only enemy cavalry, which

Frederick points out are merely on reconnaissance. Then, enemy infantry appear, shattering royal omniscience. It is clear that the enemy is marching on Pettstädt. It is also clear that the Prussians will attack him. Frederick orders tents struck, the infantry to wheel left and form line behind Lunstädt, cavalry to the front, Mayr in front of Brunswick's right wing to screen Saint-Germain and Loudon. Seydlitz, at thirty-six the youngest cavalry general present, will command the vital thirty-eight squadrons ordered to cut the enemy's march. Senior eyebrows belonging to Generals Peter von Meinicke and Baron Schönaich are raised when Seydlitz takes command. He settles matters with a simple statement: "Gentlemen, I obey the king, and you obey me."[3] The Prussian army is ready to march at two-thirty P.M.

The burning question, to attack or not to attack, is still being debated by Hildburghausen, Soubise, and their generals. But as they argue, Prussian tents begin disappearing. They vanish in less than two minutes, "as if they had been a stage set in a theater," an onlooker later wrote.[4] Obviously the Prussians are retiring to cross the Saale at Merseburg; this is soon confirmed by a reconnaissance report that the entire Prussian army is on the march. All agree that the Prussians must be attacked as soon as possible. The Duke of Broglie's reserve cavalry and four of Count Augustin Mailly's cavalry regiments march forward to strengthen the advance guard of hussars and cavalry. The march continues.

Frederick is watching the enemy. His own infantry form as ordered. He orders Colonel Moller to mount twelve heavy cannon on Janus Hill.

Moller opens fire on Broglie and Mailly north of Reichardtswerben. The fire is effective, but the cavalry continue forward. Prussian infantry complete their deployment. Seydlitz forms two lines of cavalry behind Pölzen Hill with hussar squadrons on his left.

Four P.M. Seydlitz attacks. The move is a complete surprise that hits the front and flank of the advance guard. A few squadrons manage to deploy, but Seydlitz's second line moves viciously on their flanks while hussars complete the havoc. Retreating squadrons block Broglie's and Mailly's approach. Seydlitz's people take advantage of the terrible confusion. In less than thirty minutes, the entire advance guard, fifty-seven squadrons, is running south from battle. Seydlitz, who is wounded, pursues only a short way, then wisely re-forms and takes a waiting position between Tagewerben and Storkau.

Frederick meanwhile orders the infantry to attack. Shielded by hills, they move out from the left in echelon, fifty paces between battalions, to close east of Lunstädt. As the extreme left climbs from a ravine north of Reichardtswerben, it sees enemy cavalry in full flight. The king or-

ders the battalions to move into line from Nahlendorf to west of Reichardtswerben. He is riding on the left. He brings several battalions to
the left to form an obtuse angle, which blocks the enemy's advance.
Moller shifts heavy cannon from Janus Hill to close support. Another
battery is mounted south of Nahlendorf.

The fast, brutal action demoralizes the enemy infantry. Hildburghausen, bleeding from a saber gash, does his best, personally leading a
regiment in a bayonet charge, a valiant if futile attempt that evokes
even Soubise's admiration. Frederick orders the entire Prussian line forward. With the left wing closing the bag, Seydlitz again attacks. French
and Imperials throw weapons to the ground, run south from battle.
Only two Swiss regiments retire in order. The Prussians pursue to Obschütz, taking numerous prisoners and most of the baggage.

Five-thirty P.M. Darkness alone saves the enemy, who are in frantic
flight south to Freiberg and beyond. The Prussians continue the pursuit, but it is dark and the men are tired. Frederick halts the infantry
just east of Obschütz. Men make cookfires from wooden stocks of captured muskets.

The king takes headquarters in the manor house at Burgwerben. He
finds the rooms filled with wounded French officers. He moves to a
nearby servant's cottage and begins dictating dispatches.

It was a fantastic tactical victory. The Prussians counted just over five
hundred casualties, of which 170 were killed. The enemy lost over ten
thousand, mostly prisoners (including eleven generals). "Heaven has
blessed the just cause," the king wrote to Podewils, instructing him to
have Te Deums sung to accompaniment of cannon and musket fire at
Berlin, Stettin, and Magdeburg. "Now I shall descend to the tomb in
peace," he told Wilhelmina, "since the reputation and honor of the
nation is preserved."

Early the following day Frederick left a regiment to sort out the
wounded while the main army marched on Freiberg. Cavalry and hussar patrols fanned out to round up enemy stragglers. Such was local
hatred of the French that farmers and peasants led the Prussians to
woods and villages that sheltered French fugitives.* Some surrendered;
others resisted and were shot. Pursuit continued to Eckartsberga.

It was also an immense strategic victory. The Imperial army was in
near dissolution, remnants cold and hungry, utterly defeated, sick and
frightened, huddling in miserable camps around Weimar and Erfurt.
Two days after the battle, the Prince of Hildburghausen asked Emperor

---

* A special "Relation" trumpeted the victory to all courts and widely publicized the French
excesses. The liberators of Saxony, it stressed, were nothing more than the rapists of Saxony.

Francis whether he could resign his command. "My martyrdom is finished," he wrote to a friend. "For if the emperor would give me a million a month, I would no longer stay here."[5] A few days later he wrote to Emperor Francis that he had never seen such a rout and such panic-stricken men. Soubise was in no better shape: "I write Your Majesty [King Louis] in the depths of despair; the rout of your army is total; I am not able to say how many officers have been killed, captured, or lost."[6] Neither Louis nor his entourage received the news graciously.* Warned that the King of Prussia might well appear at the gates of Paris, the Duchess of Orléans wryly exclaimed, "Thank God, at last I shall see a man."

Victory at Rossbach eliminated a major threat from the west but also brought another important gain. King George of England's son the Duke of Cumberland was in disgrace; his somewhat fragmented and demoralized army was in winter quarters at Stade. A month earlier the Prussian king had offered to send Marshal Lehwaldt's corps — once it had chased the Swedes from Pomerania — to join the Hanoverian army and push the French from Germany. Although the British monarch had realized that the Convention of Kloster-Zeven was worthless, since the French had continued to plunder Hanover, he was not ready to renew the continental war, despite William Pitt's urgings that he do so. Frederick's fantastic victory changed his mind. Andrew Mitchell now asked Frederick whether he would permit Prince Ferdinand of Brunswick to take command of the Hanoverian army. Frederick was delighted to "lend" Ferdinand's services, and in mid-November the prince was on his way to Stade.

80

WITH THE WESTERN FRONT QUIET, the King of Prussia turned east. The situation in Silesia was neither good nor bad. General Nádasdy was besieging Schweidnitz with twenty thousand troops, but Frederick believed that this fortress should hold out for at least six weeks to two months. Prince Charles and Marshal Daun, with an army of sixty thousand at Lissa, showed little inclination to move on the Duke of Bevern, who held the left bank of the Oder near Breslau. Indeed, Bevern seemed bent on attacking Charles at the first opportunity,

---

* Soubise nevertheless was soon given a marshal's baton through Madame de Pompadour's influence.

an attitude applauded by the king, who cautioned him against being talked out of it by "timid people." Frederick intended to raise the siege of Schweidnitz and then assist Bevern in driving the Austrians out of Silesia. "This will decide everything," he wrote to Wilhelmina, "and then we must negotiate, if it is possible, in order to have the peace [treaty] this winter." Prince Henry, who had been slightly wounded, would remain in Leipzig to command operations in Magdeburg and Halberstadt. Jacob Keith with a larger force would march to Bohemia and make a feint at Prague to draw General Marschall from Lusatia.

The king marched on November 13 with only eighteen battalions and twenty-nine squadrons, about thirteen thousand troops. There was no doubt that he was looking for another "decisive battle." From Torgau he asked Bevern to send exact information on enemy location, but the best intelligence, he added, would be word that Bevern had defeated Charles or at least pushed him in Frederick's direction.

Three days later Frederick learned that Nádasdy had unsuccessfully stormed fortress Schweidnitz, at a cost of six to eight thousand casualties. But the following morning, for no apparent reason, its commandant capitulated, losing ten battalions, ten hussar squadrons, valuable magazines, artillery, ammunition, and a war chest of 350,000 thalers. "I am blaming you for the loss of Schweidnitz," the king informed Bevern; had Bevern attacked the enemy, this never would have happened. If Generals Friedrich Kyau and Johann Lestwitz continued to act "like old whores," they would answer with their heads, as would all other generals who allowed themselves to be ruled by cowardice and weakness. Bevern was to attack Prince Charles at once, before he and the king were overrun and "all was lost." He himself was marching on Breslau. If Charles attacked him, then Bevern would instantly pursue. If he failed to do so, it would cost him his head.

Only five days later Frederick was informed that Prince Charles had attacked Bevern and been totally defeated. Various *Feldjäger* had galloped off with victory dispatches when a second report followed: although Bevern had inflicted an immense number of casualties on the enemy, he had been beaten and had retired across the Oder. Frederick ordered him to reoccupy Breslau and to send the bulk of his army to join the king at Parchwitz. Frederick continued his march, only to learn that Bevern had been captured, Lestwitz had surrendered Breslau, and Kyau was retreating on Glogau.* He put the generals under arrest and named General von Zieten to replace Bevern; Zieten was to join him as soon as possible.

---

* Bevern had made a late night reconnaissance accompanied only by a groom and in the moonlight had mistaken an enemy outpost for one of his own and was taken prisoner. He was subsequently well treated, being related to the Habsburgs, and eventually exchanged. Frederick appointed him governor of Stettin, but he never regained royal favor.

Meanwhile the army enjoyed a well-deserved rest, having marched over two hundred miles through difficult country in fifteen days. Once Zieten arrived, the army would number thirty-nine thousand, and Frederick would attack Charles behind Lissa. He wrote a secret testament, which called for his commanders, in case of his death, to swear fealty to the Prince of Prussia. If the battle was won, the prince was to open peace negotiations immediately with France. "For what concerns me, I wish to be buried at night at Sans-Souci without pomp or circumstance; I do not wish my body to be opened, but rather that I be buried without any fuss."

The Austrian army numbered considerably more than Frederick believed. Instead of something under fifty thousand, Charles counted sixty-five thousand men including five thousand light troops. Instead of pursuing and presumably capturing Bevern's demoralized army or attacking the king's meager corps, Charles and Daun tucked in behind the Lohe River to await their enemy's next move. Learning that Frederick was at Parchwitz, soon to be joined by Zieten, Charles called a council of war: Charles overruled divergent command opinions to decide that the army would advance through Neumarkt in order to strike Frederick before he could fortify his position. To prepare the way, Charles sent his bake ovens and a corps under Count Georg Nostitz to Neumarkt. That the king, despite numerical weakness, would attack him apparently did not occur to Charles.

Zieten's army trickled into Parchwitz at more of a slouch than a march. Defeat at Breslau showed on weary faces as march, countermarch, and finally retreat in cold rain showed on tired and hungry bodies. Yet victory depended on the newcomers. The king's corps counted only thirteen thousand, the newcomers twenty-six thousand. Somehow they had to regain belief in themselves — and in a very short time.

It was a command problem, and it would have tested a healthy commander. Frederick was not well; approaching exhaustion, he was a stooped, tired figure who could have been forgiven for taking to bed. Instead, he set an army on fire. First the troops. While others slept, the king walked snow-dusted ground from company to company, from campfire to campfire. Orderlies carried casks of wine and baskets of bread and meat, and by the campfires he ate and drank with his soldiers, listened to their tales, heard their complaints. It was drunken talk in part, certainly coarse talk, often humorous, decidedly human. He was a soldier among soldiers. That was part of the kindling process. His real secret was to challenge individual courage. *The enemy is over there to the east; he is two or three times stronger than we are. But we are going to attack him, we are going to beat him. Is this not so?* Promotion could be won by daring deeds, he suggested; so could money. He would pay "one hundred ducats for each captured cannon."

Then came the officers. He promoted those who had fought well at Rossbach and Breslau, a clear message to others who were about to fight. The first officers over the barricades, he promised, would earn the coveted Order of Merit. The night before the army marched, he called in generals and staff officers and delivered a military sermon whose title could have been borrowed from *King Henry V:* "We few, we happy few, we band of brothers." [1]

Nothing less than Germany's future was at stake, he stressed. To attack an enemy as strong as the Austrians was against all rules of warfare. Not to attack was to invite certain ruin. The danger was immense; anyone who did not wish to share it could leave the army at once without reproach. The king waited, but no one spoke and he continued. His generals were to inform the troops that the cavalry regiment which fails to attack instantly will become an unhorsed garrison regiment; the infantry battalion that hesitates a moment will lose its colors and swords. Finally, if the Prussian army was defeated, he would not again see those now before him.

Sunday, December 4, 1757. The Prussians march before daybreak. Prussian hussars collide with enemy hussars a few kilometers from Neumarkt, chase them into town, kill a hundred, capture five hundred, seize Austrian bake ovens and eighty thousand welcome loaves. The advance guard camps northeast, the main army slightly west of Neumarkt.

Evening comes cold and snow-flecked. Frederick learns that the Austrian army is across the Weistritz River without tents or baggage. So much the better. He and many of his officers know almost every foot of this ground from years of maneuvers. "The fox has left his lair," he tells an aide, "now I shall punish his insolence." [2] The troops spend a cold night under arms. Shivering sentries enviously watch enemy fires. The army is awake at four A.M. The advance guard marches thirty minutes later.

The Austrians also march early. The advance guard is crossing the Weistritz when Prince Charles learns that the Prussians are in Neumarkt. He and Daun are surprised by Frederick's rapid advance. The attacker becomes the attacked. Charles orders the army to camp in battle formation, two lines, the right wing east of Nippern, the left wing south of Leuthen, a long front of four to five miles. Nádasdy's corps and the army reserve form a third line to the rear.

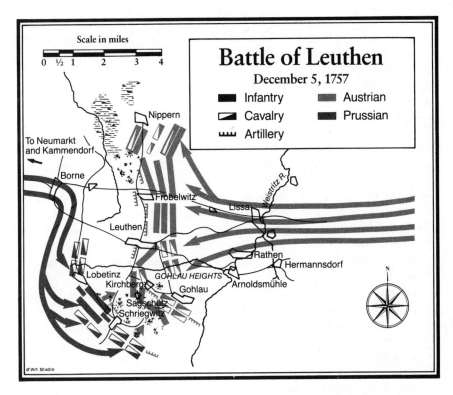

Scale in miles

0 ½ 1   2   3   4

Battle of Leuthen
December 5, 1757

■ Infantry   ■ Austrian
▱ Cavalry   ■ Prussian
Artillery

Nippern

To Neumarkt
and Kammendorf

Borne

Frobelwitz

Weistritz R.

Lissa

Leuthen

Rathen

Hermannsdorf

Lobetinz   GOHLAU HEIGHTS

Kirchberg   Arnoldsmühle

Gohlau

Sagschütz

Schriegwitz

N

d'Art Studio

Cavalry and infantry duly come up, but units are delayed. Suddenly it is dark; deployment is not complete. Charles and Daun nonetheless prepare for battle. The troops are ordered to be in defensive position before dawn. A staff officer later wrote that "great disorder ruled the camp. Food, wood, and straw are lacking." He spent the night looking for Charles and Daun in order to receive their commands — in vain.[3]

Monday, December 5, 1757. It is a cold, foggy morning with light snow on frozen earth. Prince Frederick Eugene of Württemberg's advance guard marches. Frederick rides with the hussars, which pull up east of Kammendorf to wait for the main army — four long columns, two of infantry inboard, the cavalry on each flank, a battery of 12-pounders, the famous *Brummer* guns in front of the infantry. The men are singing a hymn. Frederick turns to an aide: "With men like these, don't you think I shall have victory this day?"[4]

The king continues forward until he sees the suggestion of a cavalry line west of Borne. He takes this as the beginning of an enemy flank and calls up some cavalry. Hussars identify the force as Saxon light horse — the same that made the devastating attack at Kolin — and Austrian hussars flanked by Croatian irregulars. A few battalions clean out the Croats; the cavalry attack. General Nostitz is completely surprised; his first line is thrown back on the second; the entire formation runs. Saxon horse are heavily loaded and sluggish, Prussian horse light and fast. The Prussians show no mercy. Many unfortunates are cut down; eleven officers and about six hundred troopers are captured. Frederick orders the prisoners marched to Neumarkt in full view of oncoming columns.

It is about six A.M. Prince Charles learns of Nostitz's retreat. He shifts his army west, right-wing cavalry in a copse southeast of Nippern and two lines of infantry east of Frobelwitz and Leuthen, the left wing hooking around Leuthen. Four batteries of heavy artillery guard the front; grenadier companies and Croats screen west of the right flank. Nádasdy's corps of infantry, cavalry, and hussars cover the left flank from the heights of Sagschütz, where Nádasdy builds a line facing southwest and fronted by two heavy batteries and log barricades. It is a strong defensive position — providing the enemy attacks from the west.

At about nine A.M. King Frederick and Prince Maurice of Dessau ride to a height east of Borne. The enemy line is so visible that it could be counted "man by man."[5] Frederick sees that Charles's right rests on marshlands and cannot be attacked. His center is too strong to attack. The Austrian left at Sagschütz is the key, he decides, and this is where he will strike. To throw off the enemy he lets one cavalry and one infantry column march north of Borne.

Prince Charles is watching the Prussian advance. He believes that Frederick will attack his right, and his belief strengthens when he sees Prussian columns north of Borne. Count Joseph Lucchesi, commanding the right wing, holds the same opinion and is barraging Charles with requests for reinforcement. Charles orders his reserve to the right wing, where he and Daun station themselves. But now they see Prussian columns turning right. So the king is not going to attack after all. "Our friends are slipping away," Charles mutters to an aide; "let them go in peace."[6]

It is noon. Prussian columns close on the target area. Zieten deploys right-wing cavalry into line southeast of Schriegwitz, his front shielded by six infantry battalions. The main army deploys northwest of Schriegwitz, where the battalions are hidden from enemy view. Colonel Karl von Wedell commands the assault battalions on the right of the first line, with the *Brummer* battery in direct support. Four other heavy batteries front the first line. To the rear of the first line are Württemberg's hussars. General Georg von Driesen's hussars and cavalry remain in reserve west of Lobetinz.

General Nádasdy on the Austrian left fears an attack and sends frantic messages to Charles. Charles does not respond. Besides, the reserve corps is over four miles away on the right wing.

Wedell marches on command at one o'clock, his target a barricaded height on Nádasdy's left. Trumpets blare and drums beat as the assault battalions advance as though "at a Berlin review," according to a twenty-year-old *Fahnenkorporal* named Ernst von Barsewich.[7] Enemy artillery opens fire. The *Brummers* reply and knock out two enemy guns. Two hundred paces from the barricade, enemy muskets speak. Barsewich is shot through the throat and left for dead but is saved by a brave drummer, who drags him to cover and dresses his wound.* Wedell's people rout three battalions with a bayonet attack and capture seven small cannon. The Prussian first line, led by Prince Maurice, follows the assault, turns sharp right, and forms into echeloned battalions. Nádasdy meanwhile attacks the Prussian right with forty-three squadrons. This is a surprise, and in the tight land the Prussians are hard put to respond. Wedell goes too far and Frederick sends an aide to slow him down. But the shielding battalions break Nádasdy's attack and send him back behind Gohlau Heights. A general assault supported by heavy artillery fire breaks the Austrian first line, which turns on the other lines to bring general retreat. This masks an Austrian battery, which Maurice charges and captures. The Prussians soon own Kirchberg — prelude to rolling up the Austrian line.

Nádasdy meanwhile re-forms his cavalry, and they try to protect retreating infantry. Zieten intercepts Nádasdy. General Hans von Krockow's squadrons are hit by enemy cavalry from the front, by hussars from the rear. They hold, but Krockow, not yet recovered from a wound in his last battle, is severely wounded and taken prisoner. Then Prussian weight tells; enemy cavalry retreat again. This time they fall back on their own reinforcing infantry, who also turn and run. General Lentulus on the right captures fifteen enemy cannon; Colonel Friedrich Wilhelm von Seelen in command of Zieten's hussars takes two thousand prisoners.

It is about two-thirty P.M., and Charles and Daun are in trouble. Charles orders the entire army to swing left and make a new front facing south. The pivot is Leuthen. Austrian reserves try to set up a defensive line south of the village. Prince Serbelloni bravely supports the desperate effort and is shot from the field. The Prussians attack, firing muskets at eighty paces. The defenders retire into Leuthen. They fight stubbornly. Frederick is watching from a height to the west. He orders in his last reserves. The village is taken.

---

*After more horrendous experiences than there is space to tell, Barsewich reached Neumarkt and was operated on by a captured Dutch surgeon using a shoemaker's knives. He was then bled generously, but at least the surgeon closed the wound instead of stuffing it with charpie or linen threads impregnated with some vile salve that virtually guaranteed infection. Barsewich survived a bout of "wound fever" with the help of opium, rest, and a good diet. He eventually returned to duty and was promoted to lieutenant. (Barsewich, *Von Rossbach bis Freiberg*.)

It is about four-thirty P.M. Count Lucchesi, standing with his cavalry, sees the Prussians advancing on the Austrian right northwest of Leuthen. Without orders (or reconnaissance), he charges what he believes is the exposed Prussian left. General Driesen sees his advance. Also without orders, the sixty-year-old general moves rapidly and charges Lucchesi's squadrons; the attack is a total surprise that rips them to shreds. While they frantically try to turn, the Prince of Württemberg's hussars charge from the south and smash the Austrian horse onto their own infantry. Lucchesi is killed; the cavalry run. Panic sweeps the Austrian right; whole battalions throw down their weapons and run for the Weistritz. A bayonet attack pushes in the Austrian center and left.

It is about five-thirty P.M. The Prussians own the field. Zieten is chasing fugitives all the way to Lissa, where Nádasdy is holding the bridges with a few fragments of infantry and cavalry.

King Frederick rides to the nearly dark field, orders heavy guns to move up and fire across the Weistritz. He comes on Prince Maurice of Dessau, a general, who has been twice wounded. "I congratulate you on the victory, Herr Field Marshal," the king says. And when Maurice seems not to hear: "Did you not hear me congratulate you, Herr Field Marshal? You have helped me with the battle as no one ever before has helped me."[8]

But Frederick is not finished. He rides the line to ask whether anyone will follow him to seize the Lissa bridges. Exhausted troops cannot believe what they hear. They are sprawled on the frozen earth, bleeding from wounds; they are thirsty; they want food, fire, and sleep. Who is this man on horseback? Well, maybe he too is thirsty and hungry, tired and cold. So far he knows what he is doing. It must be important now. So a few men reason; not many, but a few. They struggle to their feet; a few more rise and pick up their heavy muskets. The remnants of three battalions will go with the king.

It is six P.M. and snowing. It could be a funeral procession, and in some ways it is. A groom holding a lantern walks by the king's horse. Infantry follow with a few small cannon; some cuirassiers join. The curious procession trudges across snow-swept ground, the men singing an old Lutheran hymn, "Nun danke Alle Gott." The rest of the army hears it; it passes from regiment to regiment, becoming a mighty chorale as the king's singers approach Lissa, brush musket fire off with cannon, move into and through the town to seize the important bridges. The king puts pickets east of the bridges. They and the artillery are to fire spasmodically the night through to refresh the enemy's panic.

The enemy's panic needs little refreshing. "Terror filled the army," a French observer later reported; "everyone was in flight."[9] Charles and Daun are trying to form a rearguard east of the Weistritz. They are getting nowhere. A hurried council of war finally agrees to total retreat to their old camp behind the Lohe River. "We trembled all night,"

Charles later informed Maria Theresa, "because we were afraid that we could not restore the regiments to order and therefore we would be cut from the roads to Schweidnitz." [10]

Back at Lissa the Prussian king at last rides to the manor house. It is full of wounded Austrians. An aide finds an empty room. Frederick dictates victory dispatches. It is nearly midnight when he summons the generals, gives his thanks to officers and men, and issues orders for the next day.

8 1

LEUTHEN was another immense victory, as Frederick's dispatches proclaimed — "one of the great victories of the century," he wrote to Wilhelmina, greatly understating his losses and greatly exaggerating those of the enemy. Still at a cost of about sixty-four hundred casualties, including twelve hundred dead, the Prussians had virtually destroyed the Austrian main army. Prince Charles lost over three thousand dead, six to seven thousand wounded, over twelve thousand prisoners, numerous flags and standards, and 131 cannon. "I venture to assure you that this battle will procure the peace," Frederick went on to his sister.

As he had not done with other victories, Frederick exploited this to its limit. The army marched early the following day. By midmorning General Zieten's advance guard had pushed Prince Serbelloni, commanding the Austrian rearguard, over the Lohe. Hussars simultaneously fanned out on wide flanks to smoke out several thousand more prisoners from villages and seize over four hundred wagons. Charles and Daun meanwhile retreated southwest toward Schweidnitz. Cold, rainy weather slowed Zieten's pursuit, but he caught an enormous convoy, captured two thousand wagons loaded with food, munitions, money, and personal baggage, and picked up fifteen hundred more prisoners. He was still too slow for Frederick's taste. Learning that he had taken a rest day, the king wrote: "One day of fatigue in these circumstances, my dear Zieten, brings us 100 rest days afterward." Despite further exhortations, the fun was really over. Shielded by hussars and irregulars, Charles crossed into Bohemia on December 20 to take up quarters around Königgrätz. Fouqué, Zieten, and Mayr pushed his light troops across the border a few days later, a brisk action that won Fouqué a new soubriquet, Imperator.

The main army was besieging fortress Breslau, no easy task in bitter cold weather, when trenches had to be hacked from frozen earth covered with four inches of snow. Conditions inside the fortress were appalling. Commandant Solomon von Sprecher's comfortable garrison had been swollen by seventy-five hundred panic-stricken fugitives, most of them without weapons, not to mention six thousand sick and wounded. Despite a severe colic, Frederick pressed the siege hard; cannon fire breached the walls in several places. By December 20 the handwriting was on the wall. Sprecher called a council of war in which only one general argued for a breakout north; the rest agreed on capitulation.* Thirteen generals, 670 officers, and seventeen thousand men became prisoners of war. The Prussians gained eighty-one field cannon, all fortress guns, a thousand horses, a large corn magazine, and a war chest of 144,000 gulden. Still not well, Frederick led a corps to push the remaining enemy from Silesia and arrange a cordon defense for the winter. Prince Maurice appeared before Liegnitz, whose garrison of thirty-four hundred soon capitulated. By year's end the only enemy left in the province was the garrison at Schweidnitz, which Lentulus had blockaded. "If ever Prussia has had occasion to sing the Te Deum, it is at this time," Frederick wrote to Podewils. And to Henry: "Fortune has returned to me; send me the best scissors you can find so that I can clip its wings."

Prince Charles had commanded an army of ninety thousand in mid-September. It had melted to about twenty-five thousand in three months. Almost forty thousand men had been taken prisoner;† a vast quantity of provisions and equipment, including over four thousand wagons, had been lost. Survivors had not been fed well; they had marched and camped in wet and cold weather, and now sickness swept through winter quarters. In late December Marshal Daun sent Emperor Francis a communication aptly entitled "Reflections the most sad . . ."[1] He feared that Frederick would yet march into Bohemia, where the Austrian army was in no position to stop him. In any event, he would be able to open the spring campaign much earlier than the Austrians.

Prussian victories had plunged Versailles and the Hofburg, Maria Theresa's city palace, into deepest gloom, but they were still not ready to conclude the peace that Frederick desired. The French foreign minister, Abbé Count François de Bernis, did believe that it was necessary

---

*Sprecher, a Protestant, was later accused of treachery for having capitulated. On his return from captivity, he was sent to the Netherlands but died on the way. (Generalstab, *Die Kriege Friedrichs des Grossen: Der Siebenjahrige Krieg,* Volume 6. Hereafter Generalstab S followed by volume number.)

† Surprisingly, the Prussians took immense care in recording the name, rank, and unit of each prisoner, including whether he was wounded or ill. (See, for example, *Politische Correspondenz,* Volume 16, Eichel to Podewils, Breslau, December 28 and 30, 1757)

for France to make peace, but he was isolated. "I seem to be the minister of foreign affairs for Limbo," he remarked.[2] The Duke of Richelieu was replaced with Marshal Count Louis de Clermont at Madame de Pompadour's suggestion, and the fiery Marshal de Belle-Isle was installed as the new minister of war. Bernis would shortly give way to Count Étienne Choiseul, "friend of Madame la Pompadour and the *philosophes* and the most brilliant of French ambassadors," in the words of André Maurois.[3]

Maria Theresa was so despondent that she reportedly wept for two days. Early in 1758 the French envoy in Vienna concluded that she was looking for peace with Prussia. But this was momentary depression, briskly relieved by her powerful political adviser, Count Kaunitz, who did not have the slightest intention of making peace. More militant than ever, Maria Theresa set about rebuilding the shattered army while opening a diplomatic offensive designed to win renewed support from France and Russia.

The fragile state of the Austrian army presented an enormous problem. One of Maria Theresa's first moves was to relieve Prince Charles of command. Charles was given a choice of remaining in Vienna as a military adviser or returning to the Netherlands. Anti-Viennese sentiment caused him to choose the Netherlands, where he died in 1780. The army suffered a major loss at this time when General Nádasdy, disgusted with senior Austrian commanders and court intrigues, voluntarily retired. Marshal Daun replaced Charles in command but could do little until replacements arrived. These came from a massive recruiting effort that included amnesty for deserters, and also from an exchange of prisoners with Prussia, which was holding eleven hundred officers and forty thousand men. But a terrible epidemic was taking a heavy toll of lives, and it began to subside only with improved diet and softer weather. As one result, the Austrian army was considerably below strength by spring. Once again Maria Theresa's light troops — hussars and irregulars — would have to screen the army while it worked to rebuild.

Her diplomatic offensive was more successful. Marshal Apraxin's withdrawal from East Prussia had upset Czarina Elizabeth, who ordered his court-martial. He died before the court convened. His command went to General Fermor, who in mid-January crossed the border into East Prussia. In the spring, the Saint Petersburg court was to increase Fermor's strength to eighty thousand and send him into Brandenburg or Silesia. Elizabeth also discovered that her long-time favorite, Count Bestushev, had been plotting with Grand Duchess Catherine to establish a regency for her three-year-old son, Paul, after Elizabeth's death. Bestushev destroyed his correspondence with her but was sentenced to death. Elizabeth changed the sentence to banishment to his estates. In late February she replaced him with Count Vorontsov, who had once accepted Prussian bribes but was now firmly attached to Austria.

Negotiations with the Versailles court proved a great deal more acrimonious. They continued all winter, but Vienna finally agreed to accept a reduced cash subsidy in return for an increase in auxiliary troops. Both courts were still firmly committed to Prussia's destruction.

While cannon slept and bells rang, the King of Prussia retired behind the walls of Breslau for a much needed rest. "I have been ill with colic for eight days," he told Henry in late December. "I can neither sleep nor eat, but I bear the illness and fatigue cheerfully, because, thank heavens, things are going well."

During this extremely cold winter Frederick followed his normal routine of hard work during the day leavened by reading, writing poetry, composing music, and playing the flute in the evening. For further amusement he established a small court, "a pleasant society," he called it, a welcome relief from the savage and terrible campaign. Finckenstein, Knyphausen, Andrew Mitchell, and d'Argens arrived; so did two nieces. He entertained his sister Emily for a week. Prince Ferdinand was there, still suffering from a recurrent fever.

His optimism soon vanished, however. Fermor's advance into East Prussia, Britain's failure to send either a fleet to the Baltic or troops to Germany, indications that the Vienna court was not interested in peace — all meant that the war would probably continue. He celebrated his forty-sixth birthday with a grand ball attended by local dignitaries (some of whom probably remembered the grand ball seventeen years earlier, before the king's departure for further conquest of Silesia), but on the same day he wrote to Henry, "If the coming year should be as cruel as that which has ended, I hope it will be the last one of my life." Two weeks later General Count Mailly, whom Frederick had released from imprisonment to sound out the Versailles court regarding a possible peace, reported from France that, although King Louis favored a just and lasting peace for Germany, he was not interested in any negotiation that might cause suspicion or mistrust of his allies.

Once again, then, military action would have to repair political failure. But this was going to be difficult. Frederick may have won two great victories, but a great many Prussian soldiers had been killed, and thousands of wounded were still convalescing in hospitals, where the epidemic familiar to Austrian camps was taking a deadly toll.*

* Frederick described it as a type of plague manifested by high fever and delirium, pustules on neck and armpits, and death within three days. Bleeding and other usual treatments were useless until someone, possibly the king, hit on treating it with a powerful emetic to induce violent vomiting and, with it, a cure. The king claimed that deaths at once dropped to less than three per hundred. (*Oeuvres*, Volumes 4 and 5, *Histoire de la Guerre de Sept Ans.*)

Home cantons supplied only limited numbers of replacements. The rest had to come from outside the kingdom. Acting on the king's orders, Prince Ferdinand scoured the electorates of Cologne and the Palatinate. Marshal Lehwaldt and Lieutenant General Count Christoph von Dohna, who replaced him in late March, recruited mercilessly in Swedish Pomerania and Mecklenburg (whose ruler unwisely had allied with France): the king demanded a thousand recruits from Swedish Pomerania, four thousand recruits from Mecklenburg, and, in addition, a thousand horses for dragoons and three thousand for artillery and ammunition and supply wagons. Even heavier levies were sent to Prince Henry in Saxony. Officers culled prison camps for volunteers. Bruno von der Hellen, envoy at the Hague, was to enlist four or five engineering officers, "if it is possible of the Protestant religion." An exchange of prisoners with Austria yielded over five hundred officers, among them eight generals, and twelve thousand men. The total effort enabled the king not only to rebuild the army but to increase it by seven thousand men, most of whom were sent to newly formed *Freibataillons,* or irregular units.* Despite this success, he remained far short of the 142,000 troops that he had hoped to have by the spring of 1758.

Prussia's finances were especially perilous. By the end of 1757 Frederick had spent over thirty-one million thalers in two campaigns. He had very little cash left and was faced with enormous expenses for 1758. As with recruits, he obtained the money only through ruthless measures. In December he had ordered Minister von Borcke and Marshal Keith to take whatever measures were necessary to raise more funds in Saxony; Keith was to turn Colonel Mayr and his irregulars loose on three or four of Count Brühl's estates around Leipzig. In early 1758 the king levied an arbitrary loan on Breslau merchants for 300,000 thalers and announced a "forced loan" of over half a million thalers from monasteries and Jesuit institutions. Mecklenburg was to come up with two million cash plus produce worth almost another million. England agreed to pay him a cash subsidy that would amount to over five million thalers for 1758. Taken together, all this gave Frederick about fifteen million thalers, not counting current income, for 1758. Although he would overrun this sum, it was sufficient to put his army in the field for the new campaign.

---

* These were called "free battalions" because they were independent of the regular establishment. There were twenty such battalions in the field by the war's end. Although at times they performed valuable service, Frederick tended to regard them as second-class troops to be used to spearhead costly assaults. (Paret, *Yorck.*)

8 2

FREDERICK'S operational plans for the campaign of 1758 have been the subject of vitriolic argument by historians for over two centuries. What was his *real* intention in the spring of 1758? Did he wish to pursue a *Vernichtungsstrategie* — a strategy of annihilation — or an *Ermattungsstrategie* — a strategy of attrition? It is a somewhat senseless argument, because by 1758 Frederick had consistently campaigned in accordance with the broad strategy laid down in *The General Principles of War,* which he adapted as necessary to meet such "accidents" as the defeat at Kolin.

As is made clear in his official correspondence and in his later history of the war, it was basically a strategic defensive that allowed for tactical offensives designed either to checkmate or to destroy enemy armies. Frederick did not open the campaign of 1758. It opened in the west, where Prince Ferdinand of Brunswick, to whom Frederick had supplied cavalry reinforcement (not to mention letters calling for aggressive operations to weaken and even destroy the French forces), marched rapidly and well against the main French army, a two-pronged effort that claimed eleven thousand French prisoners and sent the Count of Clermont's army heading for the Rhine. Prince Henry with a small corps simultaneously moved on Brunswick's left, an operation so skillfully conducted that the French estimated his force at twice its actual size and believed that the Prussian king was personally leading it. Brunswick wanted more troops to expand the operation, and Henry wanted to march farther west, but the king, though delighted with the results, refused to send more troops and peremptorily ordered Henry back to Saxony: "It is not a question of going to the Rhine but of defending the electorate [Saxony], which will certainly be endangered if you do not rejoin the corps of Marshal Keith."

Ferdinand's successful offensive greatly eased Frederick's position. With Clermont pushed back to the Rhine, he could remain on the defensive in Saxony and Pomerania while yielding East Prussia to the Russian enemy. His primary target was the Austrian army, which he assumed would attack him in Silesia in conjunction with Marshal Count Peter Shuvalov's Russian corps, forming at Grodno. He further assumed that Shuvalov would not reach Silesia until late June. "This obliges me to strike a great blow against the Austrians," he told Prince Henry in early March, "while I have all my forces assembled and before this reinforcement, if it arrives, forces me to break away."

Despite the poor state of Daun's army, Frederick did not want to attack him in Bohemia. Daun was a master of defense and delaying tactics, and Frederick could not afford a replay of the disastrous 1744 campaign, which now would mire him deep in Bohemia while the Russians invaded Silesia. Instead:

> If I march straight on Olmütz, the enemy will come to defend it; then we shall have a battle in terrain not of his choice. If I beat him, as it must be hoped, I shall besiege Olmütz; then the enemy, forced to cover Vienna, will move all his forces in that direction and, Olmütz taken, your [Henry's] army will be assigned to take Prague and hold Bohemia in respect. After which, let the Russians or whoever come, I shall be able to make the necessary detachment.

It was an ambitious plan — too ambitious, Field Marshal Keith warned. Either operation, the siege of Olmütz or the move on the Russians, would not be easy. The king was wrong to regard the Russians as "rabble." In discipline and training, they were at least equal to the Prussians.[1]

"It's a dog's life." The statement was made to a new member of the household, Henri de Catt, the king's reader. (The Abbé de Prades, who had held the position, had been arrested as a French spy the previous November, found guilty of espionage, and sent to prison.) The two had met earlier in Holland, where Catt, who was Swiss, was studying law. Now thirty years old, Catt arrived in Breslau and passed his first audience with flying colors, according to the Marquis d'Argens and Andrew Mitchell, whose subsequent advice to the newcomer tells us a good deal about the king. D'Argens advised him to "say little . . . enter as little as possible into jests; show small eagerness for the confidences that he may make to you. . . . Do not, for God's sake, criticize either his prose or his verse; don't ask him for anything, no money."[2] Andrew Mitchell counseled: "Without becoming too familiar with this Prince, be yet frank and open . . . always bring to the fore questions of literature, of philosophy, and especially of metaphysics, which he likes very much. Discuss the French poets with him, and if he shows you any of his verses, criticize only in so far as he requires. Allow him to speak rather than speak yourself."[3]

Catt was next received at the convent of Grüssau, where the king was supervising the siege of Schweidnitz. The audience lasted three and a half hours, during which the king warned Catt to keep his counsel at all times. He was not to become intimate with the king's military aides, who were jealous of each other and assumed far too much authority. He was to see Andrew Mitchell, on the other hand, as often as possible: "He is sincerely attached to me, and is a man of very solid and wide education. He is integrity itself."

Catt enjoyed royal favor from the beginning, but it must often have been hard going. He saw the king frequently in a variety of good, bad, and indifferent humors and health. Frederick was often nostalgic, telling Catt the most intimate details from the past, mixing self-pity with sardonic, often mordant humor. (One wonders whether the king subconsciously identified Catt with von Katte.) Frederick frequently complained of subordinates, sometimes even of himself. His verbosity alternated with a grim humor, on occasion cruel. One victim, a prelate of the local convent, was a permanent dinner guest, because he "amuses me, particularly by his ineptitude. During the whole meal, he is the object of my persiflage. I put thorny questions to him that he cannot solve." A young scholar turned soldier, Captain Karl Guichard, unwisely lectured the king on the endurance of Roman soldiers who marched with heavy packs and equipment. Frederick loaded him with the equipment and arms carried by a Prussian soldier and stood him at attention until he admitted that the Romans had nothing on the Prussians. Frederick henceforth called him Quintus Icilius, gave him a battalion of irregulars, and frequently kept him at headquarters, where he was a butt of the king's humor.

Fortunately, in Catt's case, the king's love of man-baiting was overshadowed by current events and by a compelling literary-poetic-musical interest shared by Catt. Frederick at this time was reading Bacon, Caesar, Tacitus, Plutarch, and Lucretius; he was completing two lengthy odes to send to Voltaire; he frequently read aloud or recited lengthy passages from French dramatists, volubly commenting on moral and philosophical points raised; and he reminisced at length about Voltaire's quarrel with Maupertuis, indeed all the personalities of the Sans-Souci days.

These were short breaks in an incredibly busy schedule concerned with military and political affairs. Andrew Mitchell and Major General Joseph Yorcke, a thirty-four-year-old British soldier and diplomat, turned up to discuss the new Treaty of Westminster. "Your Lordship will believe that I was very much pleased to find His Prussian Majesty in such good health and humor," Yorcke reported to Lord Holdernesse; "indeed I can't say enough of the Gracious Reception he has given me, nor of the free and cordial Manner in which he has talked."[4] Yorcke found the king bursting with political and military ideas, all of which he transmitted to London in detail. Privately, he complained to Mitchell "that his Majesty had talked so much, and suffered him [Yorcke] to say so little."[5]

Frederick also began indoctrinating Catt in military affairs so that he could keep careful notes for the king's future reference. He carefully explained the siege of Schweidnitz. This had begun badly because of the "shilly-shallying" of his artillery officers, whose "negligence and ignorance" finally forced him to subordinate them to the engineers. Once under way, the siege went better, and it ended in mid-April with the surrender of nearly five thousand men and fifty-one cannon. The king was so pleased with Colonel Balbi's siege works that he wrote a celebratory epistle, which he personally delivered to his chief engineer. On April 19 the king told Catt, "I am now at the beginning of my campaign. God knows how it or I will end."

The King of Prussia with about half the army marched in late April on fortress Neisse. He was in good humor, holding long talks with Catt, warning some Cistercian monks who gave him dinner that if they told the enemy of his march, "I will have you all hanged without mercy." (One monk said to an aide, "His Majesty is very gracious; it is a pity he is so ready to have people hanged.") His suspicions against *all* Catholic clergy in Silesia had been heightened by the treachery of the Bishop of Breslau, Count Philip Schaffgotsch, a favorite who had escaped to Austria. He repeated his warning at Neisse to what he called "this cowled race."

Marshal Keith followed with another corps. To shield the movement and also to mislead Marshal Daun, Frederick left strong corps under Zieten at Landeshut and Fouqué west of Glatz. He himself paid a quick visit to Glatz, where he ostentatiously reconnoitered roads as if he would march into Bohemia. The ninety-mile march to Olmütz began at Neisse. From Troppau he confidently wrote to Prince Ferdinand, "I've gained nine days [on Marshal Daun]. So much for the opening of the campaign; it is now a matter of ending it as it has begun." Yorcke described him as fully occupied with the coming operation. "I can see that he casts a wishful Eye to the Banks of the Danube. . . . It is astonishing what he goes thro', how he goes thro' it, and the Activity both of Body and Mind that he shows upon every occasion, and he is at present in the most perfect health."[6]

The difficult march through the border mountains to the great Olmütz Plain was uncontested. Yorcke found the infantry "in surprising good Order, new cloathed, and supplied with everything. It is true that there are a great many Recruits among them. . . . The Cavalry has more Old Soldiers amongst them, but has not upon the whole the look of such good order as the Foot."[7] The advance guard pushed enemy hussars out of Littau. By May 11 Frederick occupied a good defensive position southwest of fortress Olmütz, and Keith, "the most experienced officer in the army," was at Littau, nine miles northwest of the fortress, preparing the actual siege. The king was very active, reconnoitering here, raiding there, lecturing Catt on virtue and morals, playing the flute, complaining of painful hemorrhoids, reading a variety of works: "Now, to rest ourselves, let us read the tragedy of *Britannicus* [Racine], but remember that I must have, after each act I read, a pinch of snuff."

Fouqué arrived with siege guns nine days later. While his corps partially encircled the fortress — he was nowhere near strong enough to completely blockade it — Colonels Dieskau and Moller, supervised by Colonel Balbi, moved the big guns into position. This was slow work, frequently interrupted by fire from the fortress. The cannon did not open fire until the last day of May. Owing to a miscalculation, the guns in the first parallel were too far away for effective fire, and the king held Balbi responsible. A general commanding the infantry in the communication trenches sourly noted that not two shots out of a hundred reached the fortress.

Prussian deceptive measures fooled Field Marshal Daun for only a few days. Frederick had certainly gained several marches on him, but the fifty-three-year-old commander was scarcely worried. Time, he realized, was on his side. His understrength army was daily gaining reinforcements. The Prussians would not readily seize fortress Olmütz. Its strong walls were defended by 324 cannon and a garrison of eighty-five hundred, ably commanded by seventy-six-year-old General Marschall and well supplied with food and ammunition. The Russians were on the march, and each day gained by Daun brought them nearer to him — and to the Prussian enemy. For these reasons he paid no attention to an order from Vienna to march to the relief of Olmütz and give battle if necessary.

Instead, he marched in leisurely fashion to Leutomischl, from where he could attack any Prussian advance on Brünn in the flank. Austrian light troops — "this swarm of brigands," Frederick called them — moved into a wide arc around the Prussian army. From there, they observed almost all movements, interdicted convoys, threatened forage parties, raided outposts, and cut communications. When it became clear that the Prussians were investing the fortress, Daun marched to Gewitsch, about twenty-five miles west of Olmütz, to await developments.

Frederick had expected to own Olmütz by mid-June. But only in mid-June did cannon begin firing from a second parallel while a third was being completed. Toward the end of the month, the besiegers had reached the glacis, cannon fire had severely damaged fortress walls and the interior, and the commandant was not sure he could withstand an attack. On the other hand, he continued to receive produce from local farmers, and he was in touch with Daun, who moved the main army only a few kilometers southeast of Olmütz.

The Prussians also had problems. Frederick lost three cups of blood from hemorrhoids and then suffered indigestion from eating too much macaroni. The combined result made him "see everything darkly," he told Catt. Keith kept coming down with fever and asthma; Fouqué was hit by a spent canister ball and was *hors de combat* for several days. Resistance from the fortress was causing casualties, not to mention a high desertion rate *into* the fortress. To revive morale, Keith was to pass the word that reinforcements would soon arrive from Silesia; he also issued a ration of wine and promised the troops a cash gratification once the siege ended. Continuing fire hindered sapping operations; in late June the king complained of their slow progress and threatened to give his engineers duncecaps. An enemy sortie surprised one detachment, captured several hundred men, and put some cannon out of action. Austrian hussars and irregulars were "on all Sides of Us," Yorcke reported, and were keeping the king tactically blind. Frederick did not know where all of Daun's army of forty-five thousand was located, much less Daun's intentions; and attempts to penetrate the screen of irregulars were futile.

Supply was also becoming a major problem. A convoy from Neisse had to travel around forty-five miles to Troppau, then another forty-plus miles over narrow, twisting mountain roads ideal for surprise attacks by irregulars, who were apt to jump out from any bend or nearby copse. Although a large convoy arrived safely on June 10, Keith's cannon were using a lot of powder and ball; on June 18 he had only a ten-day supply left. Frederick learned this on the same day that he learned of the Prince of Prussia's death. William's death upset him more than Keith's problem.* He was occupying a strong defensive position from where he could check any foreseeable move by Daun. An enormous convoy of four thousand wagons, including nearly a thousand munition wagons, was expected from Neisse in late June. There were already indications that the fortress was yielding. Once the convoy arrived, Keith would deliver the coup de grâce in a matter of days.

The vital convoy never arrived. Hearing of its march, General Buccow sent Major General Gideon von Loudon, with a corps of about four thousand hussars and irregulars, to intercept it. Loudon was supported by irregular commanders Major General Count Joseph Saint-Ignon and Major General Baron Joseph von Siskovics, who marched north from Prerau with another four thousand irregulars. Loudon first jumped the convoy when its advance guard was leaving Bautsch. Its commander, Lieutenant Colonel von Mosel, ably defended and finally counterattacked, sending Loudon limping back to Bärn. General Zie-

---

* Thirty-six-year-old William died at Oranienburg, according to some of "a broken heart," but in reality from a brain tumor. The king wrote long and sad letters to his family. Henry could not accept the royal words, "but respect and sadness impose [my] silence." He never forgave the king for having treated William so harshly.

ten's support corps now arrived, and he took command for the final leg of the long journey. Outside of Altliebe, some twenty miles from Olmütz, he was attacked from the south by Siskovics, from the north by Loudon. In one of the most successful ambushes in history, the Austrians sent Zieten's corps in wild retreat, with the convoy escort, toward Troppau. They seized over three thousand loaded wagons, took what could be carried, and burned the rest — including all of the precious munition wagons.*

Only a hundred wagons reached their goal. General Krockow delivered them to the main army at midnight on June 30, along with remnants of nine battalions and a few squadrons of cavalry and hussars. The convoy had been wiped out, he reported, over twenty-four hundred Prussian casualties, twelve cannon and over three thousand wagons lost, convoy escort of nine thousand — mostly recruits and convalescents — last seen running toward Troppau in company with Zieten's shattered corps.

Frederick took the news calmly. Catt was impressed with his "serene and tranquil air." Here was an "accident" of war of the kind he had dwelled on in *The General Principles*. It had brought an unpleasant moment of truth, but "it is better to make an unpleasant decision," he now wrote to Keith, "than no decision at all." Keith was to lift the siege immediately; the entire army was to begin the long march back to Silesia. Any officer showing anything but confidence would be cashiered and imprisoned.

The difficult retreat through rolling rich country rising from cereal plains came off surprisingly well.† Wet foggy weather helped the early stages, as did Daun's decision not to follow immediately with the main army. Light troops harassed the army during the next few weeks, particularly Keith's columns, which moved more slowly because of an enormous train — four thousand wagons that stretched over thirteen miles — carrying siege guns, fifteen hundred sick and wounded, provisions, and equipment. Frederick halted the march at Königgrätz, where he hoped Daun would attack him. Despite pressure from Vienna, Daun did not want a battle. He knew that the king would have to march very soon to meet the Russian threat. When that happened, he would take

---

* I recently visited this area, now in Czechoslovakia (to find myself uncomfortably close to a military reservation tucked away in the hills). About eighteen miles northeast of Olmütz the entire great plain comes into view. The hilly road continues through a rolling tableland with numerous twists, turns, forests, and streams. I was there on a chilly July day with rains so heavy that secondary roads were flooded. What they must have been in 1758 defies imagination.

† Prince Henry, no great admirer of his brother's military talents, called it the king's best-managed maneuver of the entire war. (Easum, *Prince Henry of Prussia*.)

the main army into Lusatia to join the Russians on the Oder, seize Berlin, or turn on Dresden. His camp west of Königgrätz was too strongly entrenched to be attacked.

Frederick remained in the Königgrätz area until July, when he reluctantly ordered the march continued. On August 9 the weary columns closed on Landeshut, from where they had marched four months earlier.

83

DURING THE KING'S RETREAT through Bohemia, hard-riding *Jägers* had brought good and bad news from far battle fronts. In early June, Prince Ferdinand crossed the Rhine, marched on Marshal Clermont's army, and three weeks later attacked and defeated him at Crefeld. Clermont retired on Cologne and was relieved by Marshal Count de Contades. In early July, the king learned that a British force commanded by General Jeffery Amherst had landed on Cape Breton in the New World and was marching on the French bastion of Louisburg, which fell a month later.

That was the favorable news. Against it had come word from Prince Henry that Wilhelmina was so ill that he dared not tell her of Prince William's death. This was confirmed by her pathetic, nearly illegible letters, which awaited him at Grüssau. His long and emotional replies begged her to get well, since she was the only person of any meaning left to him. More bad news came from Pomerania. The king for weeks had been urging General Dohna to attack General Fermor's corps. Dohna instead had moved west of the Oder and was passively waiting for Fermor's next move. On July 30, the king wrote that he would soon join him with reinforcements; he hoped that Dohna meanwhile would give the Russians a "right good" beating.

Only a day after reaching Grüssau, the king informed Prince Henry that he was marching to the Oder, where he hoped to beat the Russians, then send Dohna against the Swedes, and himself either return to Silesia or march on Lusatia if Daun had penetrated there. The letter confirmed Henry's regency in case of Frederick's death. On August 10 he transferred command of the Silesian army (along with several pages of orders) to Margrave Charles — Marshal Keith was ill — and marched with fourteen battalions and thirty-eight squadrons (altogether some 15,000 men) plus forty heavy cannon. The march was ruthless — fifteen miles a day under hot sun by already tired soldiers, some of whom died on the way. From Liegnitz the king confirmed his plan to Dohna, who was to advertise his intentions of returning to fight the Swedes while in reality marching southeast to join the king. Frederick next learned that the Russians had bombarded and burned the town of Cüstrin to the ground, that they were besieging the fortress and were preparing to cross the Oder.

Frederick caught up with Dohna on August 22. There was no time to waste. Prince Ferdinand had been forced back across the Rhine by the French. The Austrians were pushing into Saxony and Lusatia. The Swedes might march at any moment. It was vital to cross the Oder, he explained to his generals that night, beat the Russians, push them out of Poland and Pomerania, then move on the Swedes and Austrians.

While cannon fired on a likely crossing a couple of miles northwest of Cüstrin, pioneers and peasants laid a pontoon bridge fifteen miles downstream at Alt-Güstebiese. The fast and efficient crossing was uncontested, but the march was sheer hell. "We marched the whole day in the most terrible heat," a survivor wrote a friend, "in the deepest sand and in a dust that hid both heaven and earth."[1] Andrew Mitchell, who accompanied the king, reported that the army was "excessively fatigued," having marched a "full two hundred English miles in fourteen days with only one day of rest."[2] The following afternoon, again under blazing sun, the army continued southeast to deploy between Darrmietzel and Neudamm-Mühle, its front facing south, with General Manteuffel's advance guard south of the Mietzel bridges. Across the Mietzel Valley the king watched Russian cavalry evidently making camp. Mitchell found him "in high spirits." Catt noted that he seemed confident of winning a victory without a great loss of life — but of course a "trifle" could ruin everything. The king completed some odes and retired to a sound sleep.

⌧

Prussian bombardment of the Oder bridges surprised General Fermor, who destroyed them and sent out Cossack patrols. These were more concerned with loot than with information — incredibly, not one patrol crossed the Oder. Only on August 23 did Fermor learn that King Frederick's corps had joined Dohna and that the Prussians were building a bridge at Alt-Güstebiese. He immediately fell back on Gross-Cammin and summoned General Count Georg Browne's corps to join him. That evening he learned that the Prussians were on the east side of the Oder with about fifty-five thousand men (there were actually about thirty-six thousand). He assumed they would advance south and southeast on Zorndorf.

Here was a chance to take his enemy in a flank attack. Early on August 24 Fermor moved the heavy baggage behind Klein-Cammin.

The army marched to Zorndorf to deploy in two lines stretching to Quartschen. Count Browne's corps arrived to give Fermor a total strength of about forty-four thousand (including thirty-two hundred Cossacks). Fermor learned of the new Prussian camp, and that evening a captured hussar reported that the king intended to march on Zicher and Batzlow the following day.

Fearing attack from the northeast, Fermor wedged his army between two long protective hollows, the Zabern-Grund south of Quartschen and the Langen-Grund south of Zicher. Its new front faced north. Cavalry screened its flanks; Cossacks probed Prussian outposts to the north. That night the troops remained under arms for the attack that Fermor was certain would come the following day.

Friday, August 25, 1758. The Prussian army marches at three A.M. At daybreak it is in the fringe of woods northwest of Batzlow. Frederick calls a halt and rides forward to reconnoiter. He sees nothing and continues the march, wanting maneuver room and hoping to get a view of

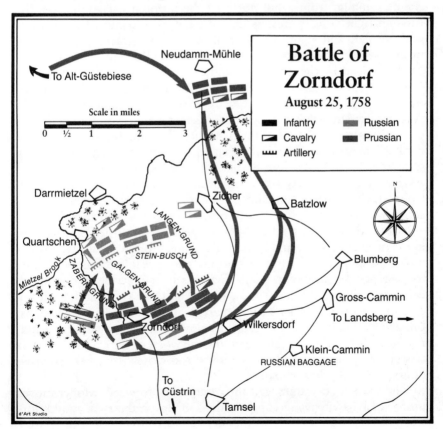

Battle of
Zorndorf
August 25, 1758

Russian lines. Hussars spot the enemy baggage dump near Klein-Cam-min. Frederick will deal with it later after the enemy army is beaten.

Fermor learns at daybreak of the Prussian march. He decides that he will be attacked from the south. He turns his army to face south and southeast in what one of his generals later describes as "a longish square."[3] This is a tactical error, because the marshy terrain to the rear blocks withdrawal in case of defeat. To secure his right he pulls in regiments from Zorndorf and extends his line to the Zabern-Grund, the long depression south of Quartschen. This is a second tactical error, because the new regiments crowd his defense. There are too many regiments on too little ground, and the lines must bend accordingly. The square fills with bodies of men and horses and the army's light baggage. Seeing the enemy marching on Zorndorf, he sets the village on fire. This is his third tactical error. Thick smoke carried by a south wind blinds his right wing.

It is about eight A.M. The Prussian army is marching on Zorndorf. The king moves from height to height but catches only glimpses of the enemy. Finally, from a hill north of the burning village, he sees the Russian right wing. Foresters describe the steep banks of the depressions on left and right. These prohibit oblique attack. This leaves a frontal attack, which will be made against the Russian right in terrain partly divided by the Zabern-Grund and still another depression, the Galgen-Grund. The king gives his orders: bombardment by Colonel Moller's heavy artillery followed by Manteuffel's eight battalions in assault; sixty-five-year-old Lieutenant General Hans von Kanitz to support with nine battalions in the first line, six in the second and on the flank. General Marschall to command one cavalry reserve of twenty squadrons behind Zorndorf, Seydlitz (now a lieutenant general) to head a larger reserve of thirty-six squadrons in the woods west of Zorndorf. Count Dohna is to command the right wing, which, aided by fifty-seven heavy cannon, will attempt to hold Fermor's center and left.

It is nearly nine A.M. when Moller opens fire on order. The cannon aim at Fermor's right and center. The guns are too far away. Moller moves them six hundred meters north. They speak with more authority. Russian guns reply in what witnesses later describe as one of the heaviest artillery actions of the entire war. Over two hundred heavy cannon are firing. Moller's cannon are beautifully sited. The Russians, blinded by smoke from Zorndorf, by powder smoke, by morning sun, and not least by the terrain, are taking the worst of the exchange. Their troops are exposed; they are deployed too closely together. For two hours they suffer heavy losses.

Manteuffel and Kanitz lead their battalions forward. Moller moves up his guns, switches to canister fire. Dohna on the right moves forward. A wide gap develops between the Prussian forces. Fermor's right wing finally sees the attack developing, moves up a second line with cavalry behind. Russian gunners also switch to canister shot. Suddenly the Russians see the attacking lines. As is their custom, they move out with bayonets. It is the high point of the attack. Now is the time for Kanitz to come up on the right and break the Russian lines.

But Kanitz is not on hand. He had earlier noticed the wide gap created by Dohna's advance. He feared an enemy attack against his exposed right flank. Without orders he shifted his attack to the right. Space now dilutes his once powerful lines. In only a few minutes a few hundred meters of enemy have grown to two thousand meters. They are under terrible crossfire by Russian batteries of the right and center. The attack falters. Manteuffel's attack is also in trouble. Somehow he persuades shredded battalions to make one more try. But Russian cavalry smash into the weak lines and fling them from the field. Infantry follow, overrunning all artillery batteries but one. Kanitz's battalions are in full retreat.

King Frederick observes the disaster from Moller's center battery. He orders Marschall and Seydlitz to attack. Prince Maurice is already leading Marschall's squadrons forward. The king takes up a standard, tries to stop panic-stricken troops. It is no use. Salvation depends on the cavalry.

Maurice is doing wonderful work with Marschall's squadrons, which throw enemy cavalry back on the infantry to check the wild counterattack. Seydlitz meanwhile picks his way across Zabern-Grund to lead thirty-six squadrons to the attack. He takes the Russian infantry by surprise. Most of them are out of ammunition; they group together in hopeless defense by bayonet. Prussian hussars charge in from behind. Once again battle turns to melee, then slaughter. What is left of the Russian battalions run, some to the Russian center, some to woods beyond Quartschen, some to the light-baggage dump and a drunken orgy on pilfered brandy. They shoot anyone who appears, including their own officers. The entire Russian right, a third of Fermor's army, is out of the battle. Maurice and Seydlitz can do no more for the moment. Their squadrons are disorganized, men and horses exhausted. They limp back to Zorndorf. The battlefield is quiet.

It is about two P.M. Frederick's position is not good. If the Russian right is *hors de combat,* his own left is shaky, his attack a costly failure. But he still has Dohna's fresh battalions, and with them he will attack Fermor's left. Dohna's artillery moves forward, opens fire; his battalions march toward Langen-Grund.

A Russian cavalry general, Thomas von Demiku, commands thirty-six squadrons south of Zicher. He sees the Prussian move and attacks. The Prussians are surprised. Dohna's valuable battery on the right is overrun; its covering battalion is surrounded and surrenders. Russian cuirassiers fall on Dohna's right but are beaten off by infantry fire. His remaining squadrons attack Lieutenant General Ludwig Schorlemer's cavalry, which counterattack to chase the intruders back to Zicher. Seydlitz's squadrons from the left wing join the action to recapture the important battery and free the covering battalion.

Dohna's attack begins about three-thirty P.M., some twenty battalions marching to the measured beat of drums. It is not far to enemy lines. Artillery supports the advance; the cavalry are on hand. Then it is hand-to-hand fighting. Prussian cavalry drive off enemy horse, turn to rip holes in the Russian lines. Browne is badly wounded and is carried off the field. To avoid capture, Fermor, already wounded, leaves the fighting. Ever so slowly the Russians yield. But their lines do not break. It is very hot; musketeers are exhausted; troopers and horses can no longer fight.

It is about six P.M. The battlefield is in dreadful and bloody disorder. Cossacks are plundering around Zorndorf and Wilkersdorf. Some Prussian infantry push to the enemy's light baggage, kill drunken Russian guardians, steal money from Fermor's war chest, and slip away from battle.

Frederick orders a final attack against the Galgen-Grund. The Russian line is scraggly. A few salvaged cannon shield it on the left, a few cavalry squadrons on the right. The Prussians attack east of Stein-Busch. Left-wing remnants are supposed to attack north from Zorndorf. Instead, they run. The attacking battalions are weary. The king is asking too much. The effort fizzles.

As darkness falls, Frederick hurriedly moves the army behind hills that stretch from Wilkersdorf northwest nearly to Quartschen, a defensive line facing southwest — a dismal scene "of horror and bloodshed," Andrew Mitchell wrote; "the country was all in flames around us."[4]

Fermor deploys what is left of his army in a defensive line facing northeast from Zorndorf. The armies are only eighteen hundred meters apart. But there is no thought of further attack, which was "fortunate," Mitchell noted, in view of the shattered condition of the Prussian army.

The battle of Zorndorf is over.

Frederick advertised Zorndorf as a great victory in order to raise morale at home and prestige abroad. Technically he was correct, since Fermor left the battlefield first and since the battle prevented his joining Daun's Austrians and also forced Lieutenant General Count Peter Rumianzov to abandon magazines on the Oder. But it was a victory that he could ill afford. It cost him nearly thirteen thousand casualties, a third of his force.

The Russians were hurt even worse — a total of over twenty-two thousand casualties, or almost half the army. The king refused Fermor's request for a three-day truce to bury the dead. The dead and wounded were his responsibility, he replied, because he owned the field of battle.

The armies faced each other for two days. Cannon fired from each side — the king was nearly killed by canister fire, Mitchell reported. Hussars skirmished here and there, but neither side was in a position to attack. Fermor gave way first. On the rainy night of August 27 the Russian army, including numerous wounded, marched to its heavy-baggage dump near Klein-Cammin.

Frederick moved south to the Tamsel area while peasants dug mass graves and special detachments cleaned the battlefield. There he learned that General Loudon's light troops had entered Lower Lusatia, followed by Daun's main Austrian army at Görlitz. Daun, he believed, intended to march on Brandenburg, possibly even Berlin. He had already urged Zieten to intercept Loudon's advance. He now sent a detachment of hussars to clear Loudon's irregulars from the Frankfurt area, and he sent Prince Francis of Brunswick with six battalions to join Zieten in covering the Mark and Berlin. He himself would march to join Margrave Charles as soon as possible. He next learned from Charles that Daun was marching from Görlitz, probably to attack Prince Henry south of Dresden. This made the situation even more critical. Although he still believed that Daun would invade Brandenburg, he could not afford to be wrong: Prince Henry's corps of twenty thousand could not hold out long against Daun's army attacking from the north and the newly constituted Imperial army attacking from the south. On the other hand, Frederick could not abandon Dohna's corps to Fermor, only a short distance away, nor could he himself risk attacking the Russian position.

To solve his dilemma it was necessary, as he wrote to Minister Count Finckenstein, "to do with the skin of the fox what I am unable to do with that of the lion," in this case a hussar attack on Fermor's wagon train at Landsberg, which, if successful, would force him to retire. But Fermor suddenly decided to withdraw to Landsberg. In early September the king with fifteen battalions and thirty-eight squadrons marched for Saxony.

84

HOPING to cross the Elbe and attack Marshal Daun in the rear, King Frederick marked up another exhausting march. But Daun, informed of Frederick's approach, abandoned his planned attack against Prince Henry in favor of a safe position at Stolpen, east of Dresden. The king accordingly closed on Elsterwerda. His columns had covered over a hundred miles in seven days; discounting one rest day, that was an astounding average of eighteen miles a day in very hot weather over sandy and dusty roads.

The immediate crisis had passed. Frederick dined with Henry in Dresden — their first meeting in nearly a year: "Excepting the short time with my sister Emily, nothing in six months has given me more pleasure," Frederick wrote to him the next day.* The problem now was to force Daun back to Bohemia. Frederick quickly rejected an attack on Daun's main position, deciding instead on a partial blockade, in the hope, as he wrote to Henry, "that hunger will do what the sword has been unable to accomplish."

In late September Frederick marched east on Bischofswerda while General Wolf von Retzow's advance corps moved on Bautzen, the idea being to threaten Daun's communications with his Zittau magazine. Loudon fell back on the main army and Prince Christoph of Baden-Durlach retreated west on Löbau. Daun's flank was now uncomfortably open. Frederick believed that food shortages would cause him to march in eight days.

It was a very tense period. On the credit side was Wedell's splendid little victory against the Swedes at Fehrbellin. Fresh reports confirmed a Turkish decision not only to break with Austria but to send an army toward the Danube. But Dohna, now in the Stargard area, was going to need help against the Russians if fortress Colberg was to be saved. And Fouqué reported from Landeshut that strong corps under Generals Count Ferdinand Harsch and Marquis Charles de Ville were threatening fortresses Glatz and Neisse.

Until Daun marched, Frederick would do nothing except suffer —

* It is doubtful whether thirty-two-year-old Henry shared the sentiment. He and Ferdinand blamed the king for William's death and also criticized him for not having made peace with France the previous summer. Such was their outspoken criticism that some members of the family feared for Henry's loyalty and Ferdinand's sanity. But Henry wore a coat of several colors and was simultaneously serving country and king very well. Judging from subsequent, intimate correspondence, Frederick apparently did not doubt his brother's loyalty or affection. While writing him in the most affectionate and laudatory terms, he did not hesitate to criticize or reprimand him in words all too familiar to other commanders. (Easum, *Prince Henry of Prussia*.)

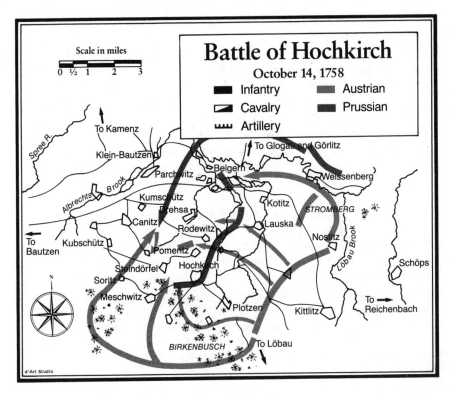

Battle of Hochkirch
October 14, 1758

Infantry Austrian
Cavalry   Prussian
Artillery

mentally from uncertainty, physically "from cruel cramps" that gave him much pain, emotionally from the death of Michael Fredersdorff the previous January, from Pierre Maupertuis's long and serious illness, from his brother Ferdinand's continued fever, and from Wilhelmina's deteriorating condition.

Daun marched toward Löbau in early October. Frederick shadowed him. On October 8 Daun was southeast of Hochkirch; Prince Christoph of Baden-Durlach's corps was further east at Reichenbach. Frederick believed that with a little more encouragement Daun would fall back on Zittau and perhaps even into Bohemia. Encouragement would come from a Prussian march on Hochkirch and Kotitz to threaten Daun's left flank while Retzow occupied a major height, the Stromberg, south of Weissenberg to threaten Daun's right. The plan foundered when Retzow, who commanded over ten thousand troops, decided it was too risky to attack the Stromberg (held by a few hundred Croats) and instead waited for the king's approach. Understandably furious, Frederick ordered him to take it at once. It was too late. Surprised by the Prussian march, Daun shifted his front from north to northwest, his right leaning on the Stromberg, which he reinforced with four battalions and a battery of heavy cannon. Frederick placed Retzow under

brief arrest and continued to fume while waiting for Keith's force and
a supply convoy to arrive.

Frederick reached Hochkirch on October 10. From this pretty little
village overlooking undulating plains, he saw most of Daun's army
deployed along rolling fields, the right resting on the Stromberg, the
front protected by marshlands, the left zigzagging south to lose itself in
wood-covered hills — altogether a formidable position rapidly growing stronger by man-made fortifications.

Frederick should have read this sight as astrologers once read a bird's
entrails for signs. What he saw was unpropitious, and should have sent
the king running back to Bautzen. But he was worried about his Silesian fortresses and was in a dangerously reckless mood. Convinced that
Daun would not attack, he decided to stand fast until Keith arrived,
then attack Baden-Durlach at Reichenbach and close on Görlitz.

His defensive position stretched nearly four miles from slightly south
of Hochkirch north to Rodewitz, the king's headquarters, and northeast to Kotitz. The terrain favored defense of left and center, which
were lightly held. The danger point was the right flank. Elevated as it
was, Hochkirch was a natural strongpoint. Marshal Keith was put in
command here with four battalions, a battery of heavy cannon, and
Zieten's cavalry. Colonel Marquis Luis Angelelli's irregulars manned
outposts in the woods that sloped from the village.

Though naturally strong, the position was not good. The line was
too long for twenty-nine thousand men to defend properly. Retzow's
corps, another ten thousand, was some four miles away. A good many
officers did not like the situation. Field Marshal Keith told his commanders that he had seen many camps in his life "but never one like
this." He said to the king, "If the Austrians do not attack us here, they
deserve to be hanged." The king replied, "We must hope that they fear
us more than the gallows."[1]

Though fearing neither the Prussians nor the gallows, Marshal Daun
respected each. He had chosen his usual passive and careful course,
designed to preserve his army until the situation favored an attack.

The present situation seemed very favorable indeed. He occupied a
virtually unassailable position opposite the enemy's fragile position.
Including Baden-Durlach's corps at Reichenbach, his forces numbered
about seventy-eight thousand, almost double those of the enemy. He
several times reconnoitered the Prussian right at Hochkirch, and he,
his generals, and staff officers considered it vulnerable. A war council
on October 12 brought a decision to attack early on October 14, the
main effort to be at Hochkirch, with supplementary attacks to hold the
Prussian center and left.

Friday–Saturday, October 13–14, 1758. Night comes early and is very dark.

Austrian drums call troops to evening parade, officers shout out watch orders, campfires burn, working parties continue to fell trees south of Hochkirch — in other words, business as usual in the Austrian camp.

The attack corps meanwhile quietly assembles — thirty-five battalions and six cavalry regiments to march in four columns on the Prussian right. Iron wheels of artillery carriages are wrapped with straw. Infantry march on prepared paths through the woods. General Loudon's corps is already south of Hochkirch and now General Count Charles O'Donell's cavalry, intended to deliver the coup de grâce, work through the dark night to position well left of Loudon.*

By four A.M., thirty thousand enemy, supported by cannon, are nestled south of Hochkirch ready to attack. On Daun's right another twenty thousand men commanded by Duke Charles of Arenberg will attack the Prussian left to wedge between the main army and Retzow's corps to the north. Retzow will be attacked by Baden-Durlach's corps, about sixteen thousand strong.

All is quiet in the Prussian camp. Soldiers listen to the enemy beat tattoo, see campfires, hear trees being felled to make more barricades. Frederick orders only normal security: tired troops to sleep in warm tents, horses to remain unsaddled. Zieten refuses the order. He, like Keith, smells danger.

During the night deserters report large troop movements in the Austrian camp. No one in the king's headquarters pays much attention; it is a known fact that Daun will not attack.

Saturday, October 14, 1758. The clock in the Hochkirch church tower strikes five.† Austrian musketeers open fire on Prussian outposts in the Birkenbusch, the birch forest southwest of Hochkirch. Angelelli's irregulars return fire.

A young artillery subaltern, Georg Friedrich von Templehof, hears the musket fire. His battery is ready for the usual morning counterfire against inquisitive pandours. When the firing continues, Templehof discharges his cannon blindly into the dark. Austrian guns reply, and a duel begins that summarily ends for Templehof when an Austrian gren-

---

* The use of foreign-born officers was common to all armies of this time. Particularly prevalent were Irish mercenaries intent on gaining fame and fortune — and probably glad to escape the Irish climate.

† I recently visited Hochkirch. The famous church was built in 1717 (to replace the original thirteenth-century structure). The clock that struck the fatal hour is on display. The southern door leading to the churchyard is scarred by musketballs from the ensuing battle. Inside the church are memorials to the fallen of both sides.

adier creeps behind him and hits him over the head with a musket butt.

Flanking battalions learn that Angelelli's outposts are overrun. Gunners rush to cannon while drummers frantically beat the call to arms. Austrian infantry are already surging in from the darkness. Loudon's cavalry charge from the left. An eyewitness will later write that "the air resounded with shouts from brave officers and men: Stand, lads! Halt comrades! — help will come! Meanwhile the earth trembled from the noise of our heavy cannon."[2]

Help does come. A regiment from north of the village counterattacks to push the enemy back to Birkenbusch. But the regiment is too small, the enemy too big. The enemy again attacks the heavy battery of twenty guns. Half-dressed grenadiers fight isolated actions against overwhelming numbers. Templehof regains consciousness and watches "an infantry fight which in murderous intensity surpasses imagination."[3] The battery is overrun; its defenders fall back on Hochkirch.

In the village Lieutenant von der Marwitz is commanding a post in the walled churchyard. His troops fire at attacking shadows. He is shot through the chest. He leans against the stone wall "commanding, encouraging, and defending his post" until the battalion commander, Major Simon von Langen, arrives with reinforcements.[4]

Enemy howitzers southwest of Hochkirch throw fire bombs into the village. Straw roofs burst into flame. A few rounds fall near Rodewitz, and now Frederick knows the unpleasant truth. He sends Prince Francis of Brunswick with three regiments to Hochkirch. A courier gallops to summon Retzow's corps. Quartermasters begin to evacuate baggage. The king rides to the action.

Zieten's hussars and Krockow's cavalry are attacking Austrian columns as they debouch from the woods. They hurt but do not stop them. The enemy is slowly encircling Hochkirch. Loudon's infantry works to heights northwest of the village; his Croats infiltrate nearby woods. General von Geist tries to recapture the heavy guns and is fatally wounded. Marshal Keith takes on the task and succeeds. But enemy grenadiers in Hochkirch fire on the battery. Keith abandons the guns to lead a fighting withdrawal. The old marshal has been shot through the groin but stays mounted. He is shot through the chest; then a cannonball knocks him, dead, from his horse.

Major von Langen meanwhile defends the churchyard with an understrength battalion, holding against seven Austrian regiments. Remnants of other battalions cling to the north edge of the village. Angelelli's irregulars chase marauding Croats from Prussian tents.

It is six A.M. Dawn breaks slowly, darkness giving way only to cold, wet, smoke-stinking fog. Prince Francis arrives with three regiments. Prince Maurice collects survivors, leads them to support Francis. The counterattack forces the enemy from the village to give Langen a brief rest in the churchyard. But suddenly the new owners are falling, hit by canister shot fired from the captured battery on the other side of the village. Prince Maurice is badly wounded and is evacuated. The newcomers seek cover in smoldering ruins and gardens.

A fresh force commanded by the king attacks in conjunction with Zieten's reorganized corps from the north. Austrians left of the village see the oncoming enemy, form a new line facing west. Fire greets fire; twenty-six-year-old Prince Francis is killed by a cannonball. An officer rides to the king, points to the fallen men around him, begs him to take shelter. "I shall do so once I see how those battalions are driven off." [5] The officer points out that His Majesty's horse is wounded. The king orders another horse.

Prussian infantry backed by cavalry again press the enemy from the burning village. But the Prussians are tired. General Hans von Krockow is fatally wounded; Colonel von Seelen, who commands Zieten's hussars, is wounded and evacuated. Musketeers are short of ammunition. Gaps appear between units. Loudon's Croats infiltrate from the left. And now General Lacy leads a devastating cavalry attack.

Langen is still defending the churchyard. He is bleeding from several wounds. The end comes. He leads the few survivors in a bayonet charge from the north door. He falls and is taken prisoner.*

The enemy owns Hochkirch. The Prussian right is a new line the king builds on the heights northeast of Pomeritz. Remnants of regiments straggle in. Ernst von Barsewich, now a lieutenant, brings fifteen men and two company flags; only 150 men of his regiment have survived. The king learns that his left, only a few battalions and a battery of thirty heavy cannon on the heights east of Rodewitz, is folding against the Duke of Arenberg's repeated, and costly, attacks. The frail battalions cannot hold. One is surrounded and forced to surrender. The rest escape to Rodewitz; the cannon fall to the enemy.

Farther north, Prince Charles of Brunswick beats off Baden-Durlach's early attack while Retzow calls his corps to arms. Retzow receives the king's orders and sends Charles with a small force as advance guard. West of Drehsa, Charles meets O'Donell's cavalry, which is to cut the roads to the northwest. O'Donell is surprised and withdraws to Steindörfel, followed by Prussian horse. Charles holds the heights southwest of Drehsa. Retzow follows with the main army to occupy the heights of Belgern and guarantee the line of retreat.

It is ten A.M. There is nothing for King Frederick but retreat. He sends cavalry northwest to hold the plains of Parchwitz. His infantry

---

* Lieutenant von der Marwitz and Major von Langen were evacuated to Bautzen, where they shortly died from their wounds. Separate memorials to Langen and to Marshal Keith are in Hochkirch church.

follow. There is no panic. General Retzow's son, an aide, finds the king, slightly wounded from a ricochet, standing on a height staring at confusion. "Daun has played me a slippery trick today," he tells the young officer. Retzow replies that His Majesty will soon put things right. Frederick agrees: "We shall manage Daun. What I regret is the number of brave men who have died this morning."[6]

The enemy virtually ignores the retreat. The new camp is built on the heights of Parchwitz, some three miles from Hochkirch.

85

DEFEAT AT HOCHKIRCH was expensive. The Prussians suffered over nine thousand casualties, most of them on the right wing — nearly a third of the army's strength. Over a hundred cannon, including sixty-seven heavy guns, were lost. Right-wing battalions lost packs and tents. Field Marshal Keith and Prince Francis of Brunswick were dead; Generals von Geist and von Krockow were soon to die. Prince Maurice would never fight again.

The king's treatment of the battle was surprisingly cavalier. "I am distressed to write to you that, the enemy having attacked me today in this area, I have been forced to retire a half league toward Bautzen." Thus wrote Frederick to Finckenstein on the evening of Hochkirch. He wrote to Fouqué in a similar vein, adding that he would not retreat one step farther and hoped for a second battle. He intended to remain where he was, he informed Prince Henry, and would like to attack Daun if possible. His brief account for publication in newspapers and foreign courts was accurate, except for losses, which he put at only three thousand. "But these are misfortunes which are sometimes inevitable in this great game of chance that is called war. . . ." he wrote. "One hopes to give better news to the public shortly."

Despite his philosophical bonhomie, the king was in trouble. Generals Harsch and de Ville had blockaded Neisse while waiting for siege artillery. Its relief at once became the most urgent task. Frederick asked Prince Ferdinand to return some borrowed cavalry regiments immediately. Prince Henry was ordered to fit out a task force of eight battalions, a detachment of hussars, and a dozen heavy cannon to join Frederick's force. General Fermor, fortunately, was withdrawing his Russian corps to Poland for the winter. Dohna was to leave a small corps in Pomerania and march at once on Torgau. General Bogislav von Tauentzien in Silesia was ordered to round up fifteen Austrian 3-pounders and eighteen 6-pounders "with the necessary ammunition, horses, and teamsters." Andrew Mitchell in Dresden was asked to notify the British crown that the King of Prussia would need another cash subsidy for 1759.

But now the king was momentarily broke. News of Wilhelmina's death arrived early on October 17. She had died on the morning of the Hochkirch battle, Frederick's last letter clutched in her hand. He had been expecting the news, but that was slight consolation. He called Catt to him and for four hours spoke almost deliriously of his loss. According to Catt the king showed him a pillbox that hung on a chain around his neck. It contained opium pills, which Frederick planned to take if captured; he spoke of them as his ultimate solution.

The king marched in late October, fought several sharp skirmishes, beat Daun to Görlitz, and carried on to Silesia. Harsch and de Ville at once raised the siege of Neisse and retired, leaving a quantity of valuable material behind.

Daun meanwhile had put Dresden to siege. Frederick did an about-face in Silesia to meet the new threat, marching in early November. He was still three marches from Dresden when Daun raised the siege and retired into Bohemia to put his army in winter quarters.

All things considered, the campaign of 1758 had not ended badly for Frederick. The enemy had been driven from Silesia and Saxony. Fortress Neisse was safe; the line of the Elbe secure. The Russian army was back in Poland; fortress Colberg remained Prussian. A bloodied and ineffectual Swedish army was huddling behind the walls of Stralsund. Both French armies were in winter quarters. Prince Ferdinand, recently promoted to field marshal, comfortably held the line of the Weser. If the Turkish army was marching, as rumored, Austria and Russia would have to shift troops to meet the threat. And if the ailing King of Spain died, Austria would have to send a large number of troops to Italy to protect its lands there.

From Frederick's view, however, debits overrode credits. Despite a terrible cost in men and money, peace seemed farther away than ever. The enemy's strategy may have differed in important ways, but the goal remained the destruction and partition of Brandenburg-Prussia. And such were enemy resources that losses, particularly in men, could easily be repaired in time for the next campaign. Indeed, from mid-December on, disturbing reports arrived at Breslau headquarters that Daun was preparing a winter campaign in Saxony.

Prussian resources, on the other hand, were sorely diminished. The last campaign had cost thousands of dead and wounded. Many of the wounded would never return to ranks that were further decimated by the twin scourges, disease and desertion. "We are very shattered," Frederick wrote to Prince Ferdinand in late December, "and our losses and our victories have carried off that flower of the infantry which formerly rendered it so brilliant." Survivors were tired; morale was shaky; officers were in short supply. Men grumbled; men deserted.

But there were some assets. Although home cantons provided only a trickle of replacements, there were still foreign recruits, returned deserters, prisoners of war, prisoners recovered by exchange with the enemy, and a good number of convalescents. Very strict measures again were successful. Ukases flew from Breslau to luckless provincial governors and area commanders: Send recruits! In addition to bringing his own units up to strength, Prince Henry was to provide three thousand Saxon recruits (none under five feet four inches). Count Dohna was peremptorily ordered to raise his quota from Mecklenburg. The king also condoned special and frequently savage recruiting parties in the Empire, such as those led by the infamous Colonel Collignon, whose methods were unusually brutal.*

An official report of early January showed a shortage of only forty-five hundred troops, which by mid-March was reduced to sixteen hundred. All told, the army numbered 123,000 — an altogether remarkable recovery. But quantity was not quality. Recruits could fill holes but could not possibly be trained and equipped to the desired level in a few months, no matter how incessant and intensive the drill.

Heavy artillery would have to make up for the loss of "the flower of the infantry." Particularly impressive were the 12-pounders, the famous *Brummer* guns used at Leuthen with such devastating effect. But these heavy guns required twelve-horse teams, which often could not negotiate tight mountain roads. The king replaced them with new 12-pounders modeled on captured Austrian pieces, lighter guns each pulled by eight horses and having an effective range of three thousand yards. He also added more howitzers, including 7-pounders issued to infantry battalions to augment the 3-pounder battalion cannon. Most of the new weapons were cast during this winter, an effort supervised by Colonel von Dieskau, who also had to arrange for necessary wagons, ammunition, teams, and teamsters. The task was enormous. In 1756 Frederick had gone to war with 120 heavy cannon. In 1759 his army would take 298 heavy cannon into the field. Mainly to prevent desertion of teamsters, the king increasingly integrated the heavy guns into the infantry, not only in camp and battle but also on the march.

---

* Collignon was a soldier of fortune who offered his services "to the Solomon of the century." The king commissioned him a colonel early in 1759, with a mission to recruit within the Empire. In a month he had enlisted a thousand men, for each of whom he received fifteen thalers. His dishonest representations and vicious ways brought complaints from many commanders on grounds that his recruits deserted at the first opportunity, but he continued operations throughout the war and remained in the army until 1771.

He next introduced a mobile field artillery unit, probably inspired by seeing Russian teamsters at Zorndorf riding the horses that pulled battalion cannon. The new battery of *reitender Artillerie* — horse-artillery — consisted of six light 6-pounders served by a forty-five-man crew. Each gun was pulled by six horses with teamsters mounted on three of them — a tactical innovation that in time would add new strength to this increasingly important arm.

86

A VERY LARGE QUESTION in King Frederick's mind was how best to use this revitalized army. Failure at Olmütz had cost him the tactical initiative. From the moment he raised the siege to trudge back to Silesia, he was no longer in charge of events. Where once he had controlled them, they now controlled him. The Russians invaded Pomerania, so he dashed there to support Count von Dohna. The Austrians invaded Saxony, so he raced there to support Prince Henry. The Austrians invaded Silesia, so he marched to the relief of Neisse. The Austrian and Imperial forces pushed back into Saxony, so he returned there.

He did not see how this defensive posture could change in 1759. He had warned King George that he would have his hands full merely to survive, and he subsequently turned down Prince Ferdinand's request to support an attack on Soubise's army. Frederick discussed his strategy with Prince Henry in early February. They agreed that the situation was very serious. Admittedly the Empress of Russia and the King of Spain were said to be at death's door, but as Frederick put it, an epidemic would have to wipe out all European rulers for Prussia to be safe. The brothers also agreed that the king, with the main army, must play a waiting game in the hope that Daun would leave the Bohemian mountains for the Silesian plains (as Prince Charles had done at Hohenfriedberg), where the king could "use the little oil that was still left in the lamp" to attack him. Frederick also persuaded Henry, not without difficulty, to make another diversion in Thuringia.

Henry marched in February and was in Naumburg in early March. While one of his generals held Erfurt to ransom, another pushed Imperial troops from Eisenach and Fulda, a brief but successful operation that won the king's limited praise. General Moritz von Wobersnow led another small corps to destroy Russian magazines in the Posen area. But such "spoiling operations" were of limited value and did not answer the main question: What was the enemy up to?

Frederick's enemies were trying to square a strategic circle. In opting for Prussia's destruction, they expressed an emotional ambition but not a workable strategic goal. Each walked different steps of the strategic ladder without recognizing, as has been pointed out, that "the single major strategic factor" was the attrition of the Prussian army.[1] Austria wanted to topple Prussia and regain Silesia and other bits and pieces. France, for whom the war was going badly against England at sea and in the colonies, wanted above all to defeat the combined English-Hanoverian army and seize Hanover for trading material. Russia wanted to keep East Prussia and as much additional Prussian territory as possible. Sweden wanted to seize all of Pomerania.

These conflicting interests had already disrupted the earlier campaigns and caused considerable distrust and dissension. In the planning for the 1759 campaign they were treated as if they did not exist. Each country went its own way, though with a diplomacy that produced surface compromise, such as a new treaty between Austria and France by which the Vienna and Swedish courts gained hefty financial subsidies without altering their private ambitions. According to the agreement finally worked out, an enormous Austrian army, over a hundred thousand troops, commanded by Marshal Daun,* would assemble along Silesian and Saxon borders while another Austrian corps of twenty-five thousand camped in Moravia. The Imperial army with an Austrian contingent, some thirty-five thousand troops, would form near Saalfeld, with the intention of seizing Leipzig. Czarina Elizabeth promised to have an army of ninety thousand at Posen by the end of May. In early July this army would march to the Oder to join Daun between Glogau and Breslau and commence operations as the situation dictated. A second Russian army of forty thousand would invade Pomerania to capture fortress Colberg. The Swedish corps was to seize fortress Stettin and press into Brandenburg.

Seemingly oblivious of this grandiose and highly fragmented plan, French commanders intended to drive Prince Ferdinand over the Weser River. Soubise's army — soon to be commanded by Duke Victor de Broglie — was to invade Hesse as support for Marshal Contades; that meant it could not support Imperial army operations in Saxony. To plaster over this awkward fact, Marshal Belle-Isle spoke grandly of joining with the Imperial army, once Daun had invaded Silesia, to carry the war "into the heart of the king's territories."[2] On the other hand

---

*Victory at Hochkirch had restored Daun's prestige at home and abroad. Pope Clement XIII sent him a consecrated hat and sword, traditional rewards for commanders of the faith who had defeated heretics. This was too much for King Frederick, who henceforth referred to him as "the consecrated hat," "the consecrated man," or simply "the hat," in addition to other pejorative titles.

the armies would not be ready to march until mid-June — which scarcely coincided with the Austrian and Russian plans.

Frederick was too good a strategist and knew his enemies too well not to gain an inkling of their various plans. In mid-March he moved his army between Schweidnitz and Jauer "in order to be ready for anything," as he told Henry. "You see by my position that I am the reserve of the army and ready to turn to where the greatest danger will draw me." He arrived at Rohnstock in a bad temper, Catt noted, partly the result of uncertainty, partly of sadness and ill health. He still had not recovered from Wilhelmina's death and frequently wept when he spoke of her to Catt. As usual he found solace in reading and writing. Voltaire sent him his new work, *Candide,* their correspondence resumed, and the king was soon showering him with a seemingly endless quantity of epistles and other verses.

If Frederick could not move tactically, Henry could. In early April the king urged him to march in Prince Ferdinand's support to push the Imperial army out of Bamberg. Henry wanted no part of the operation, and the king finally agreed to let him return to raids in Bohemia. In mid-April Henry opened a ten-day campaign in which he captured over two thousand enemy and seized or burned several valuable magazines. But meanwhile Ferdinand had been repulsed by the French (now under the Duke of Broglie) at Bergen and needed moral support. After acrimonious correspondence, Frederick *ordered* his reluctant brother to march against the Imperial army. He himself marched with a force to join General Fouqué in the hope of attacking General de Ville's Austrian corps, which again approached fortress Neisse. When de Ville retreated south, Frederick returned to Landeshut, "very fatigued and ill-pleased with the result of his march," Catt noted. He recovered quickly. "His superiority of talent, the readiness and fertility of his invention, fill me with confidence," Mitchell reported at this time. "No sooner does one project fail than he is ready with another, no disappointment discourages him, nor no success elates him beyond measure." [3] He believed that Fermor's Russians, about fifty-seven thousand strong, would invade Pomerania, besiege Colberg, and march into the New Mark. Dohna's corps, temporarily commanded by Lieutenant General Heinrich von Manteuffel, was to march as soon as possible to meet this enemy. A separate corps under General Wobersnow would observe any Russian march on Posen. Frederick would continue to watch Daun, "my big blessed beef," whose delay had allowed him to have a battle-ready army by mid-May.

It was another nervous period, "the results of a defensive war," he complained to Fouqué. "It is necessary to think of a hundred thousand things and make plans for every event." The events are described in detail in his vast correspondence of this spring. He analyzed various enemy moves, real or rumored, in tiresome detail, frequently writing to commanders two or three times a day, repeating and often contradicting himself to an astonishing degree. Andrew Mitchell, who had a lengthy audience on May 19, reported that "it is impossible to describe the fatigue of body and mind which this hero King daily undergoes, and that with an appearance of perfect tranquillity, even in the most unfavorable and perplexing circumstances."[4] The king expressed his most ardent desire for peace, Mitchell wrote. He also told Mitchell that the Grand Vizir of Turkey was ready to sign a treaty with Prussia but insisted that England either join or guarantee it (which the envoy warned would be very difficult to achieve).

Prince Henry meanwhile was pushing the Imperial army out of Saxony, a successful expedition that captured at least two thousand prisoners and destroyed enough magazines to keep Prince Friedrich of Zweibrücken quiet for a couple of months. Having relieved that pressure, Henry was ordered to prepare a corps for Manteuffel's support. Reports from Prussia continued to be confusing, but the king was beginning to believe that Fermor intended to invade Silesia from one side while Daun struck from the other. Manteuffel accordingly was ordered to march on Landsberg. Frederick next learned that Fermor was being relieved by Marshal Count Peter Saltikov, a royal favorite who had fought only one campaign in the Ukraine and was reputed to be "more sluggish and stupid than any Russian rustic."[5] The Russian army was also reported to be in a poor state, with much fighting among the senior commanders. Just as important, it was divided into separate corps.

In late June Frederick approved an operation suggested by General Wobersnow. The general would march along the Warthe River with Posen on the right, cross the river, and move on Thorn. The Russians would have to return to the Weichsel to protect the Thorn magazines, whereupon Wobersnow could possibly attack in the open. If the plan worked, Frederick enthusiastically wrote, not only would Pomerania and New Mark be retained, but the entire campaign would be won. If the Russians did not reach Glogau, Daun would not know what to do next. Once the Russians were driven across the Vistula, a matter of two or three weeks, Dohna's corps could reinforce either Henry or the king, as circumstances dictated. The plan seemed almost to mesmerize the king, already nervous and tired, certainly insecure — and here was the genesis of an immense tactical disaster.

The first inkling arrived in early July, when Wobersnow reported that the enemy had got wind of the Prussian march and pulled his corps into strongly fortified positions in Posen. Wobersnow was now going to gain the Russian flank to worry Saltikov's communications with Thorn. Frederick furiously replied that lack of speed and security had ruined the operation and that Wobersnow must now defend the New Mark.* "Prepare yourself for a very difficult campaign," he wrote to Henry. "Dohna, instead of carrying out the operation with celerity, has moved like a tortoise. . . . I shall do my task here, but if some foolish mistakes are made at Posen, I am finished."

Dohna's failure had already been compounded in the west by Prince Ferdinand, who, shaken by an earlier defeat at Bergen, was falling back toward the Weser. "For the love of God, pull yourself together," the king told him, "and do not look at things so darkly: the first step backward makes a poor impression in the army, the second step is dangerous, and the third becomes fatal."

And now Daun advanced into Lusatia, his orders from Maria Theresa to fight the Prussians if a favorable opportunity arrived. Even if he were defeated, he would not be held accountable! Frederick countered by leaving Fouqué with eighteen thousand troops at Landeshut and marching to Lähn on the Bober, from where he hoped to attack Daun's army. This move was in vain. Austrian records speak of Daun, who was crawling along at six miles a day, as advancing "with heavy heart." [6] "His fat Excellency who has lead in his ass marches like a tortoise," Frederick complained to Ferdinand. Noting that Henry was free of enemy, he ordered him to move on Bautzen to threaten Daun's rear. After a good deal of argument the prince grudgingly dispatched General Friedrich von Finck with a corps. Daun meanwhile was *fortifying* his new camp at Marklissa: "I believe that he opens the [siege] trench to take Silesia," Frederick wrote to Ferdinand; "if he continues like this, he will need four years to reach Bunzlau." Frederick meanwhile had moved camp to Schmottseifen, where, still hoping for battle, he had learned to know the terrain as well "as my garden of Sans-Souci." †

The impasse was broken by Saltikov, who in late July marched from Posen toward Crossen on the left bank of the Oder. Frederick responded by sending Lieutenant General von Wedell to relieve Dohna of command; Wedell would be to this corps "what a dictator was in Roman times." ‡ He was to stop the Russian advance, then attack "in my style." Wedell arrived in time to be beaten at Kay, in part because

---

*This was the first of several severe reprimands. The last such, written on July 19, was particularly insulting: Wobersnow had committed every fault possible and his campaign deserved to be treated as a perpetual example of what not to do.

†The king learned here that Major General Bredow, "who was as honorable a man as he was a bad officer," had died in Dresden. General Marwitz and Field Marshal Kalkstein had recently died. "My generals cross the Acheron at a fast gallop," he noted to Henry, "and soon there won't be any more."

‡Dohna was relieved on grounds of poor health. It is difficult to understand why the king failed to relieve him earlier. Perhaps he thought that Manteuffel was not up to the command or that Wobersnow, despite being junior to both, could put things right. The king's orders to Wedell can also be criticized as confusing and somewhat irresolute, and Prince Henry also complained to the king of conflicting orders at this time — with some justification.

of the precipitate retreat by two regiments that had suffered no casualties, in part for lack of sufficient cannon, in part for attacking under
unfavorable circumstances. Wedell, having lost some six thousand
men — including Wobersnow, who was killed — to Saltikov's seven
thousand, retired across the Oder, followed by the enemy. The enemy
then occupied Crossen.

Frederick accepted the news philosophically; he wrote sympathetically to Wedell and optimistically to Prince Henry. Despite the "critical
and awkward" state of affairs, one should not believe that all was lost:
"A single favorable day can restore everything to order." Nothing remained but to collect as many troops as possible and march to Wedell's
relief. "The chief object at present is to rid ourselves of the Russians,"
he told Henry, to whom he shortly turned over command at Schmottseifen.

87

THE KING marched in late July, briskly put Count Andreas Hadik's
Austrian corps out of action, but failed to prevent Loudon from joining
Saltikov's Russians at Frankfurt. He was marching as fast as possible
in this "furious crisis," he told Henry. A day later he arrived in Bees-
kow "after cruel and terrible marches," he informed Finckenstein. "I
am very tired, not having slept for six nights." He was cheered at Müllrose by a report of Prince Ferdinand's victory over the French at Minden. "But my Russians are not French," he wrote to Finckenstein, "and
Saltikov's artillery is a hundred times better than that of Contades."

While waiting at Müllrose for Wedell's and Finck's corps, he confirmed that the Russians had crossed the Oder and were camped near
Kunersdorf. That would "delay the decisive moment for some days,"
he complained to Henry. Wedell and Finck duly arrived, along with
supplies from Cüstrin. "I shall cross the Oder this night," Frederick
wrote to Finckenstein on August 10, "to advance on the enemy in order to attack him early the day after tomorrow. . . . A damned soul
in purgatory is in no more abominable situation than this in which I
find myself."

Friday, August 10, 1759. Marshal Saltikov occupies a strong defensive
position on the heights of Kunersdorf, a beautiful little village over-

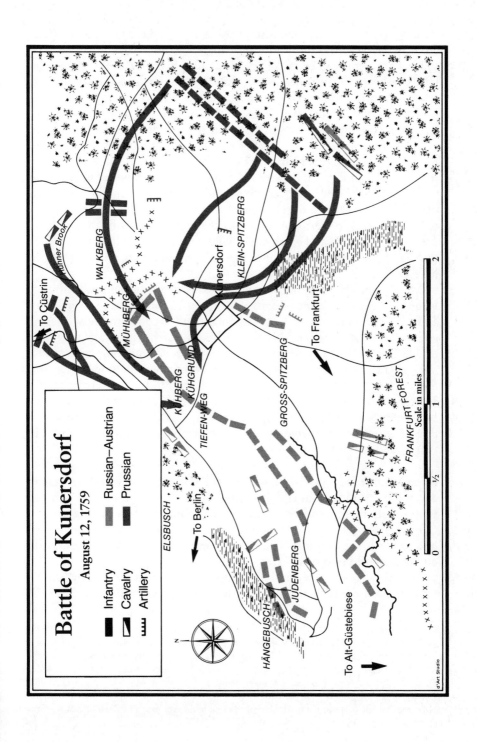

Battle of Kunersdorf
August 12, 1759

Infantry
Cavalry
Artillery

Russian–Austrian
Prussian

WALKBERG
MÜHLBERG
Kunersdorf
KLEIN-SPITZBERG
KUHBERG
KÜHGRUND
TIEFEN-WEG
GROSS-SPITZBERG
ELSBUSCH
HÄNGEBUSCH
JUDENBERG
FRANKFURT FOREST

To Cüstrin
Hühner Brook
To Frankfurt
To Berlin
To Alt-Güstebiese

Scale in miles

0   ½   1   2

d'Art Studio

looking the Oder Valley, about five miles east of Frankfurt.* The Russians, some seventy-nine thousand (including forty-six hundred Cossacks), are deployed in two lines stretching from the Kühberg on the left, southeast behind the village, then folding back to the southwest, where Croatian and Cossack irregulars carry it to the Oder. General Loudon's corps of just over nineteen thousand (including six thousand Croatian irregulars) is tucked between the left flank and the sparsely wooded Judenberg, facing north-northeast. Prince Galitsin's corps of fourteen battalions and fifty-six heavy cannon occupies the Mühlberg in front of Saltikov's left. Log barricades and earthworks protect the Mühlberg. Saltikov has over two hundred heavy cannon, which are placed in five batteries, the strongest being on the Gross-Spitzberg, which is fronted by *Wolfsgruben,* or concealed pits. The elongated right is covered by cavalry and earthworks where necessary. Saltikov and Loudon have good reason to believe that a Prussian attack will be severely defeated.

Saltikov holds a council of war on this beautiful sunny morning. Loudon argues for a move across the Oder to join Daun, sweep away Prussian resistance, seize Glogau, and spend a comfortable winter at enemy expense in Silesia. Neither Saltikov nor his generals are interested. This is the only Russian army in existence; as long as it exists, the generals will have a job and East Prussia will belong to Russia. Supplies are short; the Turks are threatening. Indeed, a retreat to the Weichsel may be in order. But Loudon's words apparently tell. A second war council that evening decides to cross the Oder within a few days. Meanwhile, Kunersdorf village will be burned in order to provide better fields of fire.

Friday–Saturday, August 10–11, 1759. While Saltikov and his generals are in evening council, the Prussian army, fifty thousand strong, with nearly three hundred cannon, is marching to the crossing area at Göritz, below Frankfurt. Pontoons and boats secretly sent from Berlin and Cüstrin are waiting. The troops enjoy a few hours of rest while engineers build two bridges.

The army crosses early in the morning, infantry and artillery by bridge, cavalry by ford. It deploys in two lines about two miles northeast of

---

* Kunersdorf (now Kunowice) is still a beautiful town, and the surrounding terrain must be similar to what it was in Frederick's day. Certainly from the heights north of the town one gains an excellent idea of the battle. My reconnaissance was somewhat labored, since a very large Russian corps was conducting maneuvers within what seemed like breathing distance. Later, in East Germany, I met several high school students from Kunowice. I remarked that I had just been there studying the battlefield. What battlefield? they asked. Incredibly, they did not know the original name of their village and had never heard of the battle of Kunersdorf!

the enemy's left flank, cavalry to the rear in a wood, Finck's corps on a height in front of the right wing. The army enjoys another rest.

Frederick reconnoiters the enemy position. He has no map, but an officer who has hunted in the area accompanies him, as does a forester. He swings his glass to the land north of Kunersdorf, which bristles with barricades, earthworks, and cannon that overlook marshy ground cut by two small roads. This is Saltikov's front, the king decides, and immediately rejects an attack here. This leaves an attack from the southeast, which he reasons will strike the Russian rear and right flank. The terrain looks far more likely here; there is room for cavalry, and thick woods will hide the army's approach. Finck will hold Saltikov while the main army attacks on both sides of the burning village of Kunersdorf. If the attack succeeds, the enemy will have no line of retreat. Saltikov will have a choice of surrender — or annihilation.

Sunday, August 12, 1759. The Prussian army marches at two A.M. Finck stays where he is to make a feigned attack. General von Wunsch in Frankfurt will fire cannon to worry Saltikov from that direction.

Frederick rides with the advance guard of hussars to some heights southeast of Kunersdorf. This time a soldier who comes from the area serves as guide, and Frederick learns the ugly truth: what he thinks is the Russian rear is the Russian front. Despite some fog, he also sees a row of ponds and swamps running from south of Kunersdorf to the great Frankfurt Forest.

He changes his plan. Instead of attacking both sides of the village, he will anchor his left east of the ponds while his right seizes the Mühlberg and rolls up the enemy flank. Aides order marching columns to turn and deploy in the woods southeast of Kunersdorf. Once this is done, the right wing will move out to join Finck in the attack.

This is not easy. It is still dark in the woods; trails are narrow and sandy. Heavy guns move slowly and are often stopped by tight turns. Teams have to be unhitched and the limbers turned. Nature otherwise is not cooperative. Lead columns strike a large depression full of pools crossed by a narrow dam impossible for the guns. The columns shift west. There is confusion; lead units go too far; time is lost. It is late morning before Colonel Moller's heavy guns are in position on the Walkberg, Klosterberg, and Klein-Spitzberg, and the battalions are deployed along the wood's edge.

The attack begins about eleven-thirty A.M. with fire from three heavy batteries that are seven hundred to fourteen hundred meters from the enemy. Russian batteries immediately reply, and for an hour the guns fight each other. The Russians are the overall loser.

The king is on the Walkberg. He watches the first line of four battalions march to the assault. A second line of four battalions follows.

The bombardment has silenced some enemy guns. A wide hollow shelters assault units from the remaining cannon. But then they are moving uphill in the open, climbing awkwardly over splintered log barricades. Enemy guns shift to canister shot, but now the Prussians close with bayonets. At a cost of two hundred casualties, they put more than twelve thousand enemy in retreat. The Mühlberg with eighty-six cannons is theirs.

Early success is deceptive. The land is such that Saltikov defends depth. Fugitives from the Mühlberg are now reinforced defenders of the Kühgrund, a pasture behind the Mühlberg. Behind the pasture are defended hills, and behind that line is General Loudon's fresh corps. The assault continues forward. Cannons cannot keep up with men on the steep, sandy trails. Infantry reach the farther side of the pasture. They are stopped; they fall back.

The main army attacks to the northwest but soon begins to shift west. Near Klein-Spitzberg the left halts to form a line facing Kunersdorf. General Friedrich von Seydlitz's and Prince Eugene of Württemberg's cavalry are in shelter behind and to the left. General von Hülsen's right follows assault units, only to run into their retreat from the Kühgrund.

There are too many troops in too tight a terrain. Order disappears, confusion sets in. Russian batteries open fire, cannonades that tear through cloth and flesh to send men reeling. The king is watching. In desperation he sends for Seydlitz. Some cannon finally come up. A new attack fares slightly better; the enemy begins to fall back. But there are no reserve battalions on hand; the left is too far away. Frederick calls in hussars and dragoons of the right. They attack west of the Kühgrund and are in turn counterattacked by Russian and Austrian dragoons. They fall back. Enemy cavalry circle the Kühgrund and fall on exhausted Prussian infantry sheltering in a gulley on the left. Seydlitz pushes in to destroy this effort and sweeps above the Kühgrund while infantry press in toward the Tiefen-Weg. Musket and canister fire drive Seydlitz back.

Finck's battalions finally reach the battlefield about three-thirty P.M. One of the first to fall is Major Christian Ewald von Kleist, famed "poet of the spring" (who later dies from his wounds). Kleist is lying wounded when his king organizes a new attack from left, center, and right that pushes the Russians from the Kühgrund to the Tiefen-Weg. Saltikov feeds in reinforcements.

Frederick moves to the left wing, which has attacked too far to the right. He sorts out units, brings up heavy guns, orders the attack to continue, and returns to the Kühgrund. The attack here falters and stops.

The Prussians are hot, thirsty, hungry, and exhausted. Some units are out of ammunition. On the right Finck's corps has been driven to

Field Marshal Jacob Keith. "If the Austrians do not attack us here," Keith told the king at Hochkirch in October 1758, "they deserve to be hanged." The king replied, "We must hope that they fear us more than the gallows."

The king at the battle of Kunersdorf, August 1759. Aides urge him to leave the field. He refuses. As a small rearguard holds off the enemy, Cossack bands close like wolves on a quarry. "We are lost," he tells a hussar officer.

retreat. The Prussian line falls back. In frantic fury Frederick orders Prince Eugene forward with cavalry. He attacks at full gallop but at some point looks around to find no one following him. He turns, is wounded, and leaves the field. Frederick orders General Puttkamer's hussars forward. Puttkamer finds death; his hussars, failure.

Frederick watches the rout unbelievingly. A fierce attack by Austrian and Russian cavalry under Loudon has shattered his left. He rides furiously from clump to clump of running soldiers, begging them to fight. They pay no heed. Aides urge him to leave the field. He refuses. As a small rearguard holds off the enemy, Cossack bands close like wolves on a quarry, sending more men in panic-stricken retreat. A detachment skirts the king's position. "We are lost," he tells a hussar officer, Captain Joachim von Prittwitz. "No, Your Majesty," Prittwitz replies.[1] He attacks with a few hussars while an aide seizes the king's bridle and gallops from the field.

⊙⊞⊙

It was the worst defeat of Prussian arms in three wars. With the exception of a few cavalry units that bravely served as rearguard, the army had lost tactical integrity. It was more than retreat, it was a rout, the survivors like frightened cattle trundling back to the Göritz bridgehead, huddling together waiting for the Russian storm to burst.

Frederick himself was shattered. That evening at Rittwein, in a filthy hut filled with bundles of straw and two badly wounded officers, he wrote to Finckenstein that though the men had fought well, they finally fell into confusion:

> I rallied them three times; at last I thought I would be captured and was obliged to yield the field of battle. My coat is riddled with bulletholes, two horses were killed under me, my misfortune is to be still alive. Our loss is very considerable: of an army of 48,000, I do not have 3000. At this moment everyone is running away and I am no longer master of my people. . . . This is a cruel reverse which I shall not survive. . . . I have no more resources, and to tell the truth I believe everything is lost. . . . Goodbye forever.

Violently ill the next day, the king ordered General Friedrich von Finck, who had also been wounded, to take command of what was left of the army, but only until the king's health improved. In a following "Instruction" to Finck, he painted a particularly gloomy picture of total military defeat. Finck, however, was to call in a small corps that was screening the Swedish army and fight when and where he could — "Time gained is very important in these dangerous circumstances." Yet Finck was to inform Prince Henry of the disaster and see that the army swore allegiance to the Prince of Prussia!

What to make of this? Was he contemplating abdication? Did he intend at last to commit suicide? He was ill with gout; he was spitting blood; and he had dizzy spells. We eliminate mental illness, suggested by some biographers. His personal secretary wrote to Finckenstein on August 15 that since the defeat, "His Majesty finds himself in a depression which causes infinite sorrow to those who have the honor to come near him." This suggests that the king was not in unsplendid isolation — the accepted version — and his letters and directives of these few days, if disconsolate and at times confused, scarcely suggest a deranged mind. It seems more logical to suggest that he was suffering from extreme exhaustion, a morbid condition that in his case was rapidly repaired by sleep.

Surface events certainly justified the king's despair. Defeat at Kunersdorf cost over eighteen thousand casualties, of whom some six thousand were killed and over eleven thousand wounded. The army had lost over 170 cannon. A lieutenant general and two major generals were killed. Prince Eugene of Württemberg and Seydlitz and several other generals were wounded, as were nearly all adjutant aides. The army on the night of defeat was easy meat for an enterprising enemy.

But that enemy also had been hurt. Total casualties came to around sixteen thousand, "which will not surprise Your Majesty," Saltikov informed Czarina Elizabeth, "who is aware that the King of Prussia sells his defeats at a dear rate."[2] Loudon was said to have argued for immediate pursuit, but Saltikov, who had thought himself beaten until the sudden dénouement, recognized a Pyrrhic victory and was not interested. Nor did Loudon, with a nearly fresh and strong corps, pursue on his own.

Left to itself, the Prussian army made a swift and remarkable recovery. Under Finck's capable direction, provos were rounding up stragglers (many of whom returned voluntarily), numerous lightly wounded reported for duty, General Johann von Wunsch's corps from Frankfurt was intact, reinforcements were marching from Pomerania, enemy deserters appeared here and there, two irregular battalions were called in, and General von Rochow was sending cartridges and cannon from Berlin (where fifty 12-pounder replacements were soon being cast by royal order). Three days later Frederick wrote that the army counted twenty-four thousand men and that the "great thunderstorm" would pass. A day later he was again in command, writing to Finckenstein and Henry of his plans and blaming a sudden panic of the infantry for the defeat: "The ridiculous fear of being taken to Siberia made them lose their heads and there was no way of stopping them." He himself was nearly back to normal; he wrote melodramatically to the Marquis d'Argens and Henry, asking the latter to imagine "all that my spirit suffers and you will easily judge that the torment of the damned does not approach it. Happy [be] the dead! They are sheltered from all concerns and sorrows." And to Finckenstein: "Luck as always will decide our fortune." Two days later the army had increased to thirty thousand and Frederick was at Fürstenwalde, screening Berlin, prepared to fight either Hadik or Loudon — or both. On August 20 he counted thirty-three thousand men, most of whom, as he complained to Finckenstein, were rogues: "I fear my troops more than the enemy." Nevertheless, he was prepared to give battle, even though his best officers were hospitalized in Stettin. Subsequent letters vacillated between desire for and fear of battle. As he wrote to Prince Ferdinand, "This is the most horrible crisis of my life."

8 8

THE CRISIS continued but never came to a boil. For King Frederick it was another difficult period that demanded a patience he did not possess. He was surrounded by large armies whose commanders harbored unknown plans of destruction. At any minute a courier could bring news that would mean battle — if Saltikov moved on Berlin, if Daun marched, if, if, if. "My problems only increase," he complained to Finckenstein on August 22, and, a day later, "Never have I found myself in such a frightful situation as this."

The Imperial army captured Halle, Leipzig, and Wittenberg, and was marching on Dresden. Frederick could send only General Wunsch with eleven "poor battalions" and a few squadrons to interfere. His request to Prince Ferdinand for a diversion was turned down. Prince Henry was on the march, momentarily out of touch.

Saltikov eased matters by marching in late August. "I announce the miracle of the House of Brandenburg," Frederick wrote to Henry, now at Sagan: instead of giving battle that could have won him the war, Saltikov "has marched from Müllrose to Lieberose." Frederick at once shifted camp to Waldow to cut Saltikov from Lusatia and food. Wunsch recaptured Wittenberg and Torgau — "the first good news that I have had in a year," Frederick noted in announcing Wunsch's promotion — and would march to the relief of Dresden once heavy guns arrived. Here General Schmettau, with a weak garrison, was besieged by thirty thousand of the enemy. The king, in informing him of the defeat at Kunersdorf, explained that he could not reinforce him; Schmettau could capitulate on condition that he be allowed to save the war chest (over five million thalers in cash) and gain free passage for his troops. Unaware that Wunsch's relief corps was on the way, and seeing no hope of holding out, Schmettau surrendered. The next day he received a second letter from the king, ordering him to hold out at all costs! Frederick informed Prince Ferdinand of the disaster, adding that "without a miracle or your aid I am lost."

The king was once again saved by the enemy's feckless and confused action. Instead of completing the destruction of the Prussian army, Marshal Daun sent General Lacy to Saltikov's headquarters to propose secondary operations that ranged from seizing Berlin to capturing fortress Glogau and taking up winter quarters in Silesia.

Saltikov was not very interested. His army had been bled white at Kay and Kunersdorf, he lacked horses, clothing, and food (Daun not having supplied the latter, though he had promised to). His one desire was to recross the Oder and return to Thorn for the winter. Nor was Daun feeling aggressive. Eight days after Kunersdorf, the French observer in his headquarters noted, "The King of Prussia is in truth too much feared."[1] Yet the Russian and Austrian courts insisted on action. Saltikov finally agreed that if Daun supported him with food, forage, and siege artillery, and also reinforced Loudon's corps, he would move on Glogau while Daun held Henry in check at Sagan.

Saltikov and Daun marched a few days later — in opposite directions. Frederick believed that Daun would soon head for Dresden and ordered Henry to join Finck and Wunsch at Torgau. He himself shadowed Saltikov's forces eastward "in order to prevent them from making some troublesome incursion, limit their foraging and oblige them to decamp as soon as possible."

This was in keeping with the king's declared strategy at the opening of the campaign: divide and conquer. But at this point it was a bold decision, in view of his weak corps of "twice-beaten troops." He was determined that Saltikov would not besiege Glogau, and if necessary he would fight a battle to prevent it. In the event, he need not have worried. When Daun failed to provide food, forage, and artillery, Saltikov informed Louden that, lacking cannon, he could not besiege Glogau. His task therefore would be to hold the king in check to give Daun a free hand in Saxony.

It was another stalemate, one army looking at the other, a relatively quiet period in which the king scribbled verses, played the flute, and wrote a not very interesting monograph on King Charles XII of Sweden, who had also campaigned in these parts.

The war of maneuver had shifted to Saxony. Throughout September Prince Friedrich Michael of Zweibrücken's Imperial army, reinforced by Count Andreas Hadik's corps, faced the Prussian corps of Generals Finck and Wunsch. Although the king criticized Finck for irresolution, the Prussians had more than held their own; indeed, Finck had just been awarded the Order of the Black Eagle for beating the enemy near Meissen. But Frederick desperately wanted Leipzig and Dresden both for winter quarters and for political reasons, and that was why he had ordered Henry to join the generals.

Henry did not want to go to Saxony, but Frederick overrode his arguments. Once under way, he was a ball of fire. With General Lentulus commanding the advance guard, the army covered fifty miles in two night marches — "the most difficult march he had ever made," Henry told the king. Skirting Daun's army east of Bautzen, Henry attacked a corps of irregulars and captured eighteen hundred, at a cost of forty-four casualties. This brought Daun running to Bautzen so rapidly that he reportedly lost three thousand men from exhaustion and desertion. Guessing Prince Henry's plan, the Austrian field marshal hurried on to join Zweibrücken at Dresden. He attacked Finck's smaller corps near Meissen and drove him back to Strehla. At this point Henry arrived, and Daun returned to Dresden.

But Henry reverted to type. He was not interested in the king's various operations designed to push Daun back to Bohemia. They did not suit his preference for a quiet war of maneuver. "Daun is mocking us," Frederick protested, again calling for vigorous action: Henry should not worry about being attacked; Henry should attack. Henry *was* worried, and now, not having slept for several nights, he momentarily lost his head. Not only did he see himself forced to retire on Torgau, but he doubted that he could remain in Saxony. The enemy was too strong, and the terrain between Torgau and Leipzig was unsuitable for battle.

Saltikov and Loudon had not yet marched, and the king had just come down with severe gout and fever when he received this thunderbolt. "Having the most beautiful of my armies," he replied, Henry should not worry about the enemy. The terrain between Torgau and Leipzig was made up of plains and was ideal for attack: "If you never wish to risk anything, it is impossible to do anything." Henry had nearly as many battalions as Daun; he should pull himself together and go after the enemy.

At this crucial point Saltikov brushed off Loudon's pleas to attack the Prussians, crossed the Oder, bypassed Glogau, and in late October began the march to Thorn. Loudon's corps, after burning several villages, began the long march through Poland to Moravia. Frederick could therefore release Hülsen's corps, which would arrive in Saxony in ten days. "Finck has filled your mind with black thoughts," he wrote to Henry. "I beg you for the love of God to think differently and with more nerve."

Henry evidently understood the unwritten warning that if he retreated, he would suffer the same fate as his brother William. A few days later, Duke Charles of Arenberg tried to outflank him and was sent running, with at least four thousand casualties. The king congratulated Henry. Frederick's health was better, and he hoped shortly to be in Torgau, "a skeleton full of good will."

The king traveled by carriage and, when that was too painful, by sedan chair, "like the relics of a saint." August Eichel found him pale and weak, wobbly on his feet, but brimming with optimism. He greeted Henry with compliments — and a tactical plan, that of pushing south with the main army while a strong detachment under Finck circled south of Dresden (as Henry had already planned). But Henry was now out of it. It was Frederick, dealing with Finck, who was to march on Freiberg and Dippoldiswalde and put a strong detachment at Maxen, from where he would interdict the enemy's baggage trains. Simultaneously Colonel Friedrich von Kleist's hussars were to burn enemy magazines at Aussig and elsewhere, along with eight or ten Bohemian villages, in revenge for Loudon's barbarity in Silesia. Daun had already withdrawn to Kesseldorf and would probably continue to the Plauengrund, west of Dresden. Finck's position and Kleist's raids would throw Daun into terrible confusion and a disorganized retreat, which could be exploited to great advantage.

That was the plan. It wasn't a bad one, but it was risky. Frederick earlier had warned Henry that Daun, who was under heavy pressure from the Vienna court, would attack an isolated detachment, so this was the time for the army to remain together. But Hülsen's corps had given the army new weight. Finck knew the Maxen area and was strong enough to be self-sufficient. His mission was interdiction. Patrols and spies would keep him informed of enemy movements and allow him to avoid a major action. Frederick subsequently warned him to remain on the alert, his corps intact; an enemy force was reportedly marching on Maxen, and the king was sending a corps under General Hülsen to Dippoldiswalde. To Finck's report that a general battle appeared imminent, the king replied that he must avoid any general action, because raids would cost the enemy far more.

It is doubtful that Finck received this final advice. Frederick was putting Ecclesiastes to verse in the style of Voltaire when the awful news arrived. Finck had been surrounded at Maxen and, after a battle of several hours, had surrendered his entire corps: sixteen battalions, thirty-six squadrons, eight generals, over five hundred officers (about a tenth of the officer corps), over twelve thousand troops.

"My God, is it possible? Have I brought my bad luck with me to Saxony?" the king asked Catt, and then raved on about his unfortunate life, the only happy period of which was at Rheinsberg. "I cannot recover from my astonishment," he wrote to d'Argens. "Astonishment, sorrow, indignation, scorn, all blended together, lacerate my soul." He received Finck's report coldly: "Up to now it is unheard of that a Prussian corps would lay down its weapons before its enemy." He was going to suspend judgment until he had all the facts.* Finckenstein was to play down the "disaster" to the public "as best he could." †

The king still did not regard the campaign as lost, and hoped that lack of food would soon force Daun to retire into Bohemia. Daun had no intention of doing so; his orders were to hold Dresden "at all costs." In this very cold winter, each tried to attack the other in vain. In mid-January both commanders went into winter quarters, Daun near Dresden with forward elements at Dippoldiswalde, Frederick immediately to the southwest with headquarters at Freiberg.

---

* After returning from imprisonment in 1763, Finck was court-martialed, cashiered, and sentenced to one year of fortress arrest. He died, at the age of forty-seven, in 1766, as a general in Danish service. King Frederick recalled his two daughters, gave them pensions, and paid for their education.

† Responsibility for Maxen has been debated through the years. The king has been criticized for unnecessarily exposing Finck. Catt later wrote that Prince Henry and many officers disputed the decision. Henry's mood is clear from his annotation of the king's letter of December 14, which as usual discussed enemy strength and intentions: "I have no confidence whatever in these reports; they are always as contradictory and uncertain as his character. He has thrown us into this cruel war, and only the valor of the generals and soldiers can extricate us. Since the day that he joined my army, he has spread confusion and misfortune in it; all my efforts in this campaign, all the good fortune which favored me, everything is lost through Frederick." (Easum, *Prince Henry of Prussia*.) This is rather silly, since Henry would still have been raiding in Bohemia but for the king's orders. Moreover, Henry had already planned to send Finck's corps south to cut Daun's communications. Finck later claimed to have been unduly influenced by the king's orders, and perhaps the king's earlier criticism of his pessimism prevented him from prudently retiring, although he seems to have been tactically blind. General Wunsch, who did defend brilliantly and who was also captured, had wished to keep fighting and laid the blame squarely on Finck. Perhaps the kindest criticism was offered by Andrew Mitchell: "If Finck had done the right thing [withdraw], he would not have dined at the king's table again for some time, but his corps would have been saved." (*Politische Correspondenz*, Volume 19.)

89

DEFEAT AT MAXEN and the pusillanimous end of the campaign had dealt the Prussian king's diplomacy an almost mortal blow. Although Austria from the beginning had regarded an Anglo-Prussian proposal for a peace conference as weakness, certain officials in Paris and Saint Petersburg were interested. But Maxen brought new strength to war parties in these courts. In early December Count Kaunitz informed the Russian court that "the King of Prussia is as good as destroyed, the English financial strength is exhausted."[1] Czarina Elizabeth agreed; she abruptly rejected a conference and pledged herself to continue the war.

Frederick nonetheless continued to work for a separate peace with France. Voltaire's efforts to bring Minister Choiseul around had failed — to no one's great surprise. But an effort by Duchess Louise Dorothea of Saxe-Gotha fared better, and Frederick grew excited with Choiseul's conciliatory reply. Neither William Pitt nor Andrew Mitchell was impressed, but Frederick refused to be discouraged. "Amidst all his great and superior qualities," Mitchell reported, the king "is by no means exempted from the common Weakness of humanity of believing with wonderful facility whatever is agreeable, and with the greatest difficulty whatever is contrary to his wishes or interest."[2] In due course the king admitted that the war party still controlled the Versailles court, but he hoped that France's lack of money and her losses on land and sea would bring her to peace.

He held no such hopes for the Russian court. On learning of the czarina's curt refusal of a conference, he again asked Pitt to send a naval squadron to the Baltic. When his request was turned down, he repeated it in February. Pitt's reply was that the British navy was already overextended, but the more probable reason was that Britain did not wish to jeopardize important Baltic trade by quarreling with Russia, Sweden, and Denmark.

Frederick had two other possible allies. One was Denmark, which tentatively offered a fleet, but negotiations dragged and he soon realized that still another effort had failed. This left Turkey. Rexin (the name still being used by Lieutenant Hand) reported that the grand vizir had been on the point of agreeing to an alliance and military action against Russia and Austria when news of an approaching general peace (spread by enemy agents) changed his mind. The king authorized Rexin to spend 500,000 thalers (he later doubled the amount) on bribes to obtain the alliance. Finckenstein was to send expensive gifts to the sultan, grand vizir, and senior officials. Once again he held high hopes for success.

y believed that any of these moves would produce
iether he was whistling in the dark is a moot ques-
sed, living almost in isolation, enjoying only his
usual outpouring of satirical verses, melodramatic
lging from his conversations with Catt and Mitch-
correspondence, he was nearing the end of his inner
st unfortunate and harsh campaign that I have ever
dispirited and ill, surrounded by enemies on every
ns, "I have lost all confidence in my fortune." "All
that I can do," he wrote a week later, "is to struggle constantly against
adversity; but I am able neither to restore fortune nor to diminish the
number of my enemies." Similar complaints went to Prince Henry and
Finckenstein. He ordered court and government to be moved back to
Magdeburg for safety.

That was one side of the king, but Mitchell caught another: "A general discouragement reigns through the whole army from the fatal effects of which he is perhaps the only person exempted. . . . Ferocity
has seized his mind and cruelty has steeled his heart." [3]

The main question in the king's mind was how best to hang on until
some fortunate event — a deus ex machina perhaps in the form of peace,
as he wrote Henry — rescued him from certain destruction. His solution, as in the previous year, was to remain on the strategic defensive
while rebuilding his shattered army, which had lost sixty thousand men
in the 1759 campaign. By mid-May he had brought it to 110,000, but
only by scraping the barrel; part of his army, as he told the British
envoy, "was fit only to be shown at a distance to the enemy. . . . The
other part was discouraged and dispirited." [4] Nevertheless he could now
begin to hit the enemy when and where possible to keep him off balance. He wanted in particular to prevent the Austrians from entering
Lusatia and joining with the Russians.

He moved carefully, reacting more than acting, hoping desperately
for peace with France, for Turkish intervention, for any miracle. "I
tremble when I see the approaching campaign," he wrote to Finckenstein in March. "I am very tired; I feel the weakness of age that hinders
me much differently than formerly," he complained to Prince Ferdinand. "War demands an old head full of experience with a young and
robust body." For the moment he would stay where he was in order to
be closer to the French negotiations, would wait for Daun to move,
attack him when he did so, then march as circumstances dictated. He
put Henry, who had returned from sick leave, in command of the Russian front; his orders were to assemble an army at Sagan, from where
he could march to Frankfurt, Pomerania, or to Fouqué at Landeshut.
Foreseeing that Daun and Zweibrücken would attack him at Freiberg,
Frederick built a fortified camp behind the Triebisch River, northwest

of Dresden, and in late April shifted his army there, his left wing resting on Meissen, where he could cross the Elbe if necessary to march to the relief of Pomerania or Silesia.

The enemy remained as divided as ever. At the Vienna court, France was rapidly becoming a military cipher while Russia grew in importance. Maria Theresa and Count Kaunitz were determined to end the war in 1760 and were increasing the army to 140,000 men. Czarina Elizabeth pledged Russia to the same goal, promising to do everything possible to make the coming campaign decisive.

Opinions differed as to how to achieve this ambitious end. Daun and Lacy proposed a modest plan of limited objectives. Loudon, backed by Maria Theresa and Kaunitz, wanted an all-out offensive to destroy the Prussian army. The plan as finally worked out called for Loudon to invade Upper Silesia with forty thousand men and join there with twenty to thirty thousand Russians. This would force the Prussian king to move from Dresden, whereupon Daun's main army and the Imperial troops would seize all of Saxony. The main Russian army was to capture Breslau. Loudon would then press the king into Lower Silesia, where his army would be destroyed.

The Russian court received the plan in early March. Marshal Saltikov put his finger on the problem, telling the French military representative "that the campaign would run a course as fruitless as the earlier ones — one will spread out on all sides without, however, operating anywhere effectively."[5] The Russian reply rejected an advance into Upper Silesia. Czarina Elizabeth promised that Saltikov would be on the Oder in mid-June, his goal to seize fortresses Glogau and Breslau. Meanwhile a strong corps under General Count Chernyshev would assemble at Posen while General Count Gottlob Tottleben's Cossacks again invaded Pomerania. Saltikov had been ordered to work closely with Marshal Daun, but Daun was expected to act aggressively and also provide the Russian army with food and siege artillery.

This delayed reply effectively put matters back to square one. How is it possible, Daun asked Maria Theresa, to work with Saltikov, a general who is "without experience, without judgment, and without determination."[6] Loudon agreed that the Russians were stalling and advised his court to proceed without them; it was already late May, and delay only favored the Prussian enemy. Loudon's march into Upper Silesia was abandoned. Instead, he moved his corps to Zittau. After learning that Prince Henry had arrived with a strong corps at Sagan, the Hofkriegsrath ordered Loudon to base on Königgrätz, where he would be reinforced to a strength of forty thousand before marching into Glatz.

With Daun playing possum at Dresden and Saltikov's army stalled on the Weichsel River, Frederick's primary concern in this dangerous spring of 1760 was Tottleben's rapacious operations in Pomerania and Loudon's burgeoning threat to Lower Silesia.

This was Prince Henry's operational responsibility. His line stretched from Landeshut, where General Fouqué commanded a small corps, to the Baltic, where General Forcade was screening fortress Colberg with another small corps of inferior quality.

Henry had not wanted this command, which he thought would result only in disaster. Having accepted it, he wished to rely on his usual careful tactics, moving against enemy supply depots rather than against the enemy himself. This was wholly unacceptable to the king under the present circumstances and soon led to another quarrel. Although Frederick had promised Henry total operational autonomy, he was soon writing one letter after another full of advice that Henry did not want and often did not follow.

Neither commander could do much about Tottleben, whose Cossacks had been prowling about in Pomerania since early May. His light troops struck everywhere, burning towns and outposts, scouring an already sad land.

Loudon's threat to Silesia was another matter. The key player here was General Fouqué at Landeshut. Frederick and Henry spent most of May speculating on Gideon Loudon's possible moves. If he invaded Silesia, Fouqué must retire northeast on Schweidnitz to cover Breslau. Frederick did not believe that Loudon would risk communications to this extent, and he was also hopeful that Turkey would invade Hungary to end this particular threat.

In late May the vice-commandant of Glatz, a Piedmontese lieutenant colonel with the unusual name of d'O, reported that Loudon was moving on Braunau. This was incorrect, but it caused Fouqué to march northeast to the Freiberg area, from where he asked Henry for reinforcements. Colonel d'O meanwhile reported that Loudon was at Frankenstein. Fouqué now evacuated Landeshut entirely and marched northeast to cover Breslau.

This displeased Henry, who had wanted Fouqué to hold Landeshut until he was in danger of being surrounded. It also displeased the king, who reprimanded Fouqué for his "too premature and precipitate" march, which might ruin everything. "My generals do me more harm than the enemy because they always move the wrong way," he added gratuitously. A few days later he ordered Fouqué to return to Landeshut and hold it to the last man.

Taken in context, the order was logical. Frederick had decided to break his own tactical impasse by crossing the Elbe to march on General Lacy's corps between Radeburg and Moritzburg. It was a dangerous but not foolhardy move, accomplished in mid-June. Though it would not lead to the decisive battle that Frederick wanted, a victory would cause Loudon to abandon the siege of Glatz (which had surprised Colonel d'O) and would allow the king to reinforce Fouqué, who was back at Landeshut "without much of an army."

The operation started well. The soldiers reminded Eichel of those of 1756, determined, looking forward to battle, not one deserter on the march, but, alas, lacking the officers of 1756. Unfortunately Lacy divined the plan and fell back toward Dresden, leaving the Prussians an empty camp.

Frederick was enormously disappointed. "I have a great desire to hang myself," he told Catt. Instead of reinforcing Fouqué, he now sent orders for him to evacuate Landeshut and fall back to screen Breslau if Loudon pressed into Silesia. At this point two reports from Rexin in Constantinople revived him. Not only was the Porte ready to sign an alliance with Prussia; it was about to send an army into Hungary. But countering this boon came news that Loudon had raised the siege of Glatz to attack Fouqué. He had taken heavy casualties at Glatz, but he still counted about thirty-five thousand against Fouqué's eleven thousand. Fouqué had made a strong defense — the enemy admitted to three thousand casualties — but was finally overwhelmed. Fouqué himself had been twice wounded and was a prisoner of war.*

90

THE CAMPAIGN OF 1760 had scarcely opened to King Frederick's liking. General Lacy's escape and General Fouqué's defeat "occasioned a sensible alteration in his temper and spirits," Andrew Mitchell reported. "He talks despondingly and with more harshness than usual, both of which have a bad effect on the army."[1] Mitchell thought that the king was trying to do more than he could and blamed a fixation on Silesia for the present situation.

The kindhearted envoy was missing the point. The king was in a countdown to defeat. He believed that the only way out was to win *une affaire décisive* over Daun — the words are constantly repeated in his letters of this time. Foreseeing that Daun would march through Lusatia to join Loudon, Frederick marched on Bautzen, a furious effort

---

* The king did not blame Fouqué, who had fought with honor and whose defense won Loudon's praise. Fouqué returned to Brandenburg in 1763, a semi-invalid who lived quietly, frequently corresponding with, and sometimes visited by, Frederick. He died in 1774.

in blazing sun that in one day cost over a hundred deaths from heat exhaustion and foul water. It was also a futile effort. The Prussians were shadowed by Daun, who offered no chance of battle. Frederick now turned west in another effort to fight Count Lacy, who, with Prince Charles of Zweibrücken and his Imperial army, merely retired south to the Pirna area. The king continued on to besiege Dresden, which he believed would fall in a few days.

It is difficult to understand his decision. Had he won the place, he could not have held it very long, so there was no foreseeable political or military gain. Siege guns had to come from Magdeburg. In the interim he relied on his own artillery, which was insufficient both in weight and quantity of ammunition. Firing continued for a week while trenches were opened and battery sites prepared. The big guns finally arrived, and the king told Mitchell that he would soon possess the city. But the garrison showed no signs of surrender. Frederick stepped up the bombardment to set the city on fire, a politically unwise move. Eichel wrote to Finckenstein that one could see little but fire and smoke and civilians streaming out by foot, horse, and cart.* Mitchell suggested that it was vindictive: "I cannot think of the bombardment of Dresden without horror, nor of many other things I have seen. Misfortunes naturally sour men's temper and long continued, without interval, at last extinguish humanity."[2]

Frederick's mood was such that the news of Count Podewils's death made little impression. "He was an honest man and a good citizen," Frederick wrote to Finckenstein. "But such are all our losses. It would appear that one becomes indifferent to everything."

His one concern was the war. While Dresden burned, Daun's army was approaching by forced marches. It camped east of the city the day after siege guns arrived. Enemy irregulars and small detachments all along had harassed Frederick's lines, once even reaching his headquarters and cutting him from all outside communication. When Regiment Anhalt-Bernburg gave way to a sally from the city, he ordered hat tresses slashed off and officers relieved of their swords; no greater insult could be imagined. He fell from his horse and the horse stepped on his foot. He barraged Prince Henry with confused and often contradictory orders. When the prince replied despondently, he was criticized for seeing the black side of things, which made him irresolute at a time when "it is far better to make a bad decision than none at all." He refused to listen to subordinates who insisted that the siege had failed.

Only in late July did he face truth and give orders to march to Meissen. As the frustrated army departed, the Austrians across the river

---

* In 1772 Dr. John Moore noted: "Many of these [Dresden] houses still lie in rubble; but the inhabitants are gradually rebuilding, and probably all the ruined streets will be repaired before a new war breaks out in Germany." (Moore, *Views of Society*.)

fired muskets and cannon in another *fête de victoire:* Loudon had captured fortress Glatz.

Dresden was not yet burning when Frederick admitted to Prince Henry that he was in "the greatest possible embarrassment. . . . All the moves that I can take are subject to great inconveniences." He had scarcely lifted the Dresden siege when he learned that Loudon was besieging Breslau. It was now a matter of trying to beat Daun to Silesia.

Leaving Hülsen with a small corps at Meissen, Frederick marched in early August with about thirty thousand men. He intended to be between the Queiss and Bober Rivers in five days; there he could have a decisive battle with Daun. Given the terrain, his already tired troops, and the heat, the march was bound to be difficult. But Daun complicated matters even more by sending irregulars to tear up the land that Frederick was to cross. Simultaneously he marched from Bischofswerda *ahead* of the Prussians while Lacy marched *behind* the Prussians, his pandours harassing the columns. In Frederick's later wry words: "A stranger seeing the movements of these armies could have been deceived. He would have surely thought that they all belonged to the same commander. Marshal Daun's army would have appeared to him the advance guard, that of Prussia the main army, and Lacy's troops the rearguard."[3]

In this dangerous situation the king marched in an almost battle-ready formation of three columns, each nearly self-sufficient (including artillery), and each ready to deploy into line of battle in case of attack. Prussian hussars and irregulars preceded and followed the first columns; dragoons, the second and third. Heavy artillery remained with brigades, aid wagons with battalions — altogether two thousand wagons rolled across the land. Pontoon carriers fronted each column, because five rivers had to be crossed. Speed was essential. Extreme heat took a high toll of lives, Mitchell noted, and caused many to desert. The Prussians covered a remarkable ninety-plus miles in five days to reach Bunzlau, where the king ordered a day of rest.

Frederick learned from intercepted letters that Daun, now at Schmottseifen, was apparently planning to besiege fortress Schweidnitz. The king intended to frustrate this plan by marching to Jauer and Striegau, thus outflanking Daun. "It will be very difficult on this occasion to avoid a general battle that will decide everything . . ." he wrote to Henry. "I believe that in a few days the quarrel between Carthage and Rome will be decided."

Frederick also learned that Henry had shaken off all doubts and had carried off his own magnificent operation. Observing that Saltikov had marched from Posen, Henry foresaw a jointure with Loudon in Silesia. He responded by a series of forced marches that averaged nearly thirty miles a day to bring his corps of about thirty-six thousand to fortress Glogau and on toward Breslau. Loudon meanwhile had closed on Breslau and demanded that it surrender or his Croats would ravish the town. He grandly remarked, "I will not spare the child in its mother's womb." General Bogislav von Tauentzien,* who was prepared for a siege, replied, "Neither I nor my soldiers are with child. Proceed if you will."[4]

Loudon was only about twenty thousand strong, and he lacked heavy artillery and supply. Saltikov, moreover, did not trust the Austrians. Although he had crossed into Silesia, he halted for two days near the border. Henry meanwhile arrived at Parchwitz, chased Loudon as far as Striegau, recrossed the Oder at Breslau, pushed off a Russian corps, and camped north of the Silesian capital. This has been accurately called "one of the most brilliant exploits of the whole war."[5] But now Henry incongruously informed the king, "If I had foreseen the difficulties that I am finding in this campaign and those that I still foresee, I would have begged you to spare me from a job that I regard as almost impossible to perform." Frederick unsympathetically replied, "It is not difficult, my dear brother, to find people who serve the state in affluent and fortunate times; good citizens are those who serve the state in a time of crisis and misfortune." He himself was near Liegnitz, he explained, about to march to Goldberg and on to Jauer, where he could get badly needed bread from Schweidnitz. But he anticipated a battle with Daun before then.

Frederick was to get more than he bargained for. Marching with his advance guard, he ran into enemy hussars on some heights near Goldberg and pushed through only to see Daun's entire army crossing to the right, or eastern, bank of the Katzbach. Blocked from Jauer, he reconnoitered Liegnitz the next day and found the enemy in his way there. Turning south again, perhaps a trifle desperately, he crossed the Katzbach, hoping to break through to Jauer, but Lacy had reached the main army and stood squarely in the way.† He neither could attack nor, because of poor roads, could he outflank the Austrians to the south. Recrossing the Katzbach in time to avoid being attacked, he took up a position southwest of Liegnitz, intending to march on Parchwitz. To free his hand, he sent two thousand empty wagons, escorted by some irregulars, back to Glogau.

Daun had gained a superior tactical position. By the evening of Au-

---

* Present as Tauentzien's secretary was thirty-one-year-old Gotthold Ephraim Lessing, whose famous play, *Minna von Barnhelm*, written in 1763, was inspired by the feeling of Prussian nationalism that emerged in the Seven Years' War.

† Prussian hussars captured a great deal of enemy baggage at Goldberg, including Lacy's entire equipage and, according to one observer, "a quite pretty Tyrolean scullery maid." Frederick later returned Lacy's baggage as a mark of courtesy "in a profession that is hard and cruel enough in itself." He retained a map showing Austrian marches until it could be copied. (Generalstab S, Volume 12.) Mitchell reported that a good many officers were criticizing the king for putting the army in a trap similar to that of Maxen. Mitchell destroyed his cipher and burned his important papers. (Mitchell, *Memoirs*.)

gust 14 his entire army, eighty thousand strong, formed an arc running from Goldberg, southwest of Liegnitz, to the Katzbach River, northeast of the city. Pressed by Loudon and by letters from Empress Maria Theresa, Daun decided to attack. Loudon reported this happy news to Marshal Saltikov, who reluctantly agreed to send Chernyshev's corps of twenty thousand across the Oder to join Loudon at Neumarkt.

Thursday, August 14, 1760. Daun's main army crosses the Katzbach at night and marches north, intending to strike the Prussian right in the morning. Lacy's corps marches northeast from Goldberg to move behind the Prussian right wing. Loudon crosses the Katzbach below Liegnitz and will attack the Prussian left flank.

A drunken Irish officer comes to the Prussian camp to report that the Austrians will attack in the morning. Frederick pays little attention. His trains are already across the Schwarzwasser. The army marches at dark. Peasants remain in the old camp to tend fires while hussars bawl out false commands. The army debouches onto a plateau northeast of Liegnitz, its left flank behind Panten, its right flank south of Hummel. Outposts and cavalry vedettes ring the small army, scarcely thirty thousand men. The night is cold and rainy. The king sits by a small fire, talking to some soldiers. The army will march again at dawn.

Friday, August 15, 1760. Loudon's corps is over the Katzbach in the area of Panten, slightly southeast of the new Prussian position. Shortly after midnight Loudon marches with his reserve regiments, his goal the heights of Pfaffendorf. In thick fog he runs into Zieten's hussars, who retire after a short and confused skirmish. Loudon continues his march.

It is three A.M. Major Herman von Hundt with a party of hussars is scouting east toward Bienowitz. From the fog and the night comes Loudon's advance guard. Austrians open fire; Prussians quickly fall back. The king hears gunfire, which is followed by Hundt's frantic arrival. He reports that Loudon's infantry is approaching. More fire sounds from the rear: the enemy has tumbled on the Prussian vedettes.

It is almost daylight. The king, already mounted, orders Brigade Schenkendorff to wheel left and march with its front against Bienowitz, its heavy battery positioned on a nearby slope. The remainder of the left wing shifts left to extend General Balthasar von Schenkendorff's new front. Troopers are still shaking sleep from their eyes when Loudon's cavalry hit from the rear. The Prussians are temporarily thrown back but manage to re-form and with three fresh regiments slowly push the enemy toward Bienowitz. It is a confused and prolonged fight in bush-covered land dotted with forest.

Frederick meanwhile orders Zieten, commanding the right wing, to prevent Daun from crossing the Katzbach and the Schwarzwasser. He

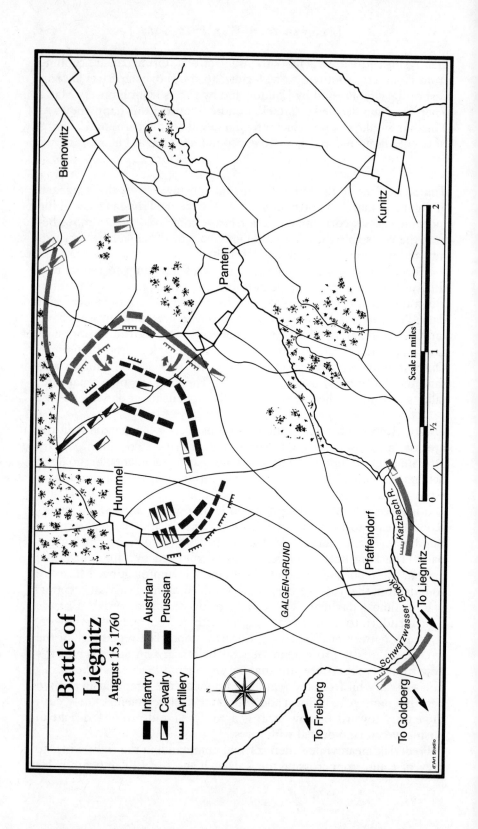

Battle of
Liegnitz
August 15, 1760

Infantry
Cavalry
Artillery

Austrian
Prussian

Bienowitz

Kunitz

Panten

Hummel

GALGEN-GRUND

Pfaffendorf

Katzbach R.

Schwarzwasser Brook

To Liegnitz

To Goldberg

To Freiberg

Scale in miles

0   ½   1   2

d'Art Studio

extends his left wing to the right toward the Katzbach. Dawn is just breaking when Loudon leads his grenadiers to an attack on the left. Schenkendorff's heavy guns greet them with canister shot. They are hurt but continue forward until stopped by musket fire. Schenkendorff is badly wounded and leaves the field. General Friedrich von Bülow moves his second line to Schenkendorff's left. Frederick orders four reserve battalions to form a new second line, which he backs by reserve cavalry. He deploys two more batteries to the front to greet the columns of Loudon's main force, now showing in early morning light.

Frederick greets the newcomers with sharp artillery fire followed by a general attack. General Wied moves out on the right to push Loudon's left back through Panten village and over the Katzbach. Enemy canister fire is taking a nasty toll. A ball smashes a man's head and covers Lieutenant Ernst Barsewich's hat with his brains. General Friedrich von Saldern offers gunners ten thalers to silence the offending battery. A gunner named Kretschmer fires a grenade that hits a powder wagon, destroying the battery and winning him an elegant reward of sixty French francs. Three battalions on Wied's left finally clean the enemy from the woods north of Panten and sweep up a number of cannon in the process. On the left Regiment Anhalt-Bernburg, the one disgraced at Dresden, moves out, officers without swords, men without hat tresses, but everyone with the humiliating memory of Dresden. Austrian guns are up now, the Austrian line holds steady, but the Bernburgers lower their muskets and, shouting *Ehre oder Tod* (Honor or death), charge with bayonets and musket butts. Regiment Ferdinand follows behind. The Austrian first line runs, the second follows. Cuirassiers gallop to charge the right. They destroy three entire regiments, seize eleven cannon and six flags.

Loudon orders retreat to Bienowitz. Frederick adjusts his lines and follows. Loudon begins to cross the Katzbach. His reserve artillery fires from west of Bienowitz, where cavalry attack the Prussian left wing. A battalion on the Prussian far left sheers from the line. Austrian cavalry see Regiment Ferdinand's exposed left, gallop to the attack, penetrate to Regiment Anhalt-Bernburg, which holds while cavalry charge to drive the intruders back to Bienowitz.

It is about five A.M. On the Prussian right Zieten's batteries fire on irregulars. Zieten and Wedell form baggage into a *Wagenburg* as they watch enemy columns approach from the south. The columns are Daun's army. Lacy's corps closes on the main army. Daun learns of Loudon's defeat and decides not to attack.

It was a victory the more dramatic because a few hours earlier the victors had faced almost certain destruction. Now the way was clear to the northeast, to Parchwitz, and to Prince Henry's army. Count

Chernyshev's Russians had gone back over the Oder on learning of Loudon's defeat, which Frederick magnified in a letter to Henry that was intentionally allowed to be intercepted by the Russians.

There was little need for exaggeration. Loudon had lost fourteen hundred dead, over twenty-two hundred wounded (including six generals), over forty-seven hundred prisoners, eighty cannons, and numerous flags and standards, not to mention a flood of deserters.* The Prussians lost over six hundred dead, twenty-five hundred wounded (including the king, whose right hip was bruised by a spent canister ball).

The king was elated. While musketeers and gunners fired victory salvos, tired men cleaned the battlefield, a task somewhat eased because Loudon had taken two thousand wounded with him.† Frederick moved from company to company, loud in praise of the soldiers who, he said, had fought "like his old infantry."

At evening parade in Parchwitz he formally thanked the army and announced a long list of promotions (Zieten was made general of cavalry) and money rewards for outstanding performance, including fifty ducats for each captured cannon. Finally he announced that Regiment Anhalt-Bernburg had removed its stain of dishonor: he was returning swords to its officers and would pay for new hat tresses for the men.

9 1

THE BATTLE OF LIEGNITZ was splendid enough, and Frederick touted it to one and all as a great victory. But as he candidly informed King George of England, "The task was not accomplished." Enemy armies were still in Silesia, Saxony, and Pomerania. The task was to clear them out before taking winter quarters. As starters he would force Russians and Austrians from Silesia in the hope of bringing Daun to a "decisive battle" in the process.

He did not look forward to the task. He was a very tired man, only too well aware of the great stroke of luck he had enjoyed at Liegnitz. "Never have we experienced such great dangers," he wrote to d'Argens

---

* Shortly after the action, Frederick wrote to Henry: "[Deserters] say that after the action he [Loudon] rolled on the ground, crying, 'My cannon, my cannon!' and cursing Daun a thousand times. I do not like heroes who roll in the sand." These and other criticisms stemmed from an innate dislike of Loudon, first because he had made his reputation as a commander of irregulars, second because he had tried to enter Prussian service originally but had been rejected by the king, who did not like the look of his eyes.

† Prussian and some enemy wounded were hauled in carts to Breslau. "Five hundred dragoons were required to dismount to give saddle transportation to the wounded," wrote one historian. (Garrison, *History of Military Medicine*.)

shortly after the battle; "never have we had more enormous fatigue." At the age of forty-eight, he was leading the life of a military monk. Like Pliny, he found consolation only in his letters: "I do not know whether I shall survive this war; but I am firmly resolved in case this happens to spend the rest of my days in seclusion, in the bosom of philosophy and friendship."

After briskly cleaning Cossack "vermin" from either side of the Oder, the king sent General Baron Karl von der Goltz with a task force of ten thousand men to shield Glogau from any new Russian threat. In late August he overrode Prince Henry's acrimonious arguments and combined the two armies to march on Schweidnitz with fifty thousand. Prince Henry went on the sicklist in Breslau with a convenient "fever," apparently at his own request and probably to avoid service close to the king.

Frederick hoped to maneuver Daun into battle or to force him from Silesia. His effort soon resembled what many historians have accepted as the eighteenth-century mode of warfare, a sort of military minuet, in this case alternating with quadrilles, waltzes, and at times a frantic czardas. Daun, of course, was not an easy partner. At Bunzelwitz, where the king was waiting for a bread delivery, he still had no idea of Daun's plans. He was ill with "a cramp so terrible that I thought I would suffocate," he wrote to Henry. He hoped his brother would soon recover and join him: "I have here a large machine to look after and I am alone. I tremble when I think of it." News from the north was bad. The Russians had converged by land and sea on fortress Colberg. If the fortress fell, Chernyshev would take up winter quarters in Pomerania and the New Mark. The king was suffering from "flying hemorrhoids" and fever. "I am like a body being dissected, each day losing one of its members," he told d'Argens. Daun was being cautious, occupying "unattackable posts" in the hills. The army continued to dance between Schweidnitz and Glatz. It won skirmishes but "nothing decisive." In late September the king, a disgruntled martial wallflower, was at Dittmansdorf, from where he wrote Henry, "This campaign appears to me more insupportable than the others; despite all my trouble and cares I cannot advance one step toward the big stakes, and I succeed only in bagatelles."

The enemy broke the impasse in early October. Pressed by the Vienna court to do *something,* Daun agreed to join the Russians in a foray against Berlin, a two-pronged effort in which Lacy would march north with fifteen thousand men and Chernyshev west with twenty thousand. Chernyshev's vanguard, three thousand men commanded by General Tottleben, closed on the capital in early October but retired on the approach of the Prince Eugene of Württemberg's corps, which was soon joined by General Hülsen. Counting only fourteen thousand, they were too weak to defend Berlin, so they retired on Spandau. The

Austrians and Russians ransacked private residences, including royal
palaces, settled for a ransom of 1.5 million thalers, and retired when
they learned that the Prussian king would soon arrive. They thoroughly
pillaged the surrounding country in the process.

Frederick was five marches from the capital when the crisis passed.
Daun meanwhile had marched to Eilenburg, southwest of Torgau in
Saxony. In an effort to bring him to battle, Frederick collected his army
and, with about forty-four thousand men, marched on Düben, which
the Prince of Zweibrücken's Imperial army hastily evacuated, moving
south. After the return of Lacy's corps, Daun's army counted about
fifty-two thousand. Daun placed the army in a defensive position just
west of Torgau. He had been ordered to give battle. Only too happy to
oblige, Frederick occupied Eilenburg and in early November marched
toward Torgau.

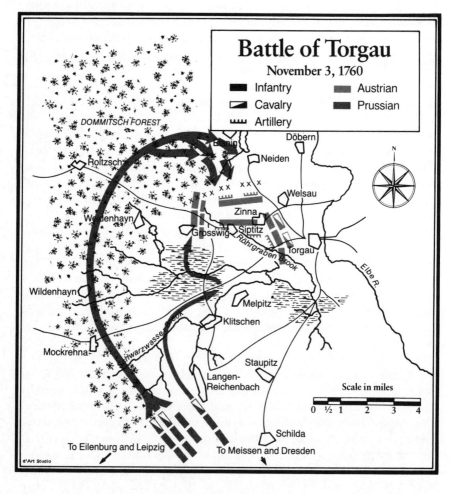

Sunday, November 2, 1760. Daun's main army is deployed about a mile west of Torgau, along the sprawling Siptitz Ridge. His long front faces almost due south, his left secure behind Röhrgraben Brook, which spills into a large pond. His right reaches west of Siptitz before folding back into pine-covered hills fronted by brooks, marshes, and pine woods, a flank that he further strengthens by reserve cavalry pushed forward in *en potence* formation. Batteries of heavy cannon cover the front.

The disadvantage of this otherwise formidable position is lack of room. Daun is crowding his men. His lines are not even three hundred yards apart. The terrain — woods and sandy soil — hinders easy movement of artillery and cavalry. There is almost no depth for maneuver.

The Prussian army advances to Schilda, southwest of Torgau. The king rides forward to study the situation. He quickly rejects an assault against either the main southern line or either flank. Instead, he will try to hold Daun in position by an attack against his center while his main force marches *around* the position to strike from the rear. Once the king attacks from the north, Zieten will attack from the south, a nutcracker play that cannot fail to roll up Daun's right flank and force him to surrender or be pushed into the Elbe — and thereby end the war.

Monday, November 3, 1760. Six-thirty A.M. The Prussians march early in four columns, Zieten with about eighteen thousand toward Daun's center, perhaps seven miles distant, Frederick with about twenty-six thousand to outflank the enemy and strike from the rear.

Things go wrong almost from the beginning. Frederick is counting on surprise, but he runs into a corps of hussars and irregulars that must be driven off with cannon fire. Daun is alerted to the Prussian march and begins to shift his main line of defense so that his second line faces north. Lacy, with twenty thousand troops, moves behind the Röhrgraben as rearguard to cover Torgau and the vital bridges.

Zieten early strikes trouble. His orders are to deploy close to Daun's main line and attack at cannon signal from the king. Zieten's advance guard runs into Lacy's outposts, which divert him to the right and bring him under heavy cannon fire. He is forced to shelter right of center while his cannon join the action.

Frederick's columns find the going very difficult. Cold rain and thick woods slow the infantry. Artillery carriages soon bog down on wet, sandy trails. The king desperately pushes ahead with only his infantry. About one in the afternoon he closes on Elsnig, almost directly north of Daun's position. But his cannon are still in the woods, Lieutenant General Hülsen's infantry are miles behind, and Prince Georg of Holstein's cavalry altogether lost. Daun's center and right are protected by marsh and brooks, which means he will have to attack farther west. The result is more delay.

The king shifts his battalions to the cover of Dommitsch Forest while aides scurry to try to locate Hülsen and Holstein. He hears cannon fire to the south and decides that Zieten must be attacking (Zieten is only exchanging cannon fire with Lacy). Fearing that Zieten will be defeated, the king decides to attack with what is on hand. Battalion 3-pounders fire from the forest edge while the king builds a first line of seven battalions, a second of General Friedrich von Ramin's brigade. As his units deploy, Daun's massed artillery opens fire along the line. Prussian cannon are blasted away. The infantry are marching toward some old log barricades about eight hundred yards away. Austrian gunners change to canister shot, which tear huge gaps in the line. A few grenadiers reach the barricades only to meet musket fire. They stumble back to the woods. Eight hundred bodies remain on the field.

It is about three P.M. Austrian infantry attack and are stopped only with difficulty by Ramin's second line. Hülsen's column finally turns up and deploys for attack. The new lines reach the barricades, silence the cursed enemy guns to their front, and are about to turn the Austrian flank when Daun's reserve falls on them. A spent ball strikes the king in the chest and knocks him out. He recovers consciousness and watches his second assault fail. Twenty-six battalions are shot to pieces; twenty heavy cannon are out of action. Some Prussian soldiers are still holding forward ground when Holstein's cavalry come up. Frederick orders him to attack from the far left. He scrapes together some infantry to launch a third assault.

It is about four-thirty P.M. Tired men struggle forward in the dusk. Austrian cavalry strike the Prussian right and roll up four battalions. General Bülow is taken prisoner, as are fifty officers and two thousand men. But Holstein's squadrons at full gallop strike surprised Austrians and send three regiments tumbling; battalion after battalion throw down arms in surrender. Daun's line turns into confused lumps of resistance. While subordinates try to sort out human knots, both commanders retire. Daun, who has been shot through the foot, claims victory in a dispatch sent to Vienna. Frederick hugs an aching chest and thinks dark thoughts.

The night holds another tactical surprise. Zieten has not attacked as ordered. He is still exchanging artillery fire with Lacy when he hears the battle peter off to the north. Fearing the worst, he begins shifting toward the main action. His far left debouches onto a critical point of Hülsen's fight. Lacy's fresh reserve is trying to save the day. Hülsen joins what infantry he can to the newcomers. He has lost several horses from under him and, unable to find another, somewhat incongruously is leading his men while standing on a gun carriage. Lacy attacks twice but is twice repulsed. Zieten's arrival is too much for the wavering

Austria[n] [fla]nk, [Rev...Aus]trians fight[i]ng in darkness chase the enemy
from t[he fie]ld, [...]t extend[i]ng to T[o]rgau and over three bridges to
the oth[er side...].

The [headquarters...the] [...] at Elsni[g]. Its rooms are full of wounded
officers. [Frederi]ck [move]s to [the] [nearb]y church. An aide lights a fire. Frederick
sits on [a bu]ndle [of straw under] [altar] candles to write a dispatch to
Fincken[stein]: ["We have beate]n Daun an[d] the Austrians; night has fallen.
Otherw[ise, I could] [report more de]ta[i]ls. We have made many prisoners."

The king arose early to walk among watch fires on a field crowded
with dead and dying, friend mixed with enemy, the soldiers cold, hungry, and thirsty. Peasants already were digging mass graves; surgeons
who had been working all night were trying to cope with new hordes
of wounded. At daybreak the king rode the lines, listening to reports
from commanders, congratulating men and units on extreme valor. He
openly embraced old Zieten, who had almost cost him the victory before finally bringing it off.

The extent of victory was clear enough. All enemy who could walk
had fled. As it turned out, Daun had suffered some nine thousand casualties. He lost over seven thousand prisoners and forty-five cannon,
or about a third of his army. Ten days after battle, Eichel reported
prisoners still coming in and suggested a total figure of eight to nine
thousand.

But the Prussian loss was so great that adjutants were forbidden to
reveal the figure: almost seventeen thousand men (including prisoners),
more than a third of the army.* The day after the battle, Frederick
apologized to the King of England for being unable to support Prince
Ferdinand's operations. But the Russians were still in the New Mark
and Pomerania; Loudon was still in Silesia. The battle "was the last
spark of a dying fire," Frederick informed Finckenstein. It was "an
event that preserves us from great misfortunes, rather than a triumph"
that would open the way to further conquests.

Although Prussian cavalry pursued the Austrians to take more pris-

---

* The figure is deceptive. As usual numerous stragglers soon returned to their regiments.
Surgeon Johann von Bilguer, who along with his distinguished colleague Johann Schmucker,
kept careful medical records, reported that of 6618 severely wounded at Torgau, he lost only
653; 5557 recovered, and 408 were discharged as invalids. Part of this and other exemplary
medical achievements probably resulted from Bilguer's and Schmucker's radical techniques.
They refused to stuff wounds with charpie, instead removing foreign objects as best they
could, then suturing the wounds and letting them drain. And they called for frequent changes
of dressing. They also rejected the prevalent French theory of immediate or primary amputation, resorting to it only when gangrene was obviously setting in. In 1761 Bilguer's dissertation on amputation won him European recognition. (Garrison, *History of Military
Medicine.*)

oners, the main army could not at once follow. Frederick wanted to recapture Dresden, but by the time he approached it the Austrians were entrenched in their former camp southwest in the Plauengrund area. "All my ability is not sufficient to dislodge them," he complained to d'Argens. He ordered all doors, windows, and ovens smashed in villages around Dresden to deprive the enemy of winter quarters. There was some hope that lack of food would force Daun to retire, he told d'Argens. If he did not, Frederick's position would be the same as the previous winter — "a sad outlook," in view of the immense labor and fatigue of the present campaign. Peace seemed more distant than ever: "In short I see everything as black as if I were in a tomb."

"It's a dog's life . . ." he wrote to an old friend. "All this marching and disorder which is not finished has aged me so much that you would have difficulty in recognizing me. The hair on the right side of my head is all gray. My teeth break and fall out; my face is as wrinkled as the folds of a skirt, my back bends like a violin bow, and my spirit is as sad and dejected as a monk of La Trappe."[1]

The king campaigned in the Dresden area for another month, pushing the Austrians from the country north and west of the capital. In mid-December he put the army in winter quarters in the Meissen-Freiberg area. Commanders were to begin recruit training to turn farmers into soldiers. Regimental commanders were to spread units to new villages in order to avoid close quarters and sickness. If the kingdom was to survive, the army had to be ready come spring.

9 2

THE KING spent the winter at Apel House in Leipzig, a comfortable if not pretentious establishment. He summoned from Berlin the Marquis d'Argens and his two nephews, Frederick William, the sixteen-year-old Prince of Prussia, and his younger brother, thirteen-year-old Prince Henry. Court musicians arrived, as did ministers, diplomats, and generals. The king's days soon conformed to earlier patterns: prodigious amounts of work leavened by reading, writing, composing, and the company of friends during long meals, walks, and concerts.

His companions were shocked to see how old the king looked, how gloomy and melancholy he had become. His manners were brusque, his words short. He received university professors in audience but gave them short shrift. Johann Christoph Gottsched, a scholar and writer, read aloud his translation of Racine's *Iphigénie,* and the king "could not understand a word of it."[1] Professor Christian Gellert fared slightly better. Forty-five years old, he was known for lectures on moral philosophy and for a book of verse fables. Quintus Icilius, now a lieutenant colonel, regarded Gellert as symbolic of a new German literature and arranged an audience with the king. Gellert kindly but firmly criticized Frederick for not encouraging German writers — and Frederick enjoyed the two-hour exchange. "That is quite another man than Gottsched," he told Icilius. Although he invited Gellert to return, the professor did not do so, nor did Frederick press the matter, but some years later he did introduce Gellert's book of fables into Prussian schools.

Despite such interludes, it was not a happy winter. The Prussian army was torn and tired, its ranks badly depleted. It lacked between ten and twelve thousand muskets and bayonets, which had to be bought secretly in Holland. It needed good generals; Prince Henry was sulking at Glogau. There was a shortage of other officers. Finances were at an all-time low; provinces were bled white of men and money. "The sufferings of the King of Prussia's subjects in Brandenbourg, Silesia, and other provinces, have been so great that I fear he will be able to draw very little from those provinces for the support of his army during the ensuing campaign," Mitchell reported. "What resources he may have to supply this defect, besides the revenues of Saxony, are unknown to me."[2]

One resource was England, but there the attitude toward war was changing. A few days after the battle of Torgau, Frederick learned of the unexpected death of King George II. That monarch, wedded to Hanover, had fully backed Pitt's direction of the war, including the alliance with Prussia. George III did not similarly respect his Hanoverian heritage. Young and inexperienced, the twenty-two-year-old king was firmly in the hands of John Stewart, the Earl of Bute, his tutor and friend, who was taken into the Cabinet, where he attacked Pitt's insistence on continuing the war. The war had been steadily growing more expensive and thus more unpopular in Great Britain. Frederick the Great, once "the Protestant hero" in British eyes, whose name and profile adorned many a country inn, was being calumniated by pamphlet and speech in late 1760. Pitt nevertheless forced through a new subsidy treaty and assured Frederick that if England came to terms with France, he would receive an additional subsidy sufficient to keep a corps of at least forty thousand auxiliaries in the field.

As in previous years the king augmented the British subsidy by further debasing domestic coinage and by ruthless requisitions of men, money, and matériel from territories still under his control. Prince Eugene of Württemberg, who was quartering in Mecklenburg, was ordered to raise three thousand recruits, six thousand *wispels* of flour (a *wispel* was twenty-four bushels), the remainder of the previous year's cash "contribution," a new contribution of a million thalers, and, in addition, two thousand oxen and six thousand sheep! Most of the recruits came from Saxony. By mid-January the army was short only five thousand men; in mid-March, sixteen hundred. But infantry and cavalry were in excellent condition, the king wrote to Henry, and eight new irregular battalions would soon be ready. Mitchell was horrified by "the very harsh manner in which the country of Saxony is treated."[3] When Leipzig merchants could not pay a tax double that of the previous year, the king imprisoned fifty of them until a suitable settlement was made. In return for the Saxon sacking of Charlottenburg palace, he ordered General Saldern to strip one of Brühl's estates. The general refused on grounds of honor. Quintus Icilius held no such scruples, and the treasury gained several hundred thousand thalers.

European courts widely criticized such draconian measures, but the king paid little attention. His back was to the wall. Prince Ferdinand of Brunswick had finally opened his winter offensive, designed to clean the French from Hanover and Hesse-Cassel. Ferdinand had a good plan and at first things went well. But then the campaign bogged down. Frederick, who offered only limited support, blamed this largely on command irresolution, but that was not altogether fair. A freak heat wave had turned frost-hardened roads into quagmires, hobbling an already inefficient supply system. In late March Ferdinand was back where he had started, on the defensive, his units restive, their morale low, discipline poor.

Peace negotiations meanwhile had become deadlocked over the vexatious subject of territorial concessions in Europe. Frederick has generally been portrayed as the villain, and it is true that he repeatedly refused to consider ceding any of his territories. But he was no more adamant than Maria Theresa, whose exaggerated claims infuriated him. France backed Maria Theresa, England backed Frederick — and there the matter remained for some months. The only hope, the king wrote to Baron von Knyphausen, now his envoy in London, was to persuade England to negotiate a peace treaty with France.

So it was that Frederick continued his ruthless policy. In his mind, any measure was defensible on grounds of survival. Despite Mitchell's pessimism and contrary to the belief of most of his enemies, he commanded an army of nearly 100,000 by early spring.

Maria Theresa and Count Kaunitz were convinced that the Prussian king was on his knees and could not possibly survive this sixth year of the war. They had spent the winter recruiting fresh troops and concerting new plans with the Russian court. If financial limitations occasioned by French penury forced the empress to release some twenty thousand troops from service that spring, she still had two strong armies at her disposal, one commanded by Marshal Daun in Saxony, the other by General Loudon in Silesia.

The primary task, the capture of Silesia — vital in case of peace talks — went to Loudon. As in previous campaigns, he was to be supported by the main Russian army, some sixty thousand troops commanded now by a new arrival on the scene, Marshal Count Alexander von Buturlin. A smaller Russian corps under Lieutenant General Count Rumianzov would invade Pomerania, capture Colberg, and turn on Berlin.

Frederick did not know where or when he would be attacked. "I am entering this campaign like a man thrown head first into the waves," he wrote to d'Argens from new headquarters in Meissen. Henry had at last eaten crow and asked to rejoin the war. He was given command of the army in Saxony. His main mission was to observe Marshal Daun; he could do little else, given his strength, thirty to thirty-five thousand, compared with Daun's sixty-five thousand. Should Daun march on Silesia, Henry was to leave a small force at Meissen and follow the king. Frederick would march to Görlitz, there to keep an eye on Loudon, Daun, and the Russians. General von der Goltz at Landeshut was covering the border with a corps about twelve thousand strong. Prince Eugene and General Paul von Werner would defend fortress Colberg. Frederick expected to know the Russian plan soon, because a spy, one Sabatky, was making General Tottleben an offer of substantial payment for this information and his promise not to ravage Pomerania as cruelly as in the past.*

Loudon made the first move; he marched in late April from Glatz with a corps of about thirty thousand, planning to capture fortress Schweidnitz. He was still considering how to outflank Goltz when Frederick reached Kunzendorf. Loudon retired to his old base near Braunau, where he was considerably reinforced by Daun while waiting for Marshal Buturlin's Russians to appear before Breslau. Frederick sent Goltz with a corps of ten thousand to screen Glogau and settled down to await events. The period was so calm, he reported to Henry, that in eight days only one hussar horse was wounded. Here he learned that Rexin, his man in Constantinople, had concluded a treaty of friendship with the Porte, but it promised no real help. Nevertheless Finckenstein was to ship presents to the value of 200,000 thalers for the sultan and other dignitaries. Rexin was to keep working for a Turkish invasion of Hungary, and Frederick also hoped the Tartars would

---

* In addition to cash, the king offered Tottleben asylum after the war. Tottleben agreed and through Sabatky steadily reported on Russian plans, strength, and movements until he was discovered in July 1761.

invade the Ukraine. France and England had at last exchanged envoys for peace negotiations. Frederick approved of the French envoy, Chevalier de Bussy, who was not "completely incorruptible." Knyphausen was to try to buy his friendship.

General von der Goltz learned in late June that the Russians were at last marching on Silesia in three widely separated columns that presumably were to rendezvous with Loudon at Breslau. Why not, Goltz suggested, attack these columns one by one? This was a tactic that Frederick had unsuccessfully urged on poor General von Wobersnow in 1759 and on Prince Henry the previous year. He at once agreed and reinforced Goltz with another ten thousand troops.

Goltz was about to march when a sudden fever killed him. His successor, Zieten, advanced as far as Fraustadt, where he attacked and defeated a Cossack corps, but meanwhile the enemy columns had joined at Posen and were marching on Militsch. This reduced Zieten to an observer's role as he slowly fell back on Breslau.

Frederick above all wanted to prevent the two enemies from joining forces. To hold what he called "a middle line," he left the mountains and began another military dance. This one, a bewildering series of maneuvers that must frequently have tested the patience of officers and men on both sides, lasted for several weeks. Contemporary descriptions of the campaign read like a military Baedeker of southern Silesia: armies and detachments scurried hither and yon, sometimes missing the mark, sometimes coming within a hair of collision, sometimes skirmishing with inconclusive results. As scores of dispatches confirm, Frederick was reacting for the most part to what he termed the "perpetual agitation" of the Austrians, who were trying to reach the Oder. Marshal Buturlin, whose army had enjoyed an orgy of rape and pillage east of the Oder, finally crossed the river to camp in and around Liegnitz. Loudon occupied Frederick's former camp on the heights of Kunzendorf. Unable to prevent his enemies from meeting, Frederick took up a defensive position between Bunzelwitz and Jauernick in order to shield fortress Schweidnitz.

Bunzelwitz soon became a *place d'armes*, a fortified camp defended in front, on the flanks, and in rear by entrenchments that used the ground so effectively that the camp later became a model for students of defensive warfare.

> All of the entrenchments were sixteen feet thick [the king later wrote], the ditches twelve feet deep and sixteen feet wide. The front was surrounded by strong palisades and the salients were mined. Pits were dug in front of the mines and to their front log barricades, sunk in the earth one next to the other, surrounded the entire exterior . . . 460 cannons defended the different works and 182 primed mines were ready to be blown on signal.[4]

With two thirds of the camp surrounded, the Prussians remained on constant alert. Tents were struck each night, defenses were manned, and the army slept under arms. The king slept each night "on straw in the great battery of Jauernick," Catt noted. Once the defenses were completed, Frederick felt reasonably optimistic, since he had retained the combined strength of infantry, cavalry, and artillery while denying it to the enemy. He expected and indeed hoped for an attack, he wrote to Henry, which he figured would cost Loudon thirty thousand casualties.

Loudon was determined to attack, but Buturlin was not so eager. He finally agreed to let Chernyshev's corps of twelve thousand make a feint against the Prussian right. The king later wrote that this decision was made at a drunken party. In the morning, Buturlin backed off entirely and, despite Loudon's exhortations, stood idly by for another ten days. Blaming Loudon for his food shortages, he then crossed the Oder to march on Berlin, although he did leave Chernyshev's corps with the Austrians. This was slight consolation to Loudon, who suffered a fit of colic for two days before retiring on Kunzendorf.

To check Buturlin's new plan, Frederick sent General Dubislav von Platen with a corps of about ten thousand across the Oder. Platen destroyed several Russian magazines and one large convoy that was carrying enough food to feed the Russian army for three weeks, and he captured some two thousand troops and five thousand wagons in the process. Buturlin now retired on Posen, where he was ordered by Czarina Elizabeth to join Rumianzov in the siege of Colberg.

Frederick would have preferred to remain at Bunzelwitz, but the Schweidnitz magazines contained enough flour for only another month, and his sicklist was daily soaring. Cossack swarms prevented meat and vegetable deliveries from the countryside, and forage parties, forced to work farther and farther from the guns, required large escorts. Skillfully dismantling the Bunzelwitz defenses, he reinforced the Schweidnitz garrison and marched southeast toward Neisse. Here he would have ample food and possibly would cause Loudon to abandon the Schweidnitz area to screen Glatz and Moravia.

The plan failed. Loudon's long and futile tactic had annoyed the Vienna court. Daun and Lacy, themselves inactive in Saxony, were freely criticizing Loudon's "partisan warfare" mentality. Wanting to recoup something from the campaign, Loudon turned to his old target of Schweidnitz. Using information smuggled out by an Austrian prisoner, he made a surprise night attack that caved in the defense and caused General von Zastrow to surrender his garrison of thirty-eight hundred.

Frederick learned the news in late September. Schweidnitz had been the key to his defensive strategy. "Never were headquarters more weighed with cares and alarms about the future," Catt wrote. "Everyone had a

long face of despair. . . . The king almost alone held firm, and kept a
good countenance." In early October Frederick marched in heavy snow
to Strehlau, another defensive position, to cover Breslau and Neisse.

Frederick planned to remain at Strehlau until Platen returned from
Pomerania to help drive Loudon from Silesia. Again the campaign became a matter of waiting, dreary hours made more unpleasant by cold
weather and limited rations, a serious attack of gout, a narrow escape
from being kidnapped by the Austrians, and bad news from Pomerania.*

Platen had reached Colberg, but instead of relieving the fortress, he
found himself besieged inside it. He and Prince Eugene finally broke
out but were in no condition to fight the Russians. Eugene's pitiful
corps trudged to winter quarters in Mecklenburg. Platen marched to
Saxony to reinforce Prince Henry. Colberg surrendered in mid-December. Loudon already had gone into winter quarters along the border
from Lusatia to Ratibor. Frederick followed by taking up quarters around
Breslau.

The king was now caught up in an unexpected twist in European
politics. After the breakdown of peace talks with England, France had
turned to King Charles III of Spain, the new and able king who was
eager for revenge on England. The result was a new "family compact,"
in essence a military alliance against England. This caused Pitt to argue
forcefully for war against Spain. Defeated by the peace faction, he resigned. Lord Bute was now in power and would, among other things,
control the matter of a renewed subsidy to Prussia.

This had not been entirely settled when Bute found himself at war
with Spain. Faced with a new challenge at sea and probably on land in
Portugal, Bute began to move away from his Prussian ally. In December he avoided asking Parliament to renew the subsidy treaty. Instead,
he assured Frederick that at the right moment he would ask for an
outright grant of money. Bute next pointed to Prussian military reverses and to his own new military obligations. He insisted that King
Frederick come to terms with Austria and "suit its terms to the means
that may be in his power of enforcing his demands by the sword"; in
other words, Frederick was to make concessions to Austria in return
for peace.

* Ever curious, particularly when it came to landowning noblemen, whom Frederick regarded
as "tenants," he befriended one Baron Warkotsch. A former Austrian officer and now a
sympathizer, Warkotsch advised the Austrians that the king's headquarters were lightly guarded
and that the king could be easily captured. A servant betrayed the plot just in time. Warkotsch and his accomplices were arrested but escaped. He was beheaded and quartered in
effigy. The king sequestered his estates and gave them to the Breslau and Glogau schools.
Loudon and the Vienna court denied knowledge of the attempt, but Loudon directed the
operation and Maria Theresa gave Warkotsch a large pension and also looked after his co-
horts. (Bernhardi, *Friedrich der Grosse*, Volume 2.)

Frederick was prepared to make no concessions, and Bute must have known this. Mitchell certainly knew it and refused to carry the message to Breslau, instead passing it to Finckenstein. When he read the dispatch, Frederick lost his temper and from that time on despised Bute.

England's defection left the king clutching at the frailest of straws: a hoped-for rising in Poland, an alliance with Denmark, a raid by the Tartars, an attack by the Turks. Despite enthusiastic dispatches about Tartar and Turk intervention, he probably did not put much stock in the possibility. His fortunes, at the start of 1762, had never been lower. In his later words, he stood "on the brink of ruin."[5]

93

"IF FORTUNE continues to pursue me as mercilessly, I shall doubtless succumb. It is only fortune that can extricate me from my present situation," Frederick wrote to d'Argens in mid-January 1762.

Fortune already had begun salvage operations. Czarina Elizabeth had collapsed a few days before Christmas. So ill as even to refuse "a saucer of cherry brandy," the fifty-three-year-old ruler had a final "spitting of blood" and died on Christmas Day — an event that the Prussian king had been anxiously anticipating for six years.[1]

"Morta la bestia, morto il veleno," he wrote to Knyphausen in London. "The death of the beast is the death of the poison." And to Finckenstein: "Behold the first gleam of light that rises; Heaven be praised for it! We must hope good weather will succeed these storms. God grant it."

It wasn't so much God as Czar Peter III who brought good weather, at least over Prussia. He wanted peace with Prussia as soon as possible, he told the British ambassador, and wished to end all engagements with the Vienna court. A few days later he ordered Marshal Buturlin to cross the Oder into Poland. He also sent a favorite, Baron Gudovich, to the king with a secret message. Gudovich found Frederick dressed in mourning in respect for the late czarina but overjoyed to see him: "I regard you as Noah regarded the dove that brought the olive branch to the ark."

Just what message Gudovich delivered is not known. Presumably it concerned Peter's desire to go to war against Denmark, and it probably entailed a partial commitment of support on Frederick's part. Frederick replied by letter and followed that by sending a twenty-six-year-old diplomat, Baron Bernhard von Goltz, to Saint Petersburg. Goltz, who was given the rank of colonel for the mission, was to secure peace with Russia and try to persuade Peter to abandon an attack on Denmark, at least for the present; if necessary he was to agree to the cession of East Prussia to Russia, providing that Frederick was compensated elsewhere.

Goltz was received by Peter with what a later historian called "enthusiastic effusiveness." Even before Gudovich had reached Breslau, the new czar not only yielded all conquests of territory in Prussia but advised his stunned allies to do the same. He provided Goltz with a magnificent equipage and mansion near the palace, visited him twice a day, and entertained him at dinner and supper. To Goltz's amazement, the czar reeled off names of Prussian regimental commanders from years back. In public he referred to Frederick as "the king, my master." The Saxon minister reported that "here at Saint Petersburg the King of Prussia *is* the emperor." Frederick responded by sending Peter the Order of the Black Eagle, returning all Russian prisoners of war to local commanders, and barraging the czar with sycophantic letters similar in tone to his initial correspondence with Voltaire. Peter replied in kind: "I recognize in Your Majesty one of the greatest heroes the world has ever seen." [2]

At this point of saccharine saturation, Peter received a lengthy and very secret report from his ambassador in London, the pro-Austrian Prince Alexander Galitsin. In a lengthy conference Lord Bute had informed him that young King George wanted peace in Europe as soon as possible. England hoped that Czar Peter would not withdraw his army from Prussia, since this would allow King Frederick to carry on the war. His Majesty and Bute wished to save "the King of Prussia from total ruin, but at the same time oblige him to make reasonable sacrifices." According to Galitsin, Bute asked him what territory Russia wanted and seemed satisfied with the reply — all of East Prussia.

Peter reacted as if Bute were personally insulting him by so treating his friend Frederick. He showed Baron Goltz the report, said he would be glad to receive peace proposals from King Frederick as soon as possible, and sent a copy of the report to Breslau!

Frederick had already been informed that England would not pay a subsidy for "the prolongation of war," but "if the subsidy should be employed toward the procurement of peace, his [Britannic] Majesty would be still ready to ask it immediately of his Parliament." [3] Here was a pressure play, pure and simple, to force Frederick to make peace on other than his own terms. Considering Prussia's contribution to six years of war that had very considerably helped England gain a vast empire, it was an unworthy act. Frederick greeted it with a prolonged silence that distressed the British court, which was already as suspicious as it was curious over his dealings with Czar Peter.

Now came Galitsin's secret report. Frederick understandably exploded in fury. "Bute deserves to be broken on the wheel," he wrote. But for Pitt's restraining influence, he probably would have recalled his envoy from London and broken relations with his ally. As it was, he complained to anyone who would listen of English infidelity, and he thenceforth refused to inform Mitchell of any negotiations with Peter.

These negotiations blossomed as a result of what a later European ruler would call "Perfidious Albion." "Make what treaties you like," Frederick grandly wrote to Peter, "and I will sign them. Your interests are mine." Goltz was instructed to "contract any obligation that the emperor may require of you. . . . He is my friend. He has only to draw up his treaties and I will sign them."

In the event, Frederick sent Peter a peace treaty that formally ended hostilities between the two countries and restored to Prussia all territory won by Russia during the past five years. Peter signed without demur in early May and soon proposed a formal defensive alliance. Its secret articles pledged Frederick to furnish an army to help Russia seize the duchy of Schleswig from Denmark, and also bound him to various diplomatic transactions, including a common policy in Poland. The proposal reached Frederick at the height of their love affair — they had recently "given" each other infantry regiments, and Frederick was dispensing expensive gifts to the czar's favorites — and the king hastened to sign. With that, Peter totally reversed Russian policy: in early June Count Zacharias Chernyshev's army marched to join Frederick in Silesia and fight the Austrians! Peter's reversal produced a side effect. Isolated and alone in the north, Sweden asked for a separate peace with Prussia, and the two powers signed a formal peace treaty before the end of June. Frederick meanwhile, by some delicate diplomatic footwork, had turned both Turks and Tartars *away* from Russia and *toward* Austria, and expected their armies to march by autumn.

By June, then, Frederick's position, both political and military, had radically changed. The ink was scarcely dry on his glistening new treaties when he took the field, his goal to recapture Schweidnitz and drive the Austrians from Silesia.

Loudon had taken winter quarters in the mountains southwest of his newly won prize, Schweidnitz. That spring Marshal Daun was transferred to Silesia. He commanded nearly eighty thousand troops. In mid-May he moved the main army to a closer defense of Schweidnitz and formed a semi-circle northeast of the bastion.

Frederick planned to attack Daun but needed Chernyshev's Russians. He now discovered something of the frustration experienced by Austrian commanders in earlier campaigns. The Russians refused to hurry. Only in late June did Chernyshev cross the Oder to camp at Lissa, on Frederick's right. With this addition, Frederick held a slight numerical superiority, but Daun frustrated his opening attack by falling back on Kunzendorf Heights. An end play designed to seize the Austrian magazine at Braunau also failed when Daun retired to his old position southwest of Schweidnitz. Unable to attack, Frederick decided to cut Daun's communications with Schweidnitz before besieging the fortress. As he was issuing orders for this move, the fortunes of war turned sharply against him.

Czar Peter III did not occupy a very secure throne. Some of his measures were well received. He continued Elizabeth's reforms by further reducing the hated salt tax and by abolishing the secret chancellery and its dreaded torture chamber. But at the same time he openly mocked institutions whose support he needed. In contrast to the devout Elizabeth, he insulted the Orthodox faith at court chapel "by lolling out his tongue at the celebrant [priest] during Mass, or by strutting about, talking and laughing loudly during divine service."[4] Even worse, he instituted a series of church reforms that even Peter the Great had shied from. He angered the army by replacing the Life Guards with one of his Holstein cavalry regiments and by appointing his Holstein uncle as commander-in-chief with orders to reorganize the army along Prussian lines, including close-order precision drill.

Peter's provocative and generally stupid behavior soon alienated important power groups that surrounded him. The grumbling might have come to nothing but for Empress Catherine, his estranged wife, who was heavy with another man's child. Catherine was a clever if calculating person who deeply resented her subordinate position. She had been thinking of a coup d'état since Elizabeth's death, and she had some powerful friends eager to put her on the throne. Peter's proposed war on Denmark played into their hands. Disgruntled in general, the army, and particularly the guards, objected to a new war against distant Denmark. This sore point was ably exploited by Catherine's lover, Gregory Orlov, and his kin. A definite conspiracy probably started as early as March 1762.

None of this was secret. Frederick himself warned Peter that "the cursed venality of a few individuals" might induce them to revolt. He advised Peter to be crowned before going off to war and also to intern known opponents. Peter refused to listen. As he continued to prepare army and country for war, the conspiracy grew to formidable proportions. In early July, when regiments were marching, Peter was summarily toppled by a group led by Catherine. A week later he was dead. By then Catherine's orders were speeding to Chernyshev in Silesia to leave the Prussian king and return to Russia.

The day before Peter was murdered by Alexei Orlov, General Chernyshev called on the King of Prussia. The move to cut Daun's communications with Schweidnitz was already under way, with troops marching on Burkersdorf, one of three well-defended posts that had to be captured. Chernyshev reported that Peter had been overthrown and that the new ruler, Czarina Catherine II, had ordered him to have his corps swear allegiance to her — and return to Poland. He added that Marshal Saltikov was to retain control of East Prussia. Catherine, however, intended to respect the recently concluded peace treaty as long as the king did nothing to cause her to break it (such as imprisoning Chernyshev's corps).

Frederick could do little but accept the fait accompli. "Judge of my confusion," he wrote to Finckenstein, "when I find myself right in the middle of our operations, which gave the greatest hopes." He did persuade Chernyshev to remain in his present position for three days, or until the attack was finished; the persuasion was enhanced by a jewel-studded sword and probably by a considerable sum of money. The attack came off as planned. The Prussians captured about a thousand prisoners and fourteen cannon, and suffered small losses. The Russians quietly observed the action and that same evening departed for Poland. Daun, plagued by a high desertion rate, began a withdrawal to Bohemia.

Chernyshev's absence was awkward but scarcely fatal to Prussian plans. More upsetting was the news that Marshal Saltikov in East Prussia was making Prussian subjects swear allegiance to the new Russian ruler. Although the new ambassador to Prussia, Prince Nicholas Repnin, arrived in Breslau to confirm the czarina's pacific intentions, Frederick was not so sure. If Catherine intended to re-enter the war in alliance with Austria, then almost nothing could save Prussia from total defeat.

Catherine's initial hostility had derived from fear that Frederick would seize Chernyshev's corps. When she discovered from her late husband's papers that Frederick had urged Peter to a conciliation, when she learned of Chernyshev's safe departure, and when she received a flattering letter of congratulations from the Prussian king, she sharply reversed her policy. She recalled the corps from Pomerania, disowned Saltikov's actions in East Prussia, and ordered him to evacuate the province at once. She also offered her good offices for the purpose of bringing about a general peace.

The siege of Schweidnitz meanwhile was proving much more difficult than either Frederick or his engineers had supposed. In mid-August he had written to Prince Henry that "the siege advances beautifully"; he hoped to take the place in less than two weeks. But inept methods, inexperienced sappers, enemy countermining, and unknown springs that flooded mining efforts slowed operations. General Count Francis Guasco showed no signs of surrender. In mid-September the king told Henry that he would soon march for Saxony. A week later he informed him that "our siege worries everyone." The weather suddenly turned cold, General Tauentzien quarreled with his chief engineer, Simon Lefebvre, whom he accused of being crazy, Lefebvre collapsed in a fit of melancholy when his *globes de compression* — his mines — failed to bring surrender, and Frederick himself took over. Guasco finally surrendered a garrison of about nine thousand in October. The siege, including Frederick's operations against Daun, cost the Prussians about three thousand casualties.

Once again Frederick possessed all of Silesia. In return for Daun's remaining in Bohemia and Glatz, he agreed to a winter truce.

He now detached General Wied with a strong corps to reinforce Prince Henry. With the border passes protected by a series of blockhouses and the rest of the army in winter quarters, he turned command over to the Duke of Bevern and departed for Saxony.

94

WHILE FREDERICK was prizing Daun out of Silesia, Prince Henry was fighting a war of maneuver in Saxony. Though considerably outnumbered by Field Marshal Prince Serbelloni, whose thirty-five thousand Austrians complemented the Imperial army, commanded now by Prince Christian von Stolberg, Henry, with the vigorous aid of General von Seydlitz, more than held his own during summer and autumn. The stand-off war infuriated Maria Theresa. When Seydlitz penetrated into Bohemia, she relieved Serbelloni in favor of General Hadik, one of Daun's favorites, who was ordered to win the southern mountains and seal Bohemia from the marauding enemy.

Hadik fought a more determined campaign. By the end of September he had forced Henry to fall back on Freiberg. Prevented by lack of tools and laborers from entrenching this camp, Henry withdrew to the Mulde while General Wied was marching to his support from Silesia. Daun, who had foreseen this reinforcement, sent a corps to parallel Wied's march.

With Wied on the way, Henry decided to attack the allied army at Freiberg before Hadik was reinforced. It was a bold decision, but he needed Freiberg for winter quarters, and he probably hoped for a victory before the king arrived. Marching at night in late October, he feinted with his extreme left, pushed hard in the center and right, a three-hour effort that drove the enemy across the Mulde. Enemy losses amounted to some eight thousand, including over four thousand prisoners. Henry listed his own casualties at between two and three thousand. He was particularly pleased with General von Seydlitz, who "rendered me the highest services." Friedrich von Kleist, the dashing hussar commander, also performed well, as did a good many officers "who have distinguished themselves and behaved with courage." The infantry "was admirable, not one battalion yielded ground." The enemy was retiring on Dresden and Dippoldiswalde; Henry was actively pursuing.

The welcome news "has made me twenty years younger," Frederick told Henry. The task now was to capture Dresden; doing that would bring peace this winter or next spring. Henry had already sent Kleist's hussars into Bohemia to burn the main Austrian magazine at Leitmeritz. When Kleist failed to break through, Henry recalled him and notified the king that in his opinion the campaign was over. Frederick reluctantly agreed that the enemy was too strong to attack at Dresden, but he persuaded Henry to send Kleist into Franconia in a terror raid designed to neutralize the estates and further isolate Austria. Kleist was also to raise 500,000 thalers in "old gold or good silver," commandeer two thousand artillery and supply horses, and bring back a few hundred recruits.

The brothers met a week later at Freiberg, "a most friendly interview," Andrew Mitchell reported, with the king emphasizing that "he came only to pay him a visit, and not to meddle in the affairs of the campaign which he had so nobly conducted." Henry and Seydlitz took the king on a tour of the battle area. Frederick confirmed all promotions made by Henry, repeatedly expressed his satisfaction, and "made him a present of certain fiefs . . . the value of which is said to be ten thousand crowns per annum."[1]

While the Prussians were campaigning in Silesia and Saxony, Prince Ferdinand was outmaneuvering the French in the west; he seized Cassel to conclude a glorious campaign. At sea the British navy had fallen on Havana, making Spain regret that it had entered the war. Throughout the autumn, Lord Bute had been actively pursuing peace negotiations, and now in early November England signed a preliminary peace with France and Spain.

The terms, insofar as they related to Prussia, were at best controversial and reflected British impatience with King Frederick's intransigence. Although the British insisted that the French evacuate Frederick's Rhenish provinces — Wesel, Cleves, and Geldern — they dodged the question of specific future ownership. Frederick deeply resented the omission of such a protective clause. If French troops evacuated these lands, Austria could occupy them with troops from the Netherlands. It was clear to him that Britain and France had made a secret deal to humble him further. "It is a hideous thing but I will speak of it no more," he wrote to Duchess Louise of Saxe-Gotha.

He had already made plans to occupy these provinces if necessary. If he proved unable to do so, he would occupy Münster and hold it hostage for return of his territories. He also sent a corps of six thousand irregulars to the border of Cleves to counterbalance the Austrian threat.

Victory at Freiberg brought a winter armistice with Austria in late November. Armies of both sides went into winter quarters, Henry remaining at Freiberg and the king establishing headquarters first in Meissen and then in Leipzig.

The king's routine was similar to that of previous winters. His nephews appeared, along with d'Argens and other old friends. But it was not a relaxing atmosphere. "I find myself still in the greatest difficulties regarding my affairs," he wrote to Prince Ferdinand in mid-December, adding that finances were one of his major problems. Peace was in the air, but one false step could destroy the efforts of seven sacrificial years. In late November the Saxon court had asked whether he wanted peace. Of course he did, he coldly replied, but on previously stated terms; that is, the return to the prewar status, with no indemnification to any party. His aggressive stand was emphasized by Kleist's predatory expedition and by ostentatious recruiting for the coming campaign.

Austria, too, was ready for peace. Daun's evacuation of Silesia and Henry's victory at Freiberg had tumbled court morale. Deserted by Russia, France, and increasingly by Empire princes, Maria Theresa was standing very nearly alone, her armies demoralized, her people tired, her treasury empty. It was true that Prussia similarly suffered. But the Prussian army continued to win battles and, judging from Frederick's militant posture, continued to *expect* to win battles.

Careful soundings made by the Vienna court in December indicated Frederick's willingness to negotiate a separate peace. After a good deal of formal diplomacy, in which the Habsburgs excelled, both rulers agreed to a peace conference. At year's end envoys from Austria, Prussia, and Saxony met at Hubertusburg castle, King August's hunting preserve southeast of Leipzig.

Maria Theresa hoped to wring two important concessions from Frederick. Her special envoy, Heinrich von Collenbach, early in the proceedings claimed Glatz for Austria and demanded compensation for Saxony. Frederick's representative, a young diplomat named Ewald von Hertzberg, duly passed these demands to the king at Leipzig.

Frederick was far less nervous than he had been. His political position was daily growing stronger. Austria was becoming isolated. An effective opposition that included Pitt had formed against Bute in England. In mid-January, Britain and France agreed to guarantee the neutrality of the Rhenish provinces and the Austrian Netherlands. "We shall have peace at the end of February or at the beginning of March," the king almost giddily informed Henry, who had returned to Berlin, "and at the beginning of April each [power] will find himself at home as in 1756."

Henry was not so optimistic. Finding the home provinces in stricken condition and Berlin rife with pessimistic rumors, and influenced by Andrew Mitchell, who held that Prussia would have to yield important territories to Austria, Henry replied in a discouraged vein. Frederick agreed that an unforeseen event could change matters. Nevertheless, he wrote, "I believe that our peace will be made before the end of February."

The king had already refused preliminary Austrian demands. He did not, however, want to push matters too far. Russia was in some ways still an unknown quantity; Catherine undoubtedly was looking askance at Prussian diplomacy in Turkey (having no idea that Frederick had almost abandoned his efforts there). His own weakness was obvious. Britain had reneged on its subsidy; he was quite alone and would have found it difficult to support another campaign. He now secretly pledged that if Maria Theresa abandoned her demands and agreed to return to the old status, he would support Archduke Joseph's claim as the next Holy Roman Emperor. Saxony, "a small accessory" to the treaty, would receive no compensation.

The Vienna court accepted the offer.

King Frederick informed Henry in early February that the peace was made. "I believe that we have made the best peace possible under the circumstances in which we find ourselves." Andrew Mitchell found it difficult to explain to his court why Vienna was willing "to submit to a treaty of the King of Prussia's dictating."[2] Frederick privately confided to Hertzberg that it is "a good peace, but we must not let them observe the fact."[3]

The last couriers returned from Poland, Vienna, and Leipzig in mid-February. On February 15, 1763, envoys signed the Treaty of Hubertusburg to end the war. British, French, and Spanish diplomats only five days earlier had signed the Peace of Paris.

Cannon were silent for the first time in seven years.

BOOK SEVEN

The Ruler and the Realm

1763–1786

*You will be surprised to learn that there is a war
in Europe in which I am not taking part.*

— *Frederick the Great to Voltaire*

95

THE KINGDOM had seen nothing like it since the Thirty Years' War, but no one alive had experienced that. Prussia in 1763 reminded its king of "a human body riddled with wounds, weakened by the loss of blood, and ready to succumb under the weight of its sufferings. . . . The nobility was impoverished, the peasants ruined, numerous villages burned, many cities destroyed. . . . A complete anarchy had upset all order in police and government; finances were in the greatest confusion; in a word, desolation was general."[1]

Of the 4.5 million subjects, about half a million had perished during the seven preceding years. The war had cost an estimated 140 million thalers. The areas that suffered had suffered badly. Silesia lost some six thousand houses and thirty-seven hundred farm buildings. Swedish and Russian armies had devastated Pomerania and the New Mark, leaving over three thousand houses burned and the estates of nobles inactive, ridden by debt. Brandenburg's damage, including destroyed factories, amounted to six million thalers. In many areas farms and estates lay fallow for want of labor, seed, and ploughhorses. East Prussia, which had been virtually a Russian province, managed to preserve most towns and cities, but the countryside had been scoured and trade losses were heavy. Trade elsewhere was almost at a standstill; inflation raged.

Repairing such extensive losses and curing such widespread evils would have taxed the most efficient government. But Frederick was in real trouble. Five senior ministers had died during the war. Lacking suitable replacements and wanting to scale down the power of the General Directory, Frederick filled only one vacancy, appointing General Karl von Wedell, who could no longer serve in the field, as minister of war. In many areas local administration had completely broken down:

> No more police in the cities [the king wrote]; a spirit of fairness and order had given way to base interest and an anarchic disorder; the departments of justice and finance had been reduced to inactivity by frequent enemy invasions; the absence of laws produced in the public a

taste for licentiousness and from that was born an avidity for illegal gain: the nobleman, merchant, farmer, laborer, manufacturer, all vied with each other in raising the price of their produce and merchandise, and seemed to work only for their mutual ruin.[2]

The man who was to put this right was fifty-one years old, an advanced age for the day — a particularly advanced age, considering his health. He had spent seven years building, maintaining, and commanding field armies in extremely challenging and active campaigns. He had ridden thousands of miles, on horseback and in spine-splitting carriages, over primitive roads and mountain trails — long, hard journeys often made in wet, cold, and often freezing weather. He had eaten ordinary rations and slept in ordinary billets or on the bare ground. For years his supper had consisted of a cup of chocolate. He had endured severe personal losses — mother, sister, brother, friends, generals, officers, and men — a prolonged obituary that darkened already shadowed emotions to leave him nearly alone in loneliness. He had conducted seven campaigns and had personally commanded thousands of men in ten major battles and scores of lesser actions. The blood of thousands covered his being; he had been wounded several times, had felt numerous horses sink beneath him. He had withstood pressure (if on occasion bending to defeat) unknown to most men.

The experience, unique in many ways, valuable in some, was scarcely salutary to an already precarious constitution. Evil humors frolicked through the thick, bent body. Demon gout time and again assaulted arms, knees, hands, fingers, legs, toes; on occasion he could neither walk nor write for the agony. Painful hemorrhoids continued to swell and rupture. Colic frequently bent him in cramp; fever bathed him in sweat and froze him in chill. Teeth had rotted, split, and fallen out — so many that he had difficulty playing his beloved flute. Depression often turned his thoughts to suicide. Less than a month before Minister Ewald von Hertzberg scrawled his signature on the Treaty of Hubertusburg, Frederick had written to Prince Henry, in what probably were honest words, "I am growing old, my dear brother; in a short time I shall be useless to the world and a burden to myself."

This was the man who now faced a task that had defied even his great-grandfather the Great Elector. Considering all the factors, the wonder is not only that he achieved a measure of success. In the sheer force of will with which he confronted the task, he resembled a dog walking on his hind legs, a performance that, as Dr. Johnson pointed out, "is not done well, but you are surprised to find it done at all."

Frederick may have been gray, bent, and beset by illness, he may have been old and tired, but he was determined to rebuild his shattered kingdom. "Princes should be like the lance of Achilles," he later wrote, "which does the harm and which cures it: if they harm many people, their duty is to rectify their wrongs." *[3]

The peace was not yet signed when he informed Henry, recuperating in Berlin, that he was going to Silesia to put things in order. Then he would do the same in his other territories while reforming the currency and paying state debts, after which "I can die when it will please me."

He returned to Berlin in late March. In part triumphal, the journey was also sad, through towns plundered and burned, where bells tolled for dead sons. The countryside was devastated; local officials presented frantic petitions for aid.

Berlin burghers were waiting to acknowledge the king with pomp and circumstance, but he avoided them by entering on back roads and going straight to the palace. Here he was welcomed by Henry and Ferdinand and a row of generals before going to the queen's apartments. He had not seen his wife for seven years. "Madame has grown plump," he greeted her, softening the words with a gift of five thousand thalers.

> The rejoicings and illuminations continued for three days after his arrival [an English correspondent reported], and on the 4th instant, he, at eight o'clock at night, went through most of the streets in an open chariot, accompanied by Prince Francis of Brunswick, to view the illuminations, and could not help admiring many of the devices invented to celebrate his virtues and his victories. On this occasion, as well as at his arrival, he was every where saluted with loud and general acclamation of, "Long live our king and father!" To which his majesty most affectionately vouchsafed to answer, "Long live my dear subjects, my beloved children!" [4]

Having paid family and civil respects, the king turned to business. His private secretary, August Eichel, was waiting at Potsdam with stacks of petitions for aid. Problems of one province were not necessarily those of another, so one or two ukases could not provide solutions, even had the administrative machinery existed to carry them out. But lack of similarity did not nullify the problems, nor would they vanish if left alone.

Despite heavy expenditures, Frederick ended the war with a treasury of eleven million thalers, admittedly in depreciated currency. He already had made emergency grants to Pomerania and the New Mark, which had suffered the worst damage. Now at Sans-Souci he continued to issue cash grants to be administered either by trusted provincial officials or by newly appointed officials, such as Franz von Brenckenhof, who directed the reconstruction in Pomerania and the New Mark.

In the early period of reconstruction the king spent only about two

---

* Frederick refers to Achilles' wounding of Telephus, King of Mysia. An oracle told Telephus that his wound could be cured only by "the wounder." Telephus went to the Greeks, who knew that they could not capture Troy without the help of Telephus. Achilles cured him with rust from his spear, and Telephus showed the Greeks the proper route.

million thalers in cash, primarily to furnish building materials and corn for food and seed. He also sent army wagons and teams to the provinces. Perhaps as many as sixty thousand artillery and commissariat horses began pulling heavy wooden ploughs that spring. He distributed twenty-five thousand *wispels* of corn and flour, seventeen thousand of oats. He demobilized some thirty thousand Prussian soldiers, peasants who returned to their cantons in time to help spring planting. Here and there he remitted taxes: a six-month remission of the contribution in Silesia, two years in Pomerania and the New Mark. In addition he lent or gave money to badly damaged towns and to individual nobles, some of whom were so impoverished that they wished to sell land to commoners, which was forbidden by law.

In late May the king spent a week in Pomerania — a favorite province because of its splendid soldiers — where he expected to find the worst. "I have traveled through the places most ruined by war," he wrote to Henry, "and I have done what I could to put things right; although certain regions have suffered a great deal, the evil is not so great as exaggeration has made it, and I flatter myself that in two years the province will be better populated and in better condition than before the war." He found people in the New Mark hard at work. One settlement of colonist farmers was flourishing, and he now planned to settle another six thousand families in the Landsberg-Cüstrin area.

He spent most of June inspecting Magdeburg, Westphalia, and the Rhenish provinces. Local administrations had suffered badly under enemy occupation, and their plight had been helped only partly by the king's hit-and-miss methods of appointment. Yet these lands were not as badly off as he had believed. In Cleves he gave the local authority 250,000 thalers toward rebuilding towns. He correctly divined that the crux of the cure rested in priming nature's pump for the all-important autumn harvest. Recovery depended in large part on getting seed in the ground, a common-sense approach that in the end paid off handsomely.

Reconstruction continued while the land came to life. In two years the king spent nearly two million thalers in Pomerania alone for rebuilding houses, supplying horses and grain, and settling new families on small farms located on crown lands. He spent even more in the New Mark, including 700,000 thalers to rebuild the burned city of Cüstrin. By 1766 he had financed the building of sixty-five hundred houses in Pomerania and the New Mark, eight thousand in Silesia. He lent large sums to Silesian nobility and founded a land mortgage bank that in time floated twenty million thalers' worth of notes. This was not sheer altruism. Silesian nobility promised not only to pay their debts but to cooperate in social reforms and to stop the nefarious practice of buying out small peasant holdings. He forced the Catholic clergy to establish industrial workshops if they wished to retain rich monasteries. Both clergy and nobility fought most of the king's reforms, but when he toured Silesia and Glatz in the spring of 1764 he found things "better than I expected."

By his own accounting, as of March 1764 Frederick had spent six million thalers for provincial relief; he later put the total cost of recovery measures at just over twenty million thalers. Of course he had other expenses, and it was a matter of careful budgeting. Recruiting from abroad to fill vacancies created by demobilization at home cost a great deal of money. So did redeeming debased metal currency. His profligacy startled some observers. Not only did he give large sums to the royal family and to his most successful generals, but he ordered work begun on a new palace at Potsdam, a six-year project conceived before the war and undertaken now to provide work and to demonstrate Prussia's healthy finances to potential enemies. Estimates vary, but the furnished palace certainly cost several million thalers.*

The king's critics have pointed to these expenditures with scorn. The ratio between sums spent on emergency relief and on extraneous items is striking, and certainly many subjects, particularly peasants, experienced a thin time for some years. Nonetheless the policy was not illogical if judged from the king's perspective. Frederick's overriding concern was not peasant prosperity but the survival of the kingdom. The problem as he saw it was not to supply as much aid as possible, but as little as was necessary to put people to work and gain a good harvest. He perhaps also reasoned that economic turbulence and administrative inefficiency would have wasted larger sums.

Critics stand on safer ground when questioning King Frederick's economic and fiscal policies, portions of which were specious and even dishonest. Depreciated currency, however necessary during war years, produced severe inflation and worked immense hardship on large sections of civil society. Minor officials were unable to pay their landlords and tradesmen; many were almost forced to accept bribes to meet their expenses. The king's vouchers, issued as a form of alleviation, were cashed by moneylenders at exorbitant fees.

At the end of the war, Frederick redeemed these vouchers and other notes with depreciated currency, quantities of which he had already used to pay for military supplies. He had also depreciated Saxon and Polish currency and allowed it to circulate in Prussia. "The numerary value [of the thaler]," Andrew Mitchell reported in spring of 1763, "is raised to upwards of 300 for the hundred, by which commerce has been thrown into the greatest confusion, and the poor and middling sort of people have been reduced to the greatest extremity, and rendered almost incapable of purchasing the bare necessities of life."[5] The

---

* The new palace is one of Potsdam's major tourist attractions today. Its dome holds three female figures — Pompadour, Maria Theresa, and Catherine — supporting the Prussian crown.

situation, Mitchell reported, could be cured only by immediate currency reform.

As all the world knows, currency reform can be a very tricky affair. Frederick's attempts may be both praised and faulted. The Mint Act of May 1763 called for a progressive two-step increase in the actual silver content of the thaler; depreciated coinage was to be "bought" out of circulation, but only at real value. This caused immense hardship to those who held large sums of "bad" money. It had another and more complicated result, however, not only in Prussia but in other countries: it further decreased an already short supply of money. That this occurred at an extremely dangerous time was beyond not only Frederick's understanding but that of most people, including the bankers.

Despite enemy action and debased currency, war had brought prosperity to a number of manufacturers, businessmen, and brokers in Berlin and elsewhere who had benefited from large army orders and from currency-exchange transactions. Splitgerber and Daum, a commercial, manufacturing, and financial firm that had long served the crown as "bankers," doubled its capital and expanded its turnover from 97,000 to 882,000 thalers in seven years. Another financial firm, Ephraim and Itzig, made high profits from the mint concession, and other merchants fared very well. Count Ernst von Lehndorff noted in his diary that foreign envoys returning to Berlin in 1763 could not find decent housing, because all the great mansions had been purchased by merchants and financiers.

Frederick's financial reforms severely hurt this merchant class. The first to suffer were those who had bought corn at inflated prices and failed to heed the king's warning to sell. When he opened magazines and granaries and simultaneously called in depreciated coins, the speculators took a fierce loss.

Far more serious, however, was the currency shortage. Even before the war, international trade and finance were growing. Amsterdam had become the commercial center of the world, and its bankers and merchants were primarily responsible for an embryonic trading system that utilized primitive credit transactions. This activity expanded during the long war, and in some instances commercial houses speculated in depreciated coinage and in land and goods, all of which involved their issuing large bills of exchange that were customarily renewed with high profits accruing from interest. But in the spring of 1763 this international banking system, if it could be called that, began to feel the strain of undercapitalization. In effect the commercial world ran out of money. Bills of exchange were considered of no value, and merchants refused to renew them, instead demanding payment in cash when the bills came due.[6] Following the bankruptcy of a leading Amsterdam money house, de Neufvilles, that summer, over thirty financial companies collapsed in Amsterdam and ninety-five in Hamburg; the panic quickly spread throughout Europe and inevitably engulfed Berlin. "Where are all these bankruptcies coming from?" Frederick asked his agent in Hamburg. "In all my life I've never heard of such."[7]

In August ten leading Berlin businessmen warned the king that some local businesses might fail if the panic spread to Prussia. They requested a recess period for the payment of bills of exchange.[8] Frederick ignored this alarming request. But then Johann Gotzkowsky, the most prominent entrepreneur in Berlin, sounded the alarm. Gotzkowsky had negotiated the Russian army out of Berlin and was one of the few merchants with whom Frederick had maintained close dealings for years. James Boswell called him "a gallant German, stupid, comely, cordial."[9] A banker, Gotzkowsky had made enormous profits during the war, importing, exporting, and manufacturing jewels, silk, and porcelain. His financial speculations finally brought him down.

In collaboration with the de Neufville brothers in Amsterdam, he had bought a large quantity of Russian army grain at high prices. Prices fell before he could sell. Lacking sufficient funds to pay creditors, he asked the king for a moratorium to give him a chance to raise money. Frederick was wary of bringing the crown into the marketplace; though realizing the need for expanded trade, he scorned its common practitioners. Now, he moved slowly. Grand Chancellor Philip von Jariges was asked to investigate relief possibilities. The king asked Ephraim and Itzig to lend the man 400,000 thalers, a request adroitly refused on the grounds that he needed far more than that to save himself. Other solvent firms also backed away; Gotzkowsky was too rich to have any friends.

Frederick could let the man go bust, lend the money himself, or declare a moratorium. Although angry with Gotzkowsky, whom he called "a madman who has foolishly handled his affairs," he could not let him go under, for fear of a general crash. Unwilling to advance the money himself, he issued a three-month moratorium and set up a special bankruptcy court. He bought Gotzkowsky's porcelain works and bought a mortgage on his silk works — in all, a matter of 500,000 thalers. In the event the special court arranged a settlement whereby the stricken man paid 50 percent of his debts.

This was scarcely a satisfactory answer but it did allow some merchants to escape disaster at a crucial period of reconstruction. "I have rescued those of our merchants who can be rescued," the king told Henry in September 1763, "and, thank God, all this is now past. The remaining horror is that all the business of exchanges is interrupted and that no money can be paid or received."

Andrew Mitchell divined Frederick's main problem in this sphere. The king complained, "Since I came into this world, I have seen nothing like it." He badly needed advice, a Prussian Colbert to reorganize the kingdom's finances. Lacking one, he stabbed in various directions and even took up with an Italian promoter who persuaded him to set up a royal lottery — "a manifest fraud," Andrew Mitchell termed it. It was one of several moneymaking schemes that failed to work. In late 1766 Mitchell reported that the king was

> in every respect in better health than he was two years ago [when Mitchell left Prussia], though at the same time I believe him very uneasy and unhappy in his own mind, from the many disappointments he has met with, arising chiefly from the adoption of the wild schemes of projectors and adventurers, for the augmentation of his revenues, most of which, upon trial, have been found to be either pernicious or impracticable; and besides the attempts to carry them into execution have already had the fatal effects of souring his temper, of alienating from him the affections of his subjects, and of hurting the credit and commerce of his countries.[10]

Frederick's naïveté in economics, both at home and abroad, was unfortunate but scarcely unique. His world was undergoing a financial metamorphosis that few recognized at the time. Adam Smith's pioneering work, *An Inquiry into the Nature and Causes of the Wealth of Nations,* was thirteen years distant and would scarcely have been applicable to backward Prussia, an agricultural, semifeudal country only beginning the transition to an industrial economy.

Frederick's real failure was in not bowing to his own lack of experience and in not recognizing that stopgap measures would not solve fundamental and deep problems. In his defense, it must be said that he lacked the experts to study these problems (although he did little to encourage their development), and his system did work, to a degree. It was the old business of *ein Plus machen* — show a profit. The kingdom not only survived under the system, it eventually prospered. At the close of his reign, the total annual revenue amounted to twenty-two million thalers and the treasury held a fifty-one-million-thaler surplus. This was five times more than he had inherited — and was more than sufficient to support the army of 200,000 men that he deemed necessary for survival.

96

ONCE THE KINGDOM was sewn with seed, once villages and towns began rebuilding, once crops were harvested, the king continued the agrarian policy begun before the Seven Years' War.

Besides encouraging farmers to increase production, he introduced new breeds of animals and such new crops as tobacco and sugar beets.

He continued to encourage cultivation of potatoes, hops for beer, and mulberry trees for silk. Farmers were encouraged and often subsidized to set up more beehives, to plant more fruit trees, and to raise more chickens to swell egg production. Forests ravaged during the war were replanted with oak, fir, spruce, and other seedlings.

Land reclamation and subsequent settlements by colonists remained tasks of foremost importance. The first principle of government, Frederick wrote in *The Political Testament* of 1768 — a new work similar in part to that written in 1752 — is "that the true strength of a state consists in its number of subjects." Earlier drainage projects along the Netze and Warthe Rivers were revived under Minister Brenckenhof's active supervision, an eight-year program that nudged the million-thaler mark in costs but yielded new lands that in time supported fifteen thousand colonists. Drainage of other areas would continue throughout his reign and bring in thousands of colonists, who were subsidized until their farms and communities became self-supporting.

It was never an easy effort.

> This nation is idle and sluggish [the king wrote in 1768]. These are two defects against which the government must unceasingly struggle. These people move only by your impulse, and will stop the moment you fail to push them. No one knows anything other than the ways of his forefathers. There is little reading, little desire to learn what we teach so that everything new frightens them. And I who have never done anything but good [for them] — they think that I am going to threaten their existence by making some useful reform or necessary change.

The key was peasant ignorance. Village schools had steadily deteriorated. Many schoolmasters could barely read or write. A reform act of 1763 required parsons to visit diocese schools twice a year and fire incompetent teachers, but there was little money to raise salaries and in turn attract capable teachers. In 1771 the king noted that most of the bad schoolmasters in the Mark were tailors and must be got rid of as soon as possible. Eight years later he was employing invalid soldiers as schoolteachers, perhaps as much to save paying their pensions as to improve educational standards. In a work on German literature, published in 1780, he stressed the need for better schools, but he seems to have done little more by the close of his reign. His excuse was always the shortage of funds necessary to obtain qualified teachers.

The nobility also often fought changes that were intended for their own good. If estates were to be preserved, the king wrote, the law of primogeniture, familiar to England, must be introduced. Yet he could not persuade fathers to leave estates to their eldest sons instead of dividing them between sons, although he hoped in time to bring this about. He hoped, too, that the nobility would in time follow his orders to ease the rigors of serfdom, which most of them refused to do. Nor could he persuade many estate owners to yield fallow lands for colonial settlements.

Despite these and other setbacks, the land recovered remarkably well, in part because of a series of good harvests. By 1768 most provinces were again paying land taxes, crown lands and forests were showing a profit, and the king was clearly optimistic about the future.

Trade and finance did not share the recovery of the countryside. Frederick's deflationary policy and currency revaluation discouraged an already feckless economy. Companies that had survived only because of a moratorium, a settlement by a special bankruptcy court, or special loans found themselves in a worse position than ever.

Strongly objecting to "financial enslavement" by the commercial centers of Hamburg and Amsterdam, and wanting "to prevent the Jews from crushing people by usurious loans," the king opened the Royal Bank of Berlin in early 1765 and followed with a branch bank at Breslau. This was a crown bank capitalized by the sale of shares, his own investment being 800,000 thalers, on which he expected to make 5 percent interest. As opponents had predicted, the general public feared that the bank would take its valuable silver in return for mere paper, so it did not exactly beat down the bank's doors. Merchants were afraid that the bank would redeem its own notes with depreciated currency, as the crown had recently done. Most of them, accordingly, invested capital abroad, exacerbating an already delicate financial situation. The bank also suffered from poor management. In time it would prosper, but its immediate effect on trade was minimal.

The king also ordered the General Directory to make an economic survey of the entire kingdom to determine the real cause of the depression. This was done by one Erhard Ursinus, a *Finanzrat,* or revenue official, whose report in the spring of 1767 gently but firmly refuted the king's economic policy, including his favorite project, the silk industry. The General Directory was sharply reprimanded for submitting such an "impertinent report." Poor Ursinus was accused of "malice and corruption" and sentenced to a year of hard labor at fortress Spandau.

Trade continued to deteriorate. In the spring of 1767 the Saxon minister reported "the wretched state of commerce in this country, where all the factories fail and where each day brings a new bankruptcy."

The king rather grandly ignored these unpleasant facts in *The Political Testament* of 1768. Instead, he confined himself to general observations, some accurate, some naïve, some wrong. He realistically pointed out that Holland, England, France, and Spain had captured overseas commerce and there was little that Prussia could do about it. Prussia should not acquire overseas possessions, "because they drain the state of people, they must be supported by a large fleet, and they constantly provide new reasons for war, as if we did not have enough already with our neighbors."

Prussia was a land power, the king continued, and not a wealthy one. She exported wood, salt, corn, wheat, horses, and textiles. She imported animals, wine, leather, cotton, wool, drugs, iron, copper, and steel. She was running a deficit trade balance, which could be corrected only by the greater manufacture of various goods. To encourage this, he subsidized various manufacturers and granted them monopoly rights to get them going. He tried to arrange a trade treaty with France to open markets in Spain and Portugal for textiles, and he tried to revive the old East Asia Trading Company. Neither effort came to anything. Despite criticism, he still subsidized the silk industry and ran one new industry himself, Johann Gotzkowsky's porcelain works. He did not mention that this enterprise, which employed over five hundred people, remained in a slump for five years before becoming prosperous.*

Prussian trade probably would have remained in deep trouble had there not been a general European recovery, a new climate exploited by merchants, financiers, and officials. In 1768 industrial production expanded in Berlin for the first time since the war, and in the following year the special bankruptcy court was closed.

The king's final concern, finances, also ran a troubled course during reconstruction. Although conditions were slowly improving in the countryside, the provinces had not recovered sufficiently to pay taxes on a prewar basis, nor did income from customs and excise duties yet achieve prewar levels. Exact figures are lacking during the early years of peace, but the royal income of 13.8 million thalers in 1768, considerably below prewar figures, suggests that the coffers were anything but full at a time when the king was spending vast sums on civil and military projects.

Frederick increased his income by establishing court monopolies on the salt, tobacco, and coffee trade. In early 1765 he invited a French writer, a friend of d'Alembert named Claude Helvétius, to survey Prussia's tax system. Helvétius had made a fortune as a member of a tax-collecting syndicate in France. To no one's surprise, the foreigner concluded that the royal treasury was losing millions of thalers through insufficient taxes, inefficient collection of taxes, corrupt officials, and smuggling. Helvétius suggested that the king farm out the tax collection system on a percentage basis to a group of Parisian capitalists. Frederick turned the idea down and established instead a new depart-

---

* He acquired the factory in 1764 and soon sent General Fouqué a breakfast set "as beautiful as any ever made at Meissen." Fouqué judiciously agreed: "The vivid colors of the tea service . . . are better than any that I have seen in Saxony. As for the mosaic cup, I fancy to see Watteau's stroke, it is so charming." Frederick continued to send sets of porcelain as state gifts and frequently sent separate pieces to friends.

ment independent of the General Directory, the General Administration of Royal Customs, or Régie. It was headed by a Frenchman, La Haye de Launay, hailed by Frederick as "Jupiter who would put an end to chaos." De Launay and four principal subordinates (later reduced to two) *each* received the unheard-of salary of fifteen thousand thalers a year — nearly four times that of a Prussian minister — and 5 percent of any net gain in excise taxes collected.

The new system came into being in mid-1766, together with higher duties on wine, beer, spirits, meat, and bread. De Launay staffed it with some two hundred Frenchmen, creating a bureaucratic framework that in time would support another eighteen hundred minor Prussian officials. Offices complete with "border brigades" sprang up in all provinces. In a situation that demanded extreme tact and patience — smuggling, after all, was a traditional way of life in Prussia — the new tax collectors struck like so many hawks. Not only did they ignore traditional provincial authorities, they made inspections and even surprise raids on private households whose owners were suspected of keeping contraband merchandise. And they zealously carried out these duties in French.

The result was predictable. Jupiter brought chaos, not order. The people — not just merchants, farmers, and peasants, but nobles and clergy as well — hated the Régie and anyone associated with it. Protests rained in from around the kingdom. When they failed to bring reform, fights broke out in Berlin and throughout the provinces; there were even murders. In Berlin a mob attacked Régie officials, and Frederick "threatened to call out the troops if this occurred again." [1]

The king had hoped that the new system would place most of the tax burden on wealthy landowners and merchants, at the same time lowering the overall tax burden by reducing smuggling. He tried to curb Régie excesses but with little success. Andrew Mitchell noted in several dispatches that Frederick was rapidly alienating "the affections of his subjects." [2] Whatever the king's intentions, much of the money collected came from the peasants, soldiers, artisans, farmers, and shopkeepers, not from the nobility or merchant class.

Despite adverse public opinion, the king was satisfied with the Régie, not so much because of the increase in revenues as because of the decrease in smuggling. He continued to rely on de Launay until the end of his reign, although he eventually complained of corruption and forbade the hiring of Frenchmen.

97

IT WAS NOT all work.

In the spring of 1763, Lord Marshal Keith returned from Neuchâtel, where, acting on Frederick's instructions, he had given the intellectual rebel Jean Jacques Rousseau sanctuary and support. He found the king tired but calm. At an intimate four-hour dinner, conversation centered on the recent war. "Not a single word escaped him in his own praise or to glorify himself," Keith wrote to Rousseau, "not a single complaint, no resentment, no bitterness against one of his enemies; you might have thought that a sensible and judicious man was arguing over some war of a thousand years ago." The king gave his seventy-seven-year-old friend apartments in the Potsdam palace, and they dined and supped frequently together. "His kindnesses are so easy," Keith wrote to a friend, "and not embarrassing, which makes them so much the more captivating." Keith went back to Scotland in August but was soon invited to return. "You will live in the bosom of friendship, liberty, and philosophy," the king promised. Keith agreed, and Frederick built a house for him next to Sans-Souci.[1]

Andrew Mitchell remained in Berlin until he was recalled to London in 1764, but what Frederick regarded as England's perfidious behavior had clouded relations between the two men and continued to do so after Mitchell's return, two years later, as Sir Andrew.* General Baron Rupert Scipio von Lentulus was on hand but was a married man and was frequently away on various missions. Karl Guichard (Quintus Icilius) remained a favorite, a disgruntled butt of royal wit but valued for his extensive knowledge of literature. Prince Henry of Anhalt, Old Dessauer's grandson, was a new favorite. Frederick regarded him as another Turenne, the most able commander in the army, next to Prince Henry, and appointed him general adjutant. Catt stayed on as reader, aided by the gossipy Baron Bielfeld. Baron Pöllnitz remained as court jester, and the Marquis d'Argens was present, in poor health as usual, while submitting to the king's sometimes cruel jokes.

Occasionally a new star flickered in the somewhat lusterless heaven of Sans-Souci. While inspecting Rhenish provinces that spring, the king collared Voltaire's close friend, the forty-six-year-old Jean le Rond d'Alembert, "a man of much learning and knowledge," in the king's words, who returned with him for a three-month stay and was asked to be president of the Academy of Sciences. Philosopher, mathemati-

* Mitchell died in 1771 and was buried in Berlin. The court attended his funeral, and the king was said to have watched the procession from his balcony with tears in his eyes. "His talents and character had wholly gained my esteem," Frederick wrote, "and he retained it to the end of his days." (Mitchell, *Memoirs.*)

Frederick's brother Prince Henry *(left)* and George Baron Keith,
Earl Marischal of Scotland. Both were the king's close confidants
in his last years.

Every evening large numbers of people walked along Berlin's
Unter den Linden, buying ices and lemonade from vendors and
listening to regimental bands. Prince Henry's palace is in the
right foreground.

cian, and collaborator with Denis Diderot on the famous *Encyclopédie*, d'Alembert was amazed by the king's knowledge of French literature; his knowledge of French poets "was as great as mine," he wrote to a friend. The court, however, displeased him: "The king is almost the only person in the kingdom with whom it is possible to converse, at least with that kind of conversation met with hardly anywhere but in France, which becomes a necessity when once it has been experienced." Apart from the king, "society is very insipid and quite worthless." Ministers, councilors, generals — "all these gentlemen say not a word and are content to laugh at some stories that we tell."[2] D'Alembert soon tired of this atmosphere and departed for Italy. "I should like to make the excursion," Frederick wrote to Keith, "if the goat was not obliged to graze where it is tethered."

He avoided Berlin society and loathed official entertaining, with its dreary protocol. When he had to receive a Turkish envoy, he found amusement only in old Baron Pöllnitz's excitement over what elegant clothes he could wear for each ceremonial occasion. Berlin's enthusiastic reception of the envoy and his extensive entourage sickened him, he told Henry: "Berlin society is presently eating dates; the fops will continue to wear turbans and those who are rich enough will establish harems. . . . I am the one who pays the piper for all this; it costs me 7000 thalers a month. The Turks are more Arabs than the Jews." The ambassador's visit to Potsdam evoked a similar reaction; the king would not have been surprised if "some of my foolish compatriots had themselves circumcised." He was not sorry to see the Turks leave, but he hoped the visit would result in an alliance.

Frederick passed a quiet and restful winter despite attacks of colic and gout. "I am at work here in writing my political and martial follies," he informed Keith in February. He was referring to a two-volume history of the Seven Years' War that would remain secret until after his death.

As he wrote in a foreword to this work, his goal was twofold: first, to prove that he could not have avoided the war and that honor and the welfare of the state prevented peace except on the stated terms; second, to detail the military operations as clearly and accurately as possible. What he called a truthful and impartial account of events contained his usual ration of errors and prejudices, but, as with his earlier histories, the work is interesting, instructive, and amusing. "These memoirs," he wrote to Keith, "convince me more than ever that to write history is to compile the follies of men and the strokes of fortune. Everything turns on these two articles, and it has always been like that. We are a poor species while we vegetate on this little atom of mud which we call the world. I am forced to revolve like a millwheel, for one is carried forward by one's destiny."

His pessimism carried over into his work: "Time, which heals and obliterates all evils, will without doubt soon restore to the Prussian states their abundance, prosperity, and former splendor; the other powers will likewise recover; other ambitious rulers will then start new wars and cause new disasters, for it is characteristic of humans that no one learns by experience: the follies of the fathers are lost on their children; each generation has to commit its own."

James Boswell visited Keith at this time and saw the king at a military parade: *

> It was a glorious sight. He was dressed in a suit of plain blue, with a star and a plain hat with a white feather. He had in his hand a cane. The sun shone bright. He stood before his palace, with an air of iron confidence that could not be opposed. As a lodestone moves needles, or a storm bows the lofty oaks, did Frederick the Great make the Prussian officers submissive bend as he walked majestic in the midst of them. I was in noble spirits. . . . I beheld the King who has astonished Europe by his warlike deeds.[3]

In 1764 Voltaire awakened a sleeping correspondence when he expressed concern over the king's health. Frederick replied somewhat cautiously, but mutual need caused them to suffer, if not overlook, the unfortunate past. Their letters once again became literary, cultural, philosophical, and even political exchanges spiced with verse, burdened by health bulletins, saddened by death notices, and lightened by often amusing and very irreverent persiflage. In general the philosopher of Sans-Souci approved of the patriarch of Ferney, sworn enemy of infamy. "You shall reach the age of Fontenelle [ninety-nine] . . . and write an epigram on your own centenary," Frederick wrote. "Finally, I see you, full of years, surfeited with glory, victor over injustice, on Olympus, supported by the genius of Lucretius, Sophocles, Virgil, and Locke, placed on a bright cloud between Newton and Epicurus."

Voltaire's subsequent and explosive defense of several victims of religious persecution in France won the king's praise in a series of lengthy, thoughtful, and generally despondent letters on the state of mankind. In 1767 he was again sending verses and essays for correction, and more than once each correspondent spoke nostalgically of happier days.

> How all has changed since the times you recall [Frederick wrote]. My feeble digestion forces me to give up suppers. I read or converse in the evening. My hair is white, my teeth are falling out, my legs are ruined by gout. I live on, daily aware of the difference between forty and fifty-six years of age. Further, since the peace I have been overloaded with prob-

---

* Keith did not altogether approve of the twenty-four-year-old Boswell, who was "full of hypochondriacal and visionary ideas," and neither he nor Andrew Mitchell asked the king to receive him. Boswell's own request for an audience was politely refused by von Catt.

lems so that I have only a little intelligence left along with a renewed passion for sciences and the fine arts. These are my consolation and joy.

Voltaire did not reply to this letter, and the correspondence languished for two years. Voltaire revived it in late 1769, probably as the result of a visit from Baron Melchior von Grimm, whose earlier satire, *Petit prophète,* and philosophical brilliance had impressed Frederick. In 1770 a group of admirers commissioned a bust of the seventy-six-year-old Voltaire by Jean Pigalle. "The finest monument has been erected by himself in his own works, which will last longer than Saint Peter's, the Louvre, and all the buildings consecrated by human vanity to eternity," Frederick wrote to Grimm as he sent a generous donation to the project. Voltaire was visibly touched, and their correspondence continued until his death, in 1778. Here are a few quotations from their final 167 extant letters:

Voltaire, October 1769: "True worship, true piety, true wisdom, consists in the worship of God as the common father of all man without distinction and in being charitable [to others]."

Frederick, January 1770: "You write for fame; I write for my amusement. . . . It will be said of me: it is a great deal that this king has not been a complete imbecile."

Voltaire, June 1770: "I have *The Essay on Prejudices* in my small library. . . . You have been far too generous in your comment, but bless you for having turned pebbles into diamonds."

Frederick, September 1770: "Youth is the time for good living; when one grows old and decrepit, one must renounce both wit and mistresses."

Voltaire, April 1771: "I do not fear death, which is rapidly approaching me . . . but I have an invincible aversion to the way of death in our Roman Catholic faith. It seems to me extremely ridiculous to be oiled for the journey to the other world as the wheels of a coach are greased for traveling."

Frederick, November 1772: "In glancing at history, I see that scarcely ten years pass without some wars breaking out. This intermittent fever can be suspended but never cured. One must seek the reason in the natural restlessness of mankind. If one person does not stir up trouble, another does; and a spark often brings on a general conflagration."

Voltaire, December 1772: "A hero, a statesman, a poet of charm, a man of universal genius, is not happy when he has the gout, no matter what the Stoics say."

Voltaire concluded his final letter, in April 1778: "You are the conqueror of superstition, just as you are the upholder of German liberty. Live much longer than I in order to consolidate all the empires that you have established. May Frederick the Great be Frederick the Immortal!"

King Frederick's family relationships in these later years were no more prosperous than in the past. He was correct enough, but it was more rote than root. He had entertained his ailing sister Louise of Schwedt and her daughters soon after his return to Potsdam in 1763. He listened to his nieces sing and gave them a ball, which didn't come off too well because of the lack of available women. He corresponded frequently and at length with Prince Henry at Rheinsberg, often unburdening economic, political, and military worries. He entertained his nephews, Prince Frederick William (the Prince of Prussia) and Prince Henry, whom he described as beautifully educated and whose company he greatly enjoyed. He equally welcomed the young and very bright Hereditary Prince Eugene of Brunswick, who had performed so well in the war, and he was very fond of his Brunswick nephews, Frederick and William.

He selected an extremely attractive bride for the Prince of Prussia. Boswell found Elizabeth so beautiful that "I talked of carrying her off . . . and so occasioning a second Trojan war." Frederick attended the celebrations of the betrothal in July 1764 and the wedding a year later. He wrote his sister Emily occasionally, but she was very ill with a mental disorder and they met only rarely. He invited his sister Charlotte of Brunswick to help with the Princess of Prussia's first delivery. A daughter was born, and at Frederick's request Czarina Catherine agreed to be godmother. He attended the wedding of his niece Wilhelmina, August William's daughter, to Prince William of Orange and thereafter they corresponded frequently and warmly. "I regard you as my own daughter and love and cherish you as such," he wrote soon after her marriage. He closely followed her many pregnancies, persuaded her to return for a visit in 1773, and generously provided for her in his will. The new palace at Potsdam opened in July 1768, and numerous relatives watched the king direct Johann Hasse's oratorio *The Conversion of Saint Augustine*. A few years later he built a temple of friendship in the palace gardens to the memory of his sister Wilhelmina. He always invited his brothers Henry and Ferdinand to Potsdam when they were in the area for reviews; he often sent Henry and his sisters fruit; he gave other relatives costly presents; he invited Ulrica to visit from Sweden and arranged for a general family reunion that came off very successfully. He made Henry's birthday "the greatest family holiday of the year," a historian noted, "the one occasion on which he would himself wear his full royal regalia and let gold plate be used for the family dinner." [4] The two brothers continued to carry on a lengthy correspondence that was informative, amusing, and on occasion ribald.

In 1769 the king wrote his will, generously providing for all his close relatives. "I leave to the queen my wife her present revenues with an increase of 10,000 thalers per year, two casks of wine per year, free wood, and game for her table [on condition that] she makes my nephew her heir." In accordance with tradition, he left everything to the Prince of Prussia on condition that he pay various legacies. These differed considerably. "To my brother Henry 200,000 thalers, 50 *antals* [2750 bottles] of Hungarian wine, and a beautiful chandelier of rock crystal . . . , the green diamond ring I wear, two riding horses with their tack, and a team of six Prussian horses."[5]

Quarrels and losses also filled the years. Count Francesco Algarotti died in Pisa in 1764; Frederick had an epitaph carved in marble placed on his tomb. His sister Sophia died in 1765. "My tears, my regrets are in vain. . . ." Frederick wrote. "Our family seems to me a forest in which a hurricane has knocked over the most beautiful trees, and where one sees at intervals some leaning pine that appears to hold on to its roots in order to watch the fall of its companions, and the damage and devastation made by the storm."[6] Also in 1766 the king quarreled with Prince Ferdinand of Brunswick, who left the army and would not be seen at Potsdam for the next six years. (Frederick maliciously told his envoy in England that it was because Ferdinand was too fat to mount his horse.) Keith quarreled with the Marquis d'Argens at Sans-Souci and openly broke with Quintus Icilius, both of whom openly criticized Frederick behind his back: "I cannot be the friend of anyone who dines every day at the king's table, and collects gall there in order to distill it."[7] Frederick and Keith would remain on intimate terms until the latter's death at ninety-two. More than anyone else, he was an unshakable friend in the final years. Prince Henry fell briefly out of favor by appearing on parade without the *sponton,* or staff, carried by regimental commanders, the inference being that he was on equal footing with His Majesty. Henry got the message and at the next parade appeared "with the hated symbol of his reduced status."[8] Henry's marriage was also awkward. He was a cold fish and had been cuckolded by his adjutant. Frederick finally talked him out of divorcing his beautiful wife, but from then on they led separate lives; she resided in one wing of Henry's palace in Berlin.

A crushing blow occurred in 1767, when young Prince Henry, the king's favorite nephew, died of smallpox. "I have loved this infant as my own son," he wrote to his brother Henry in a letter spattered with tears. Duchess Louise of Saxe-Gotha died the same year. Eichel, his confidential secretary for twenty-eight years, died in 1768, and d'Argens departed for France, where he died three years later.

The Prince of Prussia was causing more sorrow. Scarcely had he married than he was in bed — with someone else. Mistress followed mistress, almost every one an actress of dubious repute who ran him deeply into debt. His wife, Princess Elizabeth, retaliated with her own affairs. The sordid competition soon became public. Princes Henry and Ferdinand — second and third in line to the throne — informed the king that they would never allow a bastard to take away their legitimate rights to succession. The king was forced to arrange a divorce. He selected Princess Frederica of Darmstadt for the new bride, and she ensured the succession by delivering a son, Frederick William, in 1770. The Prince of Prussia did not, however, mend his dissolute and spendthrift ways, and incurred his uncle's growing anger. "The debts his Royal Highness has contracted for his extraordinary expenses surpass all imagination," the English envoy, James Harris, reported in 1775.[9] This was only part of the trouble. Frederick William was "the rising sun." His popularity in the army and kingdom added to the difficult relationship, which eventually became near total estrangement.

Frederick's relationships with family or friends could never really deepen. He had neither time nor inclination for them, he trusted almost no one, nor did his status permit the necessary intimacy. Ulrica spent most of her time in Berlin during her visit, and the king was busy at Potsdam. His appearances at weddings and christenings were brief; while others played, he worked. He loathed most social gatherings and forever refused to allow expensive celebrations of his own birthday.

He preferred to devote what free time he had to private pursuits, to reading, writing, and gardening, to expanding his five libraries, to building his impressive art collection,* and to relaxing at supper with a few friends who were wise enough not to forget that he was king. Baron Bielfeld wrote glowingly of Sans-Souci in 1764, "I doubt whether there is in all Europe a conversation more witty, more agreeable, more instructive, or more animated than at this table." The king continued to enjoy conversation — providing that much of it was his own.

98

WAR had taken a terrible toll of the Prussian army. Its ranks, further depleted by the thirty thousand men released to the farms, had to be filled. Some replacements came from home cantons, but most were recruited abroad and paid for by a special enlistment fund. Recruiting was active and generally successful; seven to eight thousand recruits, some with wives and children, arrived each year. The effort was maintained; in 1769 Frederick offered one German prince twenty thalers for each recruit of "the requisite size."

Officers, of whom the army had been very short in the last years of the war, were not so easily replaced. Over fifteen hundred had been

---

* By 1771 Frederick had added three paintings by Leonardo, five by Raphael, and nine by Titian. The overall worth of his collection would be anybody's guess. In 1983 the Getty Museum offered over twelve million dollars for one of his Watteaus, *L'Embarquement pour Cythère*, which he had acquired in 1763.

killed and a great many badly wounded and discharged. For some years the king had been forced to take "recourse to the ignoble," as he indelicately put it, meaning commoners, whom he now purged, retaining only a few engineers and artillery officers. To bring the officer corps to strength, he turned to young noblemen at home and abroad, particularly from Saxony, Mecklenburg, and the Empire. "In general the nobility cannot distinguish themselves except by the sword; if they forfeit their honor they cannot find refuge at home," he later wrote. "A commoner, on the other hand, having committed the most base acts, returns to his father's occupation without blushing or without believing himself dishonored." [1]

The school of cadets had deteriorated so badly during the war that graduates could neither read nor write. It was transformed into the Academy of Nobles by Major General Hans von Buddenbrock, who brought in competent teachers to teach an impressive curriculum spelled out by the king in an "Instruction" of 1765: "The intention of the king and the goal of this institution is to train young gentlemen so that they are properly qualified for either a military or political career." The king established another military academy in Stolpe, where fifty-six young and impoverished Pomeranian nobles "were maintained, clothed, and taught at his expense." The top fifteen graduates continued studies at the Academy of Nobles, where they were taught by "the most able professors" in Europe. [2]

Frederick had often been displeased with generals who commanded independent detachments in the war. Too often infantry generals did not properly utilize cavalry, or cavalry generals mishandled infantry. Senior generals now received copies of *The General Principles of War*, which was supplemented by new "Instructions" and in 1771 by a lengthy dissertation on tactics and terrain. [3] The "Instructions" covered garrison duties, discipline, field exercises, supervision and education of junior officers, and financial management; they were also issued to regimental and battalion commanders.

After returning from Silesia in the spring of 1764, the king wrote to General Fouqué that he was working body and soul to re-form the army, which, phoenixlike, was reappearing from the ashes. The common soldier was not much of a problem, he went on, and would be returned to prewar excellence within a year. It was officer training that he was concentrating on.

"We have held some maneuvers that have succeeded after a fashion," he told Fouqué in the autumn of 1764. "Staff officers are still not up to scratch; some years will be required to put the army on its former footing." In the spring of 1767 the king noted continuing improvement in discipline and wrote to Henry, "In three years the army will have recovered the solidity that it had before the war, and that courageous assurance which has been lost in the last campaigns."

One primary task was to restore discipline, the hallmark of Prussian arms. The king wrote, "Sternness was necessary to make the soldier obedient, training to make him skillful, and lengthy practice to teach him to fire his musket four times a minute, to march in a straight line, and to perform all the maneuvers that might be needed in different situations of war."[4]

There would be no reasoning on the part of subordinates: "When the commander orders, others must obey." The private soldier must "fear his officers more than the danger to which he is exposed, or no one will be able to lead him to the charge through a storm of three hundred thundering cannon. The common soldier will never willingly accept such dangers; it must be a matter of fear." The war had shown that "battles are won by fire superiority. . . . The infantry that charges the fastest will without question prevail over that which charges slowly." For this reason training stressed "the speed of the charge" in both infantry and cavalry. In addition to their usual services, irregulars of the free or volunteer battalions should lead the attack in open order to draw enemy fire from the battalions attacking in close order. Hussars also were to be trained in cavalry tactics.[5]

Frederick continued to rely on reviews and maneuvers to produce a cohesive army that fought by a standard tactical code. But now, years ahead of his time, he appointed provincial inspectors general for both infantry and cavalry "so as to renew order, accuracy, and strict discipline in order to attain perfect equality in the army, and that both officers and soldiers in all regiments would have the same training."[6]

Strong discipline, daily exercise, speed, precision, shock — the formula for infantry and cavalry. It was up to the officers to achieve it, which was why the training of subordinate officers was so vital. Regimental and battalion commanders were in large part responsible for this training, but the inspectors general reported directly to the king about the conduct of officers, criticizing some, recommending others. By 1768 the king seemed reasonably satisfied with officer training, except that of the staff officers.

Commissariat, quartermaster, and engineer functions had caused enormous problems in the war and would continue to do so. Once funds were available, the king had restored two large magazines, each of thirty-six thousand *wispels* of corn, in Brandenburg and Silesia. These had to be replaced every year, the task of General Wartenberg, who supervised a corps of commissars, military and civilian — "no worse rogues in the world," the king called them. Wartenberg was also in charge of two military funds, one to remount cavalry and hussars in time of war, and one to maintain reserve muskets, cloth for tents, and supplies of leather.

Having suffered from lack of qualified quartermasters during the war, Frederick introduced another innovation by ordering twelve specially selected officers to Potsdam, where he personally trained them as the cadre of a new quartermaster corps. "They were taught to survey the land, mark out camps, fortify villages, entrench heights, build stockades, plan column marches, and above all personally to sound [the depths of] all marshes and rivers."[7]

This training course of gifted young officers was not a complete success. "The great frivolity and spirit of debauchery of these young men retarded their progress," he later grumbled. He did not say what he did to counter "this unfortunate spirit of licentiousness," which was contrary to standing regulations.[8] A more successful effort resulted from winter engineer training schools in the provinces that concentrated on teaching subalterns terrain appreciation and fortification of camps.

The most glaring deficiency in the army was the treatment of veterans, many of them retired because of wounds. Only a handful, some six hundred, could be looked after in the Berlin invalid home. Others were given minor jobs in the various bureaucracies, and in time a few were hired as schoolteachers. Still others were paid one thaler a month from a special war fund, but some were paid nothing. Outstanding generals in the war had been awarded estates and generous pensions. Other generals received pensions that ranged from twelve hundred to two thousand thalers a year; still others held important jobs in the bureaucracies or on crown lands. Invalid officers received a pittance of a few thalers a month, for which the king made no apology. Even more cruel, invalid officers and men from regiments that had fought poorly, such as the East Prussian regiments at Zorndorf, received no benefits of any sort, "because punishments and rewards should be proportional to services."

Frederick wrote in *The Political Testament* of 1768 that he wanted to give more money to invalid soldiers and also pensions to widows and orphans of officers who lacked other means. The problem here, as in other spheres, was twofold: to find the money to finance these various charitable institutions; then to find honest and efficient officials to run them.

The king appended *The General Principles of War* to the new *Political Testament,* even though the last war had caused some fundamental changes in his strategic and tactical thinking. He still believed in planning grand military projects in the hope that one would work, but he seems to have weaned himself, if not from the *Vernichtungs-*, or annihilation, strategy of old, at least from his belief in "the decisive battle," the fantasy that he had pursued throughout the war. If he once had preferred offensive warfare in flat country, he had long since realized that the Austrian ability to use mass heavy artillery made this too costly. Nor would the Austrians willingly fight in such terrain because of superior Prussian cavalry and infantry mobility. In fighting the Austrians, the *real* enemy, it was necessary to occupy strong posts in the mountains and to make more sophisticated attacks. Rather than fighting a general engagement, he would now prefer to destroy detached corps, since it is easier to beat fifteen thousand men than eighty thousand, and the risks are less to gain the same goal: "To multiply small successes is precisely to build one treasure after another. In time one becomes rich without realizing how it has come about."

Defensive warfare, the king warned, is the most difficult of all. If a general chooses passive tactics, if he remains inactive and undertakes nothing, the enemy will force him from the area he wishes to defend.

> The best defensive war should be conducted with such a superior art that the enemy is unable to divine that one wishes to avoid general engagements. . . . One works by detachments. When possible one should defeat those of the enemy, make war on his supplies, seize his convoys, destroy his magazines, disrupt his forages, harass him at every opportunity.

This was nothing less than guerrilla warfare, once condemned by the king, now accepted with the fervor of a religious convert. Light troops were vital to such a campaign, he wrote. Although he did not maintain free battalions in peacetime, he called for no less than twenty-two such units for the next war.

The army continued to improve each year. In 1769 the king wrote to Fouqué, "All these troops [in Silesia] are in such condition that almost nothing more is wanted than their preservation." In 1770 he informed Henry that in case of need, the army would perform well. He later noted that the required precision in maneuvers "began to show itself only after 1770," from which time the army became more ready than ever to wage war.

99

AS FREDERICK realistically noted in his *Mémoires,* the war had left Prussia dangerously isolated. Destitute of allies, he needed to fashion a new foreign policy that met two traditional criteria. It had to offer maximum security to a kingdom of long, exposed borders, and it had to open the way for possible territorial acquisitions at the expense of weaker neighbors. Part of it, therefore, had to be an alliance with a suitable great power.

There were not many possibilities. France was immediately ruled out. She had been a dreadful ally in the Silesian wars; she was now almost bankrupt; and she would not abandon her alliance with Austria or Spain. Frederick felt betrayed by England, whose finances, moreover, were as shaky as her government was fragile. King George III "changes his mind as he changes his shirts," he complained, and Lord Bute remained the major influence at court.[1] (Visitors to Potsdam were surprised to see a beautiful horse teamed with a mule pulling a plough. The horse's name was Lord Bute.) Holland was not much use — an unwilling ally in the past with little of value for the future. A proposed alliance with Denmark had come to nothing and, in any event, would ,have harmed relations with Sweden and Russia. Sweden was not strong enough to make a valuable ally, and a fragmented political structure, in part dominated by France, would continue to hold her down. Austria was out of the question as long as Maria Theresa and Count Kaunitz ruled, for they would never forgive him for seizing Silesia. The Saxon court shared Austria's hatred. Turkey was a better possibility, but her archaic government and primitive army could not be expected to produce dramatic results on Prussia's behalf, although Frederick believed that an alliance with her would prolong the peace for several years.

The possibilities of territorial acquisition were also limited. He could move nowhere in the west without starting a general war, which he could not sustain. He had formally yielded Saxony, and any attempt to recover it would mean war with Austria and France. Russia would block any move he made in the north. Only in the northeast was there a possibility: big but confused Poland could never be a fruitful ally, but there was no reason that she couldn't be a prize — as he had suggested when he was crown prince and when he wrote *The Political Testament* of 1752.

That would mean alliance with Russia, which could provide other advantages as well. It would not only protect his exposed eastern borders; it would check whatever aggressive notions Austria or France had about him. Depending on developments, the alliance could lead to territorial gains at Poland's expense.

Frederick already had this in mind when he signed the 1762 treaty with Czar Peter III. Among the secret articles were those calling for a common policy in Poland designed to put a native Pole on the throne (once August III died) and to support the Polish Dissidents — the Greek Orthodox and Lutheran subjects — against the Polish Catholics.

Although Peter's demise nullified this treaty, and although Czarina Catherine adopted an anti-Prussian tone, postwar circumstances made a new alliance attractive to the Russian court, itself politically isolated at a dangerous time.

As early as mid-February of 1763, Frederick had sent a copy of the treaty to Catherine with a letter pointing to dangerous intrigues that would follow King August's death. He wanted to cooperate with Russia regarding a successor and would himself oppose only an Austrian prince. He supposed that a genuine Polish aristocrat, a Piast, "would suit both of us best."

Catherine welcomed the proposal on condition that the Prussian king agree to reject any candidate sponsored by France. A Piast would indeed be suitable, providing he was young enough and not corruptible by Austria or France. She also wondered whether Frederick would agree to bar the entry of Saxon troops into Poland at the time of the election. Frederick quickly agreed and proposed a defensive alliance similar to that arranged with Peter, whereby each country would furnish a specific number of troops or an equivalent money subsidy if the other was attacked.

King August died in October 1763 and was succeeded by his eldest son, Frederick Christian, a cripple, who died two months later. He was succeeded by his son, thirteen-year-old Frederick August, who, as Elector of Saxony, became an aspirant for the Polish throne. Another candidate was put forward by the powerful Radziwill and Potocki families. The Czartoryskis, a powerful landowning "family," opposed this faction, as did Catherine and Frederick. Catherine had secretly informed Frederick that she wished to have Stanislaus Augustus Poniatowski on the Polish throne.

A member of the "family" (the Czartoryskis were his uncles), Stanislaus was a worldly and charming young man who had spent two years in Paris.[2] He had been taken to Saint Petersburg by the English diplomat Charles Hanbury-Williams. Williams had quickly won over the Grand Duchess Catherine, a gain consolidated by the skillful insertion of Stanislaus into her bed. At twenty-two, Stanislaus was allegedly a virgin (though there was talk about his relationship with his fifty-year-old mentor). Catherine at twenty-six had had a torrid affair with a hot-blooded libertine courtier that resulted in two miscarriages, and she had had a son, presumably by her drunken and half-witted husband, Peter. Her affair with Stanislaus, which turned into a *ménage à quatre* with her husband and his mistress, Elizabeth Vorontsov, lasted three years. Stanislaus was the first to tire of the fun and games and departed for Poland. He was replaced by Gregory Orlov, who thoughtfully arranged for Peter's later dethronement and murder.

Czarina Catherine had many fond memories of, and no hard feelings toward, Stanislaus. Just as important, he would not represent a threat to Russian aspirations in the untidy Kingdom of Poland; indeed, his rule would ensure what Catherine called "the happy anarchy" that for so long had afflicted this tragic land.

Frederick welcomed the candidature largely for the same reasons as Catherine. In agreeing to support Stanislaus, he again urged her to an alliance. He did not believe that he would live long, he wrote, and he wanted to leave his successor a happy and secure country. "Thus I desire to form some satisfactory alliances. There, madame, is my entire policy. . . . I rely on you [to set] the time for the conclusion of the alliance."

In January 1764, Catherine replied favorably to Frederick's proposals. Three months later, the two powers signed an eight-year defensive alliance, the Treaty of Saint Petersburg, which mutually guaranteed their territories. Secret articles pledged each ruler to support the election of Stanislaus as the next Polish king, with troops if necessary, and to maintain the Polish constitution, which prohibited a hereditary monarchy. Finally, and very important, each ruler pledged to support the Polish Dissidents against the Polish Catholics, a step that could not but further divide the country.

Frederick believed that the treaty favored him more than Catherine in that it gave him much-needed security for the internal task of reconstruction at a time when army and finances were wanting. "May this alliance be as durable as I desire!" he wrote to Catherine. "May it be eternal!"

By virtually granting Catherine hegemony in Poland, however, he brought Russian influence uncomfortably close to Prussia, and he also placed himself in an awkward situation vis-à-vis the Turks. But he believed that the advantage of security, even if temporary, outweighed such disadvantages, particularly since he hoped to counter them by astute diplomacy. Prussia's good relations with Turkey might prevent Turkey from going to war against Russia. Austrian suspicions might restrain Catherine in Poland. No matter how precarious the peace, each year that it lasted would see Prussia more fully recovered, more able to influence future events.

When a Polish emissary appeared in Berlin that summer to nominate Prince Henry for Polish king, he was hustled from the country, his lips presumably sealed with cash. When Catherine moved troops into Poland, Frederick ostentatiously transferred regiments to the Polish border while his ambassador supported Russian demands in Warsaw. Threatened with troops and seduced with bribes — Catherine spent an alleged £300,000 buying Polish votes — the Polish Diet in September 1764 elected Stanislaus the king. "In all our history there was no example of an election so tranquil and so unanimous," the new monarch wrote to a friend.[3]

To attain temporary security, Frederick was fanning political winds that would influence the direction of his foreign policy for over a decade.

He and Catherine wanted different things from Poland. Catherine was following a policy established by Peter the Great, who regarded Poland chiefly as "a highway to the Turkish lands." Although she wanted to settle border differences and would insist on equal rights for Polish Orthodox believers, she did not want Poland eliminated. She wanted hegemony, not partition: "All Poland, in short, would be a dependency of Russia, and, in the next war as in the last, might give her a military base."[4] Her envoy in Warsaw, Prince Nicholas Repnin, was backed by Russian troops and was soon acting as virtual ruler.

This was about the last development Frederick wanted. In light of the rapid shifting of political alliances, Russia could easily be tomorrow's enemy. If Catherine permitted internal reforms in return for Russian suzerainty, Poland might revive to threaten Prussia. A strong Poland, with or without Russia, was not desirable.

Russia and Prussia were thus on a collision course. If they agreed that Stanislaus should not be allowed to implement such major reforms as eliminating the *liberum veto* — an insane procedure whereby a single member of the Diet could instantly nullify any bill — or introducing a hereditary, nonelective monarchy, they disagreed on minor reforms that Catherine was ready to accept. Frederick would permit nothing that in his opinion strengthened Poland, and the czarina's attitude annoyed him. When she allowed Stanislaus to introduce a general customs service, Frederick arbitrarily imposed a tax on Polish shipping on the Lower Vistula and made strong representations to Saint Petersburg. He removed the tax at Catherine's urging, but she then persuaded Stanislaus to abolish the new system. Frederick also stressed to her Turkey's fear of internal reforms in Poland, and he submitted proof of Stanislaus's overtures to France and Austria.

More conflict emerged soon after Stanislaus's election, when Catherine opened a diplomatic offensive that thoroughly alarmed her new ally. Influenced by her minister of foreign affairs, Count Nikita Panin, whose diplomacy paralleled his taste "for all ostentatious and striking things," the czarina attempted to create a northern confederation by inviting England, Sweden, Denmark, and Saxony to join the Treaty of Saint Petersburg. Count Kaspar von Saldern brought the proposal to Berlin in 1766. Frederick did not like the huge Holsteiner, "who had neither manners nor versatile thought [and] took the tone of a Roman dictator," nor did he like the proposal, which was "entirely contrary to Prussian interests."[5] He would never again ally with England. Sweden, Denmark, and Saxony would be useless allies, nor did he want them to become influential and dilute his influence at Saint Petersburg.

Frederick's new alliance might well have foundered on such political shoals had not a larger issue cropped up in Poland. Russian and Prussian insistence on full rights for the Polish Dissidents was totally unacceptable not only to King Stanislaus and the Czartoryski "family" but to all conservative Polish elements.

The issue exploded at the Diet of 1766. Stanislaus by now was tired of Prince Repnin's various ukases, but he probably would have accepted this demand in return for constitutional reforms. The Catholic bishops of Cracow and Vilna, however, had stopped at nothing in their attempts to inflame the public. Not only did the Diet refuse equal rights to the Dissidents, it confirmed laws unfavorable to them. When Catherine threatened to intervene militarily, the "family" dissolved the Diet by the *liberum veto*. The Dissidents now formed confederations, and other confederations of landowners sprang up, all as prelude to armed anarchy. France and Austria at once exploited the situation. France could not afford to go to war, but her agents actively worked with anti-Russian elements inside Poland and also worked to persuade Turkey to invade the Ukraine. Austria went so far as to concentrate troops in her eastern provinces. None of this unduly upset Frederick. "I am resigned to anything," he told Henry in late February 1767. "If I must make war, I shall make it; if I must maintain peace, I shall maintain it."

Catherine was not to be intimidated. In the spring of 1767 she persuaded the reluctant Prussian king to extend their alliance by a new secret treaty: "If the court of Vienna sends troops to Poland to combat the Russians, His [Prussian] Majesty would protest . . . [and make] a powerful diversion in their states." In such an event, Catherine would provide a corps of troops "and procure him a suitable compensation after the conclusion of peace."[6]

Thus bolstered, the czarina pursued her divisive policy against increasing Polish resistance. In October the Diet assembled almost under Russian bayonets. Repnin at once demanded that senators appoint a delegation to discuss the burning issue of the Dissenters. When the Bishop of Cracow resisted, Repnin had him arrested and deported to Russia, together with other clergymen and civil officials. Russian troops blockaded Warsaw, the Diet appointed the delegation demanded by Repnin, and in early 1768 it approved the delegation's resolutions confirming Poland's status as a Russian vassal state.

This was too much for the more militant confederates of Radom; they fled to Bar, only thirty-five miles from the Turkish border. Many of them now joined the Knights of the Holy Cross, an army organized and commanded by sixty-four-year-old Joseph Pulaski. Supported by most of the landowners, the Confederation of Bar also attracted a peasant following that fought both with and independently of the knights. The joint effort in early 1768 bore all the characteristics of guerrilla warfare. Although Russian troops captured Bar and dispersed confederation units, resistance continued to spread in and around Cracow, Lithuania, and Byelorussia. Ukrainian peasants who years before had been brutally "pacified" by Cossacks and who were now being methodically proselytized by Polish Catholic gentry, seized on the confusion to start their own uprising, a brutal affair that cost thousands of lives, mostly those of gentry and Jews, and was put down with equal brutality at a terrible cost to the peasants.

While Russians, Poles, and Ukrainians were thus fighting, French diplomats remained active in Constantinople. In September a Cossack force chasing peasant insurgents crossed the border into Turkish Moldavia and burned the town of Balta. The sultan retaliated by throwing the Russian ambassador into jail.

In October 1768, Turkey and Russia were at war.

100

THE WAR placed Frederick in an awkward position. He was allied with both powers and did not wish to offend either Russia or Turkey. Yet his alliance with Russia called for Prussian support by troops or money. Troops were out of the question, but open payment of what soon became "these cursed subsidies" would offend the Porte — and the sum, 480,000 thalers a year, was too large to disgorge without reasonable return.* He honored his word by secretly paying the subsidy, but in return he wanted the alliance extended for ten years, with Russia guaranteeing Prussian rights to Ansbach and Bayreuth or a satisfactory equivalent.

Frederick was supporting a war that he did not like in the least. Czarina Catherine had already upset him by her autocratic behavior in Poland. Now she was plainly bent on a war of expansion that would realize Peter the Great's old dream of seizing Constantinople. "This is a dreadful power," he complained to Henry, "which in half a century will cause all Europe to tremble." Turkish defeat would cause Russia to collide with Austria in the Balkans and probably bring on a general war that would involve Prussia as Russia's ally.

Frederick's long-term goal was to bring about peace before the war spread, naturally with some reward from Russia for his support. An able Saxon diplomat suggested to him that Poland could be used to keep the war from spreading: a partition of Poland by Russia, Austria, and Prussia would prevent a collision between Russia and Austria over the Polish question. "The plan has a certain *éclat*," Frederick wrote to his current envoy in Saint Petersburg, Count Victor Solms. Frederick had Solms submit this plan to Count Panin, who replied that Russia had sufficient land without taking part of Poland — but if Prussia and

---

* Frederick informed Voltaire in the spring of 1770, "I no longer buy paintings now that I am paying subsidies."

Austria would help Russia expel the Turks from Europe, then Russia saw no reason why *they* should not be rewarded with part of Poland. Poland could be compensated by giving her Moldavia and Wallachia.

The Austrian court had been keeping a sharp eye on both Prussia and Russia, and events in 1769 began bringing Poland into sharper focus. Frederick's overtures to extend his alliance with Catherine, taken with the expected Russian victory over the Turks, spelled only danger to Austria, which infinitely preferred Turkey to Russia as close neighbor. It was time to signal Saint Petersburg that Vienna frowned on Russian expansion, particularly to the southwest, and the Austrian court chose two ways to send the message.

It took the first in spring of 1769, when a Russian corps had forced some Polish confederates to seek refuge in the district of Zips on the Hungarian-Polish frontier. The Polish king asked Vienna to intervene and deprive the confederates of sanctuary. On the pretext of history — the Hungarian crown claimed to have mortgaged Zips to Poland in 1412 — reinforced by Prussian encouragement, Austrian army units occupied several trading towns in the contested territory.

Further Russian gains that summer prompted the second method for relaying the message, a meeting between King Frederick and Emperor Joseph in Silesia. Not long after Emperor Francis's death, in 1765, Frederick had proposed a meeting with the young successor, but Maria Theresa and Count Kaunitz had vetoed it. The rulers now met at fortress Neisse in late August, Frederick having invited Joseph to attend military maneuvers. The meeting was supposedly secret, a rather ridiculous pretense, considering their all-too-visible entourages. Frederick's party included Prince Henry, the Prince of Prussia (Frederick William), and assorted ministers and generals. In Joseph's group were Marshals Lacy and Loudon and Joseph's brother-in-law Prince Albert of Saxony. Joseph traveled as a Count von Falkenstein and refused to occupy Imperial apartments or even to ride in the royal carriage, a transparent disguise that fooled no one.

The fifty-seven-year-old king and the twenty-eight-year-old emperor hit it off from the beginning; Frederick went so far as to wear an Austrian uniform and abstain from eating meat in respect of Lent. Elaborate entertainment included military maneuvers each morning and opera each evening. Frederick's generous hospitality and ostentatious flattery did not stop with Joseph but extended to the members of his party as well. "At supper the king talked steadily for three hours," wrote Prince Albert of Saxony. "The Prussian princes and generals dared not open their mouths . . . but some of our Austrian generals slept peacefully."[1] The rulers frequently conferred tête-à-tête in the royal apartments, in Joseph's suite, or while walking arm in arm in the garden.

The talks apparently remained general, each man assuring the other that past animosities were buried. Aware of Joseph's admiration of Frederick, Kaunitz had placed him on guard, and the political situation was still too fluid to allow detailed conclusions. From Frederick's standpoint the importance of the meeting was its physical fact. He wanted to size up Joseph and he wanted further meetings to encourage rapprochement as a buffer to Russian ambition. He stressed his own pacific intentions repeatedly and called for a new supportive relationship between the two Houses. Joseph replied in kind, assuring the king that Silesia was a forgotten subject, but that neither he nor his mother would allow the Russians to remain in possession of Moldavia and Wallachia. He believed that Russia was bent on all-out aggression and that "all of Europe" would have to mobilize to stop her. He further suggested that if a new war broke out between France and England, as seemed possible, Austria and Prussia should enforce an exact neutrality in Germany. Frederick agreed, and they signed a secret engagement to this effect.

There was an amusing postscript. Joseph wrote that the king was a genius, but underneath a pacific exterior he retained his distrust of Austria. He "was a very curious object to see one time," Joseph wrote, "but God preserve [me] from a second; he threatens to visit me at Kolin."[2] Frederick informed Finckenstein, "He [Joseph] has invited me so politely to come see his troops in Bohemia that I have promised to go there next year." He also confided that Joseph "is a man devoured by ambition who is brooding over some great plan; who, currently restrained by his mother, is becoming impatient under the maternal yoke. . . . Rest assured that once he is his own master, all Europe will be set on fire." Frederick noted in his later *Mémoires:*

> This young prince affected a frankness that seemed natural; his friendly disposition was marked by gaiety and much liveliness. While wanting to learn he lacked patience for self-education . . . but what really denoted his character were traits that escaped him despite himself, and that revealed the unbounded ambition with which he burned.

Swinging hard the helm of state, Frederick next concluded the ten-year extension of the treaty with Russia. Catherine agreed to guarantee his rights to Ansbach and Bayreuth; in return he agreed to invade Swedish Pomerania if the Swedish senate overthrew the constitution of 1720 or if Sweden attacked Russia.*

---

* The German historian Gerhard Ritter argued that Russia won far more than Prussia by this new treaty. To the contrary: the fact of alliance was Frederick's major concern and the guarantee of the principalities was a bonus. Nor was the Swedish bit onerous. Swedish Pomerania ranked high on his future hit-list in both *Political Testaments*, though he hoped to acquire it by other than war — in 1765 he had even made a cash offer. The main danger to Prussia of the renewal was that it might involve her in a war against Austria, France, and Spain before army and treasury were ready. (Koser, *Geschichte*, Volume 3; Ritter, *Frederick the Great*.)

The war meanwhile was going very well for Russia. Count Peter Rumianzov, "the Russian Turenne" as Catherine called him, chalked up a string of impressive victories. Other armies pressed into the Crimea to seize Azov and Taganrog, once the proud possessions of Peter the Great. In a master move, a Russian fleet sailed to the Mediterranean and sank the Turkish fleet at the battle of Chesme Bay. By autumn of 1770 it seemed as if Russian armies would soon occupy the entire Crimea and would march from Moldavia and Wallachia across the Danube to the gates of Constantinople.

Prussian diplomacy meanwhile had taken a new and rather bizarre twist. Frederick wanted Queen Ulrica of Sweden to know the secret portion of his Russian alliance so that she would not anger Saint Petersburg by strengthening the Swedish monarchy with French support. In June 1770, Prince Henry carried this message to Stockholm.

Prince Henry was a new ingredient in the diplomatic stew. At forty-four, he was morose, totally estranged from his wife, fond of pretty young men, and resentful of his brother. A devious man of dangerous intrigue, he was also worldly, urbane, and extremely intelligent. Henry had shared in some of the talks at Neisse and had been far more impressed by Joseph than had the king. Frederick hoped the embryonic rapprochement might lead to a check on Russia. Henry saw it as a beginning of a dual alliance. "Why," Henry asked, "should not Frederick and Joseph, like Octavius and Anthony, divide Germany between them?"[3] Frederick replied that Maria Theresa would never accept such a plan and that he himself was too old for any more adventures. What Prussia needed was peace between Russia and Turkey to free him from these "cursed subsidies" and from danger of being drawn into a general war.

Henry believed that the situation could be milked for much more profit to Prussia. Without Frederick's knowledge, he informed Czarina Catherine, whom he had known as a girl, that he would be in Stockholm in the summer and would like to visit her. She readily agreed and promised to write to Frederick at the appropriate time.

A new twist occurred that spring, when the Austrian ambassador, in making his departure, wondered whether the Prussian king had given any thought to acquiring West Prussia and Ermeland, an enclave close to East Prussia. He wisely did not add that Count Kaunitz would agree to this in return for the recovery of Silesia. Frederick paid little attention to the matter but some weeks later mentioned it to Henry, then in Stockholm. Henry grabbed at the notion, which, if only a vague vision, "is nonetheless such a pleasant one that I find it very difficult to renounce it. I want to see you lord of the Baltic coast, sharing with the most formidable power in Germany the influence which these two, combined, could have in Europe."[4] Frederick replied cordially but negatively, yet when Henry pressed more arguments on him he conceded that Henry's ideas, if carried out, could bring "great advantages to the state."

Henry was in Stockholm when the czarina informed Frederick that she would like Henry to visit her. Frederick was delighted and at once asked his brother to make the journey, no matter how disagreeable it appeared to him; he would happily send him eight thousand thalers. He wanted Henry to try to reconcile Catherine and Ulrica. More important, he hoped that Henry would persuade Catherine to make a reasonable peace with Turkey, an effort that he believed would be helped by his own forthcoming visit with Emperor Joseph: "My little journey to Moravia will make more pacific impressions on the Russian empress than all the troops and all the reviews in the world."

Frederick met Joseph in early September at Neustadt in Moravia. But this time Count Kaunitz was present and left little doubt as to who was in charge of Austrian foreign policy. Kaunitz, along with the rest of the Austrian party, was violently anti-Russian, green with envy over Russian successes against the Turks. Kaunitz told the king that Maria Theresa would never permit the Russians to retain Moldavia and Wallachia or cross the Danube: "He added that the union of Prussia and Austria was the sole barrier that could oppose this overflowing torrent which threatened to inundate all Europe."[5] Although agreeing that the threat was very real, and expressing desire for friendship with Austria, Frederick explained that his present alliance with Catherine precluded a formal pact with Austria. He would continue, however, to respect agreements made at last year's Neisse meeting, and he also promised to inform Vienna of any overtures France made in Berlin.

During the meeting Frederick received a dispatch from Constantinople: the sultan wanted Prussia and Austria to mediate a peace between Turkey and Russia. Kaunitz tentatively agreed, providing that Frederick make the overture. Frederick found Kaunitz an extremely intelligent man: "He has sound and clear judgment, but he is so taken with himself that he believes he is an oracle in politics, and we others are novices whom he must indoctrinate." Only on Frederick's insistence was Emperor Joseph, whom Kaunitz treated more "as subaltern than master," informed of their talks. Joseph seemed more interested in his troops, though he overwhelmed Frederick with friendly gestures. Frederick described him to Voltaire as "an amiable and very meritorious prince, an emperor such as has not long been seen in Germany."

Czarina Catherine greeted Prince Henry in a manner not unlike Czar Peter's reception of Baron von Goltz in 1762. He was given a magnificent palace and showered with expensive gifts, among them a fur coat trimmed with sable and black fox. He received an open invitation for dinner and supper with his hostess, who honored him with magnificent banquets, balls, and fêtes of every description. They spent hours together discussing philosophy, literature, music, painting, sculpture, government. He was appointed honorary president of the new Academy of Sciences. Every palace and mansion was opened to him. The brother of Frederick the Great, in his own right a famous military commander, cultured friend of Voltaire and Melchior Grimm, worldly and polished, he was the toast of Saint Petersburg.

But he soon discovered that neither Catherine nor Count Panin was inclined to make an easy peace. She would not accept Austrian mediation, she insisted on Russian occupation or at least on complete independence of Moldavia and Wallachia, and she expected Frederick to continue to support her Polish policy.

Frederick did not take kindly to these dictates. "It was difficult to deal with the Russians," he later wrote, "because they understood nothing of the art of negotiation. They thought only of their own interests and ignored those of others."[6] He instructed his brother to make it clear to Panin that he was an ally, not a toady. The Russian court "may or may not accept us as mediators, but they should not openly make fools of us." By mid-November he was disgusted with the Russian court's intransigence and was on the point of refusing to pay further subsidies. England and Spain were close to war — Spain was sending an expedition to chase an English settlement from the Falkland Islands — which would involve Austria, France, and Prussia, to her ruin. Frederick wanted peace, "peace as promptly as possible without proposals of intolerable and humiliating conditions on the Turks."

Henry was frying bigger fish. Aware that his brother would welcome a settlement in Poland, he drew up a peace plan that directly involved Russia, Prussia, and Austria in Polish affairs. He followed by suggesting that a triple alliance might solve the Polish question and also force Turkey to a quick peace. The suggestion was well received by Russia and Austria.

Catherine made the first proposal, albeit obliquely. Remarking to Henry that Austria had occupied two fiefdoms in Poland, she asked: "But why should everyone not take something else?"[7] She saw nothing wrong in Frederick's occupying West Prussia, and Count Zacharias Chernyshev, one of her more hawkish generals, suggested that Prussia take Ermeland.

Frederick wanted nothing to do with it — or so he insisted. Ermeland was not worth the taking. "Polish Prussia, though, would be worthwhile," he told Henry, "even if Danzig were not included, for we should have the Vistula and free communication with [East Prussia], which would be an important item." But he was terrified of a new war, and such aggression was far too risky at this time. His real interest, he insisted, was seeing Russia at peace with Turkey. He had already been upset by the harsh terms insisted on by Count Panin for that peace. In his mind, Henry's mission had failed and it was time for his return.

Henry reached Potsdam in mid-February 1771 and forcefully presented his case for the safe acquisition of West Prussia, Ermeland, and Danzig. He found a willing convert, and one must suspect that this had been in the king's mind all along. Finckenstein drew up a draft agreement for Catherine's study — the beginning of protracted negotiations, "which, if they succeed, my dear brother, will be entirely due to you," the king wrote in March. Henry continued to involve himself in the necessary diplomacy — he and Catherine carried on a long and warm correspondence — but by autumn Frederick was claiming equal credit. It was probably because of his special brand of diplomacy that all hurdles, including Count Panin's and Maria Theresa's lengthy remonstrances, were overcome and a formal treaty was signed in August 1772.

Under its terms Poland lost over a fourth of her land area, including some five million people. Russia received over 100,000 square kilometers that held nearly two million people, Austria some 70,000 square kilometers with a population of 2.7 million. Prussia acquired West Prussia (but not Danzig and Thorn), about 16,000 square miles with 416,000 people, an area small in comparison but rich in political and strategic importance.

The Polish king and Diet still had to accept the treaty, more or less a formality, in view of the ten thousand troops that each court simultaneously sent to Poland. King Stanislaus delayed negotiations for nearly a year but after an "allied" threat of total dismemberment, he formally accepted what virtually was a fait accompli.

Thus the first treaty of partition, which set the scene for further partitions and, finally, Poland's temporary disappearance from the European map. Catherine and Frederick were delighted, and so was Prince Henry, to whom the king awarded an annual twelve thousand thalers from the new province. Emperor Joseph and Count Kaunitz in Vienna were equally pleased. Only Maria Theresa continued to have misgivings. But these bothered no one. When informed that the empress-queen had been reduced to tears by the deed, Frederick coldly noted, "Yes, always weeping — and always annexing."

101

FREDERICK'S NEW ACQUISITION, West Prussia, was both a prize and a challenge. "I have been given a bit of anarchy to reform," he sardonically noted.[1] In the spring of 1772, on his return from an inspection of the new territory, he wrote to Henry: "This is a very valuable and highly advantageous acquisition as much from the political as from the financial point of view; but to cause less jealousy I am telling those who wish to listen that all I have seen is sand, pine trees, heather, and Jews."

The chief advantage was strategic. East Prussia was no longer an isolated outpost but an integral part of the kingdom. Frederick's eastern borders were still exposed, but now they lay behind a defensible buffer zone, the key to which was the Vistula River. Once fortified, this zone would become the eastern main line of resistance. Where earlier the army in East Prussia could fall back only on Königsberg and there perish, now, with the Niemen as the first line of defense, it could make a fighting withdrawal back to a second line, that of the Pregel, and finally to the Vistula.

Further, as master of the Vistula the king virtually controlled Polish commerce while enjoying a tidy profit from shipping tolls. The new province also paid revenues of five million thalers a year and it came equipped with an army whose cavalry was equal to Prussian cavalry. The infantry needed shaping up, as did staff officers, but these tasks would soon be accomplished.

On the debit side he had acquired an impoverished and backward land of barbarians "crouching under the yoke of ignorance and stupidity," in his later words.[2] Although it behooved him (and future German apologists) to present the land in the worst possible light, there is no doubt that conditions were generally appalling. The country peasants, even "rich" ones, lived in primitive huts, subsisted on gruel, and cultivated their fields with rude wooden ploughs often pulled by women and dogs. Few villages had bake ovens, many peasants had never tasted bread, weaving looms were rare, spinning wheels unknown. Towns were equally pathetic. The plague of 1709 had killed most of the artisans, and they had never been replaced. Public buildings had fallen to ruin, schools did not exist, corrupt courts enforced unfair laws. "The towns are in a wretched state," Frederick reported. "Culm, for example, should hold eight hundred houses; there are not a hundred standing, and they are inhabited by either Jews or monks, and there are still even more miserable people there."

Having probed the rotting corpse of state, the king decided to bury most of it in favor of a Prussian resurrection. "He has taken possession of Polish Prussia with an amazing rapidity," reported the English envoy, James Harris, in October, "and the effects of his government are already felt through every part of his new requisition."[3] Prussian officials soon abrogated a quantity of laws "as bizarre as extravagant," in the king's later words. A new court and police system slowly emerged. A public works program began restoring towns and cities. Tailors, apothecaries, blacksmiths, carpenters, and masons were settled in the new province. A hundred and eighty teachers, Protestant and Catholic, opened schools where there had been none. Tax surveyors ploughed through domains to assess holdings and levy the land tax on the same basis as in East Prussia. The church and its prelates were taxed at the same rate as in Silesia. Frederick claimed certain fiefdoms as crown lands, made a lump sum payment of 500,000 thalers for them, and henceforth received their revenues. In what Frederick saw as a purifying touch, four thousand itinerant Jews, accused of begging from or robbing peasants, were banished to Poland.

Thwarted in his desire to obtain Danzig and Thorn, Frederick hoped to promote Elbing into a major trading center that would steal Danzig's commercial wealth. Toward this end, he financed construction of a canal, a project that cost 700,000 thalers. Completed in a year, it not only connected the Vistula to the Oder, Havel, and Elbe Rivers, which increased trade and river tolls; it also produced large acreages of reclaimed marshlands that in time supported new agricultural settlements.

The treaty of partition, or the first rape of Poland, did not alter the Prussian king's long-range diplomatic goal. He still wanted to end the war between Russia and Turkey before it spread to a general war that would involve Prussia. Frederick had accepted Vienna's greedy territorial demands in Poland because that court had promised to join Prussia in persuading the Porte to accept Russian peace terms.

Peace talks, begun at a conference in August 1772, were quickly dissolved; they resumed again two months later in Bucharest. In a nutshell, the Turks were not prepared to accept Catherine's hard terms. As the Austrians refused to allow a permanent Russian presence on the Danube, the Turks understandably wished to avoid that same presence in the Crimea, which Catherine insisted on. The contretemps would have been difficult to resolve even under favorable circumstances. But Catherine was not inclined favorably toward Austrian and Prussian mediation, and France did everything possible to stir up trouble, not only between the Porte and Petersburg, but between Russia and Prussia. This disruptive effort brought England into the act to complicate negotiations further. The Bucharest conference ended in March 1773 with no agreement.

The unstable temperament of the forty-four-year-old czarina was largely responsible for the impasse. Panin's restraining influence had been dampened by Prince Gregory Orlov's return to all offices "except that of fucking," as the king wrote to Henry. Orlov soon replaced the favorite in this essential office. "It is a terrible business," Frederick told Henry in July 1773, "when the prick and the cunt decide the interests of Europe."

Whatever the inspiration, Catherine reverted to a military solution, the idea being for Marshal Rumianzov to cross the Danube and work south through Bulgaria to Adrianople and Constantinople. His several efforts to do this were dismal failures. Catherine had been paying the price of fighting a difficult war. Stern measures followed one after the other and in spring of 1773 led to a major uprising of the Cossacks under Emelian Pugachev, who cloaked his rebellion in one of the most bizarre garments in history. To win peasant support, he claimed to be Catherine's assassinated husband, Czar Peter III, who had returned from death to lead his people from bondage. That he bore no resemblance to Peter did not matter. The peasantry flocked to his army, which, about fifteen thousand strong, swept across western Russia, storming army posts and killing nobles, landlords, and officers in a full-blown insurrection that was put down only with extreme difficulty.[4]

Though Catherine described Pugachev's rebellion to Melchior von Grimm as "a farce," added to Rumianzov's failures it worried her, and she asked Frederick to accept the role of peacemaker with the Turks. He quickly agreed, but the effort failed. As he later wrote, "These two powers were too exalted and haughty for anyone to bring them to agreement."

Rumianzov meanwhile had finally crossed the Danube and pressed into Bulgaria. The Turkish sultan, Mustapha III, died in January 1774 and was replaced by his brother, Abdul-Hamid (familiar "only with the harem," Frederick noted). A splendid Russian victory at Kozludji in early July on top of other Turkish losses brought about the Turks' capitulation in the same year.

The subsequent Treaty of Kuchuk-Kainardji guaranteed the independence of the Crimea and Russian possession of territory east of it, including Peter the Great's old fortresses of Azov, Kuban, and Terek, thus giving Catherine access to the Black Sea. The Turks also guaranteed free navigation of the Hellespont, a large cash indemnity, protection for Orthodox Christians in Constantinople, and a protectorate over the Christian population of Moldavia on the Danube — a package that would have pleased even Peter the Great.

The end of the Russo-Turkish War, though it relieved Frederick of the worry of a larger war, left an unsettled and potentially dangerous political situation. He was clearly apprehensive of what he regarded as Catherine's irrational foreign policy. Prince Orlov had been replaced as her lover by Lieutenant General Gregory Potemkin, a one-eyed veteran of the Turkish war, a religious mystic as ambitious as his new bedmate.* Frederick did not approve of "Tapukin," as he referred to him, or of Catherine's numerous affairs. It was clear from her behav-

---

* Prince Orlov visited Berlin in 1775. "He has a sincere and candid air," Frederick wrote to Henry; "[he is] a very sensible man."

ior, he wrote to Henry in October 1774, "that a woman is always a woman and that in a feminine government the cunt has more influence than a firm policy guided by straight reason."

Catherine and her court resented Frederick's limited rapprochement with the Vienna court and blamed him in part for forcing the return of the Danubian principalities, Moldavia and Wallachia, to Turkey. No sooner had the peace treaty been signed than Austria seized these principalities, ignoring Prussian and Russian protests. Austria now held a knife over the major supply line of the Dniester River in any future war between Russia and Turkey.

Catherine held other grievances against her ally. She correctly recognized that Frederick had foiled her attempts to establish a valid "northern system" — a power bloc — and that he would stand in the way of her further advance southward as well. She had also formally objected to additional territorial claims in Poland by Austria and Prussia, and Frederick was involved in delicate negotiations with her as a result.

Frederick regarded his alliance with Russia as more important than ever. His flirtation with Vienna had come to very little. Emperor Joseph was proving to be a hawk. Not only had he seized lands in the Balkans and Poland; he was looking at the large duchy of Friuli at the top of the Adriatic, at Bosnia in the Balkans, at Silesia, at Alsace and Lorraine. Joseph's avidity for territory and his immeasurable ambition were great cause for concern. King Frederick kept a portrait of the emperor on his desk at Sans-Souci, not out of admiration but because, as he explained to a friend, "There is a man to be watched."

More potential trouble lay in the west. France and England had been sparring since signing the unsatisfactory Peace of Paris in 1763. Had their respective treasuries not been so empty, had the internal government of each not been so divisive, war undoubtedly would have occurred earlier. As it was, neither country made any secret of its animosity toward the other.

French fortunes had declined enormously in twelve years. Louis XV was well on his way to becoming one of the most hated kings France had had. A handsome, virile man, intelligent according to some, Louis lacked the drive necessary to raise France's fortunes. He resented the duties of government, which interrupted delightful days of hunting and exhausting nights of mistresses. The court remained torn by cabal and intrigue, with policy more or less dictated by the predominant faction. His minister of foreign affairs, Duke Étienne François de Choiseul, served him well, reorganizing the army and navy, strengthening alliances with Austria and Spain, establishing new bases in the West Indies, stealing Corsica from Genoa, arranging the marriage of the sixteen-year-old dauphin to Maria Theresa's daughter, fifteen-year-old Marie Antoinette. But in 1770 Choiseul backed Spain against England when they clashed over the Falkland Islands and only just avoided a calamitous war. Choiseul was followed by Chancellor René de Maupeou, whose financial reforms were gaining ground when Louis died in 1774.

His grandson and successor, Louis XVI, was a good argument for the guillotine. Devoted to hunting, he had little to offer his country. Heavy and ugly, he ate and drank excessively. When forced to tend to business, he showed himself stupid and uncomprehending, weak and vacillating, qualities that unfortunately overrode an alleged kindness and honesty and even a certain piety unusual in the Versailles court. His marriage was a disaster. He was impotent and remained so, despite Maria Theresa's lengthy instructions to Marie Antoinette on how to arouse him.*

As crown princess, Marie had gone out of her way to antagonize King Louis's mistress, Madame du Barry, stirring up a social crisis that was solved only by Maria Theresa's blunt strictures to the child to behave herself. Marie Antoinette behaved no better as Queen of France. Surrounded by favorites, she spent her time gambling, dancing, and acting, remote from France and its problems, disdainful of her still impotent husband, whom she called "the poor man." Louis meanwhile was running a disaster course. He had replaced the able chancellor, René de Maupeou, with the seventy-three-year-old Count Jean de Maurepas, a tired and cynical man who wanted to avoid trouble and, in so doing, only courted it. Louis "spoke as master and acted as slave," Frederick wrote in disgust, "for he did only what Maurepas approved."[5] Louis's new foreign minister, Count Charles de Vergennes, followed this lead, his main effort being to support the American colonies in their incipient rebellion against British rule.

Turbulent politics also ruled the English court, mainly the result of the rebellious North American colonies. The Sugar Act of 1764, the Stamp Act of 1765, and the American Import Duties Act of 1767, familiar to American schoolchildren as the Townshend Acts, were repressive laws that caused an uproar in the colonies. In 1770 the newly appointed prime minister, Lord North, repealed all duties levied by the Townshend Act except for that on tea, but it was too late to quiet opposition voices. Insurgency continued: the Boston Massacre in 1770, the burning of a British revenue cutter by smugglers in 1772, the Boston Tea Party in 1773. Each insult hardened North's attitude and the views of his fellows. Velvet glove yielded to hard fist: the Intolerable Acts of 1774. Americans answered in kind, politically by Committees of Correspondence (hotbeds of sedition, as seen in England), then in

---

* The instructions failed to work because poor Louis was a victim of phimosis. Louis XV had earlier discovered this, but the dauphin was unwilling to submit to the painful cure of circumcision. In 1777 Emperor Joseph visited the French court and persuaded him to have the operation. The Parisians circulated a bawdy poem on Louis's prepuce, a copy of which Frederick gleefully sent Henry.

1774 by the First Continental Congress, which demanded, among other things, repeal of all restrictive legislation passed during the last decade and a boycott of British goods.

War was not far away. In April 1775, British troops clashed with American militia at Lexington and Concord. Two months later redcoats defeated the colonists at the battle of Bunker Hill. The American Revolution had begun.

While George III of England wrestled with Parliament to retain royal prerogatives, while Lord North continued to infuriate American colonists, while Louis XVI hunted away the days, while Queen Marie Antoinette gambled away the nights, while Maria Theresa counted her beads, and Czarina Catherine counted her lovers — the King of Prussia continued to build an army and treasury and to keep a sharp eye on the vagaries of European politics.

Frederick did not understand the nuances of either English or French politics. He was incapable of grasping the notion of democracy. A parliament to him was as dismaying an idea as ministerial authority in government. This did not prevent him, however, from recognizing governmental weaknesses, assessing them, and applying the lessons to the general political situation.

Of the two western powers, he held England in the greater contempt. The war in North America was a disaster — a "ruinous war," he called it — all the work of Lord Bute, whom he inaccurately insisted was still in power at Whitehall. How the English believed that they could subjugate America with an army of only seven thousand men, he could not imagine. King George obviously would have to recruit and equip a large force if he meant to wage war thousands of miles from home in a hostile climate, an effort that would largely negate British influence in Europe.

Frederick also held the French throne in contempt. Count Maurepas was not the man to return France to her former greatness. France stood in danger of becoming completely bankrupt while its complaisant ruler was the captive of his disastrous queen. Frederick understood French desire for revenge against England and accepted French intervention in North America as natural. Nor did he object: French embroilment in the American war would significantly reduce her influence in Europe and thereby weaken her allies, Austria and Spain.

Austria remained the real enemy. Emperor Joseph was making his aggressive intentions all too clear, and in 1775 he added an uncomfortable exclamation point by seizing the Balkan province of Bukovina. Czarina Catherine asked Frederick to intervene. To fight Austria he needed allies, and Russia was temporarily exhausted. In view of this, he wrote to Catherine, "it was improper that he should announce himself as the Don Quixote of the Turks."

It was not a healthy situation and perhaps James Harris was correct to report that from all accounts

his Prussian Majesty was never, at any one period of his life, known to be so uncommonly out of humour as at present. This appears not only from his conversation, but from his actions. He broke his flute, a few days ago, on the head of his favorite hussar, and is very liberal in kicking and cuffing those employed about his person. He is peevish at his meals, says little in his evening conversations, and is affable to nobody.[6]

102

FREDERICK had described himself to Voltaire as the hermit of Sans-Souci. On occasion he did shut himself away, particularly during periods of ill health, to work on the usual variety of public and private projects. He was nevertheless amazingly active when the occasion demanded, presiding over various royal marriages and baptisms or the annual carnival or receiving foreign visitors, some of whom have left their impressions of king and kingdom.

Early in 1772 James Harris, then twenty-six and newly appointed as British envoy, sat in an antechamber of the Potsdam palace listening to the king play his flute. He was eventually called to the royal presence to deliver his credentials: "After His Majesty had made a very polite answer to the few words I said . . . he made me a very flattering personal compliment, entered very freely into an easy conversation, and kept me with him for some time."[1]

Harris described Potsdam as a very pretty town, although it lacked sufficient inhabitants. "Nothing can equal the splendour and magnificence of the new palace. . . . It is superior to Versailles, to the Escorial, to everything I ever saw or heard. . . . The costliness of the furniture exceeds all belief." Lord Marshal Keith later took him around Sans-Souci, "a most agreeable retreat. . . . I never saw a greater abundance of fruits of all kinds; [the king] is a great lover of them, and spares no expense in having them in as great perfection as the climate will allow, and at all seasons." Harris rented a house "as big as the Atlantic Ocean" in Berlin, a beautiful but underpopulated city filled with soldiers. As for society in general, "A total corruption of morals reigns throughout both sexes in every class of life. . . . The men are constantly occupied in how to make straitened means support the extravagances of their life. The women are harpies, debauched through want of modesty, rather than from want of anything else. They prostitute their persons to the best payer, and all delicacy of manners or sentiment of affection are unknown to them."[2]

Colonel Count Jacques de Guibert turned up in Potsdam in 1773. Twenty-nine years old, he had just published *Essai de Tactique Générale* and had been recommended to the king by d'Alembert. Guibert was also struck by Potsdam, its straight and wide streets bordered by new houses with Italianate façades, but most of all by a civil population of only six thousand compared with a garrison of twelve thousand! Guibert did not know what to expect from an audience with the king, but he had heard rumblings of dissatisfaction. Quintus Icilius, who would die two years later, was highly critical of the king's military record in the Seven Years' War and was collecting material for a book on the subject; the Abbé Bastiani, sometimes the king's reader, was bitter and disillusioned. "The king," he said, "has never known friendship and he is incapable of feeling it." Guibert should have seen a cross old man in a snuff-stained uniform surrounded by spoiled whippets. He saw no such thing. "A kind of magical vapor," he wrote, "seemed to me to surround his person."[3]

The following year a British officer, Field Marshal Henry Conway, nephew of Sir Robert Walpole, was introduced by Lord Marshal Keith. Conway had fought well under Prince Ferdinand of Brunswick in the Seven Years' War. He arrived when the king was attending a private concert, "but the moment he was told I was there," Conway wrote to his brother, "he came out from his company, and gave me a most flattering gracious audience of more than half an hour; talking on a great variety of things, with an ease and freedom the very reverse of what I had been made to expect. . . . I asked and received permission to visit the Silesian Camps next month." Conway was invited to watch the Potsdam Guards drill: "I could have conceived nothing so perfect and so exact as all I saw." He was shown Sans-Souci: "On a table in his Cabinet there, I saw, I believe, twenty boxes with a German flute in each; in his Bed-Chamber, twice as many boxes of Spanish snuff; and, alike in Cabinet and in Bed-Chamber, three arm-chairs in a row for three favorite dogs, each with a little stool by way of step, that the getting up might be easy."[4]

Conway saw the king at maneuvers in Silesia six weeks later. The king's headquarters were in a clay hovel of a house "in the middle of a miserable Village. I saw all the Troops pass him as they arrived in Camp. They made a very fine appearance really, though it rained hard the whole time we were out; and as his Majesty did not cloak, we were all heartily wet."[5]

A visitor to Berlin in spring of 1775 later wrote of "soldiers parading, and officers hurrying backwards and forwards. The town looked more like the cantonment of a great army, than the capital of a kingdom in time of profound peace." The words came from John Moore, a forty-six-year-old surgeon and military veteran from Edinburgh who was escorting the Scottish Duke of Hamilton, nineteen years old, on a European tour. "The court itself resembled the levee of a general in the field," Moore continued, "except the foreign ministers, and a few strangers, every man there (for there were no women) was dressed in a military uniform." The newcomers were presented to King Frederick by the court chamberlain. He received them graciously: "His countenance and manner are exceedingly animated. He seemed that day in very high spirits, and spoke to all his officers in an easy style, and with a kind of gay affability. On their part, they appear before their master with an erect military boldness, free from that cringing address which prevails in many courts, but would not succeed here."[6]

For the next three mornings they watched the king inspect four to five thousand troops a day in the park, "and it is incredible with what accuracy and minute attention he did examine them." There followed three days of maneuvers with some thirty-six thousand troops. These culminated in the attack of a village defended by eight thousand men: "The right wing of the army made the attack . . . all the drums and fifes struck up at once. The soldiers advanced with a rapid pace. A numerous train of large fieldpieces, placed at proper intervals, advanced with equal velocity, and kept in a line with the front rank. The rapidity with which they were charged and discharged, as they advanced, was astonishing." The attack was repulsed and fighting retreat ensued: "It is hardly possible for any words of mine to convey an adequate idea of the perfect manner in which these evolutions were executed."[7]

The evening after the reviews the visitors were invited to Prince Henry's palace, "one of the most magnificent buildings in Berlin. No subject of the king of Prussia lives in a more sumptuous manner than this prince, who keeps a numerous establishment of servants, mostly handsome young men, very richly dressed."[8]

The Prussian discipline on a general review is beautiful [Moore wrote], in detail it is shocking. . . . In the park at Berlin, every morning may be seen the lieutenants of the different regiments exercising, with the greatest assiduity, sometimes a single man, at other times three or four together. . . . If the young recruit shows neglect or remissness, his attention is roused by the officer's cane, which is applied with augmenting energy, till he has acquired the full command of his firelock. He is taught steadiness under arms, and the immobility of a statue; he is informed, that all his members are to move only at the word of command, and not at his own pleasure: that speaking, coughing, sneezing, are all unpardonable crimes; and when the poor lad is accomplished to their mind, they give him to understand, that now it is perfectly known what he can do, and therefore the smallest deficiency will be punished with rigour. And although he should destine every moment of his time, and all his attention, to cleaning his arms, taking care of his clothes, and practising the manual exercise, it is but barely possible for him to escape punishment; and if his captain happens to be of a capricious or cruel disposition, the ill-fated soldier loses the poor chance of that possibility.

"We never cease to recollect that we are in a country where, from the sovereign to the peasant, every man is born a soldier," Nathaniel Wraxall, another English visitor to Berlin, wrote two years later. Wraxall attended Sunday service in the garrison church.

> Nothing in ancient Rome, or Sparta, could have been more ably and artfully calculated to mix the love of glory with the rites of religious worship. Nothing can be more calculated to raise the Prussian soldier in his own estimation, above those of other European States. No relics, saints, or shrines are there to be found: the music, ornaments, and decorations are all military, and all appropriate. Trophies and ensigns, gained in battle, float from the roof in every part of the edifice. They remind the veteran of his past exploits, and carry him, in the midst of devotion, to the scene of his valour at Rossbach, at Lissa [Leuthen], or at Torgau. They soften the anguish of his wounds, awaken the most grateful recollections in his bosom, and render him a participator in the name of his Sovereign. The four heroes of the Prussian monarchy who fell in battle, Schwerin, Keith, Winterfeldt, and Kleist, are elevated on four pedestals, surmounted with emblems of war and victory.[9]

John Moore described Berlin as "certainly one of the most beautiful cities in Europe." Long, wide streets were backed by white stone houses one or two stories high (with soldiers quartered in the lower floor). The royal palace, Prince Henry's palace, and the arsenal (built in the form of a square and said to contain arms for 200,000 men) were the most elegant buildings. The opera house was much lauded, as was the new Roman Catholic church, as much for religious tolerance as for elegance.*

Every evening large numbers of people walked along Unter den Linden, buying ices and lemonade from vendors, listening to regimental bands. Prostitutes "are more numerous here than in any town in Europe . . ." Moore noted. "They appear openly at the windows in the daytime, beckon to passengers as they walk in the streets, and ply for employment in any way they please. . . . Nobody is allowed to molest or abuse [them] . . . and as little attention is paid to customers, who frequent the chambers of these ladies, as if they stept into any other house or shop, to purchase any other commodity." Moore also hinted at a prevalence of homosexuality without offering details "on that nauseous subject."

Moore found Berlin society unostentatious and rather dull. He en-

---

* The papacy also praised Frederick for allowing this church to be built. But he refused to publish the papal edict of 1773 that abolished the Jesuit order, not only because he was committed to religious freedom, as he wrote to Voltaire, but because he needed the Jesuits as teachers in Silesia.

King Frederick reviewing his troops. "We never cease to recollect that we are in a country where from the sovereign to the peasant, every man is born a soldier," wrote a visitor to Berlin in 1777. "Nothing in ancient Rome, or Sparta, could have been more ably and artfully calculated to mix the love of glory with the rites of religious worship."

King Frederick the Great of Prussia, 1712–1786.

joyed a day at Prince Ferdinand of Prussia's villa outside Berlin and suppers with Prince Frederick of Brunswick and his very pretty wife. Frederica Louise, the Princess of Prussia, gave a breakfast in the garden for a large company; there was dancing all morning: "I saw none of that state and ceremony of which the Germans are accused. Those of the highest rank behaved with the greatest ease and affability to every person present, and joined in the country dances, without observing any form or etiquette." Finckenstein and other officials gave dinners and balls, but "the chief and permanent society is to be found at the houses of the foreign ministers who reside here." Queen Elizabeth had a "public day" twice a week at Monbijou and once a week at Schön-hausen, where she moved for the summer: "The princes, the nobility, the foreign ministers, and strangers, generally attend on these occasions at five in the evening. After her majesty has walked round the circle, and spoke a few words to every one, she sits down to cards."

The king, Moore noticed, very seldom appeared at the queen's court or at any place where women formed part of the assembly. "I once said to a lady of this court, that it was a pity his majesty did not love women. Considering his time of life, said she, we could dispense with his love, but it is hard that he cannot endure us." Berlin morals were extremely loose, Moore discovered, with husbands and wives openly going separate ways and divorcing with very little trouble or expense, providing there were no children. Speech was frank and open, government and king freely criticized:

> I have heard political topics, and others which I should have thought still more ticklish, discussed here with as little ceremony as at a London coffeehouse. The same freedom appears in the booksellers' shops, where literary productions of all kinds are sold openly. The pamphlet lately published on the division of Poland, wherein the king is very roughly treated, is to be had without difficulty, as well as other performances, which attack some of the most conspicuous characters with all the bitterness of satire.

Moore was surprised in Potsdam "to see buff-belts, breeches, and waistcoats hanging to dry from the genteelest-looking houses," until he learned that each house was forced to quarter at least two soldiers. The old palace struck him as "a very noble building, with magnificent gardens adjacent." The finest apartment was the study, with exquisite silver décor and library. He was shown the king's wardrobe: "two blue coats, faced with red, the lining of one a little torn; two yellow waistcoats, a good deal soiled with Spanish snuff; three pair of yellow breeches, and a suit of blue velvet, embroidered with silver, for grand occasions." These, along with two uniforms kept at Sans-Souci, constituted the entire royal wardrobe!

Sans-Souci struck Moore as "a very noble and splendid work" though "the gilding [inside and out] is laid on with a very lavish hand." When by himself, the king lived very simply; there were no more than a dozen people, including staff, in the palace. There was no military guard, only an orderly who returned to Potsdam every evening.

At this time the king was entertaining some visiting nobility. French actors, including the celebrated Henri Lekain, and Italian singers provided the main entertainment given in the small playhouse of Sans-Souci, where there were neither boxes nor a pit but a series of semicircular benches ascending from the stage. Moore and his young ward attended some of the performances. "The king generally seats himself in the third or fourth [row]. The piece then begins, and is usually finished about nine, after which all the company return to the large apartment, where the king remains conversing in a familiar manner till supper is ready. He . . . goes to bed at ten." There were no comedies, both because Lekain refused to perform them and because the king preferred tragedies. An opera was performed every other night; the king displayed "in his countenance that extreme sensibility to music, which forms part of his character."

Moore shared several conversations with the king and the Duke of Hamilton, and he carefully observed him during the theatricals. He even watched him drilling a battalion, mounted with sword drawn:

> He made them wheel, march, form a square, and fire by divisions, and in platoons, observing all their motions with infinite attention; and, on account of some blunder, put two officers of the Prince of Prussia's regiment in arrest. In short, he seemed to exert himself with all the spirit of a young officer, eager to attract the notice of his general by uncommon alertness.

Frederick was sixty-three years old,

> below the middle size, well made, and remarkably active for his time of life. . . . His look announces spirit and penetration. He has fine blue eyes . . . his countenance upon the whole is agreeable. . . . His features acquire a wonderful degree of animation while he converses. . . . He stoops considerably, and inclines his head almost constantly to one side. His tone of voice is the clearest and most agreeable in conversation I ever heard. He speaks a great deal; yet those who hear him, regret that he does not speak a great deal more. His observations are always lively, very often just, and few men possess the talent of repartee in greater perfection. . . . He uses a very large gold snuff-box, the lid ornamented with diamonds, and takes an immoderate quantity of Spanish snuff, the marks of which very often appear on his waistcoat and breeches. These are also liable to be soiled by the paws of two or three Italian greyhounds, which he often caresses.

The king continued to astonish his observant visitor.

> He reconciles qualities which I used to think incompatible. I once was of opinion that the mind which stoops to very small objects is incapable of

embracing great ones; I am now convinced that he is an exception; for while few objects are too great for his genius, none seem too small for his attention. . . . Other monarchs acquire importance from their station; this prince gives importance to his. The traveller in other countries has a wish to see the king, because he admires his kingdom: here the object of curiosity is reversed: and let us suppose the palaces, and the towns, and the country, and the army of Prussia ever so fine, yet your chief interest in them will arise from their belonging to Frederick II, the man who, without an ally but Britain, repelled the united force of Austria, France, Russia, and Sweden. Count Nesselrode, talking with me on this subject, had an expression equally lively and just: "It is in adversity that he shines; when he is really down he has an irresistible buoyancy."

103

THE MILITARY ACTIVITY that interested Colonel Guibert, Marshal Conway, Dr. Moore, and other visitors and envoys was steadily assuming a greater importance in Frederick's mind. While John Moore was jotting careful observations in a notebook, Frederick was writing to Prince Henry: "The emperor will go so far as to force every prince who loves German independence and freedom to unite against him. One can foresee that he is preparing for a cruel war, that perhaps will be as bitter as the last. If the Elector of Bavaria dies before I do, if the bugle sounds, we must again mount our horses."

Shortly after returning from Silesia in autumn of 1775, the king came down with a particularly vicious attack of gout. "I write so badly because I have gout in the right hand," he informed Voltaire in late September. A month later: "Gout has bound and tied me for four weeks. . . . Understand that I have had it in both knees, both hands, and, as an additional favor, in the elbow. The fever and pains have presently ceased and I suffer no more than a great exhaustion of strength." He suffered attack after attack that autumn and winter — in December he complained of his fourteenth attack. His nerves were shattered; he was bedridden and suffering from fever and hemorrhoids. So intense was his illness that the Austrian envoy in Berlin reported it as dropsy, implying that the king would die, a prognosis in which the British envoy concurred.

The news delighted Emperor Joseph, who ordered regiments to assemble in Bohemia, presumably to offer Frederick's successor a choice of being invaded or of returning Silesia to Austrian rule. Austrian regiments were still on the march when the king's partial recovery shattered this plan, leaving Joseph looking rather silly. Early in the new year Frederick replied to a concerned Henry:

What you have heard concerning the Austrians has some truth. . . . They believe that my end is near and are reinforcing their troops in Bohemia in order to seize Saxony and invade us. This will certainly happen if I die, and my big idiot of a nephew will be in trouble if he does not exert himself and act vigorously. But nothing can overcome his natural indolence and I must leave the care of the future to your prudence.

The king was still very ill when he invited Henry to Potsdam in February: "I shall not die calmly as regards state interests until you are in some way its guardian. I consider you as the only person who can maintain the glory of our House and become in every way the pillar of our country." No record exists of the meeting, which could not have solved very much in any case; Frederick William, the Prince of Prussia, on accession could rule as he wished. The king's subsequent and highly dubious policy, as explained in various letters, was to keep Henry informed of everything and the Prince of Prussia of nothing so as to make Henry an indispensable adviser in case of Frederick's death.

Henry's star was about to rise higher. Czarina Catherine invited him to pay a second visit to Saint Petersburg. He had remained in warm correspondence with her and, with the king's support, had been instrumental in arranging for the marriage of Princess Wilhelmina of Hesse-Darmstadt to Grand Duke Paul, her son and heir. Only two weeks after Henry's arrival in Saint Petersburg in spring of 1776, Princess Natalia (as she had become) died in childbirth. Frederick arranged for a new bride, his grandniece Princess Sophia Dorothea of Württemberg, and Henry scored a tremendous diplomatic coup by bringing Paul to Berlin for the betrothal ceremony.

The king had not been so happy and excited in years. Nothing could be a greater blow to Austrian and French diplomacy than this. "Everything that we have of magnificence will be used," he wrote to Henry. General Lentulus with a guard of honor plus servants, chefs, and pages would meet the party in East Prussia. Cavalry would turn out in Königsberg, and cannon would salute Paul along the way. Despite another severe illness, the king personally planned the reception. Balls, fêtes, illuminations, military exhibitions, operas, theater — he was like a bride expecting the boss to dinner. What would be the most suitable apartments for the grand duke? How many footmen and valets would he require? Were eight horses sufficient for his carriage? Would twenty courses per meal suffice or should there be forty?

"The commotion this unexpected visit makes in this place is beyond all description," James Harris reported, "the King himself having set an example of magnificence not heard of in this country since Frederick I's time."[1]

Paul arrived in late July. "Nothing can exceed the attention and even court His Prussian Majesty pays to the Grand Duke," Harris wrote, "nor the pains he takes to captivate and please him, in which I am convinced he has succeeded so well as to be able to make him subscribe implicitly to whatever he chooses."[2] The king and the grand duke got on extremely well, Paul approved of Sophia Dorothea, the marriage was agreed to, and Paul returned to Russia. Frederick was delighted with the outcome of Henry's mission; the czarina's confidence in him was "the surest guarantee of the union of the Russians and the Prussians."

Nevertheless the unsettled political situation continued to worry him. In September he informed Henry: "The Austrians are determined to embroil us with Russia so that with my death they can fall more heavily on our tall nincompoop [the Prince of Prussia]. Good God, what will come of all this if the good Lord does not preserve your life and health!"

In the event, the King of Prussia was very much alive when Emperor Joseph began the War of the Bavarian Succession.

Emperor Joseph for some time had shown an unhealthful interest in Bavaria. A large, rich, and beautiful country, it was governed by a weak and greedy elector, Max Joseph, who had inherited it from his father, the luckless Emperor Charles VII.

Max Joseph had made a number of important reforms. He had adopted a new civil and criminal code in imitation of Prussia, he had established an academy of sciences, and had decreed compulsory education. Unfortunately these enlightened moves carried more glitter than substance. He did almost nothing to curb the power of the Catholic Church, and he did little to lessen the general misery of his peoples. At the same time he presided over a luxurious court in which "music and debauchery," the British envoy reported, "stood on a par with the rest of Europe."[3] Nymphenburg, the summer palace, was "a miniature Versailles, a world of Watteau and Dresden china," wrote a modern historian. "In Munich the scene was equally bright, and there was the additional joy of a French opera and of card-parties at which huge sums could be lost."[4] Max Joseph's father had left an enormous number of bastards, each of whom received a crown pension. "Father Max," as he was known, contributed more recipients; Temperley estimated an annual expenditure of 200,000 florins on pensions alone.

The revenues needed to support these heavy expenditures did not exist, and the court suffered chronic financial difficulty. In trying to make ends meet, the elector cut military expenses to the bone. At a time when Bavaria was surrounded by potential enemies, the British envoy reported that the Bavarian army, only about five thousand strong, was "upon the worst footing of any I have seen in Germany."[5]

Internal weakness, coupled with the elector's failure to produce a legitimate heir, made the country a natural target in case of the elector's death. In 1764 Joseph married the elector's sister, Josepha; the union marked the beginning of a strong Austrian influence. The Vienna court continued to pour funds into the country and spent large sums in bribes to form a pro-Austrian party of Bavarian nobility. When Joseph paid an incognito visit to Munich in 1777, he undoubtedly envisaged Bavaria as a future Austrian province, and it is probable that his court legalists were already preparing a justification to his dynastic claims as Holy Roman Emperor and legitimate heir through marriage. (Josepha died the same year.)

To the emperor's distaste, others shared these claims. The foremost was the Elector Palatine, Charles Theodor, who was Max Joseph's closest relative. The two electors had signed a secret family compact in 1766 that would unite the electorates on the death of either of them, and this was several times confirmed in subsequent years. In 1777 Charles Theodor pledged himself to an additional pact with his nephew and heir, Duke Charles of Pfalz-Zweibrücken, to ensure an orderly succession. But Zweibrücken learned that Charles was secretly negotiating with the Austrians, a fact duly reported to Max Joseph, who was attempting to take countermeasures when he suddenly died in December 1777.

Charles Theodor inherited Bavaria under the terms of the elector's will. But he had secretly agreed to give Emperor Joseph more than a third of his legacy in return for large subsidies so that he could leave pensions to *his* numerous bastards. A partition treaty, soon signed and ratified, stipulated that Charles yield almost all of Lower Bavaria and Straubing, the richest and most fertile part of Bavaria, which made Joseph virtual military, political, and economic overlord of Bavaria.

Before diplomats in Vienna learned of these harsh details, Austrian troops had occupied Straubing, from where they threatened both Regensburg and Munich as well as the Upper Palatinate. A hurriedly issued manifesto explained that they would remain only "until an amicable settlement could be adjusted."

By such precipitate action Joseph (the admiring student of Frederician politics) had clearly won the first round. Even Maria Theresa, who did not wish to upset the fragile peace of Europe, was impressed. Joseph in late January informed his brother, Grand Duke Leopold of Tuscany, in words familiar to Frederick's of nearly four decades earlier, "Our decision was a good one, and will bring as much solid advantage to us as honor and renown." He did not believe that France could interfere, since she was close to war with England. The King of Prussia, finding no allies to support him, would not dare intervene. "So, unless I am mistaken," Joseph concluded, "this matter, to everyone's astonishment, will be settled very peacefully." [6]

The Austrian bugle sounded when the Prussian king was struck by another attack of gout. In mid-January the new British envoy in Berlin, young Hugh Elliot, reported the king "in high spirits, almost unnaturally so," and suggested that a medicine of wine and spice might be the cause. In early February he reported improvement in Frederick's health and concluded that he intended "to take the field in the spring" — whether to attack Austria or "to seize on neighboring territory as an equivalent," he could not say.[7]

Elliot had correctly divined the situation in part: Frederick intended to take *some* action. Several factors would determine its nature, the most important being the attitude of the great powers and of the German princes.

Frederick's single great power ally, Russia, could not be counted on for more than passive support, because she was skirmishing with Turkey. Catherine, however, would lend moral support; she feared Joseph's ambitions just as Frederick and other rulers feared hers.

The attitude of France was of utmost importance in light of her long alliance with the Vienna court. But France was in no position to uphold Austrian pretensions in Bavaria. She was heavily in debt; her subjects had no desire to support another disastrous war in Germany. Her first interest was the North American rebellion, through which she might gain desired vengeance against England. Her Austrian ally, moreover, had grown much too formidable and was taking too much for granted. Not only did the French foreign minister, the Count de Vergennes, declare that he would *not* support Austrian pretensions to Bavaria; he opened negotiations with Frederick and agreed on a future friendly relationship, though declining any sort of alliance. In short, France would observe "a strict and inflexible neutrality."

England was also of special concern to Frederick at this critical time. Unlike France, she was ill equipped to intervene militarily in Europe. Her small army had enough on its hands in North America, where General "Gentleman Johnny" Burgoyne would shortly suffer a devastating defeat. But Frederick still did not want Vienna strengthened by an alliance that undoubtedly would entail a cash subsidy, nor did he want to be in an awkward situation in relation to Hanover.

Up to this time he had made little secret of his contempt for England, and he had allowed a North American agent, Arthur Lee, to reside in Berlin while trying, unsuccessfully, to negotiate a treaty of commerce on behalf of the rebellious colonies. Although he would remain neutral until it was clear who would win, he had for some time treated the current British envoy, Hugh Elliot, with studied rudeness. He became very angry when Elliot broke into Lee's lodgings and stole confidential papers, and allowed him to stay at his post only because he thought that the operation had failed. "The worthy student of Bute . . . this goddamned Elliot," he wrote to his envoy in London. "In truth the English should blush with shame at sending such ministers to foreign courts." He sharply refused to allow German princes to march auxiliary troops across his dominions to fight for England in the New World.

He agreed to recognize American independence once France had done so, and he allowed Arthur Lee to buy eight hundred muskets, which turned out to be old and useless.

Emperor Joseph's aggression sharply changed Frederick's attitude. When Elliot requested permission to leave Berlin owing to the king's coldness, Frederick sent an emissary to dissuade him. He even promised that he would no longer aid the American rebels and that he would respect Hanover's neutrality if war broke out in Germany. These were not serious concessions, and if they kept England from alliance with Austria, they would be more than worthwhile.

Frederick also approached the German rulers with considerable dexterity. He sent a special emissary to the Duke of Zweibrücken, who, assured of Prussian support, refused to accept the partition treaty and presented the issue to the Imperial Diet at Regensburg. In early March the Prussian king bluntly contested Austrian grounds for the partition of Bavaria in a letter to Count von Kaunitz and in mid-March informed the Diet of his deed, warning that if the Austrian action were not checked, "there can be no security for the weaker members of the Empire whose territories may unfortunately be situated in the neighborhood of powerful Princes, and the Constitution of the Empire will only exist in the Records of the Diet."

The words hit home in several places. In mid-March, Saxony and Prussia signed a formal alliance that committed the elector's thirty-thousand-man army, the third largest in Germany, to the Prussian cause. The king's stand was approved by other Protestant and Catholic states, although the latter were frightened and did not openly declare themselves.

The diplomatic war continued into spring of 1778. While Prussian and Austrian scribes showered European courts with reams of broadsheets, each proclaiming the justness of the respective cause, the rulers mobilized forces in earnest. In mid-April Frederick was in headquarters at Schönwalde in Silesia, his armies assembling there and in Brandenburg. Joseph was in headquarters at Olmütz, one army assembling in the north facing the Silesian border, the other in the west facing the Saxon border.

Neither opponent seemed to want war, yet neither seemed willing to avoid it. Joseph offered several concessions, none very worthwhile. Frederick later wrote that Joseph was negotiating only to gain time to strengthen his border defenses, but that he went along in order to appease France and Russia. In late June, however, he lost patience and sent the emperor an ultimatum: Joseph's refusal to return Bavarian lands to the Elector Palatine would mean war.

When no answer arrived from Vienna, Frederick broke off negotiations. The Prussians marched in early July.

I 0 4

FREDERICK'S operational plan was relatively simple. Leaving twenty thousand men to defend the Glatz area, he would march with sixty thousand into Moravia and attack and defeat the enemy covering Olmütz. He would then send a strong detachment southeast toward Pressburg to cut Austrian communications with Hungary and threaten Vienna. Henry meanwhile would have attacked Loudon's army, some seventy thousand men concentrated northeast of Leitmeritz along the Saxon border. Joseph would have to weaken his armies in order to defend Vienna, thus opening Prague and southern Bohemia to Henry's force.

This aggressive plan, fully in keeping with Frederick's character, never got off the ground. Although Joseph did not know the king's precise intentions, he apparently smelled a rat. Shortly before Frederick marched, the Austrian emperor left a detachment to cover Olmütz while concentrating his main army, 128,000 strong, in northeastern Bohemia to set up a tactical swinging door. If Frederick moved into Moravia, Joseph could easily push through the Glatz defenses to bring the war into Silesia. Just as dangerous, he could ignore Silesia and strike into Saxony before Prince Henry's army of eighty thousand had joined with the Saxon army, an attack that the Saxon elector feared — and one that would have removed him from the war.

Frederick was thus forced to march, not into Moravia, but into Bohemia through the traditional Nachod Pass. By applying pressure to Joseph's main army, Frederick now reasoned, he would prevent him from reinforcing Loudon, thus clearing the way for Henry's advance.

Frederick's vanguard reached the Nachod area within a day and spilled to the northwest toward Arnau. He personally reconnoitered the enemy position, a line stretching along the Elbe from Königgrätz to Jaromirz, where it turned sharply northwest to terminate in the mountains beyond Arnau. Königgrätz, he discovered, was so well fortified that it could sustain a lengthy siege. Defenses northeast of Königgrätz resembled "a fortified city rather than field entrenchments." A corps about thirty thousand strong northwest of Jaromirz was "covered by ditches eight feet deep, sixteen feet wide, embellished with fraises and palisades, and . . . surrounded by log barricades which linked the separate works together." [1] Triple redoubts defended all the Elbe passages and they were bolstered by a thousand cannon and three hundred mines. Surveying all this through a spyglass, the king asked his nephew Prince Charles of Brunswick whether he thought it was possible to attack. It was possible, the prince replied, "and we shall win a victory, but most of the army will be done for." [2]

Forced to abandon direct attack, the king investigated the possibility that he might "win by cunning what can't be taken by force." But this came to naught when he discovered more strong defenses on the enemy left. Nothing remained but to assume the defensive, a line running from Nachod northwest to Arnau. His situation was frustrating in the extreme, and reports that reached Berlin of his terrible temper were probably not exaggerated.

Had Loudon's voice carried in Austrian war councils, Frederick would have been attacked. Aware that Prince Henry could not reach his area for ten days, Loudon proposed a daring plan to the emperor. Let him split his force, march with forty thousand men to Arnau, join the thirteen thousand there, and attack the Prussian right while Marshal Lacy struck center and left with over seventy thousand men. This would eliminate one army before the other got within striking distance. Neither Joseph nor Lacy could accept the plan, any more than Field Marshal Daun could have done in his day. As a result, Frederick escaped what could only have been tactical embarrassment and might well have led to serious strategic defeat.

Maria Theresa had still another plan. Anguished by having three sons in the field, she went behind the emperor's back to appeal directly to Frederick ("that wicked man") to end the war.* Frederick replied that he was ready to negotiate. Joseph learned of the effort, flew into a rage, and had to be persuaded to retain supreme command.

Prince Henry fared considerably better. After marching from Dresden, he disguised his intentions by feinting in several directions. He then crossed the Elbe above Pirna, which reinforced Loudon's belief that he would march down both sides of the Elbe. Instead, screened by forest, he marched over narrow, muddy roads, pushed back Loudon's surprised outposts, and was safely in Bohemia at a cost of four dead and a dozen wounded.[3]

Loudon had been fooled, and now he paid. Abandoning the Aussig defense, he yielded the whole line of the Elbe, a rash, impulsive, and probably frightened move that meant the sacrifice of Leitmeritz and its magazines and put him behind the Iser River. While Henry's main army moved cautiously south, General Platen shadowed Loudon's retreat, occupied Leitmeritz, and moved on toward Budin, his advance guard

---

* Nathaniel Wraxall wrote from Vienna on March 19, 1778, "It is no longer a secret that she [Maria Theresa] deprecates a rupture, and is reluctantly dragged forward by her son. . . . Those who have access to her witness the dejection of her spirits, and the agitation of her mind on the arrival of every courier; they see her eyes perpetually red with weeping, or suffused in tears. . . . She averts her eyes from every display of her military strength. . . . She passes half her time in prayer; and yesterday she remained for three hours on her knees, in the cathedral, invoking the divine blessing to aid her efforts for maintaining the peace of Germany." (Wraxall, *Memoirs*.)

pushing to less than fifteen miles from Prague, a move that caused the nobility there to evacuate the city in large numbers.

Loudon wrote to Joseph that he could not adequately defend the fifty-five-mile line of the Iser with seventy thousand troops when the enemy outnumbered him: he had to be reinforced or he would ask to be relieved of command. Joseph sent him eight battalions and ordered him to hold the Iser at all costs. A few days later when the emperor visited Loudon, he "found him in great dejection, and came back criticizing both general and army."[4]

The king wanted Henry to push across the Iser. Loudon's retreat would cause Joseph to fall back, thereby solving the Prussian army's supply problem. Henry would have no part of it. He was on the defensive, content to leave Loudon alone. He saw his own position as critical, with only ten to twelve days' supply of bread on hand. Retreat could easily become necessary, he insisted. "Once we lose the roads leading to Lusatia, retreat is impossible," he wrote to Frederick in mid-August. "One does not pass through this neighborhood twice unpunished."[5]

Frederick now decided to cross the Elbe, join Henry, and strike Lacy in flank and rear. This time he chose the lightly defended Hohenelbe area. But the terrain proved almost impassable. By the time cursing troops had manhandled heavy artillery over narrow twisting trails that had to be widened — backbreaking work that moved the guns only four miles a day — Lacy had learned of the move and reinforced the area, thus continuing the stalemate.

Neither Frederick nor Henry could deal with static warfare. The quartermaster corps functioned no more brilliantly than it had in the past. Food was scarce. "The potato war," the troops called it in reference to the main item of food. Despite augmented rations, illness and desertion had been plaguing Henry for some time. No fewer than six of his senior generals had given way to age and infirmity. Henry had lost perhaps ten thousand troops by early September when he notified the king that, owing to lack of forage and a growing sicklist, he could not hold his position longer than mid-September. His withdrawal was a disaster. "Our horses, our wagons, are broken and ruined," he told the king on September 13.[6] He was out of bread. By the end of the month he had lost two thousand more men through desertion; three thousand horses were dead.

Plagued by shortage of supplies and an epidemic of dysentery from which no one escaped, Frederick ordered a slow withdrawal, scorching the earth to prevent Austrian armies from camping on Silesian and Saxon borders during the winter. Henry and the Saxons withdrew to Saxony and Lusatia. Frederick's army moved slowly northeast, eating everything in sight; in mid-November he put the dispirited army in winter quarters and transferred his headquarters to Breslau. The campaign had cost perhaps twenty thousand troops, most of them victims of disease.

It also brought a serious turnabout in the king's relations with Henry, who had been against the war from the beginning, his argument being that Prussia could have gained territory by making a deal with Joseph over Bavaria just as a deal had been made over Poland. Frederick had refused to accept this on the grounds that Joseph had violated the laws of the Empire and could not go unpunished. "It is not a matter of acquisition or aggrandizement," Frederick wrote to Henry in February 1778, "but to check in good time the Austrian ambition so that its authority does not become despotic in the Empire, which would be to our greatest detriment." Henry's continued doubts plainly annoyed the king, who had finally told him to stay home if he wanted to. After Henry's successful opening of the campaign, he angered the king by refusing to march over the Iser. Nor did Frederick fail to criticize him for heavy losses of men, horses, and wagons during the withdrawal. Henry's resentment grew to the extent that in December he pleaded ill health and asked to resign his command. Frederick persuaded him to remain until the Prince of Brunswick could replace him, and he was still in command of the Saxon army when the war ended.

The end of the war did not end the quarrel. Henry criticized the peace terms and attempted to intervene in further negotiations. This spelled the end of royal favor for several years. His fall left him dangerously embittered. He wrote to Melchior Grimm that he had had so much experience of injustice in thirty-nine years "that he should have learned to bear it without indignation, but had not. Never again would he draw his sword for such a king."[7] He would not be asked to. Although time repaired relations enough so that there was a renewal of correspondence and an occasional meeting, the rupture was never completely healed. Henry's resentment, one modern biographer wrote, was "an obsession of the ugliest and most hateful sort. . . . He thrust it upon strangers and shocked and offended distinguished foreigners by parading it before them. He nourished it and cherished it, and let it twine itself about him until it choked out of his life the happiness he might otherwise have known."[8]

The inconclusive campaign seemed on the surface to favor Austrian arms more than Prussian. Austrian diplomacy also seemed superior. In late September the Vienna court had presented its case to the Imperial Diet at Regensburg: Vienna would restore Bavaria to the Elector Palatine if the Prussian king would renounce claims to the Ansbach-Bayreuth succession.

Vienna realized that the two issues were not related, but Frederick's linking them made him seem to minor princes the real stumbling block to peace. Probably the work of Count Kaunitz, the proposal was seen by the Vienna court as "a master stroke in politics." The British envoy in Vienna, Sir Robert Keith, informed Whitehall at end of September, "After having announced himself as the Protector and Defender of the Germanic system, [Frederick] may (over and above the expenses he has incurred) find himself reproached, deserted, perhaps attacked even by his friends, as the grand enemy and disturber of the Publick Tranquillity." [9]

Frederick did not take this lying down. More than other major rulers he had fitted Russia into the European scheme of things since the Seven Years' War. At the outbreak of the present war, he had invoked his alliance with Catherine, who, pointing to the Prussian invasion of Bohemia, had refused to send either troops or money. However, suspicious and frightened of Joseph's growing ambitions, she did express sympathy for the Prussian king's stand. Frederick recognized that her reticence was caused primarily by fear of another war with Turkey and cunningly charged Versailles with mediating the Russian-Turkish quarrel. Meanwhile he played on his allies at Saint Petersburg, notably the heir apparent, Grand Duke Paul, and Count Panin, who was in Prussian pay. Catherine would not at first yield, but when French mediation brought a Russian-Turkish agreement, her attitude began to change. Prodded by Prince Gregor Potemkin, she began to see herself as the peacemaker of Europe.

The dénouement to this diplomatic drama came in November. Russian envoys in Vienna and Regensburg announced that if Austria did not satisfactorily settle the present difficulty, the czarina would honor her treaty with Prussia and send "a body of auxiliary troops." She named Prince Repnin commander of this corps, whose first contingent, some fifteen thousand troops, ominously marched close to the Austrian border.

Catherine's bellicosity reversed the situation to Frederick's advantage. Fearing a larger war, Maria Theresa overrode vehement objections from Joseph and Kaunitz to request mediation by France *and* Russia. Frederick agreed to accept mediation by France and informed Catherine that he would welcome her mediation. She quickly accepted, having agreed with Count Panin's dictum that "Germany, as much by its position as by its power, is the center of all the affairs and all the interests of Europe." It followed that any fundamental change in the German constitution affected all European nations. She emphasized this in formal instructions to Prince Repnin, and enjoined him to support Frederick in maintaining the rights and liberties of the German kingdom:

In this way we shall have the honor, in the eyes of all Germany, of having produced the necessary dénouement, and perhaps even of having united many princes in one system. This result will produce for Russia the advantage it has so long desired, of being named Guarantor for the future of the Germanic Constitution, a position to which France owes its preponderant influence in affairs.[10]

Count Panin added a realistic footnote to the czarina's instructions by authorizing Prince Repnin to compensate Austria if that court would confirm the Prussian claim to Ansbach and Bayreuth.

King Frederick did not take kindly to Nicholas Repnin, who arrived in Breslau, he later wrote, more as a minister "who came to dictate the laws of Germany on behalf of his court" than as commander of a small auxiliary corps. The exorbitant price demanded for the auxiliaries also displeased the king: "On the one hand the weakness of the Versailles ministry, and on the other the ignorance of that of Petersburg, put the king in great embarrassment and increased his anxieties."[11] The Vienna court objected to peace preliminaries presented by the French and Russian envoys as being biased in Prussia's favor. Joseph exorcised his fury by extensive military skirmishing in February. "Never did there exist so strange a mixture of warfare and negotiation," Keith reported to London.[12] In the end Maria Theresa's pacific sentiments prevailed and the diplomats converged on Teschen for a formal peace conference.

Acrimony almost at once marred proceedings. Austria proved particularly obstructive but the Saxon elector and the Duke of Zweibrücken did not help matters by pushing extravagant and greedy land claims. Cacophany threatened to replace negotiation, and more than once Frederick feared that the congress would dissolve. Arguments and counterarguments filled the air for over two months before the great powers brought their lesser brethren in line.

Final settlement closely resembled preliminary terms. The Saxon elector received a piece of land and four million thalers in cash. Austria received a piece of land, the Innviertel, and recognition of some claims in Lusatia should the Saxon line become extinct. Frederick's rights to Ansbach and Bayreuth were upheld (and in 1791 Prussia gained these territories). Bavaria was guaranteed to the Elector Palatine and, on his death, to his nephew and heir, the Duke of Zweibrücken.

The Peace of Teschen, signed in mid-May, was guaranteed by France and Russia and eventually ratified by the Diet at Regensburg. Frederick himself, though he regarded the treaty more "as a truce than a lasting peace," was not dissatisfied. In early March he had written to Henry: "Although this restitution is not as complete as one would have liked, nevertheless it is the first unsuccessful project of the Emperor's unrestrained ambition, and we gain the great advantage that we shall be regarded in the Empire as a counterweight to Austrian despotism." The true importance of the war, as the historian George Gooch has assessed it, was that "Prussia was no longer a rebel, but a rival, the recognized champion of other German interests as well as of her own. Military glory there was none, but the political dividends were high."[13]

These dividends were evident not only in foreign chancelleries. Perhaps the most grateful of all were Bavarian peasants, who had escaped the Austrian yoke. For many years candles burned in huts beside the picture of Frederick the Great.

105

FREDERICK THE GREAT was sixty-seven years old when he returned from Breslau in May 1779. Although not entirely optimistic about the peace, he was pleased to have funded the war without touching the main treasury. Shortly after his return, he allocated eight hundred thousand thalers to agricultural and colonization projects and two million thalers to new buildings. By the end of June he had finished writing a history of his reign from 1774 to 1778. He wrote a history of the recent war and in the following year would publish a dissertation on German literature that, as a modern scholar has pointed out, blithely ignored the German enlightenment being brought to a peak by Goethe, Lessing, Moses, Mendelssohn, Herde, and others.[1] He unwisely involved himself in a complicated legal action, the famous Arnold Miller case, in which contrary to his written pledge he not only overrode court authority but dismissed and jailed several magistrates who upheld the law. Though frequently ill with gout, he continued to make inspections and hold reviews. But such was the dubious peace of Europe that these activities were secondary to his political interests.

Frederick was correct in regarding the Peace of Teschen as a truce, not a lasting peace. It would probably survive as long as Maria Theresa lived, and even after her death Joseph would be constrained to act against the Turks or in Italy as long as Prussia was allied with Russia and France.

Frederick's new and tentative alliance was not altogether realistic. Had it come to full fruition, it would have created a totally different power situation in Europe, one in which Austria would have occupied a perilous position until a new balance of power emerged.

This was a major hindrance to the forging of such an alliance. Another objection was a common interest shared by Russia and Austria. Each court desired the breakup of the Turkish empire, and it was perhaps inevitable that Czarina Catherine had begun moving toward rapprochement with Austria, which sooner or later would bring her into conflict with Prussia and France.

Frederick had tried to keep his alliance with Catherine in good repair. Since she was one of the vainest rulers of all time, flattery had helped. Shortly after the Peace of Teschen, he had written her that all Germany owed her the recently concluded peace: "some words from you have checked the entire ambition of Austria." Her friendship with Prince Henry also played a part, as did her son and heir, Grand Duke Paul, who worshipped the Prussian monarch, and Count Panin, who remained loyal to the Prussian alliance while attempting to neutralize Potemkin's increasing influence on the czarina. French diplomacy in Saint Petersburg favored matters, since the Versailles court wanted to keep Joseph quiet in the west while France struggled in its overseas war against England.

All this was not sufficiently strong to deter Catherine's grandiose territorial ambitions, which Potemkin encouraged. She was slowly moving toward a diplomacy that would isolate Prussia. Her key role in the settlement of the recent war had made her realize that Frederick needed her more than she needed him. She also knew that he would not readily accept Russian expansion at Turkey's expense. Her growing estrangement from Grand Duke Paul provided another worrisome clue, as did a sharp decline in her correspondence with Henry. In 1780 she signed the Armed Neutrality Act to join Sweden, Denmark, Austria, and Portugal in denying England the right to stop and search neutral ships believed to be carrying contraband cargo to the American colonies. Having thus courted France, she invited Emperor Joseph to visit her.

Joseph arrived at Mogilev on the Dnieper in the spring of 1780. In long talks there and at Saint Petersburg, the two rulers planned to attack and partition Turkey. Catherine agreed not to keep Constantinople and to maintain Dacia (Rumania) as a buffer state under an Orthodox ruler. Joseph agreed to aid Russia if she was attacked by Turkey. Less than a year later the two rulers signed a treaty that effectively freed the Russian hand in the east, the Austrian hand in the west. It also spelled the end of Russia's alliance with Prussia.

Frederick was wary of Joseph's visit but was not unduly alarmed. He tried to counter it by sending his own special envoy to the czarina. Henry might have succeeded, but his relations with Frederick were distant, and his correspondence with Catherine had almost ceased. Instead, Frederick sent his nephew and heir, Frederick William, the Prince of Prussia, who had come into favor during the recent war. Catherine found him singularly unattractive. "How different from his uncles," she told Melchior Grimm.[2] His friendly reception by Grand Duke Paul only worsened matters.

Despite this diplomatic failure, Frederick did not believe that Catherine would forsake their alliance. Neither Russia nor Austria was yet strong enough to take on the Turks, and he believed that Maria Theresa would continue to restrain Joseph's ambitions.

Maria Theresa's death, in November 1780, shattered this thought. It would now be a matter of time, the king realized, before he faced the threat of another powerful coalition. "Here, then, is a new order of things," he nervously wrote to Finckenstein.

The political situation did not immediately heat up. Although Catherine refused to renew her alliance with Prussia and was in warm correspondence with the Vienna court, financial limitations prevented her embarking on a new war with Turkey. Any delay benefited Frederick; once the American Revolution ended, France would again exert a major influence in Europe. Frederick meanwhile remained on excellent terms with the Versailles court, going so far as to join the League of Armed Neutrality against England.

He was nevertheless a worried man. "The emperor [Joseph] weighs on my septuagenarian shoulders," he wrote his nephew Prince Charles of Brunswick, in January 1782. Numerous letters in the following months reflect apprehension and melancholy. Prince Frederick William, his heir, had returned to his dissolute ways and was again out of favor. In spring of 1782 the king wrote a brief and secret memorandum on the political state of Europe: Emperor Joseph proposed with Russia's help to crush the Prussian monarchy "in order then to establish his despotism in Germany without opposition." He would do his best to check Joseph's actions,

> but if, after my death, monsieur my nephew drifts into indolence; if he takes no interest in things; if, extravagant as he is, he squanders state funds, and if he does not revive his intellectual faculties — I foresee that Monsieur Joseph will outrun him and that within thirty years there will no longer be either a Prussia or a House of Brandenburg; that the emperor, having swallowed everything, will end by dominating Germany, where he will eliminate all the sovereign princes in order to form a monarchy like that of France.

The king's pessimism was at the same time an indictment of enlightened absolutism. One-man rule was only as effective as the ruler. Lacking a qualified and energetic ruler, the kingdom would have to find salvation in some form of constitutional government or *Rechtstaat*, which in theory protected a state by distributing the authority. But this was totally beyond Frederick's ken, even had there been the vaguest kind of machinery to bring it about. Autocracy not permitting dilution, it followed that a weak autocrat would mean weak government.

That was in the future. At the moment, Frederick's best agent in thwarting Joseph's machinations was time. Catherine and Joseph may have decided on Turkey's demise, but they had not entirely agreed on details. These were the subject of acrimonious discussion for another two years. In the end Catherine not only rejected Joseph's territorial demands, particularly the acquisition of Venice, but in summer of 1783 she annexed the Crimea without consulting her new ally.

Joseph could do little about this power play except to come up with one of his own. He had never ceased looking westward and had been manipulating various German princes to create a favorable climate for a major diplomatic coup. This was nothing less than a territorial swap of major proportions. Elector Charles Theodor of Bavaria would cede his country to Austria in return for most of the Austrian Netherlands, the title of King of Burgundy, and £100,00 in cash. A second and equally disturbing project concerned the navigation of the Scheldt River, which was controlled by Holland under the Barrier Treaty of 1715. Joseph had already abrogated this treaty in 1781, when he forced the Dutch to abandon the border fortresses. He now demanded free passage for Austrian ships on the Scheldt, which would allow him to control Maestricht, and thus make the Austrian Netherlands more tempting to the Bavarian elector.

Joseph's diplomatic offensives only confirmed Frederick's blackest thoughts. Already out of temper with the bumptious emperor's manipulations in minor German courts, Frederick decided to try to form another confederation of German princes to oppose him, a project outlined to Ministers Finckenstein and Hertzberg in October 1784. This was a matter first of approaching individual courts, a task zealously and in general successfully carried out by Ewald von Hertzberg.

Frederick also needed a powerful ally to check Joseph. The Treaty of Paris in 1782, which ended the American Revolution, had revived English and French influence in Europe. Frederick had remained on good terms with the Versailles court, a policy strongly supported by Prince Henry and Finckenstein. But a two-month visit to France by Henry in 1784 brought only the limited political result of helping to frustrate Joseph's actions against Holland.

England was also looking for a continental ally, and Hertzberg, increasingly influential in foreign affairs, leaned toward a new alliance with her, as did the Duke of Brunswick.

Frederick's hostility of twenty years toward England had begun slowly to change. The War of the Bavarian Succession had suggested areas of common interest. The real thaw began in 1782, when the clever but disruptive Hugh Elliot was recalled from Berlin and replaced by Sir John Stepney. Stepney returned to England in spring of 1784 after a relatively calm embassy, and his role was temporarily filled by his secretary, twenty-five-year-old Joseph Ewart. Ewart remained in this post after the younger Pitt came to power a few months later and astutely conducted a series of negotiations designed to forge a new alliance with Prussia. There were two areas of mutual interest. Bavaria was one. When Hertzberg set about recruiting German rulers for the proposed confederation, he found not only keen interest but active support in Hanover. Moreover, Britain and Prussia presented a combined front in Saint Petersburg, where their envoys urged Catherine to oppose Joseph's plan to acquire Bavaria.

The second area was the United Provinces, whose stadtholder, William V, the Prince of Orange, was married to Frederick's favorite niece, Wilhelmina. William held only tenuous control of the squabbling provinces, and France was working to undermine his power. If the republicans gained control, they would ally with France. Prussia wished to prevent this, and so did England.

It was to England's benefit to support Frederick's burgeoning confederation, but Frederick was not compelled to support the English king, nor did he wish to alienate France. In his mind the major goal was to stop Joseph's aggressions. France and the United Provinces formed a secondary problem.

The peculiar situation demanded limited rapprochement, however, and Hertzberg continued to plough ground made the more fertile by Kaunitz's exhortations to German princes not to oppose Austrian plans. The upshot was a secret meeting in late June in Berlin between Prussia, Saxon, and Hanoverian envoys, who wrote a charter for a *Fürstenbund,* or confederation, of Imperial princes.

This document was published in late July and attracted widespread support from both Protestant and Catholic rulers. Taken with Czarina Catherine's refusal to approve Joseph's planned takeover of Bavaria, the *Fürstenbund* effectively ended his diplomatic foray. Some historians have marked it as the beginning of the German *Reich,* and this is permissible. But Frederick himself was too scornful of these weak, frightened, and vacillating princes, and too mindful of fluctuating diplomacy, to lend much hope to lasting confederation.

He spelled out his attitude in part to Lord Charles Cornwallis that September at the autumn reviews. Contrary to Frederick's wishes, the new foreign secretary in England, Lord Carmarthen, had asked Cornwallis to sound out the Prussian king concerning an alliance. As usual, Frederick did most of the talking. Cornwallis reported that "however the strength of his body may be impaired, the faculties of his mind are still perfect." The king was plainly apprehensive of forming the "more close and intimate connection" that Carmarthen seemed to have in mind.* While recognizing mutual interests, such as the need to check Austrian aspirations in Bavaria and French ambitions in Holland, the king pointed to the isolated position of England and Prussia. The balance of European power was lopsided, he told Cornwallis, because France, Spain, Austria, and Russia were allied, no matter how loosely, and Holland was virtually under French control. How could Britain and Prussia stand against this coalition? He had fought one Seven Years' War and did not want to fight another. However, "detach Russia and I will join the triple alliance tomorrow."[3]

A sudden and severe illness prevented a further audience, which would have been pointless in any case. Frederick realized that neither he nor King George could detach Catherine from her alliance with Austria, at least until the two powers had despoiled Turkey. Also, he wished to keep the door open to a French alliance, though he denied this intention to Cornwallis. Meanwhile he had to remain on guard, treasury full, army ready to move when and where the situation demanded.

106

THE ARMY was never far from the king's mind. He never gave up trying to make it an invincible instrument, guardian of the state, protector of its existence, promoter of its will.

But like its master, the army was old and tired. It no longer willingly accepted his ministrations. He was an unwanted suitor, visiting garrisons and holding reviews and maneuvers, inspecting, scolding, punishing, reforming, teaching. He praised some commanders, warned others, relieved a few, and promoted a few. At an autumn maneuver in 1781 an observer wrote that "the king galloped about in his ordinary way, and seemed in tolerable health. The first day he was in good humour, and was satisfied with everything, but the second and third he found great fault with the cavalry. . . . General Prittwitz was most handsomely scolded, and [General] Platen . . . had near a quarter of an hour's trimming."[1] But he could not be everywhere at once; he could not improve morale as long as officers and men received a pit-

---

* Cornwallis's diplomatic mission apparently originated with representations made by the Prussian envoy in London, Count Lusi. Carmarthen's goal was not an alliance, but rather making the court of Berlin "as useful to us as possible, without ever trusting it for a moment." Frederick severely reprimanded Lusi for having brought the mission about. (Cornwallis, *Correspondence*.)

tance for pay, as long as brutality ruled the ranks, as long as he refused to inject new blood into an army as autocratic and antiquated as his reign.

In autumn of 1784 the king traveled to Silesia, his "Peru" of riches, where as usual he poked into civil and military activities with a zeal terrifying to local officials. On the occasion the army scored a massive negative. "Were I to make cobblers or tailors into generals," he wrote to Bogislav von Tauentzien, his inspector general of infantry in Silesia, "the regiments could not be worse." Maneuvers at Neisse and Breslau were disasters. The king had no intention of losing battles "by the base conduct of my generals." Tauentzien had one year to put things right.

Seventeen eighty-five was not a good year. The Vistula, Oder, and Warthe flooded the countryside. The king spent a half-million thalers to repair dikes and damage to private holdings, and would have spent more had it been possible to remove the mountains of sand that covered estates along the Oder. Despite a poor harvest, he held down the price of corn while continuing to export it in considerable quantity.

On the credit side, Prussian manufactures rose to thirty million thalers (and would reach thirty-four million in 1786). The king signed a ten-year treaty of friendship and commerce with the United States of America and called for free trade on a "most favored" basis between the two countries.* The population continued to grow. Frederick had inherited a kingdom of 2.24 million people. It now counted about six million, about a third of whom came from new territories. He had nearly tripled the original population.

As his *Political Testaments* made clear, there was a great deal more to do. The educational system was still weak and in need of radical improvement. The kingdom needed further civil, legal, and social reforms. Frederick had shown the way; indeed, his grand chancellor had already prepared a new legal code that in 1794 would become the *Allgemeine Preussische Landrecht*, "a real constitution in the ordinary sense of the word," as Alexis de Tocqueville called it.† It would be up to Frederick's successor to continue the work of reform. The army too needed some improvements, but meanwhile it was strong enough to keep enemies at a distance.

---

*The treaty was signed by Friedrich Wilhem von Thulemeier for Prussia and by Thomas Jefferson (at Paris), Benjamin Franklin (at Passy), and John Adams (at London) for the United States.
†The modern historian H. W. Koch has described it as the final phase of the judiciary reforms initiated by King Frederick William. King Frederick was astounded with the size of the first draft: "But this is very thick; laws must be short and not copious." (Koch, *A History of Prussia*.)

In 1785 the treasury was full, the army was read
kingdom continued to grow.

Frederick returned to Silesia in the autumn of 1785. After visiting several towns and inspecting various fortresses, he attended a three-day
review witnessed by his distinguished guests, the young Duke Frederick
of York, Lord Cornwallis, and the Marquis de Lafayette. He had received them briefly at Sans-Souci. "Notwithstanding what I had heard
of him," wrote the twenty-eight-year-old Lafayette to General George
Washington, "[I] could not help being struck by that dress and appearance of an old, broken, dirty Corporal, covered all over with Spanish
snuff, with his head almost leaning on one shoulder, and fingers quite
distorted by the gout. But what surprised me much more is the fire and
some times the softness of the most beautiful eyes I ever saw, which
give as charming an expression to his physiognomy as he can take a
rough and threatening one at the head of his troops."[2] Lafayette had
been particularly well received and in one audience had spoken enthusiastically of constitutions, the franchise, and legislative bodies of government. "I used to know a young man who spoke as you have done,"
the king told him. "Do you know what happened to him?" "No, Your
Majesty," Lafayette stammered, taken aback. "Why, sir, he was
hanged!"[3]

The king's warning to General von Tauentzien had paid off, and the
regiments performed to his satisfaction. Cornwallis, who was miffed
because the king paid a great deal of attention to Lafayette, wrote that
"the cavalry is very fine; the infantry exactly like the Hessian, only
taller and better set up, but much slower in their movements. Their
maneuvers were such as the worst general in England would be hooted
at for practicing; two lines coming up within six yards of one another,
and firing in another's face till they had no ammunition left: nothing
could be more ridiculous."[4]

Lafayette contrarily informed General Washington that "nothing can
be compared to the beauty of the troops, the discipline that is diffused
throughout, the simplicity of their motions, the uniformity of their regiments. It is a plain regular machine that has been set these forty years,
and undergoes no alteration but what make it simpler and lighter."[5]

A heavy rain began early on the third day and lasted until dark. The
king remained mounted and refused cover, though he was soon drenched
and chilled. That evening he was feverish but nonetheless hosted a formal dinner for his guests. After a restless night of heavy sweating, he
finished the review, traveled on to inspect fortresses Neisse and Brieg,
and returned to Breslau for three days of festivities in honor of the
Duke of York.

He returned to Potsdam, worked hard for ten days, and attended an artillery review in Berlin. Back at Potsdam, he suffered a severe night attack of a choking catarrh that lasted for several hours and from which he recovered only with difficulty. The day after his political discussion with Cornwallis, he suffered an attack of apoplexy. Gout followed, and so did fever. He was confined to bed and could not attend the important Potsdam review in late September. "I think it very doubtful whether he will live out the winter," Cornwallis wrote to a friend.[6]

Frederick recovered but slowly. At a review of Pomeranian troops he could not mount his horse. Instead, as various regiments passed he raised his worn hat to the colors. In a weak voice he ordered his "dear Pomeranians" to march past once more, and this time he remained uncovered, as if giving his favorite infantry a last look at their king.[7]

The seventy-three-year-old king left Sans-Souci in November to live in the old palace at Potsdam. He conducted state business as usual, but he did not go out and he received only a few people. He held his usual court on Christmas and was visibly affected when old General Zieten appeared. Frederick crossed the chamber to the veteran warrior and insisted that he be seated, an almost unheard-of honor to the veteran cavalry general.

The king's isolation caused numerous rumors to circulate in European courts. Envoys continually reported his ill health and imminent death. In early January 1786, he suffered setbacks of dropsy and asthma, the latter probably explaining a continual short cough that left him breathless. Like many asthmatics, he could not sleep lying down but was forced to rest in an easy chair.

He remained very ill throughout the winter. Henry saw him in March and later told a friend that he was "almost daily expecting 'a great event' which, while it would 'interrupt all his pleasures,' would work a great change in his status."[8] But to general astonishment, and possibly Henry's disappointment, the king moved back to Sans-Souci in April. Count Gabriel Mirabeau received an audience on the day he moved. "My dialogue with the king was very lively," he later wrote, "but the king was in such suffering, and so straitened for breath, I was myself anxious to shorten it."[9] Another visitor was upset to see him sitting on the terrace, "downcast, crushed by illness, his face blanched and altered by suffering"; the coughing "echoed even in my own chest."[10] The audience lasted only five minutes before Frederick signaled attendants to carry him off.

Soft spring air and his beloved Sans-Souci worked a cure of sorts. Not once but several times he ordered his favorite horse, Condé, saddled for short rides in the countryside. The outings seemed to do him good, or at least to give him respite from misery. By now asthma and dropsy had been joined by gout, erysipelas, and large abscesses on ear and leg. What little faith he had left in his own doctor, Christian Selle, had vanished. In June he dismissed him and wrote to Dr. Chevalier Johann Zimmermann, a famous physician at Hanover, who agreed to come to him. In the interim he continued to work and dine with a few councilors, including Minister Ewald von Hertzberg.

> Though much swollen and incommoded with the dropsy, so that he could not move without assistance, from a chair in which he rested day and night [Hertzberg later wrote] . . . though it was evident he suffered dreadfully, he never betrayed the least symptom of uneasiness, or any disagreeable sensation; but preserving always his serene, contented, and tranquil air . . . he conversed with us on the ordinary topics of the day, in the most cordial and agreeable manner; on literature, ancient and modern history, rural affairs, and particularly gardening, to which he was greatly devoted.[11]

Zimmermann arrived in late June. His alleged expertise failed with Frederick. He remained at Potsdam for over two weeks, seeing his patient twice a day — a monotonous series of conversations that he later embellished and published — and prescribing copious quantities of dandelion soup. Frederick, whose appetite remained healthy, preferred spiced foods, and apparently Zimmermann made no real effort to interfere. Most likely he recognized terminal symptoms, and he may have so informed the king, because shortly before Zimmermann's departure von Hertzberg moved permanently to Potsdam, from where he daily communicated with the Prince of Prussia. Zimmermann returned by way of Brunswick to report on the king's condition to his sister Charlotte. She at once wrote to her brother, who replied from Sans-Souci: "The doctor from Hanover has wished to impress you, my good sister; in truth he has done me no good. The old must give way to the young so that each generation may find its place. . . . Meanwhile I find myself a trifle relieved during the past few days."[12]

He had entered his last week of life. A day or two later fever set in. To the queen's written condolences he replied, "Madame, I am very obliged for your good wishes, but a heavy fever prevents me from replying."

Incredibly, he continued his administrative routine almost to the end, bombarding secretaries and officers with orders — military vacancies to be filled, a new corps of irregulars to be formed, books to be bought for his library, a more detailed report from the director of customs, instructions for the forthcoming reviews in Silesia, plans for land reclamation in Pomerania, a four-page directive to a new ambassador, orders to bring three hundred sheep and rams from Spain. A day's work was topped off by fresh herring, an eel pie, and a lobster washed down with champagne.

The routine abruptly ceased on Wednesday morning. The king awakened only with difficulty. Although he tried, he could not give the Potsdam commandant the day's password. He remained that day in a semicoma. Dr. Selle, hastily summoned from Berlin, arrived in midafternoon. He found Frederick conscious but with flushed face and painful breathing. Toward evening the fever abated and he slept, perspiring heavily, as usual. On awakening, he complained of the cold. Selle found his legs cold up to the knees.

The doctor could do nothing, nor could anyone. Frederick dozed, his breath short, chest rattling. At midnight he noticed that one of his hounds was shivering and had his valet place a blanket over him. This set him to a severe fit of coughing. Sinking weakly in his chair, he murmured, *"La montagne est passée; nous irons mieux"* ("We have crossed the mountain; things will go better now").

He found it increasingly difficult to breathe. To free his chest, the valet knelt on one knee and supported the king on the other, his arm around the king's back. He maintained this position for over two hours. At a little past two A.M. on August 17, 1786, Frederick the Great died.

Frederick had wished to be buried without ceremony at Sans-Souci. But privacy is not for royalty. His body was examined by a corps of physicians and surgeons, and after a suitably royal funeral he was buried next to his father in the garrison church at Potsdam.

The church was destroyed in World War Two.

Acknowledgments
Sources and Notes
Selected Bibliography
Index

ACKNOWLEDGMENTS

I am greatly indebted to a large number of people and institutions for helping me with this book. I want to thank the staffs of the Bodleian Library, the Codrington Library of All Souls College, and the New College Library, all at Oxford; the London Library, the Reading Room and the Department of Manuscripts of the British Library, the Department of Prints of the British Museum, and the Library of the Royal Army Medical College, all in London; the Public Records Office, now at Kew Gardens; the Royal Archives at Windsor; the New York City Public Library; the Library of Congress; the Vassar College Library; the Rigsarkivet of the Regsarkiv in Copenhagen; the Rigsarkivet in the Hague; the Austrian Nationalbibliothek, the Kriegsarchiv, the Haus-, Hof-, und Staatsarchivs of the Oesterreichische Staatsarchiv, the University of Vienna Library and its special Medical Library, all in Vienna; the Armee Museum in Potsdam, the Military Museum of fortress Königstein, the City Museum in Dresden, and the Church Museum in Hochkirch, all in East Germany.

I am particularly indebted to Robert Evans, fellow of Brasenose College, Eric Christiansen and Alex de Jonge, fellows of New College, Professor Norman Gibbs of All Souls College, all of Oxford University; Sir Oliver Millar, Keeper of the Queen's Pictures, Buckingham Palace; Sir Mackworth Young, Royal Librarian, Windsor Castle; Dr. Norman Higson, Archivist of the University of Hull; Lord and Lady Hotham of Dalton Hall, Yorkshire; the Controller of Her Majesty's Stationery Office, who has kindly permitted me to quote from documents in the crown copyright; Professor John Hattendorf of the United States Naval War College; Mr. Georges Borchardt, my literary agent; Belle Griffith and the late Samuel B. Griffith, to whom this book is dedicated; Professor Winifred Asprey, who has bestowed her usual boundless hospitality and encouragement; Mr. and Mrs. Arthur Wittenstein; Commander and Mrs. Ian Langlands-Pearse; Mr. and Mrs. John Backman; Dr. and Mrs. Gordon Seaver; Colonel and Mrs. David Sutherland; and

Mr. and Mrs. Graham Rosser — all of whom have lived with Frederick for a very long time.

Professor Margaret McKenzie, Dr. Dieter Poetzsch, and Mr. Graham Rosser, O.B.E., have spent many hours vetting and often correcting my translations of German and French sources, and I am extremely grateful. I owe particular thanks to my editor, Katrina Kenison, and to her able and indefatigable colleagues, Laurie Parsons, Frances Apt, and Katarina Rice, for their many helpful comments and corrections. As King Frederick would have insisted, any remaining errors are the fault of cruel Providence.

Dr. Samuel Johnson wrote that "the greatest part of a writer's time is spent in reading, in order to write; a man will turn over half a library to make one book."

This was certainly the case with this biography. In trying to let Frederick tell his own story, which I corrected, amplified, and expanded to the best of my ability, I have relied primarily on official records: the thirty volumes of his historical, philosophical, and military writings, his poetry and personal correspondence edited by J. D. E. Preuss; the numerous subsequent collections of his vast correspondence with particular individuals; the magnificent forty-six-volume collection of his political correspondence; the bureaucratic effusions of the *Acta Borussica;* archival sources either quoted in earlier works by German, Austrian, French, British, and American writers or contained today in archives in England, France, Germany, Austria, Denmark, and Holland; the superb nineteen-volume study of his campaigns by the German General Staff; the official nine-volume study of the War of the Austrian Succession by the Austrian General Staff; the neglected two-volume official study by the German General Staff of his military experiments, refinements, and innovations between the wars; the equally neglected writings on "small war," the eighteenth-century term for guerrilla warfare; and, not least, the fascinating volumes of contemporary ambassadorial reports in British, Austrian, Danish, and Dutch archives. Austrian, Prussian, French, British, Saxon, and Bavarian official and quasi-official histories of Frederick's wars, along with analyses and memoirs by participants and later commentators, complemented my basic research sources. I have also used a variety of German, Austrian, French, British, and American secondary sources.

Extensive reliance on foreign-language sources presented a problem in a work written primarily for the general reader. It seemed pointless to cite them in detail, not only for linguistic and space reasons but because most of these works are difficult to come by, especially in the

United States. Accordingly, I have made "blanket" citations for a large number of textual quotations. And I have used short titles in notes but have given complete documentation in the Selected Bibliography. The following sources for textual quotations will be cited in individual chapter notes only when clarification is necessary.

Sources

Krauske, *Die Briefe König Wilhelms I,* for King Frederick William's correspondence with Prince Leopold of Anhalt-Dessau (Old Dessauer).

Wilhelmina, *Memoirs.*

Pöllnitz, *Memoirs.*

Bielfeld, *Letters of Baron Bielfeld.*

Friedrich der Grosse, *Die Briefe . . . an den Fürsten Leopold und die Prinzen von Anhalt-Dessau,* for Frederick's peacetime correspondence with Old Dessauer and his sons.

Frédéric le Grand, *Oeuvres Historiques,* thirty volumes, hereafter *Oeuvres* followed by volume number:

Oeuvres (16) for Frederick's correspondence with Madame de Roucoulle; Natzmer; Madame de Schöning; Camas; Manteuffel; Suhm; Beausobre; Schaumburg-Lippe; Eller.

Oeuvres (16) and Friedrich der Grosse, *Briefwechsel Friedrichs des Grossen mit Grumbkow und Maupertuis,* for Frederick's correspondence with Grumbkow, Seckendorff, the Grumbkow-Seckendorff correspondence, and Frederick's correspondence with Maupertuis. Förster, *Friedrich Wilhelm I,* vol. 3, for forty-nine letters of the Frederick-Grumbkow correspondence from 1732 to 1733.

Oeuvres (17) for Frederick's correspondence with Jordan and Duhan.

Oeuvres (18) for Frederick's correspondence with Algarotti, the Duchess of Saxe-Gotha, and Madame de Camas.

Oeuvres (19) for Frederick's correspondence with d'Argens.

Oeuvres (21–23) and Koser-Droysen, *Briefwechsel Friedrichs des Grossen mit Voltaire* (three volumes), for Frederick's correspondence with Voltaire.

Oeuvres (26) for Frederick's correspondence with Queen Elizabeth and with the dowager queen.

Oeuvres (26) and Volz, *Briefwechsel Friedrichs des Grossen mit seinem Bruder Prinz August Wilhelm,* for Frederick's correspondence with Prince August William.

Oeuvres (26) and Easum, *Prince Henry of Prussia,* for Frederick's correspondence with Prince Henry.

Oeuvres (27) and Volz-Oppeln-Bronikowski, *Friedrich der Grosse und Wilhelmina,* for Frederick's correspondence with Wilhelmina.

Oeuvres (27) for Frederick's correspondence with King Frederick William; von Hacke; Duke Charles of Brunswick, Prince Albert of Brunswick.

Oeuvres (28–30) for Frederick's military regulations and instructions.

Politische Correspondenz for Frederick's and Eichel's official correspondence, unless otherwise attributed.

Orlich, *Geschichte der schlesischen Kriege,* two volumes, for Frederick's wartime correspondence with Old Dessauer, including orders and reports.

Valory, *Mémoires des négociations,* for Valory's numerous observations on King Frederick and his campaigns.

Friedrich der Grosse, *Die Briefe Friedrichs des Grossen an seinen vormaligen Kammerdiener Fredersdorff,* for Frederick's correspondence with Fredersdorff.

Catt, *Frederick the Great,* for the king's conversations with Henri de Catt.

Notes

INTRODUCTION

1. Churchill, *Marlborough.*
2. Arneth, *Prinz Eugen von Savoyen.*

CHAPTER 1

1. Koser, *Kronprinz.*
2. Great Britain, Public Records Office, State Papers, Prussia and Poland, Foreign Office Volume 90/7. Hereafter British Foreign Office followed by specific designation for British diplomatic reports.
3. Lavisse, *Youth.*

CHAPTER 2

1. Lavisse, *Youth.*
2. Förster, *Friedrich Wilhelm I,* Volume 1.
3. Droysen, *Geschichte,* Volume 4.
4. Ergang, *Führer.*
5. Förster, *Friedrich Wilhelm I,* Volume 2.
6. For this and the following account: Förster, *Friedrich Wilhelm I,* Volume 1; Lavisse, *Youth.*
7. Ergang, *Führer.* The translation is mine.
8. Laurence Sterne, *Tristram Shandy* (Chicago: University of Chicago Press, 1952).

CHAPTER 3

1. William Shakespeare, *Julius Caesar,* Act II, Scene 1.
2. Cramer, *Geschichte.*
3. Cramer, *Geschichte.* I have taken "Br..." in his text to mean *Brunst,* which in this case would translate as "lust."
4. Cramer, *Geschichte,* which offers several of Frederick's missives.
5. Förster, *Friedrich Wilhelm I,* Volume 1.
6. Carlyle, *History of Frederick II,* Volume 1.

7. Goldsmith, *Frederick the Great.*
8. Förster, *Friedrich Wilhelm I,* Volume 1.

CHAPTER 4

1. G. Schmoller, "Eine Schilderung Berlins aus dem Jahre 1723." *Forschungen zur brandenburgischen und preussischen Geschichte,* Volume 3, 1890.
2. British Museum, Department of Manuscripts, Additional Manuscript 37392, Folio 25/7.
3. Lavisse, *Youth.*
4. Förster, *Friedrich Wilhelm I,* Urkundenbuch.
5. Cramer, *Geschichte.*
6. Lavisse, *Youth.*
7. Reddaway, *Frederick the Great.*
8. For Seckendorff's correspondence: Förster, *Friedrich Wilhelm I,* Urkundenbuch. For further details of the bribery of Grumbkow and others: Braubach, *Geheim-Diplomatie.*
9. Denmark, Rigsarkivet, TKUA, Brandenburg-Prussia: *Relation am Preussen.* Hereafter Denmark, Rigsarkivet.
10. Förster, *Friedrich Wilhelm I,* Volume 2 and Urkundenbuch.
11. Lavisse, *Youth.*
12. British Foreign Office, 90/21.

CHAPTER 5

1. Förster, *Friedrich Wilhelm I,* Volume 1.
2. Lavisse, *Youth.*
3. Lavisse, *Youth;* Albert Waddington, ed., *Recueil des instructions,* Volume 16, *Prusse.*
4. British Foreign Office, 90/21.
5. For Seckendorff's activities and reports: Förster, *Friedrich Wilhelm I,* Urkundenbuch. For the fraudulent letters: Lavisse, *Youth.*
6. Förster, *Friedrich Wilhelm I,* Urkundenbuch.
7. Förster, *Friedrich Wilhelm I,* Urkundenbuch.
8. Förster, *Friedrich Wilhelm I,* Urkundenbuch.
9. Förster, *Friedrich Wilhelm I,* Urkundenbuch.
10. British Foreign Office, 90/22. For excellent coverage of this period: Chance, *The Alliance of Hanover* and *George I.*
11. British Foreign Office, 90/22.
12. Förster, *Friedrich Wilhelm I,* Volume 1 and Urkundenbuch.
13. Preuss, *Friedrich . . . eine Lebensgeschichte,* Volume 1.
14. For Seckendorff's and Suhm's reports: Förster, *Friedrich Wilhelm I,* Urkundenbuch.
15. William Shakespeare, *King Lear,* Act One, Scene 1.

CHAPTER 6

1. For the king's instructions: Förster, *Friedrich Wilhelm I*, Volume 1; Koser, *Kronprinz;* Ergang, *Führer.* For the king's warning to Lieutenant Borcke: Lavisse, *Youth.*
2. Ranke, *Memoirs*, Volume 1.
3. British Foreign Office, 90/22.
4. British Foreign Office, 90/23.
5. Pöllnitz, *Memoirs.*
6. British Foreign Office, 90/23.
7. British Foreign Office, 90/23.
8. Margotte, *Medicine.*
9. Zimmermann, *Conversations.* For allegations of Frederick's impotency and homosexuality: Voltaire, *Mémoires;* Simon, *Frederick the Great;* Reiners, *Frederick the Great.* For refutations of Zimmermann et al.: Volz, "Friedrich der Grosse und seine sittlichen Ankläger," Lange-Eichbaum, *Genie;* Vorberg, *Klatsch;* Selle, *Krankheitsgeschichte;* Mamlock, *Ärzten.*
10. Preuss, *Friedrich . . . eine Lebensgeschichte*, Volume 1; Förster, *Friedrich Wilhelm I*, Volume 1; Koser, *Kronprinz;* British Foreign Office, 90/23.

CHAPTER 7

1. Lavisse, *Youth.*
2. Koser, *Kronprinz;* Lavisse, *Youth.*
3. Koser, *Kronprinz.*
4. British Foreign Office, 90/23.
5. Bartholdy, *Friedrich II.*
6. British Foreign Office, 90/23.
7. British Foreign Office, 90/23.

CHAPTER 8

1. British Foreign Office, 90/24.
2. British Foreign Office, 90/24.
3. British Foreign Office, 90/24.
4. British Foreign Office, 90/24.
5. Ranke, *Memoirs*, Volume 1.
6. British Foreign Office, 90/23.
7. British Foreign Office, 90/24 and 90/25.
8. British Foreign Office, 90/24.
9. Denmark, Rigsarkivet.
10. British Foreign Office, 90/25.
11. British Foreign Office, 90/25.
12. British Foreign Office, 90/25.
13. British Foreign Office, 90/25.

14. British Foreign Office, 90/25.
15. Lavisse, *Youth.*
16. Bartholdy, *Friedrich II.*
17. British Foreign Office, 90/25.

CHAPTER 9

Hotham's reports are in British Foreign Office, 90/28, and University of Hull, Hotham Archives.
1. British Foreign Office, 90/26.
2. British Foreign Office, 90/26.
3. British Foreign Office, 90/26.
4. British Foreign Office, 90/26.
5. Lavisse, *Youth;* Stirling, *Hothams.*
6. British Foreign Office, 90/27.
7. British Foreign Office, 90/27; University of Hull, Hotham Archives.
8. British Foreign Office, 90/52.
9. Koser, *Kronprinz.*

CHAPTER 10

Hotham's reports are in British Foreign Office, 90/28, and University of Hull, Hotham Archives.
1. British Foreign Office, 90/28.
2. Ranke, *Memoirs,* Volume 1.

CHAPTER 11

1. Koser, *Kronprinz.*
2. Koser, *Kronprinz.*
3. Förster, *Friedrich Wilhelm I,* Volume 3; Bartholdy, *Friedrich II.*
4. Ranke, *Memoirs,* Volume 1.
5. British Foreign Office, 90/24.
6. British Foreign Office, 90/24.
7. Wilhelmina, *Memoirs.*
8. Förster, *Friedrich Wilhelm I,* Volume 3.
9. British Foreign Office, 90/29.

CHAPTER 12

Major sources for the details of Frederick's imprisonment and Katte's execution are: Förster, *Friedrich Wilhelm I,* Volume 3; Preuss, *Friedrich . . . eine Lebens-*

geschichte, Volume 1; Ranke, *Memoirs,* Volume 1; Koser, *Kronprinz;* Lavisse, *Youth;* Gaxotte, *Frederick the Great.*

1. Koser, *Kronprinz.*
2. Koser, *Kronprinz.*
3. British Foreign Office, 90/29.
4. British Foreign Office, 90/29.
5. For excellent accounts of the trial and the king's reaction: Koser, *Kronprinz;* Hinrichs, *Kronprinzenprozess;* Fontane, *Wanderungen.*
6. Koser, *Kronprinz,* for the king's instructions.
7. Lavisse, *Youth.*
8. Förster, *Friedrich Wilhelm I,* Volume 3.
9. Ranke, *Memoirs,* 1.

CHAPTER 13

1. For Muller's reports and an extensive discussion of Katte's letter: Preuss, *Friedrich . . . eine Lebensgeschichte,* Volume 1.
2. British Foreign Office, 90/29.
3. Preuss, *Friedrich . . . eine Lebensgeschichte,* Urkundenbuch.
4. For the king's correspondence with Wolden and Hille: Förster, *Friedrich Wilhelm I,* Volume 3; Koser, *Kronprinz.* For the Hille-Wolden-Grumbkow correspondence: Volz, *Spiegel,* Volume 1; Gooch, *Frederick.*
5. Koser, *Kronprinz.*
6. For Frederick's relationship with Natzmer: Natzmer, "Jugendfreund"; Berney, *Friedrich.*

CHAPTER 14

1. Förster, *Friedrich Wilhelm I,* Volume 3.
2. Förster, *Friedrich Wilhelm I,* Volume 3.
3. Förster, *Friedrich Wilhelm I,* Volume 3.
4. Förster, *Friedrich Wilhelm I,* Volume 3.
5. British Foreign Office, 90/31.
6. Förster, *Friedrich Wilhelm I,* Volume 3.
7. Förster, *Friedrich Wilhelm I,* Volume 3.

CHAPTER 15

1. Ranke, *Memoirs,* Volume 1.
2. Frederick the Great, *Regulations for the Prussian Infantry,* translated by W. Faucitt (London, 1754).
3. Ergang, *Führer.*
4. Förster, *Friedrich Wilhelm I,* Volume 3.

CHAPTER 16

1. Förster, *Friedrich Wilhelm I*, Volume 3.
2. Carlyle, *History*, Volume 3.
3. Förster, *Friedrich Wilhelm I*, Volume 3.

CHAPTER 17

1. British Foreign Office, 90/38.

CHAPTER 18

1. Koser, *Kronprinz.*
2. Ergang, *Führer.*
3. Förster, *Friedrich Wilhelm I*, Urkundenbuch.
4. Seckendorff, *Journal Secret.*
5. Koser, *Kronprinz.*
6. Durant, *Voltaire.*

CHAPTER 19

1. Volz, *Spiegel,* Volume 1.
2. Meinicke, "Ruler Before Philosopher."
3. Besterman, *Voltaire.* See also Parton, *Life of Voltaire.*
4. Hytier, "Frédéric II."
5. Gaxotte, *Frederick.*
6. British Foreign Office, 90/42.

CHAPTER 20

1. British Foreign Office, 90/44.
2. This work is in Frédéric le Grand, *Oeuvres historiques de Frédéric II Roi de Prusse,* Volume 8. Hereafter *Oeuvres* followed by volume number. For a detailed discussion of the work: Gooch, *Frederick;* Meinicke, "Ruler Before Philosopher"; Dorn, "Conflict."
3. *Considérations sur les causes de la grandeur des Romains et de leur décadence.*
4. Durant, *Voltaire.*

CHAPTER 21

1. Carlyle, *History,* Volume 3.
2. British Foreign Office, 90/44.

3. British Foreign Office, 90/45.
4. British Foreign Office, 90/44.
5. British Foreign Office, 90/44.
6. Koser, *Kronprinz.*

CHAPTER 22

1. Meinicke, "Ruler Before Philosopher."
2. Cowie, *Hanoverian England.*
3. British Foreign Office, 90/46.
4. Koser, *Kronprinz.*
5. Koser, *Kronprinz.*

CHAPTER 23

1. *Oeuvres*, Volume 1, *Du Militaire sous le roi Frédéric-Guillaume I.*
2. *Oeuvres*, Volume 2, *Histoire de mon temps.*
3. Volz, *Spiegel*, Volume 1.
4. Volz, *Spiegel*, Volume 1.
5. Ranke, *Memoirs*, Volume 2.
6. *Oeuvres*, Volume 3, and Taysen, ed., *Friedrich der Grosse.*
7. For Frederick's orders to the provincial administrations: Preuss, *Friedrich . . . eine Lebensgeschichte*, Volume 1; Droysen, *Geschichte*, Volume 5-(1); Ranke, *Memoirs*, Volume 2.
8. For Frederick's reforms: Preuss, *Friedrich . . . eine Lebensgeschichte*, Volume 1; Droysen, *Geschichte*, Volume 5-(1); Koser, *Geschichte*, Volume 1.
9. Droysen, *Geschichte*, Volume 5-(1), and Dilthey, "Frederick."
10. Bielfeld, *Letters.*
11. Preuss, *Friedrich . . . eine Lebensgeschichte*, Volume 1.
12. Droysen, *Geschichte*, Volume 5-(1).

CHAPTER 24

Friedrich der Grosse, *Politische Correspondenz*, Volume 1 (June–November 1740). Hereafter *Politische Correspondenz* followed by volume number and time span.
1. British Foreign Office, 90/47.
2. Gooch, *Frederick the Great.*

CHAPTER 25

Politische Correspondenz, Volume 1, November 1740.
1. *Oeuvres*, Volume 2, *Histoire de mon temps.*
2. *Oeuvres*, Volume 2, *Histoire de mon temps.*

3. Crankshaw, *Maria Theresa*. See also Arneth, *Geschichte*, Volume 1; Coxe, *History*, Volume 1; Pick, *Empress Maria Theresa*.
4. William Shakespeare, *Julius Caesar*, Act III, Scene 1.

CHAPTER 26

Politische Correspondenz, Volume 1, November–December 1740.
1. Waddington, ed., *Recueil*.
2. Droysen, *Geschichte*, Volume 5-(1).
3. British Foreign Office, 90/47.
4. Gooch, *Frederick the Great*.
5. Broglie, *Frederick*, Volume 1.
6. Hearsay, *Voltaire*.
7. Koser, *Geschichte*, Volume 1.
8. Droysen, *Geschichte*, Volume 5-(1); Ranke, *Memoirs*, Volume 2; *Oeuvres*, Volume 2, *Histoire de mon temps*.
9. *Oeuvres*, Volume 2, *Histoire de mon temps*.
10. British Foreign Office, 90/48.
11. Broglie, *Frederick*, Volume 1.
12. *Oeuvres*, Volume 2, *Histoire de mon temps*.

CHAPTER 27

Politische Correspondenz, Volume 1, December 1740.
1. Generalstab, *Die Kriege Friedrichs des Grossen*. Erster Theil: *Der Erste Schlesische Krieg, 1740–1742*, Volume 1. Hereafter Generalstab I followed by volume number.
2. Koser, *Geschichte*, Volume 1.
3. Koser, *Geschichte*, Volume 1.
4. Koser, *Geschichte*, Volume 1, and Raumer, *Contributions*.
5. *Oeuvres*, Volume 2, *Histoire de mon temps*.
6. Crankshaw, *Maria Theresa*.
7. For the defense of Silesia and subsequent Austrian deliberations: Duncker, "Die Invasion Silesiens"; *Oesterreich Kriegsarchiv, Oesterreichischer Erbfolge-Krieg, 1740–1748*, hereafter *Erbfolge-Krieg* followed by volume number; Christopher Duffy, *Wild Goose;* Arneth, *Geschichte*, Volume 1; Coxe, *History*, Volume 1; Orlich, *Geschichte*, Volume 1.
8. Droysen, *Geschichte*, Volume 5-(1).

CHAPTER 28

Politische Correspondenz, Volume 1, January 1741.
1. Generalstab I, Volume 1.
2. *Erbfolge-Krieg*, Volume 1. See also Generalstab I, Volume 1; Duncker, "Der Ueberfall."
3. Broglie, *Frederick*, Volume 1. See also Koser, *Geschichte*, Volume 1.

CHAPTER 29

Politische Correspondenz, Volume 1, March 1741.
1. Rothenburg, *Austrian Military Border*.
2. Droysen, *Geschichte*, Volume 5-(1).
3. Duffy, *Wild Goose*.
4. Schwerin, *Feldmarschal Schwerin*.
5. *Erbfolge-Krieg*, Volume 1.
6. *Oeuvres*, Volume 2, *Histoire de mon temps*.
7. Duncker, "Der Ueberfall."
8. Valory, *Mémoires*.
9. *Gentleman's Magazine*, Volume 11, March–April 1741.

CHAPTER 30

Politische Correspondenz, Volume 1, March–April 1741.
1. Generalstab I, Volume 1.
2. British Foreign Office, 90/49.
3. Droysen, *Geschichte*, Volume 5-(1).
4. *Oeuvres*, Volume 2, *Histoire de mon temps*.
5. Duncker, "Militärische und politische Aktenstücke."

CHAPTER 31

1. *Erbfolge-Krieg*, Volume 1.
2. Duncker, "Invasion Schlesiens" and "Militärische und politische Aktenstücke."
3. Generalstab I, Volume 1.
4. Duncker, "Militärische und politische Aktenstücke."
5. *Erbfolge-Krieg*, Volume 1.
6. Generalstab I, Volume 1.
7. Generalstab I, Volume 1.
8. Duncker, "Militärische und politische Aktenstücke."

CHAPTER 32

Politische Correspondenz, Volume 1, April–August, 1741.
1. *Oeuvres*, Volume 2, *Histoire de mon temps*.
2. Duncker, "Militärische und politische Aktenstücke."
3. Duncker, "Militärische und politische Aktenstücke."
4. Duncker, "Militärische und politische Aktenstücke."
5. Förster, *Friedrich Wilhelm I*, Urkundenbuch.
6. *Oeuvres*, Volume 2, *Histoire de mon temps*.
7. Warnery, *Campagnes de Frédéric II*.
8. Orlich, *Geschichte*, Volume 1.

9. Sonntag, *Trenck.*
10. British Foreign Office, 90/50.

CHAPTER 33

Politische Correspondenz, Volume 1, April–August 1741.
1. Generalstab I, Volume 2.
2. *Oeuvres,* Volume 2, *Histoire de mon temps.*
3. Droysen, *Geschichte,* Volume 5-(1).
4. Raumer, *Contributions.*
5. *Erbfolge-Krieg,* Volume 1.
6. Raumer, *Contributions.*
7. Raumer, *Contributions.*
8. British Foreign Office, 90/50.

CHAPTER 34

Politische Correspondenz, Volume 1, June–September 1741.
1. Generalstab I, Volume 2.
2. Koser, *Geschichte,* Volume 1.
3. Broglie, *Frederick,* Volume 1.

CHAPTER 35

Politische Correspondenz, Volume 1, January–February 1742.
1. Koser, *Geschichte,* Volume 1.
2. Generalstab I, Volume 2.
3. British Foreign Office, 90/51.

CHAPTER 36

Politische Correspondenz, Volume 1, January–February 1742.
1. *Oeuvres,* Volume 2, *Histoire de mon temps.*
2. *Oeuvres,* Volume 2, *Histoire de mon temps.*

CHAPTER 37

Politische Correspondenz, Volume 1, March 1742.

CHAPTER 38

Politische Correspondenz, Volume 1, February–May 1742.
1. British Foreign Office, 90/53. See also British Library, Department of Manu-

scripts, Additional Manuscripts, 35,452, Hardwicke Papers.
2. Valory, *Mémoires*, Volume 1.

CHAPTER 39

Politische Correspondenz, Volume 1, May 1742.
1. *Oeuvres*, Volume 2, *Histoire de mon temps*.
2. Koser, *Geschichte*, Volume 1. See also Generalstab I, Volume 3.
3. *Erbfolge-Krieg*, Volume 3.

CHAPTER 40

Politische Correspondenz, Volume 1, May–June 1742.
1. Generalstab I, Volume 3.

CHAPTER 41

Politische Correspondenz, Volume 1, March–December 1742; Volume 2, January–November 1743.
1. British Foreign Office, 90/55.

CHAPTER 42

Politische Correspondenz, Volume 2, January–November 1743.
1. Carlyle, *History*, Volume 3.

CHAPTER 43

Politische Correspondenz, Volume 2, June–December 1743.
1. British Foreign Office, 90/57.
2. Arneth, *Geschichte*, Volume 2.
3. British Foreign Office, 90/60.

CHAPTER 44

Politische Correspondenz, Volume 2, June–December 1743; Volume 3, January–August 1744.
1. Generalstab, *Die Kriege Friedrichs des Grossen. Zweiten Theil: Der Zweite Schlesische Krieg, 1744–1745*, Volume 1. Hereafter Generalstab II, followed by volume number.
2. *Oeuvres*, Volume 30, for the 1743 "Instructions" and "Regulations."

3. *Oeuvres,* Volume 30, for the 1743 "Instructions" and "Regulations."
4. *Oeuvres,* Volume 30, for the 1743 "Instructions" and "Regulations."
5. Droysen, *Geschichte,* Volume 5-(2).
6. British Foreign Office, 90/57.

CHAPTER 45

Politische Correspondenz, Volume 3, August–September 1744.
1. Ranke, *Memoirs,* Volume 3.
2. *Erbfolge-Krieg,* Volume 7.
3. *Erbfolge-Krieg,* Volume 7.
4. *Erbfolge-Krieg,* Volume 7.

CHAPTER 46

Politische Correspondenz, Volume 3, September–October 1744.
1. *Oeuvres,* Volume 2, *Histoire de mon temps.*
2. *Oeuvres,* Volume 2, *Histoire de mon temps.*
3. *Oeuvres,* Volume 2, *Histoire de mon temps.*
4. *Erbfolge-Krieg,* Volume 7.

CHAPTER 47

Politische Correspondenz, Volume 3, October–November 1744.
1. Generalstab II, Volume 1.
2. *Erbfolge-Krieg,* Volume 7.

CHAPTER 48

Politische Correspondenz, Volume 3, November–December 1744; Volume 4, January–February 1745.
1. *Erbfolge-Krieg,* Volume 7.
2. Arneth, *Geschichte,* Volume 2.
3. Arneth, *Geschichte,* Volume 2; *Erbfolge-Krieg,* Volume 7.

CHAPTER 49

Politische Correspondenz, Volume 3, September–December 1744; Volume 4, January–March 1745.
1. *Oeuvres,* Volume 2, *Histoire de mon temps.*
2. *Oeuvres,* Volume 2, *Histoire de mon temps.*
3. *Erbfolge-Krieg,* Volume 7.
4. Generalstab II, Volume 1.

CHAPTER 50

Politische Correspondenz, Volume 4, February–May 1745.
1. *Oeuvres,* Volume 2, *Histoire de mon temps.*
2. Droysen, *Geschichte,* Volume 5-(2).

CHAPTER 51

Politische Correspondenz, Volume 4, May–June 1745.
1. Generalstab II, Volume 1.
2. Generalstab II, Volume 1.
3. Generalstab II, Volume 1.
4. Generalstab II, Volume 1.
5. Generalstab II, Volume 1. See also *Erbfolge-Krieg,* Volume 7, for a slightly different version.
6. Generalstab II, Volume 1.
7. Valory, *Mémoires,* Volume 1.
8. Ranke, *Memoirs,* Volume 3.
9. Valory, *Mémoires,* Volume 1.
10. Generalstab II, Volume 1.
11. *Erbfolge-Krieg,* Volume 7.

CHAPTER 52

Politische Correspondenz, Volume 4, June–July 1745.
1. *Oeuvres,* Volume 2, *Histoire de mon temps.*
2. Friedrich der Grosse, *Briefe . . . an . . . Fredersdorff.*
3. Orlich, *Geschichte,* Volume 2.
4. Generalstab II, Volume 1.
5. *Erbfolge-Krieg,* Volume 7.
6. Arneth, *Geschichte,* Volume 3.

CHAPTER 53

Politische Correspondenz, Volume 4, June–September 1740.
1. Hron, *Der Parteigänger-Krieg.*
2. *Erbfolge-Krieg,* Volume 7.

CHAPTER 54

Politische Correspondenz, Volume 4, September–October 1745.
1. *Erbfolge-Krieg,* Volume 7.

CHAPTER 55

Politische Correspondenz, Volume 4, October–December 1745.
1. *Oeuvres*, Volume 2, *Histoire de mon temps*.
2. *Erbfolge-Krieg*, Volume 7.

CHAPTER 56

Politische Correspondenz, Volume 4, November–December 1745.
1. Arneth, *Geschichte*, Volume 3.
2. British Foreign Office, 88/68.
3. Ranke, *Memoirs*, Volume 3.

CHAPTER 57

Politische Correspondenz, Volume 5, 1746–1747; *Acta Borussica*, Volumes 7 and 8.
1. British Foreign Office, 90/62.
2. Rosenberg, *Prussian Experience*.
3. Ranke, *Memoirs*, Volume 3.
4. Preuss, *Friedrich . . . eine Lebensgeschichte*, Volume 1.

CHAPTER 58

Politische Correspondenz, Volume 5, 1746–1747; *Ergänzungsband: Die Politischen Testamente Friedrichs des Grossen; Acta Borussica*, Volumes 7 and 8.

CHAPTER 59

Politische Correspondenz, Volume 5, 1746–1747; *Die Politischen Testamente; Acta Borussica*, Volume 7.
1. Weill, "Frederick."
2. Ranke, *Memoirs*, Volume 3.
3. Weill, "Frederick."
4. *Oeuvres*, Volumes 4 and 5, *Histoire de la Guerre de Sept Ans*.
5. Weill, "Frederick."
6. Weill, "Frederick."
7. Weill, "Frederick."

CHAPTER 60

Politische Correspondenz, Volume 5, 1746–47; *Die Politischen Testamente; Oeuvres*, Volume 2, *Histoire de mon temps*.

1. *Oeuvres,* Volume 2, *Histoire de mon temps.*
2. *Oeuvres,* Volume 28.

CHAPTER 61

Politische Correspondenz, Volume 5, 1746–47; Volume 6, 1748–49; *Die Politischen Testamente.*
1. *Oeuvres,* Volumes 29 and 30.
2. *Oeuvres,* Volumes 4 and 5, *Histoire de la Guerre de Sept Ans.*
3. Generalstab, *Kriegsgeschichtliche Einzelschriften.*
4. Generalstab, *Kriegsgeschichtliche Einzelschriften.*

CHAPTER 62

Politische Correspondenz, Volume 5, 1746–47.
1. British Foreign Office, 88/68.
2. British Foreign Office, 90/64.

CHAPTER 63

Politische Correspondenz, Volume 6, 1748–49; Volume 7, 1749–50; Volume 8, 1750–51.
1. British Foreign Office, 90/64.
2. British Foreign Office, 88/71.
3. Koser, "Aus der Korrespondenz."
4. Preuss, *Friedrich . . . eine Lebensgeschichte,* Volume 1.
5. *Oeuvres,* Volumes 4 and 5, *Histoire de la Guerre de Sept Ans.*

CHAPTER 64

Politische Correspondenz, Volumes 5–11; *Die Politischen Testamente.*
1. Lehndorff, *Dreissig Jahre.*
2. Ilchester, *Sir Charles Hanbury-Williams.*

CHAPTER 65

Politische Correspondenz, Volumes 7–9.
1. Thiérot, *Voltaire en Prusse.* See also Parton, *Life of Voltaire.*
2. Thiérot, *Voltaire en Prusse.*
3. Thiérot, *Voltaire en Prusse.*
4. Thiérot, *Voltaire en Prusse.*

CHAPTER 66

1. Thiérot, *Voltaire en Prusse.*
2. Besterman, *Voltaire.*
3. Durant, *Age of Voltaire.*
4. Parton, *Life of Voltaire.*
5. Thiérot, *Voltaire en Prusse.*
6. Thiérot, *Voltaire en Prusse.*
7. Thiérot, *Voltaire en Prusse.*
8. Parton, *Life of Voltaire.*
9. Gooch, *Frederick the Great.*
10. Parton, *Life of Voltaire.*

CHAPTER 67

Die Politischen Testamente.

CHAPTER 68

Politische Correspondenz, Volumes 9–11, 1752–55.

CHAPTER 69

Politische Correspondenz, Volume 12, January–June 1756.
1. Koser, *Geschichte,* Volume 2.
2. Mitchell, *Memoirs.*
3. British Foreign Office, 90/65.
4. British Foreign Office, 90/65.
5. British Foreign Office, 90/65.
6. British Foreign Office, 90/65.
7. British Foreign Office, 90/65.

CHAPTER 70

Politische Correspondenz, Volume 13, July–October 1756.
1. British Foreign Office, 90/65.
2. Miguel de Cervantes, *Don Quixote,* tr. by T. M. Cohen (London: Penguin, 1950).
3. British Foreign Office, 90/65.
4. British Foreign Office, 90/65.
5. British Foreign Office, 90/65.

CHAPTER 71

Politische Correspondenz, Volume 13, July–October 1756.
1. British Foreign Office, 90/66.
2. *Oeuvres,* Volumes 4 and 5, *Histoire de la Guerre de Sept Ans.*
3. British Foreign Office, 90/66.
4. Generalstab, *Die Kriege Friedrichs des Grossen: Der Siebenjährige Krieg,* Volume 1. Hereafter Generalstab S followed by volume number.
5. Generalstab S, Volume 1.
6. Duffy, *The Wild Goose.*
7. Generalstab S, Volume 1.
8. Generalstab S, Volume 1.

CHAPTER 72

Politische Correspondenz, Volumes 13 and 14, October–November 1756.
1. Duffy, *The Wild Goose.*

CHAPTER 73

Politische Correspondenz, Volumes 13 and 14, November 1756–April 1757.
1. *Politische Correspondenz,* Volume 14.
2. Generalstab S, Volume 2.
3. *Politische Correspondenz,* Volume 14.

CHAPTER 74

Politische Correspondenz, Volumes 14 and 15, April–May 1757.
1. Generalstab S, Volume 2.
2. Duffy, *The Wild Goose.*

CHAPTER 75

Politische Correspondenz, Volume 15, May 1757.
1. Koser, *Geschichte,* Volume 2.

CHAPTER 76

Politische Correspondenz, Volume 15, May–June 1757.
1. *Gentleman's Magazine,* Volume 27, 1757.
2. Carlyle, *History,* Volume 5.

CHAPTER 77

Politische Correspondenz, Volume 15, June–July 1757.
1. British Foreign Office, 90/69.
2. Carlyle, *History,* Volume 5.
3. Bernhardi, *Friedrich der Grosse,* Volume 1.
4. Waddington, *La Guerre de Sept Ans,* Volume 1.
5. *Politische Correspondenz,* Volume 15; British Foreign Office, 90/69.
6. British Foreign Office, 90/69.

CHAPTER 78

Politische Correspondenz, Volume 15, August–October 1757.
1. British Foreign Office, 90/70.

CHAPTER 79

Politische Correspondenz, Volume 16, November 1757
1. Generalstab S, Volume 5.
2. Generalstab S, Volume 5.
3. Generalstab S, Volume 5.
4. Koser, *Geschichte,* Volume 2.
5. Generalstab S, Volume 5.
6. Generalstab S, Volume 5.

CHAPTER 80

Politische Correspondenz, Volume 16, November–December 1757.
1. William Shakespeare, *King Henry V,* Act IV, Scene 3.
2. Generalstab S, Volume 6.
3. Generalstab S, Volume 6.
4. Carlyle, *History,* Volume 5.
5. *Oeuvres,* Volumes 4 and 5, *Histoire de la Guerre de Sept Ans.*
6. Generalstab S, Volume 6.
7. Barsewich, *Von Rossbach bis Freiberg.*
8. Generalstab S, Volume 6.
9. Generalstab S, Volume 6.
10. Generalstab S, Volume 6.

CHAPTER 81

Politische Correspondenz, Volume 16, December 1757.
1. Generalstab S, Volume 6.

2. André Maurois, *History of France.*
3. André Maurois, *History of France.*

CHAPTER 82

Politische Correspondenz, Volumes 16 and 17, December 1757–July 1758.
1. Varnhagen, *Feldmarschall Jakob Keith.*
2. Catt, *Memoirs,* Volume 1.
3. Catt, *Memoirs,* Volume 1.
4. British Foreign Office, 90/71.
5. Mitchell, *Memoirs,* Volume 2.
6. British Foreign Office, 90/71.
7. British Foreign Office, 90/71.

CHAPTER 83

Politische Correspondenz, Volume 17, August 1758.
1. Generalstab S, Volume 8.
2. British Foreign Office, 90/72.
3. Bernhardi, *Friedrich der Grosse,* Volume 1.
4. Mitchell, *Memoirs,* Volume 2.

CHAPTER 84

Politische Correspondenz, Volume 17, September–October 1758.
1. Varnhagen, *Feldmarschall Jakob Keith.*
2. Generalstab S, Volume 8.
3. Carlyle, *History,* Volume 5.
4. Generalstab S, Volume 8.
5. Generalstab S, Volume 8.
6. Carlyle, *History,* Volume 5.

CHAPTER 85

Politische Correspondenz, Volumes 17–18, October 1758–March 1759.

CHAPTER 86

Politische Correspondenz, Volume 18, December–July 1759.
1. Bernhardi, *Friedrich der Grosse,* Volume 1.
2. Generalstab S, Volume 9.
3. Mitchell, *Memoirs,* Volume 2.
4. *Politische Correspondenz,* Volume 18.

5. Bernhardi, *Friedrich der Grosse*, Volume 1.
6. Bernhardi, *Friedrich der Grosse*, Volume 1.

CHAPTER 87

Politische Correspondenz, Volume 18, August 1759.
1. Generalstab S, Volume 10.
2. Carlyle, *History*, Volume 5.

CHAPTER 88

Politische Correspondenz, Volume 18, August–December 1759.
1. Bernhardi, *Friedrich der Grosse*, Volume 1.

CHAPTER 89

Politische Correspondenz, Volumes 18 and 19, December 1759–May 1760.
1. Generalstab S, Volume 12.
2. Mitchell, *Memoirs*, Volume 2.
3. Gooch, *Frederick the Great*.
4. *Politische Correspondenz*, Volume 19.
5. Generalstab S, Volume 12.
6. Generalstab S, Volume 12.

CHAPTER 90

Politische Correspondenz, Volume 19, June–August 1760.
1. Mitchell, *Memoirs*, Volume 2.
2. Mitchell, *Memoirs*, Volume 2.
3. *Oeuvres*, Volumes 4 and 5, *Histoire de la Guerre de Sept Ans*.
4. Carlyle, *History*, Volume 6.
5. Easum, *Prince Henry*.

CHAPTER 91

Politische Correspondenz, Volumes 19 and 20, August–December 1760.
1. *Oeuvres*, Volume 18, Frederick–Camas correspondence.

CHAPTER 92

Politische Correspondenz, Volumes 20 and 21, December 1760–January 1762.
1. Preuss, *Friedrich . . . eine Lebensgeschichte*, Volume 2; Carlyle, *History*, Volume 6.

2. Mitchell, *Memoirs*, Volume 2.
3. Mitchell, *Memoirs*, Volume 2.
4. *Oeuvres*, Volumes 4 and 5, *Histoire de la Guerre de Sept Ans.*
5. *Oeuvres*, Volumes 4 and 5, *Histoire de la Guerre de Sept Ans.*

CHAPTER 93

Politische Correspondenz, Volumes 21 and 22, January–September 1762.
1. Reddaway, *Frederick the Great.*
2. Bain, *Peter III.*
3. Mitchell, *Memoirs*, Volume 2.
4. Bain, *Peter III.*

CHAPTER 94

Politische Correspondenz, Volume 22, September 1762–February 1763.
1. *Mitchell, Memoirs*, Volume 2.
2. *Mitchell, Memoirs*, Volume 2.
3. Reddaway, *Frederick the Great.*

CHAPTER 95

Politische Correspondenz, Volume 23, April 1763–September 1764.
1. *Oeuvres*, Volumes 4 and 5, *Histoire de la Guerre de Sept Ans.*
2. *Oeuvres*, Volumes 4 and 5, *Histoire de la Guerre de Sept Ans.*
3. *Oeuvres*, Volumes 4 and 5, *Histoire de la Guerre de Sept Ans.*
4. *Annual Register*, 1763.
5. Mitchell, *Memoirs*, Volume 2.
6. Henderson, *Studies in the Economic Policy of Frederick the Great.*
7. Koser, *Geschichte*, Volume 3.
8. Henderson, *Studies.*
9. Pottle, ed., *Boswell.*
10. Mitchell, *Memoirs*, Volume 2.

CHAPTER 96

Politische Correspondenz, Volumes 23 and 24; *Die Politischen Testamente.*
1. Henderson, *Studies.*
2. Mitchell, *Memoirs*, Volume 2.

CHAPTER 97

1. Cuthell, *Scottish Friend.*
2. Gaxotte, *Frederick.*

3. Pottle, ed., *Boswell.*
4. Easum, *Prince Henry.*
5. *Oeuvres*, Volume 6.
6. *Oeuvres*, Volume 18, Frederick–Camas correspondence.
7. Cuthell, *Scottish Friend.*
8. Easum, *Prince Henry.*
9. Harris, *Diaries.*

CHAPTER 98

Politische Correspondenz, Volumes 23 ff.
1. *Oeuvres*, Volume 6, *Mémoires depuis la Paix de Hubertsbourg jusqu'à la Fin du Partage de la Pologne.* Hereafter *Oeuvres*, Volume 6, *Mémoires.*
2. *Oeuvres*, Volume 9.
3. *Oeuvres*, Volume 29. "Éléments de Castrametrie et de Tactique."
4. *Oeuvres*, Volume 6, *Mémoires.*
5. *Oeuvres*, Volume 6, *Mémoires.*
6. *Oeuvres*, Volume 6, *Mémoires.*
7. *Oeuvres*, Volume 6, *Mémoires.*
8. *Oeuvres*, Volume 6, *Mémoires.*

CHAPTER 99

Politische Correspondenz, Volumes 23–28, April 1763–July 1768; *Die Politischen Testamente.*
1. Lodge, *Great Britain and Prussia.*
2. Perkins, "Partition of Poland."
3. Perkins, "Partition of Poland."
4. Perkins, "Partition of Poland."
5. *Oeuvres*, Volume 6, *Mémoires.*
6. *Oeuvres*, Volume 6, *Mémoires.*

CHAPTER 100

Politische Correspondenz, Volumes 28–32, January 1768–October 1772.
1. Perkins, "Partition of Poland."
2. Temperley, *Frederick the Great.*
3. Easum, *Prince Henry.*
4. Koser, *Geschichte*, Volume 3.
5. *Oeuvres*, Volume 6, *Mémoires.*
6. *Oeuvres*, Volume 6, *Mémoires.*
7. Easum, *Prince Henry.*

CHAPTER 101

Politische Correspondenz, Volumes 31–36, March 1771–April 1775.
1. Gooch, *Frederick the Great.*
2. *Oeuvres*, Volume 6, *Mémoires.*
3. Harris, *Diaries.*
4. Oldenburg, *Catherine the Great.*
5. *Oeuvres*, Volume 6, *Mémoires.*
6. Harris, *Diaries.*

CHAPTER 102

Politische Correspondenz, Volumes 32–37, March 1772–March 1776.
1. Harris, *Diaries.*
2. Harris, *Diaries.*
3. Gaxotte, *Frederick.*
4. Cuthell, *Scottish Friend.*
5. Cuthell, *Scottish Friend.*
6. Moore, *Society.*
7. Moore, *Society.*
8. Moore, *Society.*
9. Wraxall, *Tour.*

CHAPTER 103

Politische Correspondenz, Volumes 36–41, September 1744–October 1778.
1. Harris, *Diaries.*
2. Harris, *Diaries.*
3. Temperley, *Frederick the Great.*
4. Temperley, *Frederick the Great.*
5. Temperley, *Frederick the Great.*
6. Temperley, *Frederick the Great.*
7. Harris, *Diaries.*

CHAPTER 104

Politische Correspondenz, Volumes 40–43, January 1778–December 1779.
1. *Oeuvres*, Volume 6, *Mémoires de la Guerre de 1778.*
2. *Oeuvres*, Volume 6, *Mémoires de la Guerre de 1778.*
3. Temperley, *Frederick the Great.*
4. Temperley, *Frederick the Great.*
5. Temperley, *Frederick the Great.*
6. Temperley, *Frederick the Great.*
7. Easum, *Prince Henry.*

8. Easum, *Prince Henry.*
9. Temperley, *Frederick the Great.*
10. Temperley, *Frederick the Great.*
11. *Oeuvres,* Volume 6, *Mémoires de la Guerre de 1778.*
12. Temperley, *Frederick the Great.*
13. Gooch, *Frederick the Great.*

CHAPTER 105

Politische Correspondenz, Volumes 43–46, April 1779–March 1782.
1. Schieder, *Friederich der Grosse.*
2. Gooch, *Frederick the Great.*
3. Lodge, *Great Britain and Prussia.*

CHAPTER 106

1. Harris, *Diaries.*
2. Lafayette, *Letters.*
3. Latzko, *Lafayette.*
4. Cornwallis, *Correspondence.*
5. Gottschalk, *Lafayette.*
6. Cornwallis, *Correspondence.*
7. Duffy, *Army of Frederick the Great.*
8. Easum, *Prince Henry.*
9. Carlyle, *History,* Volume 6.
10. Gaxotte, *Frederick.*
11. Hertzberg, *Recueil.* See also Hertzberg, *Mémoire historique.*
12. *Oeuvres,* Volume 27.

SELECTED BIBLIOGRAPHY

Acta Borussica: Die Behördenorganisation und die allgemeine Staatsverwaltung Preussens im 18. Jahrhundert. Volumes 6–10. Berlin, 1896–1911.

Alembert, Jean le Rond de. *Trois mois à la cour de Frédéric: Lettres inédites de d'Alembert.* Edited by G. Maugras. Paris, 1866.

Alexich, Hauptmann. "Die Freiwilligen Aufgebote aus den Ländern der Ungarischen Krone im Ersten Schlesischen Krieg." *Mittheilungen des KK Kriegsarchiv.* Volume 4. Vienna, 1889.

Archenholtz, J. W. H. von. *Geschichte des siebenjährigen Krieges in Deutschland.* Berlin, 1840.

Arneth, A. *Prinz Eugen von Savoyen.* Three volumes. Vienna, 1858.

———. *Geschichte Maria Theresas.* Ten volumes. Vienna, 1863–79.

Bain, R. Nisbet. *Peter III, Emperor of Russia: The Story of a Crisis and a Crime.* Westminster: Constable, 1902.

Barsewich, Ernst Friedrich Rudolf von. *Von Rossbach bis Freiberg, 1757–1763: Tagebuch Blätter eines friderizianischen Fahnjunker und Offizier.* Edited by Jürgen Olmes. Krefeld, 1759.

Bartholdy, G. M. *Friedrich II. . . . in seinen Briefen und Erlassen, sowie in zeitgenössischen Briefen, Berichten und Anekdoten.* Munich, 1912.

Berney, Arnold. *Friedrich der Grosse: Entwicklungsgeschichte eines Staatsmannes.* Tübingen: Mohr, 1934.

Bernhardi, F. T. von. *Friedrich der Grosse als Feldherr.* Two volumes. Berlin, 1881.

Besterman, Theodore. *Voltaire.* London: Longmans, 1969.

Bielfeld, Jacob F. *Letters of Baron Bielfeld.* Four volumes. Translated by Mr. Hooker. London, 1768–70.

Blumenthal, J. L. von. *Lebensbeschreibung Hans Joachim von Zieten.* Two volumes. Berlin, 1797.

Boswell, James. *Life of Johnson.* Edited by R. W. Chapman. London: Oxford University Press, 1970.

Braubach, Max. *Die Geheim-Diplomatie des Prinzen Eugen von Savoyen.* Cologne: Westdeutscher Verlag, 1962.

British Library, Department of Manuscripts. *Additional Manuscripts* (Newcastle, Polwarth, Harris, Elliott, Stepney, Eward, Dalrymple, Whitworth, Dickinson, Robinson, Egerton, Carteret, West, Liverpool, and Hardwicke papers).

Broglie, Albert. *Frederick the Great and Maria Theresa.* Two volumes. Translated by C. Hoey and J. Lillie. London, 1883.

Buttner, G. A. *Mémoires du Baron de La Motte Fouqué . . .* Two volumes. Berlin, 1788.

Carlyle, Thomas. *History of Frederick II of Prussia, Called Frederick the Great.* Six volumes. London: Hall, 1886.

Catt, Henri de. *Frederick the Great: The Memoirs of His Reader Henri de Catt (1758–1760).* Two volumes. Translated by F. S. Flint. London, 1916.

Chance, J. F. *George I and the Northern War.* London, 1909.

———. *The Alliance of Hanover.* London, 1923.

Churchill, Winston S. *Marlborough: His Life and Times.* Two volumes. London: Harrap, 1936.

Cogniazzo, Jacob. *Geständnisse eines Oesterreiches Veterans in politische-militärische Hinsicht auf die interessantesten Verhältnisse zwischen Oesterreich und Preussen während der Regierung des Grossen Königs der Preussen der Zweyten . . .* Four volumes. Breslau, 1788.

Colin, J. *The Transformation of War.* Translated by L. H. R. Pope-Hennessy. London: Pall Mall, 1912.

Cornwallis, Charles Marquis of. *Correspondence.* Edited by Charles Ross. Three volumes. London, 1859.

Cowie, L. W. *Eighteenth Century Europe.* London: Bell, 1966.

———. *Hanoverian England, 1714–1837.* London: Bell, 1969.

Coxe, William. *History of the House of Austria from the Foundation of the Monarchy by Rhodolph of Hapsburgh to the Death of Leopold the Second, 1218 to 1792.* Two volumes. London, 1807.

Cramer, Friedrich. *Zur Geschichte Friedrich Wilhelms I. und Friedrichs II.* Leipzig, 1833.

Crankshaw, Edward. *Maria Theresa.* London: Longmans, 1969.

Crousatz, A. von. *Die Organisations des von 1640 bis 1865 brandenburgischen und preussischen Heeres.* Berlin, 1865.

Cuthell, Edith E. *The Scottish Friend of Frederick the Great, the last Earl Marischall . . .* London, 1915.

Delbrück, H. *Geschichte der Kriegskunst im Rahmen der politischen Geschichte.* Volume 5. Berlin, 1920.

Dilthey, Wilhelm. "Frederick and the Academy." In Peter Paret, editor and translator, *Frederick the Great: A Profile.* New York: Macmillan, 1972.

Dorn, Walter L. "The Conflict of Humanitarianism and Reasons of State in the Youth of Frederick the Great." Ph.D. dissertation, University of Chicago, 1925.

———. "The Prussian Bureaucracy in the Eighteenth Century." *Political Science Quarterly.* Volume 46, 1931; Volume 47, 1932.

Droysen, J. G. *Geschichte der Preussischen Politik.* Five volumes. Berlin, 1855–86.

Duffy, Christopher. *The Wild Goose and the Eagle: A Life of Marshal von Browne.* London: Chatto and Windus, 1964.

———. *The Army of Frederick the Great.* London: David and Charles, 1974.

Duncker, Carl von. "Die Invasion Schlesiens durch die königlich preussischen Truppen im Monate December, 1740." *Mittheilungen des KK Kriegs-Archiv.* Vienna, 1885.

————. "Beiträge zur Geschichte des ersten schlesischen Krieges 1741." *Mittheilungen des KK Kriegs-Archiv.* Vienna, 1886.

————. "Militärische und politische Aktenstücke zur Geschichte des ersten schlesischen Krieges, 1741." *Mittheilungen des KK Kriegs-Archiv.* New series. Volumes 1–6. Vienna, 1887–92.

————. "Der Ueberfall Bei Baumgarten am 27. Februar 1741." *Mittheilungen des KK Kriegs-Archiv.* Vienna, 1889.

Durant, W. and A. *The Age of Voltaire.* New York: Simon and Schuster, 1965.

Easum, Chester V. *Prince Henry of Prussia: Brother of Frederick the Great.* Madison: University of Wisconsin Press, 1941.

Elliot, Hugh. *Memoirs of Hugh Elliot.* Edited by Lady Minto. London, 1853.

Ergang, Robert. *The Potsdam Führer: Frederick William I, Father of Prussian Militarism.* New York: Columbia University Press, 1941.

Fontane, Theodore. *Wanderungen durch die Mark Brandenburg.* Two volumes. Berlin, 1899.

Förster, Friedrich. *Friedrich Wilhelm I: König von Preussen.* Three volumes including Nachträge and Urkundenbuch. Potsdam, 1834.

Fouqué, Baron Heinrich August La Motte de. *Der Feldzug des königlich Preussischen Generals der Infanterie H. A. Baron de la M. F. im Schlesien, 1760.* N.p., 1862.

Frederick the Great. *Regulations for the Prussian Infantry.* Translated by William Faucitt, Esq. London, 1754.

Frédéric le Grand. *Correspondance Familière et Amicale de Frédéric Second, Roi de Prusse, avec U.F. de Suhm, Conseiller intime de l'Electeur de Saxe . . .* Two volumes. Berlin, 1787.

————. *Oeuvres Historiques de Frédéric II Roi de Prusse.* Thirty volumes. Edited by J. D. E. Preuss. Berlin, 1864 ff.

Friedrich der Grosse. *Politische Correspondenz Friedrichs der Grossen.* Forty-six volumes and Ergänzungsband, *Die Politischen Testamente.* Chief editors, R. Koser and G. Volz. Berlin, 1879–1939.

————. "Die Briefe des Kronprinzen Friedrich von Preussen an den Fürsten Leopold und an die Prinzen von Anhalt-Dessau." *Forschungen zur brandenburgischen und preussischen Geschichte.* Volume 7. Edited by Otto Krauske. 1894.

————. *Briefwechsel Friedrichs des Grossen mit Grumbkow und Maupertuis (1731–1759).* Edited by Reinhold Koser. Leipzig, 1898.

————. *Briefwechsel Friedrichs des Grossen mit Voltaire.* Three volumes. Edited by R. Koser and G. Droysen. Leipzig, 1908–1911.

————. *Die Briefe Friedrichs des Grossen an seinen vormaligen Kammerdiener Fredersdorff.* Edited by Johannes Richter. Berlin, 1927.

————. *Friedrichs des Grossen Korrespondenz mit Ärzten.* Edited by G. L. Mamlock. Stuttgart, 1907.

————. *Friedrich der Grosse und Wilhelmina von Baireuth: Jugendbriefe 1728–1740.* Edited by G. Volz and F. Oppeln-Bronikowski. Leipzig, 1924.

————. *Briefwechsel Friedrichs des Grossen mit seinem Bruder Prince August Wilhelm.* Edited by G. Volz. Leipzig, 1927.

Friedrich Wilhelm I. *Die Briefe König Friedrich Wilhelm I. an den Fürsten Leopold zu Anhalt-Dessau.* Edited by Otto Krauske. Berlin, 1905.

Garrison, Fielding H. *Notes on the History of Military Medicine.* Washington: Association of Military Surgeons, 1922.

Gaudi, Colonel von. *Tagebuch des Obersten von Gaudi über die Ereignisse des seibenjährigen Krieges.* Ten volumes. Wesel, 1778.

Gaxotte, Pierre. *Frederick the Great.* Translated by R. A. Bell. New York: Yale University Press, 1942.

Generalstab, Der grosse [Deutsche]. *Die Kriege Friedrichs des Grossen.* Erster Theil: *Der Erste Schlesische Krieg, 1740–1742.* Three volumes. Berlin, 1890 ff.

———. *Die Kriege Friedrichs des Grossen.* Zweiter Theil: *Der Zweite Schlesische Krieg 1744–1745.* Three volumes. Berlin, 1895 ff.

———. *Kriegsgeschlichtliche Einzelschriften: Friedrich des Grossen Anschauung vom Kriege in ihrer Entwickelung von 1745 bis 1756.* Number 27. Berlin, 1899.

———. *Kriegsgeschichtliche Einzelschriften: Die taktische Schulung der Preussischen Armee durch König Friedrich den Grossen während der Friedenzeit 1745 bis 1746.* Numbers 28–30. Berlin, 1900.

———. *Die Kriege Friedrichs des Grossen. Der Siebenjährige Krieg, 1756–1763.* Twelve volumes. Berlin, 1901 ff.

Goldsmith, Margaret. *Frederick the Great.* New York: Boni, 1929.

Gooch, George P. *Frederick the Great, the Ruler, the Writer, the Man.* New York, 1947.

Grandmaison, Capitaine de. *La Petite Guerre ou Traité du Service Des Troupes Légères en Campagne.* Paris, 1756.

Granier, Herman. "Die Kronprinzlichen Schulden Friedrichs des Grossen." *Forschungen zur brandenburgischen und preussischen Geschichte.* Volume 8, 1894.

Great Britain, Public Records Office, State Papers, Foreign Office, Prussia and Poland, Volumes 90/7–90/72.

Guibert, J. A. H., Comte de. *Journal d'un voyage en Allemagne fait en 1773.* Two volumes. Paris, 1803.

Haake, Paul. *August der Starke im Urteil seiner Zeit und der Nachwelt.* Dresden, 1921.

Hamilton, Andrew. *Rheinsberg: Memorials of Frederick the Great and Prince Henry of Prussia.* London, 1880.

Harris, James E. *Political Diaries and Correspondence of the First Earl of Malmesbury.* Four volumes. Edited by the Earl of Malmesbury. London, 1844.

Hearsay, John. *Voltaire.* London: Constable, 1976.

Heigel, Karl Theodor, ed. *Das Tagebuch Kaiser Karl's VII aus der Zeit des oesterreichischen Erbfolgekrieg.* Munich, 1883.

Henderson, W. O., *The State and the Industrial Revolution in Prussia, 1740–1870.* Liverpool: Liverpool University Press, 1958.

———. "The Berlin Commercial Crisis of 1767." *Economic History Review.* Volume 15, Number 1, 1962.

———. *Studies in the Economic Policy of Frederick the Great.* London: Cass, 1963.

Hertzberg, E. F., Comte de. *Mémoire historique sur la dernière année de la vie privée de Frederick II, Roi de Prusse.* Berlin, 1787.

———. *Recueil des déductions, manifestes, déclarations, traités, et autres actes et écrits publics . . . depuis l'année 1756 jusqu'à l'année 1790.* Two volumes. Berlin, 1789–1790.

Hillbrand, Erich. *Die Einschliessung von Linz 1741/42.* Militärhistorische Schriftenreihe, Number 15. Heeresgeschichtlichen Museum, Vienna, 1970.

Hinrichs, Karl. *Friedrich Wilhelm I, König in Preussen: Eine Biographie.* Hamburg: Hanseatische Verlageanstalt, 1941.

————, ed. *Der Kronprinzenprozess, Friedrich und Katte.* Hamburg, 1936.

Hoen, Maximilian von. *Die Kriege Friedrichs des Grossen, 1740–1763.* Berlin: Verlag der Vossischen Buchhandlung, 1908.

Hoyer, J. G. *Allgemeine Wörterbuch der Artillerie.* Two volumes. Tübingen, 1805.

Hron, Karl. *Der Parteigänger-Krieg.* Vienna, 1885.

Hubatsch, Walther. *Frederick the Great: Absolutism and Administration.* London: Thames and Hudson, 1975.

Hull, University of. Hotham Archives.

Hytier, Adrienne. "Frédéric II et les Philosophes Recalcitrants." *Romantic Review.* Volume 57, October 1966.

Ilchester, Earl of, and Mrs. Langford-Brooke. *The Life of Sir Charles Hanbury-Williams, Poet, Wit and Diplomatist.* London: Butterworth, 1929.

Jähns, Max. *Geschichte der Kriegswissenschaften vornehmlich in Deutschland.* Three volumes. Munich, 1890–91.

Janko, Wilhelm von. *Laudon's Leben — nach original Akten des K.K. Haus-, Hof-, Staats- und Kriegs-Archivs: Correspondenzen und Quellen.* Vienna, 1869.

Jany, Curt. "Die Kantonverfassung Friedrich Wilhelm I." *Forschungen zur brandenburgischen und preussischen Geschichte.* Volume 38, 1925.

————. *Geschichte der Königlich Preussischen Armee bis zum Jahre 1807.* Three volumes. Berlin: Siegesmund, 1928–29.

Jeney, Herr von. *Der Partheygänger oder die Kunst den kleinen Krieg zu führen.* Vienna, 1785.

Jihn, Friedrich. "Der Feldzug 1761 in Schlesien und Sachsen." *Mittheilungen des K.K. Kriegs-Archiv.* Vienna, 1884.

Johnson, Hubert C. "Politics of Discord: The Domestic Leadership of Frederick II of Prussia, 1740–1756." Ph.D. dissertation, University of California, 1962.

————. *Frederick the Great and His Officials.* New Haven: Yale University Press, 1975.

Karl VII, Kaiser. *Das Tagebuch Kaiser Karl's VII aus der Zeit des oesterreichischen Erbfolgekriegs.* Munich, 1883.

Kerler, Dietrich, ed. *Aus dem Siebenjährigen Krieg: Tagebuch des preussischen Musketiers Dominicus.* Munich: 1891.

Koser, Reinhold. *Friedrich der Grosse als Kronprinz.* Stuttgart, 1886.

————. *Geschichte Friedrichs des Grossen.* Four volumes. Berlin, 1912–14.

————. "Aus der Korrespondenz der französischen Gesandtschaft zu Berlin, 1746–1756." *Forschungen zur brandenburgischen und preussischen Geschichte.* Volume 7, 1894.

Krieger, Bogdan. *Friedrich der Grosse und sein Bücher.* Berlin, 1914.

Lafayette, Marquis de. *The Letters of Lafayette to Washington, 1777–1779.* Edited by Louis Gottschalk. New York, 1944.

Lange-Eichbaum, Wilhelm. *Genie, Irsinn und Ruhm.* Munich: Reinhardt, 1942.

Latzko, Andreas. *Lafayette: A Soldier of Liberty.* Translated by E. W. Dickes. London: Methuen, 1936.

Lavisse, Ernest. *The Youth of Frederick the Great.* Translated by S. L. Simeon. London, 1891.

Lehndorff, E. A. H., Count von. *Dreissig Jahre am Hofe Friedrichs des Grossen* . . . Edited by Karl Eduard Schmidt-Lotzen. Gotha, 1907.

Lippe-Weissenfeld, Ernst Graf zur. *Husaren-Buch.* Berlin, 1863.

——. *Hans Joachim von Zieten: Eine Lebensgeschichte.* Berlin, 1880.

Lodge, Sir Richard. *Great Britain and Prussia in the Eighteenth Century.* Oxford: Milford, 1923.

——. *Studies in Eighteenth Century Diplomacy, 1740–1748.* London: Murray, 1730.

Mamlock, L. von and Bonin, R. *Geschichte der brandenburgisch-preussischen Artillerie.* Two volumes. Berlin, 1840–42.

Mamlock, G. L. *Friedrichs des Grossen Beziehungen zur Medizin.* Berlin, 1902.

——. *Friedrichs des Grossen Korrespondenz mit Ärtzen.* Stuttgart, 1907.

Margotte, Roberto. *An Illustrated History of Medicine.* Milan: Hamlyn, 1968.

Maurois, André. *A History of France.* New York: Farrar, Straus and Cudahy, 1956.

Meinicke, Friedrich. "Ruler Before Philosopher." Translated by Douglas Scott. In Peter Paret, ed., *Frederick the Great: A Profile.* London: Macmillan, 1972.

Mirabeau, Honoré Gabriel Riquetti, Count de. *The Secret History of the Court of Berlin.* Two volumes. Translated from the French. London, 1895.

Mitchell, Sir Andrew. *Memoirs and Papers of Sir Andrew Mitchell.* Two volumes. Edited by Andrew Bisset. London, 1850.

Moore, Doctor John. *View of Society and Manners in France, Switzerland, and Germany.* Two volumes. London, 1789.

Mylius, C. O., ed. *Corpus Constitutionam Marchicarum.* Twenty volumes. Berlin, 1737 ff.

Natzmer, G. E. "Ein Jugendfreund Friedrichs des Grossen, Carl Dubislav von Natzmer." *Forschungen zur brandenburgischen und preussischen Geschichte.* Volume 3. Leipzig, 1890.

Oesterreich Kriegsarchiv, *Oesterreichischer Erbfolge-Krieg 1740–1748.* Nine volumes. Vienna, 1896 ff.

Oldenburg, Zoe. *Catherine the Great.* Translated by Anne Carter. London: Heinemann, 1965.

Orlich, Leopold von. *Geschichte der schlesischen Kriege mit Plänen und Operationskarte.* Two volumes. Berlin, 1841.

Pares, Bernard. *A History of Russia.* London, 1962.

Paret, Peter. *Yorck and the Era of Prussian Reform, 1807–1815.* Princeton, N.J.: Princeton University Press, 1966.

Paret, Peter, ed. *Frederick the Great: A Profile.* New York: Macmillan, 1972.

Parton, James. *Life of Voltaire.* Two volumes. Boston, 1881.

Pauli, Carl Friedrich. *Leben grosser Helden des gegenwärtigen Krieges.* Four volumes. Halle, 1759–64.

Perkins, James. "The Partition of Poland." *American Historical Review.* Volume 2, Number 1, October 1896.

Pfeiffer, Ernst. "Die Revuereisen Friedrichs des Grossen, besonders die Schlesischen nach 1763 und der Zustand Schlesiens von 1763–1786." Doctoral dissertation, Berlin, 1903.

Pick, Robert. *Empress Maria Theresa: The Earlier Years, 1717–1757.* London: Weidenfeld and Nicolson, 1966.

Pöllnitz, Baron de. *The Memoirs of Charles-Lewis, Baron de Pöllnitz . . .* Four volumes. Translated from the French. London, 1745 ff.

Pottle, Frederick, ed. *Boswell on the Grand Tour: Germany and Switzerland, 1764.* London: Heinemann, 1953.

Preradovich, Nikolaus von. *Des Kaisers Grenzer.* Vienna, 1970.

Preuss, J. D. E. *Friedrich der Grosse, eine Lebensgeschichte.* Four volumes plus Urkundenbuch. Berlin, 1832–34.

———. *Friedrich der Grosse als Schriftsteller.* Berlin, 1837.

———. *Friedrich der Grosse mit seinen Verwandten und Freunden.* Berlin, 1838.

Ranke, Leopold von. *Memoirs of the House of Brandenburg and History of Prussia.* Three volumes. Translated by Sir Alexander and Lady Duff-Gordon. London, 1849.

———. *Der Ursprung des siebenjährigen Krieges.* Leipzig, 1871.

Raumer, Friedrich von. *Contributions to Modern History from the British Museum and the State Paper Office: Frederick II and His Times.* London, 1837.

Reddaway, W. F. *Frederick the Great and the Rise of Prussia.* London: Putnams, 1925.

———. *A History of Europe, 1715–1784.* London: Methuen, 1957.

Reiners, Ludwig. *Frederick the Great: A Biography.* Translated by L. P. R. Wilson. New York: Putnams, 1960.

Retzow, Friedrich A. *Charakteristik der wichtigsten Ereignisse des siebenjährigen Krieges, in Rücksicht auf Ursachen und Wirkungen.* Two volumes. Berlin, 1802.

Richter, Adolph L. *Geschichte des Medezinal-Wesens der Königlichen Preussischen Armee bis zur Gegenwart.* Erlangen, 1860.

Ritter, Gerhard. *Frederick the Great.* Translated by Peter Paret. London: Eyre and Spottiswoode, 1968.

———. "Frederician Warfare." Translated by Peter Paret. In Peter Paret, ed., *Frederick the Great: A Profile.* New York: Macmillan, 1972.

Rosenberg, Hans. *Bureaucracy, Aristocracy and Autocracy: The Prussian Experience, 1660–1815.* Cambridge, 1958.

Rothenburg, Gunther E., *The Austrian Military Border in Croatia, 1522–1747.* Urbana: University of Illinois Press, 1960.

———. *The Military Border in Croatia, 1740–1881: A Study of an Imperial Institution.* Chicago: University of Chicago Press, 1966.

Saint-Geniés, M. *L'Officier Partisan.* Paris, 1763–69.

Schevill, Ferdinand. *The Making of Modern Germany.* Chicago: McClurg, 1916.

———. *The Great Elector.* Chicago: University of Chicago Press, 1947.

Schieder, Theodor. *Friedrich der Grosse: Ein Königtum der Widersprüche.* Cologne: Propyläen Verlag, 1983.

Schlözer, Kurd von. *General Graf Chasot: Zur Geschichte Friedrichs des Grossen und Seiner Zeit.* Berlin, 1878.

Schmoller, G. "Eine Schilderung Berlins aus dem Jahre 1723." *Forschungen zur brandenburgischen und preussischen Geschichte.* Volume 3, 1890.

Schmucker, Johann Leberecht. *Chirurgische Wahrnehmungen, welche meistens während dem von 1756–1763 gedauerten Krieg . . .* Two volumes. Berlin, 1774.

Schöning, Kurt Wolfgang von. *Historisch-biographische Nachrichten zur Geschichte der Brandenburgisch-Preussischen Artillerie.* Three volumes. Berlin, 1844.

————. *Militärische Correspondenz des Königs Friedrich des Grossen mit dem Prinzen Heinrich von Preussen*. Four volumes. Berlin, 1851 ff.

Schwerin, Dettlof von. *Feldmarschall Schwerin: Ein Lebensbild aus Preussens grosser Zeit*. Berlin: Mittler, 1928.

Seckendorff, Christoph Louis, Baron de. *Journal Secret du Baron de Seckendorff*. Tübingen, 1811.

Selle, C. G. *Krankheitsgeschichte des höchstseeligen Königs von Preussen Friedrichs des Zweyten Majestät*. Berlin, 1786.

Simon, Edith. *The Making of Frederick the Great*. Boston: Little, Brown, 1963.

Sonntag, Kurt. *Trenck der Pandur und die Brandschatzung Bayerns*. Munich: Nusser, 1976.

Steinhausen, Georg, ed. *Georg Liebe: Der Soldat in der deutschen Vergangenheit*. Leipzig, 1899.

Stirling, A. M. *The Hothams . . .* Two volumes. London: Jenkins, 1918.

Taysen, A. von, ed. *Friedrich der Grosse: Militärischen Schriften*. Berlin, 1882.

Temperley, Harold. *Frederick the Great and Kaiser Joseph*. London: Frank Cass, 1968.

Teuber, Oscar, and Ottenfeld, Rudolf von. *Die Oesterreichische Armee von 1700 bis 1867*. Vienna, 1895.

Thiérot, Albert. *Voltaire en Prusse*. Paris, 1878.

Valory, Marquis de. *Mémoires des négociations du marquis de Valori*. Two volumes. Edited by Count H. de Valori. Paris, 1820.

Varnhagen, Karl August von Ense. *Biographische Denkmale: Fürste Leopold von Anhalt-Dessau, General Freiherr von Seydlitz*. Leipzig, 1872.

————. *Biographische Denkmale: General Hans von Winterfeldt, Feld-Marschall Graf von Schwerin*. Leipzig, 1873.

————. *Biographische Denkmale: Feldmarschall Jakob Keith, Hans von Held*. Leipzig, 1873.

Voltaire, François-Marie Arouet de. *Mémoires Pour Servir à La Vie de M. de Voltaire*. Volume 1 of *Oeuvres Complètes*. Paris, 1883.

————. *The Love Letters of Voltaire to his Niece*. Edited and translated by Theodore Besterman. London: Kimber, 1958.

Volz, G. B. *Friedrich der Grosse im Spiegel seiner Zeit*. Three volumes. Berlin: Reimar Hobbing, 1901.

————. "Friedrich der Grosse und seine sittlichen Ankläger." *Forschungen zur brandenburgischen und preussischen Geschichte*. Volume 41, 1928.

Vorberg, Gaston. *Der Klatsch über das Geschlechtsleben Friedrichs II*. Bonn: Marcus and Webors, 1921.

Waddington, Albert. *Histoire de Prusse*. Two volumes. Paris: Plon, 1911.

————, ed. *Recueil des instructions donnée aux Ambassadeurs et Ministres de la France*. Volume 16, *Prusse*. Paris, 1901.

Waddington, Richard. *La Guerre de Sept Ans*. Five volumes. Paris, 1899–1914.

Warnery, Charles Emmanuel de. *Campagnes de Frédéric II, Roi de Prusse, de 1757 à 1762*. N.p., 1788.

Weill, Herman N. "Frederick the Great and His Grand Chancellor Samuel von Cocceji: A Study in the Reform of the Prussian Judicial Administration, 1740–1755." Ph.D. dissertation, University of Illinois, 1959.

Wilhelmina, Margravine of Bayreuth. *Memoirs.* Translated from the French. London, 1812.

———. *Memoirs of Wilhelmine, Margravine of Baireuth.* Translated and edited by Princess Christian of Schleswig-Holstein. London, 1877.

Wraxall, N. W. *A Tour Through Some of the Northern Parts of Europe.* Two volumes. London, 1776.

Zimmermann, J. G. *Dr. Zimmermann's Conversations with the Late King of Prussia, When He Attended Him in His Last Illness a Little Before His Death . . .* London, 1791.

INDEX

Frederician Law Code, The (Cocceji), 367

Frederick I, elector of Brandenburg (as Frederick III) and king in Prussia, xiv, xvii, 24, 148; and baptism of Frederick, 3; death of, 4, 10; court of, 6; character of, 9; and upbringing of Fred. Wil. I, 9-10

Frederick II, king of Prussia

CROWN PRINCE: birth and infancy of, 3-4; molding influences, 4-6; bonding with sister Wilhelmina, 4-5; marriage plans to cousin Emily, 6, 28, 46-47, 55-62; maternal influence on, 8-9; and Tabagie, 15; early relations with father, 15-16, 18-19, 22-24, 28-29, 34-35, 42-47, 53; education, 17-21, 23; religious training, 17; moral training, 18; learning of foreign languages, 19; francophilia, 19-21; flute playing, 21; early library of, 21, 34-35, 67; foppishness, 21, 23; relations with Rothenburg, 27, 29; trip to Dresden, 36-39; Order of the Saxon Eagle, 38, 62; venereal illness, speculation on, 39-40; relations with von Keith, 42, 51; and Wusterhausen hunting parties, 44-45; and crisis between father and Hanover, 50-51; promoted to lt. col., 50; escape from court, 59-60, 61, 62-64; arrest and imprisonment, 64-70; military trial of associates, 69; and execution of von Katte, 70, 75; pressure from European courts to pardon, 76; swears fealty to king, 76-77; rehabilitation program at Cüstrin, 77-80; at Chamber of War and Domains, 77; and predestination doctrine, 75, 78, 81-82, 109; manners in prison, 78; quality of life at Cüstrin, 78-79; studies, 79; on territorial needs of Prussia, 79-80; marriage plans to Elizabeth, 80-81, 87; pardon and reconciliation with father, 81-89; new regimen at Cüstrin, 82-84, 85; relations with Louise von Wreech, 83-84; coolness over Wilhelmina's marriage, 84-85; reinstated in army, 85; letters to father, 85-86; reads "Infantry Regulations," 85, 86; opinions of his new character, 86-87; dissatisfaction with Elizabeth, 87-89, 94-95; appointed colonel of Regiment Goltz, 89-90; first reaction to drill, 93; payment of Cüstrin debts, 93-94; marriage, 94-98; on

love, sex, and married life, 95; wedding presents to, 98; mobilized with Regiment Goltz, 99-100; reaction to father's apoplexy, 100-103; and regimental review, 103-6; wish to join Rhine campaign, 105-6; first symphony of, 106; Amalthée garden, 106; tour of Prussia, 106-8; on misgovernment, 107; meets with King Stanislaus, 107; philosophical inquiries, 109-10; court and companions at Rheinsberg, 111-13; relations with Elizabeth, 113-15; barren marriage, 113-14; and Enlightenment, 115; readings, 115; influence of Voltaire on, 115-17; political life at Rheinsberg, 117-18; debts, 118-19; relations with father, 119-20, 126-27; intellectual pursuits, 120-21; writes *Reflections on the Present State of European Politics*, 123-25, 132; on France and balance of power, 123-24; joins Freemasons, 126; loan from George II, 127-28; reads Machiavelli, 130, 132; writes *The Refutation of the Prince of Machiavelli* (later *L'Anti-Macchiavel*), 131-33; on justifiable wars, 133; on Austrian-Turkish war, 134n; and final illness of father, 135-38

ASCENT TO THRONE: reaction to father's death, 141; and army, 143; foreign policy and alliances, 143-44, 150-52; popularity of, 144; swearing of allegiance to, 144-45; promises reforms, 144-46; religious toleration, 145; bans censorship, 145; invites intellectuals to court, 146; disbands Potsdam brigade of giants, 146; relations with family, 146-47; relations with officials, 147; becomes parsimonious, 148; takes to wearing uniform, 148; visits Strasbourg, 148-49; diplomacy of, 149-52; Herstal crisis, 152-53; meeting with Voltaire, 153; revises *L'Anti-Macchiavel*, 153, 161, 230; assessment of balance of power at Charles VI's death, 154-58

FIRST SILESIAN WAR: plans for Silesian offensive, 158-64; Corps I, 170-71; proposals to Austria, 174-75; march to Breslau, 176-77; march to Neisse fortress, 178-79; European response to blitzkrieg, 180-83; at Schweidnitz headquarters, 188-89; kidnap attempt